SECRET INGREDIENTS

"It's broccoli, dear."
"I say it's spinach, and I say the hell with it."

SECRET
INGREDIENTS

THE NEW YORKER BOOK
OF FOOD AND DRINK

EDITED BY
DAVID REMNICK

RANDOM HOUSE NEW YORK

Published in the United States by Random House, an imprint of
The Random House Publishing Group, a division of Random House, Inc., New York.

RANDOM HOUSE and colophon are registered trademarks of Random House, Inc.

All pieces in this collection were originally published in *The New Yorker.*
The publication dates are given at the end of each piece.

Grateful acknowledgment is made to Scribner, an imprint of Simon & Schuster,
for permission to reprint an excerpt from *Underworld* by Don DeLillo, copyright
© 1997 by Don DeLillo. First published as "Sputnick" in *The New Yorker,*
September 8, 1997. All rights reserved. Reprinted by permission.

ISBN 978-1-4000-6547-9

Library of Congress Cataloging-in-Publication Data

Secret ingredients: the New Yorker book of food and drink / edited by David Remnick.
    p.   cm.
Includes bibliographical references.
ISBN 978-1-4000-6547-9
1. Gastronomy—Literary collections.   2. Food—Literary collections.
3. Food habits—Literary collections.   I. Remnick, David.
II. New Yorker (New York, N.Y. : 1925)
PN6071.G3N49 2007
809'.933559—dc22   2007014490

Printed in the United States of America on acid-free paper

www.atrandom.com

12 14 16 18 19 17 15 13

Book design by Susan Turner

CONTENTS

FICTION

"Thank goodness you're here. His dish is empty."

"Very classy choice for a guy who's eating solo."

INTRODUCTION

DAVID REMNICK

To his colleagues, Harold Ross, the founding editor of *The New Yorker*, was a tireless editorial engine fueled by a steady diet of high anxiety and unfiltered cigarettes. But while the magazine over the years employed its share of gourmands (Alexander Woollcott, A. J. Liebling), Ross himself was of circumscribed appetite. For the fun of it, he had a $3,500 stake in the famous Los Angeles hangout run by his friend Dave Chasen—he provided suggestions on everything from proofreading the menu to the optimal way to brine a turkey—and yet his own diet was abstemious. It wasn't his fault. Ross suffered from debilitating ulcers. Stress, particularly the stress of inventing *The New Yorker*, keeping it afloat during the Depression, and then elaborating its original principles into a literary and commercial success, was his perpetual state, warm milk and hot broth his diet. On this meager nourishment, he kept himself going. He was shambling, stooped, and in no way an athlete, yet he was strong enough for the job. As E. B. White once said, Ross was "an Atlas who lacked muscle tone."

Some limited salvation came to Ross's innards when he befriended Sara Murray Jordan, a renowned gastroenterologist at the Lahey Clinic in Boston. Thanks to Dr. Jordan, Ross's ulcer pain eased somewhat and he even began to eat his share of solid foods. Ross's gut, an unerring, if pained, precinct, now provided him with yet another editorial idea: Dr. Jordan was not only a superb physician but a competent cook, and so

Ross put her together with his culinary expert at the magazine, Sheila Hibben, and bid them to collaborate on a recipe compendium for the gastrointestinally challenged, to be called "Good Food for Bad Stomachs." In his first bylined piece since his days as a newspaperman during the First World War, Ross contributed an introduction that began, "I write as a duodenum-scarred veteran of many years of guerrilla service in the Hydrochloric War." Ross also paid tribute to Dr. Jordan, who at dinner one night urged him to pass on his usual fruit compote and to try the digestively more daring *meringue glacée.*

"Now *meringue glacée* has a French name, which is bad, and it is an ornamental concoction, which is bad," Ross wrote. "Although I regard it as essentially a sissy proposition and nothing for a full-grown man to lose his head over, I have it now and then when I'm in the ulcer victim's nearest approach to a devil-may-care mood."

Ross's longtime deputy and eventual successor, William Shawn, neither smoked nor drank and enjoyed relatively good health to the end of a long life, yet he, too, is recalled by his colleagues not only for his editorial intelligence and preternatural generosity but also for his curious modesty at table. At his regular lunches with writers at the Algonquin Hotel, Shawn would usually order nothing more than a slice of toasted pound cake (and barely touch it) or a bowl of cornflakes in milk (and leave the flakes floating). His interest was solely with the writer across the table.

While Ross and Shawn did not distinguish themselves as *fressers,* they did build a magazine that welcomed some of the greatest eaters and also some of the greatest writers *about* eating who have ever picked up pen or fork. This anthology comprises those men and women of appetite and their successors, writers who have taken an interest in food and drink as a source of pleasure, sustenance, metaphor, portraiture, adventure, comedy, and fiction.

A. J. Liebling, who came to the magazine in 1935 from the *New York World-Telegram,* was surely the first among equals in the field. Liebling's food writing was as much about memory as it was about food, and his last book, *Between Meals,* which appeared serially in the magazine, was a memoir about the Paris of his youth. Paris, for him, was the capital of pleasure. "There would come a time," he wrote, "when if I had compared my life to a cake, the sojourns in Paris would have presented the chocolate filling. The intervening layers were plain sponge."

Like so many of his models, Rabelais included, Liebling was a prodigious writer—life being short, he valued speed and volume; he used to say that he could write better than anyone who wrote faster and faster than anyone who wrote better—but his indulgences away from the desk exacted a price. He died at the age of fifty-nine. His *Times* obituary remarked, "Mr. Liebling bore the marks of the gourmet: an extended waistline and rosy cheeks. 'I used to be shy about ordering a steak after I had eaten a steak sandwich,' he once said, 'but I got used to it.' "

Liebling habitually apprenticed himself to a cast of elders: in boxing to the trainer Whitey Bimstein, in writing to Camus and Pierce Egan, and, in the restaurants of Paris, to a playwright and heroic eater of his acquaintance, Yves Mirande, who often presided at a favorite restaurant on the Rue Saint-Augustin. In "A Good Appetite," one of the many full plates served up here, Liebling recalls Mirande's admirable capacities and, in doing so, provides a catalogue of particulars no less vivid than Homer's ships and a seminar on the virtues (however fleeting) of abandon. Mirande, Liebling wrote, would "dazzle" his fellow diners "by dispatching a lunch of raw Bayonne ham and fresh figs, a hot sausage in crust, spindles of filleted pike in a rich rose *sauce Nantua,* a leg of lamb larded with anchovies, artichokes on a pedestal of foie gras, and four or five kinds of cheese, with a good bottle of Bordeaux and one of champagne, after which he would call for the Armagnac and remind Madame to have ready for dinner the larks and ortolans she had promised him, with a few *langoustes* and a turbot—and, of course, a fine *civet* made from the *marcassin,* or young wild boar, that the lover of the leading lady in his current production had sent up from his estate in the Sologne. 'And while I think of it,' I once heard him say, 'we haven't had any woodcock for days, or truffles baked in the ashes, and the cellar is becoming a disgrace—no more '34s and hardly any '37s. Last week, I had to offer my publisher a bottle that was far too good for him, simply because there was nothing between the insulting and the superlative.' "

It is unclear whether Liebling could write faster than Proust, and certainly he could not write better, but he did dare a gibe at the master by mock-wondering if perhaps *In Search of Lost Time* would have been improved had its author fed on a heartier stimulus than the bland madeleine. "On a dozen Gardiners Island oysters, a bowl of clam chowder, a peck of steamers, some bay scallops, three sautéed soft-shelled crabs, a few ears of fresh-picked corn, a thin swordfish steak of generous area, a pair of lobsters, and a Long Island duck, he might have written a masterpiece." It was in the same spirit of gastronomic challenge that one of Liebling's heroes, Jean-Anthelme Brillat-Savarin, addressed Adam and Eve: "First parents of the human race . . . you lost all for an apple, what would you not have done for a truffled turkey?"

Adam Gopnik, one of our chief epicures, once wrote that food writing can usually be broken down into the "mock epic" and the "mystical microcosm." If Liebling was the master of the mock epic, his inheritors surely include Calvin Trillin, who goes out in search of the "magic" bagel, the perfect barbecued mutton, dim sum good enough to impress Mao Zedong. And just as Liebling insisted that the true eater subsist on a limited budget (the principle being that it takes no skill at all to walk into Le Bernardin armed with a corporate credit card), Trillin declares Kansas City his Paris and insists (as an inveterate beer drinker) that positively no one, not even the most devoted oenophile, can, in a blindfold test, tell the difference between red wine and white. Although his research is done with reliable professors in the Napa Valley, Trillin warns the reader, "I have never denied that when I'm trying to select a bottle of wine in a liquor store I'm strongly influenced by the picture on the label. (I like a nice mountain, preferably in the middle distance.)" Trillin has pursued American vernacular cuisine with the reporting energy of Seymour Hersh and the deadpan panache of Stan Laurel. The morning after bingeing on Buffalo chicken wings with a local expert, "I got out my preliminary research notes for analysis. They amounted to three sentences I was unable to make out, plus what appeared to be a chicken-wing stain."

M.F.K. Fisher is an exemplar of the mystical school, in which the secrets of life, of survival, of the nature of time and generational knowledge, are found in a clear-eyed concentration on the stuff of life, the things we eat—or should. In "The Secret Ingredient," she talks about the cooks of her acquaintance who have been in possession of seemingly magical properties. What was the secret of Bertie Bastalizzo's dumplings and casseroles? What of Fisher's mother's mustard pickles? "Where are the witches of yesteryear, the strange old women with their dogged involvement, their loyalty to true flavor and changeless quality?"

And yet it is hard, as one considers the many profiles, travel pieces, literary essays, personal memoirs, short stories, and poems assembled here in *Secret Ingredients*, to limit the categories to the mock epic or the mystical. Roger Angell's rumination on the perfect martini is personal, domestic, and sharp—mock epic *and* mystical—where Viktor Erofeyev's essay on "the Russian god," vodka, is a way of seeing (hazily) the history and psychology of a vast country, Dostoyevsky in a glass or straight from the bottle. Pursuing food is often a means of exploring a place and its inhabitants; this was certainly true of Liebling's great confederate Joseph Mitchell, who loved to roam the quays and fish markets of southern Manhattan and Long Island. Mitchell ordinarily put the focus on characters, on others, but he was not averse to determined personal research, the risk of hepatitis be damned: "One Sunday afternoon in August 1937, I placed third in a clam-eating tournament at a Block Island clambake, eating eighty-four cherries." This, Mitchell says, was "one of the few worthwhile achievements of my life." In the same spirit, Susan Orlean gets to know the Cubans by visiting the Centro Vasco in Havana; Bill Buford, a participatory eater and reporter in the mold of George Plimpton, roams the Long Island beaches with its finest oystermen; Peter Hessler, a resident of Beijing for many years, eats rat in rural China and *likes* it; Adam Gopnik, who appraises "the role of food as anxious social theatre," takes the temperature of contemporary French culture, its insularity and reaction to world trends, by reporting on the high-end kitchens of Paris; Calvin Tomkins describes a coming revolution in American taste by portraying an unlikely revolutionary, the emerging Julia Child; and John McPhee's profile of Euell Gibbons, who forces his portraitist to eat boiled dandelions and much worse, portends the coming of the natural-foods movement.

Sometimes writers go too far in advertising the difficulty of their craft, but here the writers concentrate on crafts beyond their doing: Burkhard Bilger on ecclesiastical cheesemaking; Malcolm Gladwell on the corporate creation of a condiment; Judith Thurman on the making of artisanal tofu ("an ivory-colored attar of bean curd that arrives on a turquoise plate") by a group of Kyoto monks; John Seabrook on the hunt for exotic fruit; and Gabrielle Hamilton on the art of slaughtering a chicken.

One New York chef, Anthony Bourdain, takes us into the kitchen and, whether we want to know or not, gives us a glimpse of the reality of a cook's life: "the cuts and burns on hands and wrists, the ghoulish kitchen humor, the free food, the pilfered booze." He even warns us that "the good stuff comes in on Tuesday: the seafood is fresh, the supply of prepared food is new, and the chef, presumably, is relaxed after his day off." Another word to the wise: the most "unlovely piece of steak—tough, riddled with nerve and connective tissue, off the hip end of the loin, and maybe a little stinky from age" is put into the category of "save for well-done."

As one reads these pieces, it becomes possible to discern recurring character traits, especially the dictatorial nature of the celebrity chef. Joseph Wechsberg's subject, the legendary French cook Fernand Point, "has thrown out American millionaires and French ex-ministers when he didn't feel like serving them"; ditto Alex Prud'homme's Manhattan autocrat, the *Seinfeld*-era Soup Nazi. Over the years, the literature of food, particularly its manuals, has also captivated our writers: Jane Kramer describes how she cooks particular recipes in order to prime herself to write, and Anthony Lane surveys the classic cookbooks, which "should ideally tell you almost everything but not all that you need to know, leaving a tiny crack of uncertainty that can become your own personal abyss."

Some of the most exotic and extraordinary meals that have ever appeared in the magazine have occurred in its fiction, including the melancholy drinkers in John Cheever, the erudite nineteenth-century eater in Julian Barnes's "Bark" who "would discourse on the point of esculence of every foodstuff from capers to woodcock," and the character in Alice McDermott whose sexual voraciousness is matched only by her taste for ice cream: "Pleasure is pleasure. If you have an appetite for it, you'll find there's plenty. Plenty to satisfy you—lick the back of the spoon. Take another, and another. Plenty. Never enough."

What the abstemious editors who, in large part, created *The New Yorker* understood is that a magazine travels not only with its mind but also, like an army, on its stomach. Food is a subject of subsistence, manners, pleasure, and diversion. "I look upon it," Dr. Johnson says, "that he who does not mind his belly will hardly mind anything else."

The New Yorker benefits from its founders' tolerance, and our latest anthology has enjoyed the ministrations of a great many chefs, sous-chefs, and line cooks. The book's greatest debt is to Leo Carey, a young editor of rare taste (he would never order fish on Monday) and galley-kitchen industry. Working with Jon Michaud and Erin Overby, who run *The New Yorker*'s library, Leo, like one of Mitchell's oystermen, combed the sands for everything of value, or, at least, all that Random House would allow us to fit between covers. Henry Finder and Pamela Maffei McCarthy, as always, were invaluable counselors, as was Dorothy Wickenden, who in recent years has edited a series of special issues about food. At Random House, Daniel Menaker, Stephanie Higgs, and Evan Camfield have been first-rate partners. Thanks to Bob Mankoff and Sumner Jaretski for their work in selecting and reproducing the cartoons, and to Kate Julian, Caroline Mailhot, and Sarah Mangerson for their advice on art and production. As ever, I am grateful for the help of Brenda Phipps and Louisa Thomas. Above all, thanks to the writers and artists, past and present, who have always been the stuff of, and the reason for, *The New Yorker*.

"René Magritte vs. Betty Crocker"

DINING OUT

"Your French is correct, sir—that item is a sneaker filled with gasoline."

"Well, pay me! He ate it."

ALL YOU CAN HOLD FOR FIVE BUCKS

JOSEPH MITCHELL

The New York steak dinner, or "beefsteak," is a form of gluttony as stylized and regional as the riverbank fish fry, the hot-rock clambake, or the Texas barbecue. Some old chefs believe it had its origin sixty or seventy years ago, when butchers from the slaughterhouses on the East River would sneak choice loin cuts into the kitchens of nearby saloons, grill them over charcoal, and feast on them during their Saturday-night sprees. In any case, the institution was essentially masculine until 1920, when it was debased by the Eighteenth and Nineteenth Amendments to the Constitution of the United States. The Eighteenth Amendment brought about mixed drinking; a year and a half after it went into effect, the salutation "We Greet Our Better Halves" began to appear on the souvenir menus of beefsteaks thrown by bowling, fishing, and chowder clubs and lodges and labor unions. The big, exuberant beefsteaks thrown by Tammany and Republican district clubs always had been strictly stag, but not long after the Nineteenth Amendment gave women the suffrage, politicians decided it would be nice to invite females over twenty-one to clubhouse beefsteaks. "Many a poor woman didn't know what a beefsteak was until she got the right to vote," an old chef once said.

It did not take women long to corrupt the beefsteak. They forced the addition of such things as Manhattan cocktails, fruit cups, and fancy salads to the traditional menu of slices of ripened steak, double lamb chops, kidneys, and beer by the pitcher. They insisted on dance orchestras instead of drunken German bands. The life of the party at a beefsteak used to be the man who let out the most ecstatic grunts, drank the most beer, ate the most steak, and got the most grease on his ears, but women do not esteem a glutton, and at a contemporary beefsteak it is unusual for a man to do away with more than three pounds of meat and twenty-five glasses of beer. Until around 1920, beefsteak etiquette was rigid. Knives, forks, napkins, and tablecloths never had been permitted; a man was supposed to eat with his hands. When beefsteaks became bisexual, the etiquette changed. For generations men had worn their second-best suits because of the inevitability of grease spots; tuxedos and women appeared simultaneously. Most beefsteaks degenerated into polite banquets at which open-face sandwiches of grilled steak happened to be the principal dish. However, despite the frills introduced by women, two schools of traditional steak-dinner devotees still flourish. They may conveniently be called the East Side and West Side schools. They disagree over matters of menu and etiquette, and both claim that their beefsteaks are the more classical or old-fashioned.

The headquarters of the East Side school is the meat market of William Wertheimer & Son, at First Avenue and Nineteenth Street. It is situated in a tenement neighborhood, but that is misleading; scores of epicures regularly order steaks, chops, and capons from Wertheimer's. The moving spirit of the East Side school is Sidney Wertheimer, the "Son" of the firm. A dozen old, slow-moving, temperamental Germans, each of whom customarily carries his own collection of knives in an oilcloth kit, are the chefs. Mr. Wertheimer is not a chef. He selects, cuts, and sells the meat used at the majority of the old-fashioned beefsteaks thrown in East Side halls, like the Central Opera House, the Grand Street Boys' clubhouse, the Manhattan Odd Fellows' Hall, and Webster Hall. The caterers for these halls get an unusual amount of service when they order meat from Mr. Wertheimer. If the caterer wishes, Mr. Wertheimer will engage a couple of the old Germans to go to the hall and broil the meat. He will also engage a crew of experienced beefsteak waiters. He owns a collection of beefsteak-cooking utensils and does not mind lending it out.

The chefs and waiters telephone or stop in at Wertheimer's about once a week and are given assignments. Most of them work in breakfast and luncheon places in the financial district, taking on beefsteaks at night as a sideline. For engaging them, Mr. Wertheimer collects no fee; he just does it to be obliging. In addition, for no charge, he will go to the hall and supervise the kitchen. He is extremely proud of the meat he cuts and likes to make sure it is cooked properly. He succeeded old "Beefsteak Tom" McGowan as the East Side's most important beefsteak functionary. Mr. McGowan was a foreman in the Department of Water Supply who arranged beefsteaks as a hobby. He was an obscure person, but in 1924 his hearse was followed by more than a thousand sorrowful members of Tammany clubs.

Mr. Wertheimer had almost finished cutting the meat for a beefsteak the last time I went to see him. Approximately 350 men and women were expected that night, and he had carved steaks off 35 steer shells and had cut up 450 double-rib lamb chops. In his icebox, 450 lamb kidneys were soaking in a wooden tub. The steaks and chops were piled up in baskets, ready to be delivered to the uptown hall in which the beefsteak was to be thrown. (Technically, a beefsteak is never "given" or "held"; it is "thrown" or "run.") Mr. Wertheimer, a pink-cheeked, well-nourished man, looked proudly at the abundantly loaded baskets and said, "The foundation of a good beefsteak is an overflowing amount of meat and beer. The tickets usually cost five bucks, and the rule is 'All you can hold for five bucks.' If you're able to hold a little more when you start home, you haven't been to a beefsteak, you've been to a banquet that they called a beefsteak."

Classical beefsteak meat is carved off the shell, a section of the hindquarter of a steer; it is called "short loin without the fillet." To order a cut of it, a housewife would ask for a thick Delmonico. "You don't always get it at a beefsteak," Mr. Wertheimer said. "Sometimes they give you bull fillets. They're no good. Not enough juice in them, and they cook out black." While I watched, Mr. Wertheimer took a shell off a hook in his icebox and laid it on a big, maple block. It had been hung for eight weeks and was blanketed with blue mold. The mold was an inch thick. He cut off the mold. Then he boned the shell and cut it into six chunks. Then he sliced off all the fat. Little strips of lean ran through the discarded fat, and he deftly carved them out and made a mound of them on the block. "These trimmings, along with the tails of the steaks, will be ground up and served as appetizers," he said. "We'll use four hundred tonight. People call them hamburgers, and that's an insult. Sometimes they're laid on top of a slice of Bermuda onion and served on bread." When he finished with the shell, six huge steaks, boneless and fatless, averaging three inches thick and ten inches long, lay on the block. They made a beautiful still life. "After they've been broiled, the steaks are sliced up, and each steak makes about ten slices," he said. "The slices are what you get at a beefsteak." Mr. Wertheimer said the baskets of meat he had prepared would be used that night at a beefsteak in the Odd Fellows' Hall on East 106th Street; the Republican Club of the Twentieth A.D. was running it. He invited me to go along.

"How's your appetite?" he asked.

I said there was nothing wrong with it.

"I hope not," he said. "When you go to a beefsteak, you got to figure on eating until it comes out of your ears. Otherwise it would be bad manners."

That night I rode up to Odd Fellows' Hall with Mr. Wertheimer, and on the way I asked him to describe a pre-Prohibition stag beefsteak.

"Oh, they were amazing functions," he said. "The men wore butcher aprons and chef hats. They used the skirt of the apron to wipe the grease off their faces. Napkins were not allowed. The name of the organization that was running the beefsteak would be printed across the bib, and the men took the aprons home for souvenirs. We still wear aprons, but now they're rented from linen-supply houses. They have numbers on them, and you turn them in at the hat-check table when you get your hat and coat. Sometimes a man gets drunk and mislays his apron and there is a big squabble.

"In the old days they didn't even use tables and chairs. They sat on beer crates and ate off the tops of beer barrels. You'd be surprised how much fun that was. Somehow it made old men feel young again. And they'd drink beer out of cans, or growlers. Those beefsteaks were run in halls or the cellars or back rooms of big saloons. There was always sawdust on the floor. Sometimes they had one in a bowling alley. They would cover the alleys with tarpaulin and set the boxes and barrels in the aisles. The men ate with their fingers. They never served potatoes in those days. Too filling. They take up room that rightfully belongs to meat and beer. A lot of those beefsteaks were testimonials. A politician would get elected to something and his friends would throw him a beefsteak. Cops ran a lot of them, too. Like when a cop became captain or inspector, he got a beefsteak. I understand Commissioner Valentine is kind of opposed to testimonials. Anyway, they don't have many cop beefsteaks these days. Theatrical people were always fond of beefsteaks. Sophie Tucker got a big one at Mecca Temple in 1934, and Bill Robinson got one last year at the Grand Street Boys' clubhouse. But the political clubs always gave the finest. When Tammany Hall got a setback, beefsteaks also got a setback. For example, the Anawanda Club, over in my neighborhood, used to give a famous beefsteak every Thanksgiving Eve. Last year they skipped it.

"At the old beefsteaks they almost always had storytellers, men who would entertain with stories in Irish and German dialect. And when the people got tired of eating and drinking, they would harmonize. You could hear them harmonizing blocks away. They would harmonize 'My Wild Irish Rose' until they got their appetite back. It was the custom to hold beefsteaks on Saturday nights or the eve of holidays, so the men would have time to recover before going to work. They used to give some fine ones in Coney Island restaurants. Webster Hall has always been a good place. Local 638 of the Steamfitters holds its beefsteaks there. They're good ones. A lot of private beefsteaks are thrown in homes. A man will invite some friends to his cellar and cook the steaks himself. I have a number of good amateur beefsteak chefs among my customers. Once, during the racing season, a big bookmaker telephoned us he wanted to throw a beefsteak, so we sent a chef and all the makings to Saratoga. The chef had a wonderful time. They made a hero out of him."

When we reached the hall, we went directly to the kitchen. Two of Mr. Wertheimer's chefs were working at a row of tremendous gas ranges. One had a pipe in his mouth; the other was smoking a cigar. There was a pitcher of beer on a nearby table and at intervals the chefs would back away from the ranges and have some beer. They were cooking the four hundred high-class hamburgers. The air was heavy with the fragrance of the meat. The steaks, chops, and kidneys were racked up, ready for the broilers. A strip of bacon had been pinned to each kidney with a toothpick. I asked a chef how many minutes the steaks were kept on the fire. "It's all according," he said. "Twelve on one side, ten on the other is about the average. Before they go in, we roll them in salt which has been mixed with pepper. The salt creates a crust that holds the juice in." In a corner, waiters were stacking up cardboard platters on each of which a dozen half-slices of trimmed bread had been placed. "This is day-old bread," one of them said. "The steak slices are laid on it just before we take them out to the tables. Day-old bread is neutral. When you lay steak on toast, you taste the toast as much as the steak."

In a little while I went out to the ballroom. The Republicans were arriving. Most of them were substantial, middle-aged people. They all seemed to know each other. At the hat-check booth, everybody, men and women, put on cloth butcher's aprons and paper chef's hats. This made them look a lot like members of the Ku Klux Klan. The hats had mottoes on them, such as IT'S HELL WHEN YOUR WIFE IS A WIDOW and PROHIBITION WAS GOOD FOR SOME. OTHERS IT PUT ON THE BUM. Before sitting down, most couples went from table to table, shaking hands and gossiping. After shaking hands, they would say, "Let's see what it says on your hat." After they read the mottoes on each other's hats, they would laugh heartily. On each table there were plates of celery and radishes, beer glasses, salt shakers, and some balloons and noisemakers. Later, a spavined old waiter told me that liquor companies send balloons and noisemakers to many beefsteaks as an advertisement. "In the old days they didn't need noisemakers," he said contemptuously. "If a man wanted some noise, he would just open his trap and howl."

While couples were still moving from table to table, a banquet photographer got up on the bandstand and asked everybody to keep still. I went over and watched him work. When he was through we talked for a while, and he said, "In an hour or so I'll bring back a sample photograph and take orders. At a beefsteak I usually take the picture at the start of the party. If I took it later on, when they get full of beer, the picture would show a lot of people with goggle eyes and their mouths gapped open."

As the photographer was lugging his equipment out, waiters streamed into the ballroom with pitchers of beer. When they caught sight of the sloshing beer, the people took seats. I joined Mr. Wertheimer, who was standing at the kitchen door surveying the scene. As soon as there was a pitcher of beer in the middle of every table, the waiters brought in platters of hamburgers. A moment later, a stout, frowning woman walked up to Mr. Wertheimer and said, "Say, listen. Who the hell ever heard of hamburgers at a beefsteak?" Mr. Wertheimer smiled. "Just be patient, lady," he said. "In a minute you'll get all the steak you can hold." "Okay," she said, "but what about the ketchup? There's no ketchup at our table." Mr. Wertheimer said he would tell a waiter to get some. When she left, he said, "Ketchup! I bet she'd put ketchup on chocolate cake." After they had finished with their hamburgers some of the diners began inflating and exploding balloons.

I heard one of the chefs back in the kitchen yell out, "Steaks ready to go!" and I went inside. One chef was slicing the big steaks with a knife that resembled a cavalry sabre and the other was dipping the slices into a pan of rich, hot sauce. "That's the best beefsteak sauce in the world," Mr. Wertheimer said. "It's melted butter, juice and drippings from the steak, and a little Worcestershire." The waiters lined up beside the slicing table. Each waiter had a couple of the cardboard platters on which bread had been arranged. As he went by the table, he held out the platters and the chef dropped a slice of the rare, dripping steak on each piece of bread. Then the waiter hurried off.

I went to the kitchen door and looked out. A waiter would go to a table and lay a loaded platter in the middle of it. Hands would reach out and the platter would be emptied. A few minutes later another platter would arrive and eager, greasy hands would reach out again. At beefsteaks, waiters are required to keep on bringing platters until every gullet is satisfied; on some beefsteak menus there is a notice: "2nd, 3rd, 4th, etc., portions permitted and invited." Every three trips or so the waiter would bring a pitcher of beer. And every time they finished a platter, the people would rub their hands on their aprons. Sometimes a man would pour a little beer in one palm and rub his hands together briskly. At a table near the kitchen door I heard a woman say to another, "Here, don't be bashful. Have a steak." "I just et six," her friend replied. The first woman said, "Wasn't you hungry? Why, you eat like a bird." Then they threw their heads back and laughed. It was pleasant to watch the happy, unrestrained beefsteak-eaters. While the platters kept coming they did little talking except to urge each other to eat more.

"Geez," said a man. "These steaks are like peanuts. Eat one, and you can't stop. Have another." Presently the waiters began to tote out platters of thick lamb chops, too. (On souvenir menus, these lamb chops are called "canapé of elephant's wrist.")

Then a man stepped up to the microphone and introduced a number of politicians. Each time he said "I'm about to introduce a man that is known and loved by each and every one of you," a beaming politician would stand and bow and the constituents would bang the tables with their noisemakers. One of the politicians was Kenneth Simpson, the Republican leader of New York County. While bowing right, left, and center, he took bites out of a chop. There were no speeches. A politician would have to be extraordinarily courageous to make a speech at a beefsteak. When all the Republican statesmen of the Twentieth A.D. had been introduced, a band went into action and two singers stepped out on the dance floor and began singing numbers from *Show Boat*. By the time they got to "Ol' Man River," the 450 double lamb chops were gone and the waiters were bringing out the kidneys. "I'm so full I'm about to pop," a man said. "Push those kidneys a little nearer, if you don't mind." Here and there a couple got up and went out on the dance floor. The lights were dimmed. Some of the couples danced the Lambeth Walk. Done by aproned, middle-aged people, ponderous with beefsteak and beer, the Lambeth Walk is a rather frightening spectacle. The waiters continued to bring out kidneys and steak to many tables. There was no dessert and no coffee. Such things are not orthodox. "Black coffee is sometimes served to straighten people out," Mr. Wertheimer said, "but I don't believe in it."

When the Republicans began dancing in earnest, the activity in the kitchen slackened, and some of the waiters gathered around the slicing table and commenced eating. While they ate, they talked shop. "You know," said one, "a fat woman don't eat so much. It's those little skinny things; you wonder where they put it." Another said, "It's the Cat'lics who can eat. I was to a beefsteak in Brooklyn last Thursday night. All good Cat'lics. So it got to be eleven-fifty, and they stopped the clock. Cat'lics can't eat meat on Friday." The two weary chefs sat down together at the other side of the room from the waiters and had a breathing spell. They had not finished a glass of beer apiece, however, before a waiter hurried in and said, "My table wants some more steak," and the chefs had to get up and put their weight on their feet again. Just before

I left, at midnight, I took a last look at the ballroom. The dance floor was packed and clouds of cigar smoke floated above the paper hats of the dancers, but at nine tables people were still stowing away meat and beer. On the stairs to the balcony, five men were harmonizing. Their faces were shiny with grease. One held a pitcher of beer in his hands and occasionally he would drink from it, spilling as much as he drank. The song was, of course, "Sweet Adeline."

The West Side school of beefsteak devotees frequents the Terminal Hotel, a for-gentlemen-only establishment at Eleventh Avenue and Twenty-third Street. Its chef is Bob Ellis, an aged, truculent Negro, whose opinion of all other beefsteak chefs is low. Of them he says, "What they call a beefsteak ain't no beefsteak; it's just a goddam mess." Mr. Ellis is also a talented clambake and green-turtle chef and used to make trips as far west as Chicago to supervise one meal. His most unusual accomplishment, however, is the ability to speak Japanese. He once worked on freighters that went to the Orient, and he sometimes reminds people who hang out around the belly-shaped Terminal bar that he has a wonderful command of the Japanese language. When someone is skeptical and says, "Well, let's hear some," he always says haughtily, "What in hell would be the use of talking Jap to you? You wouldn't comprehend a word I was saying."

Among the groups of rough-and-ready gourmands for whom Mr. Ellis is official chef are the I.D.K. ("I Don't Know") Bowling Club, a hoary outfit from Chelsea, and the Old Hoboken Turtle Club. This club was founded in 1796, and Alexander Hamilton and Aaron Burr were charter members; now it is an exclusive association of West Side and Jersey butchers, brewers, saloonkeepers, boss stevedores, and businessmen. Most of the members are elderly. Mr. Ellis has cooked for them since 1879. In 1929 they gave him a badge with a green turtle and a diamond on it and made him a Brother Turtle. The Turtles and the I.D.K.'s and many similar West Side organizations always hold their beefsteaks in the Terminal cellar, which is called the Hollings Beefsteak Keller after John Hollings, a former owner of the hotel, who sold out in disgust and moved to Weehawken when Prohibition was voted in. He used to store his coal in the cellar. Mr. Ellis refuses to call it a *Keller;* he calls it "my dungeon."

"In the old days all steak cellars were called dungeons," he told me. "To me they're still dungeons."

The dungeon has a steel door on which is printed the initials O.I.C. U.R.M.T. That is a good sample of beefsteak humor. Also on the door is a sign: WHEN YOU ENTER THIS KELLER YOU FIND A GOOD FELLER. The dungeon has a cement floor, over which sawdust has been scattered. The ceiling is low. On the trellised walls are yellowed beefsteak photographs ranging from an 1898 view of the M. E. Blankmeyer Clam Bake Club to a picture of a beefsteak thrown in 1932 by the New York Post Office Holy Name Society. Over the light switch is a warning: HANDS OFF THE THIRD RAIL. In one corner is a piano and a platform for a German band. The dungeon will hold 125 persons. "When a hundred and twenty-five big, heavy men get full of beer, it does seem a little crowded in here," Mr. Ellis said. Beer crates and barrels were once used, but now people sit on slat-backed chairs and eat off small, individual tables. Down a subterranean hall from the dungeon is the ancient brick oven, over which Mr. Ellis presides with great dignity.

"I'm not one of these hit-or-miss beefsteak chefs," he said. "I grill my steaks on hickory embers. The efflorescence of seasoned hardwood is in the steak when you eat it. My beefsteaks are genuine old-fashioned. I'll give you the official lineup. First we lay out celery, radishes, olives, and scallions. Then we lay out the crabmeat cocktails. Some people say that's not old-fashioned. I'm eighty-three years old and I ought to know what's old-fashioned. Then we lay out some skewered kidney shells. Lamb or pig—what's the difference?

"Then comes the resistance—cuts of seasoned loin of beef on hot toast with butter gravy. Sure, I use toast. None of this day-old-bread stuff for me. I know what I'm doing. Then we lay out some baked Idahoes. I let them have paper forks for the crabmeat and the Idahoes; everything else should be attended to with fingers. A man who don't like to eat with his fingers hasn't got any business at a beefsteak. Then we lay out the broiled duplex lamb chops. All during the beefsteak we are laying out pitchers of refreshment. By that I mean beer."

Mr. Ellis lives in the Bronx. Whenever Herman Von Twistern, the proprietor of the Terminal, books a beefsteak, he gets Mr. Ellis on the telephone and gives him the date. Usually he also telephones Charles

V. Havican, a portly ex–vaudeville actor, who calls himself "the Senator from Hoboken." He took the title during Prohibition, when everything connected with Hoboken was considered funny. Mr. Havican is a celebrated beefsteak entertainer. Most often he sits down with the guests and impersonates a windy, drunken senator. He also tells dialect stories and gives recitations on such topics as "The High Cost of Meat Is What's the Matter with the World, My Friends" and "The Traffic Problem Is Bad."

"If I am not previously known to the people at a beefsteak, I sometimes impersonate a dumb waiter," Mr. Havican told me, listing his accomplishments. "I spill beer on people, bump into them, step on them, and hit them with my elbows. All the time I look dumb. It is a very funny act to a person with a keen sense of humor. Once a cranky old guy could not understand the humor of it. He wouldn't let me explain. He just kicked me, and I had to spend three weeks in the hospital."

1939

"Fusilli, you crazy bastard! How are you?"

THE FINEST BUTTER AND
LOTS OF TIME

JOSEPH WECHSBERG

When I went to France this summer, after an absence of more than a year, I was pleased to find that, for the first time since the end of the war, my Parisian friends had stopped griping about the black market and rationing and were again discussing, passionately and at great length, the heady mysteries of *la grande cuisine*, which, next to women, has always been their favorite topic of conversation in times of content. Once more, with the air of brokers divulging something hot in the market, they were confiding to each other the addresses of good restaurants.

The finest restaurant in France, and perhaps anywhere, it was agreed by my always well-informed friends, is not in Paris. If I wanted to have the epicurean experience of my life, they assured me, I would have to go to Vienne, a town of twenty-three thousand inhabitants in the Department of Isère, seventeen miles south of Lyon, at the confluence of the Rhône and Gère rivers. There I would find the Restaurant de la Pyramide and its proprietor, the great, the formidable, the one and only M. Point.

"Ah, Fernand Point!" said one of my French friends with a deep sigh. "The greatest epicures in France and Navarre sing his praises. His *gratin d'écrevisses* reaches perfection. The yearbook of the Club des Sans-Club awards him the mark of Excellent—its highest. I once had a *volaille en vessie* there that . . ."

"Point's hors d'oeuvres alone are worth a trip from New York," someone else said. "He calls them hors d'oeuvres but they are a meal in themselves—and what a meal! There is a pâté. . . ."

"Last year at Point's I had the best lunch I've had since Escoffier left the Ritz," a third gourmet friend told me. This friend is a man of seventy-four years and 320 pounds, and he has spent most of the former in increasing the latter with good food. "In short, you *must* go to Point's restaurant."

I objected mildly that I wasn't much interested in the show places of *la grande cuisine.* Since the disappearance of the black market, France's restaurants have returned to their prewar standard, which is, by and large, the best in the world. I could see no reason, I said, for patronizing fancy establishments when there is such an astonishing number of small restaurants all over the country where one can get a delicious omelet, a succulent veal stew, a fine cheese, and a bottle of honest *vin du pays* for less than six hundred francs, or something under two dollars.

"Ah, but Point's restaurant is not a show place," my old friend said. "It is a temple for gastronomes who know that *la grande cuisine* must be well orchestrated, that it must be surrounded by careful details, ranging from the temperature of the dining room to that of the wines, from the thinness of the pastry shells to that of the glasses, from the color of the fruits to that of—"

"All right," I said. "I'll go."

"But it's not a question of whether or not you will *go*," my friend said. "The question is will M. Point let you eat in his place? He has thrown out American millionaires and French ex-ministers when he didn't feel like serving them. Only last week, a friend of mine called M. Point long distance and asked him to reserve a table for the next day. That, of course, was a mistake, because M. Point usually insists on being notified at least three days beforehand. My friend gave his name—a *very* important name in French politics, I assure you. Ha! M. Point pretended to be totally unimpressed and kept saying, 'Would you mind repeating the name?' Before long, my friend had lost his celebrated poise and could only mumble that he was being recommended by M. Léon Blum. And what do you think M. Point said to that? He said, 'And who is M. Blum, if I may ask?' "

My friend chuckled. "But I think I can help you out with an introduction. I have a British friend, M. Piperno, who happened to be among the Allied troops that liberated Vienne, and I'll have him give you a letter that will open all doors to you. Any friend of M. Piperno's is treated royally at Point's. But be sure to call M. Point well in advance to reserve your table. And for heaven's sake, don't think of ordering your meal! You don't order at Point's. *He* tells *you* what to eat."

A few days later, I received a note from my friend enclosing an amiable letter of introduction from a Mr. T. H. Piperno, and decided to put in a person-to-person call to M. Point without delay to reserve a table

for lunch some day the following week. Finally, after some misunder-
standings involving Point's name, my name, and the name of a girl,
Denise Something, who had a lovely way of yawning and seemed to be
the long-distance operator in Vienne, I got hold of a man with a high,
querulous voice who said yes, he was Point, and there were no tables
available for the next week—or the next two weeks, for that matter. I
quickly said that I was a friend of Mr. Piperno's. M. Point's voice
abruptly dropped several notes as he said "Oh!" Then he precipitately
told me that I might come any day I liked, absolutely, it would be a
pleasure, and how about tomorrow? And in whose name should the
table be reserved? I began to spell out my name, but M. Point must
have got restless, because he said not to bother with the name—there
would be a table. He hung up forthwith, without a goodbye.

My friends in Paris had urged me to prepare myself for my monumental lunch by eating only extremely light food, and very little of it, during the preceding twenty-four hours, and I was hungry and cross when
my overnight train pulled into Vienne early the following morning. A
gentle rain was misting down upon the green trees of the town's miniature boulevards and blurring the outlines of the narrow streets bordered
by old houses and small, dark shops. I set out for the nearby Grand
Hôtel du Nord, where, again on the advice of my friends, I had engaged
a room. "You'd better plan to spend the night," they had said. "No use
trying to rush away. You have to relax after a meal at Point's." There
were only a few people on the street—pale, stockingless girls who were
carrying small lunch boxes, and shabbily dressed men who looked as
though they surely had never lunched or dined at Point's.

The Grand Hôtel du Nord was, despite its name, an unassuming
establishment that did not indulge in such extravagances as elevators, a
bathroom on every floor, and warm water after nine in the morning, but
my room was clean and the comforter on my bed was filled with eider-
down. I had a pleasant view of two sides of a square—on one flank the
town museum, on the other the Café du Commerce et des Voyageurs
and its clients, all of them, I was sure, busy in lively discussions of politics, soccer, and the high cost of living. I washed up, read a newspaper
I had bought at the station (politics, soccer, and the high cost of living),
and finished my interrupted sleep. When I awoke, it was getting on

toward twelve o'clock, and nearly time for me to present myself at the Restaurant de la Pyramide. As I stepped into the street, I was stopped by a young man wearing a raincoat and a beret and carrying a pipe. He smiled at me like a Fuller Brush man, asked my pardon for his presumption, and informed me that he was Jean Lecutiez, an archeologist who had been sent to Vienne by the Ministry of National Education to dig up the ruins of the houses, temples, aqueducts, baths, and assorted monuments that the Romans left there two thousand years ago.

"I happened to be visiting my friend the desk clerk of your hotel as you came in, and I saw on the registration blotter that you were a writer," M. Lecutiez said. "Right away, I told myself that I would make it my business to take you around." I tried to protest, but he said, "Oh, don't worry—no bother at all. My two colleagues will carry on with the work. There are three of us archeologists here—a very old man, *un homme mûr* [a mature man], and myself." M. Lecutiez prodded me energetically with the stem of his pipe. "You must realize, Monsieur, that Vienne, the old Vienna Allobrogum, was the capital of the Allobroges in the first century B.C. Julius Caesar established a colony here. Later, the Romans went up north and founded Lugdunum, which eventually became Lyon. Naturally, the people in Lyon don't like to hear this, but it's true—"

"I'm sorry," I said. "That's wonderfully interesting, but I have a luncheon engagement at . . ."

M. Lecutiez ignored this interruption. "Vienne, like Rome, is built around seven hills," he went on as he grasped my arm and relentlessly walked me away. "They are Levau, Mont Salomon, Mont Arnaud, Mont Pipet, Sainte-Blandine, Coupe Jarret, and Mont Saint-Just. I'll take you up on every one of them. Now, this afternoon we're going to start with—"

"It's almost lunchtime," I said. "How about an aperitif? Then I'll really have to run for my appointment."

"Thank you, I never drink," he said. "Would you like to see the pyramid?"

"Ah," I said. "That's exactly where I'm going. I'm lunching at Point's."

"The restaurant, *je m'en fiche*," said M. Lecutiez. "I mean the real pyramid, which for hundreds of years was commonly, and erroneously, thought to be the grave of Pontius Pilate. There is nothing like it anywhere. Come, it's no distance at all." As we crossed the street, a wild bicyclist almost ran us down, but M. Lecutiez seemed not to notice. "It was the great French architect Delorme who first stated that the pyramid dates from the fourth century and was the domed center of the spina, or longitudinal center wall, of a Roman circus, where chariot races were held. Now we turn here, and *voilà!*"

There before us, an island in the middle of the street, was the pyramid, a monument, perhaps fifty feet high, that looks like a giant metronome. Its square base is pierced by four arches. The thoroughfare it stands in is one of those drab, deserted side streets that one sees in so many small French towns.

"Excavations undertaken in 1854 by Constant Dufeu proved Delorme completely right," M. Lecutiez went on, hardly pausing for breath. "We are indeed standing in the middle of what was once a vast Roman circus. It was a big arena, fifteen hundred feet long and . . ."

On the other side of the street, set in a ten-foot wall, was a gate, and beside it a black marble plate inscribed in red letters FERNAND POINT, RESTAURATEUR.

". . . and the chariots must have come from over there," M. Lecutiez was saying, pointing up the street. "They would pass right where we're standing, and then—"

"It's been a tremendously instructive talk," I broke in, "and I am most grateful to you, but I must go." M. Lecutiez looked at me with a hurt expression, but I walked firmly across the street toward the gate in the wall. On the left, the wall connected with a decrepit three-story building that looked as if it should have been condemned long before the Renaissance; on the right it joined a house that was considerably newer but seemed rather run-down and in need of a coat of paint. The rain had stopped and the sun had come out, but even under these favorable conditions the exterior of M. Point's temple for gastronomes presented an unprepossessing appearance. I walked through the gate and found myself suddenly, without any transition, in another world. I was in a garden with clean gravel paths, green lawns, beds of flowers, and a terrace shaded by old maples and chestnuts and covered with white tables and wicker chairs still wet from the rain. The courtyard walls of the building that I had thought should have been condemned were completely cloaked with ivy, which blended admirably with the beautifully landscaped grounds. To my right was a two-story house—the one that

from the front I had thought was run-down. Its garden side was immaculate. The frames of its wide windows were freshly painted, and the
whole building looked as clean and spruce as a Dutch sugar house. I
walked up three steps, scuffed my shoes on a mat, opened the big door,
and entered the hall of what seemed to be a handsome country residence. On the wall were paintings and an old print of the pyramid,
bearing the caption UN MONUMENT ANTIQUE, VULGAIREMENT APPELÉ
LE TOMBEAU DE PILATE.

A man in a white jacket approached from the rear of the house,
greeted me cheerfully, and took my raincoat and hung it on a hanger in
the hall, as is the custom in French homes. I said I wanted to see
M. Point, and was ushered into a small, pleasantly furnished salon. The
walls were hung with paintings and mirrors, a gold pendulum clock
stood on a buffet, and a large glass-topped table sat in the middle of the
room. On the table were champagne glasses and a half-empty magnum
of champagne, and behind it was standing a huge man. He must have
been six feet three and weighed three hundred pounds. He had a
longish, sad face, a vast double chin, a high forehead, dark hair, and
melancholy eyes. I couldn't help thinking that one of M. Lecutiez's
sybaritic Roman emperors had come to life. He wore a comfortably
large suit, and a big bow tie of black silk ornamented with a flowery
design, like those the eccentric citizens of Montparnasse and flamboyant Italian tenors wore in the old days.

I introduced myself and we shook hands. I gave him Mr. Piperno's
letter. M. Point read it casually and shook hands with me again. "Sit
down!" he commanded with a magnificent gesture. "For the next few
hours, this house will be your home. I'm delighted you came early.
Gives us a chance to talk and drink champagne. Quiet, Véronique!" On
a chair beside him, a precisely clipped brown poodle was making hos-
tile noises. "Véronique belongs to the family," he said. "We also have a
nine-year-old daughter, Marie-Josette. *Enfin!*" He filled two of the
champagne glasses and said, "*À votre santé.*"

We drank. "I like to start off my day with a glass of champagne,"
M. Point said. "I like to wind it up with champagne, too. To be frank, I
also like a glass or two in between. It may not be the universal medicine
for every disease, as my friends the champagne people in Reims and
Épernay so often tell me, but it does you less harm than any other liquid. Pierre—our sommelier—and Mme. Point and I go to the cham-

pagne district every year to buy. And, of course, to Burgundy, too. Last week, we visited a great friend, the Marquise de la Tourette, the proprietor of one of the great Hermitage vineyards." M. Point filled the glasses again. "*Ah, quelle grande dame!* She won't sell her wines in the commercial market. You have to be her friend, and you must literally force her into selling the stuff. She is over eighty, and every day she walks from her château to the church and back. Permit me to drink the health of the Marquise de la Tourette!"

While we were solemnly drinking the health of the Marquise, a man wearing a beret and the light-blue overalls and apron that are the uniform of France's winegrowers and sommeliers came in. He had a shriveled face that looked as though it had been chiseled out of a piece of seasoned wood.

"Ah, Pierre," said M. Point. "Monsieur, this is Pierre Chauvon, our sommelier and a great connoisseur of that ever-new miracle, wine."

The old man scratched his head under his beret with his left hand as he gave me his right. *"Allons, allons, Chef!"* he said, embarrassed but quite pleased. "You know a lot about wines yourself, and Mme. Point knows even more. Ah, I assure you, Monsieur," he said to me, "Madame is *épatante.* She is *très, très forte.* When we go to the vineyards and taste the wines, the winegrowers always look at her first. She's better than I am, and I certainly know my business." He smiled, revealing a few side teeth and almost none in the front. "Unfortunately, Madame always gets hungry around noon, and once you've eaten, your taste and judgment aren't reliable anymore. I don't eat when we're out. Mustn't make a mistake, eh, *Chef*?"

"Everybody calls me '*Chef*' here," M. Point explained to me. "Never '*Patron.*' They just won't forget that I used to be my own chef in the kitchen. Now I merely supervise things there, and my wife takes care of the clients in the dining room. Well, Pierre, why don't we show our friend the cellar? Nothing to be ashamed of, is it?"

M. Point led the way out into the hall, around a few corners, and down a stairway into a big, brightly lighted wine cellar with earthen walls. It was cool, and the dirt floor was as clean as much sweeping could make it. All along the walls were shelves on which bottles were stacked horizontally. Tacked to the lower-left-hand corner of each shelf was a small label giving the place of origin and the vintage of the wine. In the center of the room was a table covered with baskets of fresh fruit—enormous pears, Calville apples, lush peaches, and aromatic *fraises de bois*. A roster of the wines in the cellar hung on one wall. It listed 219 names, in four columns. Glancing at random down the second column, I saw Richebourg '42, Romanée-Conti '35, Corton Charlemagne '38, Les Grands Echézeaux '42, Hermitage '98, Romanée-Conti '43, La Tache '43, Hermitage la Cour Blanche '06, Clos de Vougeot '37, Vosne-Romanée '93, Corton Charlemagne '42, La Tache '37, Romanée St. Vivant '40, Pouilly '40, Montrachet '29, Richebourg '29, Chambolle Musigny '21, Hermitage Blanc '70, Marc de Bourgogne '29, and Vire Chapitre '26.

"What a mess!" said M. Point, waving at the chart. "We've always mixed them up—don't know why. Anyway, it's not a bad selection. We have all the great vintage years of Château d'Yquem, back to 1908, and a lot of the fine years of Château Margaux and Château Lafite-Rothschild. You can see we're crowded in here. I had to rent a place down the street for Pierre to keep his champagnes in."

He pointed to a section of the shelves at my right. "How do you like our cognacs?" They were impressive—cobweb-covered bottles of eighty-year-old Otard and *hors-d'âge* Camus, along with batteries of gin, Scotch, aperitifs, and liqueurs. M. Point slapped his stomach. "Before the war, I refused to serve cocktails. Now they bring their own bottles if I don't serve them. My God, after a couple of those concoctions your palate can't distinguish an 1899 Château Mouton-Rothschild from 1949 fountain-pen ink! What's that you have, Pierre?"

The sommelier was examining a small bottle of the sort in which winegrowers send samples to merchants and restaurateurs. "The new Moulin-à-Vent," he said.

"We buy many wines by the barrel—*la pièce*," M. Point said, "and Pierre 'works' the wine, draining it from one barrel into another three times a year. The dregs remain in the old barrel. Pierre knows what he's doing. He wouldn't make a *soutirage*—as the process is called—while a south wind is blowing. The wind must be from the north. Right, Pierre?"

"*Bien sûr, Chef.* I make three *soutirages* a year—in January, March, and September. Each barrel of Burgundy contains 225 liters, and each barrel of Beaujolais 218 liters. When the wine is ready, I bottle it myself in my workroom. I've always done it. Had my own *bistro* in Lyon and would go to Burgundy three times a year to buy wines. Those were nice times, before my wife—" He stopped and scratched his chin. "Ah, why warm up those old stories? I'm happy here now. I'm sixty-seven, and I hope to stay here until I die."

"*Allons, allons,* Pierre!" M. Point cried, and his high-pitched voice almost cracked. "What kind of talk is that? Go on, tell me how the wine is."

Pierre uncorked the sample bottle and took a big mouthful of the wine. He let it roll over and under his tongue, closed his eyes, and made a gargling sound. Then he spat on the floor. "It'll be all right in three years," he said with authority.

"Good!" M. Point took my arm. "Let's go up to the kitchen and give some thought to your lunch."

The kitchen was large and cheery, with a white-tiled floor and walls. Copper pots hung from hooks on the ceiling, and silver trays were stacked on broad white tables. The ranges and slicing machines were so highly polished that they looked brand-new. M. Point told me that coal was used to cook everything except pastry, which was baked in an electric oven. At the rear of the kitchen were four refrigerators. Through their glass doors I could see hors d'oeuvres and butter in the first, rows of dressed chickens in the second, fillets of beef and veal tenderloins in the third, and potatoes, bunches of white asparagus, and other vegetables in the fourth. The room was a busy place. Cooks and apprentices were washing vegetables, cutting meat, mixing sauces, and doing various other chores, but there was a total absence of haste or nervousness.

A plump and elegant gray-mustached man in a spotless chef's outfit joined us and was introduced to me as M. Paul Mercier, the *chef de cuisine.* "Do you like chicken, Monsieur?" he asked me. He picked one up from a nearby table. "All of ours come from the region of Bresse, the best in France for poultry. Each is tagged with a silver label and a serial number. We store them in the refrigerator for four or five days after getting them, but we don't freeze them. They do a lot of freezing in America, don't they?"

"*Malheureux, malheureux!*" M. Point exclaimed, clasping his hands in deep unhappiness. "Of course they do a lot of freezing. It's such a hot country they have to, I am told. But you can't expect to get a good piece of chicken from a freezer. Here we keep everything just above the freezing point." As he talked, his eyes roved over the kitchen, taking note of every bit of activity. "The main thing about cooking is to see to it that only the very best ingredients are used, and used as they should be. When you are interested in *la grande cuisine,* you can't think of money, or you are licked from the start. And you have to go out yourself and get the ingredients. At six o'clock this morning, M. Mercier himself went to Lyon to buy the very freshest strawberries and asparagus he could find in the markets. And butter, naturally. How can anybody expect to cook well without using the finest butter? *Du beurre, du beurre, du beurre,* I keep telling my men—that's the secret of good cooking. And time, lots of time."

I noticed that the bustle in the kitchen had subsided and that most of the undercooks were listening to M. Point with hushed attention. M. Point solemnly raised his right hand and proclaimed, "*La grande cuisine* doesn't wait for the client. It is the client who must wait for *la grande cuisine.*" He stopped and looked around the kitchen. "*Allons, mes enfants!*" he said, clapping his hands. "Let us go back to work." Ushering me through a doorway, he took me into a small courtyard. "I want to show you our aquarium," he said. The aquarium consisted of two square tanks. In one I saw a couple of dozen brook trout swimming around, and in the other a number of crayfish. The water in each tank was kept fresh by a flowing faucet. M. Mercier joined us. "Are we going to serve Monsieur a trout?" he asked. "*Au bleu,* perhaps?"

"I haven't decided yet," M. Point said. He turned to me. "So often our clients ask for what they call 'difficult' things, with long and fancy names. People don't know that the most difficult and also the best dishes are the simple ones. What did you cook for your family on your last day off, Paul?"

"A *choucroute,*" M. Mercier said.

"There you are. Here is a great chef, who can cook a chicken in champagne with truffles the like of which has never before been tasted, and what does he cook for himself at home? A *choucroute*—cabbage, delicious soft ham, Alsatian sausage, and very young potatoes—and what could be better?" He swallowed, and I found myself swallowing, too. My stomach was gnawing. "But it takes experience. What looks easier to make than a *sauce béarnaise*? Butter, egg yolks, chopped shallots—nothing to it, is there? But years of practice are needed before you can do it right. Forget to watch it for a single instant and it's gone, finished, lost. Everybody thinks he can fry eggs, and I suppose anybody can, but to fry them so they are soft and mellow throughout, not burned on the bottom and raw on top—*that* is art, my friend. Isn't that right, Paul?"

"Absolutely," said M. Mercier.

"Absolutely. Now, Monsieur, let us return to the salon and think seriously about your lunch."

In the hall, we encountered a slim, middle-aged, efficient-looking woman in a gray tailored suit who was carrying an order pad under her arm. M. Point introduced her to me as his wife, Marie-Louise. She smiled at me briefly and then whispered in M. Point's ear. "Madame *who?*" he said. "No, no. Tell her we have no table. I don't want her. She smokes before dessert. The last time she was here, she even smoked after the hors d'oeuvres." He escorted me into his salon. The magnum was empty, and he called loudly for another. It was quickly brought in an ice bucket by a frightened young waiter. M. Point watched the youth sternly as he worked out the cork and stopped the flow of foam by pressing a silver spoon over the mouth of the bottle. "A little trick," M. Point said. "Metal will stop the flow. Don't pour yet, Marcel. Always leave the bottle open in the ice bucket for a few minutes." A drop of champagne had spilled on the tabletop, and the waiter, before leaving, carefully wiped it away with his napkin. M. Point nodded in approval. "So many otherwise good restaurants in France don't teach their personnel the importance of the attention to detail that makes for flawless service," he said. I saw Mme. Point greeting four guests, and a waiter or two scurrying by in the hall. In a minute, a boy in a white apron put his head in the door and said that a M. Godet was calling from Lyon about a reservation, and would M. Point— For some reason, this seemed to infuriate M. Point. He shooed the boy away, went to the door, and announced down the hall in a loud voice that he was about to have a glass of champagne and that he would be grateful if the world would leave him in peace for a few minutes. Then he shut the door, came back, and sat down.

"Too many people," he said. "Vienne is halfway between Paris and the Riviera, and everybody wants to stop over to break the monotony of the trip. Not many Vienne people come here; most of my clients are from the outside world. It's been that way ever since I opened the restaurant, twenty-six years ago, when I was twenty-six years old." He poured us each a glass of champagne and looked thoughtfully into his.

"I was born near here, and I always wanted to cook. My father was a chef. A very good chef. He made me start from the beginning—washing dishes, waiting on tables, peeling potatoes. It's quite important to peel them right, believe me. Then I learned to cook vegetables and make soups and things like that, and after that I went to Paris. Remember Foyot's? Ah, they had a great *saucier!* He taught me a lot. And for a long time I worked at the Hôtel Bristol. I came back home in 1923 and bought this place with my savings. It was just a shack and a few trees then. In time, Father and I added the second floor and a new kitchen, the wine cellar, and the terrace. We had the garden landscaped and bought the adjoining lot. Father died a few years ago. All this time I was doing the cuisine myself, always learning, always trying to improve a little, always eating well. You've got to love to eat well if you want to cook well. Whenever I stop at a restaurant while traveling, I go and look at the chef. If he's a thin fellow, I don't eat there. I've learned much about cooking, but I still have far to go."

M. Point leaned back, reached into the drawer of a table behind him, and pulled out a leather-bound book with a gold inscription on its cover: F. POINT, LIVRE D'OR. "I started keeping this on the restaurant's tenth anniversary, in September 1933," he said. He handed it to me. On page one was a short note, *"Quel excellent déjeuner!,"* signed by the Aga Khan. "He really knows how to eat well," M. Point said. A couple of pages on, the Fratellinis, France's most famous clowns, had written "Today we have eaten at Lucullus's," and Colette had written "The trout was rosy, the wine was sparkling, the pâtisserie went straight to my heart—and I am trying to lose weight! This is definitely the last time I come here—*on ne m'y reprendra pas!"* Farther along there was an unfinished sentence by Léon Blum: *"Si j'en trouve encore la force après un tel déjeuner . . . ,"* a drawing by Jean Cocteau, and an observation by Curnonsky (the *nom de table* of Maurice Edmond Sailland, who in 1925 was elected Prince of Gastronomes by a group of Paris newspapers): "Since cooking is without doubt the greatest art, I salute my dear Fernand Point as one of the greatest artists of our time!"

Nothing was entered from January 1940 until September 2, 1944. On the latter date, someone had written *"Premières Troupes Alliées—Merci 1000 Fois!"* over an excited, illegible signature. Below was the exclamation *"Vive la France!"* and the signatures of, among others, the Abbé de Pélissier, F.F.I., and Lieutenant Colonel H. C. Lodge, Jr., and

Carl F. Gooding, "American jeep driver." Several pages beyond, I came upon a pasted-in letter, dated December 3, 1946, and typed on the stationery of the War Office (Room 900), Whitehall, London S.W. 1. It read "Mr. Fernand Point: I have the honor to inform you that His Majesty the King has approved the award to you of the King's Medal for Courage in the Cause of Freedom, for your good services in France. . . ."

I asked M. Point about the letter. He shrugged and took the *livre d'or* away from me and threw it back into the drawer. "No time for that," he said. "Time for lunch. If you will go into the dining room, I'll step into the kitchen and see what can be done. I've thought it all out."

At the entrance to the dining room, I was taken in tow by a cheerful headwaiter, who led me to a table. Mme. Point came up with the order pad still under her arm. She gave me a long, speculative glance—the kind of glance that wives so often give their husbands' drinking companions—and then she smiled and said that she hoped I would have a nice lunch. She went off, and I looked around the dining room. I had the feeling of being in a comfortable home in the country. The room wasn't so small as to give one a sense of being cooped up with a lot of other people (there were perhaps fifteen or twenty other clients), and not so large as to give a feeling of mass production. There were pretty white curtains on all the windows, and on every table was a vase of fresh flowers. In the center of the room stood a long buffet covered with stacks of big, ivory-colored plates, piles of silver, and rows of glasses, and against one wall was a grandfather's clock. When I opened my white napkin of rough linen, it turned out to be almost the size of a small bedspread, and exhaled the fragrance of fresh air and of the grass on which it had been dried in the sun.

A waiter placed one of the ivory-colored plates in front of me, and another waiter served me the first hors d'oeuvre, an excellent *pâté campagne en croûte*. French cooks are generally expert at baking an extremely light, buttery dough called *croûte*, but never before had I eaten *croûte* that almost dissolved in my mouth. When I had finished, the first waiter replaced my plate, fork, and knife with clean ones, and a third waiter served me a slice of *foie gras naturel truffé* embedded in a ring of *crème de foie gras*. The ritual of changing plates and silver was repeated after each hors d'oeuvre—hot sausage baked in a light pastry shell, accompanied by delicious *sauce piquante;* a pâte of pheasant; crackling hot cheese croissants; fresh asparagus (which M. Mercier must have bought in Lyon that morning), set off by a truly perfect hollandaise sauce. A bottle of wine—an elegant, airy Montrachet—was brought in an ice bucket; the waiter filled my glass half full and gave it a gentle swirl to spread the bouquet. It was a great show and a fine wine. The last hors d'oeuvre was followed in person by M. Point, who informed me that I had now completed the "overture." "The overture merely indicates the themes that will turn up later," he said. "A good meal must be as harmonious as a symphony and as well constructed as a good play. As it progresses, it should gain in intensity, with the wines getting older and more full-bodied." Having delivered himself of this pronouncement, he returned to the kitchen.

Whenever I think back to that lunch, I feel contentedly well fed; the memory of it alone seems almost enough to sustain life. The next course was *truite au porto,* which, the headwaiter told me, had been prepared by M. Point himself: brook trout boiled in water to which vinegar, pepper, salt, and bay leaf had been added, and then skinned, split in half, and filled with a ragout of truffles, mushrooms, and vegetables. With it came a sauce made of butter, cream, and port wine. It was a masterpiece; I was by then entirely willing to take the word of my friends in Paris that Fernand Point is today France's greatest chef. The trout was followed by a breast of guinea hen with morels, in an egg sauce; a splendid Pont-l'Evêque; strawberry ice cream, made of *fraises de bois* that had been picked the day before; and an array of pâtisserie. M. Point had chosen as a wine for the guinea hen a rich, full-bodied Château Lafite-Rothschild '24. And at the end of the meal, with my coffee, there was a Grande Fine Champagne '04, the taste of which I still remember vividly.

Later, M. Point sat down at my table. The smell of good coffee and good cigars and the sound of soft, relaxed conversation drifted through the room. M. Point acknowledged my praises with the casual air of a seasoned virtuoso who had expected nothing else. "We always strive for near-perfection," he said. The inevitable bottle of champagne in its ice bucket was whisked up to the table by the headwaiter, and two glasses were filled. "Of course, I know that there is no such thing as perfection. But I always try to make every meal"—he closed his eyes, searching for the right words—"*une petite merveille.* Now, you won't believe it, but I gave a lot of thought to your lunch. I said to myself, 'Maybe he should have a *sole aux nouilles* instead of the *truite au porto.*' I decided against it. It might have been too much, and I don't want my clients to eat too much. Only in bad restaurants is one urged to order a lot. *Enfin,* you are satisfied."

I said he could probably make a fortune if he opened a restaurant in Paris. He nodded glumly. "My friends have been telling me that for years. But why should I leave? I belong here. My men like to work for me. We have thirteen men here in the dining room, and eight cooks and two pâtissiers, under Paul Mercier, in the kitchen. Many of them have been with me for over ten years, and some have been here a lot longer than that. They don't quit, as they do in Paris. Look at Vincent, here. He's been with me for twenty years—or is it twenty-one, Vincent?"

The headwaiter filled the glasses again and gave the champagne bottle a twirl as he replaced it in its bucket. "Twenty-one, *Chef,*" he said.

"You can't get rid of them," said M. Point. "I could throw Vincent out the door and he would come right back in through the window. No, *mon cher ami.* Point stays at the Pyramide." He lifted his glass. "Let us drink to the Pyramide!"

"To the Pyramide!" I said.

We drank a considerable number of toasts afterward—to France; to the United States; to Escoffier; to Dom Pérignon, who put the bubbles in champagne; and to the memorable day when M. Point prepared his first *truite au porto*—and it was with a feeling of light-headedness and supreme contentment that, late in the afternoon, I paid my bill (which came to no more than the price of a good meal in a good restaurant in New York), bid farewell to M. Point, and went out into the garden. It had rained again, but now the sun was shining. The earth had a strong smell of mushrooms and flowers. I headed back to my hotel. At the corner of the Cours Président Wilson, I ran smack into M. Lecutiez. He was talking to an unworldly-looking patriarch, who I presumed was the oldest of the three archeologists, but M. Lecutiez introduced him to me as *l'homme mûr,* the mature man. He said goodbye to his colleague and seized my arm with great enthusiasm. "I've been waiting for you!" he said, waving his pipe happily. "We've got lots of things to do. We still have time to climb at least three of Vienne's seven hills."

I said that he must excuse me, because I was hardly able to make the Grand Hôtel du Nord, having just had lunch at M. Point's.

"M. Point has a very interesting place," M. Lecutiez said.

"Interesting?" I said. "They say it's the best restaurant in this country. It's the most remarkable—"

"Oh, I don't mean that," M. Lecutiez broke in. "I don't give a damn about the restaurant. I care only for antiquities, you know, and M. Point has plenty of them buried under his place. When they landscaped his garden ten years ago, they came across a couple of first-class Roman sculptures. I wish we could take over M. Point's place and start digging in earnest. I'll bet there are any number of marvelous relics under his wine cellar."

1949

"I'd like to tell you about our specials this evening."

A GOOD APPETITE

A. J. LIEBLING

The Proust *madeleine* phenomenon is now as firmly established in folklore as Newton's apple or Watt's steam kettle. The man ate a tea biscuit, the taste evoked memories, he wrote a book. This is capable of expression by the formula TMB, for Taste > Memory > Book. Some time ago, when I began to read a book called *The Food of France*, by Waverley Root, I had an inverse experience: BMT, for Book > Memory > Taste. Happily, the tastes that *The Food of France* re-created for me—small birds, stewed rabbit, stuffed tripe, Côte Rôtie, and Tavel—were more robust than that of the *madeleine*, which Larousse defines as "a light cake made with sugar, flour, lemon juice, brandy, and eggs." (The quantity of brandy in a *madeleine* would not furnish a gnat with an alcohol rub.) In the light of what Proust wrote with so mild a stimulus, it is the world's loss that he did not have a heartier appetite. On a dozen Gardiners Island oysters, a bowl of clam chowder, a peck of steamers, some bay scallops, three sautéed soft-shelled crabs, a few ears of fresh-picked corn, a thin swordfish steak of generous area, a pair of lobsters, and a Long Island duck, he might have written a masterpiece.

The primary requisite for writing well about food is a good appetite. Without this, it is impossible to accumulate, within the allotted span, enough experience of eating to have anything worth setting down. Each day brings only two opportunities for field work, and they are not to be wasted minimizing the intake of cholesterol. They are indispensable, like a prizefighter's hours on the road. (I have read that the late French professional gourmand Maurice Curnonsky ate but one meal a day—dinner. But that was late in his life, and I have always suspected his attainments anyway; so many mediocre witticisms are attributed to him that he could not have had much time for eating.) A good appetite gives an eater room to turn around in. For example, a non-professional eater I know went to the Restaurant Pierre, in the Place Gaillon, a couple of years ago, his mind set on a sensibly light meal: a dozen, or possibly eighteen, oysters, and a thick chunk of steak topped with beef marrow, which M. Pierre calls a "Délice de la Villette"—the equivalent of a "Stockyard's Delight." But as he arrived, he heard M. Pierre say to his headwaiter, "Here comes Monsieur L. Those two portions of *cassoulet* that are left—put them aside for him." A *cassoulet* is a substantial dish, of a complexity precluding its discussion here. (Mr. Root devotes three pages to the great controversy over what it should contain.) M. Pierre is the most amiable of restaurateurs, who prides himself on knowing in advance what his friends will like. A client of limited appetite would be obliged either to forgo his steak or to hurt M. Pierre's feelings. Monsieur L., however, was in no difficulty. He ate the two *cassoulets,* as was his normal practice; if he had consumed only one, his host would have feared that it wasn't up to standard. He then enjoyed his steak. The oysters offered no problem, since they present no bulk.

In the heroic age before the First World War, there were men and women who ate, in addition to a whacking lunch and a glorious dinner, a voluminous *souper* after the theatre or the other amusements of the evening. I have known some of the survivors, octogenarians of unblemished appetite and unfailing good humor—spry, wry, and free of the ulcers that come from worrying about a balanced diet—but they have had no emulators in France since the doctors there discovered the existence of the human liver. From that time on, French life has been built to an increasing extent around that organ, and a niggling caution has replaced the old recklessness; the liver was the seat of the Maginot mentality. One of the last of the great around-the-clock gastronomes of France was Yves Mirande, a small, merry author of farces and musical-comedy books. In 1955, Mirande celebrated his eightieth birthday with a speech before the curtain of the Théâtre Antoine, in the management of which he was associated with Mme. B., a protégée of his, forty years younger than himself. But the theatre was only half of his life. In addition, M. Mirande was an unofficial director of a restaurant on the Rue Saint-Augustin, which he had founded for another protégée, also forty years younger than himself; this was Mme. G., a Gasconne and a magnificent cook. In the restaurant on the Rue Saint-Augustin, M. Mirande would dazzle his juniors, French and American, by dispatching a lunch of raw Bayonne ham and fresh figs, a hot sausage in crust, spindles of filleted pike in a rich rose *sauce Nantua,* a leg of lamb larded with anchovies, artichokes on a pedestal of foie gras, and four or five kinds of cheese, with a good bottle of Bordeaux and one of champagne, after which he would call for the Armagnac and remind Madame to have ready for dinner the larks and ortolans she had promised him, with a few *langoustes* and a turbot—and, of course, a fine *civet* made from the *marcassin*, or young wild boar, that the lover of the leading lady in his current production had sent up from his estate in the Sologne. "And while I think of it," I once heard him say, "we haven't had any woodcock for days, or truffles baked in the ashes, and the cellar is becoming a disgrace—no more '34s and hardly any '37s. Last week, I had to offer my publisher a bottle that was far too good for him, simply because there was nothing between the insulting and the superlative."

M. Mirande had to his credit a hundred produced plays, including a number of great Paris hits, but he had just written his first book for print, so he said "my publisher" in a special mock-impressive tone. "An informal sketch for my definitive autobiography," he would say of this production. The informal sketch, which I cherish, begins with the most important decision in Mirande's life. He was almost seventeen and living in the small Breton port of Lannion—his offstage family name was Le Querrec—when his father, a retired naval officer, said to him, "It is time to decide your future career. Which will it be, the Navy or the Church?" No other choice was conceivable in Lannion. At dawn, Yves ran away to Paris. There, he had read a thousand times, all the famous wits and cocottes frequented the tables in front of the Café Napolitain, on the Boulevard des Capucines. He presented himself at the café at nine the next morning—late in the day for Lannion—and found that the place had not yet opened. Soon he became a newspaperman. It was a newspaper era as cynically animated as the corresponding period of the Bennett-Pulitzer-Hearst competition in New York, and in his second or third job he worked for a press lord who was as notional and niggardly as most press lords are; the publisher insisted that his reporters be well turned out, but did not pay them salaries that permitted cab fares when it rained. Mirande lived near the fashionable Montmartre cemetery and solved his rainy-day pants-crease problem by crashing funeral parties as they broke up and riding, gratis, in the carriages returning to the center of town. Early in his career, he became personal secretary to Clemenceau and then to Briand, but the gay theatre attracted him more than politics, and he made the second great decision of his life after one of his political patrons had caused him to be appointed *sous-préfet* in a provincial city. A *sous-préfet* is the administrator of one of the districts into which each of the ninety *départements* of France is divided, and a young *sous-préfet* is often headed for a precocious rise to high positions of state. Mirande, attired in the magnificent uniform that was then de rigueur, went to his "capital," spent one night there, and then ran off to Paris again to direct a one-act farce. Nevertheless, his connections with the serious world remained cordial. In the restaurant on the Rue Saint-Augustin, he introduced me to Colette, by that time a national glory of letters.

The regimen fabricated by Mirande's culinary protégée, Mme. G., maintained him *en pleine forme*. When I first met him, in the restaurant during the summer of the Liberation, he was a sprightly sixty-nine. In the spring of 1955, when we renewed a friendship that had begun in admiration of each other's appetite, he was as good as ever. On the occasion of our reunion, we began with a *truite au bleu*—a live trout simply done to death in hot water, like a Roman emperor in his bath. It was served up doused with enough melted butter to thrombose a regiment of Paul Dudley Whites, and accompanied, as was right, by an Alsatian wine—a Lacrimae Sanctae Odiliae, which once contributed slightly to my education. Long ago, when I was very young, I took out a woman in Strasbourg, and, wishing to impress her with my knowledge of local customs, ordered a bottle of Ste. Odile. I was making the same mistake as if I had taken out a girl in Boston and offered her baked beans. "How quaint!" the woman in Strasbourg said. "I haven't drunk that for years." She excused herself to go to the telephone, and never came back.

After the trout, Mirande and I had two meat courses, since we could not decide in advance which we preferred. We had a magnificent *daube provençale*, because we were faithful to *la cuisine bourgeoise*, and then *pintadous*—young guinea hens, simply and tenderly roasted—with the first asparagus of the year, to show our fidelity to *la cuisine classique*. We had clarets with both courses—a Pétrus with the *daube*, a Cheval Blanc with the guineas. Mirande said that his doctor had discounseled Burgundies. It was the first time in our acquaintance that I had heard him admit he had a doctor, but I was reassured when he drank a bottle and a half of Krug after luncheon. We had three bottles between us— one to our loves, one to our countries, and one for symmetry, the last being on the house.

Mirande was a small, alert man with the face of a Celtic terrier—salient eyebrows and an upturned nose. He looked like an intelligent Lloyd George. That summer, in association with Mme. B., his theatrical protégée, he planned to produce a new play of Sartre's. His mind kept young by the theatre of Mme. B., his metabolism protected by the restaurant of Mme. G., Mirande seemed fortified against all eventualities for at least another twenty years. Then, perhaps, he would have to recruit new protégées. The Sunday following our reunion, I encountered him at Longchamp, a racecourse where the restaurant does not face the horses, and diners can keep first things first. There he sat, radiant, surrounded by celebrities and champagne buckets, sending out a relay team of commissionaires to bet for him on the successive tips that the proprietors of stables were ravished to furnish him between races. He was the embodiment of a happy man. (I myself had a nice thing at 27 to 1.)

The first alteration in Mirande's fortunes affected me so directly that I did not at once sense its gravity for him. Six weeks later, I was again in Paris. (That year, I was shuttling frequently between there and London.) I was alone on the evening I arrived, and looked forward to a pleasant dinner at Mme. G.'s, which was within two hundred meters of the hotel, in the Square Louvois, where I always stop. Madame's was more than a place to eat, although one ate superbly there. Arriving, I would have a bit of talk with the proprietress, then with the waitresses—Germaine and Lucienne—who had composed the original staff. Waiters had been added as the house prospered, but they were of less marked personality. Madame was a bosomy woman—voluble, tawny, with a big nose and lank black hair—who made one think of a Saracen. (The Saracens reached Gascony in the eighth century.) Her conversation was a chronicle of letters and the theatre—as good as a subscription to *Figaro Littéraire*, but more advanced. It was somewhere between the avant-garde and the main body, but within hailing distance of both and enriched with the names of the great people who had been in recently—M. Cocteau, Gene Kelly, la Comtesse de Vogüé. It was always well to give an appearance of listening, lest she someday fail to save for you the last order of larks *en brochette* and bestow them on a more attentive customer. With Germaine and Lucienne, whom I had known when we were all younger, in 1939, the year of the *drôle de guerre*, flirtation was now perfunctory, but the *carte du jour* was still the serious topic—for example, how the fat Belgian industrialist from Tournai had reacted to the *caille vendangeuse*, or quail potted with fresh grapes. "You know the man," Germaine would say. "If it isn't dazzling, he takes only two portions. But when he has three, then you can say to yourself . . ." She and Lucienne looked alike—compact little women, with high foreheads and cheekbones and solid, muscular legs, who walked like *chasseurs à pied*, 130 steps to the minute. In 1939, and again in 1944, Germaine had been a brunette and Lucienne a blonde, but in 1955 Germaine had become a blonde, too, and I found it hard to tell them apart.

Among my fellow customers at Mme. G.'s I was always likely to see some friend out of the past. It is a risk to make an engagement for an entire evening with somebody you haven't seen for years. This is particularly true in France now. The almost embarrassingly pro-American acquaintance of the Liberation may be by now a Communist Party–line hack; the idealistic young Resistance journalist may have become an editorial writer for the reactionary newspaper of a textile magnate. The Vichy apologist you met in Washington in 1941, who called de Gaulle a traitor and the creation of the British Intelligence Service, may now tell you that the general is the best thing ever, while the fellow you knew as a de Gaulle aide in London may now compare him to Sulla destroying the Roman Republic. As for the women, who is to say which of them has resisted the years? But in a good restaurant that all have frequented, you are likely to meet any of them again, for good restaurants are not so many nowadays that a Frenchman will permanently desert one—unless, of course, he is broke, and in that case it would depress you to learn of his misfortunes. If you happen to encounter your old friends when they are already established at their tables, you have the opportunity to greet them cordially and to size them up. If you still like them, you can make a further engagement.

On the ghastly evening I speak of—a beautiful one in June—I perceived no change in the undistinguished exterior of Mme. G.'s restaurant. The name—something like Prospéria—was the same, and since the plate-glass windows were backed with scrim, it was impossible to see inside. Nor, indeed, did I notice any difference when I first entered. The bar, the tables, the banquettes covered with leatherette, the simple décor of mirrors and pink-marble slabs were the same. The premises had been a business employees' bar-and-café before Mme. G., succeeding a long string of obscure proprietors, made it illustrious. She had changed the fare and the clientele but not the cadre. There are hundreds of identical fronts and interiors in Paris, turned out by some mass producer in the late twenties. I might have been warned by the fact that the room was empty, but it was only eight o'clock and still light outdoors. I had come unusually early because I was so hungry. A man whom I did not recognize came to meet me, rubbing his hands and hailing me as an old acquaintance. I thought he might be a waiter who had served me. (The waiters, as I have said, were not the marked personalities of the place.) He had me at a table before I sensed the trap.

"Madame goes well?" I asked politely.

"No, Madame is lightly ill," he said, with what I now realize was a guilty air.

He presented me with a *carte du jour* written in the familiar purple ink on the familiar wide sheet of paper with the name and telephone number of the restaurant at the top. The content of the menu, however, had become Italianized, the spelling had deteriorated, and the prices had diminished to a point where it would be a miracle if the food continued distinguished.

"Madame still conducts the restaurant?" I asked sharply.

I could now see that he was a Piedmontese of the most evasive description. From rubbing his hands he had switched to twisting them.

"Not exactly," he said, "but we make the same cuisine."

I could not descry anything in the smudged ink but misspelled noodles and unorthographical *"escaloppinis"*; Italians writing French by ear produce a regression to an unknown ancestor of both languages.

"Try us," my man pleaded, and, like a fool, I did. I was hungry. Forty minutes later, I stamped out into the street as purple as an *aubergine* with rage. The minestrone had been cabbage scraps in greasy water. I had chosen *côtes d'agneau* as the safest item in the mediocre catalogue that the Prospéria's prospectus of bliss had turned into overnight. They had been cut from a tired Alpine billy goat and seared in machine oil, and the *haricots verts* with which they were served resembled decomposed whiskers from a theatrical-costume beard.

"The same cuisine?" I thundered as I flung my money on the falsified *addition* that I was too angry to verify. "You take me for a jackass!"

I am sure that as soon as I turned my back the scoundrel nodded. The restaurant has changed hands at least once since then.

In the morning, I telephoned Mirande. He confirmed the disaster. Mme. G., ill, had closed the restaurant. Worse, she had sold the lease and the goodwill, and had definitely retired.

"What is the matter with her?" I asked, in a tone appropriate to fatal disease.

"I think it was trying to read Simone de Beauvoir," he said. "A syncope."

Mme. G. still lives, but Mirande is dead. When I met him in Paris the following November, his appearance gave no hint of decline. It was the season for his sable-lined overcoat *à l'impresario*, and a hat that was a furry cross between a porkpie and a homburg. Since the restaurant on the Rue Saint-Augustin no longer existed, I had invited him to lunch with me at a very small place called the Gratin Dauphinois, on the Rue Chabanais, directly across from the building that once housed the most celebrated sporting house in Paris. The Rue Chabanais is a short street that runs from the Square Louvois to the Rue des Petits Champs—perhaps a hundred yards—but before the reform wave stimulated by a municipal councillor named Marthe Richard at the end of the Second World War, the name Chabanais had a cachet all its own. Mme. Richard will go down in history as the Carry Nation of sex. Now the house is closed, and the premises are devoted to some low commercial purpose. The walls of the midget Gratin Dauphinois are hung with cartoons that have a nostalgic reference to the past glories of the street.

Mirande, when he arrived, crackled with jokes about the locale. He taunted me with being a criminal who haunts the scene of his misdeeds. The fare at the Gratin is robust, as it is in Dauphiné, but it did not daunt Mirande. The wine card, similarly, is limited to the strong, rough wines of Arbois and the like, with a couple of Burgundies for clients who want to show off. There are no clarets; the proprietor hasn't heard of them. There are, of course, a few champagnes, for wedding parties or anniversaries, so Mirande, with Burgundies discounseled by his doctor, decided on champagne throughout the meal. This was a *drôle* combination with the mountain food, but I had forgotten about the lack of claret when I invited him.

We ordered a couple of dozen *escargots en pots de chambre* to begin with. These are snails baked and served, for the client's convenience, in individual earthenware crocks, instead of being forced back into shells. The snail, of course, has to be taken out of his shell to be prepared for cooking. The shell he is forced back into may not be his own. There is thus not even a sentimental justification for his reincarceration. The frankness of the service *en pot* does not improve the preparation of the snail, nor does it detract from it, but it does facilitate and accelerate his consumption. (The notion that the shell proves the snail's authenticity, like the head left on a woodcock, is invalid, as even a suburban housewife knows nowadays; you can buy a tin of snail shells in a supermarket and fill them with a mixture of nutted cream cheese and chopped olives.)

Mirande finished his dozen first, meticulously swabbing out the garlicky butter in each *pot* with a bit of bread that was fitted to the bore of the crock as precisely as a bullet to a rifle barrel. Tearing bread like that takes practice. We had emptied the first bottle of champagne when he placed his right hand delicately on the point of his waistcoat farthest removed from his spinal column.

"Liebling," he said, "I am not well."

It was like the moment when I first saw Joe Louis draped on the ropes. A great pity filled my heart. *"Maître,"* I said, "I will take you home."

The dismayed *patronne* waved to her husband in the kitchen (he could see her through the opening he pushed the dishes through) to suspend the preparation of the *gendarme de Morteau*—the great smoked sausage in its tough skin—that we had proposed to follow the snails with. ("Short and broad in shape, it is made of pure pork and . . . is likely to be accompanied . . . by hot potato salad."—Root, page 217.) We had decided to substitute for the *pommes à l'huile* the *gratin dauphinois* itself. ("Thinly sliced potatoes are moistened with boiled milk and beaten egg, seasoned with salt, pepper, and nutmeg, and mixed with grated cheese, of the Gruyère type. The potatoes are then put into an earthenware dish which has been rubbed with garlic and then buttered, spotted with little dabs of butter, and sprinkled with more grated cheese. It is then cooked slowly in not too hot an oven."—Root, page 228.) After that, we were going to have a fowl in cream with *morilles*—wild black mushrooms of the mountains. We abandoned all.

I led Mirande into the street and hailed a taxi.

"I am not well, Liebling," he said. "I grow old."

He lived far from the restaurant, beyond the Place de l'Etoile, in the Paris of the successful. From time to time on our way, he would say, "It is nothing. You must excuse me. I am not well."

The apartment house in which he and Mme. B. lived resembled one of the chic modern museums of the quarter, with entrance gained through a maze of garden patches sheathed in glass. Successive metal grilles swung open before us as I pushed buttons that Mirande indicated—in these modern palaces there are no visible flunkies—until we reached an elevator that smoothly shot us upward to his apartment, which was rather larger in area than the Square Louvois. The décor, with basalt columns and floors covered with the skins of jumbo Siberian tigers—a special strain force-fed to supply old-style movie stars—reminded me of the sets for *Belphégor*, a French serial of silent days that I enjoyed when I was a student at the Sorbonne in 1926. (It was, I think, about an ancient Egyptian high priest who came to life and set up bachelor quarters in Paris in the style of the Temple of Karnak.) Three or four maids rushed to relieve Mirande of his sable-lined coat, his hat, and his cane, topped with the horn of an albino chamois. I helped him to a divan on which two Theda Baras could have defended their honor simultaneously against two villains of the silents without either couple's getting in the other's way. Most of the horizontal surfaces in the room were covered with sculpture and most of the vertical ones with large paintings. In pain though he was, Mirande called my attention to these works of art.

"All the sculptures are by Renoir," he said. "It was his hobby. And all the paintings are by Maillol. It was *his* hobby. If it were the other way around, I would be one of the richest chaps in France. Both men were my friends. But then one doesn't give one's friends one's bread and butter. And, after all, it's less banal as it is."

After a minute, he asked me to help him to his bedroom, which was in a wing of the apartment all his own. When we got there, one of the maids came in and took his shoes off.

"I am in good hands now, Liebling," he said. "Farewell until next time. It is nothing."

I telephoned the next noon, and he said that his doctor, who was a fool, insisted that he was ill.

Again I left Paris, and when I returned, late the following January, I neglected Mirande. A Father William is a comforting companion for the middle-aged—he reminds you that the best is yet to be and that there's a dance in the old dame yet—but a sick old man is discouraging. My conscience stirred when I read in a gossip column in *France-Dimanche* that Toto Mirande was convalescing nicely and was devouring caviar at a great rate—with champagne, of course. (I had never thought of Mirande as Toto, which is baby slang for "little kid," but from then on I never referred to him in any other way; I didn't want anybody to think I wasn't in the know.) So the next day I sent him a pound of fresh caviar from Kaspia, in the Place de la Madeleine. It was the kind of medication I approved of.

I received a note from Mirande by tube next morning, reproaching me for spoiling him. He was going better, he wrote, and would telephone in a day or two to make an appointment for a return bout. When he called, he said that the idiotic doctor would not yet permit him to go out to a restaurant, and he invited me, instead, to a family dinner at Mme. B.'s. "Only a few old friends, and not the cuisine I hope to give you at Maxim's next time," he said. "But one makes out."

On the appointed evening, I arrived early—or on time, which amounts to the same thing—*chez* Mme. B.; you take taxis when you can get them in Paris at the rush hours. The handsome quarter overlooking the Seine above the Trocadéro is so dull that when my taxi deposited me before my host's door, I had no inclination to stroll to kill time. It is like Park Avenue or the near North Side of Chicago. So I was the first or second guest to arrive, and Mme. B.'s fourteen-year-old daughter, by a past marriage, received me in the Belphégor room, apologizing because her mother was still with Toto—she called him that. She need not have told me, for at that moment I heard Madame, who is famous for her determined voice, storming at an unmistakable someone: "You go too far, Toto. It's disgusting. People all over Paris are kind enough to send you caviar, and because you call it monotonous, you throw it at the maid! If you think servants are easy to come by . . ."

When they entered the room a few minutes later, my old friend was all smiles. "How did you know I adore caviar to such a point?" he asked me. But I was worried because of what I had heard; the Mirande I remembered would never have been irritated by the obligation to eat a few extra kilos of fresh caviar. The little girl, who hoped I had not heard, embraced Toto. "Don't be angry with *Maman!*" she implored him. It was a gathering so familial that it recalled the home scenes in *Gigi.*

My fellow guests included the youngish new wife of an old former premier, who was unavoidably detained in Lille at a congress of the party he now headed; it mustered four deputies, of whom two formed a Left Wing and two a Right Wing. ("If they had elected a fifth at the last election, or if, by good luck, one had been defeated, they could afford the luxury of a Center," Mirande told me in identifying the lady. "*C'est malheureux,* a party without a Center. It limits the possibilities of maneuver.") There was also an amiable couple in their advanced sixties or beginning seventies, of whom the husband was the grand manitou of Veuve Clicquot champagne. Mirande introduced them by their right name, which I forget, and during the rest of the evening addressed them as M. and Mme. Clicquot. There was a forceful, black-haired man from the Midi, in the youth of middle age—square-shouldered, stocky, decisive, blatantly virile—who, I was told, managed Mme. B.'s vinicultural enterprises in Provence. There were two guests of less decided individuality, whom I barely remember, and filling out the party were the young girl—shy, carefully unsophisticated, and unadorned— Mme. B., Mirande, and me. Mme. B. had a strong triangular face on a strong triangular base—a strong chin, high cheekbones, and a wide, strong jaw, but full of stormy good nature. She was a woman who, if she had been a man, would have wanted to be called Honest John. She had a high color and an iron handgrip, and repeatedly affirmed that there was no affectation about her, that she was *sans façon,* that she called her shots as she saw them. "I won't apologize," she said to me. "I know you're a great feeder, like Toto here, but I won't offer you the sort of menu he used to get in that restaurant you know of, where he ruined his plumbing. Oh, that woman! I used to be so jealous. I can offer only a simple home dinner." And she waved us toward a marble table about twenty-two feet long. Unfortunately for me, she meant it. The dinner began with a kidney-and-mushroom mince served in a giant popover— the kind of thing you might get at a literary hotel in New York. The inner side of the pastry had the feeling of a baby's palm, in the true tea- room tradition.

"It is savory but healthy," Madame said firmly, setting an example by taking a large second helping before starting the dish on its second round. Mirande regarded the untouched doughy fabric on his plate with diaphanously veiled horror, but he had an excuse in the state of his health. "It's still a little rich for me, darling," he murmured. The others, including me, delivered salvos of compliments. I do not squander my moral courage on minor crises. M. Clicquot said, "Impossible to obtain anything like this *chez* Lapérouse!" Mme. Clicquot said, "Not even at the Tour d'Argent!"

"And what do you think of my little wine?" Mme. B. asked M. Clicquot. "I'm so anxious for your professional opinion—as a rival producer, you know."

The wine was a thin *rosé* in an Art Nouveau bottle with a label that was a triumph of lithography; it had spires and monks and troubadours and blondes in wimples on it, and the name of the *cru* was spelled out in letters with Gothic curlicues and pennons. The name was something like Château Guillaume d'Aquitaine, *grand vin.*

"What a madly gay little wine, my dear!" M. Clicquot said, repressing, but not soon enough, a grimace of pain.

"One would say a Tavel of a good year," I cried, "if one were a complete bloody fool." I did not say the second clause aloud.

My old friend looked at me with new respect. He was discovering in me a capacity for hypocrisy that he had never credited me with before.

The main course was a shoulder of mutton with white beans—the poor relation of a gigot, and an excellent dish in its way, when not too dry. This was.

For the second wine, the man from the Midi proudly produced a red, in a bottle without a label, which he offered to M. Clicquot with the air of a tomcat bringing a field mouse to its master's feet. "Tell me what you think of this," he said as he filled the champagne-man's glass.

M. Clicquot—a veteran of such challenges, I could well imagine— held the glass against the light, dramatically inhaled the bouquet, and then drank, after a slight stiffening of the features that indicated to me that he knew what he was in for. Having emptied half the glass, he deliberated.

"It has a lovely color," he said.

"But what is it? What is it?" the man from the Midi insisted.

"There are things about it that remind me of a Beaujolais,"

M. Clicquot said (he must have meant that it was wet), "but on the whole I should compare it to a Bordeaux" (without doubt unfavorably).

Mme. B.'s agent was beside himself with triumph. "Not one or the other!" he crowed. "It's from the *domaine*—the Château Guillaume d'Aquitaine!"

The admirable M. Clicquot professed astonishment, and I, when I had emptied a glass, said that there would be a vast market for the wine in America if it could be properly presented. "Unfortunately," I said, "the cost of advertising . . ." and I rolled my eyes skyward.

"Ah, yes," Mme. B. cried sadly. "The cost of advertising!"

I caught Mirande looking at me again, and thought of the Pétrus and the Cheval Blanc of our last meal together *chez* Mme. G. He drank a glass of the red. After all, he wasn't going to die of thirst.

For dessert, we had a simple fruit tart with milk—just the thing for an invalid's stomach, although Mirande didn't eat it.

M. Clicquot retrieved the evening, oenologically, by producing two bottles of a wine "impossible to find in the cellars of any restaurant in France"—Veuve Clicquot '19. There is at present a great to-do among wine merchants in France and the United States about young wines, and an accompanying tendency to cry down the "legend" of the old. For that matter, hardware clerks, when you ask for a can opener with a wooden handle that is thick enough to give a grip and long enough for leverage, try to sell you complicated mechanical folderols, and, when you go on insisting, tell you that effectual things are out of fashion. The motivation in both cases is the same—simple greed. To deal in wines of varied ages requires judgment, the sum of experience and flair. It involves the risk of money, because every lot of wine, like every human being, has a life span, and it is this that the good vintner must estimate. His object should be to sell his wine at its moment of maximum value—to the drinker as well as the merchant. The vintner who handles only young wines is like an insurance company that will write policies only on children; the unqualified dealer wants to risk nothing and at the same time wants to avoid tying up his money. The client misled by brochures warning him off clarets and champagnes that are over ten years old and assuring him that Beaujolais should be drunk green will miss the major pleasures of wine drinking. To deal wisely in wines and merely to sell them are things as different as being an expert in ancient coins and selling Indian-head pennies over a souvenir counter.

Despite these convictions of mine about wine, I should never have tried a thirty-seven-year-old champagne on the recommendation of a lesser authority than the blessed M. Clicquot. It is the oldest by far that I have ever drunk. (H. Warner Allen, in *The Wines of France,* published circa 1924, which is my personal wine bible, says, "In the matter of age, champagne is a capricious wine. As a general rule, it has passed its best between fifteen and twenty, yet a bottle thirty years old may prove excellent, though all its fellows may be quite undrinkable." He cites Saintsbury's note that "a Perrier Jouet of 1857 was still majestical in 1884," adding, "And all wine-drinkers know of such amazing discoveries." Mr. Root, whose book is not a foolish panegyric of everything French, is hard on champagne, in my opinion. He falls into a critical error more common among writers less intelligent: he attacks it for not being something else. Because its excellences are not those of Burgundy or Bordeaux, he underrates the peculiar qualities it does not share with them, as one who would chide Dickens for not being Stendhal, or Marciano for not being Benny Leonard.)

The Veuve Clicquot '19 was tart without brashness—a refined but effective understatement of younger champagnes, which run too much to rhetoric, at best. Even so, the force was all there, to judge from the two glasses that were a shade more than my share. The wine still had a discrete *cordon*—the ring of bubbles that forms inside the glass—and it had developed the color known as "partridge eye." I have never seen a partridge's eye, because the bird, unlike woodcock, is served without the head, but the color the term indicates is that of serous blood or a maple leaf on the turn.

"How nice it was, life in 1919, eh, M. Clicquot?" Mirande said as he sipped his second glass.

After we had finished M. Clicquot's offering, we played a game called lying poker for table stakes, each player being allowed a capital of five hundred francs, not to be replenished under any circumstances. When Mme. B. had won everybody's five hundred francs, the party broke up. Mirande promised me that he would be up and about soon, and would show me how men reveled in the heroic days of *la belle époque,* but I had a feeling that the bell was cracked.

I left Paris and came back to it seven times during the next year, but never saw him. Once, being in his quarter in the company of a remarkably pretty woman, I called him up, simply because I knew he would like to look at her, but he was too tired. I forget when I last talked to him on the telephone. During the next winter, while I was away in Egypt or Jordan or someplace where French papers don't circulate, he died, and I did not learn of it until I returned to Europe.

When Mirande first faltered, in the Rue Chabanais, I had failed to correlate cause and effect. I had even felt a certain selfish alarm. If eating well was beginning to affect Mirande at eighty, I thought, I had better begin taking in sail. After all, I was only thirty years his junior. But after the dinner at Mme. B.'s, and in the light of subsequent reflection, I saw that what had undermined his constitution was Mme. G.'s defection from the restaurant business. For years, he had been able to escape Mme. B.'s solicitude for his health by lunching and dining in the restaurant of Mme. G., the sight of whom Mme. B. could not support. Entranced by Mme. G.'s magnificent food, he had continued to live "like a cock in a pie"—eating as well, and very nearly as much, as when he was thirty. The organs of the interior—never very intelligent, in spite of what the psychosomatic quacks say—received each day the amount of pleasure to which they were accustomed, and never marked the passage of time; it was the indispensable roadwork of the prize-fighter. When Mme. G., good soul, retired, moderation began its fatal inroads on his resistance. My old friend's appetite, insufficiently stimulated, started to loaf—the insidious result, no doubt, of the advice of the doctor whose existence he had revealed to me by that slip of the tongue about why he no longer drank Burgundy. Mirande commenced, perhaps, by omitting the fish course after the oysters, or the oysters before the fish, then began neglecting his cheeses and skipping the second bottle of wine on odd Wednesdays. What he called his pipes ("*ma tuyauterie*"), being insufficiently exercised, lost their tone, like the leg muscles of a retired champion. When, in his kindly effort to please me, he challenged the *escargots en pots de chambre,* he was like an old fighter who tries a comeback without training for it. That, however, was only the revelation of the rot that had already taken place. What always happens happened. The damage was done, but it could so easily have been averted had he been warned against the fatal trap of abstinence.

1959

"Do you want to be vaguely dissatisfied with Italian or Korean?"

THE AFTERGLOW

A. J. LIEBLING

When I returned to Paris in the fall of 1939, after an absence of twelve years, I noticed a decline in the serious quality of restaurants that could not be blamed on a war then one month old. The decline, I later learned, had been going on even in the twenties, when I made my first studies in eating, but I had had no standard of comparison then; what I had taken for a Golden Age was in fact Late Silver. Like me, Waverley Root, author of a recent book called *The Food of France*, made his first soundings in the subject in 1927, both of us being unaware that the watershed was behind us and that we were on a long, historic downslope. Enough of the glory remained to furnish us with memories by which to judge the punier times ahead, though; the food of

France in 1926–27 still constituted the greatest corpus of culinary thought and practice anywhere. The only touted challenger for the lead then was China, and the only touts were people who wanted to let you know they had been there. When you got these Orientalized *fines gueules* to a table where they had to use a knife and fork instead of chopsticks, they could not tell the difference between a Western sandwich and a *darne de saumon froid sauce verte*. In most cases, their sole preparation for gourmandizing had been a diet of institutional macaroni in a Midwestern seminary for medical missionaries, and any pasture the Lord led them to was bound to be better.

Chinese *haute cuisine* is unlikely to improve under the austere regime of Mao. The food of France, although it has gone off disastrously, is still the best there is. But we are headed for a gastronomic Dark Time, such as followed the breakup of classical civilization, and nobody younger than Root, who is fifty-six, can remember the twilight. My lamented mentor Yves Mirande, the author of a hundred successful farces and one of the last great gastronomes of France, could remember the full glow of the sun, before the First World War. "After the First War, everything had already changed," Mirande wrote me in 1952, when he was seventy-seven. "The mentality of today began to show the tip of its ear." One thing that changed early was the position of the women he called *les courtisanes de marque*—the famous women of the town—and this had a prodigious, if indirect, effect upon the sumptuary arts. "Yes, Paris was radiant, elegant, and refined," Mirande wrote of his heaven before 1914. "In the world and in the half-world, feasts followed upon feasts, wild nights upon vertiginous suppers. It was the courtesans' *grande époque*. Innocent of preoccupation with the future, they had no trace of a desire to build up an income for old age. They were gamblers, beautiful gamblers, with a certain natural distinction in their ways and a *je ne sais quoi* of good breeding—the bonnet thrown over the windmill, but without falling into vulgarity or coarseness. They had a tone—a tone as distinct from the society woman's as from the fancy girl's. All the successful demimondaines ordered their clothes from the great couturiers. Their carriages were splendid, better turned out for a drive in the Bois than those of duchesses and ambassadors." Moreover, these town toasts ate magnificently, and boasted of the quality of the meals their admirers provided for them. It was the age not only of the dazzling public supper but of the *cabinet particulier*, where even a bourgeois seduction was preceded by an eleven-course meal. With these altruistic sensualists, a menu of superior imagination could prove more effective than a gift of Suez shares; besides, the ladies' hosts had the pleasure of sharing the meals they had to pay for. The *courtisanes de marque* were substantial in a Venus de Milo–y, just short of billowy way. Waists and ankles tapered, but their owners provided a lot for them to taper from. Eating was a *soin de beauté* that the girls enjoyed.

The successful Frenchman of the early 1900s was fat; it was the evidence of his success, an economic caste mark. To be thin at thirty was a handicap in the world of affairs, the equivalent in our culture of driving a year-before-last automobile shorter than a Coast Guard cutter. It indicated that one had never been in a position to eat one's fill. Caricature accents but does not reverse reality, and I cherish a special twenty-four-page number of *L'Assiette au Beurre,* a journal of savage caricature, printed in 1902 and devoted to *le singe,* which was, and is, argot for "the employer." Every successful *singe* in the issue—rapacious, lecherous, murderous—is fat. The only unfat *singe* is the one on the last page—an obviously unsuccessful pimp who is beating up a thin girl, clearly not a *courtisane de marque.*

By 1927, however, the celebrated belles, amateur and professional, had become even more skeletal than they are today. Lady Diana Manners and Rosamond Pinchot, the international beauties paired in Max Reinhardt's *The Miracle,* for example, were as leggy and flat as a pair of handsome young giraffes. It was no longer any use taking a woman to a great restaurant except to show her off. She would not eat, and, out of ill temper disguised as solicitude for her escort's health, she would put him off his feed as well. The chic restaurants of Paris—which were none of my or Root's concern at the moment—were already beginning their transition from shrines of *dégustation* to showcases for the flapper figure. The men, too, had turned to the mortification of the flesh, though less drastically. Without exception, the chaps who emerged from the trenches at the end of the war had lost weight, and at such a time everyone wants to resemble a hero. Of the victorious commanders, only Joffre and Sarrail had figures like Napoleon's, and they had not been conspicuously successful. Foch and Pétain were ramrods, like Pershing. Also, *le sport,* which before the war had been considered a form of eccentricity, was

now taken seriously. When Lacoste, Cochet, and Borotra beat the
United States for the Davis Cup that very spring, the sensation was
greater than when Lindbergh completed his transatlantic flight. There
was also a wave of that endemic European malady *americo-mimesis;* the
attack in the twenties is often forgotten by contemporary Europeans in
their rage against the bigger one now in progress. The infection then
was carried by jazz and by American silent moving pictures, which had
nearly wiped out European films. (The injection of the human voice
into movies and the resultant language barrier gave the foreign cinema a
decade of reprieve.) And, finally, there was the legend of the Perpetual
Boom. America, it appeared, was the country that had discovered an infallible system for beating the races. This made Americans, in the abstract, as unpopular as we eventually became in the forties, but it also
spurred imitative identification. The silent-film comedian Harold Lloyd,
who played go-getting young-businessman types, energetic to the point
of acrobacy, was the pattern-symbol of the Frenchman disgusted with
old methods. Even a dilettante can still spot Frenchmen of that vintage
by their tortoise-shell glasses and their briskness. (Jacques Soustelle is a
classic specimen.) Their costume has become fixed, like the Sikh's tur-
ban. The crash of 1929 discredited the original motivation of the mimesis, but the Frenchman trapped by habit behind his tortoise-shells had
forgotten why he put them on.

In 1927, these changes were beginning to be reflected in the composition of the restaurant world. The 1925 edition of the *Guide du Gourmand à Paris,* a Baedeker for the aspiring eater, listed six restaurants as
its *"peloton de tête,"* or leading platoon—Montagné, Larue, Foyot, Voisin,
Paillard, and La Tour d'Argent, all "temples of gastronomy" for serious
feeders. (Of the first five, all venerable, four ceased to exist even before
the declaration of the Second World War. Larue maintained its majes-
tic style through the winter of the *drôle de guerre,* 1939–40, but has disappeared since, to be replaced by an establishment called Queenie's,
whose name, as the French say, is a program. La Tour d'Argent, in order
to continue, has gone in heavily for public relations, and floodlights itself at night, like a national monument. Such expedients may be justified
as being necessary to survival, but they cast a shadow on the age that
renders them necessary.) The specialties that the *Guide* listed as the glories of these great houses in their declining years were not of a sort to
accord with low-calorie diets or with the new cult of the human liver.

Before the First World War, the doctors of France had been a submissive and well-mannered breed, who recognized that their role was to facilitate gluttony, not discourage it. They returned to civilian life full of a new sense of authority, gained from the habit of amputation. Instead of continuing, as in the past, to alleviate indigestion, assuage dyspepsia, and solace attacks of gout, they proposed the amputation of three or four courses from their patients' habitual repasts. Since the innovators were, as always, the doctors most in fashion, the first patients to be affected were the most fashionable—precisely those who patronized the most expensive restaurants. The *Guide* listed Montagné's greatest attractions as "meats and fish under a crust of pastry; salmon, turbot, prepared *à l'ancienne*, in a sheath of dough; venerable Louis-Philippe brandy. And the coffee!!!" This is a catalogue of horrors for a man worried about his weight and works, but it was a program of delight for an eater of Mirande's *grande époque*.

The constant diminution of the public that was interested in flamboyant food ended the economic justification of the restaurants staffed to supply it; the new doctrines had the same effect on temples of gastronomy that the Reformation had on the demand for *style-flamboyant* cathedrals. At first, the disappearance of the expensive restaurants was not felt at the lower levels where Root and I reveled, but it slowly became evident, as the disappearance of the great opera houses would become evident in the standards of professional singing; with no Metropolitan to aspire to, the child soprano of Boulder, Colorado, would have no incentive to work on her scales. As a career for the artistically ambitious, cooking became less attractive just at the moment when alternative means of earning a living grew more numerous for the offspring of the proletariat. Child-labor laws and compulsory education were additional obstacles in the way of the early apprenticeship that forms great cooks. One of the last of the Fratellini family of clowns, an old man, made a television address in Paris a few years ago in which he blamed the same conjunction of circumstances for the dearth of good young circus clowns. "When I was a child, my father, bless him, broke my legs, so that I would walk comically, as a clown should," the old man said. (I approximate his remarks from memory.) "Now there are people who would take a poor view of that sort of thing." In another area of the arts, Rocky Marciano's preceptor, Charlie Goldman, a septuagenarian, says that there will never again be great boxers, because such must begin their professional careers before the age of puberty, while they can keep their minds on their business. (Marciano, who began late, was a fighter, not a boxer, and fighting is more a knack than an art.) When Persian carpets were at their best, weavers began at the age of four and were master workmen at eleven.

During the twenties and thirties, the proportion of French restaurants that called themselves *auberges* and *relais* increased, keeping pace with the motorization of the French gullet. They depended for their subsistence on Sunday and holiday drivers, who might never come over the road again, and the *Guide Michelin,* the organ of a manufacturer of automobile tires, ominously began to be the arbiter of where to dine—a depressing example of the subordination of art to business. By 1939, the shiny new "medieval" joints along the equally new highways had begun to supplant the old hotels, across the road from the railroad stations, that in the first quarter of the century had been the centers of good, solid provincial eating. The hotel proprietors' living depended on the patronage of traveling salesmen, whose robust appetites and experienced palates had combined with their economical natures to maintain the standards of honest catering. But the drummers no longer moved by train, doing one large town or small city a day and staying overnight at the Hôtel du Commerce or the Lion d'Or. They were now motorized, and scooted about the highways in minute Citroëns and Arondes, managing to get home to their bases in the larger provincial cities at the day's end. They lunched in a hurry—"like Americans"—and the rural hotels began to die. When the peasants, too, started to become motorized, the small towns themselves began to die. The small-town and small-city merchants had pushed a bill through the Chamber of Deputies prohibiting the great retail chains, like Monoprix, from opening stores in cities of less than ten thousand population, and one result was to accelerate the desertion of the small towns by shoppers; to get the variety and lower prices of the chain stores, they passed up the old centers altogether.

By 1939, the country coyness of the *auberges* and *relais,* with their pastiche medieval décors and their menus edited with fake-archaic whimsey—the equivalent of "ye" and "shoppe"—had even invaded the capital. *"Humectez vos gousiers avec les bons vins du noble pays du patron en actendant les chatouille-gencives du Maistre Queux,"* a Paris restaurant menu was likely to read, in place of the 1926–27 *"Vins en carafe—rouge ou blanc, 50 centimes. Saucissons d'ail, 50 centimes. Sardines . . .*" The new baby-talk Rabelais was about as appetizing as, and on a level with, some of our own bill-of-fare prose: "Irrigate the li'l ol' red lane with some of our prime drinkin' whiskey and branch water while the Chef Supreme rustles up an Infra-Red Popover Salad Bowl."

The Rue Sainte-Anne is a medium-long street, narrow and totally without distinction, that begins near the Rue de Rivoli end of the Avenue de l'Opéra and runs north toward the Grands Boulevards; it roughly parallels the Rue de Richelieu, at a remove of a couple of squalid blocks, but it has no Comédie Française to illustrate its beginning and no Bibliothèque Nationale to lend dignity to its middle. A block or two before it reaches the Boulevards, it takes the name of the Rue de Gramont. It is lined with uninviting hotels, cobbler's shops, neighborhood hairdressers, and establishments that sell the drab sundries of wholesale businesses— wooden buttons and hat blocks, patterns for dresses, office supplies— and with restaurants that feed office workers at noon. Among all the restaurants, there is frequently a good one, but it never lasts long. The Rue Sainte-Anne is the kind of street that seems to attract independent spirits. A talented cook who opens there is an Expressionist; he feels no need of a public. In 1927, one such cook had been a man named Maillabuau. He practiced his art behind a dour street façade (he was a horse-player, and a losing one), but his restaurant, despite its threadbare aspect, was listed right behind the *peloton de tête* of the *Guide du Gourmand à Paris.* In 1939, on my first evening in wartime Paris, I headed straight for Maillabuau's, but it had disappeared; I walked the length of the Rue Sainte-Anne twice to make sure. Yielding to hunger, I entered another restaurant, of the same unpromising aspect—a storefront muffled in curtains against air raids but extruding a finger of light to show that it was open for business. (Everybody in France, at that stage, waged a war of small compromises.) A shabby exterior is no guarantee of good food— perhaps more often it is the contrary—but I was too hungry by then to leave the neighborhood. Nor were the streets hospitable in the dimout. There were no cruising taxis.

Thus it was that I stumbled into the family circle of M. Louis Bouillon, a native of Bourg-en-Bresse, which is the eating-poultry capital of France and in the home province of the great Brillat-Savarin, who was born in Belley. M. Bouillon was a small man with bright, liquid eyes, a long nose, like a woodcock's, and a limp, drooping mustache that looked as if it had been steamed over cook pots until it was permanently of the consistency of spinach. When I entered, he was sitting with his elbows on a table and his head in his hands, contemplating a tumbler of *marc de Bourgogne* as if trying to read the fate of France in an ink pool. Around the table, with newspapers and coffee, were seated Mme. Bouillon; Marie-Louise, the waitress; the Bouillons' daughter, Dominique, a handsome girl of eighteen; and their son, not yet called up for service. (I did not know their individual identities yet, but I soon learned them.) Mme. Bouillon brightened, and Marie-Louise rose and came to meet me. "Sit where you wish, Monsieur," she said. "You have your choice."

There had been a scare at the very beginning of the war, and a great many people had left Paris, expecting it to be bombarded. They had not yet quite decided to come back—it was in the first week of October 1939—and business was, in consequence, dead. I have seldom been so welcome anywhere, or got so quickly acquainted. And I had fallen luckily. M. Bouillon was a great cook. His son was in apprenticeship at the Café de Paris, one of the few remaining big classic restaurants. His daughter, that paragon, could make a soufflé Grand Marnier that *stood up on a flat plate.* M. Bouillon told me that he had only recently taken over the restaurant. The rickety cane chairs and oak sideboard looked bad enough to have come from Maillabuau's dispersal sale. But there was food. "The markets are full," M. Bouillon said. "Game, shellfish—everything you can think of. It's customers that lack." I forget what I had at that first meal—a steak *marchand de vin,* or a *civet* of hare, perhaps, before the soufflé, which I ordered to see Dominique do her trick. Then I settled down to drinking with M. Bouillon. He was sombre at first. What kind of a war was this, he wanted to know. When would we go out and give them a crack on the snout? In *his* war, the horizon-blue war, the Boche had come as far as the Marne and been stopped within six weeks of the beginning. That put people in the proper cadence. This war set one's nerves on edge. It was the British, he felt sure, who were responsible for the delay; they were perhaps negotiating with Fritz. A war that could not make up its mind had a funereal effect on commerce. The Americans were different from the English, but they weren't in the war. M. Bouillon and I grew sentimental, optimistic, bellicose, and, finally, maudlin. I had a hard time finding my way home, although my hotel, the Louvois, was only 150 yards away—a straight line with one turn to the right.

After that, M. Bouillon's restaurant became my advanced field headquarters while I vainly tried to get an *ordre de mission* to go to the front, where nothing was happening anyway. Conditions rapidly simulated normal. The Parisians came back. An ill-founded feeling of satisfaction succeeded the alarm and puzzlement of the first days; the Allies might not be hurting the Nazis, but at least the Nazis weren't hurting the Allies. There was a growing public hunch that the "real" war would never begin. Often, M. Bouillon took me with him on his buying trips to Les Halles, so I could see that the Germans weren't starving Paris. On these trips, we would carry a number of baskets and, as we filled one after another with oysters, artichokes, or pheasants, we would leave them at a series of bars, in each of which we had one or two *Calvas*. The new Calvados sold at the market bars was like a stab with a penknife, and at some bars we would drink Pouilly-Fumé by the glass for a change of pace. The markets were overflowing; I recall that there was fruit from Mussolini's Italy and fine poultry from Prince Paul's Yugoslavia. M. Bouillon drew my attention to the chickens, which he said were as handsome as those of Bresse but inferior in flavor. There was transport, apparently, for everything but war materials. (I drew the wrong conclusion, naturally; if there was transport for the superfluous, I inferred, the essential must already have been taken care of.) The Bouillon theory was that when we had completed our round of Les Halles, we would circle back on our course to pick up the baskets, with a courtesy round at each port of call, and thus avoid a lot of useless toting. It worked all right when we could remember the bars where we had left the various things, but sometimes we couldn't, and on such occasions M. Bouillon would cry that *restauration* was a cursed *métier*, and that if the government would permit, he would take up his old Lebel rifle and leave for the front. But they would have to let him wear horizon blue; he could not stand the sight of khaki, because it reminded him of the English.

Of all the dishes that M. Bouillon made for me, I remember with most affection a *salmis* of woodcock in Armagnac with which I astounded a French friend—a champagne man—whom I entertained in the little restaurant. I'm sure that it was the best I've had in my life, and M. Bouillon could do almost as well with a partridge, a beef stew, or a blood pudding with mashed potatoes. My Frenchman, as a partner in a good firm of champagne-makers, had to get around to an enormous number of restaurants in a normal year, so when he acknowledged M. Bouillon's greatness, I felt the same gratification that I felt much later when Spink's, of London, authenticated a coin of Hadrian, minted at Gaza, that I had bought from an Arab in Gaza itself. M. Bouillon was my discovery, and the enjoyment of a woodcock signed "Bouillon" was an irreplaceable privilege.

Like most fine cooks, M. Bouillon flew into rages and wept easily; the heat of kitchens perhaps affects cooks' tear ducts as well as their tempers. Whenever we returned to the restaurant from Les Halles minus some item that M. Bouillon had paid for and that Madame had already inscribed on the menu, there would be a scene, but on the whole the Bouillons were a happy family—Madame and the children respected Monsieur as a great artist, though the son and daughter may have thought that he carried temperament a bit far. It was an ideal family unit to assure the future of a small restaurant; unfortunately, the war wiped it out. When the fighting began in earnest, in May 1940, the customers again left Paris. The son was mobilized, and the rest of the family went away to work in the canteen of a munitions factory. When I reentered Paris at the Liberation, in 1944, I looked them up and found that they had returned to the quarter but that they no longer had the restaurant. To conduct a restaurant successfully under the Occupation had called for a gift of connivance that poor M. Bouillon didn't have. Since August 1944, I have lost sight of them.

It was in 1939, too, that I was first introduced to M. Pierre and his establishment on the Place Gaillon. (The fact that the restaurant is not on the Rue Sainte-Anne but some two hundred meters from that street of transition perhaps accounts for the fact that M. Pierre is still in business.) It is my favorite middle-sized restaurant; the cuisine has a robust, classic clarity, like a boxing style based on the straight left. Everything is done the way it says in the book, without neologisms or deviations. The matériel is of the best, the service is deft, and the prices are rather stiff. M. Pierre has the appearance of a distinguished sinner in a René Clair movie; in 1939 he had prematurely white hair (to which his age now entitles him), a high complexion, and an upright backbone. His elegance was acquired not at the Quai d'Orsay but in the métier in which he made his debut, at fourteen. Our first bond was my discovery that he is a Norman, and from the proper part of Normandy—he is from Avranches, across from Mont-Saint-Michel—and, consequently, an amateur of Calvados, which, to my taste, is the best alcohol in the world. He sometimes spends weekends calling on peasants in his automobile and trying to wheedle from them a few bottles or—wild dream—a small keg of the veritable elixir of Eden. (Every Norman knows that the apple of the Bible is symbolic; it stands for the distilled cider that will turn the head of any woman.) Good Calvados is never sold legally. The tax leaves a taste that the Norman finds intolerable, like the stuff that wives put in whiskey to cure alcoholics. And only a few of Pierre's clients know what they are drinking from his precious bottles; not everybody has had the advantage of a good early soaking in the blessed liquid. Millions of Frenchmen are obtuse enough to prefer cognac, and of late a lot have switched to Scotch.

Even in 1939, Pierre, master of the whole classic repertoire of cooking, admitted that the elaborate numbers in it were no longer in demand. At noon, his restaurant sometimes had the aspect of what Americans were just beginning to call a steak house. "Only twenty-five percent of my customers order a *plat du jour*," he said to me one day. "The rest take grilled things. It's the doctors, you know. People think only of the liver and the figure. The stomach is forgotten." He tried his best to modify the rigors of this cowboy diet—like a modiste adding a button or a ribbon to soften what the fashion writers call a stark line— by offering superb steak *au poivre*, steak *Diane*, steak *maison* (with a sauce made on a white-wine base), and steak *marchand de vin* (red-wine ditto), but a growing number of customers kept demanding their steak *nature*. "Oysters and a steak, a bit of *langouste* and a mixed grill, a *salade niçoise* and a lamb chop—it's to die of monotony," Pierre said. "If it were not for you and a few like you, I'd drop the *cassoulet* on Tuesday—it's a loser."

The trend has continued since. One evening in 1956, I entered M. Pierre's honest, soothing precincts. The headwaiter—old, gentle, dignified, with the face of a scholarly marquis—led me into the largest room, and in passing I observed a group of six (doubtless three couples) around a table at which a waiter was serving a magnificent *plate côte de boeuf*, while a colleague, following in his wake with the casserole from which the meat had been recovered, ladled onto each plate the leeks, the carrots, the onions, and the broth to which the beef had given its essential tone. The men, I could see, had acquired their jowls, their plump hands, and their globular outlines, uninterrupted by necks—as well as their happy faces—in an age before the doctors had spread the infection of fear; the wives had won their husbands' love, and learned to feel secure in it, before the emergence of the woman with a flat basic figure, on which she simulates a pectoral bulge when Balenciaga's designs call for it, and a caudal swelling when fashion goes into reverse.

When I arrived at my table, I did not even look at the *carte du jour;* my nose was full of the delectable steam of the boiled beef. I said, "For me, a dozen *pleines mers"*—oysters that are a specialty of Pierre's *écailleurs,* the men who stand out in the cold and open them—"and the *plate côte.*"

An expression of sorrow elongated the old-ivory face of the maître d'hôtel. "I am desolated, M. Liebling," he said, "but the boiled beef is not on the menu. It was prepared *sur commande*—the party over there ordered it two days in advance."

That the humble glory of the classic French kitchen should have to be ordered two days in advance in one of the best restaurants in Paris is evidence of how far *la cuisine française* has slipped in the direction of short-order cooking. Beef boiled in its bouillon was the one thing that in the seventeenth and eighteenth centuries, before the development of true restaurants, the traveler was sure of finding at the lowliest inn, where the "eternal pot," drawn upon and replenished but never emptied, bubbled on the low fire that was never allowed to die. "Soup [the pot-au-feu] is at the base of the French national diet, and the experience of centuries has inevitably brought it to its perfection," the divine Brillat-Savarin once wrote.

"If there is any left over," the maître d'hôtel told me, looking toward the table of the happy six, "I will be glad to bring it to you. But I strongly doubt there will be."

And now one final instance of lost love on the Rue Sainte-Anne. In June of 1955, I discovered a small establishment there, completely without charm and crowded at noon with employees of neighboring business houses, which posted prices so low that I knew the fare could not be out of the ordinary, though it must have been good value to attract so many people. In the evening, however, when the quarter was quiet and customers few, the proprietor, I learned, could perform marvels. He was a Greek, born in Cairo, who had served his apprenticeship in the kitchens of Shepheard's Hotel and then worked in good restaurants in France before the First World War. Enlisting in the French army, he had won naturalization, he said, and after the war he had worked in most of the good kitchens that he had not been in earlier. On sampling his work, I gave his story full credence, although it was not apparent to me why he had not risen higher in his profession. His explanation was that he had always been an independent soul—*une forte tête*—and had preferred to launch out for himself. He had mounted small restaurants in Paris, in Le Havre, in Granville—a little bit of everywhere. He liked to be his own boss. An imposing man, he must have measured six feet eight inches from the soles of his shoes to the top of the chef's toque that he always wore—one of the starched kind, shaped like an Orthodox priest's hat. He had a face that a primitive Greek sculptor might have intended for either a satyr or a god—terra-cotta red under an iron-gray thatch. His hands were as big and as strong as a stonecutter's, and his manner in the kitchen was irascible and commanding. He could be observed in the opening in the top half of the kitchen door, through which he thrust the steaming *plats* when they were ready to serve—and also often thrust his head, toque first, to bellow at the waitress when she did not come quickly to retrieve the evening masterpieces he extended. He would have to duck, naturally, to get the toque through. The round white top would appear in the aperture first, like a circular white cloud, and then, as he moved his neck to the vertical, his face would shine out like the sun—round, radiant, terrible—to transfix the waitress. The girl, bearing the deliciously heavy trays to table, would murmur, to excuse him, "By day, you know, he isn't at all like that. What he cooks for the day customers doesn't excite him—and then it must be said that he hasn't the same quantity of cognac in him, either. The level mounts." The Greek must have been in his middle sixties; his wife, an attractive Frenchwoman some twenty years younger, minded the bar and the cash and the social relations of the establishment; she, too, was fond of brandy. He could produce an astonishing *langouste à l'américaine* and a faultless pilaf to accompany it; I have never known a man who could work with such equal mastery in the two idioms, classic and Levantine.

The preeminent feature of any kind of lobster prepared *à l'américaine* is the sauce, which, according to *The Food of France*, contains white wine, cognac, fish bouillon, garlic, tomatoes, a number of herbs, the juices of the lobster itself, and the oil in which the lobster has been cooked before immersion in the liquid. (I have never personally inquired into the mysteries of its fabrication; I am content to love a masterpiece of painting without asking how the artist mixed his colors.) Early in his great work, Root disposes magisterially of the chauvinistic legend, invented by followers of Charles Maurras, that lobster *à l'américaine* should be called *à l'armoricaine* (from "Armorica," the ancient name for Brittany), simply because there are lobsters (*langoustes* as well as *homards*) on the coast of Brittany. "The purists," he says, employing a typically mild designation for these idiots, "do not seem to have been gastronomes, however, or they might have looked at the dish itself, which is obviously not Breton but Provençal, the lobster being cooked in oil and accompanied lavishly with tomatoes—and, indeed, until the middle of the nineteenth century, virtually the same dish was known as *homard à la provençale*. The most reasonable explanation for this name seems to be the one which ascribes it to a now vanished Parisian restaurant called the Américain, which is supposed to have made a specialty of it."

In general, the Bretons practice only one method of preparing their lobsters, true or spiny—boiling them in sea water, which is fine if what you want to taste is lobster. In lobster *à l'américaine*, on the other hand, the sauce, which cannot be produced without the lobster, is the justification of the indignity inflicted on him. If the strength of this dish, then, lies in the sauce (as I deem indisputable), its weakness, from a non-French point of view, lies in the necessity of mopping up the sauce with at least three linear meters of bread. Bread is a good medium for carrying gravy as far as the face, but it is a diluent, not an added magnificence; it stands to the sauce of lobster *à l'américaine* in the same relationship as soda to Scotch. But a good pilaf—each grain of rice developed separately in broth to the size of a pistachio kernel—is a fine thing in its own right. Heaped on the plate and receiving the sauce *à l'américaine* as the waitress serves the lobster, the grains drink it up as avidly as nymphs quenching their thirst. The grains do not lose form or identity, although they take on a bit of *rondeur*. Mere rice cooked any old way won't do the trick; it turns to wallpaperer's paste. The French in general are almost as bad with rice as the Chinese, who are the very worst. The Armenians, Greeks, and Turks are the best with it. The conjunction of my Greek cook's *langouste* and his pilaf was a cultural milestone, like the wedding of the oyster and the lemon.

At the end of July, six weeks and several dozen *langoustes* after making the Greek's acquaintance, I left Paris. I came back in November, arriving at the Hôtel Louvois on a chill evening. I left my bags unopened and hurried through the chill to the little shrine I had discovered. *Langouste* was too much to hope for at that season, but the Greek also made an excellent couscous—a warming dish on a cold night, because of the fiery sauce you tip into the broth—and he was sure to have that on the bill. The aspect of the restaurant had not changed. There were still paper tablecloths, a zinc bar, a lettered sign on the window proclaiming GRANDE SPÉCIALITÉ DE COUSCOUS. But the faces—one behind the bar and the other framed in the kitchen window—were not the same. They were amiable faces, man and wife, but amiability is no substitute for genius. I ordered couscous, but it was a mere cream of wheat with hot sauce and a garniture of overcooked fowl—a *couscous de Paris*, not of North Africa, where the Greek had learned to make his. I had a drink with the new *patron* and his wife when I had finished. They were younger than their predecessors, and said that they knew and admired them. They would "maintain the same formula," they promised. But restaurants don't run by formula. The Greek had sold out to them, they told me, because he and his wife had quarreled.

"Why did they quarrel?" I asked.

"Because of their art," the new woman said, and smiled fondly at her husband, as if to assure him that nothing so trivial would come between them.

In 1927, the crepuscular quality of French cooking was not discernible to Root and me, because the decline was not evident at the levels at which we ate. (We ate independently, for we did not know each other then. Root was a copyreader on the Paris edition of the Chicago *Tribune*, earning fifteen dollars a week, and I was a combination Sorbonne student and remittance man, living on my father's monthly bounty.) The cheap and medium-priced restaurants that we patronized held good; slimming and other eccentricities affected only the upper strata, and only the rich had automobiles. Motoring and eating were still separate departments. Root, remaining in France during the dozen years that followed, was perhaps less aware than I of what my lamented Dublin friend Arthur McWeeney would have called the "disimprovement" of French cooking. The experiences of an individual do not follow precisely the descending

curve of a culture. A man as wily as Root—gastronomically speaking—
might eat so well every day that he would be insensible to the decreas-
ing number of good restaurants. The number was still high then—and is
even now, although, naturally, there are fewer today, and the best aren't
as good as the best used to be, or the next-to-best as good as the next-
to-best used to be, and so on down the line. Good bottles, however,
persist, especially among the classified growths of the Bordelais. The
proprietor of a legally delimited vineyard, constrained to produce his
wine on the same few acres every year, cannot change his ingredients to
fit deteriorating public taste. Good year, bad year, the character of his
wine, if not its quality, remains constant, and the ratio of good and bad
years is about the same every century. (The quantity of bad wine sold
annually in France has certainly increased, but that is another matter; it
is sold under labels of vague or purely humorous significance, or *en carafe*
as something it isn't.) When the maligned Second Empire delimited
and classified the vineyards of Médoc in 1855, it furnished French culture with a factor of stability, such as it furnished Paris when it made a
park of the Bois de Boulogne. Both were ramparts against encroach-
ment. Wine drinking is more subjective than horse racing and nearly as
subjective as love, but the gamble is less; you get something for your
money no matter what you pick.

So Root the individual was eating voraciously and perceptively, and
with total recall, all during that twelve-year interval, and laying the basis
for his masterpiece. (I don't think he will ever write a book on the food
of Britain. In his monumental treatise, he says, "I used to think . . . that
the English cook the way they do because, through sheer technical defi-
ciency, they had not been able to master the art of cooking. I have discovered to my stupefaction that the English cook that way because that
is the way they like it.") Root and I met in the winter of 1939–40, during the *drôle de guerre,* and we shared some good meals; then for a
month, between May 10, when the Germans invaded the Low Countries, and June 11, when the French government quit Paris, we had more
pressing preoccupations. (I still remember with gratitude, though, a
meal of fresh brook trout and still champagne taken at Saint-Dizier, behind the crumbling front; a good meal in troubled times is always that
much salvaged from disaster.) When the government pulled out, Root
invited me to accompany him in pursuit of it in a small French automobile. "Maybe we can find some good regional food on the way," he said.

I left France for the United States eleven days later; Root, with his French wife and their infant daughter, followed in a month. He returned to France when the war was over, and has spent most of his time there since. *The Food of France* is a monument to his affection for a country as well as for its art.

The originality of Root's approach to his subject is based on two propositions. The first is that regions compel the nature of the foods produced in them, which is only partly and sketchily true, and, by extension, that the characters of the foods, the wines, and the inhabitants of any one region interact and correspond, which makes for good anecdote but is pure whimsey. (De Gaulle has not a poor mind, although his province, Flanders, has a relatively poor and restricted cuisine; Camus's mind is balanced, not overseasoned like the food of his native Algeria; Mauriac's is thin and astringent, not voluptuous like his native *cuisine bordelaise*, which he adores.) Root's erudition is superior everywhere but at its best south of the Loire. Alsace and Normandy haven't his heart, although he tries to be fair, and he doesn't perform a sufficient obeisance to Anjou; on Provence, Nice, and the Central Plateau he is superb, and in his attack on the cooking of the Lyonnais heroic. Still, to call the cuisine of Alsace an offshoot of German cooking, as he does, is as unfair as it would be to dismiss French culture as an offshoot of Roman civilization. A lot has happened since the shooting in both cases.

In Provence, though, where he has sunned his well-covered bones during much of the past decade, Root is without peer:

> The grease in which the food of a country is cooked is the ultimate shaper of its whole cuisine. The olive is thus the creator of the cooking of Provence. A local saying points this up. "A fish," it runs, "is an animal that is found alive in water and dead in oil." . . . Garlic may not belong to Provence alone, but at least it gets special recognition there. It has even been called "the truffle of Provence." A third element must be noted as particularly typical of Provençal cooking—the tomato, which manages to get into almost everything. . . . The rabbits of this area hardly need herbs; having fed all their lives on thyme, they have inbred seasoning. . . . Artichokes . . . are ubiquitous in the region. . . . In the Vaucluse area you may be surprised if you order something listed on the bill of fare as *asperge vauclusienne,* for it is a joking name in the tradition of Scotch woodcock or prairie oysters, and what you will get is not asparagus at all but artichoke. It will be a very festive ar-

tichoke, however, stuffed with chopped ham and highly seasoned with a mixture of those herbs that seem to develop particular pungency in the dry, hilly terrain of upper Provence.

This is the lyric portion of the book; it is in Provence, I think, that Root's New England heart now lies.

The sounder of Root's two propositions, in my opinion, is his division of all French cooking into three great "domains," in accordance with his dictum that the grease in which food is cooked is the "ultimate shaper" of the cuisine. Root's "domains" are that of butter (northeastern and northern France, the Atlantic coast to below Bordeaux, and the center as far south as Lyon), that of fat (Lorraine, Alsace, and the Central Plateau), and that of oil (Provence and the County of Nice). The Basque coast has a mixed cuisine based on all three media and so refutes the universality of the system. It is true that the old division of France by orthodox *fines gueules* into gastronomic "regions" (in many cases smaller than *départements*, of which there are ninety in Continental France) has been in the process of breaking down since the remote date when the abolition of serfdom made it legitimate for the population to move around. The Revolution, the diligence, the railroad, and, finally, the automobile ended the pinpoint localization of dishes and recipes—and in any case, as Root shows, these traditional ascriptions of dishes to places are often apocryphal. Repeatedly, as he leads the reader about France, he points out instances where adjoining provinces dispute the invention of a dish, and where a province that didn't invent a dish does it rather better than the one that did. There are, however, broad similarities in the cooking of certain subdivisions of France that are larger than the old provinces or the modern *départements*. These similarities (and differences) do not follow any purely geographic lines, and Root's "domains" are an ingenious beginning of a new taxonomy; he is like the zoologist who first began to group species into genera, observing that while a cat, a monkey, a man, and a tiger are different things, a man is rather more like a monkey than like a cat, and a cat rather more like a tiger than like a man. Somebody had to start, and Root is a true innovator. Whether the cooking of Périgord really is more like the cooking of Alsace (because both use the fat of the goose and the pig) than like that of the southwest (which, like Périgord, uses garlic) is another question; some future scientist of taste may attempt a new grouping on the basis of seasoning. If the inventor of the new system has as much love for his subject and as much learning as

Root, the result can only be another good book, as rich in the marrow of argument as *The Food of France.*

Now that Root's monument has been erected for the ages—a picture of a cultural achievement, fixed to history's page before the snack bars and cafeterias and drive-ins could efface it from men's minds—he seems a trifle melancholy. "It's hard to find such good eating in the provinces nowadays, even at the present high rates—or maybe I'm just getting old and cranky," he wrote me not long ago. "The fact is that it's a long while since I have come upon one of those bottles of wine that make you sit up and take notice, and it's even pretty rare nowadays to have a memorable meal." Here, however, he was unduly sombre. There will still be enough good bottles and good meals to last us all a few more decades; it is only that they are becoming harder to find. The rise and fall of an art takes time. The full arc is seldom manifest to a single generation.

1959

"It started out with lactose, but now he's intolerant of everything."

IS THERE A CRISIS IN
FRENCH COOKING?

ADAM GOPNIK

Nine o'clock on a Friday morning, and David Angelot, the *commis* at the restaurant Arpège, on the Rue de Varenne, has begun to braise tomatoes for dessert. The *tomate confite farcie aux douze saveurs* is one of the few dishes in the Michelin red guide whose place on the menu has to be clarified with a parenthesis (*dessert*), indicating that though it sounds like a veggie, it eats like a sweet. It is a specialty of the kitchen of the great chef Alain Passard, which a lot of people think is the best and most poetic in Paris, and probably all France; it requires a hair-raising amount of work by the *commis*, the kitchen cabin boy; and many people who care about French cooking believe that it is a kind of hopeful portent—a sign that the creative superiority of French cooking may yet be extended indefinitely. Normally, a braised tomato becomes tomato sauce. ("The limitations of this insight," one of Passard's admirers has noted gravely, "describe the limitations of Italian cuisine.") To make a tomato get sweeter without falling apart not only is technically demanding but demonstrates, with a stubborn, sublime logic, an extremely abstract botanical point. Tomatoes are not vegetables; they are fruit.

For David, who may not see M. Passard all day long, they are work. David, who is eighteen, and who studied cooking at a government school just outside Lyon, cuts the tomatoes open (about fifty of them, from Morocco, in the winter), scoops them out, and makes a *farce*, a stuffing of finely chopped orange and lemon zest, sugar, ginger, mint, pistachios, star anise, cloves; then he makes a big pot of vanilla-scented caramel and braises the stuffed tomatoes in it, beating the caramel around the tomatoes vigorously for forty-five minutes without actually touching them. The tomato is a fruit, and can be treated like one, but it helps to beat a lot of caramel into its body, to underline the point.

While he works, he thinks about his girlfriend (who is also a cook, and with whom he lives in an apartment in north Paris), his future, and his desire to someday visit Japan. He works in a tiny basement room in the small, two-story space of the kitchen, and he shares that room with another, more experienced assistant, Guilhem, who spends his mornings making bread. (All the bread at Arpège is made by hand.) Guilhem, while he works, thinks of going back to Washington—he calls it "D.C."—where he has been before, where there is a constant demand for good French food, and where he has an offer to work in a French bakery. If David's job at Arpège embodies one of the principles of high French cooking—the gift of making things far more original than anyone can imagine—Guilhem's embodies the opposite but complementary principle: the necessity of making things much better than anybody needs. This morning, he will make three kinds of bread: a sourdough raisin-and-nut loaf; trays of beautiful long white rolls; and a rough, round peasant bread. All the bread will be sliced and placed in baskets to be presented upstairs in the dining room, and then mostly pushed around absentmindedly on the plates of people who are looking at their menus and deciding what they really want to eat. This knowledge makes Guilhem a little bitter. He thinks about D.C.

In the main kitchen, a short flight up, Pascal Barbot, the sous-chef, is keeping things under control. The atmosphere there, with eleven serious short men in white uniforms going about intricate tasks in a cramped space, does not so much resemble the bridge of a nuclear submarine in an action movie as it does the bridge of a nuclear submarine in an action movie after it has been taken over by the Euroterrorists led by Alan Rickman: that kind of intensity, scared purposefulness, quickness, and heavy, whispered French. The kitchen is white and silver, with a few well-scrubbed copper pots hanging high up—not like the lacquered copper you see in rusticated, beam-heavy restaurant interiors but dull and scrubbed and penny-colored. The richest colors in the kitchen are those of French produce, which is always several glazes darker than American: the birds (chickens, pigeons, quail) are yellow and veined with deep violet, instead of the American white and rose. The assistant chefs start at nine o'clock, and will remain at their *stages* until one o'clock the next morning. When the service begins, around twelve-thirty, they will experience an almost unendurable din, which, after a few days of work, they learn to break down into three or four distinct sounds: the *thwonk* of metal in water hitting the sides of a sink as a pot is washed by one of the Malinese *plongeurs;* the higher, harsh *clank* of one clean saucepan being placed on another; the surprisingly tinny, machine-gun *rat-a-tat* of a wire whisk in a copper pot; and the crashing, the-tent-just-fell-down-on-your-head sound of hot soiled pans being thrown down onto tile to be washed again. (In a good kitchen, the pans are constantly being recycled by the *plongeurs.*)

The kitchen crew includes three Americans. They have worked mostly at California and New York restaurants of the kind that one of them describes as "grill-and-garnish joints." They are all converts to Passardism. There is never anything entirely new in cooking, but Passard's technique is not like anybody else's. Instead of browning something over high heat in a saucepan and then roasting it in an oven, in the old French manner, or grilling it quickly over charcoal, in the new American one, Passard cooks his birds and joints *sur la plaque:* right on the stove, over extremely low heat in big braising pans, sometimes slow-cooking a baby gigot or a milk-fed pig in a pot for four or five hours on a bed of sweet onions and butter. "He's just *sweating* those babies," one of the Americans marvels under his breath, looking at the joints on the stoves. "Makes them cook themselves in their own fat. It's like he does everything but make them pluck their own feathers and jump into the pan. Fucking genius."

Downstairs, another of the Americans is slicing butter and teasing Guilhem about his D.C. plans. "Look at this butter," he says to himself. "That's not fucking Land O'Lakes." He turns to Guilhem. "Hey, forget about D.C.," he says. "It's cold. There are no women. Where you want to go is California. That's the promised land. Man, that's a place where you can cook *and* have a life."

Guilhem looks genuinely startled, and turns to speak. "You can?" he says, softly at first, and then louder, calling out to the back of the American cook as he races up the stairs with the butter pats for the dining room. "You *can?*"

Most people who love Paris love it because the first time they came they ate something better than they had ever eaten before, and kept coming back to eat it again. My first night in Paris, twenty-five years ago, I ate dinner with my enormous family in a little corner brasserie somewhere down on the unfashionable fringes of the sixteenth arrondissement. We were on the cut-rate, American-academic version of the Grand Tour, and we had been in London for the previous two days,

where we had eaten *steamed* hamburgers and fish-and-chips in which
the batter seemed to be snubbing the fish inside it as if they had never
been properly introduced. On that first night in Paris, we arrived late
on the train, checked in to a cheap hotel, and went to eat (party of
eight—no, party of nine, one of my sisters having brought along a
boyfriend), without much hope, at the restaurant at the corner, called
something like Le Bar-B-Que. The prix-fixe menu was fifteen francs,
about three dollars then. I ordered a *salade niçoise,* trout baked in foil,
and a cassis sorbet. It was so much better than anything I had ever
eaten that I nearly wept. (My mother, I am compelled at gunpoint to
add, made food like that all the time, too, but a mother's cooking is a
current of life, not an episode of taste.) My feelings at Le Bar-B-Que
were a bit like those of Stendhal, I think it was, the first time he went
to a brothel: I knew that it could be done, but I didn't know there was
a place on any corner where you could walk in, pay three dollars, and
get it.

That first meal in Paris was for a long time one of the few completely reliable pleasures for an American in Europe. "It was the green
beans," a hardened New Yorker recalled not long ago, remembering his
first meal in Paris, back in the late forties. "The green beans were like
nothing I had ever known," he went on. He sat suddenly bolt upright,
his eyes alight with memory.

Now, though, for the first time in several hundred years, a lot of
people who live in France are worried about French cooking, and so are
a lot of people who don't. The French themselves are, or claim to be,
worried mostly about the high end—the end that is crowded into the
Passard kitchen—and the low end. The word *crise* in connection with
cooking appeared in *Le Monde* about a year ago, with the news that a
restaurant near Lyon, which had earned three Michelin stars, was about
to close. Meanwhile, a number of worrying polls have suggested that
the old pyramid of French food, in which the base of plain dishes
shared by the population pointed upward to the higher reaches of the
Grande Cuisine, is collapsing. Thirty-six percent of the French people
polled in one survey thought that you make mayonnaise with whole
eggs (you use only yolks), 17 percent thought that you put a *travers de
porc* in a pot-au-feu (you use beef), and 7 percent believed that Lucas
Carton, the Paris restaurant that for a century has been one of the holiest of holies of haute cuisine, is a name for badly cooked meat. More
ominously, fully 71 percent of Frenchmen named the banal steak-frites

as their favorite *plat;* only people past sixty preferred a *blanquette de veau,* or a *gigot d'agneau,* or even a pot-au-feu, all real French cooking. (The French solution to this has been, inevitably, to create a National Council of Culinary Arts, connected to the Ministry of Culture.)

To an outsider, the real *crise* lies in the middle. That Paris first-night experience seems harder to come by. It is the unforced superiority of the cooking in the ordinary corner bistro—the *prix-fixe ordinaire*—that seems to be passing. This is partly a tribute to the international power of French cooking, and to the great catching-up that has been going on in the rest of the world for the past quarter century. The new visitor, trying out the trout baked in foil on his first night in Paris, will probably be comparing it with the trout baked in foil back home at, oh, Le Lac de Feu, in Cleveland—or even back home at Chez Alfie, in Leeds, or Matilda Qui Danse, in Adelaide—and the trout back home may just be better: raised wild or caught on the line. Even the cassis sorbet may not be quite as good as the kind he makes at home with his Sorbet-o-matic.

The fear—first unspoken, then whispered, then cautiously enunciated, and now loudly insisted on by certain competitors—is that the muse of cooking has migrated across the ocean to a spot in Berkeley, with occasional trips to New York and, of all places, Great Britain. People in London will even tell you, flatly, that the cooking there now is the best in the world, and they will publish this thought as though it were a statement of fact, and as though the steamed hamburger and the stiff fish had been made long ago in another country. Two of the best chefs in the London cooking renaissance said to a reporter not long ago that London, along with Sydney and San Francisco, is one of the capitals of good food, and that the food in Paris—"heavy, lazy, lacking in imagination"—is now among the worst in the world.

All this makes a Francophile eating in Paris feel a little like a turn-of-the-century clergyman who has just read Robert Ingersoll: you try to keep the faith, but Doubts keep creeping in. Even the most ardent Paris lover, who once blessed himself at every dinner for having escaped Schrafft's, may now find himself—as he gazes down one more unvarying menu of *boudin noir* and *saumon unilatéral* and *entrecôte bordelaise* and *poulet rôti,* eats one more bland and buttery dish—feeling a slight pang for that Cuban-Vietnamese-California grill on Amsterdam Avenue, or wondering whether he might, just possibly, enjoy the New Sardinian Cooking, as featured that week on the cover of *New York.*

I would still rather eat in Paris than anywhere else in the world. The best places in Paris, like the Brasserie Balzar, on the Rue des Écoles, don't just feed you well; they make you happy in a way that no other city's restaurants can. (The Balzar is the place that plays Gallant to the more famous Brasserie Lipp's Goofus.) Even in a mediocre Paris restaurant, you are part of the richest commonplace civilization that has ever been created, and that extends back visibly to the previous century. In Paris, restaurants can actually go into a kind of hibernation for years, and awaken in a new generation: Lapérouse, the famous swanky nineteenth-century spot, has, after a long stretch of being overlooked, just come back to life, and is a good place to eat again. Reading Olivier Todd's biography of Camus, you discover that the places where Camus went to dinner in the forties (Aux Charpentiers, Le Petit St. Benoît, Aux Assassins) are places where you can go to dinner tonight. Some of Liebling's joints are still in business, too: the Beaux-Arts, the Pierre à la Place Gaillon, the Closerie des Lilas.

These continuities suggest that a strong allegiance to the past acts as a drag on the present. But, after several months of painstaking, tie-staining research, I think that the real problem lies in the French genius for laying the intellectual foundation for a revolution that takes place somewhere else. With movies (Méliès and the Lumière brothers invented the form, and then couldn't build the industry), with airplanes, and now even with cooking, France has again and again made the first breakthrough and then gotten stalled. All the elements of the new cooking, as it exists today in America and in London—the openness to new techniques, the suspicion of the overelaborate, the love of surprising juxtapositions—were invented in Paris long before they emigrated to London and New York and Berkeley. But in France they never coalesced into something entirely new. The Enlightenment took place here, and the Revolution worked out better somewhere else.

The early seventies, when I was first in France, were, I realize now, a kind of Indian summer of French haute cuisine, the last exhalation of a tradition that had been in place for several hundred years. The atmosphere of French cooking was everywhere in Paris then: thick smells and posted purple mimeographed menus; the sounds of cutlery on tables and the jowly look of professional eaters emerging blinking into the light at four o'clock.

The standard, practical account of the superiority of French cooking was that it had been established in the sixteenth century, when
Caterina de' Medici brought Italian cooks, then the best in the world,
to Paris. It was not until after the French Revolution, though, when the
breakup of the great aristocratic houses sent chefs out onto the street
looking for someone to feed, that the style of French cooking went
public. The most famous and influential figure of this period—the first
great chef in European history—was Antonin Carême, who worked, by
turns, for Talleyrand, the future George IV, Czar Alexander I, and the
Baroness de Rothschild. He invented "presentation." His cooking looked
a lot like architecture, with the dishes fitted into vast, beautiful neoclas-
sical structures.

The unique superiority of French cooking for the next hundred
years depended on the invention of the cooking associated with the
name Auguste Escoffier. Escoffier's formula for food was, in essence,
the same as Jasper Johns's formula for Dada art: take something; do
something to it; then do something else to it. It was cooking that
rested, above all, on the idea of the master sauce: a lump of protein was
cooked in a pan, and what was left behind in the pan was "deglazed"
with wine or stock, ornamented with butter or cream, and then poured
back over the lump of protein. Escoffier was largely the creature of
courtiers and aristocratic patrons; the great hoteliers of Europe, and
particularly César Ritz, sealed in place the master-sauce approach that
remains the unchallenged basis of haute cuisine.

It was also an article of faith, dating, perhaps, to Alexandre Dumas
père's famous *Grand Dictionnaire de Cuisine,* that the cooking of Carême
and Escoffier had evolved from a set of provincial folk techniques. At
the heart of French food lay the pot-au-feu, the bouillon pot that every
peasant wife was supposed to keep on her hearth, and into which, according to legend, she threw whatever she had, to stew for the day's
meal. French classic cooking was French provincial cooking gone to
town.

I heard another, more weirdly philosophical account of this history,
from a professor named Eugenio Donato, who was the most passionately intellectual eater I have ever known. Armenian-Italian, reared in
Egypt and educated in France, he spoke five languages, each with a

nearly opaque Akim Tamiroff accent. ("It could have been worse," he said to me once, expertly removing one mussel with the shell of another as we ate *moules marinière* somewhere on the Place de la Sorbonne. "I had a friend whose parents were ardent Esperantists. He spoke five languages, each with an impenetrable Esperanto accent.") Eugenio was a literary critic whom we would now call a post-structuralist, though he called what he did "philosophical criticism."

Most of the time, he wandered from one American university to another—the Johnny Appleseed or Typhoid Mary of deconstruction, depending on your point of view. He had a deeply tragic personal life, though, and I think that his happiest hours were spent in Paris, eating and thinking and talking. His favorite subject was French food, and his favorite theory was that "French cooking" was foreign to France, not something that had percolated up from the old pot-au-feu but something that had been invented by fanatics at the top, as a series of powerful "metaphors"—ideas about France and Frenchness—which had then moved downward to organize the menus and, retrospectively, colonize the past. "The idea of the French chef precedes French cooking" was how he put it. Cooking for him was a form of writing—Carême and Escoffier had earned their reputations by publishing cookbooks—with literature's ability to make something up and then pretend it had been there all along.

The invention of the French restaurant, Eugenio believed, depended largely on what every assistant professor would now call an "essentialized" idea of France. One proof of this was that if the best French restaurants tended to be in Paris, the most "typical" ones tended to be in New York. Yet the more abstract and self-enclosed haute cuisine became, the more inclined its lovers were to pretend that it was a folk art, risen from the French earth unbidden. For Eugenio, the key date in this masquerade was 1855, when the wines of Médoc were classified into the famous five growths in which they remain today. "The form of metropolitan rationalization being extended to the provincial earth, *in the guise of the reflection of an order locked in the earth itself*," he announced once, bringing his fist down on the tablecloth. He was a big man, who looked uncannily like John Madden, the football coach.

On that occasion, we were eating lunch in one of the heavy, dark, smoky Lyon places that were popular in Paris then. (There is always one provincial region singled out for favor in Paris at any moment—

"privileged" would have been Eugenio's word. Then it was Burgundy; now it is the southwest. This fact was grist for his thesis that the countryside was made in the city.) The restaurant was, I think, someplace over in the seventh—it may have been Pantagruel, or La Bourgogne. At lunch, in those days, Eugenio would usually begin with twelve escargots in Chablis, then go on to something like a *filet aux moelles*—a fillet with bone marrow and Madeira sauce—and end, whenever he could, with a mille-feuille.

The food in those places wasn't so much "rich" as deep, dense. Each *plat* arrived looking mellow and varnished, like an old violin. Each mouthful registered like a fat organ chord in a tall church, hitting you hard and then echoing around the room: there's the bass note (the beef), there's the middle note (the marrow), and there's the treble (the Madeira in the sauce).

It couldn't last. "We have landed in the moment when the metaphors begin to devour themselves, the moment of rhetorical self-annihilation," Eugenio once said cheerfully. This meant that the food had become so rich as to be practically inedible. A recipe from the restaurant Lucas Carton I found among a collection of menus of the time which Eugenio bequeathed to me suggests the problem. The recipe is for a *timbale des homards*. You take three lobsters, season them with salt and pepper and a little curry, sauté them in a light *mirepoix*—a mixture of chopped onions and carrots—and then simmer them with cognac, port, double cream, and fish stock for twenty minutes. Then you take out the lobsters and, keeping them warm, reduce the cooking liquid and add two egg yolks and 150 grams of sweet butter. Metaphors like that can kill you.

Something had to give, and it did. The "nouvelle cuisine" that replaced the old style has by now been reduced to a set of clichés, and become a licensed subject of satire: the tiny portion on the big oval plate; the raspberry-vinegar infusion; the kiwi. This makes it difficult to remember how fundamental a revolution it worked in the way people cooked. At the same moment in the early seventies, a handful of new chefs—Michel Guérard, Paul Bocuse, Alain Senderens—began to question the do-something-to-it-then-do-something-else-to-it basis of the classic cooking. They emphasized, instead, fresh ingredients, simple treatment, an openness to Oriental techniques and spices, and a general reformist air of lightness and airiness.

The new chefs had little places all around Paris, in the outlying arrondissements, where, before, no one would have traveled for a first-rate meal: Michel Guérard was at Le Pot-au-Feu, way out in Asnières; Alain Dutournier, a little later, settled his first restaurant, Au Trou Gascon, in the extremely unfashionable twelfth. In the sad, sedate seventh arrondissement, Alain Senderens opened Archestrate, first in a little space on the Rue de l'Exposition, in the shadow of the Eiffel Tower, and then on the Rue de Varenne.

From the beginning, the new cooking divided into two styles, into what Eugenio identified as "two rhetorics," a rhetoric of *terroirs* and a rhetoric of *épices*—soil and spice. The rhetoric of the *terroirs* emphasized the allegiance of new cooking to French soil; the rhetoric of the *épices* emphasized its openness to the world beyond the hexagon. The soil boys wanted to return French cooking to its roots in the regions; the spice boys wanted to take it forward to the new regions of *outre-mer*. Even as the new cooking tried to look outward, it had to reassure its audience (and itself) that it was really looking inward.

On the surface, the beautiful orderly pattern continues. Alain Senderens is now in Michel Comby's place at Lucas Carton and has replaced the *timbale des homards* cooking with his own style. Senderens's Rue de Varenne Archestrate is now occupied by Alain Passard, the Senderens of his generation, while the original Archestrate is occupied by a talented young chef and his wife, just starting out, who have named the restaurant after their little girl: La Maison de Cosima.

But, twenty-five years later, the great leap forward seems to have stalled. A large part of the *crise* is economic: a hundred-dollar lunch is a splurge, a four-hundred-dollar lunch a moral dubiety. Worse, because of the expense, the cooking at the top places in Paris is no longer a higher extension of a commonplace civilization. It is just three-star cooking, a thing unto itself, like grand opera in the age of the microphone. Like grand opera, it is something that will soon need a subsidy to survive—the kitchen at Arpège depends on regular infusions of range-struck Americans to fill the space left by the French kids who no longer want to work eighteen-hour days for very little money while they train.

And it is like grand opera in this, also: you can get too much of it, easily. It is, truth be told, often a challenge to eat—a happy challenge, and sometimes a welcome one, but a challenge nonetheless. It is just too rich, and there is just too much. The new cooking in France has become a version of the old.

At Lucas Carton, you begin with, say, a plate of vegetables so young they seem dewy, beautifully done, but so bathed in butter and transformed that they are no longer particularly vegetal; and then you move on to the new lobster dish that has taken the place of the old one. Where the old lobsters were done in a cowshedful of cream, the new lobsters are done, *épice* style, with Madagascar vanilla bean. This is delicious, with the natural sugar of the lobster revealing the vanilla as a spice—although, for an American, the custard-colored sauce, dotted with specks of black vanilla, disconcertingly calls to mind melted lunchroom ice cream. For dessert, you might have a roasted pineapple, which is done on the same principles on which Passard's tomatoes are braised: it ends up encrusted in caramel. This is delicious, too, though intensely sweet. Lunch at Lucas these days can fairly be called Napoleonic or Empire: the references to the revolutionary principles are there, but finally it's in thrall to the same old aristocratic values.

Lucas is hardly representative, but even at the lesser, less ambitious places the cooking seems stuck in a rut: a chunk of boned protein, a reduced sauce; maybe a fruit complement, to establish its "inventive" bona fides; and a purée. The style has become formulaic: a disk of meat, a disk of complement, a sauce on top. The new cooking seems to have produced less a new freedom than a revived orthodoxy—a new essentialized form of French cooking, which seems less pleasing, and certainly a lot less "modern," than the cooking that evolved at the same time from the French new cooking in other countries. The hold of the master sauté pan, and the master sauce, and the thing-in-the-middle-of-the-plate, is still intact.

Thinking it over, I suspect that Eugenio put his finger on the problem with the new cooking in France when it first appeared. "A revolution can sweep clean," he said. "But a reformation points forward and backward at the same time." The new cooking was, as Eugenio said, a reformation, not a revolution: it worked within the same system of Michelin stars and fifteen-man kitchens and wealthy clients that the old cooking did; it didn't make a new audience; it tried to appropriate the old one.

In America—and in England, too, where the only thing you wanted to do with the national culinary tradition was lose it—the division between soil and spice wasn't a problem. You could first create the recipes and then put the ingredients in the earth yourself. The American cooks who have followed in Alice Waters's path-making footsteps at Chez Panisse, in Berkeley—the generation whom a lot of people think of as the children of M.F.K. Fisher—created a freewheeling, eclectic cosmopolitan cuisine: a risotto preceding a stir-fry leading to a *sabayon*. Then they went out and persuaded the local farmers to grow the things they needed.

In France, the soil boys won easily. Some of what they stood for is positive and even inspiring: the *terroirs* movement has a green, organic, earth-conscious element that is very good news. The *marché biologique* every Sunday morning on the Boulevard Raspail has become one of the weekly Parisian wonders, full of ugly, honest fruit and rough, tasty country meat. And it is rare for any restaurant in Paris to succeed now without presenting itself as a "regional" spot—a southwest, or Provençal, or Savoyard place. (Even at the exquisite Grand Véfour, at the Palais-Royal, the most beautiful restaurant in the world and a cathedral of the cosmopolitan tradition, it is thought necessary to parade around a plate of the cheeses of the chef's native Savoy.)

Yet the insistence on national, or local, tradition—on truth to *terroirs*—can give even to the best new Paris restaurants a predictability that the good new places in London and New York don't share. The French, who invented the tradition of taking things over and then insisting that they were yours all along, are now shy about doing it. The cooking at a French restaurant must now, for the first time, be French. This tendency came to a head last spring, when a group of important French chefs actually issued a manifesto protesting the spread of exotic food combinations and alien spices in French cooking, and calling for a return to the *terroirs*.

Peter Hoffman, the owner and chef of the influential Savoy, in New York, is one of those American chefs who went to France in the early eighties, were dazzled, and now find that the light has dimmed. He likes to tell about his most recent dinner at the three-star restaurant L'Ambroisie, on the Place des Vosges. "We went to L'Ambroisie and had a classic French dish: hare with blood sauce. It was fabulous, everything you want rabbit with blood to be. But then I got talked into ordering one of the chef's specialties, a mille-feuille of langoustines with curry, and it was infuriating. It was a French dish with powder. It was such an insular approach, as though nobody understood that curry isn't a powder that you apply cosmetically. Nobody had read Madhur Jaffrey, or really understood that curry isn't just a spice you shake but a whole technique of cooking you have to understand."

As the writer Catharine Reynolds points out, the new cooking in America and England alike is really Mediterranean cooking, inspired by Italy, Tunisia, and Greece. It suits the fat-allergic modern palate better than the old butter-and-cream cooking of the north. France, which has a big window south, ought to be open to its influence, yet remains resistant. The real national dish of the French right now—the cheap, available food—is couscous. But North African cooking remains segregated in couscous parlors, and has not been brought into the main current. A fossilized metropolitan tradition should have been replaced by a modernized metropolitan tradition, yet what took its place was sentimental nationalism.

It was the invasion of American fast food, as much as anything, that made the French turn back to their own tradition and, for the first time, see it as something in need of self-conscious protection. Looking at America, the French don't see the children of M.F.K. Fisher; they just see the flood tides of McDonald's, which, understandably, strike fear into their hearts. The bistro became an endangered species. To make still one more *blanquette de veau* suddenly became not a habit of commonplace civilization but a form of self-defense.

Waverley Root once divided all Gaul into three fats—lard, olive oil, and butter—and said that they determined the shape of French cooking. That you might be able to cook without putting any fat in the pan at all was an unthinkable notion. The charcoal grill, the brick oven, and all the other nonfat ways of cooking now seem normal everywhere except in France. People who look at cooking more practically than philosophically think that that technical lag is the heart of the problem.

"It's deglaze or die" is how Alexandra Guarnaschelli, an American cook in Paris, puts it. The master-sauce approach remains the basis of French cooking, whereas elsewhere it has been overthrown by the grill. The pan and the pot have always been the basic utensils of French cooking—just what was there—in the same way that the grill was the primary element of American-vernacular backyard cooking. For Americans, grilled food wasn't new but familiar, and good cooking is made up of familiar things done right. As the excellent American chefs Chris Schlesinger and John Willoughby have pointed out, grilling forced an entirely new approach to sauce-making: with no residue to deglaze, the cook had to think in terms of savory complements rather than subtle echoes. Grilling demanded chutney, fruit mustards, spice mixes. Although the French tradition included these things, they weren't part of the vernacular.

Alex has seen some of the predicament at first hand. She is twenty-seven; she arrived in France five years ago and, after training in Burgundy, became a *commis* at Guy Savoy's two-star place in the seventeenth arrondissement. Within a couple of years, she had worked her way up to fish chef, and, a little while later, Savoy appointed her second-in-command at his bistro, La Butte Chaillot. (This is like a young Frenchman arriving in New York, all enthusiastic about baseball, and ending up five years later as the third baseman of the Yankees.)

The other day, over coffee on the Avenue Kléber, Alex, who is from New York (she went to Barnard, Mom's an editor at Scribner, Dad's a professor), said, "I decided I wanted to chop onions, so I tried the C.I.A."—the Culinary Institute of America, the M.I.T. of American cooking—"but it was like eighteen thousand a year, *tout compris*, so I decided to go to Burgundy and chop. I started learning the French way, which is half beautiful beyond belief and half 'Please shoot me.' It's by the book. Really, there's a book, and you learn it. There's a system for everything, a way to do it. You can't cut the fish that way, because *ça n'est pas bon*. You can't bone a chicken that way, because *that's* not good. 'We do it the way it's always been done in France.' When I first started at Savoy, there was one old stager who, every time I did something, would just frown and shake his head and say, 'It won't do, it won't do.' Finally, I did *exactly* what he did, and he said, 'Good, now, always do it exactly the same way.' So I did. You never get a real attempt to innovate, or to use new flavors. You can change an adjective, but the sentence stays the same.

"Whenever we make a classic sauce, everybody gathers around and *argues* about it. Once, we got into a two-hour argument about whether you use chervil as well as tarragon in a true béarnaise. There are certain things these days that I will not do. I will not do mayonnaise or béarnaise. Uh-uh. I don't have time for the postgame analysis.

"Of course, there's that tomato at Passard's place," she went on. "But have you seen the way the poor kid has to work to make it?"

Alex's existence helps to explain why the new cooking went deeper in America than it could in France: in America the cooking revolution was above all a middle-class revolution, even an upper-middle-class revolution. A lot of the people who made the cooking revolution in America were doing it as a second career. At the very least, they were doing it after a liberal-arts degree; David Angelot started slicing carrots at fifteen. The most mocked of all modern American restaurant manners—the waiter who introduces himself by name—is, on reflection, a sign of something very positive. "I'm Henry, and I'll be your waiter tonight" means, really, "You and I belong to the same social class. Tomorrow night, I could be sitting there, and you could be standing here."

The French system of education, unrenovated for a long time, locks people in place. Kids emerge with an impressive respect for learning and erudition, and intimidated by it, too. For an American, getting a Ph.D. is a preliminary, before you go someplace else and find your real work, like opening a restaurant. Nobody thinks of changing *métiers* in France, because it's just too hard. In America, not only the consumers of the new cooking but, more important, the producers and dealers were college-educated. I once met a pair of American academics who had gone off to live with a flock of goats and make goat cheese. They had named the goats Emily, Virginia, Jessamyn, Willa, and Ursula. It was terrific goat cheese, too.

Beyond these reasons—the missing grill, the resurgent nationalism, the educational trap—there may be an even deeper reason for the lull in French cooking. A new book, *L'Amateur de Cuisine*, by an unknown author, Jean-Philippe Derenne, which was published last year, offers an anatomy of French cooking—an effort to organize the materials, forms, and manners of the subject in a systematic way. "This cookbook is a book," the author writes on the first page, and then attempts to create a whole taxonomy of cooking based not on folk tradition or cosmopolitan recipes but on an analysis of plants and animals and the chemistry of what happens when you apply different kinds of heat and cold to them before you eat them. He begins his market section with the minerals (a crisp page and a half), and then passes to the plants (more than a hundred pages) and the animals, divided into those of the earth and the sky and those of fresh and salt water. (Even "Serpents, Sauriens, Lézards, etc." get their moment in the sun.) He gives a precise biological description of every imaginable thing there is to eat, then presents an exact analysis of every imaginable method of cooking it and shows how all the glories of cuisine rise out of the limitless intersections of these two forces. It is a vast, eleven-hundred-page volume, comprehensive and radiant; it resembles less a cookbook than a medieval almanac, offering a timeless, secure, benevolent universe of food. Its subject isn't cooking. It's *plenty*.

Derenne is a modest and gentle scholar, not a cook or a critic, or even a gourmand. He is a doctor, the head of the pulmonary department at a Paris hospital. Over lunch one afternoon at Arpège, Derenne, who is a small, good-natured man, with the open face and happy appetites of a Benedictine monk, said, "The same week that *L'Amateur de Cuisine* came out, I published another book, called *Acute Respiratory Failure of Chronic Obstructive Pulmonary Disease*." That was another thousand pages. This, surely, is a record for total weight by one author published in one week.

Derenne wrote the cookbook in seclusion, in the garden of his little house near Fontainebleau, only to find himself, on its publication, a new lion of the French culinary establishment: the man who wrote the book. He gets reverential, *cher maître*–type letters from Paul Bocuse. Passard himself sees him as a friend. Dr. Derenne doesn't know quite what to make of it all.

"My editor said to me, when I gave him the manuscript, 'Why, you've written the first humanist history of food.' I said, 'No, not humanist. It's a religious book, really.' I was inspired by a history of religion by Mircea Eliade, which attempted the same kind of logical organization: rising upward from the types of religious apparition into the possibilities of organized faith. I've done for cooking what that author did for belief: shown an underlying logic without attempting to make it logical."

He went on to talk about a second volume, which he's just started: "It may be called *Free Cuisine*, but really it will be about the rejected cuisine. About everything the world throws out. Shells and guts and

leaves—the whole world of the rejected. This is religious, too, because
religion depends on being able to find the holy in the ordinary. It's
putting together things banal in themselves which nonetheless become
transformed into something transcendent. You know who else has this
quality? Duke Ellington—he simply used what he had."

There was something surprising about Derenne's talk, an expansive, open, embracing ardor that a hundred years ago would have
seemed more American than French. It seems possible that the different fates of the new cooking in France and America are a sign of a new
relation between the two places.

A century ago, Americans used to say that what brought them to
Europe was its history. At home, there was "no sovereign, no court . . .
no aristocracy . . . nor ivied ruins; no cathedrals," as Henry James's famous list has it. What really brought Americans to the Old World,
though, was the allure of power: cultural power, political power, military power—imperial power, as it existed in Europe and only there.
What fascinated Whistler and James in the Old World was not its age
but the extreme self-consciousness that comes with power, the way that
power could be seen to shimmer through manners—the way that what
you wore or how you stood (or what you ate) spelled out your place in
a complicated and potent social hierarchy.

Now that that power has passed into American—or, anyway,
English-speaking—hands, the trappings of power which come from
extreme self-consciousness are ours, too. Even our cooking—especially
our cooking—has become involved with power. Where you stand on,
say, the spread of McDonald's is a political issue, just as where you
stood on the outdoor café was in France a century ago. Even the smaller
issues of the palate count: most American women define their femi-
nism, at least in part, in terms of their attitude toward the kitchen. A
century ago, the modern form of that self-consciousness was invented
in Paris. The limitlessly complicated relation of what you eat and where
you eat it to where you stand in the social order is the subject of, for instance, the first two chapters of Maupassant's *Bel-Ami*. But now food
and cooking in France have begun to take at least a small half turn back
toward their other role, as sources of nourishment, comfort, cohesion.
The role of food as anxious social theatre, seen at its crudest in the endless worry in Los Angeles and New York about power tables—where
you sit at Spago, what time you leave the Four Seasons—is diminishing

in France. We are the worldly, corrupt ones at the table now, and the Europeans, in this regard at least, are the innocents. Even their philosophers eat for pleasure.

When the *tomate confite*, which David Angelot had been working on since nine o'clock, came out at last, Derenne tasted it. Then he said, "You see, he demonstrates for us what we knew from the first, that the tomato is a fruit. Would you call that arrogance or modesty?"

Not long after that, I finally did what I had dreaded doing, though it would have been the practical thing to do all along, which was to go back to that first restaurant and see what it was like now. I walked back and found both the hotel and the restaurant, though both had changed their names—the hotel belonged now to the Best Western chain—and, while in memory I had kept them on the same street, they were in fact a street apart. But the exterior of the restaurant was unmistakable; I found it by getting the Eiffel Tower in exactly the same area of my eye as it had occupied when I was fourteen. It was not far from—I am not making this up—the Avenue Marcel-Proust. The restaurant is now called the Tournesol, and the less expensive prix fixe is 114 francs, or about twenty dollars. I ate à la carte. I had a little foie gras, sole meunière, and a cassis sorbet.

The food was even better than I had remembered. This proves either that (a) Proust was wrong, and you can always recapture the pleasures of your youth if you just go back to the places where you had them, or (b) there is more good cooking left in Paris than I knew, or (c) I went to the wrong place. Anyway, there's hope.

1997

DON'T EAT BEFORE READING THIS

ANTHONY BOURDAIN

Good food, good eating, is all about blood and organs, cruelty and decay. It's about sodium-loaded pork fat, stinky triple-cream cheeses, the tender thymus glands and distended livers of young animals. It's about danger—risking the dark, bacterial forces of beef, chicken, cheese, and shellfish. Your first 207 Wellfleet oysters may transport you to a state of rapture, but your 208th may send you to bed with the sweats, chills, and vomits.

Gastronomy is the science of pain. Professional cooks belong to a secret society whose ancient rituals derive from the principles of stoicism in the face of humiliation, injury, fatigue, and the threat of illness. The members of a tight, well-greased kitchen staff are a lot like a submarine crew. Confined for most of their waking hours in hot, airless spaces and ruled by despotic leaders, they often acquire the characteristics of the poor saps who were press-ganged into the royal navies of Napoleonic times—superstition, a contempt for outsiders, and a loyalty to no flag but their own.

A good deal has changed since Orwell's memoir of the months he spent as a dishwasher in *Down and Out in Paris and London*. Gas ranges and exhaust fans have gone a long way toward increasing the life span of the working culinarian. Nowadays, most aspiring cooks come into the business because they want to: they have chosen this life, studied for it. Today's top chefs are like star athletes. They bounce from kitchen to kitchen—free agents in search of more money, more acclaim.

I've been a chef in New York for more than ten years, and, for the decade before that, a dishwasher, a prep drone, a line cook, and a sous-chef. I came into the business when cooks still smoked on the line and wore headbands. A few years ago, I wasn't surprised to hear rumors of a study of the nation's prison population which reportedly found that the leading civilian occupation among inmates before they were put behind bars was "cook." As most of us in the restaurant business know, there is a powerful strain of criminality in the industry, ranging from the dope-dealing busboy with beeper and cell phone to the restaurant owner who has two sets of accounting books. In fact, it was the unsavory side of professional cooking that attracted me to it in the first place. In the early seventies, I dropped out of college and transferred to the Culinary Institute of America. I wanted it all: the cuts and burns on hands and wrists, the ghoulish kitchen humor, the free food, the pilfered booze, the camaraderie that flourished within rigid order and nerve-shattering chaos. I would climb the chain of command from *mal carne* (meaning "bad meat," or "new guy") to chefdom—doing whatever it took until I ran my own kitchen and had my own crew of cutthroats, the culinary equivalent of *The Wild Bunch*.

A year ago, my latest, doomed mission—a high-profile restaurant in the Times Square area—went out of business. The meat, fish, and produce purveyors got the news that they were going to take it in the neck for yet another ill-conceived enterprise. When customers called for reservations, they were informed by a prerecorded announcement that our doors had closed. Fresh from that experience, I began thinking about becoming a traitor to my profession.

Say it's a quiet Monday night, and you've just checked your coat in that swanky Art Deco update in the Flatiron district, and you're looking to tuck into a thick slab of pepper-crusted yellowfin tuna or a twenty-ounce cut of certified Black Angus beef, well-done—what are you in for?

The fish specialty is reasonably priced, and the place got two stars in the *Times*. Why not go for it? If you like four-day-old fish, be my guest. Here's how things usually work. The chef orders his seafood for the weekend on Thursday night. It arrives on Friday morning. He's hoping to sell the bulk of it on Friday and Saturday nights, when he knows that the restaurant will be busy, and he'd like to run out of the last few orders by Sunday evening. Many fish purveyors don't deliver on Saturday, so the chances are that the Monday-night tuna you want has been kicking around in the kitchen since Friday morning, under God knows what conditions. When a kitchen is in full swing, proper refrigeration is almost nonexistent, what with the many openings of the refrigerator door as the cooks rummage frantically during the rush, mingling your tuna with the chicken, the lamb, or the beef. Even if the chef has ordered just the right amount of tuna for the weekend, and has had to reorder it for a Monday delivery, the only safeguard against the seafood supplier's off-loading junk is the presence of a vigilant chef who can make sure that the delivery is fresh from *Sunday* night's market.

Generally speaking, the good stuff comes in on Tuesday: the seafood is fresh, the supply of prepared food is new, and the chef, presumably, is relaxed after his day off. (Most chefs don't work on Monday.) Chefs prefer to cook for weekday customers rather than for weekenders, and they like to start the new week with their most creative dishes. In New York, locals dine during the week. Weekends are considered amateur nights—for tourists, rubes, and the well-done-ordering pretheatre hordes. The fish may be just as fresh on Friday, but it's on Tuesday that you've got the goodwill of the kitchen on your side.

People who order their meat well-done perform a valuable service for those of us in the business who are cost-conscious: they pay for the privilege of eating our garbage. In many kitchens, there's a time-honored practice called "save for well-done." When one of the cooks finds a particularly unlovely piece of steak—tough, riddled with nerve and connective tissue, off the hip end of the loin, and maybe a little stinky from age—he'll dangle it in the air and say, "Hey, Chef, whaddya want me to do with *this?*" Now, the chef has three options. He can tell the cook to throw the offending item into the trash, but that means a total loss, and in the restaurant business every item of cut, fabricated, or prepared food should earn at least three times the amount it originally cost if the chef is to make his correct food-cost percentage. Or he can decide to serve that steak to "the family"—that is, the floor staff—though that, economically, is the same as throwing it out. But no. What he's going to do is repeat the mantra of cost-conscious chefs everywhere: "Save for well-done." The way he figures it, the philistine who orders his food well-done is not likely to notice the difference between food and flotsam.

Then there are the People Who Brunch. The "B" word is dreaded by all dedicated cooks. We hate the smell and spatter of omelettes. We despise hollandaise, home fries, those pathetic fruit garnishes, and all the other cliché accompaniments designed to induce a credulous public into paying $12.95 for two eggs. Nothing demoralizes an aspiring Escoffier faster than requiring him to cook egg-white omelettes or eggs over easy with bacon. You can dress brunch up with all the focaccia, smoked salmon, and caviar in the world, but it's still breakfast.

Even more despised than the Brunch People are the vegetarians.

Serious cooks regard these members of the dining public—and their Hezbollah-like splinter faction, the vegans—as enemies of everything that's good and decent in the human spirit. To live life without veal or chicken stock, fish cheeks, sausages, cheese, or organ meats is treasonous.

Like most other chefs I know, I'm amused when I hear people object to pork on nonreligious grounds. "Swine are filthy animals," they say. These people have obviously never visited a poultry farm. Chicken—America's favorite food—goes bad quickly; handled carelessly, it infects other foods with salmonella; and it bores the hell out of chefs. It occupies its ubiquitous place on menus as an option for customers who can't decide what they want to eat. Most chefs believe that supermarket chickens in this country are slimy and tasteless compared with European varieties. Pork, on the other hand, is cool. Farmers stopped feeding garbage to pigs decades ago, and even if you eat pork rare you're more likely to win the Lotto than to contract trichinosis. Pork tastes different, depending on what you do with it, but chicken always tastes like chicken.

Another much maligned food these days is butter. In the world of chefs, however, butter is in *everything*. Even non-French restaurants—the Northern Italian; the new American, the ones where the chef brags about how he's "getting away from butter and cream"—throw butter around like crazy. In almost every restaurant worth patronizing, sauces are enriched with mellowing, emulsifying butter. Pastas are tightened with it. Meat and fish are seared with a mixture of butter and oil. Shallots and chicken are caramelized with butter. It's the first and last thing in almost every pan: the final hit is called *monter au beurre*. In a good restaurant, what this all adds up to is that you could be putting away almost a stick of butter with every meal.

If you are one of those people who cringe at the thought of strangers fondling your food, you shouldn't go out to eat. As the author and former chef Nicolas Freeling notes in his definitive book *The Kitchen*, the better the restaurant, the more your food has been prodded, poked, handled, and tasted. By the time a three-star crew has finished carving and arranging your saddle of monkfish with dried cherries and wild-herb-infused *nage* into a Parthenon or a Space Needle, it's had dozens of sweaty fingers all over it. Gloves? You'll find a box of surgical gloves—in my kitchen we call them "anal-research gloves"—over every station on the line, for the benefit of the health inspectors, but does anyone actually use them? Yes, a cook will slip a pair on every now and then, especially when he's handling something with a lingering odor, like salmon. But during the hours of service gloves are clumsy and dangerous. When you're using your hands constantly, latex will make you drop things, which is the last thing you want to do.

Finding a hair in your food will make anyone gag. But just about the only place you'll see anyone in the kitchen wearing a hat or a hairnet is Blimpie. For most chefs, wearing anything on their head, especially one of those picturesque paper toques—they're often referred to as "coffee filters"—is a nuisance: they dissolve when you sweat, bump into range hoods, burst into flame.

The fact is that most good kitchens are far less septic than your kitchen at home. I run a scrupulously clean, orderly restaurant kitchen, where food is rotated and handled and stored very conscientiously. But if the city's Department of Health or the EPA decided to enforce every aspect of its codes, most of us would be out on the street. Recently, there was a news report about the practice of recycling bread. By means of a hidden camera in a restaurant, the reporter was horrified to see returned bread being sent right back out to the floor. This, to me, wasn't news: the reuse of bread has been an open secret—and a fairly standard practice—in the industry for years. It makes more sense to worry about what happens to the leftover table butter—many restaurants recycle it for hollandaise.

What do I like to eat after hours? Strange things. Oysters are my favorite, especially at three in the morning, in the company of my crew. Focaccia pizza with robiola cheese and white truffle oil is good, especially at Le Madri on a summer afternoon in the outdoor patio. Frozen vodka at Siberia Bar is also good, particularly if a cook from one of the big hotels shows up with beluga. At Indigo, on Tenth Street, I love the mushroom strudel and the daube of beef. At my own place, I love a spicy *boudin noir* that squirts blood in your mouth; the braised fennel the way my sous-chef makes it; scraps from duck confit; and fresh cockles steamed with greasy Portuguese sausage.

I love the sheer weirdness of the kitchen life: the dreamers, the crack-pots, the refugees, and the sociopaths with whom I continue to work; the ever-present smells of roasting bones, searing fish, and simmering liquids; the noise and clatter, the hiss and spray, the flames, the smoke, and the steam. Admittedly, it's a life that grinds you down. Most of us who live and operate in the culinary underworld are in some funda-mental way dysfunctional. We've all chosen to turn our backs on the nine-to-five, on ever having a Friday or Saturday night off, on ever hav-ing a normal relationship with a noncook.

Being a chef is a lot like being an air traffic controller: you are con-stantly dealing with the threat of disaster. You've got to be Mom and Dad, drill sergeant, detective, psychiatrist, and priest to a crew of op-portunistic, mercenary hooligans, whom you must protect from the ne-farious and often foolish strategies of owners. Year after year, cooks contend with bouncing paychecks, irate purveyors, desperate owners looking for the masterstroke that will cure their restaurant's ills: Live Cabaret! Free Shrimp! New Orleans Brunch!

In America, the professional kitchen is the last refuge of the misfit. It's a place for people with bad pasts to find a new family. It's a haven for foreigners—Ecuadorians, Mexicans, Chinese, Senegalese, Egyp-tians, Poles. In New York, the main linguistic spice is Spanish. "Hey, *maricón! Chupa mis huevos*" means, roughly, "How are you, valued com-rade? I hope all is well." And you hear "Hey, *baboso*! Put some more brown jiz on the fire and check your meez before the sous comes back there and fucks you in the *culo*!," which means "Please reduce some ad-ditional demi-glace, brother, and reexamine your *mise en place*, because the sous-chef is concerned about your state of readiness."

Since we work in close quarters, and so many blunt and sharp ob-jects are at hand, you'd think that cooks would kill one another with regularity. I've seen guys duking it out in the waiter station over who gets a table for six. I've seen a chef clamp his teeth on a waiter's nose. And I've seen plates thrown—I've even thrown a few myself—but I've never heard of one cook jamming a boning knife into another cook's rib cage or braining him with a meat mallet. Line cooking, done well, is a dance—a high-speed, Balanchine collaboration.

I used to be a terror toward my floor staff, particularly in the final months of my last restaurant. But not anymore. Recently, my career has taken an eerily appropriate turn: these days, I'm the *chef de cuisine* of a much loved, old-school French brasserie/bistro where the customers eat their meat rare, vegetarians are scarce, and every part of the animal—hooves, snout, cheeks, skin, and organs—is avidly and appreciatively prepared and consumed. Cassoulet, pigs' feet, tripe, and charcuterie sell like crazy. We thicken many sauces with foie gras and pork blood, and proudly hurl around spoonfuls of duck fat and butter, and thick hunks of country bacon. I made a traditional French pot-au-feu a few weeks ago, and some of my French colleagues—hardened veterans of the business all—came into my kitchen to watch the first order go out. As they gazed upon the intimidating heap of short ribs, oxtail, beef shoulder, cabbage, turnips, carrots, and potatoes, the expressions on their faces were those of religious supplicants. I have come home.

1999

"I'll have the dog's breakfast, please."

A REALLY BIG LUNCH

JIM HARRISON

On our frequent American road trips, my friend Guy de la Valdène has invariably said at lunch, "These French fries are filthy," but he always eats them anyway, and some of mine, too. Another friend, the painter Russell Chatham, likes to remind me that we pioneered the idea of ordering multiple entrées in restaurants back in the seventies— the theory being that if you order several entrées you can then avoid the terrible disappointment of having ordered the wrong thing while others at the table have inevitably ordered the right thing. The results can't have been all that bad, since both of us are still more or less alive, though neither of us owns any spandex.

Is there an interior logic to overeating, or does gluttony, like sex, wander around in a messy void, utterly resistant to our attempts to make sense of it? Not very deep within us, the hungry heart howls, "Supersize me." When I was a boy, in northern Michigan, feeding my grandfather's pigs, I was amazed at their capacity. Before I was caught in the act and chided by my elders, I had empirically determined that the appetite of pigs was limitless. As I dawdled in the barnyard, the animals gazed at me as fondly as many of us do at great chefs. Life is brutishly short and we wish to eat well, and for this we must generally travel to large cities, or, better yet, to France.

Never before have the American people had their noses so deeply in one another's business. If I announce that I and eleven other diners shared a thirty-seven-course lunch that likely cost as much as a new Volvo station wagon, those of a critical nature will let their minds run in tiny, aghast circles of condemnation. My response to them is that none of us twelve disciples of gourmandise wanted a new Volvo. We wanted only lunch, and since lunch lasted approximately eleven hours we saved money by not having to buy dinner. The defense rests.

Some would also think it excessive to travel all the way from Montana to Marc Meneau's L'Espérance, in Burgundy, for lunch, but I don't. Although there are signs of a culinary revolution in the United States, this much-bandied renaissance is for people in cities such as

New York, San Francisco, Seattle, and Chicago. When traveling across America over the past forty years, I've repeatedly sought extreme unction of a sort while in the midst of digestive death in the parking lots of restaurants. I've found it best, in these situations, to get some distance—to drive for a while, pull over, take a walk, fall to my knees, and pray for better food in the future.

I suspect that it's inappropriate to strand myself on a high horse when it comes to what people eat. We have proved ourselves inept fools on so many mortal fronts—from our utter disregard of the natural world to our notions of ethnic virtue to the hellish marriage of politics and war—that perhaps we should be allowed to pick at garbage like happy crows. When I was growing up in the Calvinist Midwest, the assumption that we eat to live, not live to eat, was part of the Gospels. (With the exception, of course, of holiday feasts. Certain women were famous for their pie-making abilities, while certain men, like my father, were admired for being able to barbecue two hundred chickens at once for a church picnic.) I recall that working in the fields for ten hours a day required an ample breakfast and three big sandwiches for lunch. At the time, I don't think I believed I was all that different from the other farm animals.

It's a long road from a childhood in rural Michigan to being the sort of man who gets invited to a thirty-seven-course lunch. But, above all, a gourmand is one who is able to keep eating when no longer hungry, and a gourmand without a rich sense of the comic is a pathetic piggy, indeed. Once, at Taillevent, in Paris (a restaurant that is always referred to as a "temple of gastronomy"), I had the uncomfortable sense that I was in a funeral parlor. I heard no laughter except from my own table. And when I wanted a taste of Calvados as an entremets the waiter actually told me that I'd have to be patient until after the cheese course, an hour distant. Luckily, an intemperate French count who was at my table told the waiter to bring my Calvados immediately or he would slap his face; at those prices, you don't want to be schooled. Haute cuisine has rules for those who love rules. Those rules have, for the most part, driven me into the arms of bistros. If I were given the dreary six months to live, I'd head at once to Lyon and make my way from bistro to bistro in a big stroller pushed by a vegetarian.

The thirty-seven-course lunch, which was held on November 17 of last year, was based on recipes by the great cooks and food writers of the past (among them Le Maréchal de Richelieu, Nicolas de Bonnefons, Pierre de Lune, Massialot, La Varenne, Marin, Grimod de La Reynière, Brillat-Savarin, Mercier, La Chapelle, Menon, and Carême), and drawn from seventeen cookbooks published between 1654 and 1823. It was food with a precise and determinable history. My host for the lunch was Gérard Oberlé, a man of unquestionable genius, whom I had met a decade earlier at a wine-and-book festival near Saumur, on the Loire. I don't recall seeing any books at the three-day party, where I was a wine judge, along with Alain Robbe-Grillet and Gérard Depardieu. (None of us was particularly startled when we were told that the wines had been "prejudged" and were there for decoration only.) Early one morning, I discovered Oberlé eating a sturdy platter of charcuterie on the patio of the château where we were staying. It took me a number of years to uncover all the aspects of his character—as if I were peeling the laminae from a giant Bermuda onion (which Gérard somewhat physically resembles, but then so does the Buddha). Gérard is a book collector and a dealer in illuminated manuscripts, a musicologist with a weekly program on Radio France, a novelist and an essayist, an "expert of experts" dealing with insurance fraud (assessing the actual value of private libraries destroyed by fire), a countertenor who once sang Purcell's "Come Ye Sons of Art" while woodcock hunting in Michigan's Upper Peninsula, a student of the history of French food who has produced a couple of what he calls "two-kilo" bibliographies on the subject, a wine and salami scholar, a former officer in a society for the protection of the integrity of fromages de tête (headcheese), a culinary eccentric, and a grand cook. Once, in Cancale, on the Brittany coast, where we were eating the rare and enormous seventy-year-old oysters known as *pieds de cheval* (horse's feet), he remarked, "These would be difficult to eat in a car."

Soon after I met Gérard, I visited his manor, in Burgundy, where he prepared a particularly interesting dish of ancient origin—a torte of fifty baby pigs' noses. "Really a simple dish," he said. As he explained it, you soak the pigs' noses overnight in clear water, then simmer them for about two hours in red wine, herbs, and garlic. Later, you add potatoes and bake the dish with the upturned noses forming a delightful mosaic on the surface. Such dishes are usually only for the extremely curious or those with an agricultural background. I recall both of my grandmothers boiling pigs' heads with herbs and onions to make a headcheese, for which the especially toothsome cheek, tongue, and neck meat was extracted, covered with the cooking liquid, and gelatinized in a glass dish.

By the time I met Gérard, I had already been exposed to excesses of every sort, including those of the film industry, and I had known a number of big eaters, myself included. But I had never met a truly refined big eater. Not long afterward, Gérard threw a dinner with fifty courses. Why? Because it was his fiftieth birthday. Why else? When I first read the menu, it seemed incomprehensible to me, though there was an interior logic—the meal was designed after one described in Petronius's *Satyricon*.

This is not to say that Gérard concentrates on the arcane and the frivolous. In my dozen or so visits to his home, I've experienced many French standards, in versions better than any I'd had before. You know you are not in a restaurant when you enter Gérard's kitchen and notice a wooden bowl with a kilo of black truffles waiting to be added to your all-time favorite dish, *poulet demi-deuil,* or "chicken in half-mourning." The dead fowl has been honored by so many truffle slices, slid under its skin, that it appears to be wearing black (not to mention the large truffle stuffed in the bird's cavity, to comfort its inner chicken). When I said, "Gérard, you shouldn't have," he replied, "I'm a bachelor. I have no heirs."

Over the years, on my visits to France, Guy de la Valdène, Gérard, and I had discussed the possibilities for a "theme" meal, and we had read the menus of several that Gérard had already given. At a certain point, it began to seem entirely reasonable to plan a lunch that began with twenty-four courses and then urged itself upward. And no restaurant was more logical a location than L'Espérance, in the village of Saint-Père-sous-Vézelay, a scant hour and a half from Gérard's home, in the Morvan. Of all the great chefs in France, Marc Meneau, a very tall man who looms above his employees as did de Gaulle above his citizenry, is one of the least aggressive, apparently devoid of any interest in becoming a public figure. His restaurant, long a required destination for gourmands, is pure country French, elegantly set in a grand garden, with nothing whatsoever in its décor to intimidate the customer. (And it would soon regain the third Michelin star that it had lost in 1999.)

Gérard had known Meneau for years, and with Guy and me safely at home in the United States he proceeded to plan the feast, using his improbable library as the source. Having once sat in on an after-lunch confab on the *vrai ancien coq au vin* (reduce seven liters of Merlot down to one, whisk in the rooster blood, et cetera), I can only imagine the countless hours of discussion that ensued between Gérard and Meneau.

When the morning of the event finally arrived, I wasn't particularly hungry. This didn't alarm me—many professional athletes before a big game feel that they would prefer to spend the day with their Tinkertoys or in the arms of Lucrezia Borgia. I had already been off my diet for two weeks, touring the French countryside with Guy and Peter Lewis, a Seattle restaurateur. Everywhere we went, we ate the best food available, with the excuse, not totally accurate, that we'd worked hard, saved our pennies, and had it coming. (The novelist Tom McGuane once noted that in the course of thirty-five years of correspondence between us I had lost a total of eighteen hundred pounds—so I was really "getting down there.")

The day dawned cool and misty. There was a certain anxiety in the air at the manor, with Gérard watching to make sure that I didn't partake of the breakfast that I thought I needed. All I wanted was a simple slab of the game pâté from the evening before, but when I tried to sneak into the kitchen from the outside pantry door he was there in front of the fridge like a three-hundred-pound albino cat.

I've always felt that there is no lovelier village in France than Vézelay, and no lovelier religious building than its cathedral on the hill, the Madeleine of Vézelay. I'm not Catholic, but I've lit candles in that church in prayer for troubled friends, and it has always worked. At least, they're all still showing vital signs. But I had no time to run up the steep hill and light a candle for my own digestion. The twelve of us sat down at noon. To my left was the vintner Didier Dagueneau, whose exquisite Pouilly-Fumé we had been drinking since our initial Krug Grande Cuvée. The first time I met Didier, I was startled by his appearance, which is that of a Minnesotan pulp cutter. During the winter downtime at his vineyard, in Pouilly, he travels far north, toward the Arctic, to run the dozens of sled dogs that he owns and whose racket irritates his neighbors. To my right was Gilles Brézol, Gérard's business partner and a man of sophisticated intelligence, who taught French for a year in Alabama and Nevada during the civil-rights upheaval. I've had dozens of meals with Gilles, who eats as much as I do but remains irritatingly slender. In fact, in this group of mostly book collectors and

journalists sworn to secrecy, no one was technically obese. Although the
lunch had originally been planned for eleven, a twelfth guest, a beautifully tailored, elderly French gentleman, unknown to all of us, had been
invited by Meneau, in accordance with the superstitious notion that
any large group should include a stranger, who might very well be an
angel in disguise.

Meneau came out of the kitchen; his only advice was *"Courage"* (or
"coo-rahj," as my phrase book likes to say). We began with a girlish delicacy—a clear soup made from poultry, diced vegetables, and crayfish—
followed by tartines of foie gras, truffles, and lard. The next soup was a
velvety cream of squab with cucumbers, served with cock-crest fritters.
Then there was a soothing crayfish bisque, and I began to wonder how
long we would be pursuing the soup motif.

But, oddly, I felt squeamish about the first of the hors d'oeuvres—
oysters and cream of Camembert on toast, which proved to be the only
course I couldn't eat. (We all have our own food phobias, and a mixture
of pungent cheese and oysters makes my little tummy recoil.) Next
came a chilled jellied loaf of poultry on sorrel cream, followed by a private joke on me—fresh Baltic herring with mayonnaise. (According to
my late mother, I was wild about herring from the age of two. Her family was Swedish, and the fish was a staple.) I loved the tart of calf's
brains with shelled peas but was not terribly fond of the omelette with
sea urchin, a dish that Louis XV liked to prepare for himself—though
it was certainly better than the cottage cheese with ketchup that
Richard Nixon favored as a snack. (There is a well-founded rumor that
George W. Bush nibbles on bologna with marshmallow bonbons.) A
fillet of sole with champagne sauce accompanied by monkfish livers
was wonderful, as was the roasted pike spiked with parsley. I did pause
to consider whether all of these hors d'oeuvres might dampen my appetite for the main courses. The wine steward noted my unrest, and a
quick goblet of Montrachet tickled my enthusiasm upward. There
were only two pure-blood Americans at the table, Peter Lewis and I,
and we had agreed not to shame our own holy empire.

We headed into the "second service" without an appropriate
break—say, a five-mile march through the mountains and an eight-
hour nap. The courses, naturally, became more substantial. First came
an oven-glazed brill served with fennel cream, anchovies, and roasted
currants, then a stew of suckling pig that had been slow-cooked in a
red-wine sauce thickened with its own blood, onions, and bacon. I

leaped forward from this into a warm terrine of hare with preserved plums, and a poached eel with chicken wing tips and testicles in a pool of tarragon butter. But I only picked at my glazed partridge breasts, which were followed by a savory of eggs poached in Chimay ale, and then a mille-feuille of puff pastry sandwiched with sardines and leeks.

Now it was halftime, though there were no prancing cheerleaders. The menu advised us to "languish" in the salon and nibble on ravioli with carrots and cumin and thick slices of "noirs eggs of puff pastry with squab hearts." Instead, I went outside, where the grass was wet and my feet seemed to sink in even farther than usual. In the walled herb garden, I began to reflect that this kind of eating might not be a wise choice in the late autumn of my life. Perhaps I should fax the menu to my cardiologist in the States before proceeding? I soon realized that this was one of the ten million insincere impulses I've had in my life. I began to walk faster for a dozen yards and almost jumped a creek, but then thought better of it.

The "third service" loaded even bigger guns, or so it seemed, with its concentration on denser, heavier specialties that tried the patience of my long-fled appetite. From Massialot, we were offered a "light" stew of veal breast in a purée of ham and oysters in a pastry-covered casserole, and a not-so-light gratin of beef cheeks. La Varenne's gray squab was boned, stuffed with sweetbreads, squab livers, and scallions, and spit-roasted. It was the Prince des Dombes who said, "Nothing arouses me but taste" ("*Je ne me pique que de goût*"). He would have been a disappointing match for a vigorous girl. You can imagine her hanging a rope ladder from her tower bedroom for knights-errant—or, better yet, woodchoppers and stable hands—to climb, while the prince aroused himself in the kitchen. From his files, we had wild duck with black olives and orange zest, a *buisson* (bush) of crayfish with little slabs of grilled goose liver, a terrine of the tips of calves' ears, hare cooked in port wine inside a calf's bladder, crispy breaded asparagus, a sponge cake with fruit preserves, and cucumbers stewed in wine.

It was consoling to begin winding down with a swirl of turnips in sweetened wine, radishes preserved in vinegar, a warm salad with almonds, cream of grilled pistachios, meringues, macaroons, and chocolate cigarettes. These were simple warm-ups to the medley of desserts served to us in the salon: a rosette of almond milk with almonds; a soft cheese of fresh cream with quince jelly; rice whipped with sweetened egg whites and lemon peel; a grand ring-shaped cake, a savarin, flamed with Old Havana rum and served with preserved pineapple; little molds of various ice creams; and a "towering structure of every fruit imaginable in every manner imaginable."

Sad to say, my notes from the meal are blurred and smeared by the cooked exudates of flora and fauna and the wines that rained down on us as if from the world's best garden sprinkler. Reading through the veil of grease, I see that my favorites among the wines served were Chablis Les Clos, Montrachet 1989, Volnay-Champans 1969, Château Latour 1989, and Côte Rôtie. Of course, any fool would love these great wines as he felt his wallet vaporize.

There. Time to do dishes. As Diderot said of a lunch at the fabulously wealthy Baron of Holbach's home, "After lunch, one takes a little walk, or one digests, if it's even possible." Night had long since fallen, and I reflected that lunch had taken the same amount of time as a Varig flight from New York to São Paulo.

In the salon, my fellow diners were yawning rather than gasping or sobbing. Was this another example of the banality of evil: a grievous sin committed—in this case, gluttony—and no one squirming with guilt? I have noticed that Frenchmen are far less susceptible to heart disease, in part because they don't seem to experience the stress of self-doubt or regret. My mother, a Swedish Lutheran, liked to ask her five children, "What have you accomplished today?" If I'd told her, "I have eaten thirty-seven courses and drunk thirteen wines," I would have been cast into outer darkness. But then this was the Iron Mom, who also said, with a tiny smile, in reference to my life's work, "You've made quite a living out of your fibs."

At midnight, while sipping a paltry brandy from the 1920s and smoking a Havana Churchill, I reflected that this was not the time to ponder eternal values. I was sitting next to Gérard, who was cherubically discussing the historical subtleties of certain courses. In a way, we were forensic anthropologists, doing arduous historical fieldwork. How could we possibly understand the present without knowing what certain of our ancestors had consumed? Marc Meneau, his lovely wife, Françoise, and thirty-nine members of his staff had led us on a sombre and all-consuming journey into the past.

At dawn or a few hours thereafter, I felt relieved, on stepping out of the bathtub, that I hadn't fallen on a hard surface and broken open like an overly mature muskmelon.

No question looms larger on a daily basis for many of us than "What's for lunch?" and, when that has been resolved, "What's for dinner?" There have been mutterings that the whole food thing has gone too far in America, but I think not. Good food is a benign weapon against the sodden way we live.

By the time I reached Paris the next afternoon and took a three-hour stroll, I was feeling a little peckish. I'd heard that certain quarrels had already arisen over our lunch, and I felt lucky that my capacity for the French language was limited to understanding only the gist of conversations—sort of the way the average American comprehends our government. On the phone, the natives were restless to the point of "scandal," and from the tornado of rumors (everyone knows that men, not women, are the masters of gossip) I learned that many had found both the food and the service disappointing, the lack of "theatre" sad. (As for myself, I couldn't make a judgment. I once helped to cook a whole steer and a barrel of corn for a picnic in Michigan and have eaten many ten-course dinners, but our French lunch had left those occasions in the numbered dust.) The most interesting rumor I heard was that the tab for the lunch had been picked up by a Louisiana billionaire, who couldn't attend because a pelican had been sucked into an engine of his Gulfstream. This detail was so extraordinary that it seemed likely to be true.

That last evening in Paris, before my flight and the tonic Chicago-style hot dog that awaited me at O'Hare, Peter and I dined at Thoumieux, my old standby restaurant, near the Invalides. We had a simple Gigondas, and I ordered two vegetable courses, then relented at the last moment and added a duck confit. Long flights are physically exhausting, and good nutrition lays the foundation of life. On Air France, I was sunk in profound thought, or so I felt at the time. Like sex, bathing, sleeping, and drinking, the effects of food don't last. The patterns are repeated but finite. Life is a near-death experience, and our devious minds will do anything to make it interesting.

2004

THE FOUR MAJOR FOOD GROUPS

Regular:

Hamburger, cola, French fries, fruit pie.

Company:

Cracker variety, canapé, "interesting" cheese, mint.

Remorse:

Plain yogurt, soybeans, mineral water, tofu.

Silly:

Space-food sticks, gelatine mold with fruit salad in it, grasshopper pie.

R. Chast

EATING IN

"It's better than my mother's cooking but not
as good as my first wife's."

"I think we overordered."

THE SECRET INGREDIENT

M.F.K. FISHER

It is common in small communities, especially if they are far from large towns, for one person or another to become known for a special power. A man may have some control over sick frightened animals, which gradually extends to his own friends and is interpreted as miraculous or divine healing. A woman may be of a hypersensitive nature, which with time develops into an intuitive "clairvoyance" about other people's dreams and hopes. In the same way, there are men and women who have a special nose for mushrooms, or an inimitable hand with pastry and jellies. At present, I myself, living less than a hundred miles from a big city and with about two thousand other townspeople, do not know of any local witches or warlocks, but there are several people who seem to have an uncanny power over food. They manage to keep to themselves whatever it is that makes their creations subtly and definitely better than any attempts to approximate them. They are even willing to make knaves and clowns of themselves to protect their recipes.

I have known one of these passionate cooks, and for many years—Bertie Bastalizzo. By now she is retired from her own kitchen: she married a man even more ancient than she who fell in love with her food and holds her and it for himself alone, to our hungry chagrin. While she was practicing on her own, I did my best in both overt and underhanded ways to learn her secret ingredients, but I remain foiled.

She had been very lonely after her first husband died, and to keep herself from the river she began to cook about three dishes for local families smart enough to recognize her superiority. The routine of ordering and then fetching one of her preparations was rigid, and involved appointments, reservations, and occasional frustrations if Bertie's schedule was full. She was very fussy about the kind of dishes her creations were to be served in, and several of us invested in large, handsome pottery baking dishes, which sit on our shelves unused since that old robber stole Bertie from us. We knew her instructions about how long to let the food "rest" before serving it, what temperature to let it rest in, and even what to do with it once it was at its peak of restedness. In fact, she dictated everything but our actual digestion, serene in her power over our palates, for she and we knew, with conditioned fatalism, that never again would we taste the likes of her delicate little dumplings of herbs and chicken, her flat tarts of thin noodles and mushrooms, her feathery mixtures of *capellini d'angelo* and a kind of pesto, which was, naturally, "secret."

One summer, I spent several weeks flattering her into letting my younger daughter, who had all the makings of a good cook as well as a private investigator, act as her kitchen helper. I kept notes unashamedly on the reports of this sorceress's apprentice, but any results I produced were nondescript. Something was simply *not there,* and neither my accomplice nor I could guess what.

Much later, Bertie offered blandly—as if to punish me for my obvious breach of trust—to write her recipe for the dumplings. I felt humbled and grateful, as if a small halo had suddenly been awarded me in spite of my sins. I have kept her large piece of pink butcher paper to remind me of these mixed emotions, for its scrawl is unintelligible to me—cryptic, completely meaningless. It lists ingredients that are never mentioned again. It notes measurements ranging from "some" to a monstrous "$10\frac{1}{2}$ pounds" (of salt!). Perhaps Bertie believed that she was giving me her true recipe. Perhaps I cannot translate it because her own English was too limited to write it. Perhaps she was simply having some fun.

I still like her and regret that since she succumbed to a second love we no longer taste her beautiful dishes. But part of me rebels at her seeming trickery. Her scribbled directive is one more exhibit in my private Hall of Gastronomical Ill Fame, for I really cannot believe that a good cook will distort a prideful recipe. I continue this stubborn and obviously naïve faith in the face of many more such pitiable little tricks, and prefer to console myself by thinking back on the wonderful odorous kitchen I would go to when it was time to pick up one of Bertie's mammoth casseroles.

This was a ritual, as well as a pleasurable ordeal, for I must be there exactly when I had been told to, or a little before, and on each of countless times I was instructed in how long to let the dish rest and was quizzed sternly about what else would be served with it. If Bertie approved, occasionally she gave me a jar of her fresh pickled zucchini as a tacit benediction. And always, as if she could not bring herself to let one more creation leave her own familiar kitchen for a stranger's, I must sit down and consume a beaker of one of the worst drinks I can remember in a long life of polite subjection to them. It was kept in a half-gallon jug in the icebox, and drunk straight, from cottage-cheese glasses with daisies on them. The recipe, always reverently accredited to the deceased Mr. Bastalizzo: pour one pint from a full jug of dark sweet vermouth made by a local vintner, add one pint of bourbon whiskey, shake a little now and then, and enjoy. Simple, near lethal, and challenging!

One time, there was some delay in getting the dish from Bertie's hands into mine; she ran out of aluminum foil to cover it and had to find a new roll. It was much like the way a mother will nearly miss the train that is to take her tender child to camp. I drank *two* tumblers of her husband's brew, and with the flash courage of unexpected inebriation I asked my friend point-blank if she had really meant ten and a half pounds of salt. She simply cackled, like a tipsy old Mona Lisa. I reeled carefully to my car, my arms filled with another example of her culinary mystique.

We are so conditioned to the threat of the Secret Ingredient, and the acceptance of trickery, that even honesty has become suspect when we are brash enough to ask for recipes. My own mother always disclosed calmly her "secret" in making the best mustard pickles in the world, but almost nobody believed her, simply because she *told* it. She made the pickles according to a fairly standard recipe, almost measure for measure like many I have read, *but* she added to it one nine-ounce jar of Crosse & Blackwell's Chow Chow. There was no substitute, she said, and it was the honest truth, as anyone could prove by trying. Here, because it seems the right place, is her method:

EDITH'S MUSTARD PICKLES

1 quart very small cucumbers, whole.
1 quart large cucumbers, sliced.
1 quart green tomatoes, sliced.
1 quart small white onions, peeled.
1 large cauliflower in small flowerlets.
1 pint green string beans, 2 inches long (cut).
4 green peppers in 1-inch cubes.

4 quarts water.
2 cups salt.

1 cup flour.
6 tablespoons Colman's mustard (dry).
1 tablespoon turmeric.
1 cup sugar.
Vinegar.
1 9-ounce bottle Crosse & Blackwell's Chow Chow.

Let vegetables stand overnight in brine of water and salt.
Heat to scalding point and drain. Make smooth paste of
flour, mustard, turmeric, sugar, and enough vinegar to make
2 quarts. Cook in double boiler until thick. Add Chow
Chow. Mix with vegetables. Heat through, and bottle.

And here, almost in refutation of my mother's candor, is the best
version I have yet evolved from Bertie's directions for her pickled zucchini:

8–12 medium zucchini.
1 cup vinegar.
1 cup brown sugar.
4 cloves garlic.
1 cup chopped parsley.
1 tablespoon oregano.
1 tablespoon salt.
1 teaspoon pepper.

Leave zucchini whole, or slice thickly, lengthwise. Brown
gently in olive oil. Pack vertically in jars. In same oily skillet,

boil vinegar and sugar. Add rest of ingredients, boil gently 5 minutes, and pour over zucchini to cover. Add more oil on top if needed to make ¼-inch cover. Keep in icebox. Serve drained and cold for antipasto or with cold meats.

Needless to say, this translation is *not* exactly right, but its result is a fresh, delicious hors d'oeuvre in the summer, kept for even a week or so in the icebox, and made if possible from vegetables fresh from the vine and preferably not more than four inches long. (It is also very good with any kind of supper entrée, hot or cold.) I honestly have no idea what the Secret Ingredient might be, but charity will excuse my obtuseness, perhaps, if I give one short example of Bertie's prose, found under my door apropos of a later rendezvous for ten dozen of her mystery dumplings: "Please If you fene time, cools me up abaut 5 pm clook up." Add measurements to this, and you have an undecipherable code!

People like Bertie—and even my honest mother—are increasingly rare, and I have a dismal feeling that they may soon disappear completely. It is not so much a question of their supplies as it is of their own unquestioning demand for quality. The things they used in their recipes were not hard to grow, or buy, and while they bowed to seasonal riches and made pickles when the vegetables were at their best, because that is the way they had to, we can buy zucchini and beans and even green tomatoes the year around in the supermarkets. We can assemble everything even cryptic directions call for, from vinegar to turmeric and, with a little effort, Crosse & Blackwell's Chow Chow (and none other!). But do we? Why bother? Why clutter the icebox with a couple of jars of chilled zucchini? Who wants a dozen bottles of mustard pickles sitting around? Who has the time, when you come right down to it, to *fuss* with such maneuvers? So-and-so is almost as good, and a lot less trouble.

There was an interesting proof of this conjecture lately in our town, when the second of two birthday parties was given for an honorable lady of ninety-eight. Ten years before, when we celebrated her comparatively youthful anniversary, we did special honor to her by blackmailing another friend of almost the same age to make hundreds of her famous sand tarts to eat with the punch. They were delicate thin little wafers, light and crisp and not the classical sand tart at all, and for decades her recipe for them was her sternly guarded secret. Perhaps it was age that softened her pride, for when I discreetly and admiringly asked if perhaps a hint of old-fashioned lemon extract might be the Secret Ingredient, she gave me a pleased nod—and later the recipe! On it she wrote at the end, ". . . and ¼ teaspoon of ???"—our private joke.

So the ten years passed, and when the time came to deputize a few of us to supply soppets for the ninety-eighth-birthday punch, I proudly produced the famous sand-tart recipe, feeling sure that the old lady who had not been able to reach that age would never begrudge it in honor of the one who had. But nobody had time enough to follow it—or, rather, it was mutually and immediately vetoed in favor of a wonderful new trick (just as good!) that involved packaged mixes of both cake and custard, frozen lemon juice, and sweet sherry. "Really fun to make . . . so quick and easy . . . and all you do is *slice* it."

That is the end of the story. Or is it? Where are the witches of yesteryear, the strange old women with their dogged involvement, their loyalty to true flavor and changeless quality? If at times they protected their "secrets" to the point of knavery, at least they had the courage to stay passionate about it. Perhaps that was the Secret Ingredient: the blind strength of timeless passion.

1968

THE TROUBLE WITH TRIPE

M.F.K. FISHER

The main trouble with tripe is that in my present dwelling place, a small town in northern California, I can count on one hand the people who will eat it with me. What is more, its careful, slow preparation is not something I feel like doing for a meal by myself at this stage of the game, or for several meals. It is one of the things that call for a big pot and plenty of hungry people. Not even my children really like it, although studiously conditioned reflexes forced them to taste it in various guises and countries and to give fair judgment, which in their case was No. Friends tell me that they hate tripe because they, in turn, were forced to eat it when young, or saw too much of it in fraternity boardinghouses as an "economy meat"—reasons like that. I myself could claim a childhood trauma if I needed to, and I admit that I did not face a dish of tripe from my grandmother's death until I was a good decade beyond it. In modern lingo, tripewise I lay fallow. The old lady, gastronomical dictator appointed by her own vision of righteous Christian living, a nervous stomach, and the fact that she more than generously shared the expenses of our exploding household, for some reason approved of eating the inner linings of an ox's first and second bellies.

In *Larousse Gastronomique*, where tripe is discussed under "Offal" in the English edition, there is news for Grandmother. (She would dismiss it as foreign nonsense, of course.) "Rich in gelatine, tripe needs prolonged cooking," says the culinary scripture, "and is not easy to digest, so that it has no place in the diet of the dyspeptic [or] sufferers from gout." I sense that my beldame was practicing upon herself and us a kind of sympathetic medicine, to request that tripe be prepared and served—to be brave, eat a lion's heart; to remain shy and timid, eat violets in a salad; and so on. Oxen are reputedly serene and docile, and she had a digestive system that ranked her among the leaders in Battle Creek's regular army of dyspeptic missionaries and would have honored her with a front seat at any late-Victorian spa in farther waters, like Vichy or Baden-Baden. The reasoning, perhaps: since an ox has not one but two pieces of equipment for his continuous ruminative consumption of the grains and grasses known also to be salubrious for man, why would partaking of some of his actual stomachs not help Mrs. Holbrook's own unhappy organ?

My grandmother unwittingly enjoyed perfect digestion, thanks to her constant attention to it, and it was no more than her due reward if she believed that her hypersensitive innards would and could assimilate this delicate honeycomb of animal muscle, with gastric gratitude if not pleasure. She did not believe in the latter, anyway, as part of a true and upright life, and as for the hinted danger of gout, only gentlemen had that in her days of rigid divisions of the sexual hazards of existence.

There was only one way to serve tripe fit to eat when I was little— that is, fit for Grandmother to eat. It was seldom prepared when my mother was feeling fit enough herself to maintain some control over the menus, but when she was low in our private pecking order we ate it fairly often. My father, quietly and successfully determined to remain cock of the roost with dignity, always found it commendable, or at least edible. The recipe for it, if I feel sturdy enough to give it in correct form, would start with boiling the rubbery reticulum in pieces, draining it casually, and dousing it with something called White Sauce, which was and will remain in the same class as my grandmother's flour-thickened Boiled Dressing. The dish was at best a faintly odorous and watery challenge to one's innate sense of the fitness of things.

I recognize that such experiences can lead to cynicism, or the analyst's couch. In my own case, they seem mainly to have stiffened my wish to prove them mistaken, and I am now a happy, if occasionally frustrated, tripe eater.

I had a good beginning, the second time around (really a kind of ghost-laying), at Crespin in Dijon. The small restaurant is gone now, but for a long time it served some of the simplest and lustiest meals I have ever eaten, especially on market days, for the wine people who came in from all that part of Burgundy to talk about casks, corks, sulfates. There were always snails at Crespin, of course, except in very hot weather, and in the cool months oysters out on the sidewalk in kelpy baskets, and both downed by the dozens. There was the classic green salad to scour the maw, and a good plain tart of seasonal fruits if one could still face it. I remember some cheeses in the winter. And then there were sealed casseroles of *tripes à la mode de Caen véritable.*

Those casseroles, for two or six or eight people, seemed to possess the inexpressible cachet of a numbered duck at the Tour d'Argent, or a small perfect octahedral diamond from Kimberley. They were unsealed at the table. The vapor hissed out, and the whole dish seethed. Plates were too hot to touch bare-handed, to keep the sauce from turning as gluey as a good ox would need it to be at a temperature more suited to his own digestion. It was served with soup spoons as well as knives and forks, and plenty of crusty bread lay alongside. It was a fine experience.

Crespin, with its hoary, monstrous old oyster opener always there on the wintry sidewalk, his hands the most scarred I have ever seen and still perhaps the surest in the way they handled the Portugaises, the green Marennes, upon their dank beds of fresh seaweed—Crespin and the old man and even the ruddy marketers are gone, except on my own mind's palate.

The last time I went there, I was alone. It was a strange feeling at first. I was in Dijon late in the 1950s, to go again to the Foire Gastronomique. The town was jumping, quasi-hysterical, injected with a mysterious supercharge of medieval pomp and Madison Avenue–via–Paris commercialism. I went to several banquets, where ornate symbols were pinned and bestowed, with dignitaries several levels above me in the ferocious protocol of eating and drinking, and then I went by myself to the restaurant I wanted to be in once more.

In the small low room there was a great hum and fume, like market day but even better, and every table but one was occupied by large, red-faced, loud, happy Burgundians. *My* table was empty, and it seemed indicated by the gods that I should come to sit at it. I had sat there many times before. It was a little apart, though not obtrusively so, up a step like the fantastic banquet boards still cluttered and heavy at the official feastings, and pleasantly enclosed on three sides, with the white window curtains at my back. If I had not come, a potted plant would have been set neatly in my place, I know. I felt pleased to be there instead, and as usual I was awed by my continuing good luck in life, especially now and then.

I think I ate a few snails, to stay in the picture. (The old scarred oysterman was not there, it being early November and very warm.) Then, although after all the banquets I felt about as hungry as a sated moth, I ordered a small and ritual casserole of *tripes*. They were as good as they had ever been some decades or centuries ago on my private calendar.

They hissed and sizzled with delicate authority. Nobody paid any attention to my introspective and alcoved sensuality, and the general noise beat with provincial lustiness in the packed room. An accordionist I had last seen in Marseille slid in from the frenzied streets and added to the wildness, somewhat hopelessly. When he saw me digging into my little pot of tripe, he nodded, recognizing me as a fellow wanderer. I asked him if he would have a drink, as he twiddled out near-logical tunes on the instrument he wore like a child on his belly. He looked full at me and said, "Sometime a *pastis* on the Old Port." I have not yet met him there again, but it is almost doubtless that I shall.

I could not know that the next time I returned, lemminglike, to the dank old town, Crespin and the white curtains and all of it would be gone, but it is. It is too bad to explain.

The classic recipes for preparing tripe can be found in any good cookbook, which someone who has read this far will already know and be able to consult. I like the French methods, but there are excellent ones in almost every culture that permit the use of this type of animal meat. Here is a good one that is fresh to the taste, adapted from the *trippa alla Petronius* served currently in a London restaurant called Tiberio:

> 3 pounds tripe, previously boiled until tender.
> 4 medium-sized carrots ⎫
> 3 sticks of celery   ⎬ chopped very fine.
> 2 large onions   ⎭
> ³/₄ cup butter.
> 4 tablespoons tomato purée.
> 1 glass (6–8 ounces) dry white wine.
> ¹/₂ glass olive oil.
> 2 cloves of garlic, minced.
> ¹/₂ cup chopped fresh parsley.
> ¹/₂ cup chopped fresh basil.

> Drain tripe and cut into 1-inch squares. Gently brown the three vegetables in the butter. Add tomato purée and wine, and stir until sauce thickens. Add tripe, and simmer slowly for 1 hour.

In separate skillet warm olive oil, and add garlic, parsley, and basil, taking care not to overheat. Cook slowly about 5 minutes, mix quickly into tripe, and serve.

This is a comparatively fast recipe (the true *tripes à la mode de Caen* take at least twelve hours of baking), and it is very simple, which explains why it is sought after in a posh Mayfair restaurant, where the clients may feel jaded. I think that the fresh herbs give it its special quality, but perhaps it could be successfully tinkered with if they proved unprocurable. Fortunately, this is seldom the case with parsley. If dried basil had to be used, one to two tablespoonfuls should be soaked in one and a half instead of one glass of wine, and I would be tempted to go a step further and use a light dry red instead of the Tiberio's white. All this would, I fear, make the whole dish more ordinary.

While I am about it, I might as well discuss why it is much easier to make things with tripe now than it was a hundred or so years ago, or when I myself was little. I do this in a missionary spirit, convinced that they can be very good to eat and should be less shunned in our country. In these days, tripe is almost always taken through its first tedious cleansings in special rooms at the wholesale butchers' factories. My friend Remo, meatman and mentor, says somewhat cryptically that the stuff is subjected to enormous pressure, which I assume means with steam. It is then trimmed to a uniform niceness, wrapped in bundles rather like large pallid grape leaves, and delivered fresh or quick-frozen to the markets where there is any demand for it.

Once the cook takes over from the butcher, this modern treatment makes it possible to prepare tripe for any dish in an hour or a little more, by washing it well and then simmering it in ample water flavored to taste with carrots, onion, celery, herbs. When tender but not too soft, it is drained—and then *avanti, en avant,* forward!

Here is the method, perhaps to shame some of us into trying our luck for a change, recommended in 1868 by the expatriate Pierre Blot, in his *Hand-Book of Practical Cookery, for Ladies and Professional Cooks. Containing the Whole Science and Art of Preparing Human Food* (D. Appleton & Co., New York):

TRIPE

How to clean and prepare. Scrape and wash it well several times in boiling water, changing the water every time, then put in very cold water for about twelve hours, changing the water two or three times; place it in a pan, cover it with cold water; season with parsley, chives, onions, one or two cloves of garlic, cloves, salt, and pepper; boil gently five hours, take out and drain.

When I was a child, I felt a somewhat macabre interest in watching our cook go through this old routine. It started in a washtub, with much sloshing with big scrub brushes and whackings at the slippery, ivory-white rubber. Then I am sure that baking soda was put into a couple of the several changes of water, making things foam in an evil way—I suppose a battle with some of the digestive juices my grandmother counted on? For the last cool soaking, handfuls of salt were thrown in, or so it now seems to me. But I am downright sure that in our house there was no fancy nonsense of herbs and suchlike in the final slow boiling. Plain fare with a good White Sauce, that is what we were served. "Eat what's set before you, and be thankful for it!" was the gastronomical motto that quivered always in the air above our table while Grandmother sat there, and with a certain amount of philosophical acceptance it can be a good one, the whole chancy way.

1968

"It was a good rotting carcass, but it wasn't a great rotting carcass."

NOR CENSURE NOR DISDAIN

M.F.K. FISHER

Casseroles are, I think, an American phenomenon, like Coke and chewing gum, and by many traditionalists they are put somewhat disdainfully into the same category. On the other hand, they are probably well on their way around the world, not far behind the ubiquitous soft drink and pacifier, as more people live hastier lives everywhere.

Webster and Larousse agree that the correct definition of a casserole is an open, deep-sided vessel in which foods may be baked and served. It can also be, in classical cooking, a mold made painstakingly of rice or mashed potato or pastry, filled and baked with vegetables or meats in various sauces. Webster says that *en casserole* can also refer to the food within one of these receptacles of earthenware or more edible starches, but it is in the American edition of the *Larousse Gastronomique* that the nearest approach is made to our own national definition: "In U.S.A. a *casserole* defines a dish made of two or more elements . . . rice . . . spaghetti, etc., in combinations with meat or fish plus a sauce or gravy, and often a variety of vegetables. This one-dish-meal can be prepared in advance and cooked and served in a decorative *casserole* . . . very popular in homes where there are no servants."

And there it is, neatly summed up! We make them every day, and write books about them, and exchange recipes for our own latest family triumphs of Matter over Time, and manufacturers sell seasonal variations on the theme of ovenproof dishes decorated by famous artists, and electric timers in millions of kitchens are set every morning to guarantee that the evening meal will be correctly crisp and bubbling by exactly six-thirty that night, and it is a good evolution, a healthy institution, an interesting gastronomical compromise.

There are some basic rules about casserole cooking that should be instinctive, but they can be *learned* by the most unskilled beginners. Naturally, such rules are guided by the cook's own quirks of taste, but they have little to do with actual prejudices. The foods used should never in any way be dubious in either looks or taste, as can happen unexpectedly to a remnant left too long at the back of the icebox—or even overnight, uncovered. One ingredient should dominate, so that the dish is plainly made of chicken, or shrimps, or lamb. There should not be a pointless mixture of flavors and textures, just to use up that cup of pimentos, that saucer of cold steak, those two chicken wings, the sour cream left from last night's cocktail party, with perhaps some chopped clams in it, all bound together with a bowl of leftover macaroni and two cans of cream-of-something soup. (Oh! Sprinkle it with grated cheese. Put plenty of paprika on top. Harry will be late, and ravenous after golf—he'll eat *anything* on Wednesdays.)

A good casserole will have clear-cut textures as well as flavor, and tired food can never stand up to the slow baking it should be given. The ingredients should be firm, if not completely fresh, and crispness can be added with thinly sliced green pepper or water chestnuts, chopped nuts, crumbled crisp ham or bacon, according to the cook's judgment. It is hard to say which is the more displeasing, a casserole made of a dozen indistinguishable hints of exhausted flavors or one that is a noxious mushy pablum resembling the predigested purées fed to helpless infants. I myself believe that it is a good thing to have the backbone of the dish completely fresh, and then perhaps to make whatever holds it together (rice or a form of *pasta* or perhaps potatoes) just before the whole is assembled. Rice, if correctly cooked and stored, will hold its texture for a few days, but most kinds of *pasta* do not improve with age, and I have found that while I am preparing the other ingredients for a dish to be served several hours later I can make fresh spaghetti or noodles or *capellini* for it, with much happier results than if I use the remains of last night's starch. In other words, it is best not to cook *pasta* with one canny eye on a leftover, although I do that with almost everything else!

The books written about this kind of cooking are interesting, if sometimes a little hazardous for one's mental digestion. The most unfortunate and at the same time most common expression of enthusiasm for the new-old branch of kitchen art is that "*anything* goes into a casserole." It is not necessary to say why I find this reasoning actively dangerous. Casseroles are here to stay for a long time, and they are, for good or ill, a part of our living patterns, and I think it is dastardly to reduce them to the botulistic mediocrity such statements condone. Oddly enough, it is our own families who live in the greatest danger, for a casserole which will perhaps serve four or five can be and most often is slapped together from good-to-shameful remnants from the icebox, whereas some truly worthy dishes are made from near scratch for the Whist Club and the Business Buffet, with real care and thought. Perhaps that is why my own personal belief in combining leftovers and fresh ingredients seems valid.

Increasingly, there are such compromises between one's knowledge of good cooking and one's harried way of life, and a friend of mine with a large family has evolved her own formula for casserole cooking: three thick layers—first cooked starch at the bottom, then meat freshly and lightly cooked (and cubed if possible), and then a juicy vegetable, preferably tomatoes. The whole is covered with grated cheese and crumbs, all having been generously buttered and seasoned, of course, and is cooked for half an hour or so, until it bubbles and sends out good whiffs. Her theory is that the juices must sink into the bottom layer. The result is pronounced eminently edible by her food-conscious crew. It is preeminently modern American, not neo- in any sense of that prefix.

Casseroles lend themselves all too easily to mass feeding, and many a schoolchild has been forever warped, gastronomically, by the two-by-two slab of stiff macaroni-tuna served him on Fridays in the cafeteria. Macaroni and tuna, prepared separately and then combined in light layers, *can* make a decent casserole marriage, I like to believe, although personally I list the strongly flavored canned fish with bananas and chocolate bars as something safely behind me—a childhood aberration.

As for macaroni, it will remind me always of the catered salad a group of us sold to our classmates in boarding school, to raise money for a new swimming pool. I have tried to find a recipe for this monstrosity in at least twenty books, mostly about American regional cooking but also in a few culinary dictionaries and manuals, and *it is not listed*. This in itself is commendably sinister. The fact remains that it is often to be found in delicatessens—a kind of cold casserole, in the slant-sided glass counters where food is kept cool in large pans that look like unmentionable hospital equipment. My surmise is that the hollow, bent *pasta* is cooked past the *al dente* stage but not to a glue, and is then cooled and tossed with a mayonnaise made of very old eggs. My interest in this salad is plainly clinical, but in 1927, when Lindbergh was loning it over the Atlantic, I was battening on the dish in Miss

Harker's School. It sold well, and I loved it, and we never had it at home.

By now, somewhat more mercifully, macaroni is one of the standbys for our national hot casseroles; it does not deteriorate as fast as other Italian-type pastes, and it feeds a lot of people with little effort. A big pan of macaroni and cheese, plain or fancy, will provide a lot of tender, tasty nourishment, as any experienced member of the Whist Club will agree, and when it is prepared with ham and tongue *alla milanese,* or with eggplant and mozzarella cheese, it can appear at the most sophisticated buffet. And I will still take any other kind of *pasta* ever invented, in or out of a casserole.

Although I subscribe frankly to the somewhat outdated ways of combining a few freshly cooked things shortly before serving them or even at the table, I often make dishes ahead of mealtime, and from so-called leftovers, which I think meet all the requirements for our national dish. It is family history that once when my father wanted to carve more meat for a guest, he begged him fervently, "Help me finish this, for God's sake, or she will make a casserole of it!" And I probably would have, for in times when I have combined going to an office and running a decently nourished household I have evolved many ways to cook more than will probably be needed for a meal, so that something will be left, to challenge what I prefer to think of as my inventiveness rather than my lazy penury.

I kept house in Whittier, California, for my father for several years after my mother's death and before his, and I came to recognize, and then fairly skillfully to cheat, his conditioned opposition to leftovers. He was very snobbish about them, and about several other kinds of food. One evening, he surprised me by spurning a tender and artful kind of patty of chopped beef that I had devised for him after he had a double set of false teeth installed and found it difficult to chew the prime sirloin steaks he was used to. When I asked him why, he said that "hamburger meat" was for roadside stands and economy measures. "I realize that times are hard," he said bitterly, "but are we reduced to *scraps,* made of God knows what?" I proved to him that I was buying his accustomed cuts of beef, boning them, and chopping them myself to make his little entrées, although, of course, I avoided my real reason for this dietary hazard. He ate the next one, but I could see that it was more with pity than pleasure, and I moved on to further disguises.

Once, in an almost unconscious protest against the ingrained snobbishness of people in general and my father in particular, I bought a low-priced beef heart. It was a young one, my slightly astonished butcher assured me. In my cookbooks it was more often than not listed as an economy meat, and I decided that I would make it into a luxury dish, to amuse myself at least. I studied every method for attaining this goal, which from the first was labeled an impossibility if I had read between the lines. I combined the results of my research, and for what seemed several days as I look back on them I turned, marinated, parboiled, skinned, soaked, and otherwise tried to change the beef heart's muscular nature. There was a tedious roasting at low heat, with too much attention demanded to baste the thing enough to keep it from becoming thick leather on the outside.

I served it on a bed of watercress, with a sauceboat of its juices alongside, and a newly sharpened knife. My father, always the carver, attacked it with only a quick glance at me on his right. My two little girls sat on his left. We were deftly served, and, according to family custom, the children got a puddle of the gravy in the pit my father made automatically in their whipped potatoes. Then, perforce, I was hoist on my own *cafard*, for nothing could be done about our cutting the slices he had so neatly hewn off. He took the carving knife, made one thin bite for himself, chewed at it, and then, while we sat watching, he asked me gently, "Just what is this?" I was damned if I would tell him, so I looked at the girls, who were aware of all my preparations, and I countered by saying, without impudence, of course, "Well now, Father, tell *me*." He put the carving tools back on the handsome platter, so brown and green, and said, "Dinosaur." And that was one of the times that happen rarely in human lives, when a wave of maniacal laughter, the kind that verges on tears or hysteria, engulfed all of us, and we lay back in our chairs from it, and then sighed, and then went howling off again. Finally we quieted, like the ocean after a storm, and we put the watercress behind our ears and ate all the whipped potatoes and decided I had found the longest way in the world to make really delicious gravy. I have read that in Paris, in 1848 or so, some gastronomers ate elephant meat from the prehistoric deep freeze of the Russian steppes, and once in Whittier, in about 1955, we ate dinosaur.

But I did not dare to make a casserole of its near petrifaction. Time has drawn its kind veil again, and I cannot remember what happened to the large dark boulder so cunningly prepared and served forth. Instead, I probably roasted or poached some little chickens the next day, and the next day made a casserole from *them*.

1968

"Let's focus on what we do best—eating out."

GOOD COOKING

CALVIN TOMKINS

The headwaiter at Kan's could not decide immediately where to seat the Child party. One table was too small, another too far from the windows. Chinese waiters flew about in response to his urgent commands. Mrs. Kan, the proprietor, hastening to the scene, exchanged ceremonious greetings with Paul and Julia Child and was introduced to Rosemary Manell and Elizabeth Bishop, who would be assisting Julia throughout the next week in a series of cooking demonstrations for the benefit of the Presbyterian Hospital in San Francisco. Mrs. Kan was deeply honored by the presence in her restaurant of Julia Child, whose television show, *The French Chef*, is well known in San Francisco, but also deeply distressed, for she had not expected the visit. At length, the Child party was seated at a large table near the center of a big, elegant second-floor room that overlooks the city's Chinese quarter.

"Julia would like it if you ordered for all of us," Mrs. Manell said to Mrs. Kan. Julia nodded, beaming. She had lost her voice two days before, in Seattle, where she had given a series of four cooking demonstrations for the benefit of St. Mark's Cathedral. At a cocktail party following one of the demonstrations, she had swallowed an hors d'oeuvre that contained a very hot pepper, and a doctor she consulted seemed to think this might have been the cause of it. She was not supposed to use her voice, and she was communicating with facial expressions, gestures, and notes written with a felt-tip pen on a white pad. Whenever she scribbled a note to Mrs. Kan, Mrs. Kan took the pad and pen and wrote out her reply. Mrs. Bishop explained that this wasn't really necessary, since Julia could hear perfectly well, but Mrs. Kan seemed to think it impolite to reply orally to a written message.

Mrs. Kan's selections began with barbecued spareribs, served as an hors d'oeuvre, and progressed to fried squid. "Fresh frying fat makes all the difference," Julia wrote when she had tasted it. Mrs. Kan wrote back, "An expert such as you knows!" The squid was followed by diced-winter-melon soup, pale green and delicately flavored ("Does it look like cat vomit?" Julia inquired in a note not shown to Mrs. Kan), and then by lemon chicken, Kan's special noodles flavored with chicken and coriander, asparagus with beef, and bean cake with barbecued pork. Two other diners sent complimentary greetings to the Childs' table, and their waiter told them that everyone wanted to know what Julia was having (nobody in America calls her anything but Julia). As the meal continued, Julia scribbled faster and faster, and asked the others to read her notes aloud, so there could be the appearance of conversation. "Isn't this far better than that hot Szechwan stuff?" she wrote. "Paul and I lived 1½ years in China and never had it. I wonder if it really exists there." The Childs lived in China during the Second World War—Kunming, in fact, was the scene of their courtship, while they were both working for the Office of Strategic Services—and they have retained ever since a keen interest in Chinese cooking. Julia Child does not do any Chinese cooking herself, because she feels that one lifetime is hardly sufficient to encompass the cuisines of France, her specialty, but she loves to go to Chinese restaurants. "I would be perfectly happy w. only Chinese food," she wrote. "Either French or Chinese. Could live w. only Chinese."

Mrs. Kan wanted the Childs to see the kitchen. She also wanted to take their picture, and she refused to let them pay for the meal. Paul Child made certain that the photo would not be used as an endorsement for Kan's—"We never do that"—and he said that they always paid for meals in restaurants. "We must be very careful, no payola," Julia wrote on her pad. "Remember Watergate!" Mrs. Kan smiled firmly. Everyone got up and went into the kitchen, where Julia inspected mysterious vessels and vats, and put her arm around the chef. The chef, who stood a good eighteen inches short of Julia's six feet one and a half, seemed absolutely delighted.

Going back to the hotel in a taxi, Paul was upset that he had not been permitted to pay for the meal. "She was so determined," he said. "I didn't want to do *battle* over it."

"We'll send her a book," Julia wrote. And a little later, in a note to Mrs. Bishop, "We must all help to cheer up Paul. He gets depressed when anything wrong w. wife."

The Childs and their associates were at about the midpoint of a demonstration tour that had begun in Seattle and would conclude in

Honolulu. There were to be eight cooking demonstrations in San Francisco, at the Kabuki Theatre, in the new Japan Center on Geary Street. They had flown in from Seattle on a Thursday, four days in advance of the first demonstration, and they needed all of the time they had to get ready. In their comfortable suite at the Clift Hotel, the Childs, Mrs. Manell, and Mrs. Bishop spent hours going over lists, schedules, and recipes in thick loose-leaf notebooks. Other lists had preceded them—lists of cooking equipment and food staples and hardware and supplies of all kinds, which the Women's Board of Presbyterian Hospital of Pacific Medical Center, co-sponsor of the event along with Liberty House, the San Francisco branch of the Honolulu department store, had agreed to provide. The Women's Board had done its job with great zeal—had provided, in fact, more than fifteen hundred separate items, from a stove and a refrigerator down to rolls of paper towels and packages of scouring pads. (Many of the utensils were going to be raffled off to ticket buyers after the demonstrations.) There were always a number of things, like fresh vegetables, that could only be bought at the last minute, however, and Mrs. Manell and Mrs. Bishop were responsible for getting those. The dishes to be cooked onstage at the Kabuki were all fairly spectacular. Having more or less invented what could be called the theatre of cooking during her twelve years on television, Julia was not going to let her audience down, and the stage, she knew, required larger effects than the home screen. She would give San Francisco her Caneton en Aspic à la Parisienne and Charlotte Malakoff, Beef Wellington and Quiche aux Asperges, Le Loup en Croûte and Crêpes à la Pagode en Flammes.

By Saturday, two days before the first demonstration, Julia's voice had returned. Her younger sister, Dorothy (Mrs. Ivan Cousins), who lives in Sausalito, had sent her to a throat specialist well known for treating opera singers and other performers, and he had painted and sprayed Julia's aggrieved larynx so skillfully that she was able to go through with a scheduled press conference at the Kabuki Theatre that morning. Julia and Paul sat for an hour at a small table in the theatre lobby, which Liberty House had turned into a festive-looking culinary boutique for the demonstrations, and replied in their quite different conversational styles—cheery, gracious, down-to-earth in Julia's case, precise and urbane in Paul's—to the not invariably stimulating questions of a dozen or so food and feature editors. Julia recommended that newcomers to cooking approach it "with courage and daring." Paul said they should not be afraid of hard work. Julia said cooking wasn't really hard once you mastered the essential techniques. Paul said that mastering the techniques required much hard work. Julia came out against the term "gourmet," which she said had lost all meaning through overuse ("We just say 'good cooking' "), and she also had harsh words for the frozen string bean. A bearded reporter who said that he was from the Gay Liberation Press announced that he and his friends were coming to all the demonstrations. ("I think it's very good they're coming out of the closet," Julia said later.) Since nobody asked her about cholesterol, Julia brought up the subject herself. It was a very bad idea, she said, to think that you could cut out all foods that were high in cholesterol, as those were often the healthiest foods. Everyone needed a balanced diet. "We've done research on this," she said, "and we've found that some doctors believe a completely cholesterol-free diet can lead to premature aging and sexual frailty."

Although the press conference was a great success, the publicity for the cooking demonstrations had been, up to this point, somewhat disappointing. Only one major story had appeared in a San Francisco paper (the *Chronicle*), and that one had printed the wrong telephone number to call for tickets and reservations. Tickets for each demonstration were priced at fifteen dollars, and advance sales had been slow— partly, it was thought, because San Franciscans were nervous about the so-called Zebra murders, and were afraid to go out in the evening. With Julia's arrival, though, the trickle of publicity became a flood, and ticket sales picked up.

"This is such an American custom, the way these affairs are run by volunteer women," Paul Child said that afternoon. "It's practically unheard of in Europe." Barbara Grant, the president of the Women's Board, and Hannah Foster, the vice president, and their colleagues had started eight months before to prepare for the 1974 benefit. It had been Mrs. Foster's idea to invite Julia Child—in previous years the Women's Board's fund-raising had centered on an annual débutante ball. Mrs. Foster, Mrs. Grant, and several others on the benefit committee put in long hours throughout the Childs' stay in San Francisco, running errands for the cooking team, washing dishes and pots from the stage kitchen, briefing volunteer ushers, selling tickets, and not infrequently pressing their husbands into service as well. Only one or two of the people connected with the Women's Board seemed to be what Julia refers to as "lady types"—the type that comes into a kitchen, sees several stacks of unwashed utensils, and asks, "Is there anything I can do?"

After inspecting the rather elaborate cooking setup that had been provided for them on the Kabuki stage—a made-to-order kitchen flanked by large hanging screens to pick up television images of what Julia would be doing from three video cameras mounted directly above the work spaces—the Childs were a little worried that the benefit committee might have spent too lavishly. "In Seattle," Paul said, "we performed in the auditorium of the cathedral, on a set put together mostly from found objects. Somebody had contributed a stove, another person a refrigerator, and there were chests of drawers for work spaces and a couple of child-sized tables under the counters for shelves. It was really very clever and workable, and it didn't cost much." The financing of these demonstrations does not directly concern the Childs, who derive no money from them personally. They donate all their fees to WGBH-TV, in Boston, the public television station where *The French Chef* originated, in 1962. The tour expenses are paid by the sponsoring group (WGBH picks up any extras), and the Childs look upon the rather considerable effort and time involved mainly as a means of generating favorable publicity for Julia's books—the monumental *Mastering the Art of French Cooking*, Volumes I and II, and a book of recipes from their television shows, called *The French Chef Cookbook*. Nevertheless, both the Childs wanted the hospital to make money from the San Francisco demonstrations, and they were somewhat alarmed to hear that the benefit committee had already spent something like thirty thousand dollars on expenses. Liberty House had donated most of the cooking equipment, and Safeway Stores had provided quantities of free staples, but there had been heavy outlays for the construction of the model kitchen on the stage of the Kabuki Theatre. An 850-seat house fitted out with tables for the audience to dine at while watching a performance, the theatre had been designed for the presentation of traditional Kabuki drama, but evidently there had not been enough Kabuki lovers in town to support it, so the management was planning to use the space for stage shows of various kinds. At one point, the management had added to the benefit committee's difficulties by trying, unsuccessfully, to cancel its one-week lease on the theatre.

The Childs refused almost all invitations to dinner or to cocktails in the days before the first demonstration. "We want to put on a good show," Julia explained, "and we just can't spare the time." Lunches for the Childs and their two assistants were cooked by Rosemary Manell in the demonstration kitchen, and they ate them at a table in the wings. (Later, when they were giving demonstrations each afternoon and evening, they had dinner there as well.) They spent the weekend at the theatre, stocking and setting up for the first show and doing the necessary precooking. A great deal of precooking is done for Julia's television series; a dish may have to be shown in three or four different stages of preparation, and since the twenty-eight minutes of allotted airtime do not allow for the completion of these stages, versions of the dish at each stage must be ready to show. In a three-hour live demonstration, much of the actual cooking does take place onstage, but puff pastry and yeast doughs must be made ahead so they can rise, backups are needed in case of onstage disasters, and cold ducks (for Caneton en Aspic) must be cooked in advance. Rosemary Manell and Elizabeth Bishop, who had both been on previous demonstration tours, knew the names that Julia and Paul assign to every item of equipment and every work space (to save time in explaining or describing), and they were even allowed access to the Sacred Bag, a phenomenally heavy black canvas satchel containing certain cooking items that Julia cannot do without (her favorite bone flour scoop, her large pastry-cutting wheel, her special knives, and so on), plus emergency items such as extension cords, of which there are never enough on hand. The Sacred Bag has been around since the beginning of the television series.

The Childs had known Rosemary Manell since 1949, when they were all together in France. Paul Child and Abram Manell, Rosemary's husband, were both with the Foreign Service then, and the two couples, who shared an interest in good food, which in Julia's case was becoming something more than an interest, used to dine together regularly in the Childs' apartment, on the Rue de l'Université, or the Manells', on the Île St.-Louis. Rosie, as the Childs and their friends (but no one else) call her, now lives in Belvedere, just across the bay from San Francisco. She is a talented painter and potter, an expert tailor, a first-class cook; she wears Scandinavian-blond hair in a thick braid down her back, and is nearly as tall as Julia.

Elizabeth Bishop, a Bostonian with close-cropped dark hair and a sense of humor that has often relieved tension at difficult moments, was one of the volunteers who came to work for *The French Chef* at WGBH. When the show started, Paul did all the behind-scenes washing up—and a good deal of the chopping, grating, mincing, and precooking as well. He had only recently resigned from the Foreign Service, after nearly twenty years, but because he has always adapted easily to changed circumstances, and suffers from no apparent insecurities of the male ego, he took, from the outset, an active and supportive part in Julia's new career. "I'm here," Paul used to say. "I'll do anything." But as the program developed, it soon became evident that more backstage help was needed, and, with no difficulty whatsoever, a crew of half a dozen volunteers was formed. Several of the women were married and had small children at home; they hired babysitters or housekeepers to come and do the dishes there while they went to the WGBH studio in Cambridge and spent the day doing the dishes for Julia. Actually, they did much of the precooking and testing for the show. Julia sometimes introduces them on the air. "Meet my associate cooks," she says. "Mary O'Brien, Liz Bishop, Bess Hopkins, Edith Seltzer, Rita Rains, Bess Coughlin, and Gladys Christopherson. It's always more fun cooking with friends, don't you think?" Mrs. Bishop lives in Cohasset, Massachusetts, with her husband and their three children, and when *The French Chef* was in production she often did not get home until one or two o'clock in the morning. Now that the Childs are taking a year off from television and the show is being seen only in reruns, she is delighted to be able to travel with them on their demonstration tours. "Cooking is the least of it," she told a friend in San Francisco. "You know, in a funny way I feel closer to Julia than I do to anyone. Of course I'm *closer* to Jack and the children, but there are things I could say to her that I couldn't say to anyone else."

Julia Child was born Julia Carolyn McWilliams in Pasadena, California, in 1912. The oldest of three children in a moderately well-to-do family—her father, John McWilliams, managed some family farming land in Arkansas and Southern California—she was entered in Smith College the day she was born. "My mother was in the Class of 1900 there," she said recently, "and there was just never any doubt that I would go. In those days, people were very enthusiastic about their college." As a member of Smith's Class of 1934, Julia was planning to be a

Great Woman Novelist. "They laughed when I sat down at the type-writer," she told an interviewer in San Francisco. "And they were right, too, because nothing much ever came of the plan. I wrote for the Smith College *Tatler,* and after I graduated I went home for a while, and then I went to New York and tried to get a job with *The New Yorker,* but they turned me down. The woman-novelist idea was very vague and un-formed. I just thought it would develop at some time or other."

After three years in New York, working in the advertising depart-ment of W. & J. Sloane and living with two Smith classmates in an apartment under the Queensboro Bridge, she went back home and spent another two years in Pasadena. "I had a very good time doing vir-tually nothing," she said. "There was always lots of fun and laughter." Then the war came, and on the advice of her friend Janie McBaine (who subsequently married Marquis Childs) she went to Washington and got what she describes as "a dreadful typing job" with a government information agency whose nickname was Mellett's Madhouse. After six months, she left and joined the Office of Strategic Services. At one point, there was a call for volunteers for overseas duty, and Julia McWilliams, reasoning that she would probably be going to Europe after the war in any case, put in for Far Eastern duty. With an oddly as-sorted group that included the anthropologists Gregory Bateson and Cora Du Bois and a congeries of explosives experts, forgers who had done time in federal prisons, and some missionaries who had been born in the Far East, she traveled by troop train across the United States and then by boat to Australia and on to Bombay, arriving the same day that two ammunition ships caught fire and blew up a large part of the Bom-bay docks. From Bombay, some of them went by train across the Indian subcontinent to Madras, and from there to Ceylon. It was at the OSS headquarters in Ceylon that she met Paul Child.

Child, who got to Ceylon a few months after Julia, was in charge of Visual Presentation for the OSS there. That meant, for the most part, setting up and maintaining a war room for the general staff, with maps and charts to show the areas, topographies, troop concentrations, and other factors on which military planning depended. (He had recently come from New Delhi, where he had set up a war room for Lord Louis Mountbatten and General Wedemeyer.) Julia was placed in charge of the Registry, a document center for messages to and from OSS agents in the field. She noticed the Visual Presentation officer because he seemed, on the whole, to be more civilized than anyone else there. Paul was ten years older than Julia, and he had seen a lot of the world. He had been a lumberman in Maine and a waiter in Hollywood, and he was a self-taught artist. During the twenties, he had knocked about Europe, spending several years in Paris, where he got to know Hemingway, Gertrude Stein, and other expatriates; that supposedly golden decade had been a rather penurious one for Child, who had made a marginal living by selling his own woodcuts and making copies of the antique furniture in the Cluny Museum. After that, he had become a schoolteacher, first in France and later at the Shady Hill School, in Cambridge, Massachusetts, and at the Avon Old Farms School, near Hartford, Connecticut, where he taught art and French. He was, in addition, an accomplished engraver and photographer, a black belt in judo, a master of several languages, and a man who could converse interestingly and amusingly on almost any subject. Although a more or less confirmed bachelor by this time, Child also noticed Julia McWilliams. "She seemed like a pretty great woman to me," he recalled recently. "She was completely competent, unflappable—just the way she is now—and running a very complicated operation with great skill."

At this stage of the war, late in 1943, the Americans and the British were planning an operation to cut off the Japanese garrison in Singapore by making a surprise landing behind enemy lines on the Malay Peninsula. This plan was abandoned when it became evident that the required naval support was not available—everything was going into the approaching invasion of Normandy. Child was sent to help set up other war rooms on the Chinese mainland, at Chungking, and then at Kunming. Julia McWilliams was also assigned to Kunming, and the friendship begun in Ceylon developed into something more serious. Kunming, which had never been in Japanese hands, was full of refugees from all parts of China. There was enough food available, and Paul and Julia were able to sample and become enthusiastic about many different Chinese cuisines. They were in Kunming when the Japanese surrendered. Soon afterward, Paul made his way home by way of Peking. Julia's detachment was scheduled to go to Shanghai, but, with the war over, the unit's morale was not what it had been. "I felt we'd lost the purity of our purpose," Julia said recently. "You can see I'm a Victorian woman at heart. Anyway, I decided to go home. They flew me over the hump to Calcutta and loaded me onto a troopship, from which I disembarked, weeks later, smelling, as somebody said, like a cattle boat."

A reunion took place several months later in Washington. "We had decided that we should look each other over in civilian clothes, and that we should meet each other's families," Julia recalls. That done, they were married in the fall of 1946. Julia was thirty-four, Paul forty-four. For the first year and a half, they lived in Washington. The Office of Strategic Services had been discontinued, but OSS people who had been in Visual Presentation were automatically absorbed into the State Department, and Paul was now doing graphic work for the government. Early in 1948, by a happy official stroke, he was assigned to the United States Information Service office in Paris.

France was not at all the way Julia had imagined it. "I'd never met any French people before," she said not long ago, "and I thought they'd be—you know, snippy, the way they always seemed in *Harper's Bazaar* or *Vogue*. I was just amazed to get off the boat at Le Havre and see all those great big beefy people. We drove to Rouen and had lunch there at the Couronne, and I was euphoric. I was practically in hysterics from the time we landed. Of course, I didn't realize how difficult it was going to be for me to learn the language. It was two years, really, before I could get along in it, and four years before I was fluent. But from the beginning I just fell in love with everything I saw. It took me a long time to get over my infatuation—now they can't fool me so easily."

The Childs found a comfortable third-floor apartment on the Rue de l'Université, behind the Chambre des Députés. Paul could walk across the Pont de la Concorde to his office, on the Faubourg du St.-Honoré. At first, Julia spent most of her time at Berlitz, struggling with the language. Both the Childs readily concede that at this point her cooking left a good deal to be desired. Paul knew and appreciated good food, but Julia, like many American women of her background, had never really learned to cook at home, and until she married Paul she had never been interested in learning. In the fall of 1949, though, she was sufficiently interested to enroll in a special early-morning course at the Cordon Bleu cooking school, where she found herself the only woman student—the twelve others were ex-GIs, learning cooking on the GI Bill of Rights. "I would leave home at seven in the morning, cook all morning with the GIs, and then rush home to make lunch for Paul," Julia remembers. "I'd give him the béarnaise or the hollandaise sauce I'd just learned, or something equally rich. In about a week we both got terribly bilious."

The Cordon Bleu, founded in the nineteenth century, once served as a cooking school for orphans, to help them make their way in life. By the 1930s, it had become a place where well-to-do housewives (many of them Americans) sent their servants to learn the techniques of the classic cuisine. In modern times, it has not been a professional school— to become a professional chef in France one has to serve as an apprentice for years in a restaurant or hotel kitchen, and that training is often supplemented by attendance at a government-sponsored technical institution. But the Cordon Bleu hired professional chefs as teachers, and when Julia enrolled, in 1949, the teaching was excellent. Two of the three chefs whom Julia had as teachers were in their seventies: Max Bugnard, who had owned his own restaurant in Brussels before the war, and Claude Thillmont, for many years the pastry chef at the Café de Paris. The third was a younger man—Pierre Mangelatte, who was the chef at an excellent small restaurant in Montmartre, the Restaurant des Artistes.

"Bugnard was a marvelous meat cook, a marvelous sauce maker, wonderful with stocks and vegetables, although not so much with desserts," Julia recalls. "As a young man, he had known Escoffier. Chef Thillmont had worked in the twenties with Mme. Saint-Ange on her great cookbook, *Le Livre de Cuisine de Mme. Saint-Ange*, now unfortunately out of print. Those two men knew just about everything there was to know. And in the afternoons we would have demonstration classes by Mangelatte, who was a brilliant technician." Julia had just enough French by this time to keep up with the instruction. Her interest in the subject, she found, was limitless. "Until I got into cooking," she once said, "I was never *really* interested in anything."

Marie-Antoine Carême (1784–1833), celebrated gastronome, personal chef (successively) to Talleyrand, Czar Alexander I, George IV, and Baron Rothschild, author of five classic books on food, is generally considered the founder of *la grande cuisine*. On the Sunday evening before the cooking demonstrations began at the Kabuki Theatre, the Chefs Association of the Pacific Coast presented its Carême Medal to Julia Child, at a dinner given in her honor in a private dining room at the

Jack Tar Hotel. The dinner began, surprisingly, with matzo-ball soup, continued with a seafood *coquille*, paused for sherbet, forged onward with beef Wellington, a potato basket, and cucumber salad, and concluded with a chocolate bombe and petits fours. In draping the Carême Medal around Julia's neck, the president of the association spoke of her as "the person who brought classic cooking into American homes" and "the one chef in the country who has the recognition that we are all striving for." A few of the chefs at the long table seemed to harbor reservations about the award's going, for the first time, to a woman— Joe Rivas, the principal chef for the Pam Pam chain of restaurants in San Francisco, said firmly that women would never make it as chefs in major restaurants, because they were not strong enough physically— but virtually every one of them, including Rivas, wanted to meet Julia and shake her hand.

There was a good deal of talk at the dinner about the shortage of qualified chefs in this country and the absence of professional cooking schools. The Pacific Coast chefs, most of whom seemed to be European-born and in their late fifties or sixties, bemoaned the fact that so few younger men were coming up to take their places. Julia said that unfortunately the same thing was now true in France. Fewer and fewer people wanted to put in the long hours that a first-class restaurant, or even a humble village bakery, demanded. Convenience foods were taking over in restaurants as well as in private households. There were some great young chefs at work, to be sure—Julia mentioned in particular Roger Vergé, whose Hostellerie Moulin de Mougins, near Cannes, had just received its third star in the *Guide Michelin*. But, as Paul Child pointed out, men like Vergé and Paul Bocuse and the Troisgros brothers did not write down what they had learned or invented, and their discoveries would probably die with them. "Nowadays, everybody likes to run down Escoffier," Julia said, "but nobody's doing what he did to preserve the great traditions."

"*She's* doing it," Paul said, pointing at his wife.

"Oh, but I'm doing it for the home. Somebody should be doing it for the profession, the way Escoffier did."

"Nobody has that kind of dedication," Paul said.

What Paul had in mind was the dedication that went into *Mastering the Art of French Cooking*, on which Julia and two collaborators worked without interruption for ten years. The book's phenomenal success—the first volume alone has sold more than a million and a quarter copies in America to date—suggests that perhaps the traditional *haute cuisine* of France may be moving not only from the restaurant to the private home (where it began) but from the Old World to the New. Only a few long-established, all-purpose cookbooks, such as Irma Rombauer's *Joy of Cooking*, have sold more copies in hardcover. There are many young couples in America who start out conjugal life with what they refer to simply as *Julia Child* and continue to use it more or less exclusively ever after. A woman who lives on the Alaskan tundra has written to say that she is cooking her way through *Julia Child*. The wife of a forest ranger in New Mexico, who lives sixty miles from the nearest town, is doing the same. Much of the book's success, of course, is directly related to the even more phenomenal success of Julia Child as a television personality, but it seems reasonable to assume that any-one who puts down $12.50 for the book is not just going to leave it out on the cocktail table. A lot of dedicated French cooking does seem to be going on.

Julia had no intention at first of getting involved in the book, which she heard about soon after a friend in Paris had introduced her to Si-mone (Simca) Beck. Mme. Beck had started to work, with another friend of hers, named Louisette Bertholle, on a book about French cooking for Americans. "Simca was very much like me," Julia has said. "A middle-class person who was extremely interested in cooking. She had gone to the Cordon Bleu in the old, prewar days, when Henri Pel-laprat was teaching there. I knew nobody then who was really *deeply* in-terested in cooking. I had nobody to talk to about it, and so when I met Simca we just fell into each other's arms. She and Louisette introduced me into the Cercle des Gourmettes, which is a French ladies' gastro-nomical society—founded, I think, in 1927. The Cercle met every two weeks, and there was a chef to give instruction. By the time I joined it, most of the members were in their seventies, and they would never ar-rive until about noon, in time for the aperitif and lunch. Simca and Louisette and I would arrive at nine-thirty, so we got what amounted to private lessons from the chef. It was my introduction to really sophis-ticated French food and living—foie gras in season, and lobster dishes, and very elaborate ways of doing things. Anyway, I knew that Simca and Louisette were working on a big book, and that they needed an American collaborator—they'd had one, a man, who didn't work out for some reason—but I had no interest in it then. The book was their affair.

"What happened next was that some friends of ours from California came to Paris and, knowing about my interest in cooking, said, 'Why don't you teach us?' Simca, who is always enthusiastic, said, 'Why not?' And so the very next day we started our school, which we called the École des Trois Gourmandes. Our apartment was the perfect place for it, because we had a big, airy kitchen on the upper floor (it was a two-floor apartment) with a dumbwaiter that brought things down to the dining room. We engaged two of my Cordon Bleu chefs, Bugnard and Thillmont, to come in once or twice a week. There were never more than six in the class—mostly Americans, but one or two French. We would cook all morning, then sit down and eat it, with Paul at the head of the table to pour the wine. If you brought a guest, you had to pay five hundred francs. We three found that we were absolutely fascinated with teaching."

Sometime in 1951, Julia was persuaded to become the American collaborator on the cookbook. She had her own ideas about the project, however, one of them being that it should be a "real teaching book" rather than a mere collection of recipes. With the shining exception of Mme. Saint-Ange's classic, most of the available books for serious students of French cooking were little more than a chef's shorthand notes for the various dishes; unless the reader knew beforehand how to make a white sauce or poach a trout, or how to add egg yolks to a hot sauce without making it curdle, the book was not much help. Julia thought that every step and every technique should be thoroughly explained, and that the reasoning behind the various techniques should also be made clear. The essence of French cooking, she has often said, is knowing the properties of each ingredient and cooking it in such a way that its best points are fully brought out. If the purpose of their book was to overcome the American fear of "elaborate" French cuisine, one of the methods would be to leave nothing out—to describe, for example, what a dish should look like and feel like at each stage in its preparation, and also to discuss some of the things that could go wrong during the process, along with corrective measures. This meant long recipes— pages and pages long in many cases. (The longest is the twenty-two- page recipe for French bread in Volume II of *Mastering the Art of French Cooking*, an adaptation of the professional baker's art to the home kitchen that Julia and Paul, who collaborated on the research, regard as probably their most important contribution so far.) It also meant a prodigious amount of research (two years on French bread alone), testing, and often impassioned argument among the three authors.

From 1952 on, much of the argument was by mail. After four years in Paris, Paul Child was transferred to Marseille, and then, two years later, to the embassy in Bonn, where he was exhibits officer, and where the Childs acquired a reputation for oddness because they did not spend much time in the embassy's housing compound or swim in the swimming pool there (they preferred a pool on the other side of the Rhine), and because Paul did not spend weekends polishing his car. Paul concedes that he never really became reconciled to the bureaucratic aspects of government service. He and Julia had been unable to have children, and their primary interests were aesthetic and culinary. Julia was always well liked by the other embassy wives—she was too delightful not to be—and her social talents were a notable asset to Paul in his career. "I can't tell you how important it is for a Foreign Service officer to have a partner like Julia," Paul said one day in San Francisco. At the same time, she was putting a great deal of time and energy into research on the book—experimenting and testing, amassing a private library and clipping file on the subject, exchanging information and ideas with her collaborators. One epic argument with Simone Beck, over the proper ingredients of the *vrai cassoulet,* consumed sixty single-spaced typewritten pages before it was finally resolved.

In the spring of 1951, Julia wrote a sample chapter and an outline of the book, had several copies made, and sent them to various friends in the United States. One of the recipients was Avis DeVoto, Bernard DeVoto's wife. Some time before, in his monthly column in *Harper's,* DeVoto had written a diatribe against the stainless-steel paring knife, which, he complained, would not take an edge or perform any useful kitchen function. Julia saw the column in Paris, wrote him a letter expressing vigorous agreement, and enclosed a French paring knife with a good, sharpenable carbon-steel blade. Avis DeVoto had written a friendly reply, and a correspondence had sprung up. "We both liked to write letters," Mrs. DeVoto said recently, "and there was a lot to write about. The McCarthy thing was heating up in Washington. Julia and Paul were bewildered and rather frightened by it. Sometimes we'd write each other three or four times a week." According to Mrs. DeVoto, Julia was a pretty bad writer at that point. The sample chapter of the cook-book struck her as "muddy, verbose, and awkward," and the spelling was atrocious. "But I knew the minute I saw it that this book on French cooking was really going to work," she said. "I'm not a bad cook, and I could see this was a whole new approach." She took it around to Houghton Mifflin, the publisher of several of her husband's books. Al-though the response there was somewhat mixed, Houghton Mifflin gave the authors a $250 advance and told them to have the book fin-ished in a year's time.

Six years later, having decided that their research demanded a mul-tivolume cookbook, the authors delivered an eight-hundred-page type-script that dealt, solely and exhaustively, with recipes for poultry and sauces. "That was my fault," Julia said last spring. "I've always done the writing, and the whole thing was much too detailed and academic. It was my conception that everyone would be interested in knowing, for example, that if you didn't happen to have a suffocated duck on hand you could get the same effect by using pig's blood." Not surprisingly, Houghton Mifflin turned it down. The Childs were in Washington at the time; Paul had been recalled from Bonn in 1956. Simone Beck had come over to visit them, and the Childs met her at the bus station with the bad news. "The despair in the waiting room could have been cut with a knife," according to Julia. "But then Simca, with her unfailing optimism, said we would just have to do it over again." The Childs left soon afterward for Paul's new post, in Oslo, and Julia spent the next year rewriting the book.

Although the second version covered more culinary ground and seemed to Avis DeVoto greatly improved in content and prose style ("I never thought anyone could really learn to write," she said, "but Julia did—she taught herself, with help from Paul and one or two other peo-ple"), Houghton Mifflin again found it unpublishable. Mrs. DeVoto submitted it next to William Koshland, at Alfred Knopf. She knew that Koshland liked to cook, and she urged him and Judith Jones, another Knopf editor interested in good food, to take it home and try out some of the recipes. Judith Jones was immediately convinced. "I was sure it was revolutionary," she said recently. "It was like having a teacher right there beside you in the kitchen, and everything really worked." Koshland liked it, too, and kept trying recipes out of it at home, but other editors at Knopf were uncertain. Time passed. From Oslo came increasingly anguished letters from Julia, inquiring whether ten years' work was down the drain. Eventually, the *fins becs* at Knopf prevailed over the doubters. The first volume of *Mastering the Art of French Cooking* came out in the fall of 1961, to virtually unanimous praise. Craig Claiborne called it "probably the most comprehensive, laudable, and monumental work on the subject," written "without compromise or condescension." The late Michael Field said that it "surpasses every other American book on French cooking in print today." The New York food establishment, which is not known for its generosity of spirit, took the book and the authors to its collective bosom, and Dione Lucas even gave a dinner for the Childs at the Egg Basket, her restaurant on East Fifty-seventh Street. Houghton Mifflin has been regretting its decision ever since.

At ten o'clock on Monday morning, Julia stood at the counter of the onstage kitchen at the Kabuki Theatre, pounding out chilled pastry dough with giant blows of a rolling pin and occasionally popping a small piece of it into her mouth. ("I love uncooked dough, don't you?") Rosie Manell was cutting green beans and red pimientos into tiny strips, with which Julia would decorate the duck aspic according to a pattern drawn in colored inks by Paul. Liz Bishop was glazing a duck, and Paul was rewriting the scripts for a group of fund-raising appeals that Julia had agreed to tape later in the week for KQED, the local public television station. In contrast with the anxious manner of some of the ladies on the benefit committee, who appeared from time to time to discuss the length of intermissions or the proper way to handle questions from the audience, the cooking team seemed calm and relaxed. On a television talk show two hours earlier, an interviewer had asked Julia whether it was necessary for her to be "quite so sloppy" in the kitchen. It was a familiar question, often asked by television viewers who do not cook or who belong to what James Beard calls "the sanitation school of cookery." As Paul Child occasionally explains, when you are trying to cook a rather complicated dish in twenty-eight minutes on camera, you do not take time to wash the pots and scour the work spaces. Onstage at the Kabuki, at any rate, a great deal of work was getting done with a minimum of fuss.

People who work with Julia Child are nearly always impressed by her sense of organization. "She may look sort of slapdash on the screen, but she's the most organized person I've ever met," according to Bess Hopkins, who now works in the office at WGBH. In the cluttered room that Julia uses as an office at home in Cambridge, her library of books on food and cooking and her extensive files of material on the subject are arranged and cross-referenced with the care and thoroughness of a major research institute, which, indeed, is what they amount to. A great deal of scholarship underlies that breezy self-assurance on camera; she can afford to appear casual, because she knows precisely what she is doing.

Some of her most ardent fans like to remember the slips and disasters of the early *French Chef* shows: the potato pancake dropped on the counter and scooped back into the skillet with the serene advice that "nobody's looking"; the spilled liquids and solids; the famous Roast Suckling Pig that defied all Julia's efforts, with several knives, to carve it up. What her co-workers remember is Julia's incredible skill at averting disasters or turning them somehow to her advantage. *The French Chef* programs have all been videotaped in continuous half-hour shooting sessions—a decision made at the beginning, because it avoided expensive editing—and only half a dozen times in more than two hundred programs taped so far has it been necessary to stop and reshoot. When a dessert began to lose its shape after unmolding on camera, Julia simply nudged it together with two spoons and urged her flock not to lose heart in similar situations. ("Never apologize—nobody knows what you're aiming at, so just bring it to the table.") When Ruth Lockwood, Julia's present producer and the person primarily responsible (with the Childs) for *The French Chef*'s style and format, forgot once to take the butter out of the refrigerator to soften before a taping, Julia improvised without a tremor: "Where's the butter? Oh, I forgot to take it out of the fridge! Well, here's what you do when that happens." And that evening she called Ruth at home, because she knew how Ruth, who never forgot anything, would be feeling. Mrs. Lockwood says that in the twelve years she has worked with Julia they have never had a real dispute about anything. One of the few times anyone has seen Julia lose her temper, in fact, was one day when there was a fire on the set. A towel flared up, a pot holder caught fire, and the cameraman stopped shooting. Julia was furious. She wanted to show the viewers just what to do at home when this happened.

Paul and Julia enjoy reminiscing about the early days of the show. They had come back from Norway in 1960—it had been Paul's decision to retire from the Foreign Service before he reached the compulsory retirement age of sixty-five—and established themselves in a comfortable old house they had bought several years before in Cambridge (the house where Josiah Royce, the philosopher, once lived). Paul planned to spend his time painting and photographing, and Julia was going to give private cooking lessons and work on Volume II of *Mastering the Art of French Cooking*. In the spring of 1962, a few months after the first volume had been published, Julia was invited to appear on a literary-interview program on WGBH to talk about it. Thinking it might liven things up, she brought along a copper bowl and a wire whip, and showed the viewers how to beat up egg whites. WGBH received twenty-seven letters about the interview, all expressing delight. As Russell Morash, *The French Chef*'s first producer-director, put it recently, twenty-seven letters might not mean very much to a major network, but to a small, noncommercial station like WGBH it was impressive. Would Mrs. Child be willing to consider doing a pilot program for a possible series of cooking shows?

They made three pilot shows in June 1962, using a basement display room of the Boston Gas Company in downtown Boston, because the WGBH studio had recently been destroyed by a fire. WGBH's director of programming, Robert Larsen, liked the pilots so much that he was willing to put the station's own funds into financing a series of twenty-six shows. They went into production in January 1963, in a makeshift set on the third floor of the Cambridge Electric Company, which had better parking facilities than Boston Gas. The early shows were all "remotes," videotaped with two cameras connected by cables to a power source in WGBH's mobile unit parked outside the building. They did four shows a week. Julia and Paul and Ruth Lockwood would spend all day Monday in the Childs' big kitchen at home, drinking oceans of tea and blocking out the rough outlines, time sequences, and opening and closing lines for the week's programs. Tuesdays and Thursdays were rehearsal days, prior to tapings on Wednesdays and Fridays. Today, neither the Childs nor Mrs. Lockwood can imagine how they kept it up. Julia and Paul, who did all the shopping for the shows, would get to the Cambridge Electric Company an hour or so ahead of the others, carrying the Sacred Bag and a huge load of groceries. Whenever it snowed, Paul had to shovel the fire escape so the crew could bring in the cables and equipment. The crew numbered twenty-four, counting volunteers, and they usually ended up eating the show. Grips and cameramen would take home dishes in one state or another for their wives to finish cooking. The last show of the first series called for Lobster à l'Américaine. Julia and Paul bought enough for everyone, and plenty of dry Riesling, and after the show they had a banquet on the set. Not a farewell banquet, because the second series was already in the works, with several "subscribers" (public television does not refer to "sponsors"), such as Safeway Stores, Hills Bros., and eventually the Polaroid Corporation, to help pay for it. They did sixty-eight shows at the Cambridge Electric Company before moving to the new WGBH studios, in Cambridge, in November 1963.

Old friends of Julia's often say that those early black-and-white shows were the best—that in spite of the mishaps, or perhaps because of them, Julia was more herself than she has appeared in the technically superior programs that followed. Julia, who is highly self-critical, does not agree at all. "I was inclined at the beginning, having been involved in writing and teaching, to be too expository, to talk too much," she has said. "Ruthie Lockwood kept reminding me that television was a visual medium and that the points had to be made visually. Also, I had no time sense to speak of, so it was very difficult for me at first. We've always worked with a system of 'idiot cards,' which they hold up to tell me when it's time to move on to the next step, but at the beginning I'd sometimes forget to look for them. And then I'd look at the wrong camera sometimes. The boys finally started putting a little hat on the camera that was shooting, and a big sign under the lens reading ME FRIEND." The videotapes of the first thirteen shows, which were made before the program started to be picked up by other noncommercial stations around the country, no longer exist—they literally wore out from overuse. Julia was rather pleased, because it gave her an opportunity to redo those programs (all basic mainstays such as Boeuf Bourguignon, Coq au Vin, and omelettes) in a more professional manner.

The unique blend of Julia's earthy humor and European sophistication, her tendency to slap and sniff and taste everything without losing a shred of her dignity, were there from the beginning. "Julia is a natural ham and a natural comic," Paul once said, "and Ruth Lockwood, with her own slightly corny sense of humor, has always encouraged that in her." Using a giant sabre to carve her Poulet Sauté Marengo, appearing in a pith helmet and firing off a popgun to bring down a squab for "Small Roast Birds," and other elements of horseplay have undoubtedly helped to build her audience, which seems, from the mail that comes in, to include a surprising number of children and husbands. Julia, moreover, is not above a little gentle baiting of her detractors, who tend to be mainly sanitationists (or "home-economics types," as Julia calls them), and those who are disturbed by her use of wine and other, more demonic spirits in cooking. "Now we'll add a quarter of a teaspoon of white wine," she will say, pouring copiously from the bottle. "The children will love it." An amazing number of people seem to think that Julia's high good humor and her occasional mishaps on the home screen can mean only that she is drunk. Cartoons have depicted her swigging from a bottle as she cooks, and some viewers insist that they have actually seen her do this on camera—a misapprehension that may stem, Julia thinks, from the time she carefully peeled, seeded, and squeezed a tomato and then drank off the juice in a cup. When the BBC was contemplating a *French Chef* series in Britain, the program that they put on the air to test audience reaction opened with Julia picking up the lids from two steaming saucepans and clashing them together like cymbals. This caused the steam lingering in both lids to fly right into her face, a painful surprise that she accepted with one of her more robust peals of laughter. The station received so many calls from distressed Britons wondering what on earth a drunken or demented American woman was doing on the Third Programme that the BBC decided not to run the series after all. Actually, as Paul sometimes points out, it is peculiar to assume that anything as complex as what Julia does on television—does with split-second timing and with explanations that make sense—could be done at all by someone under the influence of liquor. "She wouldn't be dropping spoons up there, she'd be falling down," Paul says. It may be that real spontaneity has become so rare that it requires an explanation. "We never really know what she's going to say on the program," Ruth Lockwood said recently. "She memorizes the opening and closing lines, and there is a sort of rough script, consisting mostly of key words and phrases, but aside from that there's just no telling what's going to happen. We always say it's the only real suspense show on television."

The last show in *The French Chef* series was taped in December

1972. There are more than two hundred of them on tape, and reruns keep the program going in most parts of the country, but after twelve years the Childs are not sure they want to continue with it. "If I ever do any more, I want them to be more professional," Julia said recently. "I want to be sure that the closeups are correct, and things like that. One time, we had a program on roasting a turkey, and at the end you couldn't see the turkey being carved, couldn't see a damn thing." She would like to be able to edit the show after each taping, though editing would add considerably to the expense. Julia thinks of herself primarily as a teacher—"*The French Chef,*" she says, "is really a continuation of L'École des Trois Gourmandes"—and she feels that her students should not have to put up with anything less than the highest standards.

It has been said that Julia Child really "made" public television. She was certainly the first major star to emerge from noncommercial programming—the first to become a nationally known figure. Wherever she goes now, people recognize her and speak to her; in restaurants, waiters ask her to sign the menu (which pleases her enormously), and other diners send over friendly notes and try to find out what she has ordered. A recent television commercial featured Julia Chicken, a fowl who spoke in the French Chef's unmistakably rich and breathy accents, until the Childs' lawyer put a stop to it, and *The Electric Company,* a children's program, has had a character named Julia Grownup. Although Julia Child has little time to savor the fruits of her fame, she clearly enjoys it—"loves every minute of it," according to Avis DeVoto—and, just as clearly, will not miss it when it recedes. She has consistently turned down all offers from commercial TV, just as she has turned down all requests to endorse products or to lend her name to promotions other than those in support of public television. Last year, she was approached by NBC, which offered her a spot at nine-thirty in the morning five days a week; she turned it down, largely because the audience at that hour would be almost entirely women, "and our audience is bigger than that." She has given back to WGBH, through fees for demonstrations, fund-raising appeals, and royalties from *The French Chef Cookbook,* far more than she has ever received from it. The Childs feel that her television exposure has been responsible in large part for the success of *Mastering the Art of French Cooking,* and that alone has made them, if not rich, at least comfortable beyond anything they had ever expected. Everyone involved, it appears, is grateful to everyone else, and the television audience seems happy enough for the time being with reruns. There has been talk about presenting *The French Chef* in a new format, based on public cooking demonstrations like the ones in San Francisco. But at present, Julia's only plans for television involve a few special shows with James Beard.

Meanwhile, Julia has completed the manuscript of another cookbook, using recipes done on the show since the first one appeared, in 1968, and she and Simone Beck may do a revised edition of *Mastering the Art of French Cooking*. Louisette Bertholle, who dropped out of the collaboration after Volume I, now lives near Bourges and is teaching and writing on her own. But the Childs and Mme. Beck and her husband, Jean Fischbacher, a perfumer, remain in close contact professionally and personally—particularly during the spring and summer, when the Childs stay in a little house they have built on some property of the Fischbachers' in the south of France. One purpose of a revision would be to bring readers up to date on some of the culinary equipment that has come along in recent years (such as nonstick pans and highly versatile electrical processors). In Volume I, the authors took a somewhat Olympian tone about utensils, in line with the traditional *hauteur du chef,* but Julia has come to feel that it is a good thing to speed matters up where possible in the kitchen, and that if the same effect that used to be produced by laborious handwork can be duplicated by a machine, then *vive la machine.*

An hour before the first San Francisco cooking demonstration was to start, at two on Monday afternoon, the Childs and their two assistants were finishing a leisurely lunch in a curtained-off area at the left side of the stage. These "working" lunches were relatively simple but far from casual occasions. During the preceding days, Rosie Manell had dished up many regional specialties, such as cracked crab, tiny bay shrimps, rex sole, and abalone (sautéed twenty seconds to a side, no more), each of which had been complemented by a chilled Muscadet or some other wine from the Liberty House boutique in the theatre lobby. Each meal began with a ritual *carillon de l'amitié,* the four wineglasses held carefully by the stems so the sound would ring out clearly. "One of the good things about getting to be sixty," Julia said that Monday, "is that you make up your mind not to drink any more rotgut wine." There was a great deal of laughter and much talk of food. "When a vegetable is as beautiful as this asparagus," Rosie Manell said at one point, "you've just got to take it seriously"—a comment that Julia liked so much she repeated it to her audience a little later. Immediately following lunch, while the others made a final check of the dozens of items that would be used during the afternoon's demonstration, Julia was left alone in the dining alcove for her "quiet time," which she used to go over her notes. She showed not the slightest hint of nervousness or stage fright.

The demonstration was twenty minutes late getting started. Heavy rains had slowed traffic, but when Julia came out from the wings the downstairs area of the Kabuki was filled nearly to capacity, the audience consisting mostly of well-dressed women, who greeted her enthusiastically. Julia introduced her "team": Rosie Manell and Liz Bishop, who would be onstage throughout the performance, and Paul, "our general manager, timekeeper, and resident ogre," sitting at a table in the front row, where he could give time signals and make suggestions to the performers. The program called for soufflé on a platter, with poached eggs; Caneton en Aspic à la Parisienne; and Charlotte Malakoff. "Nobody in their right mind would want to serve all three at the same meal," Julia explained, "but each could be the centerpiece of a memorable meal. Now then, where are my glasses?"

The difference between Julia on television and Julia live onstage is mainly a difference in timing. Without the minute-to-minute pressure and the time cards held up to tell her to move on, she can be a little more expansive, and better able to savor the amusement and delight of whatever she happens to be doing. Volunteer hostesses in stylish aprons, instructed by the benefit committee to bring portable microphones to anyone who wanted to ask a question, never did so, because nobody needed them; when someone had a question, she would ask it, and Julia would glance up from her work, grin, and answer while continuing to work. She was in her kitchen and about eight hundred people were there with her. "I know what it is about her," an attractive San Franciscan said during the intermission. "She's just like a child playing. Anybody who has that much fun just has to be irresistible."

Julia's explanations of what she was doing and why were interspersed with items of general information. French ducks, she observed, tended to be less fatty than American ducks, which made them better for *Caneton en Aspic*. Raffle tickets would be sold during intermission for all the food cooked onstage, including the duck bones, which could be used for stock. ("Just think, somebody's going to win all these lovely duck bones.") If you wanted to, you could use "the other spread" in the soufflé, but it wouldn't taste as good as it did with butter. "But then who am I to tell you what to use?" she went on. "It's the method that counts, really. You can substitute any ingredients you want." That morning, Rosie and Liz had cleaned out the local Safeway's entire stock of sweet butter—thirty pounds, which they would use up before the week was out. Nobody catches Julia Child using the other spread.

"All this looks a little terrible until you get it done," she noted in passing.

"Let's just taste and see if it's any good," she said a little later, dipping a spoon into the just-blended duck mousse. She tasted, paused, cast her eyes upward. "It's pretty good," she said, adding a touch more cognac. Another taste, and a nod of the head. "I think," she said, patting the cognac bottle, "that that's what makes the difference between an American meat loaf and a French pâté, don't you?"

Rosie and Liz moved in and out of the work space, helping where needed. Julia chatted with them and with the audience. From his seat out front, Paul occasionally offered a suggestion, telling Julia, for example, to move to the right or the left so the overhead television cameras could pick up what she was doing and relay it to the screens on either side. "They can't see what you're doing, J.C.," Paul would say. "Hold up the pan."

James Beard spoke recently of the "all-embracing quality" that draws people to Julia Child. "She has the kind of bigness that all great artists have," he said. "Singers especially. She just sweeps everyone up and carries them away. I think she could run for political office and do very well." The choreographer Merce Cunningham, a great fan of Julia's program, has observed that she moves like a dancer. "Everything is direct and clear—no superfluous gestures," Cunningham said. "That must be how she gets through all that complicated business within the time limit, and it's one reason she's so fascinating to watch." She is also very good at building to a dramatic climax.

The Charlotte Malakoff provided the climax of the first day's demonstrations. Instead of serving the velvety almond-cream dessert (flavored with chocolate and rum) molded in homemade ladyfingers, as the printed program had said she would, Julia decided to serve it in a cage of spun caramel. Donning a thick red rubber glove from the Sacred Bag to keep from burning her hand, she took a small cake pan, held it upside down, carefully buttered the exterior surface, then set to work covering it with molten caramel dripped from a spoon. The skeins of caramel glittered in the stage lights. It took several minutes for her to cover the pan. She let it cool, then carefully began to work the caramel loose, chatting the while about the need for patience in cooking. After a tense interval, the caramel slid free, and she held up a gossamer cage. Applause from the audience. "Don't clap yet," Julia warned. She thought the cage needed fixing in a couple of spots, so she slipped it back over the bottom of the cake pan and added more hot caramel. "Anything you spill you can turn into taffy," she said. Again the cage was delicately pried loose from the pan. Julia started to hold it up for all to see, and in doing so dropped it. Gasps and groans from the audience; the cage was in smithereens. Julia put her head back and laughed. "We'll just have to do it all over again," she said, and did it all over again, successfully, to thunderous applause.

The same thing happened at the second performance, that evening, except that she broke the cage when she went to put it in the freezer. "Never give up!" she cried. "This is a fine illustration of not getting discouraged." The audience, which this time included a substantial number of men, was limp with delight. Fifty or more people stayed on after the show to stand in line and have their copies of *Mastering the Art of French Cooking* autographed by Julia and Paul, and nearly all of them wanted to talk with the Childs, to say something about what Julia had meant in their lives and how grateful they were. Julia asked questions about each person's home or family or kitchen. They were signing autographs until after midnight.

Later, back at the hotel, the team gathered in the Childs' suite for a nightcap. They had ridden up in the elevator with Rudolf Nureyev, who was in town with the National Ballet of Canada and was staying at the same hotel; the two "superstars," as Herb Caen referred to them in his column in the *Chronicle*, rode up together silently, without a sign of recognition, but afterward Julia commented with interest on Nureyev's costume, which consisted of knee-length snakeskin boots and a snakeskin shirt. It looked, Liz Bishop said, as though the snake were eating him. The conversation in the suite flowed without effort. Julia and Paul talked about Norway, which they had both adored. They liked the Norwegians and their way of life, they liked the countryside, and they even liked, in moderation, the food. "You have to learn how to order there," Julia said. "Their poached sea trout is delicious. The fried food is awful. And their idea of vegetables is four kinds of potato and some parsley." Julia learned more Norwegian than Paul did, because Paul was too busy at the embassy to give full attention to lessons. Julia has been known to sing the Norwegian national anthem at parties, her great, plummy voice swooping up and down the scale with utter confidence, though in no discernible key.

Before going to bed, they talked a little about the various groups, mainly in California, that were now dedicating themselves to mysticism, psychic experimentation, and the transformation of consciousness. Julia didn't seem to know much about the new consciousness, but she thought it sounded interesting. "I just hope," she said at one point, "that good food is a part of it."

1974

"It's the waiter at the restaurant where we ate tonight. He wants to know if everything is still all right."

LOOK BACK IN HUNGER

ANTHONY LANE

R eady? Ready. Okay, here we go. "Fold the wings akimbo, tucking the wing ends under the shoulders as shown here." Lovely. "Then, on the same side of the chicken where you came out from the second knee . . ." Umm. "Poke the needle through the upper arm of the wing." Wings with arms, like a bat's. Cool. "Catch the neck skin, if there . . ." Hang on. *If there?* If not there, where? Whose neck is this, anyway? ". . . and pin it to the backbone, and come out through the second wing." And go for a walk in the snow, and don't come back till next year.

This wing-stitching drill, as any cook will tell you, is from the celebrated "To Truss a Chicken" section of Julia Child's *The Way to Cook.* It's a pretty easy routine, really, as long as you take it slow, run through a batch of test poultry first, have a professional chef on hand to help you through the bad times, and feel no shame when you get arrested and charged with satanic drumstick abuse. Julia Child is a good woman, with no desire to faze or scald us; she genuinely wants us to bard that bird, to cook it, and to carve it. ("Fork-grab under the knee. . . . Soon you'll see the ball joint where the leg-thigh meets the small of the back.") Hell, she wouldn't mind if we went ahead and *ate* the damn thing.

I don't know what it is about cookbooks, but they really drain my giblets. I buy them, and use them, and study them with the micro-attentive care of a papyrologist, and still they make me feel that I am missing out. I follow instructions, and cook dinner for friends, and the friends are usually friends again by the next morning, but what they consume at my table bears no more than a fleeting, tragically half-assed resemblance to the dish that I read about in the recipe. Although I am not a good cook, I am not a dreadful one, either; I once had a go at *mouclade d'Aunis*, once made a brave fist of *cul de veau braisé Angevin,* and once came very close to buying a carp. Last summer, I did something difficult with monkfish tails; the dish took two days to prepare, a full nine minutes to eat, and three days to wash up after. But an hour in front of my cookbooks is enough to slash my ambitions to the bone—

to convince me that in terms of culinary evolution I remain a scowling tree dweller whose idea of haute cuisine is to grub for larvae under dead bark.

And we all know the name of the highly developed being standing tall at the other end of the scale. Super-skilled, free of fear, the last word in human efficiency, Martha Stewart is the woman who convinced a million Americans that they have the time, the means, the right, and— damn it—the *duty* to pipe a little squirt of soft cheese into the middle of a snow pea, and to continue piping until there are "fifty to sixty" stuffed peas raring to go. Never mind the taste; one glance at this woman's quantities is enough to spirit you into a different and a cleaner world. "I discovered a fantastic thing when preparing 1,500 potatoes for the Folk Art Show," Martha writes in her latest book. *The Martha Stewart Cookbook* is a magisterial compendium of nine previous books, and offers her fans another chance to sample Martha's wacky punch lines ("Tie securely with a single chive") and her naughtiest promises ("This hearty soup is simple to assemble"). So coolly thrown off, that last line, and you read right through it without picking up the outrageous implication. Since when did you "assemble" a soup? Even the ingredients are a fright. "Three pounds fish frames from flounder or fluke," Martha says brightly, sounding like Henry Higgins. To the rest of humanity, soup is something that involves five pans, two dented strainers, scattered bones that would baffle a forensic pathologist, and the unpleasant sensation of hot stock rising from the pot, condensing on your forehead, and running down into the pot again as lightly flavored sweat.

Martha does not perspire. There is not a squeak of panic in the woman's soul. She knows exactly where the two layers of cheesecloth can be found when the time comes to strain the stock. She assembles her fish chowder as if it were a model airplane. Moreover, she does so without appearing to spend any time in the kitchen. "One of the most important moments on which to expend extra effort is the beginning of a party, often an awkward time, when guests feel tentative and insecure," she says. The *guests* are insecure? How about the frigging cook? Believe me, Martha, I'm not handing round the phyllo triangles with lobster filling during that awkward time; I'm out back, holding on to the sink, finishing off the Côtes du Rhône that was supposed to go into the stew. But Martha Stewart is an idealist who has cunningly disguised herself as a helping hand; readers look up to her as a conservative angel who keeps the dream house tidy, radiant, ready for pals, and filled with family. "If I had to choose one essential element for the success of an Easter brunch, it would be children," she writes, as if preparing to grill the kids over a high flame.

Yet the conservative image won't quite fit. The Stewart paean to the joys of Thanksgiving ("To not cook and entertain on this day would seem tantamount to treason") is itself rather joyless in its zealotry; you keep hitting something sharp and steely in her writings—a demiglace intolerance of ordinary mortals. Her kitchen is bewitched, and she's Samantha. You won't see it on her TV shows, but I bet Martha Stewart can wiggle her nose and turn any chauvinist Darrin into crabmeat. If you're planning to fork-grab her under the knee, forget it. Was it the spirit of the season or a quiet celebration of dominant female power that led to the baked-ham recipe at the start of *Martha Stewart's Menus for Entertaining*? It looks succulent in the accompanying photograph, and I have long yearned to make it, but three factors have restrained me. First, it serves sixteen, and I don't know that many people who would be happy to munch ham at one another. Second, you need "one bunch chervil with flowers." (That's plain silly, if not quite as ridiculous as a recipe that I came across at the peak of nouvelle cuisine, in the 1980s—a recipe that demanded *thirty-four* chervil leaves.) Third, the ham must be baked for five and a half hours in a pan lined with fresh-cut grass. As in meadow. "Locate an area in advance with tender, young, organically grown grass that has not yet been cut," our guide advises. "It is best to cut it very early in the morning while the dew is still evident." I'm sorry, Martha, but it just won't do. I have inspected the grass in my backyard, and I am not prepared to serve Baked Ham with Cat Whiff and Chopped Worms.

There must be millions of other people who refuse to get up at dawn and mow the lawn for dinner. This fellow feeling should be a comfort to me, yet somehow it makes no difference. Cooking, for all the apple-cheeked, home-baked community spirit in which food writers try to enfold it, is essentially a solitary art—or, at least, a guarantee of lonely distress. When your hollandaise is starting to curdle and you've tried the miraculous ice-cube trick and you've tried beating a fresh egg yolk and folding in the curdled stuff and the result still looks like the climactic scene of a David Cronenberg picture, it doesn't really help to know that someone is having the very same problem in Pittsburgh. Your only friend, in fact, is that shelf of cookbooks just out of reach. Leaving the sauce to its own devices, you grab each volume in turn, frantic for advice, and make your fatal mistake: you start to read. Two yards away, the sauce is separating fast—the lemon is pursing its lips, the eggs are halfway back to the fridge—but you don't care. By now, determined to find out where you went wrong, and already dreaming of a perfect future sauce, you are deep into Georges-Auguste Escoffier's recipe for hollandaise: "Remove the pan to the side of the stove or place it in a bain-marie." Well, which?

In that simple "or" reside both the delight and the frustration of the classic cookbook. It should ideally tell you almost everything but not all that you need to know, leaving a tiny crack of uncertainty that can become your own personal abyss. If any text counts as a classic, it is Escoffier's *Le Guide Culinaire*, which was published in 1903. Escoffier was a colleague of César Ritz, and a man of such pantry-stocking initiative that when Paris was besieged in the Franco-Prussian War he fed the starving troops on zoo animals and stray pets. I eagerly scanned the *Guide* for pan-seared hartebeest or poodle mousse à la Fifi sauvage, but all I could find was this unflinching recipe for clear turtle soup:

> To kill the turtle, lay it on its back at the edge of the table with the head hanging over the side. Take a double meat hook and place one hook into the upper jaw and suspend a sufficiently heavy weight in the hook at the other end so as to make the animal extend its neck. . . .

It goes without saying that the flippers should be blanched, and that "the green fat which is used for making the soup must be collected carefully." But where, exactly, does this green fat come from? The author doesn't tell us. Somewhere between the carapace and the plastron, presumably, but I'm not sure that I really want to know.

Whether cooks still use Escoffier—or Larousse, or Carême, or any of the other touchstones of French cuisine—is open to question. It is not just the encyclopedic spread of these Frenchmen's interests, their desire to chew on something that we would prefer to watch in a wildlife documentary, that feels out of date; it is also their unshakable conviction that we already know our worldly way around a kitchen, that they are merely grinding a little fresh information into our basic stock of knowledge. When Escoffier tells us to "stud the fattened pullet with pieces of truffle and poach it in the usual manner," he presumes that we habitually spend our weekends looking for pullets to fatten and that we can poach them in our sleep. Many readers are scared off by this assumption; I feel flattered and consoled by it, all the more so because I know it to be dead wrong. I am not a truffle stud, nor was meant to be. Yet I willingly dream myself into a time when you could "quickly fry 10 blackbirds in hot butter"—just because I relish the imaginative jump required to get there, not because I particularly want a blackbird-lettuce-and-tomato sandwich for my lunch.

In other words, the great cookbooks are more like novels than like home-improvement manuals. What these culinary bibles tell you to do is far less beguiling than the thought of a world in which such things might be done. A single line, for instance, from Benjamin Renaudet's *Secrets de la Bonne Table*, published at the beginning of this century, effortlessly summons up the century that had just ended: "When the first partridges are shot in the early morning, send them down to the house." If that grabs you, take a look at *Culinary Jottings for Madras*, a collection of recipes by Deputy Assistant Quartermaster-General Arthur Robert Kenney-Herbert. First published in 1878, the book tells you more about the nature of imperial rule in India than any number of political histories. If you can feed a party of eight on snipe soup, fish fillets à la Peg Woffington, mutton cutlets à la Moscovite, oyster Kramouskys, braised capon, and a brace of wild ducks with bigarade sauce, if you can finish off with prune jelly, iced molded pudding with strawberries, and cheese, and if you can serve and eat all that when it's ninety-five degrees in the shade, then you can conquer any country you like. Nothing can stand up to Peg Woffington.

There is a pinch of snob nostalgia in reading this stuff, of course, but I don't think it ruins the flavor. What is attractive about cookbooks, after all—what prickles the glands like vinegar—is not luxury but otherness. I have a particular weakness for the chunky, old-style block-busters that sit in every kitchen, offering reams of advice that is seldom taken, or even required. Endlessly updated with new editions, these masterworks are doomed never to be up to date. Craig Claiborne's *New York Times Cook Book*, which has slowly acquired the gravitas of Holy

Writ, was first published in 1961. I found an early edition, and smiled at the hors d'oeuvres suggestions that are arrayed for our delectation in the first section of the book: how to serve oysters on the half shell, how to serve caviar, how to serve foie gras. It was a time capsule of America in the late fifties and early sixties; it made me want to watch *Pillow Talk* all over again. With a sigh of regret, I turned to the latest edition. How would it start in the nineties? Char-grilled calamari with arugula and flat-leaf parsley? Stuffed snow peas à la Martha? Shiitake tarts? But no, there it was again: how to serve oysters on the half shell, et cetera. What was once an accurate index of national taste has now become a museum piece. It's the same story with Irma S. Rombauer and Marion Rombauer Becker's *The Joy of Cooking*, which began life in 1931 and reads as if it had never got past 1945. Social historians should head straight for the "Pies and Pastries" section and check out the crusty jokes: "No wonder pictures of leggy starlets are called cheesecake!" Ba-boom.

Down below caviar, even farther down than cheesecake, there is a place where the joy of cooking gives way to the joy of not bothering to cook at all. Yet even here, on the ocean floor of *cuisine en bas*, among such primitive life forms as the Fried Peanut Butter and Banana Sand-wich, there is food for thought. To discover this sandwich in Brenda Arlene Butler's *Are You Hungry Tonight?: Elvis' Favorite Recipes* is to be transported, without warning, to an age of innocence. The book's final chapter offers readers the chance to re-create the giant six-tier wedding cake that Elvis and Priscilla cut together on that happy day in 1967: the words "Eleven pounds hydrogenated vegetable shortening (such as Sweetex or Crisco)" speak to me as directly, and as movingly, as the par-tridges that Renaudet called for in the early morning.

There are times when this need to look elsewhere—to reach into the ovens of another age, or another culture, and pull out whatever you can—grows from a well-fed fancy into a moral necessity. Hence the in-valuable contribution of Elizabeth David, whose name remains as revered in England as that of M.F.K. Fisher in America. (Why do women make such great cookery writers? Partly, I suspect, because they realize that it is enough to be a great cook, whereas men, larded with pride in their own accomplishment, invariably go one step too far and try to be great *chefs*—a grander calling, though somehow less respectable, and certainly less responsive to human need.) Both David and Fisher were spurred to action by the Second World War: Fisher's *How to Cook a Wolf* was published in 1942, when food shortages were beginning to bite, and David's *A Book of Mediterranean Food* appeared in 1950, when England was still rationed, undernourished, and keen on suet.

Elizabeth David's mission was to find the modern equivalent of Renaudet's partridges, to resuscitate flagging and amnesiac palates with the prospect of unthinkable dishes. Such food had no need to be rich; it simply had to taste of something, to bear recognizable links to natural produce, and, most important, to be non-gray. Whether it ever saw the light of day, or the candlelight of evening, was beside the point; the mere promise of it, David herself confessed, was a form of nourishment. "Even if people could not very often make the dishes here described," she pointed out, "it was stimulating to think about them." And so on the first page of *A Book of Mediterranean Food* she kicked off with *soupe au pistou* and its accompanying dollop of *aïllade*. The garlicky stink of Nice hit England full in the face, and the nation—or, at any rate, the middle classes—came back to life.

Nowadays, the situation is reversed. We know too much about food. Your principal obligation when you sit down at a restaurant in New York is to play it cool. Black spaghettini with cuttlefish and fennel tops? Been there. *Soupe au pistou?* Wake me up when it's over. In the past year, I have eaten both reindeer (a fun Christmas dish) and ostrich (better baked in sand, I guess), but they hardly count as exotic anymore. Cookbooks have followed the lead of restaurants and delicatessens: specialist works abound, the narrower the better. I gave up reading Sara Slavin and Karl Petzke's *Champagne: The Spirit of Celebration*, a book devoted to cooking with and for champagne, at the point where it instructed me to "roll each cheese-coated grape in the garlic-almond mixture." Isn't there some kind of Grape Protection Society that should be fighting this stuff? As for *365 Ways to Cook Hamburger and Other Ground Meats*, by Rick Rodgers, what can I say? Welcome to the most disgusting book on earth. It's not the dishes themselves that I object to—not even Ed Debevic's Burnt Meatloaf, or the Transylvanian Pork and Sauerkraut Bake—but the grueling way in which one recipe after another resounds with the same mournful litany: "One pound ground round." Remember the wise words of M.F.K. Fisher: "The first thing to know about ground round steak is that it should not be that at all."

Far more cheering and plausible is Nick Malgieri's *How to Bake*, which runs for 276 pages before it even gets to "Plain Cakes." Should you find the book a little too broad in scope, you could always play the sacred card and go for *The Secrets of Jesuit Breadmaking*, by Brother Rick Curry, S.J. This alternates clear spiritual homilies with yeasty advice about cooling racks. Sometimes, with a brilliant flourish, Brother Curry kneads his twin passions into one phrase: "As we begin the most austere week in Christianity, tasty rich biscuits remind us that Jesus is coming." I suspect that such highly sophisticated reasoning may have been the downfall of Gerard Manley Hopkins, poet and Jesuit, who suffered what was reputed to be one of the worst cases of constipation in the nineteenth century.

If you really intend to be the star of your own cookbook, you need to watch out. (The finest cooks, such as Escoffier, are godlike, everywhere in the text yet nowhere to be seen.) Brother Curry, schooled in humility, gets it about right: when he says that his Loyola Academy Buttermilk Bread "goes great with peanut butter," we instinctively believe that he's plugging a good idea rather than himself. The trouble starts with celebrity cookbooks and tie-ins; try as I might, I cannot conceive of a time when I will want to concoct a meal from the pages of *The Bubba Gump Shrimp Co. Cookbook* or its literate successor, *Forrest Gump: My Favorite Chocolate Recipes*. *Entertaining with Regis and Kathie Lee* is remarkable less for the quality of the cuisine than for the photographs of Kathie Lee, who seems to spend half her time with her mouth wide open, as if to catch any mouthfuls flying by. Then there's Rosie Daley, whose food looks perfectly nice, but whose *In the Kitchen with Rosie* might not have reached the bestseller lists were she not employed as a cook by Oprah Winfrey. It's kind of hard to concentrate on the ingredients, what with Oprah's cheerleading ringing out at regular intervals. "I have thrived on pasta. I can eat it every day and practically do." You'd never guess.

Whether such works can be relied upon in the kitchen is of little consequence. Cookbooks, it should be stressed, do not belong in the kitchen at all. We keep them there for the sake of appearances; occasionally, we smear their pages together with vibrant green glazes or crimson compotes, in order to delude ourselves, and any passing browsers, that we are practicing cooks; but, in all honesty, a cookbook is something that you read in the living room, or in the bathroom, or in bed. The purpose is not to nurture nightmares of suckling pig, or to lull ourselves into a fantasy of trimly bearded oysters, but simply to baste our rested brains with common sense, and with the prospect of common pleasures to come. Take this romantic interlude from *'Tis the Season: A Vegetarian Christmas Cookbook*, by Nanette Blanchard: "Turn down the lights, light all the candles you can find, throw a log on the fire, turn up the music, and toast each other with a Sparkling Grape Goblet." Oh, oh, Nanette. On the other hand, what could be sweeter than to retire with *Smoke & Spice*, by Cheryl Alters Jamison and Bill Jamison, whose High Plains Jerky would be an ornament to any barbecue? Those in search of distant horizons could always caress their senses with *The Art of Polish Cooking*, in which Alina Żeranska offers her triumphant recipe for "Nothing" Soup (*Zupa "Nic"*), adding darkly, "This is an all-time children's favorite."

If I could share a Sparkling Grape Goblet with anyone—not just any cook but any person in recorded history—it might well be with Jean-Anthelme Brillat-Savarin. Magistrate, mayor, violinist, judge, and ravenous slayer of wild turkeys during his visit to America, Brillat-Savarin is now remembered for *The Physiology of Taste*, which was first published in 1825. There is a good paperback version, translated by Anne Drayton, but devotees may wish to seek out the translation by M.F.K. Fisher herself; it has now been reissued in a luxurious new edition, with illustrations by Wayne Thiebaud. To say that *The Physiology of Taste* is a cookbook is like saying that Turgenev's *Sportsman's Sketches* is a guide to hunting. "When I came to consider the pleasures of the table in all their aspects, I soon perceived that something better than a mere cookery book might be made of such a subject," Brillat-Savarin writes. It is a perception that few have shared; the closest modern equivalent, perhaps, is in the work of A. J. Liebling, a man whose delicately gluttonous writings on food keep wandering off (when he can tear himself away) into such equally pressing areas as Paris, boxing, and sex. Brillat-Savarin, like Liebling, gives few recipes, though he muses on innumerable dishes, on the scientific reasons for their effect on the metabolism, and on the glow of sociable well-being that is their ideal result. He sprinkles anecdotes like salt, and he defines and defends *gourmandisme* ("It shows implicit obedience to the commands of the Creator"), following it through the various stages of delight and surfeit to its logical conclusion. There is a chapter on "The Theory of Frying" and a wonderful disquisition on death, embellished with gloomy good cheer: "I would recall the words of the dying Fontenelle, who on being asked what he could feel, replied: 'Nothing but a certain difficulty in living.'"

The lasting achievement of Brillat-Savarin is that he endowed living with a certain ease. Intricately versed in the difficulties of existence, he came to the unorthodox conclusion that a cookbook—a bastard form, but a wealthy, happy bastard—could offer the widest and most tender range of remedies. I'm not sure whether he knew how to fold the wings of a chicken akimbo, and if you'd handed him a snow pea and told him to stuff it he would have responded in kind; but it takes someone like Brillat-Savarin to remind us that cooking need not be the fraught, perfectionist, slightly paranoid struggle that it has latterly become. His love of food is bound up with a taste for human error and indulgence, and that is why *The Physiology of Taste* is still the most civilized cookbook ever written. I suspect that Brillat-Savarin might have been bemused by Martha Stewart, but that he would have gotten on just fine with Ed Debevic and his Burnt Meatloaf.

I sure wish that he had been on hand for my terrine of sardines and potatoes. There I was—apron on, gin in hand, closely following the recipe of the French chef Raymond Blanc. All went well until I got to the harmless words "a piece of cardboard." Apparently, I needed cardboard to lay on the terrine mold; the cardboard then had to be covered with "evenly distributed weights" for twelve hours. Weights? Cardboard? Twelve hours? They weren't listed with the ingredients. I had my sardines; I had my twenty capers and my freshly grated nutmeg; but I had no cardboard. Frankly, it would have been easier to kill a turtle.

That's the trouble with cookbooks. Like sex education and nuclear physics, they are founded on an illusion. They bespeak order, but they end in tears.

1995

"Cook regrets to state, Ma'am, that she's trod on the pudding."

THE REPORTER'S KITCHEN

JANE KRAMER

The kitchen where I'm making dinner is a New York kitchen. Nice light, way too small, nowhere to put anything unless the stove goes. My stove is huge, but it will never go. My stove is where my head clears, my impressions settle, my reporter's life gets folded into *my* life, and whatever I've just learned, or think I've learned—whatever it was, out there in the world, that had seemed so different and surprising—bubbles away in the very small pot of what I think I know and, if I'm lucky, produces something like perspective. A few years ago, I had a chance to interview Brenda Milner, the neuropsychologist who helped trace the process by which the brain turns information into memory, and memory into the particular consciousness called a life, or, you could say, into the signature of the person. Professor Milner was nearly eighty when I met her, in Montreal, at the neurological institute at McGill, where she'd worked for close to fifty years, and one of the things we talked about was how some people, even at her great age, persist in "seeing" memory the way children do—as a cupboard or a drawer or a box of treasures underneath the bed, a box that gets full and has to be cleaned out every now and then to make room for new treasures they collect. Professor Milner wasn't one of those people, but I am. The memory I "see" is a kind of kitchen, where the thoughts and characters I bring home go straight into a stockpot on my big stove, reducing old flavors, distilling new ones, making a soup that never tastes the same as it did the day before, and feeds the voice that, for better or worse, is *me* writing, and not some woman from another kitchen.

I knew nothing about stockpots as a child. My mother was an awful cook, or, more accurately, she didn't cook, since in her day it was fashionable not to go anywhere near a kitchen if you didn't have to. Her one creation, apart from a fluffy spinach soufflé that for some reason always appeared with the overcooked turkey when she made Thanksgiving dinner (a task she undertook mainly to avoid sitting in the cold with the rest of us at the Brown Thanksgiving Day home football game), would probably count today as haute-fusion family cooking: matzo-meal-and-Rhode-Island-johnnycake-mix pancakes, topped with thick bacon, sour cream, and maple syrup. Not even our housekeeper and occasional cook could cook—beyond a tepid, sherried stew that was always presented at parties, grandly, as lobster thermidor, and a passable apple filling that you could spoon out, undetected, through the large steam holes of an otherwise tasteless pie. I don't think I ever saw my father cook anything, unless you can call sprinkling sugar on a grapefruit, or boiling syringes in an enamel pan, the way doctors did in those days, cooking. (I use the pan now for roasting chickens.) The only man in my family with a recipe of his own was my brother Bobby, who had mastered a pretty dessert called pumpkin chiffon while courting an Amish girl who liked pumpkins. My own experience in the kitchen was pretty much limited to reheating the Sunday-night Chinese takeout early on Monday mornings, before anyone else was awake to eat it first.

I started cooking when I started writing. My first dish was tuna curry (a can of Bumble Bee, a can of Campbell's cream-of-mushroom soup, a big spoonful of Durkee's curry powder, and a cup of instant Carolina rice), and the recipe, such as it was, came from my friend Mary Clay, who claimed to have gotten it directly from the cook at her family's Kentucky farm. It counted for me as triply exotic, being at once the product of a New York supermarket chain, the bluegrass South, and India. And never mind that the stove I cooked on then was tiny, or that "dining" meant a couple of plates and a candle on my old toy chest, transformed into the coffee table of a graduate school rental, near Columbia; the feeling was high sixties, meaning that a nice girl from Providence could look forward to enjoying literature, sex, and cooking in the space of a single day. I don't remember whom I was making the curry for, though I must have liked him, because I raced home from Frederick Dupee's famous lecture on symbolism in *Light in August* to make it. What I do remember is how comforting it was to be standing at that tiny stove, pinched into a Merry Widow and stirring yellow powder into Campbell's soup, when I might have been pacing the stacks at Butler Library, trying to resolve the very serious question of whether, after Dupee on Faulkner, there was anything left to say about literature, and, more precisely, the question of whether *I'd* find anything to say in a review—one of my first assignments in the real world—of a book of poems written by Norman Mailer on the occasion of having stabbed his second wife. I remember this because as I stood there, stirring powder and a soupçon of Acapulco Gold into my tuna curry, I began to accept that, while whatever I did say wasn't going to be the last word on the poetics of domestic violence, it would be *my* word, a lot of Rhode Island still in it, a little New York, and, to my real surprise, a couple of certainties: I was angry at Norman Mailer; I was twenty-one and didn't think that you should stab your wife. Mailer, on the other hand, had produced some very good lines of poetry. He must have been happy (or startled) to be taken for a poet at all, because a few weeks after my review ran—in a neighborhood paper you could pick up free in apartment-house lobbies—his friend Dan Wolf, the editor of what was then a twelve-page downtown alternative weekly called *The Village Voice,* phoned to offer me a job.

I bought a madeleine mold, at a kitchen shop near the old *Voice* offices, on Sheridan Square. It was my first purchase as a reporter who cooked—a long, narrow pan of shallow, ridged shells, waiting to produce a Proust—but though I liked madeleines, they didn't collect my world in a mouthful, the way the taste of warm apples, licked from the cool tingle of a silver spoon, still does, or, for that matter, the way the terrible chicken curry at the old brasserie La Coupole, in Paris, always reminded me of Norman Mailer's wife. The mold sat in my various kitchens for ten years before I moved to the kitchen I cook in now, and tried madeleines again, and discovered that, for me, they were just another cookie—which is to say, not the kind of cookie that belonged in the ritual that for years has kept me commuting between my study and my stove, stirring or beating or chopping or sifting my way through false starts and strained transitions and sticky sentences.

The cookies I like to make when I'm writing are called "dream cookies." I made my first batch in my friend John Tillinger's kitchen, in Roxbury, Connecticut, at one in the morning, in a mood perhaps best described by the fact that I'd just been awakened by the weight of a large cat settling on my head. The cookies were a kind of sand tart. They had a dry, gritty, burned-butter taste, and I must have associated them with the taste of deliverance from sweet, smooth, treacherous things like purring cats. I say this because a few years later I found myself making them again, in North Africa, in the middle of reporting a story about a tribal feud that involved a Berber wedding and was encrypted—at least, for me—in platters of syrupy honeyed pastries, sugared couscous, and sweet mint tea.

At the time, my kitchen was in the Moroccan city of Meknès, where my husband was doing ethnographic research, but my story took me to a village a couple of hours up into the foothills of the Middle Atlas Mountains. It was a wild, unpleasant place. Even today, some thirty years, a couple of wars and revolutions, and an assortment of arguably more unpleasant places later, I would call it scary. The wedding in question, a three-day, her-house-to-his-house traveling celebration, was about to begin in the bride's village—which had every reason to celebrate, having already provided the groom's village with a large number of pretty virgins and, in the process, profited considerably from the bride-prices those virgins had commanded: goats, chickens, silver necklaces, brass plates, and simple, practical, hard cash, some of it in negotiable European currencies. The problem was that none of the young men in the bride's village were at all interested in the virgins available in the groom's village, whose own supply of goats, chickens, necklaces, plates, and money was consequently quite depleted. All that village had was an abundance of homely daughters—or, you could say, the bad end of the balance of trade in brides. As a result, the men in the groom's village were getting ready to fight the men in the bride's village, a situation that left the women in both villages cooking day and night, in a frantic effort to turn their enemies into guests.

By then, I was close to being an enemy myself, having already broken one serious taboo: I had asked the name of somebody's aunt in a conversation where the naming of paternal aunts in the company of certain female relatives was tantamount to calling catastrophe down on the entire family, and the women had had to abandon their cooking in order to purge the premises, which they did by circling the village, ululating loudly, while I sat there in the blazing sun, under strict orders to keep the flies off a platter of dripping honey cakes. It hadn't helped any that, in a spirit of apology (or perhaps it was malice), I then invited the villagers to Meknès and served them my special Julia Child's *boeuf bourguignon,* which made them all quite ill. A few days later, I went to the medina and bought some almonds for dream cookies. I don't know why I did it. Maybe I was homesick. Certainly, I was being spoiled, knowing that Malika, the young Arab woman who worked for me and became my friend, would grind those almonds into a sandy paste as quickly as she had just peeled peaches for my breakfast—which is to say, in less time than it took me to check for scorpions underneath the two cushions and copper tray that were then my dining room. But I think now that I was mainly trying to find my voice in a country where some women couldn't mention an aunt to a relative—where the voices of most women, in fact, were confined to their ululations. Once, I heard that same shrill, flutey cry coming from my own kitchen and rushed in to find Malika shaking with pain and bleeding; she was sixteen, and had taken something or done something to herself to end a pregnancy that I had never even suspected. After that, I would sometimes hear the cry again, and find her huddled in a corner of the room, struck with a terror she could not describe. No one had ever asked her to describe it, not even the man she'd married when, by her own reckoning, she was twelve years old.

I never finished the story about the Berber bride. I was a bride myself, and this posed something of a problem for my erstwhile village friends, who had wanted to find me a husband from the tribe and thus assure themselves of the continued use of, if not actually the title to, my new Volkswagen. In the event, one night, after we'd been trading recipes, the women sent me home with a complicated (and fairly revolting) "love recipe" to try out on the husband I already had, and it turned out—at least, according to the neighbors who warned me not to make it—to be a bit of black magic whose purpose was, to put it discreetly, less amorous than incapacitating. I took this as a sign that it was time to come down from the mountains. I wrote a book about an Arab wedding instead, and I waited until I was back in my study in New York to finish it. The lesson for me, as a writer, was that I had to burrow back into my own life before I could even start thinking clearly about someone else's, or come to terms with the kinds of violence that are part of any reporter's working life, or with the tangles of outrage that women reporters, almost inevitably, carry home with their notes.

In New York, I cook a lot of Moroccan food. I keep a *couscousière* on the shelf that used to hold the madeleine mold, and then the Swedish pancake skillet and the French crêpe pan and the Swiss fondue set and the electric wok that my husband's secretary sent for Christmas during a year when I was stir-frying everything in sesame oil—something I gave up because stir-frying was always over in a few fraught seconds and did nothing at all for my writing. The cooking that helps my writing is slow cooking, the kind of cooking where you take control of your ingredients so that whatever it is you're making doesn't run away with you, the way words can run away with you in a muddled or unruly sentence. Cooking like that—nudging my disordered thoughts into the stately measure of, say, a good risotto simmering slowly in a homemade broth—gives me confidence and at least the illusion of clarity. And I find that for clarity, the kind that actually lasts until I'm back at my desk, poised over a sentence with my red marker, there is nothing to equal a couscous steaming in its colander pot, with the smell of cumin and coriander rising with the steam. That's when the words I was sure I'd lost come slipping into my head, one by one, and with them even the courage to dip my fingers in and separate the grains.

Some of the food I learned to cook in Morocco didn't translate to New York. I have yet to find a hen in New York with fertilized eggs still inside it—a delicacy that the Meknasi would produce for their guests in moments of truly serious hospitality—not at the halal markets on Atlantic Avenue or even at International Poultry, on Fifty-fourth Street, poulterer to the Orthodox carriage trade. I cannot imagine slaughtering a goat on Central Park West and then skinning it on the sidewalk, if for no reason other than that I'm an ocean away from the old *f'qui* who could take that skin before it stiffened and stretch it into a nearly transparent head for a clay drum with a personal prayer baked into it. I have never again squatted on my heels, knees apart and back straight, for the hours it takes to sift wheat through a wooden sieve and then slap water into it for a flat-bread dough, though in the course of various assignments I have made chapati with Ugandan Asian immigrants in London, stirred mealie-mealie with Bushmen in Botswana, and rolled *pâte feuilletée* with Slovenian autoworkers in the projects of Södertälje, Sweden. And I am still waiting for permission to dig a charcoal pit in Central Park for the baby lamb that I will then smother in mint and cumin, cover with earth, and bake to such tenderness that you could scoop it out and eat it with your fingers.

But when I'm starting a piece about politics, especially French politics, I will often begin by preserving the lemons for a chicken *tagine,* perhaps because a forkful of good *tagine* inevitably takes me back to the home of the French-speaking sheikh whose wives taught me how to make it (to the sound of Tom Jones singing "Delilah" on a shortwave radio), and from there to the small restaurant in Paris where I ate my first *tagine* outside Morocco, and from *there* to the flat of a surly French politician named Jean-Pierre Chevènement, who lived near the restaurant, and who unnerved me entirely during our one interview by balancing cups of espresso on the breasts of a hideous brass coffee table that appeared to be cast as a woman's torso, while barking at me about French nuclear policy. Similarly, I make choucroute whenever I'm starting a piece that has to do with music, because my first proper choucroute—the kind where you put fresh sauerkraut through five changes of cold water, squeeze it dry, strand by strand, and then braise it in gin and homemade stock, with a ham hock and smoked pork and sausages buried inside it—was a labor of love for the eightieth birthday of the composer George Perle; and since then the smell of sausage, gin, and sauerkraut mingling in my oven has always reminded me of the impossible art of composition, and set my standards at the level of his luminous woodwind suites.

On the other hand, when I write about art I like to cook a rabbit. My first rabbit was also, unhappily, my daughter's pet rabbit, and I cooked it with understandable misgiving, one summer in the Vaucluse, after an old peasant sorcerer who used to come over during the full moon to do the ironing took it from its hutch and presented it to her, freshly slaughtered and stuffed with rosemary, on the morning of her first birthday, saying that once she ate it she would have her friend with her "forever." We had named the rabbit Julien Nibble, in honor of our summer neighbor Julien Levy, a man otherwise known as the dealer who had introduced Ernst and Gorky and most of the great surrealists to New York, and my daughter, who is thirty-one now, has refused to eat rabbit since we told her the story, when she was six or seven. But I have kept on cooking rabbit, changing recipes as the art world changes, and always asking myself what Julien would have made of those changes, and, of course, whether he would have liked the dinner. There was the saddle of rabbit in a cognac-cream sauce that smoothed out my clotted thoughts about a middle-aged Italian painter with what I'd called "an unrequited sense of history." There was the *lapin niçoise*, with olives, garlic, and tomatoes, that saw me through the first paragraphs of a story about the politics of public sculpture in the South Bronx. There was the rich, bitter rabbit ragout—a recipe from the Croatian grandmother of the Berlin artist Renata Stih—that got me started after a couple of earthquakes hit Assisi, shattering the frescoes on the ceiling of San Francesco into a million pieces. Dishes like these become invocations, little rituals you invent for yourself, in the hope that your life and your work will eventually taste the same.

Good cooking is much easier to master than good writing. But great cooking is something different, and during the years that I've stood at my stove, stirring and sprinkling and tasting, waiting for a sauce to thicken and a drab sentence to settle—if not precisely into echoing, Wordsworthian chords, at least into a turn of phrase that will tell you something you didn't already know about Gerhard Schröder, say, or Silvio Berlusconi—my cooking has leaped ahead by several stars, leaving my writing in the shade. Some dishes have disappeared from my repertoire; tuna curry, for example, has been replaced by the crab-and-spun-coconut-cream curry I first tasted in Hong Kong in 1990 and have been working on ever since, and never mind that the crab in Hong Kong turned out to be doctored tofu, while mine arrives from a Broadway fishmonger with its claws scissoring through the paper bag. Some dishes I've sampled in the course (and cause) of duty are memorable mainly because I've tried so hard to forget them. For one, the crudités I managed to get down at Jean-Marie Le Pen's gaudy and heavily guarded Saint-Cloud villa, with M. Le Pen spinning an outsize plastic globe that held a barely concealed tape recorder, and a couple of Dobermans sniffing at my plate. For another, the rat stew I was served in the Guyana jungle by a visibly unstable interior minister, who had accompanied me there (en route to a "model farm" hacked out of the clearing that had once been Jonestown) in a battered Britten-Norman Islander with no radar or landing lights and a thirteen-year-old Air Force colonel for a pilot. Some dishes I've repressed, like the cauliflower soup that was ladled into my plate in the dining room of a Belfast hotel just as a terrorist's bomb went off and a wing of the building crumbled, leaving me, the friend whose couch I'd been using for the past week, and a couple of other diners perched in the middle of the sky—"like saints on poles," a man at the next table said, returning to his smoked salmon. Some dishes I've loved but would not risk trying myself, like the pork roast with crackling that Pat Hume, the wife of the politician and soon-to-be Nobel peace laureate John Hume, was in the process of carving, one Sunday lunch in Derry, when a stray bullet shattered the window and lodged in the wall behind her; she didn't stop carving, or even pause in her conversation, which, as I remember, had to do with whether the New York subways were so dangerous as to preclude her visiting with the children while John was in Washington, advising Teddy Kennedy on how to get through a family crisis.

Some dishes I've left in better hands. It's clear to me that I'm no match for the sausage vendor at the Frankfurt Bahnhof when it comes to grilling a bratwurst to precisely that stage where the skin is charred and just greasy enough to hold the mustard and then stuffing the bratwurst into just enough roll to get a grip on, but not *so* much roll that you miss the sport of trying to eat it with anything fewer than four paper napkins and the business section of the *Frankfurter Allgemeine Zeitung*. In the same way, I know that I will never equal my friend Duke, a Herero tribesman known from the Kalahari Desert to the Okavango Delta by his *Dukes of Hazzard* T-shirt, in the art of thickening a sauce for a guinea fowl or a spur-winged goose in the absence of anything resembling flour. Duke was the cook at my fly camp when I was out in the delta researching a piece about "bush housekeeping," and he thickened his sauces there by grating roots he called desert potatoes into boiling fat. But the secret was how many potatoes and, indeed, how to distinguish those potatoes from all the other roots that looked like potatoes but were something you'd rather not ingest. I never found out, because the day we'd planned to fly to the desert to dig some up a tourist camping on a nearby game preserve was eaten by a lion, and my pilot volunteered to collect the bones. Food like that is, as they say in the art world, site-specific.

Take the dish I have called *Canard sauvage rue du Cherche Midi.* I cooked my first wild duck in a kitchen on Cherche Midi in 1982, and during the sixteen years that I lived between Paris and New York I tuned the recipe to what my friends assured me was perfection. But it has never produced the same frisson at my New York dinner table that it did at the picnic table in my Paris garden, if for no reason other than that my neighbors across the court in New York do not punctuate my dinner parties with well-aimed rotten eggs accompanied by shouts of "Savages!" the way one of my Paris neighbors—a local crank by the name of Jude—always did, and that consequently my New York guests know nothing of the pleasure that comes from pausing between bites of a perfect duck in order to turn a hose full blast on the open window of someone who dislikes them.

Some dishes just don't travel, no matter how obvious or easy they seem. I know this because I tried for a year to duplicate the magical fried chicken known to aficionados as Fernand Point's Poulet Améri-cain—a recipe so simple in itself that no one since that legendary Vi-enne chef has ever dared to put it on a menu. I have never even attempted to duplicate the spicy chicken stew that the actor Michael Goldman heats up on a Sterno stove in his damp, smelly Paris *cave*, sur-rounded by the moldy bottles of Lafite and Yquem and Grands Echezeaux that you know he's planning to open as the night wears on. Nor have I attempted the Indonesian rijsttafel—which is basically just a platter of rice with little bowls of condiments and sauces—that my late friend George Hoff, a Dutch kendo master and nightclub bouncer, tossed off one night, in London, after a long and strenuous demonstra-tion that involved raising a long pole and slamming it down to within a centimeter of my husband's head. Or the fish grilled by a group of young Portuguese commandos in the early summer of 1974—I was covering their revolution; they were taking a break from it—over a campfire on a deserted Cabo de São Vicente beach. Or, for that matter, the s'mores my favorite counselor roasted over a campfire at Camp Fern-wood, in Poland, Maine (and never mind that I hated Camp Fernwood). Or even popcorn at the movies.

But most things do travel, if you know the secret. A lot of cooks don't share their secrets, or more often lie, the way my mother-in-law lied about the proportion of flour to chocolate in her famous "yum-yum cake," thereby ending whatever relationship we had. *My* best secret dates from a dinner party at Gracie Mansion when Ed Koch was the mayor of New York. I had known Koch from his Village Independent Democrat days, when he pretty much starved unless his mother fed him. But now that he was Hizzoner the Mayor of New York City he could, as he repeatedly told his guests, order anything he wanted to eat, no matter what the hour or the season or inconvenience to a staff best trained in trimming the crusts off tea sandwiches. The dinner in ques-tion got off to an awkward start—"You're Puerto Rican? You don't *look* Puerto Rican" is how, if I remember correctly, he greeted the beautiful curator of the Museo del Barrio—and it was frequently interrupted by phone calls from his relatives, who seemed to be having some sort of business crisis. But everybody agreed that the food was delicious. It wasn't elaborate food, or even much different from what you'd cook for yourself on a rainy night at home: pasta in a tomato sauce, good steaks, and hot-chocolate sundaes for dessert. But the meal itself was so oddly remarkable that I went back to the kitchen afterward and asked the cook how he'd made it, and he told me, "Whatever Ed likes, whatever he says he never got as a kid, I double the quantity. I doubled the Parmesan on the pasta. I *tripled* the hot-chocolate sauce on the ice cream." Ed's principle was "More is more."

It's not a principle I would apply to writing, but it's definitely the one I cook by now, on my way from excess in the kitchen to a manuscript where less is more. If my couscous is now the best couscous on the Upper West Side, it's because, with a nod to Ed, I take my favorite ingredients from every couscous I've ever eaten—the chickpeas and raisins and turnips and carrots and almonds and prunes—double the quantity, toss them into the broth, and then go back to my desk and cut some adverbs. I put too many eggs in my matzo balls, too much basil in my pesto, too much saffron in my paella. I have no patience with the kind of recipe that says "¼ teaspoon thyme" or "2 ounces chopped pancetta." I drown my carrots in chervil, because I like the way chervil sweetens carrots. I even drown my halibut in chervil, because I like what it does to the reduction of wine and cream in a white fish sauce— though, now that I think of it, when I'm on a bandwagon, when I'm really mad at the world I'm writing about and the people in it, I will usually switch to sorrel.

The first time I cooked halibut on a bed of sorrel, I was in New York, laboring over a long piece about liberation theology in South America and, in particular, about a young priest whose parish was in a favela with the unlikely name of Campos Elísios, about an hour north of Rio de Janeiro. I wasn't mad at my Brazilian priest—I loved the priest. I was mad at the Bishop of Rio, who was on the priest's back for ignoring orders to keep his parishioners out of politics. At first, I thought I could solve the problem by taking the afternoon off to make *moqueca*, which was not only my favorite Brazilian dish but, in my experience, an immensely soothing one—a gratin of rice, shrimp, lime, and coconut cream, served with (and this is essential, if you're serious) a sprinkling of toasted manioc flour—which provides the comforts of a *brandade* without the terrible nursery taste of cod and potatoes mushed together. I made *moqueca* a lot in Rio, because I was angry a lot in Rio. Angry at the poverty, at the politics, at the easy brutality of people in power and the desperate brutality of people without it. But it's hard to make my *moqueca* in New York unless you have a source of manioc flour, and the closest I came to that was the seven-foot-long flexible straw funnel leaning against a beam in my living room—an object devised by the Amerindians, centuries ago, to squeeze the poison out of manioc so that they wouldn't die eating it. I had wasted the better part of the afternoon on Amsterdam Avenue, searching for manioc flour, when I happened to pass a greengrocer with a special on sorrel. I bought him out, and a couple of hours later I discovered that the patient preparation of sorrel—the blanching and chopping and puréeing and braising in butter—had taken the diatribe in my head and turned it into a story I could tell.

There are, of course, moments in writing when even the most devoted cook stops cooking. Those are the moments that, in sex, are called "transporting" but in journalism are known as an empty fridge, an irritable family, and the beginnings of a first-name friendship with the woman who answers the phone at Empire Szechuan. When I am lost in one of those moments, I subsist on takeout and jasmine tea, or if takeout is truly beyond me—the doorbell, the change, the tip, the mismatched chopsticks, the arguments when I won't share—on chili-lime tortilla chips and Diet Coke. If the hour is decent, I'll mix a Bloody Mary or a *caipirinha* like the ones that the priest and I used to sneak in the kitchen of the parish house of Campos Elísios on evenings when the Seventh-Day Adventists would arrive at the favela in force, pitch a tent in a field, and call the poor to salvation through amps rented by the hour from a Copacabana beach band. But moments like those are rare.

My normal state when beginning a piece is panic, and by now my friends and family are able to gauge that panic by the food I feed them. This past spring, in the course of a few weeks of serious fretting over the lead of a story about an Afghan refugee, I cooked a small Thanksgiving turkey, two Christmas rib roasts, and an Easter lamb. I cooked them with all the fixings, from the corn-bread-and-sausage stuffing to the Yorkshire pudding and horseradish cream—though I stopped short of the Greek Easter cheesecake that three cookbooks assured me had to be made in a clean flowerpot. My excuse was that I'd worked through Thanksgiving and been snowbound in Berlin through Christmas, and, of course, it *was* nearly Easter when I began my holiday cooking. Easter, actually, went well. No one mentioned the fact that we were celebrating it on a Saturday night, or, for that matter, that at noon on Sunday we were due, as always, for our annual Easter lunch at the home of some old friends. But Thanksgiving in April brought strained smiles all around, especially since my next-door neighbor had already cooked a lovely Thanksgiving dinner for me in February. And while my first Christmas was a big success—one of the guests brought presents and a box of chocolate mushrooms left over from a *bûche de Noël*—my second Christmas, a few days later, ended badly, when my daughter suggested that I "see someone" to discuss my block, my husband announced to a room full of people that I was "poisoning" him with saturated fats, and my son-in-law accused me of neglecting the dog. But I did end up with a paragraph. In fact, I thought it was a pretty good paragraph. And I finished the piece the way I usually finish pieces, with notes and cookbooks piled on the floor, working for a few hours, sorting the Post-its on my desk into meaningless, neat stacks, and then heading for my big stove to do more cooking—in this case, to add the tomatoes to a Bolognese sauce, because my last paragraph was too tricky to handle without a slow, comfortable Italian sauce, and I'd been using Bolognese for tricky characters since I first tackled the subject of François Mitterrand, in a story on his inauguration, in 1981.

It seems to me that there is something very sensible about keeping your memories in the kitchen, with the pots and the spices, especially in New York. They take up no space; they do not crash with your computer; and they collect the voice that you can't quite hear—in tastes and smells and small gestures that, with any luck, will eventually start to sound like you. I'm not in New York right now. The dinner I was cooking twenty-five pages ago—the clam-and-pork stew with plenty of garlic and *piri-piri* that I first ate in a Portuguese fishermen's tavern near Salem, the day I tacked wrong and sailed my boyfriend's sixteen-footer into a very big ketch and broke his mast and, with it, whatever interest he had in me—is not the dinner I am cooking today, at a farmhouse in Umbria. My stove is smaller here (though my pots are bigger). I do not write easily about myself. I am not as tasty or exotic as the characters I usually choose. My first attempt at anything like autobiography was a thinly disguised short story, and it was returned with the gentle suggestion that I replace myself with someone "a little less like the kind of person we know everything about already." But twenty years later I did manage to produce a reminiscence of sorts. It was about my mother and my daughter and about being a feminist, and it ended where I am writing now, in Umbria, looking across a pond to a field of wheat and watching a family of pheasants cross my garden. It occurred to me, worrying over *this* ending—not quite a panic but enough of a problem to have already produced a Sardinian saffron-and-sausage pasta, a cold pepper soup with garlic croutons, nightly platters of chicken-liver-and-anchovy bruschetta, pressed through my grandmother's hand mill, and twenty jars of brandied apricot jam—that I might possibly solve the problem by cooking the same dinner that I'd cooked then. It turns out to be one meal I can't remember.

2002

"If she says 'Yummy,' it's bonuses right down the line."

FISHING AND FORAGING

"We don't know what it is, but it's fresh."

"*Dog meat has been eaten in every major German crisis at least since the time of Frederick the Great, and is commonly referred to as 'blockade mutton.' It is tough, gamy, strong-flavored.*"
—Time, *November 25th.*

A MESS OF CLAMS

JOSEPH MITCHELL

Practically all the littleneck and cherrystone clams served on the half shell in New York restaurants come out of the black mud of the Long Island bays. They are the saltiest, cleanest, and biggest-bellied clams in the world. The most abundant beds are in Great South Bay and are owned by the towns of Islip and Babylon. Right after dawn every weekday about seventy licensed clammers from these towns go out on the Bay in a fleet of dilapidated sloops and catboats and spread out over the beds. They work over the sides of their anchored boats, using long-handled tongs and rakes; the clams are bedded in bottoms which lie under eight to ten feet of water. At noon the buy-boats of two clam-shipping firms—Still & Clock of Bay Shore and G. Vander Borgh & Son of West Sayville—go out and anchor near the fleet, and from then until 4 P.M. the clammers bring their catches to the buy-boats in bushel bags and sell them over the rail for cash.

One muggy day last week I made a trip to the South Bay beds with Captain Archie M. Clock, who commands the Still & Clock buy-boat. This boat is the *Jennie Tucker*, a battered, stripped-down, thirty-eight-foot sloop powered with a motor the Captain took out of an old Chrysler. Captain Clock and his partner, Louis Still, are members of families which have fished, oyster-farmed, and clammed on the South Shore since the middle of the eighteenth century. I arrived at their weather-beaten clam shed on Homan Avenue Creek in Bay Shore at ten in the morning and found Captain Clock on the narrow wharf at the rear. He was sitting on an overturned clam bucket, smoking his pipe. A man I know who runs a wholesale shellfish business in Fulton Fish Market had written me a note of introduction to the Captain, and I handed it to him. He read it, grunted, and said, "You picked a good day to see the beds. We're going out a little early." He motioned toward a bucket with the stem of his pipe. "Have a seat and make yourself at home," he said. "Do you care much for clams?"

I sat down on the bucket and told him that one Sunday afternoon in August 1937, I placed third in a clam-eating tournament at a Block Island clambake, eating eighty-four cherries. I told him that I regard this as one of the few worthwhile achievements of my life.

"Well, you can eat yourself a bellyful today," he said. "I feel like having a few myself. They tell me brewers sometimes get so they hate beer, and sometimes I get so I can't stand the sight of a clam, but I'm real hungry this morning."

The *Jennie Tucker* was lying alongside the wharf, and the mate, a muscular young man named Charlie Bollinger, was sloshing down her decks with buckets of water. "Give her plenty of water, Charlie," the Captain told him. He turned to me and said, "You have to be double-extra clean when you're handling clams. Let a few dead clams lie around and you'll breed up a smell that'll knock you off your feet." He stood up, yawned, and went into a little office in the shed. When he returned he carried an armful of gear which included a lunch bucket, a tattered old ledger, and a green metal box. Later I learned that this box contained the cash with which he would buy the day's load.

"Everything okay, Charlie?" he asked.

"She's clean as a whistle, Archie," said the mate.

"Let's get going then," he said. We went aboard and the Captain stored his gear in the sloop's tiny cabin. The Captain was stocky, slow-moving, and sleepy-eyed. He was deeply tanned, but he had smeared some white salve on his nose and ears to guard against sunburn. He was roughly dressed; he wore patched pants, a blue work shirt, and a long-visored swordfisherman's cap. He took the tiller, which he handled expertly, until we were well out in the Bay. Then he turned it over to Bollinger, got his ledger, and sat down beside me on the hatch. "The beds they're clamming lie about four miles down the Bay," he said, motioning with his head in the direction of Babylon. He opened the ledger and got a new page ready, writing down the names of the clammers. The wind from the ocean ruffled the pages as he worked. Most of the names he wrote down were old Long Island ones, like Doxsee, Ricketts, Baldwin, Crowell, and Tooker.

"Most of the clammers come from families that have been around this bay so many generations they long since lost track," he said. "The bulk of them are of English descent or Holland Dutch, and there's quite a few squareheads. They know the bottom of the Bay like they know their wife's face. Clamming is back-breaking, but a man can get a living if his muscle holds out. I looked through this ledger last night and figured I paid one clammer eighty-some-odd dollars last week, but that's unusual. Most of them average between five and ten bucks a day. It's all according to how good a man can handle the tongs."

He laid his ledger on the hatch, stretched his arms, and yawned. The morning had been cloudy, but the sun came out soon after we left the wharf and now it was burning off the haze on the Bay. After it had been shining fifteen minutes, we could see the striped Fire Island lighthouse and the long, glistening dunes on Oak and Captree Islands. I asked the Captain if any bayman can go out to the beds and clam.

"He cannot," the Captain said. "He has to get a Conservation Department license that costs two and a half, and he has to be a resident of the town that owns the beds he works. A Babylon man can't clam in Islip water, and vice versa. In fact, they're always fussing among themselves about the division line. That's a fuss that'll go on as long as there's a clam left in the mud."

"How much do you pay for a bushel?" I asked.

"The price is based on the size of the clam and the demand in Fulton Market," the Captain said. "Prices may fluctuate as much as fifty cents in a single season, but right now I'm paying the boys two dollars a bushel for littlenecks and a dollar and a half for cherrystones. That's for the half-shell trade. For the big ones—what we call chowders— I pay a dollar a bushel.

"The bulk of the clams in South Bay are hard-shells—they're called quahogs in New England. There's a few soft-shells, or steamers, around the shores of the Bay, but we don't bother with them. Most of the steam clams you see in the city come from New England. The hard-shell is the king of the clams. He can be baked, fried, steamed, put into chowder, or served on the half shell. I *will* say that the best chowder is made with a mixture of softs and hards. Out here we believe in Manhattan-style chowder, a couple of tomatoes to every quart of shucked clams. Our chowder clams are around four years old, a couple of years older than littlenecks. We truck our necks and cherries to dealers in Fulton Market and to restaurants in Manhattan and Brooklyn, and we truck the chowders to the Campbell's soup factory in Camden, New Jersey. They take around fifteen hundred bushels of chowders off us every week." He turned to the mate. "I'll take her now, Charlie," he said.

Soon after Captain Clock took the tiller, we approached the fleet. The little boats were laying with the wind and the tide about two miles southeast of Babylon. Captain Clock said the majority of the boats were anchored near the imaginary line dividing the beds, and that some were hugging it. "Human nature," he said. "The boys from Islip just itch to work the Babylon water, and the Babylon boys think they could tong up twice as many if they could get over on the Islip territory." A few of the boats carried two clammers, one for each side, but one man to a boat seemed to be the rule. When we were about fifty yards from the nearest clammer, the Captain ducked into the cabin and cut off the motor. Bollinger hurried to the bow and threw out the anchor.

"Now I'll show you how to clam," said Captain Clock. "We'll tong up a few pecks for us to eat."

He rolled up his shirtsleeves and picked up a pair of tongs, an implement with two sets of teeth fixed to the ends of two fourteen-foot handles. He lowered the tongs into the water, which was nine feet deep, and pushed the opened teeth into the mud; then he brought the handles together scissors-fashion, closing the teeth. Just before hauling the tongs over the rail, he doused the closed teeth in the water several times, washing out the mud. He opened the teeth on the deck and out dropped a dazed spider crab, two bunches of scarlet oyster sponge, a handful of empty shells, and twelve beautiful clams. The shells of the clams were steel blue, the color of the Bay water.

"A good haul," he said. "I got four cherries, two necks, two chowders, and four peanuts." He said that a state law forbids the sale of clams less than an inch thick and that such undersized clams are called peanuts. He tossed the peanuts and the crab back into the water. Then he put the tongs overboard again. He sent the teeth into the mud seven times and brought up forty-three clams. Then he laid aside the tongs and got two clam knives off a shelf in the cabin. He gave me one and we squatted on the deck and went to work opening the cherries. When the valves were pried apart, the rich clam liquor dribbled out. The flesh of the cherries was a delicate pink. On the cups of some of the shells were splotches of deep purple; Indians used to hack such splotches out of clamshells for wampum. Fresh from the coal-black mud and uncontaminated by ketchup or sauce, they were the best clams I have ever eaten. The mate sat on the hatch and watched us.

"Aren't you going to have any?" I asked.

"I wouldn't put one of them goddamn things in my mouth if I was perishing to death," he said. "I'm working on this buy-boat ten years and I'm yet to eat a clam."

He scornfully watched us eat for a few moments; then he went into the cabin and came out with a portable radio, which he placed on the cabin roof, and tuned in on a news broadcast. While the Captain and I opened and ate clams we looked out at the fleet and watched the clammers. The Captain said that a clammer works both sides of his boat until the tongs start coming up empty; then he lets out slack in his anchor cable and drifts into unworked territory. "Most of them are patient," he said, "but some will be lifting and dropping their anchors all day long. When a man does that we say he's got the runs." The fleet was made up largely of catboats stripped of their rigs and powered with old automobile motors. The majority of the men were tonging, but here and there a man worked with a rake. The Captain said that rakes are used only on stretches of soft bottom. "The handle of a rake is twenty-two feet long," he said, "and it takes a Joe Louis to pull it." Some of the clammers were stripped to their belts, but most of them worked in their undershirts. Occasionally a man would lay aside his tongs or rake and squat in the bottom of the boat and bag up his clams. Captain Clock said it is customary for the clammers to sell their catches in the early afternoon hours, so the shippers will have time to cull and barrel the clams for trucking in the evening.

The Captain and I were finishing the last of the forty-three clams when a whistle in Babylon blew for noon. "We better eat dinner, Archie," Bollinger said. "They'll start bringing their loads over pretty soon now."

Intent on his last clam, the Captain nodded. Bollinger brought out their lunch buckets and a thermos jug of iced tea. I had bought a couple of sandwiches in Bay Shore and I got them out of my raincoat. Bollinger tuned in on a program of waltzes broadcast from a Manhattan hotel. We sat on peck baskets in the hot sun and ate and listened to the waltzes. We were drinking tea out of tin cups when the first of the clammers came alongside. Bollinger jumped up, tossed the clammer a rope, and helped him make fast to the *Jennie Tucker*. The clammer was a small, spry old man in hip boots.

"What you got?" Captain Clock asked him.

"Nothing to speak of," he said. "Just a mess of clams. I been scratch-raking off Grass Island. I got two bushels of cherries, a bushel of necks, and two bushels of chowders." Gripping the bags by their ears, he passed them to Bollinger. Captain Clock took a five and two ones out of his cashbox and handed them to the clammer, who carefully placed them in an old-fashioned snap purse. Then he picked up two conches from the bottom of his boat and tossed them to Bollinger.

"I was about to forget your konks," he said. He threw aside the ropes, pushed off, and started his engine.

"Be good," yelled Captain Clock.

"I'm getting so old," the clammer said, "I can't be anything else."

Captain Clock laughed. "That's Captain Charlie Smith," he said. "He's known from Florida to Maine. More of a fisherman than a clammer. He's in his seventies, but he'll take that thirty-foot boat and go anywhere. Once a nor'wester caught him off Block Island, and he just crawled inside and rode her for three days and nights. When he finally got in, they say, he looked fresh as ever. They say he looked like he'd just had a shave and a haircut."

Bollinger deposited the conches in a rusty wire basket. "Konks are my racket," he said. "They get caught in the tongs and the boys save them for me instead of throwing them back. One of the truck drivers takes them in and sells them to Italian clam stands in downtown New York and we divvy up. It's just cigarette money. The Italians boil the konks and make something called *scungili*."

We drank some more tea, and then another clammer, a gloomy-eyed, sunburned young man, pulled alongside. He was in a catboat that had been patched with tin in a dozen places.

"Hello, Tarzan," said Bollinger. "Didn't that old eelpot sink yet? How many clams you got?"

"I been croshaying the mud for six hours and I barely took enough to bait a hook," the young man said. "They was thin where I was tonging."

"Quit bellyaching," said Bollinger. "If it was to rain clams, you wouldn't be satisfied." The young man passed over a bushel of necks, two bushels of cherries, a scanty peck of chowders, and three conches. Captain Clock handed him five ones and twenty cents. He folded the bills into a wad and stuffed it in his watch pocket. "Another day, another dollar," he said. "My back feels like it was run over by a load of bricks." He cranked his engine and moved off, heading for Babylon. "He'll get drunk tonight," Captain Clock said. "I can tell by the way he was talking." The Captain bent over a bag of cherries. He scooped a double handful out of the mouth of the bag and spread them on the deck. "Beauties," he said. "Uniform as peas in a pod. The shells are blue now, but they'll turn gray or white before we get them to town." He opened a cherry and balanced it on his palm. He looked at it admiringly. "A spawner," he said. "Now, that's the beauty of a clam. He doesn't make a bit of fuss about spawning. An oyster's just the opposite. He spawns from May through August—the months without an 'r' in them—and he gets so milky you can't eat him on the half shell. You can fry him, but you can't eat him raw. A clam is better behaved. He never gets milky enough to notice and he's just as good in the midsummer months, when he's spawning, as he is on the coldest day of the winter."

Captain Clock said that last year the town of Islip bought two thousand dollars' worth of hard-shells from Massachusetts and New Jersey and scattered them in its beds. "Foreign clams put new blood in the natives," he said. "They improve the breed. The spawn mixes and we get a better set. Hey, Charlie, hand me a knife. I'm going to try some of these chowders." The Captain opened a dozen chowders and arranged them in a semicircle on the hatch. We were eating them when Bollinger suddenly shouted, "Here come the cops!" He pointed in the direction of Babylon, and I saw a launch flying a green flag. In a minute it cut the water just off our bow, heading for the fleet. The clammers stopped work and commenced yelling. "They're warning each other," Bollinger said. "That's the police boat from Babylon. The cops go through the beds every day or so. You never know when they'll show up. If they spy an Islip man in Babylon water, they give him a ticket and he has to go to court and get fined." The clammers leaned on their tong and rake handles while the police boat slowly picked its way through the fleet. It did not halt; evidently the clammers were behaving themselves.

Presently another clammer called it a day and came alongside. He was a gaunt, stooped man, who silently handed over four bushels of necks, three bushels of cherries, and a bushel and a peck of chowders. He collected $13.75, bit a chew of tobacco off a plug he took from his hip pocket, mumbled, "Good night, Cap," and pushed off. "He's one of the best clammers on Long Island," said Captain Clock. "I bet he's got ten thousand dollars in the bank, and he's so saving he gets his wife to cut his hair." The gaunt clammer's departure from the beds appeared to be a signal to the others. Soon after he left, they began moving toward the buy-boat in twos and threes. In twenty minutes the *Jennie Tucker* was surrounded by loaded boats, waiting their turns to come alongside. "They all have to come at once," Bollinger said indignantly. Captain Clock stood at the stern, hunched over his ledger, which he had placed on the cabin roof. Bollinger helped the clammers heft their bags over the rail. He piled the chowders aft, the cherries on the hatch, and the necks forward. When a boat finished unloading he would call out the number of bushels, and the Captain would make a notation in his ledger and then pay off the clammer.

To get out of Bollinger's way, I went to the bow and sat on a bale of empty bags. Standing in their boats, the waiting clammers smoked cigarettes and shouted insults at each other. I couldn't tell if the insults were good-natured or genuine. "If I was you, I'd take that old cement-mixer home and set fire to it," one yelled at his neighbor. "I wouldn't be caught dead in that dirty old boat." "Well, it's paid for," said the master of the cement-mixer, "and that's more'n you can say." "Paid for!" screamed the first man. "You mean you stole it off the beach. Nothing's safe when you're around. Why, by God, you'd steal a tick off a widow's belly!" Most of the clammers seemed to be quite surly. I heard a young clammer ask the man in the next boat, a sullen old man in wet overalls, how many clams he had. "None of your business," said the old man. "Well, I was just asking to pass the time," said the young clammer. The old man grunted. "Fare better if you keep your trap shut," he said.

At a quarter after four the last clammer finished unloading, cast off, and made for home. The Captain snapped his cashbox shut and we sat down and drained the iced tea in the thermos jug. Then Bollinger hoisted the anchor, started the motor, and pointed the *Jennie Tucker* for her wharf. The decks were piled high. "A regular floating clam mountain," said Bollinger. The Captain rearranged some bags on the hatch, clearing away a space to sit. He lit his pipe and added up the row of figures in his ledger.

"We took a hundred and forty-five bushels," he said. "One day I took two hundred bushels. I emptied my cashbox for that load. The stern was awash on the trip in." He pointed toward Oak Island. "See those boats over there? Some of the boys are still out, but they don't sell over the rail like the others. They have bigger boats and they stay out until late in the afternoon and bring their loads right to our shed. We buy every clam that's offered, no matter if there's a glut in New York or a big demand. Some days we buy more clams than we can get rid of, and we take the surplus out to some lots of water we lease from the town of Islip and shovel them overboard. In the last five weeks we've planted thirteen hundred bushels of cherries and five hundred bushels of necks in those lots. When we need them, we go out and tong them up. No waste that way. In the old days, when clams were very dear, we used to have clam pirates. They would steal up at night and tong our lots, but not anymore. We keep a watchman, just in case."

At five o'clock, the *Jennie Tucker* puttered up to her wharf. Mr. Still, the senior partner of the firm, was standing in the back doorway of the shed, waiting. He looks after the office end of the business. He is a shellfish expert and belongs to the family which once ran Still's, a renowned seafood restaurant and hangout for Tammany gluttons on Third Avenue, and which still runs a thriving oyster business in a scow anchored in Pike Slip, beneath Manhattan Bridge. When the *Jennie Tucker* scraped against the wharf, Mr. Still shouted, "Here she is," and four men came out of the shed. The moment the buy-boat was tied up, two of these men leaped aboard and began lifting the bags to the wharf. The others placed them on handtrucks and wheeled them into the culling room. This was a long, cool room, which smelled like a clean cellar. There the clams were poured in great heaps on tables built against the walls. The tables and the cement floor had recently been hosed down and they were wet and immaculate. Captain Clock, Mr. Still, and Bollinger took places at the tables and culled the clams, tossing aside those with broken shells or gapped-open lips.

After they had been culled, the clams were poured into woven-wire baskets and dipped in a tank of tap water into which an antiseptic solution had been poured. Then some were emptied into great, three-bushel barrels and others into tubs holding three pecks. Soon the room was crowded with loaded barrels, and Mr. Still got a hammer out of the roll-top desk in the little office adjoining the culling room. He tacked tags on the heads of the barrels, addressing them to various restaurants and Fulton Market dealers. Then they were wheeled into one of the company's three trucks. At seven o'clock, this truck contained sixty-five barrels and twenty-two tubs. "She's ready to roll," said Mr. Still. "If you're a mind to, you can ride into the city with this load." He introduced me to Paul Boice, the driver, and I climbed into the cab of the truck. It was one of those massive, aluminum-painted trucks.

We took the Sunrise Highway. At Valley Stream, we stopped at a diner for hamburgers and coffee. The counterman knew Boice. "Care for some clams tonight, Paul?" he asked, grinning. "How about a dozen nice clams for supper?" The driver laughed perfunctorily. Evidently it was an old joke. "When I want clams for supper," he said, "I'll notify you. Fix me a hamburger." We did not tarry long in the diner. In Brooklyn the driver deftly guided the heavy truck through a maze of side streets. "I've been hauling clams over this route eight years and I know every shortcut there is," he said. "Clams are nowhere near as perishable as oysters, but I don't like to dawdle." When we rolled off Manhattan Bridge he glanced at his watch. "Took less than two hours," he said. "That's good time."

He made his first delivery at Vincent's Clam Bar, at Mott and Hester streets, unloading three clam tubs and the basket of *scungili* conches Bollinger had gathered during the day. The proprietor brought Boice a goblet of red wine. "I get a drink on the house every time I hit this place," he said. He drove down Mott Street, passing slowly through Chinatown. Entering South Street, he had to climb out of the cab and drag a sleeping drunk out of the road. "Truck drivers have to go slow down here just because of drunks," he said. "I drag one out of my way practically every night." The Fulton Market sheds were dark, deserted, and locked up when we arrived. "I make four deliveries in the Market," Boice said, "and then I head uptown and make stops at big restaurants in the theatrical district." He backed the truck up to the door of a shellfish wholesaler and we climbed out of the cab. We looked up and down the street and did not see a soul. "There's a night watchman down here who helps me unload," Boice said, "and I always have to wait for him to show up." We sat down on the steps of the wholesale house and lit cigarettes. Across the street, on top of a pile of empty flounder crates, three overfed fishhouse cats were screeching at each other. We sat for fifteen minutes, watching the cats screech and fight, and then I said goodbye. "If you order clams or chowder tomorrow," Boice said, peering up the dark street for the night watchman, "like as not you'll eat some of the ones we hauled in tonight."

1939

"It tastes fine to me."

A FORAGER

JOHN McPHEE

Euell Theophilus Gibbons, who has written four books on the gathering and preparation of wild food, once reached through the fence that surrounds the White House and harvested four edible weeds from the president's garden. Gibbons has found light but satisfying snacks in concrete flower tubs in the mall at Rockefeller Center, and he once bagged fifteen wild foods in a vacant lot in Chicago. Foraging in Central Park, he collected materials for a three-course dinner, which he prepared and ate in a friend's apartment on East Eighty-second Street. Gibbons seldom goes out of his way to perform these urban wonders, however. His milieu is open country. He lives and writes in a farmhouse near Troxelville, Pennsylvania, in the center of the state, where thousands of acres of forest rise behind his land and a wide valley of farms slopes away from his front door. He is a Quaker. He has been, among other things, a schoolteacher. All his life he has been a forager as well, becoming, in pursuit of this interest, an excellent general naturalist. But the publication of his first book, *Stalking the Wild Asparagus,* in 1962, was not so much the by-product of a lifetime of gathering wild food as it was the long-delayed justification for what had, until then, been a lifetime of disappointment as a writer. While moving from job to job and from school to school, he had written sonnets, light verse, short stories, and several kinds of novel, including a biblical epic, which he abandoned in order to write a whimsical romance about a poor schoolteacher who gives up his profession, buys rural land, builds with his own hands a home made from native materials, and creates the impression that he is a millionaire by purchasing a dinner jacket from the Salvation Army and inviting professors and potentates to black-tie banquets at tables laden with sunfish caviar, cattail wafers, pickled top bulbs of wild garlic, wild-cherry olives, wild-grape juice, blueberry juice, dandelion wine, sautéed blue-eyed scallops, crappies cooked in tempura batter and served with mint and sassafras jellies, day-lily buds with pasture mushrooms, sautéed oyster mushrooms, buttered dandelion hearts, buttered cattail bloom spikes, wild asparagus, scalded milkweed buds, wild salads (made from Jerusalem artichokes, ground-cherries, wild mustard, watercress, wood sorrel, purslane, and green-briar under wild-leek dressing), hot biscuits of cattail-root flour, May-apple marmalade, chokecherry jelly, dandelion-chicory coffee, candied mint leaves, candied wild ginger, wild cranberries glacés, candied calamus roots, hickory-maple chiffon pie, and sweet blackberry wine. Gibbons, who was fifty at the time, sent the novel to a New York literary agent he had met, and she soon indicated to him that she felt he was not yet ready as a fiction writer. Tactfully, she suggested that he trim out the plot, characters, and dialogue; she urged him to reshape the manuscript as a straightforward book on wild food. That was seven years ago. Today, Gibbons is buoyant with royalties. He has followed his *Wild Asparagus* with *Stalking the Blue-Eyed Scallop, Stalking the Healthful Herbs,* and *Euell Gibbons' Beachcomber's Handbook.* He is at work on a definitive volume covering every edible plant in North America from the Rio Grande to the Arctic Circle, and his papers—all his sonnets, short stories, notes, novels, outlines, and marginalia—are under lock and key in the Boston University Library, which has established a Euell Gibbons Collection.

Gibbons's interest in wild food suggests but does not actually approach madness. He eats acorns because he likes them. He is neither an ascetic nor an obsessed nutritionist. He is not trying to prove that wild food is better than tame food, or that he can survive without the assistance of a grocer. He is apparently not trying to prove anything at all except that there is a marvelous variety of good food in the world and that only a modest part of the whole can be found in even the most super of supermarkets. He is a gourmet with wild predilections. Inadvertently, the knowledge that he has acquired through years of studying edible wild plants has made him an expert on the nourishment aspects of survival in the wilderness, but the subject holds no great interest for him and in some ways he finds it repellent, since survival is usually taught by the military and he is a conscientious objector. Nonetheless, he has given his time to assist, in an unofficial way, at the United States Navy's survival school in Brunswick, Maine. He has also taught survival techniques at the Hurricane Island Outward Bound School, off the Maine coast. It was in Maine that I first met him—in summer and only briefly—and not long thereafter I wrote to him and asked if he would like to take a week or so and make a late-fall trip in central Pennsylvania living off the land. I apologized that I would not be able to make such a trip sooner than November, and I asked him if he thought we could find enough to eat at that time. His response was that we could stuff ourselves, if we wanted to, right up until the time of the first heavy snowfall. During the early autumn, through letters and telephone calls, we framed a plan for a six-day trip, in part by canoe on the Susquehanna River and in part on the Appalachian Trail. We decided to start out with no market food of any kind, and we also decided not to take fishing rods or shotguns. With a regimen like that, we clearly weren't going to eat the way Gibbons frequently eats at home, where his *haute cuisine sauvage* depends on liberal admixtures of such ingredients as eggs and butter, and on the advanced equipment of a contemporary kitchen. Mere survival, however, was incidental to our plans. We intended to spend the first couple of days on a survival diet, and then, gradually extending the number of ways in which we would prepare our foraged foods, we planned to introduce, a meal at a time, certain fundamental substances—salt and cooking oil, for example—that we would pick up in country stores. Thus, we would use survival foraging not as an end in itself but possibly as a metaphor, a device through which we would put ourselves in an appropriate frame of mind to recapitulate, in a sense, the earliest beginnings of human gastronomy.

While these plans were taking shape, Gibbons seemed to be full of enthusiasm, so far as I could judge from the letters of a man I scarcely knew, but then it occurred to him that the weather might be forbidding and that one result of his efforts on the river could be a soaking with cold spray. He wrote to say that even though we would almost certainly not go hungry, we might very well find ourselves beset by wind and rain, and perhaps snow. He said, "I wonder if you have considered that a survival trip might involve some pretty acute discomfort, maybe even to the extent that it could be called suffering." He suggested that we forage near his home and do our cooking in his kitchen, forgetting survival in favor of gluttony. I telephoned him and urged him to stay with the plan, saying that the foraging we would be doing, in territory relatively unfamiliar to him, would be a much more interesting challenge for him. He said, for the first time, that he could not be completely certain that we would find enough to eat, explaining that there would be plenty of wild food in that part of the state in November but not necessarily in the specific places where we might happen to look for it. I had the advantage, in this exchange, of complete ignorance, which had given me a reckless confidence. When I pressed for the trip, Gibbons said okay, he was willing to try it.

In November, I went to Troxelville, and on the morning of the fourth Gibbons and I started by car for the river. He remarked that no Indian, except perhaps a frightened Indian, would ever have set out on such a trip without gathering provisions first, so we foraged the countryside for an hour or two and collected an initial supply of Jerusalem artichokes, persimmons, hickory nuts, black walnuts, and several kinds of mint, which we stored in plastic bags in a pack basket. The weather had become unseasonably raw, and we were under a snow sky, but sunlight came through the clouds at intervals. A wind was blowing. The air temperature, according to an outdoor thermometer we had with us, was just below freezing. The canoe we had, a borrowed one, was an Old Town Guide, and it was strapped to the roof of Gibbons's Volkswagen bus. We planned to put in about fifty miles north of Harrisburg at a point just outside of Selinsgrove. Selinsgrove is a small town where a bronze plaque of the Ten Commandments is set up at eye level on the main street. In a hardware store there, we weighed ourselves on what we were assured was an accurate scale. Gibbons, who was wearing a red jacket, a red bandanna around his neck, a red hat, dungarees, and sneakers, weighed 198 pounds. No one in Selinsgrove gave us a second glance, for we were obviously hunters. In woods by the river as we prepared to shove off, with no guns and a pack basket full of nuts and tubers, a passerby might well have wondered what kind of hunting we intended to do.

Before going onto the river, we ate the first of sixteen wild meals. It was an agreeable cold lunch, and the principal utensil was a hammer. Gibbons set out a mound of walnuts and hickory nuts and a small bucket full of persimmons. "This is the wildest bunch of supplies that were ever taken on a camping trip," he said. His voice was soft and seemed to have traces of a drawl. He picked up the hammer and pounded a hickory nut, using as an anvil a water-smoothed stone. The shell split. With a nutpick, he flipped out two intact halves of hickory meat. He picked up another nut and held it on the stone between his thumb and forefinger, its point at the top; then he tilted it about ten degrees on its axis, explaining that this was the optimum angle. He paused for a moment before he brought the hammer down, then split the nut perfectly. "Indians used to boil these and make a kind of beverage called *pawcohiccora*," he said. " 'Hickory' derives from that word." He tilted another nut and studied it as if he were about to split a ninety-carat diamond. He pounded it. "Ouch! Goddamn it!" he said, and he handed me the hammer while he rubbed the end of his thumb. We went on cracking hickories and walnuts for about an hour. To be comfortable, we had stretched out on a narrow beach of smooth stones by the edge of the water, and it was pleasant there in the sunlight, although the breeze off the river was cold, and in the middle of lunch our joints began to stiffen. Gibbons showed me the best way to disassemble a black walnut, reducing it to eighths with seven blows, and while I was having my walnuts he ate persimmons. The persimmons were soft and sticky—almost but not perfectly ripe. Dark orange and about the size of large grapes, they were full of sugar and tasted something like fresh apricots, but because they were not quite ready they had an astringent aftertaste. Gibbons put three of them into his mouth, chewed them up, and spat out the seeds. "We're going to scatter persimmon seeds from hell to breakfast," he said. "You know, I think I could eat a hamburger now, but not a whole filet mignon." He put his hand back into the persimmon bucket in order to rout his retreating hunger. I was eager to get onto the river while the sun was still fairly high. Gibbons was looking out over the water, and it apparently appealed to him less than ever. "Why don't we stay here tonight?" he said. "Then we can get a good early start in the morning." I pointed out to him that it was only two-thirty in the afternoon. Forlornly, he got into the canoe.

The Susquehanna was about three-quarters of a mile wide, and the water level on that day was so low that in most places the river was only a foot deep. As we began to move downstream, we picked our way among hundreds of islands. Around the small ones the current made rips, where the canoe rocked slightly and picked up speed. Every two or three miles, we came to long, low mountains—Hooflander Mountain, Fisher Ridge, Mahantango Mountain. The mountains ran with level summits to the eastern and western horizons and stood like successive walls before us. When these mountains first folded into existence, Gibbons said, the river was already there, and it cut through the mountains as they formed, creating a series of portals for its own passage. The mountains, when young, were vastly higher than they are now. In the course of eons, they have almost wholly disintegrated and been carried away by the river. The small mountains that remain today are the foundation stubs of fantastic peaks. As we moved along, we could see the stratification lines in the water gaps tilting one toward another, and, extending these lines into the air, we could all but see the high silhouettes of the mountains when they were new. The remnants, the forested mountains of central Pennsylvania, with their flat ridgelines, looked as soft as Scottish wool—their trees gray and bare against a background of fallen leaves on rising ground—and the implied mountains of Pennsylvania, miles high between the actual ones, cast a kind of shadow that was colder than the wind on the river. Near the west bank of the river, there was a highway that now and again came into view. Tractor trailers moved in and out of sight, flying streamers of diesel smoke from their stack exhausts. Two or three times, we saw black carriages, drawn slowly up the highway by single horses. These Amish carriages swayed in the wind made by the big trucks.

The paddling had made us warm. The canoe was dry, and the clouds had spread enough to give us a steady afternoon sun. Gibbons saw a promising section of riverbank, and we stopped for a snack—sheep sorrel, peppergrass, and winter cress. "You don't need vinegar with a salad if you've got sheep sorrel," he said, and he moved along until he found some dandelions, which he wanted to have for supper. He dug them up with something that he called a dibble stick. It was actually a dock-and-thistle killer—a kind of spade with an extremely narrow blade. Although we found groves of riparian dandelions, he applied the dibble stick with considerable selectivity, bending over and studying one plant after another, excluding multiheaded dandelions and ramming the stick home when he found single-headed specimens, which have larger integral roots and crowns. "I must say these dandelions look excellent," Gibbons said. "They should be good now. In summer, they get so damned bitter you can't take them." As he put more and more dandelions into one of his plastic bags, his regard for the world became brighter. "Gosh, they're a delicacy!" he went on. When one bag was full, he started on another.

"You act like a man who's finding money," I told him.

"That's exactly it," he said. "That's exactly the way I feel."

Gibbons is a tall man—six feet two. His posture is poor, and he says that this is the result of fifty years of bending to forage. His head is a high and narrow one, with a long stretch from chin to forehead but a short distance from ear to ear, as if he had somehow successfully grown up in the space between two city buildings. His hair is brown, turning to gray, and is wavy. Now, after several hours in the open, it was standing almost straight on end. On the way back to the canoe, he collected a bagful of pennyroyal, and, pointing to a small clump of plants, he said, "That's sage there, but I don't know what the hell we would do with that, since we're not going to cook meat."

On a promising weed near the sage I found a small fruit that resembled a yellow cherry tomato. I asked him if it was edible.

"That's a horse nettle," he said. "It's deadly poisonous."

Covered with beggar's-ticks—as Gibbons calls the small seedpods that cling to clothing—we moved on downstream, he in the bow, I in the stern. The sun was still bright and the sky blue. "Well, I certainly am glad that we decided to make this trip on the river," he said. "We're not suffering like the early Christians." He paddled on for a while, looking from bank to bank and up at the mountains. At a little after four, he began to sing. We stopped for the night at five.

At that first campsite, which was on flat and wooded ground, four great paddle wheels from steamers long gone from the river were leaning aimlessly against tree trunks, and near them was a colony of ground-cherry plants, close to the water's edge. A small stream that ran into the river there was almost dammed with watercress. We still had daylight, and we cut a pile of cress and collected a peck of unhusked ground-cherries. While Gibbons, in boots he had brought along, was standing in the stream bagging the watercress, he became irritated at the thought of people who fear to take watercress from just any stream. "People say, 'Is it growing in polluted water?'" he told me. "For gosh sakes, what difference would that make? Your own vegetable garden is polluted when you put manure on it. The important thing is to wash the cress in pure water, or boil it, which we're going to do. We'll have this for breakfast." Ground-cherries, members of the nightshade family, are sometimes called strawberry tomatoes, and they hang from vinelike plants in small tan husks that become lacy with age. The husks are about an inch high, and are shaped and ribbed like Japanese lanterns. Inside each lantern is a berry that is yellow green and resembles a cherry only in that it is smooth and round. It has no pit. It looks like a small tomato, half an inch in diameter. Like many wild foods, ground-cherries are good as hors d'oeuvres, and we ate some as we gathered them. Their flavor is much like the flavor of tomatoes, with a wild, musky undertone. Fifty yards upstream was a swampy lowland where the shoreline was imprecise because it was overgrown with cattails. Gibbons waded in among the cattails, leaned over, and reached down into the freezing water until his arm was submerged to the shoulder. He came up with the leading end of a cattail root, from which a short white sprout was protruding. He broke off the sprout and reached into the water again. The second sprout he found was as short as the first one, and Gibbons was disappointed. "I've seen them eight inches long," he said, and tried again. When he had about ten short white sprouts, he gave up. He calls the cattail the supermarket of the swamps, since it has half a dozen edible parts (not all edible at the same time of year), in a range from the soft green bloom spikes to a rootstock flour that makes excellent drop biscuits. On his way back to the campsite, he paused at a remarkable weed that had a leaf large enough to wrap groceries in. "Burdock," he said, and he dug it up with the dibble stick. As we dug six or seven more, I discovered that burdock is the plant that produces the spherical bristly burrs I had been picking up inadvertently all my life—the burrs that look like communications satellites and will hang on to almost anything but glass. Just beyond the burdock was a group of plants that looked to me like dandelions, but each one had a dry stalk rising from its center. "Chicory," Gibbons said. "It's getting dark. Let's just take the greens." So we cut a pile of chicory greens, and Gibbons sorted them. He threw away the outside leaves and kept the young and tender ones.

We had a nest of pots with us, and a Coleman stove, which we used part of the time in supplement to wood fires. It was six o'clock when Gibbons began to prepare dinner that night, and the air temperature was thirty-three degrees. While we talked, we breathed out shafts of vapor, which swirled into the steam that was rising from the pots. As Gibbons bent forward intently over his cooking, light flickered up against his face—the benevolent face of a kind and religious man that seemed to have in it, as well, a look that was gleamingly satanic. He said that he thought that in this kind of encounter with nature—or in any other kind of encounter with nature—human beings make a sorry mistake if they feel that nature is something to be conquered. "The product I gather out here means something different to me than food from a store, but I don't feel that I have made nature stand and pay tribute. I know that when I disturb the earth to get these plants I will almost always cause more of them to grow. I don't like to eat Indian cucumbers, because I have to destroy the plants to get them. I don't want to destroy; I want to play the part I am supposed to play in relation to plants. I come to a persimmon tree and the tree is growing something sweet, so I'll eat it and scatter the seed. When I do that, I'm carrying out the role I'm supposed to be carrying out. Nature has many, many balances, and we have to find a balance that includes man. If man accepts that he has to be a part of the balance, he must reject the idea of the conquest of nature. Whenever I read that phrase 'conquest of nature,' I feel a little depressed. Man is a part of the total ecology. He has a role to play, and he can't play it if he doesn't know what it is—or if he thinks that he is conquering something." While Gibbons speaks, he characteristically averts his eyes from the path of his words, but from time to time, as he reaches a key word, his eyes open wide and focus directly on the listener. He seems to be checking to see that the listener is still there. Light and rapid smiles and frowns follow one another across his face. "The idea that we are engaged in a conquest of nature is a fallacy that is causing all kinds of trouble," he went on. "We're covering the earth with concrete, filling swamps, leveling hills. Some of these things have to be done, but we should do these things with knowledge. The conquest of nature has to stop. When Orientals climb a mountain, they believe that the mountain lifts them, not that they have conquered the mountain. Here. You're going to have to peel your own artichokes. I cooked them in their jackets tonight."

For dinner, we had boiled Jerusalem artichokes, boiled whole dandelions, ground-cherry salad, a dessert of persimmons, and pennyroyal tea. Jerusalem artichokes are tubers of wild sunflowers. They look like small sweet potatoes, since they are bumpy and elongated and are covered with red jackets. The flesh inside, however, is delicate and white. Boiled, it has the consistency of boiled young turnips or summer squash, and the taste suggests the taste of hearts of artichokes. Gibbons said that Jerusalem artichokes are native American plants. Indians sometimes cultivated them. They were well known to colonists, and the word "Jerusalem," in this instance, is apparently an English corruption of the Spanish word for sunflower—*girasol*. Gibbons also said he was

sorry that Jerusalem artichokes and a number of other wild foods—
such as ground-cherries and wild rice—had been named for more familiar foods. "These things are not substitutes for tame foods," he went
on. "They have flavors of their own, and it is not fair to them to call
them by the name of something else. These are not artichokes. They're
sunflower tubers." With a knife and fork, he laid one open and then
scooped up a mound of the white flesh. It was steaming hot. "Boy!" he
said. "That goes down very gratefully. Just eating greens, you can get
awfully damn hungry. We'll eat plenty of greens, but we need these,
too." For a while, we ate without speaking, because the artichokes were
so good. Gibbons ran his fork into the root of a dandelion and drew the
rest of the plant—a long streamer of leaves—away from a heaping
mound of dandelions on his plate. With Italian skill, he rotated the fork
until the plant was curled around it like spaghetti. I imitated him, and
we both began to wolf down dandelions. Gibbons was a little disappointed. "These dandelions are tough," he said. "Too bad. They get better and better the colder it gets. With this weather, we may get some
better ones in the next few days." The dandelions were also somewhat
bitter, but Gibbons seemed to find them just right in this respect. Ordinarily, he would have boiled them in three waters, he explained, but
he had used only one pot of water this time, because, as he put it, "we're
using no salt and we got to taste *something.*" If I had been a little less
hungry, I think I would have left the dandelion leaves on my plate. The
crowns and the roots, however, were mild and delicious. When we had
finished dinner, Gibbons said that his hunger was satisfied but that he
did feel a longing for meat or fish. "Right now I wish I had a big plate
of sea-urchin roe," he said. Then he rolled a cigarette and lit it, and that
seemed to kill off the thought.

I boiled water in the largest pot, dropped a cake of soap into it, and
began to wash up the dinnerware. Gibbons rolled another cigarette.
He said that he was trying to cut down on his smoking and that was
why he had reverted to a custom of his youth and was rolling his own.
He was so good at it—just a turn of his fingers and a fast lick at the
paper—that his rolled cigarettes looked machine-made. I asked him
how many Pennsylvania Quakers he knew who could roll a smoke like
that.

"I'm not a birthright Quaker," he said. "I'm a convinced Quaker. I
was born in Clarksville, Texas—in Red River County."

The date of his birth was September 8, 1911. At that time, his father, who was also born in Clarksville, was a blacksmith and a grocer, pursuing both careers in a single store. Gibbons's father was also a dreamer. His horizons were wicketed with rainbows, and before long he would become an irremediable drifter, taking his family with him as he moved around the Southwest, making one fresh start after another—now a carpenter, now a contractor, now a rancher, a farmer, a sawyer, a builder of culverts, a bit-sharpener in oil fields. Gibbons's mother was from Dresden, Tennessee, where she had grown up on a hill farm. Her mother taught her to hunt and to trap and to eat wild greens, wild fruits, wild lettuce, and pokeweed salads. When Gibbons's mother was a little girl, she provisioned her dollhouse not with mud pies but with wild food. In Texas, years later, she passed along her knowledge to her children, three boys and a girl. Euell, the second child, was by far the most interested. "Red River County isn't like Texas at all," he told me. "It's more like Pennsylvania. There were woods there, and river bottoms, and hills. The whole idea that you could go out into the woods and gather good things was tremendously exciting to me. When I was five, I thought up my first wild recipe. I took hickory nuts and hackberries and pounded them up in a cloth and made a wild confection. Wild food was our calendar—a signal of the time of year. In the spring, we had wild asparagus and poke and all the early greens. Lamb's-quarters came in the late spring and strawberries in the early summer, then mulberries and blackberries. In late summer, we had purslane, wild plums, maypops—that's a kind of hard-shell passion fruit—and in the fall there were plenty of muscadines, wild pecans, hickory nuts, black walnuts. As it got a little colder, there were persimmons, hackberries, and black haws. Wherever we went, I asked what the Indians ate. We considered all these things delicacies, and we would not have *not* gathered them, any more than we would have let things in the garden go to waste."

I asked what his brothers do now, and he said that both live in Albuquerque, and one is a cabinetmaker and the other is a driver for the Navajo Freight Lines. His mother, who is eighty, lives in Albuquerque, too. His father and his sister are both dead.

Gibbons snapped a last cigarette off his fingers and into the river. A few minutes later, he got into his sleeping bag and began to wrap himself in a new space blanket. He said, "Let's see if we can get through the night without dreaming about food. That will determine how successful we have been today."

When we got up, at 6 A.M., the temperature was twenty-five degrees and there were panes of ice around pools at the edge of the river. The river surface was absolutely smooth, and twists of vapor were rising from it. Families of coot swam in zigzags in the mist. We had a collapsible bucksaw with us. I set that up, cut logs from a fallen birch, and made a good-sized fire while Gibbons got together the materials for breakfast. The first thing he made was water-mint tea. I had three cups in quick succession. The cups we had were made of aluminum, and the heat coming through the handle of mine burned my fingers, while the rest of my hand was red with cold. Gibbons said, "In Troxelville, mint is called tea, so you know what they do with it." The night before, I had been full of compliments for the dinner he had cooked, and now he seemed a little sensitive about the breakfast he was about to serve. He warned me that breakfast is the roughest meal to get through on any survival trip, because that is usually the time when the wild foods are most dissimilar from the foods one is used to at home. He then filled two plates with a medley of steaming watercress, chicory greens, cattail sprouts, and burdock roots. It was, frankly, a pretty unusual breakfast. The boiled watercress was delicious, and the cattail sprouts were sweet and tender. The chicory greens, being even bitterer than the dandelion greens of the night before, were a little strong for that hour in the day. The burdock roots, which he had sliced into discs, were undistinguished in flavor, and tough. "One thing we won't need on this trip is vitamin pills," Gibbons said. "This watercress, for example, has more vitamin C in it—weight for weight—than there is in orange juice. Spinach is the only garden vegetable I know of that has more vitamin A than these chicory greens. On the whole, people might be better off if they threw away the crops they so tenderly raise and ate the weeds they spend so much time exterminating. The stinging nettle has more protein than any other leafy material ever tested. Cooked nettles don't sting. Nettle beer is very good." Neither of us finished the chicory greens, and we flipped the leftovers off our plates onto the ground. Gibbons said, "When we throw away garbage, it goes right back into the earth." We ended the breakfast with several handfuls of persimmons, which tasted as sweet and as bland as dates following the bitter greens.

After breakfast, we heard shotgun blasts up and down the river, some quite close, and I said, "What are they shooting at?"

Gibbons said, "Duck, I think."

I began to think of roast duck stuffed with oranges. Gibbons must have started to think about roast duck at that moment, too. "There's a difference between being hungry for foods that you're used to eating and being just plain hungry," he said, and he added, "I've been both." Then he went off foraging while I cleaned up and packed the gear. When he came back, he was carrying a bag full of winter cress and three bags full of oyster mushrooms. The winter cress looked like magnified watercress, but its taste, Gibbons said, would be altogether different. The oyster mushrooms were gray and floppy and made me think of the gills of sharks. Gibbons told me that he had found them growing on a dead birch and a dead willow, and he said, "When they steam, they smell like oysters."

"How do you tell the difference between an edible mushroom and a poisonous mushroom?" I asked him.

"You can't," he said. "A family in New Jersey died two weeks ago from eating *Amanita verna*—you know, the death angel. A reporter at the Philadelphia *Inquirer* called me up and said, 'How do you tell the difference between mushrooms and toadstools?' You don't. There are too many of them. Some are neither edible nor poisonous. You learn to recognize the edible species. It is exactly like recognizing someone's face; once you know a person, you know that person from all other people. If you came home at night and a woman you had never seen was standing there in your house, you wouldn't think it was your wife. God help you, anyway, if you would. Oyster mushrooms, meadow mushrooms, chanterelles, shaggymanes, puffballs—you get to know each one, and you never forget them. I don't just go out, find a mushroom, eat it, and see if it's going to kill me. I know what I'm looking for."

A boy hunter walked into the campsite. He was about twelve years old, and he was wearing a red cotton parka. A shotgun slanted down from the bend in his right arm. He had short-cropped blond hair. His left hand was bright with blood.

"Hello. What did you kill?" I said to him.

"Rabbit. You get anything?"

"Yes," said Gibbons.

"What did you get?"

"Winter cress."

"Don't you hunt?" the boy said.

"Sometimes," Gibbons told him. "Have you seen any ducks this morning?"

"No, but I shot five coot down there, on the water."

"What did you do with them?"

"What did I *do* with them? I'm not going to wade out after coot. I'm not going to get wet for coot—not when it's this cold."

The boy moved on up the riverbank. Gibbons and I looked at each other for a moment, and each saw all reserves about hunted game crumbling away. We threw all our stuff into the canoe and shoved off. A coot is a ducklike bird—not a delicacy, but edible.

We searched the river for the five dead birds. Perhaps to give his appetite every possible consideration, Gibbons began to refer to the coots as ducks, and he began to shape a menu in his mind that included not only ducks but also freshwater clams. "Watch the bottom," he said. "I want ducks and clams. If we had ducks and clams, we could have clam-and-mushroom stuffing for the duck." So we began to scan the bed of the river as well as the surface. The water was clear and it flowed along over ribs of stratified rock that were partly covered with leaves and algae but not with clams. On the surface all around us were gliding coots but no dead ones. We slanted back and forth in angled patterns down the western side of the river. It seemed impossible, on such a still morning, that we could not see the birds.

"That little kid was lying," I said. "He didn't shoot any coots."

"There's a clam!" Gibbons shouted.

"Where?"

"Right there, Goddamn it. Stop the canoe!"

We backwatered hard, and then I pried the canoe broadside to the current and jammed my paddle against the river bottom on the down-stream side. While I hung on, Gibbons plunged his arm into the water, soaking part of the sleeve of his jacket. When he drew out his arm, he had a muddy half shell in his hand.

We drifted on, still searching, and we began to feel the chill of the morning. Above us was a mackerel sky, and no warmth was coming

through it. The current gradually took us close to the bank, and after we
had gone along beside it for a while, alternately drifting and paddling,
we came to another hunter, in a semi-blind—an adult this time, all red
and brown and crouched and ready.

"Get anything?" Gibbons said to him.

"One pintail duck," said the hunter. "They're scarce today."

"You're telling me," said Gibbons.

We paddled steadily for a long stretch, all but giving up the search,
and we began to feel warm. Around noon, the sun broke through. "You
couldn't say we were suffering like the early Christians," Gibbons said.
"We've got a pretty good sun there now."

"What else could we ask for?" I said.

"A duck."

We shot through a little rip and stopped paddling at the end of it
to drift and eat persimmons. While I ate mine, I leaned back on the
gunwales, so that the sun could hit me full in the face, and I closed my
eyes and spat the seeds into the air. "What were you before you were a
Quaker?" I asked him.

"I was raised up a Southern Baptist—no dancing, no card playing,
picayunish piety—and that produced all kinds of problems, many of
which I still have with me. That part of Texas where I first lived was
some micro-culture. Puritanism in theory. Tobacco Road in practice."

The canoe moved quietly around a small island. Two white-tailed
deer, from cover in the middle of the island, jumped and ran. When
they entered the shallow water of the river, spray flew up from their
feet. It happened that there was a deep channel between the island they
had left and a much larger island in the center of the river. The deer
slowed down, then lost touch with the bottom and began to swim. Instinctively, Gibbons and I took our paddles and made boiling eddies in
a race to catch the deer. This was bizarre. What on earth did we intend
to do if we caught up with them? Were we going to jump out of the
canoe and drown them or knife them in the river? There was no logic,
and there had been no second or even first thoughts. But we were both
paddling as if our lives depended on it. Apparently, just the sight of all
that meat was enough to make us move. For a time, we gained on the
deer. Then their feet found the bottom again and they moved a little
faster as the water shallowed. Soon they were skimming along over a
few inches of water, spray flying. They ran up onto the big island and

sprinted along its central ridge. When they had moved several hundred yards down the ridge, they disappeared from sight.

"Lunch?" Gibbons said, and we beached the canoe on the big island. We could find no stones there, so we went into the river and picked up two flat ones. For an hour, we cracked walnuts and hickory nuts, exchanging the hammer, and when we were not pounding or picking at the nuts we ate watercress and persimmons. Like people in all parts of the country, we were eating essentially the same lunch we had had the day before, and it was not much of a thrill. We were tired, so we stretched out and propped ourselves on our elbows while we worked. The ground was cold. Over lunch, Gibbons told me this story:

In 1922, his father took the family to the Estancia Valley, in New Mexico, to establish a homestead. The state of New Mexico was ten years old, and was having unpromising beginnings, for a four-year drought of appalling severity had discouraged homesteaders in the state, and many of them were giving up and moving away. Euell's father was a man of such unnerving optimism that he saw the drought as an opportunity. Surely rains were near, and meanwhile departing people were all but giving away their homes and goods. He traded the family car to a defeated homesteader for a cow, a calf, a colt, two mares, a mule colt, twelve hens, farm tools, a set of harness, a woodstove, and an axe. The family moved into a half dugout, which had a dirt floor and, above ground level, was made of logs. Water was carried from a spring several hundred yards away. Euell's father found work with a new company that had been established in the valley salt flats to make salt. This, he said, would be his permanent career. Gibbons remembers that his father described as permanent every job he started. The salt of the valley had not been tested, and cattle died wherever the salt was sold. The company collapsed. The drought continued, and since there was no other work for Euell's father, the mule colt was sold and the money was used to buy food. Soon his father left the valley, on foot, to search for a job, and the mother and four children in the half dugout had no idea where he was going, how long he would be gone, or whether he would come back. The remaining animals began to starve. Euell's mother got sick, apparently from malnutrition. A mare died, and Euell's dog ate the carcass. Wood, out there in the semi-desert, was difficult to find, and Euell, who was twelve years old, began to take posts from an old pole corral a half mile away. The cow, in her hunger, ate yucca and died.

Euell skinned the cow and sold the hide in Cedarvale, the nearest town. The chickens ate the flesh of the cow, and the family, who had been living on lard, pinto beans, flour, and syrup, began to eat the chickens, one by one. When Euell killed the last hen, he found an egg inside it, and for many weeks after that the egg sat on a shelf because no one would be the one to eat it. It was eventually thrown away. Meanwhile, pinto beans had become the family's diet morning, noon, and night. At the sight of pinto beans, they sometimes vomited. About a mile and a half away, there was a house that stood empty. Its owners were to be gone indefinitely, and Euell went there to see if they had left any food. He found the front door swinging in the wind on one hinge. Sandstorms had blown drifts of sand into the house and had knocked a stovepipe chimney from the roof as well. There was no food inside. A few yards from the house was a dugout shelter, and it was locked. Euell thought for a while, then broke in. Inside, he found two hundred pounds of pinto beans.

Outside, his dog began to bark. Euell went out and saw that the dog was concentrating on the stovepipe chimney that had blown off the house. He picked up one end of the chimney and squinted into it. A pair of rabbits was in there, and after he had killed them he began to wonder—for the first time in this strange, dry, and unpromising landscape—about wild food. Soon after the last of the family's livestock had died, there had been some rainfall in the Estancia Valley, and, as will happen in desert country, things were suddenly green. On his way home with the rabbits, he found Russian thistles growing along a fence row, and he also found wild garlic, lamb's-quarters, and wild potatoes. All these ingredients were used that evening in rabbit stew. The next day, Euell put a pack on his back and went to the edge of the valley, where he found puffball mushrooms growing under cedar trees, piñon nuts, and fruits of the yellow prickly pear. He made long daily hikes in search of provisions. He found buffalo berries on the margins of sand hills. He found a way to fish the ground for rabbits—pushing barbed wire into rabbit holes and rotating the wire so that the barbs would work their way into the rabbits' fur. His father returned, with money, about a month later. Until then, the family lived on the wild food Euell foraged.

Now, on the island in the Susquehanna, Gibbons stopped talking for a few minutes and cracked a number of walnuts. He hunted around

for his nutpick, found it, and ate the nuts. "Wild food has meant different things to me at different times," he said. "Right then it was a means
of salvation, a way to keep from dying."

I asked him if his family had been able to stay in the Estancia Valley.

"Oh, no," he said. "It was a whale of an unstable situation when I
was growing up. But my father finally did homestead a place in north-
western New Mexico, about a hundred miles from Albuquerque, near a
town called Cuba. We had four hundred and six acres. It was a very,
very small spread, but you had the use of a lot of free range. When I was
fifteen, I left home. I didn't run away, I just left. I always sent money
home. I worked the wheat harvest in Texas. I worked in a dairy. I
worked in boll-pulling fields. I knew carpentry from my father, and I
helped build a church. I spent seven weeks trapping on the Red River.
With some others, I panned gold. We could get a little bit of color
along the Tonque. In Logan, New Mexico, I worked for the LE Ranch,
and later for the Bell Ranch. And after that I worked for Blumen-
shine's, near Albuquerque. These were all straight riding jobs—yayuh,
a cowboy. Just a general cow nurse—riding fences, working cattle. I
spent nearly every day all day in the saddle, but I never was a good rider.
I've always said the reason I learned to ride was all that cactus out
there—you had no place to fall if you were thrown. I was never badly
hurt, though. A cowboy also does an awful lot of digging postholes,
stringing fences, fixing windmills. I earned extra money bronc-stomping,
and I got pretty good with a rope. I can still do it. Every once in a while,
I lasso a whole bunch of children at once, just to give them some fun. I
learned a lot about nature from the Navajos. They were semi-agricultural.
They were lean in the spring, and when they killed a horse they ate
everything. When I was twenty-one, I caught a freight for California."

As Gibbons finished telling me these things, I found that I was
looking at the red bandanna around his neck. His long, spare, unpos-
tured frame seemed suddenly just right for the resigned slouch of a
cowboy in the saddle, although that was the last thing I would have
imagined before then. And I thought I could see now why he had apparently been so timorous about starting out in the first place. He had
had his share of discomforts years ago, and the idea of artificially creating them, or even running the risk of creating them, must have seemed
bleak to him. I, for my part, had been sure that Gibbons would take

care of the food and that luck would take care of the November weather, so I had been full of energy when we started out, and had thought that I was going to have to rally Gibbons to get him through the trip. What was happening, though, was that I was losing energy now and Gibbons was visibly getting stronger as he settled into the routine, accepted the conditions we had set up, and relaxed in the momentum of fifty years' experience.

A stiff, cold wind began to blow north up the river, and a heavily layered sky closed out the sun for the rest of the day. We wanted to end the river part of our trip six or eight miles downstream, near Clarks Ferry, where the Appalachian Trail crosses the river, and we had planned to arrive there that afternoon. "Well, if we're fixing to get there before dark, we had better get going," Gibbons said, and he got lightly to his feet and walked to the edge of the water. He looked back at me. "Let's go," he said. I had been stretched out on the ground for almost an hour—as he had—and I got up slowly. I felt stiff and chilled. Gibbons was waiting in the bow, and I got into the stern and shoved off. All afternoon, we pushed the canoe into the cold headwind, and conversation was impossible. When we had covered about a mile, however, Gibbons began to sing:

> "When the north winds blow
> And we're going to have snow
> And the rain and the hail come bouncin',
> Then I'll wrap myself in a buffalo robe,
> Away out on the mountain."

The dusk was deep when we took the canoe out of the river, at a windswept and deserted picnic ground that had stone fireplaces. As we had planned, I hitchhiked back to pick up Gibbons's Volkswagen, then returned to the campsite. On the way, I stopped in a general store and bought a box of salt, for that evening's meal, and cooking oil, for the following night. The counter was covered with cinnamon buns and chocolate cupcakes, but, oddly, they did not appeal to me at all. What I really wanted was eight ounces of undiluted whiskey; but whiskey was not on our menu, either. Feeling cold and miserable, I went back to the campsite. Gibbons was digging up dandelions in the dark, and he was whistling.

Dinner revived me. Gibbons had found some catnip, and he made catnip tea. He said that catnip is a mild sedative, and I drank all I could hold. We built a high bonfire that whipped in the wind. The dandelions, boiled in three waters, were much better than they had been the night before, and the oyster mushrooms might have been taken from a banquet for the Olympian gods. Each mushroom was at least six inches across and, in the center, nearly an inch thick. As they steamed, the vapor from the pot did seem to carry the essences of oyster stew. Their taste, however, was fantastically like the taste of broiled steak.

The simple ingredients of that dinner—dandelions and mushrooms, no dessert—were splendid in themselves, but they were made transcendent by the presence of salt. This was the first of the kitchen staples that we would introduce, one at a time, during the rest of the trip, and, perhaps a little expansively, we had the feeling that we had repeated the experience of some inspired Cro-Magnon who first thought to crush the white substance and sprinkle it on his food. After dinner, Gibbons rolled a cigarette and said, "What I could sure eat right now is a praline." We planned to introduce sugar at breakfast the next morning (in the car Gibbons had a large block of maple sugar he had made from a neighbor's trees in Troxelville), and his remark about the praline set a pattern that he repeated many times, concentrating his fantasies on kinds of food that were on the horizon of our diet. "Roadside stands sell terrible pralines," he went on. "They use corn syrup. I make pralines out of maple syrup, hickory nuts, and cream."

Unfortunately, Gibbons did not make pralines for breakfast. As unappealing as pralines might have been at that time of day, nothing edible could have been worse than what we had. The meal began with peppermint tea, which was very good in itself and was excellent with chunks of maple sugar in it. The substance of that breakfast, however, was a great mound of hot persimmons, which had been stewed in maple sugar and were now glued together with concentrated maple syrup. We stuffed them eagerly into our mouths, because they looked good, but we found that all the astringency of slightly unripe persimmons seems to be brought out powerfully when they are stewed. They puckered not only our mouths but also our throats. Gibbons observed, without apparent alarm, that he thought that his esophagus was going to close. Nonetheless, he kept shoveling in the styptic persimmons, and I followed his lead. There was enough carbohydrate fuel in the stewed fruit to keep us going all day, and we needed it. Each mouthful tasted fine on entry but quickly turned into something like a glut of blotting paper, requiring a half dozen forced swallows to squeeze it down. Gibbons had told me that in all his experience of cooking wild food for others no one had ever gotten sick. In order to preserve his record, I excused myself and went for a walk, taking deep breaths, until I was sure that the persimmons were going to stay with me.

We spent the morning foraging near the river, for Gibbons had become nervous about the Appalachian Trail. "Nut trees bear very little in dense forest," he said. "A dense forest is a famine area. Along a river, sun may get in, but I have walked for miles in dense forest without finding one damned thing I could eat. It is possible to eat the inner bark of trees, but there's almost nothing else." A short walk into a valley west of the river calmed him completely. This was dry, brown, beautifully autumnal pheasant country, with corn stubble in the open and the clustered stalks of the summer's weeds fringing ditches, streams, and fields. In such fringes, Gibbons is truly happy, for more concentrated foraging can be done in them than in any other kind of area north of the tropics or far from the sea, and for sheer concentrated provender the only comparable areas in the United States are the food-laden zones between high and low tide. About a quarter of a mile from the Susquehanna, a small rivulet ran along one side of a cornfield and then under a blacktop road. The curving plow of the farmer had spared a fifth of an acre in the angle where the stream met the road, and there we found wild mustard, lamb's-quarters, chickweed, wild spearmint, catnip, winter cress, dandelions, and groundnuts. Gibbons ignored the first three, because they were past their prime. We almost ignored the dandelions, too, since we had had so many, but Gibbons dug up a few with the dibble stick to see how they were, and announced with excitement that they were the largest dandelions he had ever found. The roots of these single-headed beauties were more than an inch thick. "This is the best dandelion field I've ever got into," he said as he pried one after another out of the earth. "I've seen *cultivated* dandelions that weren't as big as this!" It was a clear, sunny morning, so we sat down right there and dressed the dandelions, deciding to have crowns for lunch and roots for dinner. The crown is the place where the leaves are joined, at the base of the plant. When the leaves are cut away, the remaining stubble resembles a coronet. We put these into one bag, and we pared the roots, which were about three inches long, and put them into another. The groundnuts in that remarkable place were also the largest he had ever found. They grow below the surface, and are discoverable at that time of year only by thin filament vines that wind upward around the stems of other plants. These groundnuts are in no way similar to peanuts, which are called groundnuts in many parts of the world. Groundnuts of the sort we found are spherical and are sometimes called Indian potatoes. They are connected underground by stringlike roots. Gibbons excavated carefully, and he brought up one, then another, then another, each separated from the next in line by a foot or so of root. His eyes were bulging. Each groundnut was about the size of a golf ball. "Captain John Smith said he found groundnuts as large as eggs," Gibbons told me. "But these are the biggest I've ever seen. You're in on the kill—

"Where the whitest lilies blow,
Where the freshest berries grow,
Where the groundnut trails its vine,
Where the wood grape's clusters shine."

Walking back to the river, we passed a persimmon tree that was four stories high. The persimmons hanging from its branches were so large that they looked almost like oranges. In fact, some were two inches in diameter. We walked right on past them without a second glance.

"There is interesting wood in a persimmon tree," Gibbons said. "It is in the same family as ebony."

Before repacking our gear and going up onto the Appalachian Trail, we had a light but hot lunch beside the river—boiled dandelion crowns, catnip tea, and walnuts. The crowns were every bit the delicacy that Gibbons had claimed they would be—easily the equal of asparagus tips or young broccoli spears. With vegetables, Gibbons has the touch of the Chinese. Each crown offered an initial crunchy resistance and then seemed to dissolve in a mild but distinguished sea of the flavor essence of dandelion. We took many long draughts of catnip, and we felt good. Sunlight was sparkling on the river. The temperature was in the middle forties. Gibbons began to talk about a tribe of Indians in the Andes. He said that when these Indians travel they take no provisions at all, and they go for three or four days on coca leaves that they chew as they move. He paused for a moment, shaved some maple sugar into his catnip, stirred it, and said, "They live on nothing but the cocaine—and their own energy. It's rough. They get thin. They're using up their own bodies when they're doing it." He drank some more catnip. "Of course, we're getting plenty of energy from this sugar," he went on. "When I tapped the trees, I made spiles out of elderberry stems and sumac stems. I cooked the sap right there in the woods, in two old bake pans. I've made sugar from the sap of red maples, silver maples, Norway maples—hell, yes—and from walnut trees, butternut trees, sycamores, black birches. This? This is sugar-maple sugar. This is living. In the Sudan, there are certain Nilotic tribesmen whose diet is insufficient and consists almost wholly of cornmeal. They start the day by eating their ration of cornmeal as fast as they can, so it will digest more slowly and prolong the feeling of being full. Let's get going."

The Appalachian Trail rose and fell in long, untiring grades through the mountains, among hardwood forests that were not at all dense and where sunlight, on that first afternoon, sprayed down through the trees. The ground all around us was yellow and red with dry leaves, and the clear sky was a bright pale blue. Along the edges of the trail for hundreds of yards at a stretch were colonies of ground pine and wintergreen. We stopped to collect wintergreen, and soon after we moved on Gibbons began to sing a song about making love to a turtle-dove. I said to him, "This is the best famine area I've ever been in." He then began to talk about fried chicken, fried pork chops, fried pota-toes—for we were going to break out the bottle of cooking oil that night and fry things for the first time. We stopped at a log lean-to that had a stone fireplace in its rear wall and, against the side walls, perma-nent bunks whose wooden frames were covered with heavy sheets of steel mesh. Behind the lean-to was a brook.

We collected wood and started our fire. The temperature fell rapidly after the sun went down. The night was going to be clear and cold, and we kept the fire high. By seven, when Gibbons had the two frying pans out and was beginning to sauté dandelion roots in one and sliced groundnuts in the other, the temperature at the open end of the lean-to was below freezing and the temperature at the closed end was almost a hundred degrees. The distance between these extremes was eight feet. Gibbons seemed at home there, cooking, with his face bak-ing and his back freezing, and the dinner he served was outstanding—

wild-spearmint tea, piles of crisp dandelion-root tidbits, and great quantities of groundnuts so skillfully done that they seemed to be a refinement of home-fried potatoes. Having fried food was an appealing novelty. We were hungry, and we ate as rapidly as Nilotic tribesmen, without conversing. Gibbons looked up once and said, "The Smithsonian has a very good man on starchy roots." Then he went on eating.

Afterward, Gibbons made another pot of spearmint tea, and he built up the fire so that it glowed all around him as he sat on a corner of his bunk and told me that he had been a tramp and a Communist—first the one, then the other—in the 1930s, in California and the Pacific Northwest. "California was a poor place for wild food. I gathered some purslane, lamb's-quarters, and black walnuts. And out near Needles I once got some prickly pear. There was not much wild stuff in California that I recognized. I foraged cultivated foods from fields and shops." His first view of the state was over the side of a coal car, which he left at San Bernardino in March 1933, hopping another freight to Los Angeles. Calling himself by the name of a friend in New Mexico, he signed in at Uncle Tom's Transient Center. "I had a road name. Lots of bums had road names. At Uncle Tom's, you got a number, and that was that from then on. But there was no work in Los Angeles. There were too many bums there. After so many days, you had to leave. I went to the railroad yards and found a train of reefers—refrigerator cars—that had been made up to go north empty. There were hatches on the tops of the cars. I raised a dozen of those hatches and men were crammed in under every one of them. I finally had to sit on the top of the train. When we left L.A., men were all over the top. There were probably a thousand guys on that one freight."

In Ventura, Gibbons stayed at the Sally (Salvation Army), and in Lompoc he begged toffins (semi-stale baked goods) from a friendly baker. He found a preacher in Lompoc who had the same size feet he had, and he built a chicken coop for the preacher in return for a pair of shoes. The preacher was so astonished at Gibbons's willingness to work hard and at his skill as a carpenter that he gave him the shoes and $2.50. "Everything was green in Lompoc. It was April. The sun was shining. Lompoc was my heaven, and I didn't need any other one. There were no more jobs, and I had to move on." He caught a freight to Surf, where he joined up with a Mexican and a Spaniard, shared his toffins with them, and spent five cents of his $2.50 on a measure of coffee, which he brewed in a No. 10 can. He slept in a bindle (bedroll) and carried it on his back during the day. "I was a bindle stiff, like the others. I had a blanket with me, and a pack made out of an old tin bread box." He rode a freight to Santa Clara and arrived on Good Friday, a day of luck. A butcher gave him a pound of hamburger, and at a packing plant he was given a bag full of prunes—"huge prunes that sold for five cents apiece in Southern Pacific Railroad dining cars." He found artichokes in Santa Clara fields, and while he was walking along a road near the artichoke fields a car driven by a woman stopped beyond him and a small boy got out, ran back, and gave him a fifty-cent piece, telling him that it was an Easter present.

Gibbons paused to say that he apparently developed in that era what some people who know him well have called his "hobo instinct." Few American hoboes of the 1930s knew much about wild food, he said, but he acknowledged nonetheless that there are hobo overtones in his approach to his specialty—his excited way of seeing wild plants as wild coins, and his affection for roadside foraging. He said, "There is nothing I would rather do than eat my way through a roadside ditch."

At times, in California, Gibbons lived in ding camps. " 'Ding' is the hobo word for bum. When you go bumming, you go dinging." In the ding camp at San Jose, he took a course in Spanish, and he worked in the camp variety show as a blackface minstrel, a juggler of vegetables, and a trick roper. The San Jose troupe traveled to other camps—in Sacramento, Oakland, San Francisco—and also played in theatres, where Gibbons got three dollars (tops) for an appearance. "The thing that broke that up was marijuana smoking. About half the guys in the troupe were hay burners. Five cents a stick."

"Were you a hay burner?" I asked.

"No, I never was a hay burner."

Gibbons pushed the logs in the fireplace closer together. "I went to a few Communist meetings with men from the transient camps. We would hear lectures on the labor situation and put money in the collection plate. But my left-wing activities really began after I got a job as a laborer for Continental Can in San Jose. I met a girl there who was a Party functionary—she was subsidized by the Party. I fell in love with her. I had a little one-room shack I had been living in, and she moved in, and we painted it white. There were fig trees beside it, and we gathered walnuts, prunes, oranges, figs, and lived on those. I sold newspapers to make dimes, and I wrote leaflets for the Party. We worked to organize Continental Can, and we finally got them out on strike. After the plant settled the strike, we were fired. They wanted the agitators out, and we were agitators. To tell you the truth, my Communism at that time was all mixed up with my love affair. I was not a member of the Party. She was a militant Communist. I was in love with her, but she was not in love with me. I was just convenient—I wrote leaflets. I finally got tired of living with Karl Marx, and in the summer of 1934 I caught a freight. I ended up in a ding camp in San Luis Obispo, where they had hot showers."

The camp in San Luis Obispo was on a vast private estate. Gibbons and the other transients built roads and bridges for the owner and were paid by the federal government—five dollars a month, plus tobacco, work clothes, and meals. Gibbons swam in the Pacific, dug clams, caught fish, and began to develop a lifelong metaphysical fondness for islands and the sea. He and other Communist sympathizers—an Englishman called London Fog, an Icelander called Whitey, an American named Sam—drifted together and discussed world revolution. One day, when they were fed sandwiches that consisted of two pieces of bread that had been dampened with gravy, they walked off the job, shouting, "We want better food!" When Whitey tried to get the whole camp to strike, he, Gibbons, Sam, and London Fog were jailed. They managed to get off a telegram to the San Francisco office of the International Labor Defense, which, in Gibbons's words, was "a non-Commie organization that was to the left of the American Civil Liberties Union and defended many Commies." An ILD lawyer came to help them. They were given suspended sentences, with the provision that they leave San Luis Obispo County. Gibbons went to Seattle and joined the army.

When his hitch was done, he worked in Seattle and Puyallup (near Tacoma) as a carpenter, a surveyor, and a boatbuilder. He formally joined the Party and became a district organizer, or "messenger boy from higher up to the local level." There were about fifty members in his district. He worked with front organizations like the American League Against War and Fascism, and he picketed Japanese ships that were hauling scrap iron out of Seattle. "We picketed the ships because we thought scrap iron would go into munitions and come back at us." He married a girl named Ann Swanson, and they had two sons. (One of them is now an electrician in Albuquerque, and the other is an airman in Vietnam.) Gibbons and his wife caught crayfish in Washington lakes and sold most of the catch. They also gathered and sold dewberries, and, just for themselves, they collected salmonberries, blackberries, raspberries, salal berries, serviceberries, sea urchins, crabs, clams, mussels, moon shells, lamb's-quarters, purslane, wild mustard, and camass ("very much a local wild food, a sweetish and smooth-flavored bulb"). During those years, he gave more time to his political activity than to his work, and more time to wild food than to politics. When the Russians attacked Finland in 1939, he resigned from the Party. "I couldn't jump through hoops. It was the peacekeeping part of Communism that had interested me. I wasn't working for any foreign power. I was working to improve things right here. When the Russians attacked Finland, it was as if the Quakers, now, suddenly decided to support the war in Vietnam." With the coming of the Second World War, he went to Pearl Harbor, as a civilian but without his family, to build small boats for the Navy.

Gibbons and I stayed up fairly late that first night on the Appalachian Trail, in part because we could feel the curtain of ice-cold air at the front of the lean-to and we wanted to keep the fire going. In the course of a long and digressive conversation, I asked him why he had wanted to become a Communist in the first place, and he said, "A thousand men in a freight train, old women digging in garbage cans—the Communists were the only people who were trying to do anything about it. The Party was legal. I didn't see that it was decent to be anything but a Communist at that time."

"Did you believe in God while you were a Communist?"

"Yes, I guess so. I would have used a different vocabulary then. I believed in a higher right. For that matter, I'd have an awfully difficult time articulating my belief in God right now."

The perforated-steel bunks in the lean-to may have been designed to give maximum ventilation, and therefore coolness, to hikers in summer; at any rate, they gave some sort of maximum that night. Cold came up through each perforation like a separate nail. Around 3 A.M., choosing what turned out to be a warmer place, I took my sleeping bag and went out and lay down on the frozen ground. Gibbons snored right through the night, in comfort, in his bunk. At 6:45, when we got up, the temperature was seventeen degrees. Ice in the big pot was an inch thick. The fire was dead, and Gibbons was cheerful. He said, "Well, you couldn't say we're suffering like the early Christians." After we had rebuilt the fire, he asked me to husk a couple of hundred ground-cherries. I threw the husks into the flames, one by one, and they blazed like Ping-Pong balls. He, meanwhile, brewed wintergreen tea, which was hot and delicious and left an aftertaste that was clean and fresh. We put in very little sugar, because Gibbons was anxious that the subtle essence of wintergreen not be lost. We ate red wintergreen berries in lieu of orange juice or grapefruit, and they were like small mints and had the same effect as the tea. Then he stewed the ground-cherries, which were flavorful and went down very gratefully, as Gibbons might have put it. That was the entire breakfast, and it was all we needed after the heavy dinner of the night before. We were in the fourth day of the trip, and we had not felt hungry after any of the meals we had had, nor were we likely to from then on, for that noon we were going to introduce flour and baking powder, and, that evening, bacon. Before we left the campsite, I cracked and shelled a cupful of hickory nuts and stowed them away while Gibbons hung a mirror on an eave of the lean-to and shaved, for the first time since leaving home. He tried to comb his hair, which was standing almost straight on end, and he seemed to be in even better spirits than he had been in the day before. He said that he almost felt ready to keep on going, foraging across the land indefinitely.

During the morning, we made a fairly long detour to buy the supplies we needed, and we rejoined the trail just before lunch. Gibbons talked all morning about breads, cakes, and muffins, and he told me that wild-rose-petal jam is outstanding in crêpes. We had lunch beside the trail. Gibbons mixed a batter with the flour and baking powder, and into it he put the cupful of hickory nuts and a large gob of mashed persimmons. Neither then nor as the trip continued did I ever see him measure anything, nor did he once fail in his eye for proportions or in his considerable understanding of the unstable relationships between time and flame. He said not to worry about the persimmons in the batter, and he was right. Pan-baked, they gave a sweet and quiet flavor to the persimmon-and-hickory-nut cakes he served that noon. We both stuffed ourselves on them and, at my request, finished the meal with wintergreen tea.

It had been a clear morning, with the temperature going up into the middle thirties, but now the sky darkened quickly and a light rain began to fall. We had intended to forage that afternoon. Instead, we went on to the nearest campsite and took shelter. We felt smug, because our previous foraging had more than taken care of our needs; we had plenty of food and could avoid the cold rain. When we had a fire going and were getting warm and dry, I asked Gibbons what was the longest time that he had ever lived on foraged food. His answer was three years. As we sat there looking out at the rain coming down through a stand of tall white pines, he told me the story of those years.

In 1946, he found himself alone in Hawaii without a job and without much inclination to find one. His marriage had been, as he termed it, a casualty of the war, and he had learned that his wife did not want him to return to Seattle. He was something of a casualty himself, he said, because he had become debilitated by alcoholism. During the previous five years, he had built and repaired boats in Pearl Harbor until a time, near the end of the war, when a hospital ship tied up at the pier where he was working and medical corpsmen needed three full days to remove all the maimed young men whose arms, legs, and faces had been blown away. Soon thereafter, Gibbons became a conscientious objector and asked to be released from his obligations to the Navy. He was told that he could work as an attendant in a mental hospital if he preferred, and he did so until he complained strongly about the way some patients were being treated—as when he saw a powerful hose turned on a man who was locked in a barred cell. Gibbons was fired. He tried boatbuilding for a time as a private contractor, and failed. After struggling within himself over what seemed to be poor prospects for building a sound future, he decided to shelve the future and become a beachcomber in the South Pacific. He soon found that he might almost as easily have secured an appointment as a United States envoy to Tahiti. It took money and contacts to become a beachcomber in the South Seas. For example, islands that were under the control of the British or the French required all beachcombers to register and to post sizable bonds. Permits were needed for beachcombing on islands under the military control of the United States. Gibbons decided to do his beachcombing in the Hawaiian Islands, where no one cared. He bought classified space in the Honolulu *Advertiser* and described himself as a writer who would exchange yard work and maintenance work for a place to live. A deal resulted, and soon he was living beyond Dia-

mond Head in a hut that had a thatched roof and siding of matted coconut leaves. The hut stood under a kamani tree that had a limb spread
of eighty feet and released frequent showers of kamani nuts (Indian almonds). He gathered, among many things, guavas, thimbleberries,
ohelo berries, coconuts, wild bananas, figs, dates, wild oranges, breadfruit, papayas, mangoes, fish, crabs, turtles, and panini (the fruit of a
Hawaiian cactus). In season, he always had baskets of pineapples in the
hut, for Hawaiian pineapples are grown to fit machines and those that
do not fit the machines are often left in the fields. He ranged the islands
hunting wild pigs, wild cattle, wild goats, wild sheep, and axis deer. At
one point, he became so successful at trapping and selling fish and lobsters that he almost lost his status as a beachcomber. He cooked over
homemade charcoal and lathered himself with homemade coconut
soap. He made swipes, the quick-fermented liquors of the islands—
pineapple swipes, panini swipes. And he gave wild luaus, at which people drank, danced, sang all night, and ate crayfish cocktail, crab salad,
broiled lobsters, charcoal-broiled teriyaki venison steaks, wild beef,
roast boar, palm-heart salads, avocados, seaweed, guava chiffon pie,
passion-fruit sherbet, and mangoes covered with whipped coconut
cream—all at a cost to the host of no dollars and no cents. He served
the food on banana leaves.

When he had been living in the hut for a couple of years, he applied
for admission to the University of Hawaii, and entered as a thirty-six-
year-old freshman. He majored in anthropology, studied creative writing as well, and won the university's creative-writing prize. Student life
gradually drew him away from the hut and ended his full-time beachcombing. He worked part-time for the Honolulu *Advertiser* and made
up crossword puzzles in the Hawaiian language, although he could not
speak it. "That's no trick," he told me. "There are only twelve letters in
the Hawaiian language—seven consonants and five vowels." In 1948,
during a summer session at the university, he met a schoolteacher
named Freda Fryer, who had come to the islands from Philadelphia.
She, too, was divorced. They were married a year or so later. Together,
they made an exhaustive effort to find a church they could agree upon,
and eventually they decided to join the Quaker Meeting. "I became a
Quaker because it was the only group I could join without pretending to
beliefs that I didn't have or concealing beliefs that I did have," Gibbons
told me. "I could be completely honest. I'm not very orthodox." Before

long, they moved to the island of Maui, where they both taught—she kindergarten and he carpentry and boatbuilding—in the Maui Vocational School. Gibbons had been given custody of his two sons, who had lived for a time with his mother in Albuquerque, and the boys joined him in the islands. He gathered more wild food on Maui than he had on Oahu, he told me, for he had more people to feed. He kept a banana calendar. He walked the woods, made notes on the condition of ripening wild bananas, went home and marked his calendar, and returned for the bananas when they were ripe. He took his wife for long, rugged hikes in the Maui brush. She worried about centipedes and scorpions while he looked for wild pomelos and wild oranges. Week in and week out, he brought home so much wild food that they had to throw at least half of it away.

The rain stopped, or nearly, and Gibbons and I had dinner—huge, steaming mounds of winter cress with interstitial bacon, and stacks of oyster mushrooms. Winter cress is as excellent a green vegetable as there could ever be. It is tender, it has a mild and pleasant flavor that is somewhere between watercress and spinach, and it is in season from late fall until early spring. Italian Americans harvest it voraciously, Gibbons said, but most people don't even know it exists. After dinner, he reached up to a bough of one of the tall pines and gathered several hundred needles. He put them into a pot and poured boiling water over them. After steeping them for perhaps five minutes, he poured out two cups of white-pine-needle tea.

In the morning, at six-thirty, the eastern sky through the pines was orange red. The temperature was twenty-nine degrees. We decided that such a splendid day deserved to start with more white-pine-needle tea. It had in its taste the tonic qualities of the scent of pine, but it was not at all bitter. I had imagined, on first trying it the night before, that I would have a feeling I was drinking turpentine. Instead, I had had the novel experience of an outstanding but unfamiliar taste that was related to a completely familiar scent—a kind of direct translation from one idiom to another. As we stood by the fire drinking the fresh morning tea, Gibbons said that in the pine needles he had used there was about five times as much vitamin C as there would be in an average lemon. For the rest of that breakfast—the best one of the trip—we had persimmon bachelor-bread covered with maple syrup (made from the remains of the maple-sugar block) and a side dish of sautéed dandelion roots. "My God, I have enjoyed the dandelion roots on this trip!" Gibbons said. While I was cleaning up the pots, he wandered around in the woods and found a witch-hazel bush in bloom. He called to me to come and see it. Witch hazel sheds its leaves in the autumn, and then, when the forest around it is bare and winter is close, it blooms. Gibbons was excited by the find. He said that a drink of witch-hazel tea was thought by American Indians to be nearly as stimulating as a draught of rum, and he suggested that we have some for lunch. The blossoms are yellow and look something like forsythia blooms. We ran several branches through our fingers and stripped them clean.

Gibbons and I left the Appalachian Trail that morning, and, having recovered his Volkswagen, we foraged overland, slowly and miscellaneously and for the sheer pleasure of it, in a generally southerly direction. He seldom went faster than twenty-five miles an hour, but the ride would have been only slightly more dangerous if he had been driving blindfolded. As the beautiful countryside spread out before him, with all its ditches and field fringes and copses of nut trees in the sun, his eyes were rarely on the road, and he wove back and forth across it, scudded past stop signs, ignored approaching traffic, and nearly overran ten or fifteen tractors. Meanwhile, he read the land as if it were language—dock, burdock, chicory, chickweed, winter cress, sheep sorrel, peppergrass, catnip—and where something particularly interested him he stopped. We had no immediate need of all the things we gathered that morning, but Gibbons, having found them, could not pass them by. He showed me how to winnow dock seed and said that dock is a relative of buckwheat. We sat in a field and ate wild carrots. He found a wild asparagus plant—just so that I could see it, for it was out of season. We gathered brandy mint, walnuts, winter cress, watercress, dandelions, sheep sorrel, chicory, and the fruits of staghorn sumac. Once, when we were working our way along a roadside ditch opposite a farm, a woman came out of the farmhouse and craftily went to her mailbox (nothing there), the better to observe us at close hand.

Gibbons greeted her, and said, "We're just trying to find out what kinds of weeds grow here."

After she had gone back to the farmhouse, I said to him, "If you had told that lady that you were looking for something to eat for lunch, she would have thought you were crazy."

He said that would not have bothered him, but that he had learned to avoid saying he was looking for food, because when he did so people tended to feel sorry for him and to insist that he go into their houses and have a hot meal.

Angling this way and that on the old crown roads of Adams County, we came, as we had hoped to, at lunchtime, to the battlefield at Gettysburg. We stopped in a wooded cul-de-sac between two pylon monuments to Berdan's U.S. Sharpshooters. The unseasonably cold weather seemed to be gone; the temperature that noon was fifty-seven degrees. The sky was three times as blue as it had been for weeks. There was a warm breeze. Oak leaves rattled in the trees, and the leaves of other trees covered the ground and formed drifts, in places a foot deep. Gibbons went into the woods, picked up a rock that weighed at least seventy-five pounds, and carried it to a patch of sunlight, where we established a walnut-shelling factory—shell buckets, meat buckets, reject buckets—and produced a cupful of walnut meat in twenty minutes. We introduced cornmeal at that lunch, and the menu was black-walnut hush puppies and witch-hazel tea. The hush puppies, hot and filling and pervaded with the savory essence of walnut, made the second-best lunch of the trip (we still had one to go). The witch-hazel tea smelled like a barbershop, stimulated nobody, but was agreeably mild in taste. Gibbons said that its flavor had a faint hint of eucalyptus and that he didn't like it. I liked it well enough, but after the white-pine-needle tea it seemed quite ordinary. As we were leaving the battlefield, Gibbons stopped beside a long row of cannons and dug up a cluster of wild garlic.

Rain—a really heavy rain this time—came in the middle of the afternoon and ended the warmth of the day, and the foraging as well. We drove north, intending to stop for the night, and to have our final dinner of the trip, in a state park. We had been riding without conversing for a while when Gibbons cleared his throat and said, "Come listen to this little tale about the lowly, humble snail. He doesn't think, as on he labors, that he is better than his neighbors, nor that he is a little god; he knows he's just a gastropod." He kept going in this vein at some length—"False pride is never his asylum; he knows Mollusca is his phylum"—and then he explained to me that he frequently writes "biological verse," and publishes it in prose form in, among other places, *Frontiers: A Magazine of Natural History.* He also said that some of his serious verse has been published in the *Friends Journal,* and that in his long search for his own phylum as a writer he had tried all kinds of things and had spun some wild tales, such as a novel he once began about spacemen returning to earth after a thermonuclear tragedy and trying to forage wild food in the wasteland. I asked him if he thought he would ever start another novel, and he said he hoped to, but that, even with regard to his wild-food writing, his mind was forever swaying on a shaky fence between confidence and fear. He went on to say candidly that this sort of vacillation was characteristic of him generally, and that he didn't mind telling me now that he had even been afraid to start out on this trip because he had had no confidence that he could bring it off. He said he had been haunted for as long as he could remember by a sense of fraudulence, and thought that he had created failure for himself time after time in hopeless servitude to this ghost. It had been all he could do to weather the success of his published books, even though he had also been haunted for years by a desire to find himself as a writer. He said he imagined that some kind of desperate restlessness arising out of these crosswinds had made him leave Hawaii in 1953.

From the fall of 1953 through the spring of 1954, he taught at a Friends school in New Jersey, and then he moved to a six-hundred-acre farm in Greenfield, Indiana, where he became a co-founder of what he hoped would be a large agriculturally based cooperative community. "I was hot on intentional communities at that time," he said. "I had studied them, and we had even considered joining specific ones in New Zealand and Costa Rica. In Indiana, I wanted to create a community that would produce its own food." The community started on perhaps too narrow a base, having a charter population of five. The other four were Gibbons's wife, his partner (whose family owned the farm), his partner's wife, and his partner's child. Gibbons developed a truck garden and explored the area's ample varieties of wild food, but his partner spent all his time raising corn. "The corn was being bought by the government and stored until it rotted," Gibbons told me. "We were getting nowhere, so I decided to go." Before he left, he became concerned about a thirteen-year-old boy whose father and two older brothers were in prison. The boy's future was in the hands of an Indiana court. Gibbons got the court's permission to take the boy with him, and the boy lived with Gibbons and his wife for five years as a foster son. Gibbons spent most of that time at Pendle Hill, a Quaker study center in suburban Philadelphia, where students from all over the world enroll to do private study, to write theses, and to take courses under teachers such as Henry J. Cadbury, a retired professor from the Harvard Divinity School, and Howard H. Brinton, the leading American authority on Quaker history. Pendle Hill is itself a kind of cooperative community, and Gibbons became a member of the staff, taking responsibility for the maintenance of the grounds and buildings, and cooking breakfast for everyone every day. He also went to Cadbury's and Brinton's lectures and took courses in Bible, literature, social studies, philosophy, and writing. He fondly remembers Pendle Hill as "a hotbed of pacifism and peacemongers." Experimentally, he grew pokeweed in a basement there, in the hope that he could serve bleached poke to the others. They didn't like it.

Gibbons went on to tell me that in 1960 his wife volunteered to support him through her teaching for as long as he needed to write— and do nothing but write—until he was satisfied that he had won or lost his long conflict with that particular genie. "Freda pushes me, and I resent it sometimes, but I couldn't get anywhere without the pushing," he said. "She is quick and simple, and I am complicated. No matter what situation she finds herself in, she can rise to the occasion and do the sensible thing, and, of course, I'm not like that at all. She doesn't like to forage, and when I come home with wild food she sometimes says, 'Euell, could you please leave that stuff on the back porch?' Yet she supported me for two years while I wrote my first book, and it never would have been written without her." They moved from Pendle Hill to an old farmhouse at Tanguy Homesteads, a rural interracial cooperative community near Philadelphia. Within a year, he had produced *Mr. Markel Retires,* his novel about the schoolteacher who retreated into a world of wild food, and another year was required for *Mr. Markel* to be boiled in three waters and utterly metamorphosed into *Stalking the Wild Asparagus.* Gibbons had been hesitant to try a straightforward handbook of wild food, mainly because several of them existed—Nelson Coon's *Using Wayside Plants,* Oliver Medsger's *Edible Wild Plants,* sections of the Boy Scout *Handbook,* and, most detailed of all, *Edible Wild Plants of Eastern North America,* by Merritt L. Fernald, Reed L. Rollins, and Alfred C. Kinsey—the same Alfred C. Kinsey who attracted a much wider audience with reports on sexual behavior. Gibbons had never been fully satisfied with any of the wild-food manuals, however. Fernald, Rollins, and Kinsey, in Gibbons's view, had written a "dry list" and may not have tried out some of the recipes they suggested. "I can't believe they ever cooked skunk cabbage," he told me. Gibbons gathered, cooked, and ate everything he wrote about, and he rejected some foods that had been generally reported to be edible because he had found them unpalatable. "I have never successfully eaten arrow arum," he said, to give me an example. "Same with golden club. Both of them prickled my throat and burned my mouth." He sent wild food to Pennsylvania State University for analysis of its nutritive values. He read *The Journal of Lewis and Clark*, *The Journal of George Vancouver*, the observations of Captain John Smith on wild food, and the work of other early observers. He read ethno-botanies of the Iroquois, the Abnaki, the Menomini, the Cherokee, and other Indian tribes. Then, as he wrote, he included his own experiences with the plant he was discussing, gracefully and relevantly weaving his autobiography into his work. When *Stalking the Wild Asparagus* was published, it quickly established him as the master of his field—which shook him up no end.

(I was to make a visit, some weeks later, to Tanguy Homesteads, and to find that while Gibbons was doing his research for the book he was a wild Hans Christian Andersen to the children there. He fed them the foods that he tested in his kitchen, took them fishing and foraging, and one day showed them twenty-five wild foods growing within a hundred feet of a supermarket. Gibbons has been gone from Tanguy for five years now, but the children there still collect meadow mushrooms, still make cattail-flour muffins, and, at his invitation, regularly visit him in Troxelville in the summertime. "Without the common weed, Euell wouldn't have his career," one child said to me. I also learned that Gibbons had run for Thornbury Township constable on the Democratic ticket while he lived at Tanguy, but his campaign ended in failure.)

Gibbons moved to Troxelville in December 1963, but he had owned his house there for some years, having noticed in the *Friends Journal* an ad offering, for five thousand dollars, a farmhouse on eleven acres, with a peach orchard and a stream. He has let the peach orchard go wild, preferring the cornucopian wilderness that has now grown up among the old trees. There are 111 houses in Troxelville. Most of them are on one street and are as close together as houses in Manhattan, and their fronts abut the sidewalks. Gibbons's house is one of the few that is remote from this compact center. The town looks European, clustered like a walled village, with miles of open land surrounding it. The country is Pennsylvania Dutch, and the people are burghers. "People have a sort of tolerant attitude toward me there," Gibbons said. "However, it took my neighbors a long time to decide that I wasn't completely crazy." (After the trip, I asked a young man in Troxelville what he thought of Gibbons's fondness for unusual foods, and the fellow said, "It's okay, if that's his interest, but to me a weed is a weed." Several doors down the street, an old man who was sweeping the sidewalk told me proudly that Gibbons had once made violet jelly for the entire town.) Gibbons's home freezer usually contains items like fresh-frozen day-lily buds, frozen seaweed, Birds Eye lima beans, Pepperidge Farm bread, frozen gooseberries, and hickory nuts, which are easier to crack when they are frozen. Next to one another on the kitchen shelves are things like Decaf, Bisquick, dried elder blow, rose-hip jam, and boneset tea. Gibbons pays taxes of seventy-five dollars a year on his Troxelville property, and he also has to pay something called an Occupation Tax. When he told the assessor what he does for a living, he was listed as a part-time day laborer.

Few people in Troxelville are Quakers, Gibbons told me, and many of the old and frequently grand meetinghouses in that part of Pennsylvania are now nearly empty on Sundays. He and his wife go to meeting at Bucknell University, in Lewisburg, twenty-five miles away. "In meeting, of course, if anyone is moved to speak he speaks, and college professors are almost always moved to speak," he said. (A couple of weeks later, I asked one of the professors for his view of Gibbons, and he said, "People are supposed to speak when the spirit moves them. Sometimes we think Euell *plans* to be moved. Sometimes he speaks like an anarchist in meeting. He has no faith in existing institutions and says that he has no use for institutions that are killing the spirit of society." Other members told me that Gibbons has "religious depth and insight to an amazing extent" and that "he's been inspired, and he is inspiring at times, but he's not like a preacher preaching down." After meeting, people sometimes thank Gibbons for sharing his thoughts and say to him, typically, "That just spoke to my condition.")

At seven that last evening of the trip, the rain was still humming on the roof of the Volkswagen, and Gibbons and I decided that it would be pointless to try to cook in a state park. As a campsite, we chose instead a motel in Mechanicsburg. After we had registered, we unloaded our luggage, and, in the room, we spread a tarpaulin on the floor and sorted things out. Then we put in a request for ice. When it came, we opened the door only enough to get the ice bucket through the crack, since we were both somewhat self-conscious about the appearance of the room. On one of the beds were several ground-cherry plants, loaded with ripe ground-cherries; a wild carrot; a big, airy, fernlike wild-asparagus plant (a souvenir for me), full of berries; and a deadly poisonous jimsonweed, heavy with seedpods (I wanted to take that home, too). On a bedside table were nutpicks and hunting knives. The Coleman stove and the cooking pots were on the bathroom floor, and on the bathroom shelves were salt, oil, wild garlic, and the hammer. Mounds of wild food were spaced out on the tarp. The large outdoor thermometer that we had been using throughout the trip was hanging by a loop of string over the wall thermostat. The temperature indoors was seventy-five degrees. We opened the windows. Gibbons took the red fruits of the staghorn sumac and soaked them and rubbed them in a pot of cold water. After sweetening the water, he poured sumac-ade into glass tumblers, over ice. "This has no food value, but it's a nice sour drink," he said. It tasted exactly like fresh lemonade.

Gibbons set me to work peeling Jerusalem artichokes while he carved chicory crowns. In a market in Gettysburg, we had foraged two porterhouse steaks as a climactic salute to the Susquehanna River and the Appalachian Trail. We had also bought some butter, and the dinner as a whole consisted of buttered mashed Jerusalem artichokes, buttered oyster mushrooms, buttered chicory crowns, porterhouse steak rubbed with the wild garlic of the Gettysburg battlefield, and a salad of watercress, sheep sorrel, brandy mint, salt, oil, wild garlic, and red wintergreen berries. The glistening greens dotted with red berries provided an extraordinary variety and balance of tastes, and I have never encountered a salad anywhere that was more attractive or delicious than that one. The chicory crowns had much sharper overtones than the dandelion crowns we had had, and, while good in themselves, served most significantly to put the steak into relief. The steak was excellent and was made trebly so by the taste of the chicory in apposition to it. Gibbons said, "People have forgotten how to use bitter things."

At breakfast, the penultimate meal, we introduced eggs, and Gibbons made a fine wild omelette containing winter cress, watercress, and wild garlic. We had bacon as well, and pennyroyal tea. Then we packed up and headed north across the mountains toward Troxelville. The first ridge was Blue Mountain, and from it we could see, about fifteen miles away, the level ridgeline of the next one, Tuscarora Mountain. Between these two was a valley so rich with dairy farms and wooded streams that there had to be, somewhere in it, an incomparable lunch. Slowly, we foraged toward Tuscarora Mountain, passing up practically everything—wild mustard, day-lily tubers, bearing hickories, poke, chicory—in a selective search for excellence. We had crossed about two-thirds of the valley when Gibbons finally stopped. From the car, he studied a colony of small plants that were growing beside a barn. "Mallow," he said. "Let's go see if they're any good." Roughly one out of ten of the plants was heavy with seed-bearing discs, and it was these that Gibbons was looking for. Each one was round, had wedgelike segments, and, although it was only a third of an inch in diameter, remarkably resembled a wheel of cheese. Gibbons said that mallow fruits are almost universally called doll cheeses but that around that part of Pennsylvania people often call them billy-buttons. We went over to the farmhouse to get the permission of the farmer, who said, "Those billy-buttons are no good to me. Take all you want." The picking was slow, and we needed about twenty minutes to get a pint of them.

Across the rest of the valley, nothing of particular interest presented itself, and soon we were moving uphill through hardwood forests on Tuscarora Mountain. The climb became quite steep. Going around one hairpin curve, which Gibbons was somehow attending to with his peripheral vision, he suddenly swung off the road and stopped. Below us, on the inside of the curve, hanging prodigally over a ravine, were hundreds of thick bunches of wild frost grapes. They were as densely concentrated as grapes in a vineyard, probably because they had little room to expand into from such a difficult purchase on the cliffside. The vines were sturdy and about two inches through. They supported us easily, and, out over the ravine, we filled bags and buckets with grapes. Then we drove on up the mountain.

At the summit, there was a turnout area, with a plank table under a stand of oaks. The ridgeline of Tuscarora Mountain is so narrow and its sides are so steep that we seemed to be standing on a wall two thousand feet high as we looked down on either side at villages, rivers, and farms. That day was as extravagantly out of season as most of the preceding days had been, but this time with sunshine and warmth. The temperature there on the ridge was seventy-one degrees. Gibbons lighted the stove and began to cook a large potful of grapes in a little water. He cooked the mallow cheeses in water, too, and as they simmered the fluid around them took on the consistency of raw egg white. "These are the fruits of round-leaf mallow," he said. "If you cook the fruits of marsh mallow like this, the same sort of stuff comes out. The original marshmallows were made from it. Now there is no more marsh mallow in marshmallows than there are Hungarians in goulash." He stirred the doll cheeses in their clear, thick sauce. "I used to do a lot of foraging with a friend of mine who was a vegetarian," he went on. "He was an Oriental, and a vegetarian for religious reasons, and he would not eat eggs, or even gelatin. I once made a May-apple chiffon pie for him, using seaweed for gelatin and mallow instead of egg whites." When the grapes had simmered for a while, he strained them into another pot, sweetened the juice, and thickened it with flour. After draining the mallow cheeses, he stirred butter into them. Then he served lunch— buttered mallow cheeses and wild-frost-grape flummery. The mallow cheeses were both crunchy and tender, and their taste was more delicate than the taste of any cultivated vegetable I could think of. The frost-grape flummery, deep in color, was quite similar to a Scandinavian fruit soup, and it was filling. Each of these dishes could have been a flourishing entry on any luncheon menu in any restaurant anywhere at all that noon, but on a mountaintop, with hundreds of square miles of forests and valleys falling away in two directions, they were served in an atmosphere appropriate to the attainments of the greatest living wild chef.

We moved on into the second valley, and followed an indirect route to Troxelville, so that we could stop again and weigh ourselves. From notes, we made sure that we were wearing exactly the same clothes that we had been wearing when we weighed ourselves at the outset, which was not difficult, since we still had them on. We found that I had gained eight ounces. Gibbons had gained two pounds.

1968

THE FRUIT DETECTIVE

JOHN SEABROOK

One hot summer day not long ago, just as the specialty-food stores around town were putting up FIRST OF THE SEASON signs to advertise their peaches, a rare and extraordinary shipment of apricots appeared in Manhattan. They were white apricots, which you almost never see in the United States. Unlike the familiar tawny-colored varieties, these had pale, almost translucent skin, with a yellow blush. And, unlike the cottony supermarket fruit, the white apricots tasted great: a rush of sugar, with a complex, slightly acidic aftertaste. The flesh almost melted in your mouth, and the juice was so plentiful that you had to bend over while eating one, to avoid staining your shirt.

The apricots were available at Citarella, which has four branches, and only at Citarella—a fact that pleased the store's produce manager, Gregg Mufson, a great deal. Like his competitors at the other high-end specialty stores around town, such as Eli's, Dean & DeLuca, and Grace's, Mufson tries to titillate his customers by giving them uncommon fruits—curiosities that they may have encountered in a restaurant, on their travels, or on the Food Network. "Anything new, anything different, and if I can get it directly from the grower it's even better, because there's no middleman," said Mufson, who is in his mid-thirties and wears a neatly trimmed goatee. "I want them to go 'Wow!' I want to blow their minds with something. They'll eat these apricots, and they won't forget that taste, and then they'll come back and buy some more of my fruit." Mufson pays attention to the food press, so that he can be sure to have the trendy fruits and vegetables in stock. "When the *Times* did an article on rambutans"—bright-red, golf-ball-size, tendril-covered fruits from Southeast Asia, with translucent, sweet-tart flesh— "we sold ten cases of them in a couple of days." Appearance, he added, is the most important quality in attracting people to new fruit—the more colorful the better—followed by sugar. "Basically, if it's sweet, people like it," he said.

At first, not many customers paid much attention to the new apricots. "That's a white apricot," one of the produce workers in the store said when a customer asked about the fruit. "First one I ever seen," he added. But the customer went for the Apriums—yellow-skinned, pink-fleshed plum-apricot hybrids, which have become popular in the past few years.

Soon, however, word about the white apricots got out. The pastry chef at Citarella thought they were one of the best fruits he'd ever tasted. The chef Daniel Boulud bought two cases of white apricots and was "crazy for them," Mufson said; Boulud used them to make apricot galettes. The owner of Citarella, Joe Gurrera, gave a white apricot to Martha Stewart when she came into the East Hampton branch of the store, and "she was blown away by it," Mufson reported. "Blown a-way." The store sold out of its supply in a couple of days; the next shipment disappeared even more rapidly. Mufson was delighted. "My boss gave me a compliment! My boss never gives me compliments. He said, 'This is the best fruit ever. We got to get more of this stuff.' All I can say is David really scored this time."

David is David Karp, a sometime "provisioner" for specialty stores like Citarella, and a noted fruit writer. He is the Fruit Detective, a persona he invented around the time he worked as a provisioner for Dean & DeLuca. His job is to range around the country and the world and find exotic fruits, or uncommon varieties of common fruits. In recent years, he has traveled to Madagascar to investigate vanilla, to Sicily to hunt for blood oranges, and to the Australian outback to research bush fruits. But most of his work is performed in California. The Fruit Detective is a familiar figure at the Santa Monica Farmers' Market—he's the one in the pith helmet with the leather chin strap, his fruit knife in a holster on his belt, looking like a slightly demented forest ranger as he interrogates farmers with rapid-fire questions and eats their fruit. Readers of Karp's articles, which appear regularly in the *Los Angeles Times* and *Gourmet,* follow him on his quest for pomelos, Asian pears, mulberries, and persimmons. Most people experience a truly great piece of fruit very rarely—that perfect peach you ate one summer day long ago, a taste you hope for in every subsequent peach you eat but never quite recapture. Karp's goal is to have that experience again and again.

I first heard about the Fruit Detective from a friend, an organic farmer in southern New Jersey named Torrey Reade.

"Anything new on the farm?" I asked her one day about a year ago.
"Well, we had a visit from the Fruit Detective."

"What's a fruit detective?"

Torrey wasn't sure, exactly, except that the fellow was passionate, almost manic, about fruit. "He left his business card—wait, I think I may
have it in my wallet."

The card said DAVID KARP, FRUIT DETECTIVE. It had raised lettering that looked slightly crooked, and it gave a residence in Venice, California. The name reminded me that I once knew a David Karp, whose
passage from brilliant Upper East Side private-school kid to heroin ad-
dict was a sad but familiar story of money, drugs, and wasted talent. I
stood there rubbing my finger over the lettering, wondering what had
become of that David Karp, while Torrey described her encounter.

"We were trying to grow Charentais melons," she explained,
"which is a French exotic, and he had heard about us from a health-
food store in Princeton. Somehow he found us and came down to see
about getting some for Dean & DeLuca. He was wearing this funny
hat and shorts—no one in South Jersey wears shorts in the summertime, because of the bugs. We showed him our melons, which he liked
but didn't love, and then he started asking, 'What else do you have?' So
we told him about the pear tree that was growing near the old privy. He
demanded to see it immediately. It produces these tiny, inedible pears,
but he thought it might be an heirloom variety and got very excited—
he was actually hopping around in the weeds."

The more she described the Fruit Detective, the more he sounded
like my David Karp. I kept the card and, over the winter, sent the Fruit
Detective an e-mail. After he confirmed that he was the person I was
thinking of, we talked on the phone and made plans to have lunch the
next time he came to New York on "fruit work."

I hadn't known David Karp well, but I had heard a lot about him from
some friends who had grown up with him in Manhattan and told
memorable Karp stories. Karp's father, Harvey Karp, was an extraordinarily successful businessman, whose house in East Hampton was reputed to be a palace. David was brilliant. He was fluent in Latin, and,
it was said, read only the poets of late antiquity. He published a translation of the sixth-century writer Venantius Fortunatus when he was

twenty. Not only did he get 800s on the SATs but he got 800s on a friend's SATs, too—and he did it while coming down from LSD. He also knew more about punk rock than any of his friends, and he was well versed in drugs.

After graduating from Wesleyan, in 1979 (word of the SAT caper had got back to the authorities, and he and his friend were suspended for a year, but he finished in three years), Karp worked on Wall Street in risk arbitrage and option trading, where he was soon making more than a hundred thousand dollars a year. He collected rare books and rare wines. He produced a Lydia Lunch album, *13.13,* in 1982, and cultivated friends in the downtown rock world. But his dabbling in heroin had turned into an every-weekend habit, and in 1984, after drugs were found in his desk at work, Karp got fired. At this point, a less apocalyptic spirit might have stepped back from the dark side; Karp moved into the Hôtel Plaza Athénée in Paris with his fashion-model girlfriend and a supply of heroin, and indulged in a life of total hedonism—sleeping all day, living off pastries from Lenôtre, getting high and staying up all night reading Saint Augustine (in Latin), and, when his drugs ran out, taking the Concorde back to New York to buy some more. Eventually, he ran through most of his money and returned to New York, where he was soon supporting his habit by selling off his book collection and by dealing heroin to friends and friends of friends.

Karp has been completely sober—no drugs, alcohol, or cigarettes—for almost twelve years. In 1990, after waking up on a floor strewn with broken glass and Cap'n Crunch cereal ("Junkies love sweet stuff"), he had allowed his parents to put him in detox at Gracie Square Hospital, and he then spent seven months in rehab in Southern California, doing the twelve-step program. On returning to the world, he called up a college friend, Eric Asimov, who writes the "$25 and Under" column for the *Times,* and proposed a freelance piece about apricots. Fruit was connected in Karp's mind to the great love of his life, a woman he had met in college, with whom he had shared an interest in collecting fruit-crate art and the elaborately decorated wrappers around blood oranges. "I thought it would intrigue her if I became a fruit expert," he explained. He'd try to find great fruit, and woo her with it. He got the fruit, but not the woman. "This is very pathetic," he told me. "The story of unrequited love. But what can I say? She was the love of my life." In the course of pursuing her, he began amassing "dossiers" on different fruits, which contained the names of thousands of fruit growers, breeders, marketers, wholesalers, and retailers. Ten years later, he is a unique source of information on the fruit industry—a vital link between the "knowers" who love obscure fruit and the "growers" who cultivate it.

Karp moved to California in 1999, because that's where so much of the nation's fruit comes from, and he lives in a small cottage in Venice with his cat, Sahara, who, he is convinced, once saved him from dying of an overdose by licking his face until he woke up. When he isn't searching for fruit, he collects books about fruit, compiles songs about fruit, and corresponds with fruit lovers all over the world—chefs, specialty stores, and amateur fruit enthusiasts who simply want to know the difference between a Pluot, an Aprium, and a plumcot. Does he have any other interests? Aardvarks, Karp says. "I love them, because most people think they're unattractive, but I think they're incredibly soulful." Once, when he was visiting the Philadelphia Zoo, he climbed into the anteater pen, hoping to commune with the animals, but instead experienced "a nasty confrontation with the business end of an anteater."

We met in April. In the intervening years, Karp had lost the hair on the top of his head. "I've grown glabrous," he said, using the term of art for a fuzzless nectarine. He looked very fit, not at all like a former junkie—more like a guy who eats a lot of fruit.

Over lunch, he told me that he had recently wrapped up a research project on bitter almonds ("I'm not, generally speaking, a nut enthusiast") and was hot on the trail of European greengage plums, which are common abroad but extremely rare in the United States. "Have you had one? Oh, my God, you'll die when you taste one—it's an atom bomb of flavor. I'm convinced there's a small planting somewhere in California, and I won't stop until I find it." He didn't eat much of his pasta, and what he did eat he liberally coated with dried chile peppers, a shaker of which he carries in his black canvas bag. He scolded me for drinking a Coke: "That stuff is bad for you. Have you ever seen what it will do to a penny?"

After he had finished his lunch, he said, "Okay, ready to eat some mind-blowing fruit?" It is Karp's custom, whenever he meets people for a meal, to bring along remarkable fruit. Eric Asimov recalls an occasion when the Fruit Detective turned up with a bright-red fruit from West Africa called a miracle fruit (*Synsepalum dulcificum*), which, Karp said, had a startling effect on the taste buds: for an hour after you've eaten it, even the sourest foods taste sweet. "I tried one, and then I ate a sour lemon," Asimov said. "I was stunned at how sweet it became."

Karp took from his bag a large, heart-shaped, scaly greenish fruit that I had never seen before—a cherimoya, a fruit native to South America. Taking out his grapefruit knife, he concentrated his full attention on slicing into the white, custardy flesh and peeling several sections for me. The focus he brought to this task, the specialized equipment he used, and the obvious tactile pleasure he took in the procedure, combined with the prospect of an imminent mind-blowing experience, were all powerfully reminiscent of the David Karp of twenty years ago. And, as promised, the fruit was amazing.

One day in 1962, a Mormon missionary walked into a Safeway in Los Angeles and asked for a Chinese gooseberry. The produce manager didn't know what that was, so he asked the main produce buyer for Safeway, who, in turn, called Frieda Caplan, the founder of Frieda's Finest, a local wholesaler of specialty produce items. She didn't know, either. A few months later, a broker representing New Zealand farmers was walking around the L.A. wholesale produce market, trying to sell Chinese gooseberries. The other produce buyers weren't interested, but Caplan, remembering the Safeway buyer's query, said, "I'll take all you've got," and that turned out to be 2,400 pounds. "No one is ever going to buy something called a Chinese gooseberry," a shipping official told Caplan. The rind of the gooseberries was kind of furry and reminded him of New Zealand's national bird, so he suggested naming the fruit after it—the kiwi.

People who grow and market unusual fruits tell that story a lot, usually as a way of illustrating the potential that exists in the American marketplace for something new. Although the United States is the most ethnically diverse country on earth, that diversity is not reflected in the fruit stocked by the average supermarket. The mango, which is one of the most popular fruits worldwide, is not among the top ten American fruits (which are, in descending order, bananas, apples, watermelons, oranges, cantaloupes, grapes, grapefruit, strawberries, peaches, and pears). Our vegetables are considerably more diverse than our fruits. Portobello mushrooms, arugula, fennel, radicchio, mesclun, Swiss chard, and jicama—all specialty items ten years ago—are now in American supermarkets across the country, but sapotes, lychees, and loquats are not. American travelers in Asia and Latin America find many delicious fruits—jackfruit, longan, and breadfruit—that are never available fresh at home. This is because the United States Department of Agriculture has outlawed the importing of certain foreign-grown tropical fruits to prevent the spread of tropical pests. But two years ago the USDA began allowing papayas and rambutans grown in Hawaii to be imported to the mainland after they had been treated with electron beams—the same process that neutralizes anthrax spores in the mail (though anthrax requires a much higher dose). The new technology, many in the exotic-fruit world believe, will greatly expand Americans' awareness of the fruit that the rest of the world eats, and bring a cornucopia of new items to the produce department.

Part of being a fruit detective means figuring out what will be the next kiwi. That's not Karp's only interest; he spends at least as much time tracking down the classic varieties of familiar fruits as he does sleuthing exotics. But the intrigue and potential payoff implicit in the next big fruit are irresistible. When I saw Karp in April, he was enthusiastic about the prospects of the pitahaya, which is grown in Central America and in Asia, where it's known as dragon fruit. He talked up dragon fruit during his meeting with Gregg Mufson, of Citarella, a few days after our lunch. "Giant, flaming-pink, spineless member of the cactus-pear family, the most spectacular-looking fruit I've ever seen," Karp told Mufson, practically spitting with excitement. He said that while some varieties aren't so tasty—"they taste like a snow cone, like they were made of gelatinized mousse with sugar"—others are much more interesting: the magenta-colored flesh has the texture and flavor of watermelon, sometimes with a hint of strawberry.

Mufson was initially skeptical about dragon fruit, but after listening to Karp he got more curious.

"Know where we can get some?" he asked.

"I have a connection," Karp said, with a manic gleam in his eye.

Karp told Mufson that although no foreign-grown pitahayas were currently allowed into the country, he knew of a "top secret" planting, which was about three hours south of Los Angeles, outside the desert town of Borrego Springs. The planting was a partnership among a specialty-produce grower, Kevin Coniff, who had propagated a variety of pitahaya for Southern California; a farmer, Thomas Antel, who owns the land where the pitahaya plants were growing; and a large wholesaler of fresh produce, D'Arrigo Brothers, which was putting up the money. The reason the pitahaya planting was secret was that the partnership, or "consortium," as Karp delighted in calling it, was trying to develop an exclusive American market for dragon fruit, and they didn't want their plans publicized before they were ready. "It's like opening a movie in L.A. or New York. They'll want to get it into fancy markets and affluent areas, with a lot of foodies and food press, and the word spreads from there."

Mufson said that D'Arrigo Brothers had done something similar with broccoli rabe. Over the past ten years, the company created hardier varieties of broccoli rabe, so that what was once a specialty item has become available year-round, with D'Arrigo Brothers controlling most of the distribution. "Nearly all the broccoli rabe that comes into New York, the D'Arrigos handle it," Mufson said.

Karp slapped his fist into his palm. "They're up to the same thing with dragon fruit!" he exclaimed. "Boy, this sounds like a case for the Fruit Detective, if ever there was one."

Mufson stared at him. He had never met anyone like the Fruit Detective before.

In mid-June, I flew out to Los Angeles and joined Karp for five days of fruit work. Before this trip, I imagined that David Karp was a man who had been redeemed by fruit—someone who had found in fruit a way of escaping his demons. What I came to realize over the course of our five days together—five very long days—was that Karp had not really banished his demons at all. He'd just found a way of channeling his particular needs and talents (the desire for esoteric knowledge, the pursuit of extreme pleasure, a sympathy for shady characters, and experience in dope dealing) into a career as a purveyor of amazing fruit—a career, it turns out, that serves those needs and talents very nicely.

Much of our time together was spent in the cramped cab of Bessie, as Karp calls his white Ford Ranger pickup truck, which became ever more cramped as it filled with fruit during our travels. Days began early and ended late, but Karp was never tired. "All I need is my morning fruit fix," he'd say cheerfully, offering me a slice of "exquisite" Snow Queen white nectarine from Reedley, California, as I blearily slid into the cab.

We stopped at farmers' markets and roadside stands along the way. Karp has been known to conduct stakeouts of certified farmers' markets that he suspects of being "cheaters" (farmers who buy fruit from wholesalers, remove the stickers, and sell it as their own); if he finds proof, he may publish the cheaters' names in the *Los Angeles Times*. We didn't catch any on our trip, but when Karp found people selling fruit that was inaccurately labeled he would instruct them on its true heritage. In one market, he found farmers from Vera Ranch, near Vallejo, selling plums called mirabelles, which, he explained to the woman behind the counter, weren't mirabelles but myrobalans. "These are much too large, totally out of season, and there is a tartness in the skin of mirabelles these don't have, and mirabelles generally have a clingstone"—a pit that is attached to the flesh.

"Wow," said the woman. "You know your stuff."

In the truck, we talked of fruit constantly. Karp is especially passionate about stone fruit—apricots, peaches, nectarines, plums, and cherries—and, because it was cherry and apricot season, we spent a lot of time on those fruits. We discussed the genealogy of different varieties, and the way the great varieties were described in the works of fruit literature that Karp most admires—chiefly, Robert Hogg's *The Fruit Manual: A Guide to the Fruits and Fruit Trees of Great Britain* (fifth edition, 1884) and Edward A. Bunyard's *The Anatomy of Dessert* (1929). Karp quoted, from memory, passages about the "melting" quality Bunyard prized; after a while, it was hard to tell when he was quoting and when he wasn't. "At its ripest, it is drunk rather than eaten," he'd say, referring to Coe's Golden Drop plum. Discussing the transparent gage, he pronounced, "A slight flush of red and then one looks into the depths of transparent amber as one looks into an opal, uncertain how far the eye can penetrate." If I got something wrong or forgot a point about fruit made in an earlier conversation, Karp was quick to correct me. By the end of five days of fruit talk in the fruitmobile, I was counting the minutes to the time I could say goodbye and not have to talk about fruit anymore.

I also watched Karp eat a lot of fruit. I saw him grazing in a cherry orchard with the farmer, who, after sampling cherries for half an hour, had to run for the bathroom. Craig Ledbetter, an apricot breeder with the Department of Agriculture, whom we met near Fresno, said, "David eats fruit that I wouldn't touch, and I eat a lot of fruit. Soft, half-rotten stuff on the ground—he has no problem putting that into his mouth."

On our first day, we drove down to Borrego Springs, in the hope of seeing the pitahaya planting. But Thomas Antel, the landowner, would let us view the plants only from across the road. Karp, clad in his pith helmet, attempted to extract information from Antel about the consortium's intentions. (When I asked later if the pith helmet was necessary, Karp said that he was always getting clobbered by falling fruit, and that last year in Hawaii he had been struck on the head from the height of twenty feet by a durian—a delicious but terrible-smelling fruit familiar in Asia. "Without my helmet, that durian would have killed me," he said.)

"So how are the plants doing?" Karp asked, taking out his notebook.

"It's a learning experience, David, a learning experience," Antel said, looking nervously at the notes Karp was taking. "What can I tell you? I wish I could show you the plants, but there's too much money involved to screw this up." He rubbed his face hard with both hands, and his mood seemed to darken. "People feel a sense of entitlement, like they can just come down here and see what we're doing."

Karp was undaunted. "Where did the breeder get his breeding stock from?" he demanded. "Because they say there are some varieties that taste better than others."

"They may be right, David, they may be right. Look, I can't talk about this. There's some very big players involved in this thing, and they don't care who gets hurt—that's just the way it is."

The agricultural landscape in which the Fruit Detective travels is made up mostly of small organic-fruit-growing operations—farms of mainly a hundred acres or less, many of which produce the older varieties of plums, apricots, peaches, and apples that were loved by generations of Americans before the coming of the hardier but flavorless supermarket varieties. These farmers survive by looking for niches. A niche could be a classic variety of fruit that the big commercial growers don't produce, such as the Blenheim apricot, which is, in the Fruit Detective's opinion, one of the best-tasting fruits in the world. Or a niche could be a brief window of time in the growing season of a particular item when the commercial producers don't have any fruit and the small farmer can name his price. But since the passage of the North American Free Trade Agreement, in 1994, many of the larger growers of commodity fruits, such as tomatoes and mangoes, are finding that they can't compete with the cheaper labor and production costs in Mexico, and so they are also looking for niches in order to survive.

"The marketing window keeps getting smaller and smaller," said Andy Mariani, who farms eighty acres, most of which are devoted to cherries—Black Republican and Rainier, among other varieties—in the Santa Clara Valley. "We used to have a window here between cherries from Stockton and cherries from Washington. First, it was a couple of weeks, then a couple of days. Now it's almost nothing. The Stockton growers use sprays to retard the ripening process, so they can sell when the price is highest." Mariani's cherry harvest was in full swing on the day we visited, and, as a result of an abrupt downturn in cherry prices caused by the Stockton farmers, he had lost his "candy bar"—an expression sometimes used in the fruit world to describe a lucrative crop. "We just lost seventy-five thousand dollars in one day," Mariani said. "I would have been better off in the stock market."

Karp worships farmers like Mariani and, as a writer, takes every opportunity to promote their efforts. Eric Asimov said recently, "David is more like a wine writer than like a food writer. He brings that level of connoisseurship and obsessive attention to detail—the importance of the soil, the cultivation methods, and the growing region. Wine writers talk about the importance of *terroir*, or place; David is the first writer to bring that concept to fruit." He added, "Grape growers make the cover of wine magazines, but you never read about the great peach or cherry growers, except in David's pieces."

Most food writing is about cooking—it's less about the ingredients than about the rendering of those ingredients, and the consuming of them in communal settings. Karp is interested in the primal act of tasting—eating fruit right from the tree, vine, or bush. ("I'm not a foodie," he says. "I'm a fruitie.") His goal is sensual pleasure, but he has a rarefied idea of what fruit should taste like. The particular kind of taste he's after is one that the nineteenth-century writers on fruit described as "high flavor"—a fecund, almost gamy taste that, according to Karp, has been all but lost as fruits have been bred for mass production and long-distance shipping. "High flavor is the flavor of a pheasant, hung until high," he said. "You bite into the fruit, you taste the sugar, the texture, the acidity, and there's an almost overpowering aroma. That's what fruit should taste like. But Americans don't know that, because most of the fruit we eat is trash fruit." A real peach, allowed to ripen on the tree, is too fragile to withstand the rigors of a cross-country journey by truck or train, and so breeders have created low-acid, high-sugar peaches, which can be picked when they're still very hard but still taste sort of sweet.

We found the white apricots on a small farm in Brentwood, about an hour east of San Francisco. The farmer was Ross Sanborn, who is eighty-two years old. He wore faded denim overalls and had a full head of white hair and a face deeply browned from years in the sun. ("Hey, looks like you're going on a safari!" he said when he saw Karp.) Sitting in the shade of his porch, Sanborn told us that he had been trying to breed white apricots for almost thirty years, working with plant material he obtained from Morocco and Iran in the 1970s. Finally, he said, he believed he had come up with what he'd hoped was "the perfect 'cot." He called it an angelcot.

After we had finished talking, we followed Sanborn out to the part of the orchard where the white apricots were growing. Karp went up to a tree, picked an angelcot from it, and held it in the tips of his long fingers, caressing the velvety "pubescence," which is the fruitie term for the fuzz. "There's something so sensuous about apricots—of all the fruits, they are the most like a woman's breast," he said, denying himself the pleasure of tasting the fruit as long as he could. He unsheathed his fruit knife, neatly halved the 'cot, and examined the pit. Then he bent at the waist and brought the pitless half up to his mouth, inhaled, and bit. The fruit melted. The juice ran down his chin. A bite, then another bite, and all that remained of the apricot were the bits of flesh sticking to the Fruit Detective's face.

2002

GONE FISHING

MARK SINGER

A poll that I recently conducted among several of David Pasternack's friends and colleagues yielded a nearly unanimous result.
The question was: If Dave were a fish, what kind would he be? The answer was: a tuna. One respondent, Artie Hoernig, a commercial fisherman who also operates a retail fish market and restaurant in Island
Park, New York, was more specific. "Absolutely a bluefin tuna," he said,
referring to a species that I'd heard Pasternack characterize as "like a
freight train swimming in the ocean." A minority opinion from his father, Mel ("striped bass—wild, big, good fighter"), dovetailed with
Dave's own measured self-appraisal: "Half tuna, half striper, I guess.
Tuna for the thrill of the chase, the hunt. I love to catch a tuna. And
striped bass is the king of the fish inshore. It's our native fish, and I
grew up catching 'em, you know." He went on, "Basically, I've fished my
whole life. I started fishing with my father when I was about five, in Jamaica Bay, off of Floyd Bennett Field, in Brooklyn. Snapper, bluefish,
blowfish, flounder. I fished regularly with a guy named Captain Lou. I
always fished with older guys. It was, like, somebody would introduce
me and they'd take me under their wing. People don't necessarily do
that anymore, which is too bad, because that's how you learn—'You're
tying it *that* way? No, you tie it *that* way.' If you wanna catch a lot of
fish, you've gotta take an aggressive approach. And what's the point of
fishing if you don't wanna catch 'em?"

Pasternack is the chef and co-creator of Esca, a five-year-old fish
restaurant on West Forty-third Street in Manhattan. His recipes are
unaffectedly refined, and he defines his culinary creativity in elliptical,
prosaic terms: "It's passion, plus knowing when something needs a little something"—the emblem of a cook, or, for that matter, any artist
who knows what to put in and what to leave out. A focused, sensible
fellow, he understands the fish business better than just about anyone,
in ways intuitive, visceral, and pragmatic. Before dawn one spring
morning at the Fulton Fish Market, as we were admiring a machete-
wielding Ecuadorean who, with the celerity of a Jedi, was quartering

and trimming a mattress-sized yellowfin tuna, Pasternack noticed a neatly pressed silver-haired gent standing nearby. He said to me softly, "A good old-fashioned 'made' guy. Nice guy. But he's notorious. The market was run by 'em for years, until they passed the RICO laws, and then these guys were supposed to be banned. I'm surprised to see him here, even though he owns the business. And if you print the name of the business I'll have no glass left in my windows."

Local climate and geography have surprisingly little bearing upon the experience of eating in New York. The foods most closely identified with the city at street level—pizza, pastrami, pretzel, dim sum, falafel—all made their way here on immigrant tides. And the past decade has witnessed an exoticism that often seems more than a little forced. When a phenomenon like Jean-Georges Vongerichten creates an empire in Manhattan, his ambition—which presumes, of course, that a critical mass of people will ante up the equivalent of a mortgage payment for a meal—reflects a high-wire determination to move far beyond his Alsatian roots. (French-Thai fusion! Malay-Thai street food!) Pasternack happens to be Jewish and Esca happens to be resolutely Italian (if unlike any other Italian restaurant in the city). Whatever. Compared with New York's other celebrated chefs, he has stayed unusually close to home; Esca is, among other things, the direct consequence of his years of experience with a rod and reel. Pasternack lives in Long Beach and, for a while, had a habit of schlepping to Esca, on the Long Island Rail Road, plastic garbage bags containing fish that he'd caught the previous day. "But I'd be exhausted by the time I made the walk from Penn Station," he said. So he persuaded his wife, Donna Peltz, to make deliveries in their 1988 Toyota sedan, which she did until two years ago, when he decided that he could justify investing in a truck. No other restaurant in the city—not now and presumably not ever—offers year-round wild game that has been personally bagged by the chef.

Before Esca ("bait," in Italian), Pasternack worked for two decades in a succession of mostly French-themed New York restaurants, bistros, and brasseries, and before that he attended culinary school at Johnson & Wales, in Providence, Rhode Island. During his year and a half in Providence, he drove every weekend to his hometown, Rockville Centre, a Nassau County suburb only a few miles inland (or only a madeleine-like sea breeze) from the South Shore of Long Island. Then,

after he found work and began living in Manhattan, he stayed connected to the old neighborhood by renting a room or an apartment
close to the beach. As often as he could manage, he spent his days off
fishing, in the bays and inlets and in the wide-open Atlantic, from the
Rockaways to Montauk Point. He took stripers, tuna, flounder, fluke,
sea bass, porgies, cod, weakfish, bluefish, mackerel, the inadvertent
shark—in his concise inventory, "whatever swam." Though there's no
mistaking Pasternack for a literary type, spending time with him got
me thinking about the way a chef's evolution can mirror that of a
novelist. In the same way that a fiction writer can rely upon the dictum "Write about what you know," Pasternack, as much as a New
York–born-and-bred chef can, has thrived by cooking best what he
knows best.

In the differentiation between executive chefs, celebrity chefs, and
working chefs, Pasternack is plainly in his element in the third category. He doesn't have a cell phone or respond to e-mail, but he's easy to
get hold of. His office, in effect, is the same spot in the kitchen where
he cuts fish, orders supplies, conceives menus, plates food, and super-
vises his staff. He's at Esca five, sometimes six days a week, typically
from 10 A.M. to 11 P.M. Though he rents a pied-à-terre on the East
Side, most nights he takes the train home to Long Beach, where he and
Donna live with their year-old daughter, Ruby, in a redbrick and rose-
stucco bungalow with a detached garage. My first glimpse inside the
garage was a moment of recognition: suspended from the rafters were
two punching bags. Days when Pasternack is neither working nor fishing, he likes to ride his bicycle along the Long Beach boardwalk—it extends nearly two and a half miles—and then spend a half hour
thumping the heavy bags. On or off the job, whether he's giving instructions in Spanglish to a fish cleaner ("Antonio, you're gonna take
this *abajo* and this *abajo* and you're gonna keep 'em *separado*, okay?") or
butchering a side of veal or setting the hook in a fish that's on the line,
he has the authority of a nimble middleweight, at once firmly grounded
and light on his feet. He's five nine, with powerful arms and shoulders
and a creeping waistline. At forty-one, he looks his age. He has short
light-brown hair that's receding and thinning at the crown, a nose you
notice, broad cheeks, a strong jaw, blue-gray eyes, and often a slightly

weary demeanor. His smile is wry and asymmetrical, listing toward starboard. About every third day, he's clean-shaven.

The kitchen at Esca is relatively small—two levels, six hundred square feet in all—but for the twenty or so prep cooks, line cooks, runners, and dishwashers who circulate during peak hours, it probably feels less crowded than others they've worked in, because the boss isn't inclined toward histrionics or harangues. He speaks in a low, even register, with an inflection and delivery that are pure South Shore, which is basically blue-collar Brooklynese that's moved farther out on Long Island. "Saint Francis said you have to speak in the vernacular, and that's Dave," Mel Pasternack, a semiretired trial attorney, told me. "When he talks to a fishmonger, he speaks fishspeak."

"The fish business is very complicated, very complicated," Dave says when the conversation turns to catch limits, size limits, quotas for different species in different jurisdictions, and the vagaries of a marketplace in which the law of supply and demand regularly conflicts with conservation laws that often strike commercial fishermen as impractical and convoluted. In general, his sympathies lie with the fishermen. Which is to say that Pasternack is a resourceful guy who has cultivated mutually beneficial relationships with certain other guys: "My striped-bass guy called this morning. . . . I was talking to a guy who just came back from Florida. He was snook fishing every day. . . . Whenever Mike goes cod fishing, I'm his guy. . . . The way they ship stuff now is pretty amazing. Here, try this opah. It's also called moonfish. Fatty, right? A lot of natural fat to it. Kinda has that tuna texture? With a completely different flavor. Very buttery, almost swordfishy. Opah comes from somewhere in the Pacific. I can speak to a guy, he'll call me at eleven or twelve o'clock, the fish'll be here when I get here the next morning. . . . A lot about buying fish is spontaneity. A guy called me yesterday and told me what he had and what he recommended. You'd have to be an idiot to buy what he didn't recommend. I talked to a guy this morning, he was unloading a boat of monkfish. I bought some of the monkfish livers from him, to make pâté. He also had big jumbo scallops. And I bought a box of blackfish from him. . . . I called my crab guy last week. To find out when he's gonna have blue claws and softshells. He told me to call him back in a month. I call guys all the time."

The great majority of restaurants in the city, from cozy to corporate, buy all their fish through a single supplier. Pasternack deals with at least fifty: brokers; wholesalers; gillnetters; dredgers; and pinhook, or rod-and-reel, anglers. On any given day, salmon might arrive from Alaska; abalone and black cod from British Columbia; giant clams from Puget Sound; mahogany clams, sea urchins, and diver scallops from Maine; spot prawns from Santa Barbara; pink snapper and John Dory from New Zealand; yellowtail from Japan or California; red snapper, pompano, mahi-mahi, and grouper from the Gulf of Mexico; sardines from Portugal or California; scorpionfish, branzino, orata, and calamari from the Mediterranean; red mullet from Senegal; Arctic char from Iceland; octopus from South Carolina, Portugal, or Thailand; halibut, hake, skate, monkfish, fluke, flounder, kingfish, weakfish, sea bass, striped bass, scallops, sole, and tuna from up and down the East Coast; oysters from Long Island, Rhode Island, Maine, the Canadian Maritimes. Almost all of it is wild, and none of it has ever been frozen, nor will it be. (The freezer at Esca, no larger than a domestic fridge, is reserved for pasta and desserts.) The fish travel by truck, express mail, air freight, courier, UPS. Some arrive at the kitchen still flopping.

Pasternack speaks almost daily with Rod Mitchell, the owner of Browne Trading Company, in Portland, Maine, where hundreds of boats a month unload at the Portland Fish Exchange, the largest display fish auction in the country. Mitchell, who has been described as the "fish purveyor to the stars" but prefers to call himself a "fish picker," combines his talent for scrutinizing individual fish with a global overview of the seafood trade, and he regards Pasternack as an ideal customer. "Dave's quest is to have as many different kinds of fish as he can and still be able to sell them all," he told me. "He wants to know every kind of fish that he can get his hands on. If I mention something he hasn't heard of before, he says, 'Send it.' He can get something new and taste it raw, and he knows exactly what to do with it. I'm about to send him a new fish from Brazil, pintado. It's also called a tigerfish. Amazing-looking. It makes you imagine that it could walk. It has no scales, and its skin is colored like a tiger's. It's never been imported to the United States before. It's a fish we found at a seafood exposition in Brussels. The minute I saw it, I thought of Dave."

Every weekday, Pasternack dispatches a buyer, Roberto Nuñez, and a driver ("Tony, the truck guy") to the Fulton Fish Market. About once a week, he shows up at the Fulton market for the predawn rounds (a ritual that, lamentably, will soon be drained of its echt-Manhattan flavor,

when the market relocates to Hunts Point, in the Bronx). Pasternack
moves briskly from stall to stall, with an open mind and the confidence
that if he doesn't see what he likes ("Some weeks the market's good,
some weeks it has shit") he'll find something else somewhere else that
will excite him. Certain dishes appear on the Esca menu 363 days a
year: Sicilian fish stew, Amalfitano fish soup, linguine with mahogany
clams, spaghetti with a whole lobster, squid-ink pasta with cuttlefish,
fritto misto, marinated anchovies and sardines, grilled octopus. But the
guiding principle is that everything is provisional—dependent upon
the quality of the available ingredients and upon Pasternack's sensibility ("There is no system; it's more about mood")—and that, of course,
there are always plenty more fish in the sea.

Invariably, when I've dropped by Esca to see Pasternack, I've found
him just inside the open doorway of the kitchen, on the ground-floor
level, armed with a very sharp knife. The first fish I watched him perform surgery on was a forty-pound halibut that had recently been
swimming in the vicinity of Portland. His workstation—situated to afford an unobstructed view of the line cooks and prep cooks at the grill,
sauté, and pasta stations, and to allow him to inspect every dish before
it leaves the kitchen—is two and a half feet deep and nine feet wide,
sufficient to accommodate the occasional four-hundred-pound tuna.
His knife was German, with a twelve-inch blade, one of a dozen of
varying sizes that he keeps in a plastic tray within easy reach. "I sharpen
my knives every Saturday," he said. "Nobody touches my knives. Not
even my wife. They're scared."

Downstairs, the halibut had already been scaled, gutted, and shorn
of its dorsal and pelvic fins. It took Pasternack about a minute to remove the first fillet, drawing the knife handle toward him in sure, even
strokes, with his left hand, as he proceeded along the spine. He lifted
and flipped the fish, reinserted the knife laterally, just behind the pectoral fin, cut to the caudal fin, and severed the second fillet. He separated the flesh from the skin of both fillets as cleanly and economically
as if he were peeling apples. The carcass was headed for the soup kettle, but not quite yet. "The head's gonna be my lunch," he said as he
harvested two plum-sized lumps of cheek meat. Then he began trimming the fillets. "Pretty nice halibut," he said. "This time of year they
can be on the spawn. The meat can be a little milky." Not in this instance, however. From each fillet he cut out the bloodline, a dark-meat

layer that extends lengthwise below the dorsal fin, and sectioned the collar into strips for fritto misto. "You know, this is a fish that you're paying six and a half dollars a pound for. You're gonna lose at least thirty-five or forty percent. So you've got to utilize the whole animal. That's where your knife really makes all the difference." The halibut's primary destiny was to be carved into seven-ounce serving portions, poached, and accompanied by smashed fava beans from Pennsylvania and a vinaigrette made with ramps from upstate New York. Twenty-seven dollars, à la carte.

Esca has seating for 60 to 110 in pleasant weather, when an outdoor patio is opened—and on a normal day each table fills four times. Pasternack fillets and slices fish throughout the morning and during lunch, breaks for a couple of hours in midafternoon, and then resumes until seven o'clock. He multitasks in a self-assured manner—announces orders to the line cooks; talks on the phone; consults with the front-of-the-house managers, nodding when he hears that there's someone in the dining room whom he should meet and greet; gives instructions to the kitchen runners, who shuttle one aluminum tray after another laden with freshly gutted fish—all the while wielding knives with the same rhythmic, delicate precision. How often does he cut himself? "Only when somebody asks me that question. No, actually, not that much. But I'm due." A wall phone with an extra-long cord rings at all hours, and Pasternack usually answers it himself, always with the same greeting: "Kitchen."

Between the moment he first looks at a fish and the moment he finishes filleting it, he often changes his mind about what he's going to do with it. If it's perfectly fresh yet doesn't look perfect (it hasn't been bled properly; it's bruised; it was caught in a net and drowned and the flesh is now too opaque; spawning season is under way and the texture seems a bit flabby or "funky"), it won't be right for the house specialty, crudo—sashimi-sized slices of raw fish that have been accented with sea salt, olive oil, and lemon juice, or with other condiments. But it would still be fine grilled or pan-seared or sautéed. I once asked him to try to articulate the process of creating a new dish. What, precisely, is he thinking when he combines raw fluke with sea beans, radish, and salt? Geoduck (a.k.a. giant clam crudo) with sugar-baby watermelon or artichoke? "I don't know, man," he replied. "It's a very hard question to answer. I think it's more experience than anything else. Experience dictates that you understand certain things about certain ingredients at certain times of year. You look in the fridge and you have to be able to work with what you have, in season. But it can't be arbitrary. That's the problem with a lot of these young cooks. They don't yet get the idea of how flavors can work, how you have to take into consideration acidity, texture, the properties of various oils. They think they're being creative but they're pushing the envelope too much. People like Daniel Boulud and Thomas Keller, what makes them so good is that their food is creative but they know the boundaries."

I suppose it's odd to say that I've been struck by Pasternack's empathy for fish, given his recurring role in their demise, but he nevertheless seems intent upon doing honor to the deceased, characteristically by doing no more than necessary to evoke essential flavors and unembellished subtleties. Not that he's unwilling to call a fish a fish. One day, as I watched him reduce an eight-pound mahi-mahi to about thirty bites of crudo, he showed me its pearly, iridescent pale-pink flesh and said, "You don't always see it this color. Sometimes the meat's a little grayer." On the other hand, mahi-mahi is "a very stupid fish. You catch one and you leave him in the water and all the others'll follow and you can catch 'em all. Not very smart. Good eating, though."

Next, he went to work on a Pacific sturgeon, scraping away a yellow adipose layer that looked like chicken fat. "Atlantic sturgeon is a protected species," he said. "This fish was caught in the Columbia River, in Washington. It's called a bullet because of the shape. Actually, they're always a little dirty. But this is one of my personal favorites. Really fatty, like eating a piece of pork."

From time to time, I would prompt him with fish names and he would respond with an off-the-cuff Pasternackian taxonomy.

Flounder: "The quintessential Long Island fish. In New England, they've got scrod. Maine, they've got haddock. Long Island, it's flounder. I was born to flounder fish. I fished for them in Jamaica Bay, South Bay, Hewlett Harbor, under the Meadowbrook Bridge, Island Park, East Rockaway. It was a really abundant fish. But the flounder haven't cooperated in the last couple of years."

Cod: "Cod is God. The Spaniards came here in search of cod. Italians, the same thing. It's a great, versatile fish. Unfortunately, none of them seem to make that right turn at Montauk anymore."

Porgy: "Ghetto fish. It's a fish that's usually associated with minorities. A great fish. But not considered your mainstream white-bread fish. I grill it. Sweet meat. Phenomenal skin."

Hake: "In the cod family but sweeter, softer in texture than cod, not as rich; half the price of cod. I like it roasted, because it can get really caramelized on the outside without doing anything. It's just got a lot of natural sugars."

Bluefish: "Godzilla. The other quintessential Long Island fish. Pound for pound, the hardest-fighting fish there is. Ferocious, eats anything, bites anything that gets in its way. Powerful, elusive. You could stick a beer can on a hook with bait inside and the fish'll bite the beer can."

Pasternack's first restaurant job was more turf than surf. At fourteen, he bused tables in a Rockville Centre steak house whose charms included the bookies who hung out at the bar and the pictures of photo finishes that hung on the walls. Not until his mid-twenties, while cooking at La Reserve, an old-school French place near Rockefeller Center, did he commit to the notion that this was what he would do with his life. By then, he'd gone to college for a year; spent a winter cooking in Vermont and a couple of years at Provence, in Greenwich Village; earned a diploma from Johnson & Wales; and worked in a hotel kitchen in Dallas long enough (less than a week) to recognize that he belonged back in New York. He left La Reserve after three years, following the death of André Gaillard, the French-Vietnamese chef who had hired him, and for the next five years stayed in motion as a line cook or sous-chef in a number of busy, trendy restaurants: Bouley, Steak Frites, Prix Fixe, and Sam's (where he met Donna Peltz, who was tending bar). He was in his early thirties and feeling that he was spinning his wheels when Terrance Brennan, a former sous-chef at Le Cirque who had also been at Prix Fixe, asked him to come to Picholine, a year-old bistro near Lincoln Center. Brennan had a clear idea of what he wanted Picholine to be and the good sense to give Pasternack plenty of latitude. When Ruth Reichl, in a 1996 review in the *Times*, awarded the restaurant three stars, it was understood that Pasternack, the *chef de cuisine*, deserved much of the credit. One of his signature dishes was seared sturgeon with caviar sauce; the fish was served with a reduction of shallots, white wine, champagne vinegar, tarragon, and peppercorns whisked

with a beurre blanc, to which malossol caviar was added at the last moment. Typical of Pasternack's cooking style at Picholine, it was labor-
intensive (that is, French) in a way that his style at Esca is decidedly
not.

While at Prix Fixe, he'd become friendly with Susan Cahn, whose
family owned Coach Farms, and who often worked at their goat-cheese
stand in the Union Square farmers' market. Through her, he met her
husband-to-be, Mario Batali, who was then merely a robustly talented
chef, not yet a food-culture demigod and conglomerateur. Batali and
his partner Joe Bastianich, who between them had interests in five
Manhattan restaurants (this was 1999; they're now up to ten), dined
frequently at Picholine. They could see that Pasternack was crazy about
fish yet otherwise demonstrably sane, and, conveniently, they had an
available location, Fricco Bar, an underperforming trattoria on Forty-
third Street west of Ninth Avenue.

"Joe and Mario kept coming into Picholine and saying, 'Come on,
let's do something,' " Pasternack recalled. "They asked me what I
wanted to do. I said a seafood restaurant, Provençal style. I wanted to
call it Rascasse. That's the name of a very important fish in the whole
Mediterranean culture. Bony, spiny, gnarly, a basic ingredient in bouillabaisse, *zuppa di pesce,* fritto misto. Joe said, 'Can you make it Italian?'
I said, 'A good cook is a good cook. I can do it Chinese if you need to.'
He said, 'Let's make a deal.' "

That fall, Pasternack accompanied Batali and Bastianich on a ten-
day excursion to Italy. Starting out in Venice, they ate and drank their
way up the Adriatic coast, toward Trieste and Istria, in northern Croa-
tia. (On a subsequent trip, Batali and Pasternack and Simon Dean, who
became a manager of and partner in Esca, spent a week in Amalfi, Sor-
rento, and Naples.) "We met my buddies who were fishmongers and
restaurateurs," Bastianich, who owns vineyards in Friuli and Tuscany
and is the co-author of a book on Italian regional wines, told me. "We
found out that everyone was eating raw fish. We had thought we were
going to come back with ideas along the lines of what you would consider classic Venetian-style food—risottos and *brodetto di pesce.* Crudo
was a revelation."

They tasted, among other things, raw scampi, orata, branzino, lobster, scallops, and sole—briny, sweet, chewy, buttery, and enhanced only
by lemon, olive oil, and sea salt. Immediately, they knew that the Esca

kitchen would become a testing laboratory for crudo—a term that Bastianich more or less coined. (The word *crudo* means "uncooked," but when it appears on a menu in Italy it typically refers to prosciutto.)

"Joe conceptualized the idea behind our crudo selections," Batali told me. "And Dave's taken the ball and run around the bases several times with it. A month before we opened, we were in the kitchen, trying this and that. Dave did a crudo that was a giant sea scallop with tangerine oil, pink peppercorns, and some Sicilian sea salt. And it was a giant moment. It was: Holy shit, this is gonna be a great restaurant."

This is, perhaps, benignly revisionist history. According to Pasternack, none of them had quite foreseen that crudo would become the hallmark of Esca, or anticipated that the restaurant would generate such instant enthusiasm. "The crudo appetizers at Esca are the freshest, most exciting thing to happen to Italian food in recent memory," William Grimes wrote in the *Times*. Nor could Pasternack have predicted that his handiwork would inspire so much mimicry. "Imitated by many, copied by few," he likes to say about the post-Esca proliferation of crudo, which has become appetizer fare in such unlikely locales as Cleveland, Denver, and St. Louis.

Each day, Esca offers a dozen or so wallet-lightening crudo options. Thirty dollars, for instance, will bankroll a tasting selection that amounts to two bites each of, say, pink snapper with black lava sea salt, weakfish with a thin sliver of preserved blood-orange rind, opah with baby fennel and wild-fennel pollen, yellowtail with Gaeta-olive aioli, kingfish with pickled fiddlehead, and fluke with sea beans and radish. "Raw fish makes a statement about quality," Pasternack told me. "People don't eat raw fish at just any restaurant." And he draws a firm distinction between crudo and ordinary American sushi and sashimi. "I always liked sushi—and I lived above a sushi place for four years—but I thought it always tasted the same. Place A was the same as Place B as Place C."

One night last spring, I observed Pasternack adroitly handling a crudo crisis that materialized as he was preparing a guest-chef banquet at the James Beard House, in Greenwich Village. (In 2004, the James Beard Foundation honored him as the New York chef of the year.) Pasternack and his crew had come expecting to serve dinner to seventy-two, but, at the last minute, the Beard House staff had allowed an extra table of eight. Not counting the oysters that were served before everyone was seated, the menu included two crudo courses. The first of these consisted of two morsels of black sea bass garnished with lemon juice, sea salt, pepper, and a sprig of salad burnet, a green that looks like parsley and tastes like cucumber. The bass had been cut by Pasternack that morning, and now eighty plates were lined up in the kitchen—eight of them empty. A loaves-and-fishes moment, of sorts. Somehow he discerned sixteen pieces of bass that could be halved, a sleight-of-knife executed so that no one in the dining room would notice. As he drizzled olive oil over each portion, he said, "How was that for creative management?" A faint smile. "They'll go home. They just won't necessarily go home full."

"For a lot of American chefs, it's hard to understand how simple things are in Italy," Batali said. "That was our idea, both with the crudo and with how Esca presents fish in general. It's all in the ingredients. When Dave talks about the difference between the fluke in Sheepshead Bay and the fluke from some other part of Long Island, you know that in fact one does taste different from the other. Dave has a real understanding of what the Italians call *materia prima*—the raw ingredients—and making them available for the palate to explore."

It hasn't proved to be a professional or interpersonal liability that Pasternack's instinctive Italian sensibility doesn't extend to actually speaking the language (though he possesses a sizable vocabulary of kitchen nouns and adjectives). One of the waitresses at the Beard House addressed him in Italian throughout the evening; he would occasionally nod, and nothing was apparently lost in translation. In the area of Long Island where he grew up there is a great deal of cultural overlap between Italian Americans and Jews. For whatever reason—and probably not merely because in the twenty-eight years since his bar mitzvah he has consumed immeasurable quantities of pork and shellfish—his diction, body language, and general affinities make him come across like a bit player in *GoodFellas*, so much so that he's occasionally prone to identity confusion. A few years ago, for an appearance with Bryant Gumbel on *The Early Show*, he prepared a crudo that consisted of ivory salmon, fresh soybeans, lemon juice, sea salt, and olive oil. Gumbel asked, "How important is it what kind of oil you use on these fish?"

"Oil is essential," Pasternack replied. "When we talk about oil, we talk only about extra-virgin olive oil. Because it's like the Japanese put the soy sauce, us Italians, we put the olive oil."

When he got home, his father, who had been watching, called and said, "What's with this 'us Italians' business? We're Jewish. Remember?"

"My wife's half Italian," Dave replied.

"Davey," Mel Pasternack felt constrained to point out, "you don't inherit that."

A spring weekday, shortly after noon. In the Esca dining room—pale-yellow walls; brown leather banquettes; brass Art Deco sconces; a floor-to-ceiling expanse of Italian wines along one wall; a cherry-blossom arrangement that would shame a Christmas tree; otherwise, no dazzle and pleasantly little noise—orders are discreetly punched into a computer. Moments later, they emerge from a small printer on the kitchen counter where Pasternack works his way through a pile of striped bass while orchestrating the lunch flow. "Four times," he informs Pablo Martínez, at the garde-manger station—meaning that a party of four have placed their orders and are now ready for their *amuse-gueules,* a plate of grilled bruschetta topped with a mélange of cannelloni beans, smoked mackerel, olive oil, red onions, and parsley. As the first-course dishes leave the kitchen, he glances at a clock, scrawls the time on the printout, and clips it to a shelf at eye level. At the appropriate moment, he will cue his crew—Sarah Ochs, the sous-chef; Katie O'Donnell, the sauté cook; Mike Sneed, at the pasta station—to mobilize the entrées.

"Pablo, you got two asparagus, two caprese, and a mindora. You got a third caprese gonna go with the oysters and you got a fourth caprese gonna go with another asparagus. . . . Give me a chicken, got an octo, I got skate with a cod. I got a snapper with an octo, I got branzino. . . . We got two stripers, a cod, a snapper, an orata, and a fett"—fettuccine. "I got two times. . . . Two, two. Misto, order branzino, order snapper, a cod, make sure you got a branzino ahead of a cod, you got a cod, two stripers, snapper, and then an orata. . . . Double octo, and make 'em look soigné, Sarah. Put up a cod in a minute. You got another big branzino, you got a pimente. Mike, order two fetts. . . . All right, Pablo, you're gonna give me two asparagus, two caprese, and a spigola. Katie, you got asparagus and a caprese. Mike, you got the fett, it goes with the caprese. . . . Two two three three two. . . . Order three stripers and a porgy, another asparagus with arugula, another asparagus with a misto. . . . All right, Mike, spaghetti pimente. You got another spaghetti following the second branzino. You got a spaghetti with an orata. You got a spigola, snapper, skate, and an orata. . . ."

The temperature literally rises, but the atmosphere remains coolly businesslike. When Simon Dean, the Esca manager, wanders in holding an envelope and a magazine and says, "Dave, here's a piece of what looks like hate mail. Also, here's your copy of the latest issue of *Private Air Magazine: Life at the Speed of Luxury*," Pasternack replies, "It's a little hard right now to be funny. I'd love to, but . . ." In fact, his mood is sanguine. A very nice piece of fish arrived that morning, a crimson shoulder cut from a seven-hundred-pound bluefin tuna—by way of Rod Mitchell, in Portland. "There's a lot of competition for these fish," he says. "I don't want to say I'm at the bottom of the pecking order. But I'm near the bottom. Plenty of people will pay a lot more than I will." At eighteen dollars a pound, the bluefin is too expensive to grill or sauté, so half of it will become crudo. The other half will go to Bistro du Vent, a calculatedly jointlike joint just around the corner, on Forty-second Street, that Pasternack and his Esca partners opened last January. There it will also be served raw, an appetizer à la steak tartare.

Four crudo plates are ready to be dispatched, but Pasternack first squirts a piece of bluefin with lemon juice, sprinkles it with pepper, sea salt, and olive oil, hands it to me, and declares, "This is the king of tuna, man. Think steak, filet mignon. This is what the Japanese'll pay exuberant prices for."

As it happens, he's just returned from Japan himself—his first visit, the highlight of which was a daily perambulation through Tsukiji, Tokyo's wholesale fish market ("like walking inside an aquarium"). He'd made the trip as the guest of Hiromi Go, an Esca regular.

"Hiromi's a very popular Japanese singer," he says. "He's like Elvis Presley over there. He's getting ready to record, like, his sixtieth album. He's been coming here for years and I'm always saying to him, 'When are you taking me to Tokyo?' So his wife set it up. I cooked two dinners, one for twelve people and one for forty. The second was in a Shinto shrine. I ate quite a few things I'd never had before."

Such as?

"Whale. It's really only fresh in Scandinavia, Russia, and Japan. Very interesting. A tuna-y texture and a liver-y finish. You know, in Japan they raise horses in the style of Kobe beef—massage it, give it sake, beer, different grains and grasses, play music for it. So I did a crudo dish that was horse, whale, and fatty tuna all on the same plate.

They all looked alike. The whale could have been the tuna and the tuna could have been the horse."

A waiter comes in with the news that a customer has requested cocktail sauce to accompany what might best be described as an order of the original crudo—a half-dozen Peconic Bay oysters. Having just seen Pasternack gracing tidbits of abalone, weakfish, and opah with, respectively, gaila melon, crushed almonds, and *olio verde*, I expect him to take offense. Instead, he reaches into a knee-level cooler and removes a mixture of horseradish, fresh chiles, lemons, ketchup, capers, and olive oil. "It's their money," he says. "Give 'em what they want, they'll come back."

So that includes tartar sauce with the fritto misto?

"No. They ask for that, which I think happens maybe twice a year, we tell 'em we don't have it." He shrugs. "What're they gonna do? Hey, we don't have it, we don't have it."

I once asked Joe Bastianich, who enjoys sportfishing for tuna, about his experiences on the water with Pasternack, and he said, "Dave's fishing, that's a little too blue-collar for me." For his part, Pasternack, who seems constitutionally incapable of condescension, has said, "I don't understand freshwater fishing. That's too Zen for me, too proper. Saltwater fishing, you know, there's a lot more blood and guts." A few years ago, Pasternack was invited, along with some other New York chefs, to a culinary event in Jackson Hole, Wyoming. While there, he went flyfishing on the Green River with Ed Artzt, a frequent Esca patron who was formerly the chief executive of Procter & Gamble. "It was my first time fly-fishing," Pasternack said. "I was good, I was a natural. I was the only guy who actually caught anything. I caught a cutthroat. After I took it off the hook, I went to open the cooler and everybody on the boat kind of looked at me like, What are you doing? I'm like, 'Dinner.' They go, 'No, everything here's catch-and-release.' I said, 'I spent the whole day to catch this one fish and we're gonna *throw it back*?' "

My recollection of my first fishing outing with Pasternack, though it took place fairly recently, is somewhat spotty. We were aboard a commercial boat called the *Sorry Charlie*, about three miles from Point Lookout, Long Island. As the tide was running out, a brisk wind was blowing in, which meant that conditions were, by my standards, insufficiently calm. I spent part of the morning in the cabin, seated atop a

cooler, resting my head against a wall, wondering when the Dram-
amine was going to kick in, and smiling weakly when my shipmates
periodically impugned my manhood. The captain, Mike Wasserman,
struggled nobly to stay anchored over an old shipwreck that was a reliable gathering spot for black sea bass. He succeeded well enough for
the group—five of us were fishing—to land about twenty-five keepers
and store them in the live well. "The Rolls-Royce of fish," Pasternack,
who caught the most, said. "Steamed, fried, poached, baked, sautéed,
grilled—I'll take a black sea bass any day over a piece of tuna." In the
afternoon, we moved close to the shore and, using clams for bait,
hauled in dozens of stripers that had been trailing a clam dredger as
it repeatedly plowed a half-mile stretch parallel to Rockaway Beach.
At the end of the trip, Pasternack bought everything in the live well
and the coolers, plus Wasserman's catch from the previous day: a hundred or so bass, and three conger eels that were headed for the *zuppa
di pesce*.

The next time I went to sea was a sultry July day, when Pasternack
was in quest of bluefish with his friend, piscatorial mentor, and supplier
Artie Hoernig, the captain of *Smokey III*, a thirty-one-foot Down
East–type cabin cruiser that he docks in Island Park. We met at 7 A.M.
in the parking lot of Artie's South Shore Fish Market, where we were
joined by Pete Hession, a retired UPS driver. Hoernig, who is in his late
fifties, has a mahogany tan, a neatly trimmed silver beard, bloodshot
blue eyes, and an inexhaustible supply of fish stories. The date, he announced, happened to be the eighteenth anniversary of one of his most
gratifying adventures, the landing of a 782-pound mako shark. That
same year, Pasternack, then in his mid-twenties, caught a three-
hundred-pound bull shark near Key West. He had the head mounted,
and it hung in his bedroom until a couple of years ago, when his wife
told him, "Either the garage or you give it away." It now occupies wall
space at Artie's market, right next to the head of the mako.

Hoernig went inside and returned with the day's bait, twenty
pounds of fresh and thirty pounds of frozen bunker, two flats of frozen
spearing that would be used as chum, and ten pounds of frozen squid.
A half hour later, this cargo got loaded onto the boat, along with three
large coolers filled with crushed ice, and by nine o'clock we'd reached
our destination, an area five miles offshore where Hoernig had planted
about forty-five lobster pots.

The ocean surface was oddly placid. Hoernig: "It's like a fucking lake."

Hession: "I hope we see a breeze."

Pasternack: "The only breeze we're gonna see out here, Pete, is thunderstorms."

Using bait-casting reels with forty-pound-test wire leaders and heavy-test monofilament backing, we tossed treble hooks baited with thick chunks of bunker into water about sixty feet deep. From the get-go, the bluefish were excitable. Pasternack quickly landed a seven-pounder, I caught one, Pasternack caught another. Then things got quiet for about fifteen minutes. "One, two, three, and that's it?" Hoernig said. "Probably a fucking mako's down there chasing these bastards."

When they resumed biting, Hoernig would say, "Davey's in!" or Hession would say, "Oh, Artie's in!" Then: "Pete's in!" Bluefish have notoriously sharp teeth and strong jaws, and the most prudent way to get one into a boat is with a gaff. As promised, there was ample gore—bluefish blood and bunker guts. At times, we had three fish on the line simultaneously. By eleven o'clock, we'd filled one cooler. A half hour later, Hoernig switched to an ultralight spinning rod and tied on a bucktail jig baited with a piece of squid, rigged for what's referred to on the South Shore as "fluking." He soon landed a two-and-a-half-pounder, and Pasternack, in a competitive spirit, got busy fluking, too. Occasionally, someone would lower a white plastic bucket over the side and fill it with water for washing our bloody hands. As the mid-day sun poured down, Pasternack and Hoernig took to cupping hand-fuls and dousing their heads. "I'm getting fucking ready to jump in, man," Pasternack said. It was not yet one o'clock when the second cooler reached capacity—mostly blues, a few fluke, a sea bass. Time to go pull lobster pots.

Citing my journalistic priorities, I managed to steer clear of the heavy lifting. As Hoernig eased the boat alongside a buoy, Pasternack would use a gaff to grab the submerged rope, and Hession would wrap a couple of turns around a small electric winch attached to the starboard gunwale. Invariably, the ropes were coated with algae the consistency of sodden shredded wheat and the lobster traps were encrusted with tiny mussels the size of split peas. The first few pots contained little Jonah and calico crabs and conch, and porgies flapping like birds, but were lobster-free. "No wonder your lobster's so expensive," Pasternack said.

"A labor of love," he said to me as he tossed clumps of algae over-board and prepared to dump putrescent bunker carcasses from the mesh bait bag inside a trap. Pasternack wore a plain white T-shirt, loose-fitting gray athletic shorts, white crew socks, calf-length white rubber boots, and an FDNY Rescue cap. Varieties of fish flesh were pasted to his clothing, but he didn't appear to mind, unlike Hession, who concluded that the best way to clean the filth from his blue jeans was to tie them to a fishing line and drag them behind the boat. Which seemed like a clever idea until the line snapped, stranding him in his green plaid boxers. ("All I can say, Pete, is you're a victim of circumstance," Hoernig told him.)

Some squid eggs—transparent Gummi worm–like masses—clung to one of the traps. I asked Pasternack whether he'd ever eaten them. He said that he hadn't, but that he'd tasted octopus eggs in Italy. Almost defensively, he added, "I ate bunker. I got Artie to eat it, too. Little ones. They fried 'em in his restaurant. We called 'em Hewlett Bay anchovies. The sardines of Long Island. It was good, right, Artie? People squirted lemon juice on 'em." He leaned over with the squid eggs, handed them to me, and said, "Here, put this in the cooler."

They hoisted twenty-two traps, good for twenty-one lobsters. As Pasternack relaunched traps by sliding them down a plank and off the rear of the boat, he whistled "I've Been Working on the Railroad."

"You like blue-fishing?" he asked me as we headed back.

Yes, I did.

He leaned against the gunwale. In the background: Atlantic Beach and the high-rises of the Rockaways. The sun was in his face, he was bloody and sweaty and due for a shave. Lunch had been a turkey-and-cheddar sub, and there were dabs of mayo at the corners of his mouth. "I told you, I don't always catch the biggest one, but I'm always catching 'em," he said. "Some guys are only about catching big fish. I've always been for quantity. I like to eat 'em. I'm a meat-and-potatoes guy."

I asked what he would do with the bluefish at Esca.

Palms up, he shook his head. "There's lots of good stuff to work with now," he said. "Lobster mushrooms. Great corn. Good tomatoes are starting to show up. This time of year it's easy to be a cook." Today, though, he'd been fishing and truly hadn't given it a thought. But tomorrow, back in the kitchen, he'd have an idea.

2005

ON THE BAY

BILL BUFORD

Mike Osinski was an acquaintance, someone I saw every now and then in the elevator of the Manhattan apartment building we'd both lived in for nearly ten years. Although I never knew what he did exactly (something in finance; he was always wearing a suit), he seemed different from the others—affable in a way I associate with people from the Southern states, less formal, with an unpretentious good-ol'-boyness. One day, I spotted Osinski walking his dog and realized I hadn't seen him for some time. He'd grown a graying goatee and was wearing baggy jeans and muddy work boots.

"I've left the city," he said. "I've given up the rat race!" He seemed giddy and made big gestures with his hands. He was now living in Greenport, a town on one of the far tines of Long Island's North Fork. "I'm working on the water! I'm a bayman!" (Baymen are the region's traditional seafood hunter-gatherers.) He motioned for me to step closer. "And I've lost thirty pounds." Osinski slapped himself to show off his abs. "Oysters did this. I harvest oysters. I'm a new man. The differences between men and women? Now I understand them. Do you know what I mean? I am a maaaaaaan!" He said the word "man" as though it should always have twelve syllables.

Osinski was born in 1954, and grew up in Mobile, Alabama, with a barefoot taste for the bounty of the intertidal beaches. (He was a youthful advocate of the Southerner's unspoken principle that, in the Gulf states, your identity is fed by what you pull out of the warm waters for dinner.) But Long Island isn't anything like the Gulf. I stared at my neighbor and thought, Oysters. Is that what happens when we get older—we take up hobbies?

I didn't see Osinski for another year, when I ran into him and his dog after a morning of deliveries. Gramercy Tavern had taken his oysters—"The chef says they're the best he's eaten in his life"—and other restaurants had followed: Esca, the Four Seasons, BLT Fish, Le Bernardin. These were some of the most respected eateries in the city. Le Bernardin was regarded by many as the best fish place in America. "And they love my oysters," Osinski said.

Greenport is a hundred miles from Manhattan, on the upper reaches of Peconic Bay, a fast-moving body of water squeezing between Shelter Island and the raggedy narrow end of New York on its way to the open sea. Osinski's home, built in the 1830s, probably by a whaling captain, sits on a sandy isthmus with views of water in two directions: in front, the Peconic; in back, a brackish inlet, fed by a creek and the bay's tides, called Widow's Hole, after one Margaret Leverage, the wife of the whaler. (He went to sea after completing the house, and never returned.) It was a mournful legacy, but one that Osinski nervously ended up drawing from.

On the East Coast, oysters derive their names from where they're found—they might be called a thousand things, but there is only one species, *Crassostrea virginica*. The names, therefore, can seem a little arbitrary, which was illustrated by a story told to me by Sandy Ingber, the chef at Grand Central's Oyster Bar, of the Pemaquid. "This Pemaquid—it was a good oyster," Ingber said. "But it didn't sell." Who knows why? The name had no magic or was difficult to pronounce. "So I started calling it a Bristol." Pemaquid is near Bristol, Maine. "I couldn't keep it on the menu." (Ingber has since gone back to calling it a Pemaquid.) By this logic, Osinski's oysters could be Peconics or Greenports, but he decided to invoke the pond behind his house and call them Widow's Holes, even though the name had some unwieldy implications: no eager, neo-oysterman really wants his shellfish to invoke mortality (Here, eat my raw shellfish and you, too, can make your wife a widow). On the other hand, what exactly is a widow's hole? "It sounds pornographic, doesn't it?" Osinski asked, as though it were the punch line to a dirty joke, not an entirely unhappy association for the world's most famous aphrodisiac. "Osinski's oysters are perfectly good," Ingber told me, "but my job is to move shellfish. Widow's Holes—that's a name I can move."

The view from Osinski's home meets just about everyone's definition of picturesque, but on a cold December morning it was remarkably uninviting. The bay was gray. The sky was gray. The trees were black and bare. There seemed to be no horizon. Out on the water, an empty ferry was leaving for Shelter Island. Overhead, and in all directions, were formations of geese—they made me think of sergeants' stripes in Second World War movies—on their way to somewhere else. In the shallow water where Osinski kept a boat, skim ice had formed. I had offered to help out, and was given oyster gear to put on: bright-orange overalls called bib pants, a top called water-proof sleeves, some giant gloves (wet inside), and an extra-thick wool hat (also wet). But the bib pants were uncomfortably snug—I learned later that Osinski had grabbed the wrong pair and given me a pair belonging to Isabel, his wife, not a small woman but much, much smaller than me—and my breakfast constricted alarmingly when I walked outside, tipping side to side like a moonwalker, because I couldn't bend my knees.

I didn't know what it meant to harvest an oyster. I had images, probably from books, of people standing in a skiff, raking the bottom and lifting dislodged shellfish with "tongs," deftly maneuvered like giant chopsticks. My suspicion is that, in earlier times, everyone knew where and how they got their oysters, because in earlier times every-one seemed to eat them. The mystery of oysters today is why people stopped.

It happened fast. "For most of the twentieth century, most people in town were involved in shellfish," the mayor of Greenport, Dave Kapell, told me when I called him looking for explanations. "There were a dozen canneries, plus shuckers and washers and packers and a barrel-making factory for the daily shipments to Fulton Fish Market. Discarded shells were everywhere, some in piles forty feet high, and always the stench of oyster tissue decomposing." According to Kapell, most of the waterfront was given over to shellfish. So was most of the water in front of the waterfront, a concept I didn't understand until I was shown a map from the fifties, a familiar enough graphic—small lots, big lots, a network of right angles—but unusual in this respect: the property was at the bottom of the bay. It is likely that Greenport underwater was more valuable than the town on land.

Today, the town is framed by the remains of two giant canner-ies—Lester & Toner Company, near Osinski's home, and the Long Island Oyster Company, on the other side of the bay, a gleaming white monster with what looked like Hellenic pillars. Both businesses went bankrupt in the sixties. Lester & Toner is now condominiums; the Hellenic pile is empty. What happened?

Overharvesting, according to Dave Relyea, an owner of Frank M.

Flower & Sons, in Oyster Bay (started in 1887, "the last of the big
boys"): people didn't know how to replace what they were taking out.
And then pestilence (Dermo and MSX, parasites that mysteriously
appeared in the fifties—no one knows from where). And predators
(starfish, mainly, which arrived in the thirties and then again in the
sixties, devouring whole bays). But people, principally. And pollution
and the pervasive unease raised by the prospect of diseased shellfish.
Oysters eat by filtering nutrients through their gills—a single oyster
cleans about two gallons of water an hour—but their health corresponds to that of the water passing through them. Good water: good
oysters. Bad water: bad oysters. Bad oysters: bad tummy ache, unless
your oysters are really bad, in which case you have a really bad tummy
ache. In Louisiana, where the fecund Gulf and the warm Mississippi
encourage all kinds of growth—including the unique *Vibrio vulnifi-
cus,* a cousin of cholera—someone dies from oysters every year.

There were other factors. Osinski blames the Catholic Church
("If only everyone still ate fish on Fridays, I'd be rich"), an unlikely explanation but not without merit: people stopped eating oysters because they stopped knowing them. My Louisiana grandfather, for
instance, a boomingly affable man (who also believed that if you're
from the Gulf you eat the Gulf), had loved oysters—along with craw-
fish and shrimp, plus swamp items like catfish and possum—and devoured them with a voracious zeal, somehow finding something in
the shellfish that confirmed his Southernness. My father, a more selective eater, didn't confuse identity with diet, and thought oysters
were repellent. It takes only one generation to turn against a thing,
and the next generation (mine) has no idea what it's missing. As a result, oysters today are mainly a nostalgia food, rarely eaten at home but
served in restaurants by members of a staff we'd like to believe won't
poison us. They are the very people Osinski sells to. Which was why
I was accompanying him out into the freezing Peconic. Le Bernardin
needed another two hundred.

Osinski's boat had dents and scratches, and was aggressively secondhand. The front was a mess. The sight conveyed disorder and reeked
of dead seaweed and rotting fish. There were bags, plastic containers,
pieces of wire, buckets, a proliferation of desiccated shells, and, some-

where, an anchor, which I eventually discovered when I was ordered to find it. (I waddled forward with great difficulty—I can't begin to describe the tidal pull that occurred when I bent over.) In the back, built up against the stern, were two platforms, like tables. This was where Osinski sorted his oysters. Le Bernardin insists on small oysters, no larger than three inches. "Women don't like the big ones," Osinski explained. "A frog waiter told me. It makes them uncomfortable."

Osinski learned that the land underwater could be owned when he took a course in oystering five years ago in nearby Southold. (It was taught by Kim Tetrault, a marine biologist of a highly romantic disposition, who seems determined single-handedly to revive the shellfish of the Peconic.) Most of the bay's underwater land now belongs to the state: you paid taxes on it like any other piece of property, but most people didn't. The previous owners of Osinski's property, though, had paid theirs, and Osinski turned out to own acres of underwater land. This was where we were now, about three hundred feet out, bobbing up and down in a higgledy-piggledy scattering of buoys.

Osinski grabbed one, wrapped the rope around a winch, and started cranking. Slowly, what looked like a giant chest emerged from the dark-gray bay, magnified by the water, getting bigger and bigger until it broke the surface, seaweed and sea creatures cascading off the sides. The boat tipped. It was a steel cage, about four feet in length and three feet high, and weighed nearly four hundred pounds. I helped Osinski pull it in and bring it to rest on the sorting table. He unlatched a hatch and pulled out a "purse," a mesh bag filled with oysters that spilled out like marbles, along with flip-floppy bluefish, many different kinds of crabs, and what looked like muddy seaweed (sea squirts, in fact, which obstruct the flow of water, an oyster's source of food, and need to be ripped out, a task I undertook with great vigor, trying to be useful, whereupon I discovered the origins of the name: my contact lenses browned over, the bay went momentarily opaque, and it was only on blinking, scratchily, that I saw how I had been covered with sea squirt). In the event, this wasn't the cage Osinski was hoping to find—the oysters had been there only since last spring and were two inches in length. By next September, they'd be "market size." (An oyster can grow two inches a year.)

He hooked another buoy. This cage wasn't one he wanted, either.

We pulled out another. He was looking for oysters from the previous year, two-year-olds, which should be Le Bernardin size.

"I know they're here somewhere." Osinski was muttering. He hooked another buoy, but the rope was tangled. "Jesus Christ," he said. "Who in the hell did that?" He yanked and pulled. Several cages appeared to have been stacked on top of each other. "Oh, I guess I did, didn't I?" And of course he had, because he was the only one working this patch of the Peconic.

The year before, Osinski had been out on Christmas Day. Le Bernardin was a new account, and he wasn't finding three-inch oysters for the busy New Year's week ahead. The inlet froze, and he had to keep plowing his boat through it, breaking the surface, to ensure he could get back in. (Everyone, I learned, respects the mortal cold of this bay in the winter.) Even on the Peconic, ice formed. When Osinski returned, with thirty oysters for his efforts, his children—Susanna (then six) and Mercator (five)—were waiting for him, jumping up and down, oblivious of the implications that Daddy was not walking up from the dock with a festive bounce. It was late afternoon, and they wanted to know what Santa Claus had brought them.

"Oh, shut up. There is no goddam Santa Claus. Leave me alone." Osinski then went to bed. Later that week, he clandestinely bought someone else's oysters (a great lapse of conviction, as if, in his exhaustion, he'd lost his raison d'être and concluded that an oyster was an oyster was an oyster, after all). A chef phoned: "We don't know what happened, but these oysters are not what we thought we were buying. We're throwing them away."

This time, Osinski eventually found a cage of the appropriate-sized shellfish and sorted through the purse's take, filling up a sack for Le Bernardin, saving the larger ones for other restaurants, and putting the smaller ones back for next year—provided he could find them again. We'd been on the water five hours. The day had yielded 170 oysters. Osinski gets seventy cents an oyster. That's $119.

Until recently, Osinski had been making much more money, hundreds of thousands a year ("I can't tell you—my neighbors hate me as it is"), but hadn't been doing what he wanted. His secret ambition had always been to be a writer—that, and to live by the sea. (His website includes poems about the Peconic, but nothing about the price of an oyster.) When he graduated from college (English literature at Florida State University), he got a job on a shrimping boat, seeming to realize one of his ambitions, but quit after the boat almost went under in a storm. Then he was hired as a reporter for a Florida newspaper called *Today*, near Cape Canaveral, but was, by his own self-denigrating account, too sloppy to be a journalist. In a story about a white sheriff, Osinski confused the name of a white community with the name of a black one. He was fired. He seemed always to be getting fired, owing to what I'm tempted to describe as his congenital messiness. In this respect, his disordered oyster boat was like his life. "I know, I know, soon you'll find me with a Coke machine in the garage and my pickup sitting out on bricks and a yard full of children." (In fact, the yard is full of the detritus of his new profession—cages and purses drying out in the sun—as well as a rusted red wagon, a broken broom, a basket of sweet potatoes, a stroller with a wheel missing, a giant plastic duck, a torn pink blanket, a traffic cone, a tricycle parked inside a shrub.) A career breakthrough came when, urgently needing money, he took a job as a computer programmer. He got fired from that one, too, but not before discovering that his affinity for numbers was protected by a computer's ability to self-correct. When I first met Osinski, he and a partner were writing a program affectionately called "the money tree" (it enabled banks to trade mortgages quickly and with a calculated risk). He made a lot of money for a lot of people, until he realized he didn't have to be in an office and got someone to buy the program. Then he was fired ("I don't know why—most people just don't like me"). He is now writing a novel of his new life—his life on the water.

My second trip to Greenport was the first day of winter. It was windy and cold—twenty-two degrees—but also bright and clear. This time, I had a horizon to look out onto—my mind, liberated by the sight, seemed to expand to the very edge—as well as a capacious pair of bib pants, also liberating. "It's the winter solstice!" I cried out. This big sky, the salty air. "What an ecstatic way to start a season!"

For Osinski, it was just another day on the bay. Dates didn't matter to him anymore, he said. "I don't pay attention. I know tide tables.

I live by the phases of the moon and by watching the sea." I wasn't sure I believed him, but I recognized the philosophical point. He killed the engine, and we pulled up a cage. Once again, there weren't many oysters that were market size, although enough for an impromptu breakfast.

There was a shucking knife on a bench, like a butter knife with more edge. Osinski grabbed a towel to hold an oyster in place, so the liquid wouldn't tip out—the "liquor" is regarded by many as the most important ingredient in the experience of a shellfish—and gently pressed the blade against the hinge. Nothing happened. He pressed again: nothing. Typically, what I'd have done at this point was increase the pressure; rebuffed, I'd respond by raising the level of attack, but the result was never pretty. For Osinski, the operation was a negotiation. The blade in position, he wiggled it up and down gently. He seemed not to be prizing open the shells but massaging the muscle that kept them closed. I thought, At any moment he's going to sing some soothing thing to coax the little fellow out. Then the muscle simply relaxed, and the shells separated.

"You don't chew, do you?" I asked. I was confirming what I knew to be the received practice. ("It's all about the mouth feel," Sandy Ingber had told me. "Slurp, never chew." But he admitted that he took a discreet bite when testing a new product.)

"You tease it," Osinski said, "you work it with your tongue. But you'd never sink your teeth into it. Goodness, no!" I watched. He slurped, swished, his cheek puffing out as the oyster, denuded of its shell only a few seconds before, was knocked around inside his mouth until it went down, and I found myself marveling at the speed with which a creature can be transported from ocean to stomach, dispatched from the dark and deep to—well, the dark and deep. Osinski emitted a sigh of pleasure. "I feel so elemental when I eat oysters. All primitive cultures ate them. The prehistory of man is in the shells they left behind." He was alluding to what archeologists call middens, piles of shells, sometimes several acres across, believed to be thousands of years old, stacked up like dirty dishes (which in effect they were). They are described by Mark Kurlansky in his elegant history of New York, *The Big Oyster:* the inside of an oyster shell is white like ivory, and piles of them, gleaming in the sun, were visible from great distances. "When I eat an oyster," Osinski declared, "I feel I'm connecting to something primordial."

It was my turn. I slurped and, before swallowing, remembered the instruction to play with my oyster-creature, and was then struck by an unexpected affinity between where I found myself and what was in my mouth. It was the briny intensity of what had crossed my palate: the food equivalent of the salty air. Whatever I was doing (I couldn't bring myself to call it eating) tasted absolutely of here—this spot on the Peconic.

Osinski opened more oysters. We ate them—or swallowed them, anyway—and sat studying the water and the million ways that a winter morning's sun was reflected on it. ("When I'm out here, I actually get quite metaphysical.") But I was left wondering: Is an oyster a primordial meal?

I asked Eric Ripert, the chef of Le Bernardin. I'd been intending to get in touch, ever since helping Osinski to eliminate three-and-a-half-inch shellfish in order to fill Le Bernardin's uniformly dimensioned order. ("No, no, bigger is not correct," Ripert told me. "It doesn't work. To have a huge chunk of something so slimy in the mouth, this mass of meat—no, no, it's disgusting.") It turns out that Ripert had thought hard about oysters and valued their primordial qualities. For a start, he was an unapologetic head-tipping slurper and a connoisseur of the liquor ("I want to say it tastes of the sea transformed—can you say that in English? It is seawater but no longer seawater"), and an enthusiast of the Long Island crop. ("I come from France and did not expect to find edible oysters here. It was the water. I feared pollution. To my surprise, the water was wonderfully fresh, and the oysters have a briny quality I associate with Normandy.") But when I asked Ripert if he chewed he surprised me.

He paused, deliberating. "Yes," he said, finally.

"How many times?"

"Well . . ." He projected an imaginary bivalve into his mouth. "A couple of times. Actually, may I make a confession? I chew once. My parents taught me this. They told me, 'Eric, you must always bite an oyster, firmly, once. Otherwise, it will be alive in your stomach.'"

I phoned Kim Tetrault, the marine biologist.

"You need to understand what happens when an oyster closes its shell," he explained. "That liquor is not just seawater. It's also part oyster. We call it extrapallial fluid. It's like the blood that bathes an oyster's tissues. When oysters close their shells, they are sealing themselves in their own environment—the world is their oyster—and they will survive as long as the extrapallial fluid doesn't dehydrate." The Romans used to ship their oysters from Britain, a journey that must have taken weeks. Tetrault confirmed that, under certain conditions, an oyster can live that long out of the water. He described his students dissecting shellfish. "If you've shucked an oyster carefully, you haven't killed it. In my classes, we continue feeding it—the gills keep working—and its heart beats for another fifteen minutes."

Maybe Osinski was right. Many foods are eaten raw. Many foods are swallowed whole. But how many raw foods are also still alive?

On my third trip to Greenport, our first cage yielded seven hundred oysters. Osinski was thrilled. "Whoopee! I knew I had some around here, I just knew it!" A second cage yielded almost as many, and by the time we pulled up a third Osinski had nearly two thousand oysters. "Oh, Daddy did well today." He was giddy—downright hot-diggety-dog kick-ass happy—as though we'd just caught something wild and rare and managed to pull it in. But we hadn't, had we? We'd merely relocated parcels that he had dropped in the water himself. (Most hunter-gatherers would call that cheating.) Of course Osinski would have no system for organizing. One of the benefits of being a messy person is that your life, in a condition of irretrievable disorder, is full of surprises.

Osinski was an underwater farmer. I'd been so caught up in his adventure—the open air, the water, the struggles to find three-inchers—that I hadn't registered what I'd been seeing. Cages don't occur in the wild. Today, you can eat a flavorless pink thing called "salmon," which arrives at its mealy texture by a form of intensive farming that didn't seem all that different from what I seemed to be witnessing here.

But an oyster is different. The commonplace (among tissue eaters) is that wild is better than farmed because a wild animal is more exercised, more oxygenated, more organically its natural self than anything grown in confinement. An oyster is not active in this wild way. Once oysters find a hard spot to settle on, they're not going anywhere: they eat and exude (having, as Osinski believes, "no brain, just a stomach and an anus—therefore it's okay to eat them while they're alive"). According to William K. Brooks, whose 1891 masterpiece, *The Oys-*

ter, is still regarded as one of the best accounts of the life of a bivalve, "the adult oyster makes no efforts to obtain its food, it has no way to escape from danger, and after its shell is entered it is perfectly helpless and at the mercy of the smallest enemy. . . . It is almost as inert and inanimate as a plant." (Left alone, oysters live for fifteen years and grow very big; Tetrault has a shell that's a foot long. I looked at it and thought, Ha! Imagine swallowing that one without chewing.)

Today, Brooks's study is interesting for its doomsday predictions. Frightened by the terrible decline of the oysters in Chesapeake Bay, he urged his colleagues to raise shellfish in hatcheries and plant them—like so many acres of potatoes. The Romans knew how to do it; so did the French. Even Colonial Americans did transplanting: by 1775, the Wellfleet, from Cape Cod, was virtually extinct; what you eat today might actually be descended from Chesapeakes.

I saw an example of Brooks's vision on a visit to Fishers Island, where Osinski buys the seed oysters that he plants in cages in his underwater plot. The Fishers Island Oyster Company is run by Steve Malinowski, an aqua-entrepreneur who has managed to raise five children while working on the water. Eight years ago, he began a nursery to ensure that he wouldn't wake up and discover he had no oysters. Today, Malinowski produces so many seed oysters—about five million a year—that he sells some to other shellfish farmers. But there has been some tension. Two years ago, Manhattan's top restaurants always offered at least one oyster from Long Island Sound: Fishers Islands, delivered by UPS the day after being harvested. Lately, you saw another: Widow's Holes, delivered by Osinski on the day he'd pulled them out of the water. "It's an interesting dilemma, to visit restaurants and find Mike Osinski's oysters grown from our seeds," Malinowski told me. "We want our buyers to succeed, but maybe not succeed too well."

Malinowski runs the only hatchery on the island, having acquired Ocean Pond Oyster Company. Ocean Pond was started in 1962, after Carey Matthiessen and his brother, the writer Peter Matthiessen, discovered that a seldom visited local pond was full of shellfish. (They'd dragged up an abandoned boat, found it was covered with oysters, and concluded that oysters had been there since the 1938 hurricane blew open a passage to the sea, and the pond, previously freshwater, had become brackish.) Oysters grow well in brackish water because their natural predators can't find them there. Brackish oysters don't have much flavor—"They were big, but bland," according to Carey Matthiessen—and, when mature, are moved to the sea to acquire that crisp salinity that gets the saliva going. But the pond was perfect for baby oysters—a low-salinity incubator.

I visited the hatchery: bubbling green vats of phytoplankton (a bivalve's dinner) and gallons of seawater heated to the temperature of early summer—an oyster's honeymoon suite. Oysters like warm water—they reproduce when it reaches seventy degrees, and at that time, according to Osinski, "they're not to be eaten because they taste of gonads." (Thus the caution against eating oysters during the "r"-less summer months—"Nobody likes shells full of sex.") In normal conditions, a male spews billions of sperm in the proximity of a female, who then releases millions of eggs—most of which never meet in the topsy-turvy open sea. But in a temperature-controlled tank the process is more efficient, and you need only a few romantic "brood" oysters to produce a few million offspring.

Malinowski introduced me to six brooders. I couldn't tell the boys from the girls, but with oysters it doesn't always matter. Oysters are not just hermaphrodite, as some people believe. They're protandrous: capable of alternating their sex. "You've got no idea what you're going to get," Matthiessen told me. "One year, an oyster produces eggs. The next year, it could be sperm." Oysters hibernate when the temperature drops below forty degrees and seem to lose their gender. "If you pull one out and open it up, its genitals are completely flat—they're not one thing or the other." And then it's anybody's guess what happens when they wake up.

I studied the six shellfish. Not a lot seemed to be happening—six oysters having sex looked a lot like six oysters not having sex. Then I noticed a barely perceptible whitish stream issuing from one. Procreation had begun.

Malinowski showed me an incubation tank with a swirling pink dust: three-day-old larvae, millions of them. Larvae become "spats," which, sheltered, grow to maturity in Ocean Pond, until they're big enough to be taken out to sea. Malinowski's spot was just off one of the island's peninsulas, looking out into the Sound.

We went there in his boat, and he opened up an oyster and gave it to me.

"You chew, don't you?" I had to ask. The question flustered Malinowski—a large-boned, big-handed, rustic sort of fellow, gap-toothed, with a rugged face and a no-nonsense manner.

"No one has ever asked me that before. What do *you* do?" (For a man who'd spent most of his life with oysters, he seemed remarkably uncertain about the etiquette.) He reflected. "Yes, I chew. I've always chewed. If you swallow, you can't taste the oyster. If you swallow, all oysters are the same."

"How many times?"

His jaws leaned left, then right, then left again. "Three times. I chew an oyster three times."

I tipped mine in, heart beating, gills working, and was struck by the liquid—both the amount (a lot) and its saltiness (also a lot). Widow's Hole oysters are briny, but this one was brinier, even though both oysters came from the same seed. The difference was in where Malinowski's had grown up—closer to the open sea. I chewed, once, twice, a third time. It was crunchy (which was curious, because there were no bones). Then, on the fifth chew, I got something I hadn't tasted before: a sweetness.

Malinowski grinned. "Yes, they say that's what's unique about our oysters. That sweetness that kicks in around your last chew."

Salt and sugar, briny and sweet, an evocation of air and clean water; the flavors of the oyster lingered as long as a minute. I asked for another and chewed it—twenty-two times—with relish.

Recently, I was visited by a memory of a trip I took with my grandfather to an ice factory when I was five years old. It was August 1959: a hot, sultry Louisiana morning and a cold ice factory. My grandfather pulled up to a loading dock—unpaved, a bright-red Louisiana clay—and a man brought us a block of ice wrapped in straw. In the early morning, lots of people were buying blocks of ice wrapped in straw. My grandfather lived in a paper-mill town, and although he had a refrigerator (we'd be making hand-cranked ice cream), most homes still had iceboxes.

The ice factory is gone and its passing is connected with what happened to oysters. My father never bought a block of ice. His was the first generation to enjoy refrigerated mass-market foods. His favorite was Salisbury steak, a factory-made meat that kept long enough to be shipped anywhere. An oyster can't be eaten this way. It needs to be kept cool by ice, because it has to be eaten when it's fresh. That's how you eat oysters—before the ice melts. You have to chew to know the difference, Malinowski told me, which is another way of saying that the difference is everything. Osinski used the word *terroir:* in an oyster, as with wine, you should be able to taste the place it came from; in this still-living creature you will find the water and the food it ate—these living, fragile, handmade creatures tasting wonderfully of the health of the planet.

2006

"I started my vegetarianism for health reasons, then it became a moral choice, and now it's just to annoy people."

"Captain, this Brie is totally out of control!"

LOCAL DELICACIES

"How's the barbecue chicken?"

"This is <u>not</u> the one I selected! I never forget a face!"

AN ATTEMPT TO COMPILE A SHORT HISTORY OF THE BUFFALO CHICKEN WING

CALVIN TRILLIN

I did not appreciate the difficulties historians must face regularly in the course of their research until I began trying to compile a short history of the Buffalo chicken wing. Since Buffalo chicken wings were invented less than twenty years ago, I had figured that I would have an ·easy task compared to, say, a medievalist whose specialty requires him to poke around in thirteenth-century Spain. Also, there is extant documentation identifying the inventor of Buffalo chicken wings as Frank Bellissimo, founder of the Anchor Bar, on Main Street—the form of the documentation being an official proclamation from the City of Buffalo declaring July 29, 1977, Chicken Wing Day. ("WHEREAS, the success of Mr. Bellissimo's tasty experiment in 1964 has grown to the point where thousands of pounds of chicken wings are consumed by Buffalonians in restaurants and taverns throughout our city each week . . .") I would not even have to rummage through some dusty archive for the document; the Anchor Bar has a copy of it laminated on the back of the dinner menu. I had the further advantage of having access to what people in the history game call "contemporary observers"—a crowd of serious chicken-wing eaters right on the scene. A college friend of mine, Leonard Katz, happens to be a Buffalonian—a native Buffalonian, in fact, who is now a dean at the medical school of the State University of New York at Buffalo. I have also known his wife, Judy, since long before the invention of the chicken wing. She is not a native Buffalonian, but she carries the special credentials that go with having been raised in New Haven, a city that claims to have been the scene of the invention of two other American specialties—the hamburger and the American pizza. Although Leonard Katz normally limits his chicken-wing consumption to downing a few as hors d'oeuvres—a policy, he assured me, that has no connection at all with the fact that his medical specialty is the gastrointestinal tract—the rest of the family think nothing of making an entire meal out of them. Not long before I arrived, Linda Katz had returned from her freshman year at Washington University, in St. Louis—a city where the unique local specialty is, for reasons lost to historians, toasted ravioli—and headed straight for her favorite chicken-wing outlet to repair a four-month deprivation. A friend of Linda's who returned from the University of Michigan at about the same time had eaten chicken wings for dinner four nights in a row before she felt fit to continue. Judy Katz told me that she herself eats chicken wings not only for dinner but, every now and then, for breakfast—a pattern of behavior that I think qualifies her as being somewhere between a contemporary observer and a fanatic.

Even a chicken-wing eater of Judy Katz's seriousness could not have tested the full variety of Buffalo chicken wings. It is said that there are now several hundred places in the area where Buffalonians can order what they usually refer to simply as "wings"—including any number of places that also offer "a bucket of wings" to go. She has, however, obviously taken what is known in social science—a field whose methods are used increasingly by modern historians—as a fair sampling. On my first evening in Buffalo, the Katz family and some other contemporary observers of their acquaintance took me on a tour of what they considered a few appropriate chicken-wing sources so that I could make some preliminary research notes for later analysis. The tour naturally included the Anchor Bar, where celebrated visitors to Buffalo—Phyllis Newman, say, or Walter Mondale's daughter—are now taken as a matter of course, the way they are driven out to see Niagara Falls. It also included a noted chicken-wing center called Duffs and a couple of places that serve beef-on-weck—a beef sandwich on a salty roll—which happens to be the local specialty that was replaced in the hearts of true Buffalonians by chicken wings. In Buffalo, chicken wings are always offered "mild" or "medium" or "hot," depending on how much of a dose of hot sauce they have been subjected to during preparation, and are always accompanied by celery and blue-cheese dressing. I sampled mild. I sampled medium. I sampled hot. As is traditional, I washed them down with a number of bottles of Genesee or Molson—particularly while I was sampling the hot. I ate celery between chicken wings. I dipped the celery into the blue-cheese dressing. I dipped chicken wings into the blue-cheese dressing. I tried a beef-on-weck. I found that I needed another order of medium. After four hours, the tour finally ended with Judy Katz apologizing for the fact that we were too late for her favorite chicken-wing place, a pizza parlor called Santora's, which closes at 1 A.M.

The next morning, I got out my preliminary research notes for analysis. They amounted to three sentences I was unable to make out, plus what appeared to be a chicken-wing stain. I showed the stain to Judy Katz. "Medium?" I asked.

"Medium or hot," she said.

Fortunately, the actual moment that Buffalo chicken wings were invented has been described by Frank Bellissimo and his son, Dom, with the sort of rich detail that any historian would value; unfortunately, they use different details. Frank Bellissimo is in his eighties now, and more or less retired; he and his wife, Teressa, are pretty much confined to an apartment above the Anchor Bar. According to the account he has given many times over the years, the invention of the Buffalo chicken wing came about because of a mistake—the delivery of some chicken wings instead of the backs and necks that were ordinarily used in making spaghetti sauce. Frank Bellissimo thought it was a shame to use the wings for sauce. "They were looking at you, like saying, 'I don't belong in the sauce,' " he has often recalled. He implored his wife, who was doing the cooking, to figure out some more dignified end for the wings. Teressa Bellissimo decided to make some hors d'oeuvres for the bar—and the Buffalo chicken wing was born.

Dom Bellissimo—a short, effusive man who now acts as the bustling host of the Anchor Bar—tells a story that does not include a mistaken delivery or, for that matter, Frank Bellissimo. According to

Dom, it was late on a Friday night in 1964, a time when Roman Catholics still confined themselves to fish and vegetables on Fridays. He was tending the bar. Some regulars had been spending a lot of money, and Dom asked his mother to make something special to pass around gratis at the stroke of midnight. Teressa Bellissimo picked up some chicken wings—parts of a chicken that most people do not consider even good enough to give away to barflies—and the Buffalo chicken wing was born.

Dom and Frank agree that Teressa Bellissimo chopped each wing in half and served two straight sections that the regulars at the bar could eat with their fingers. (The two straight pieces, one of which looks like a miniature drumstick and is known locally as a drumette, became one of the major characteristics of the dish; in Buffalo, a plate of wings does not look like a plate of wings but like an order of fried chicken that has, for some reason, been reduced drastically in scale.) She "deep-fried" them, applied some hot sauce, and served them on a plate that included some celery from the Anchor Bar's regular antipasto and some of the blue-cheese dressing normally used as the house dressing for salads. Dom and Frank also agree that the wings were an immediate success—famous throughout Buffalo within weeks. Before long, they say, chicken wings were on the dinner menu instead of being served gratis at the bar—and were beginning to nudge aside the Italian food that had always been the Anchor Bar's specialty. In the clipping libraries of the Buffalo newspapers, I could find only one article that dealt with the Bellissimo family and their restaurant in that period—a long piece on Frank and Teressa in the *Courier-Express* in 1969, five years after the invention of the chicken wing. It talks a lot about the musicians who had appeared at the Bellissimos' restaurant over the years and about the entertainers who used to drop in after road shows. It mentions the custom Teressa and Frank had in times gone by of offering a few songs themselves late on a Saturday night—Teressa emerging from the kitchen to belt out "Oh Marie" or "Tell Me that You Love Me." It does not mention chicken wings. Perhaps the interviewer simply happened to be more interested in jazz drummers than tasty experiments. Perhaps Frank and Dom Bellissimo are, like most people, fuzzy on dates. By chance, my most trusted contemporary observers, the Katzes, were living out of the city during the crucial period; Linda Katz looked surprised to hear that there had ever been a time when people did not eat chicken wings. The exact date of the discovery seemed a small matter, though, compared to the central historical fact, common to both Bellissimo stories, that the first plate of Buffalo chicken wings emerged from the kitchen of the Anchor Bar. It seemed to me that if a pack of revisionist historians descended on Buffalo, itching to get their hands on some piece of conventional wisdom, they would have no serious quarrel with the basic story of how the Buffalo chicken wing was invented—although the feminists among them might point out that the City of Buffalo's proclamation would have been more exact if it had named as the inventor Teressa Bellissimo. The inventor of the airplane, after all, was not the person who told Wilbur and Orville Wright that it might be nice to have a machine that could fly.

"A blue-collar dish for a blue-collar town," one of the Buffalonians who joined the Katz family and me on our chicken-wing tour said, reminding me that historians are obligated to put events in the context of their setting. Buffalo does have the reputation of being a blue-collar town and, particularly after the extraordinary winter in 1977, of being a blue-collar town permanently white with snow. Buffalonians who do much traveling have resigned themselves to the fact that the standard response to hearing that someone comes from Buffalo is a Polish joke or some line like "Has the snow melted yet?" Buffalo has always had a civic-morale problem. Could the problem have been exacerbated by making a local specialty out of a part of the chicken that somebody in San Francisco or Houston might throw away? Frank Bellissimo seemed to argue against that interpretation. "Anybody can sell steak," he told me. "But if you can sell odds and ends of one thing or another, then you're doing something." The celebrated visitors who troop through the Anchor Bar are, after all, almost always favorably impressed by Buffalo chicken wings. Craig Claiborne proclaimed them "excellent" in one of his columns—although he may have undercut the compliment a bit by saying in the same paragraph that he had remained in Buffalo for only three hours.

One way that the invention of the chicken wing seems to have improved morale is that there now exists among Buffalonians a widespread commercial fantasy of hitting it rich by introducing Buffalo chicken wings to some virgin territory. People in Buffalo are always talking about trying wings out on Southern California or testing the waters in Providence. While I was on my tour with the Katz family, Andy Katz, who is fifteen, had one question about my opinion of the local delicacy: "Do you think these would go over in Toronto?" There are already some attempts to sell wings outside of western New York. A former Buffalonian is serving wings in the Paco's Tacos outlets of Boston. It is said that wings are available in Fort Lauderdale—where so many Buffalonians have retired that the annual events include a beef-on-weck banquet. This summer, in the new Harborplace shopping complex in the inner harbor of Baltimore, a place called Wings 'n Things opened with the announced intention of dealing in the sort of volume hitherto common only within Buffalo itself—a couple of tons of wings a week. "It takes money to make money," Dom Bellissimo told me while reflecting on the fact that his family did not parlay the invention of chicken wings into a franchise fortune. Sometimes he thinks that the opportunity has not been lost forever. "I would like to go with a chain," he told me. "I'm so ready for it. I wish I could get involved with some money people. I'd show them how to go with this thing."

About two years ago, a Buffalo stockbroker named Robert M. Budin wrote a piece for the *Courier-Express* Sunday magazine suggesting, in a lighthearted way, that the city adopt the chicken wing as its symbol. Budin's piece begins with two Buffalonians discussing what had happened when one of them was at a party in Memphis and was asked by a local where he was from. Deciding to "take him face on," the visiting Buffalonian had said, "I'm from Buffalo." Instead of asking if the snow had melted yet, the local had said, "Where those dynamite chicken wings come from?"

"You mean positive recognition?" the friend who is hearing the story asks. It becomes obvious to the two of them that Buffalonians should "mount a campaign to associate Buffalo with chicken wings and rid ourselves of the negatives of snow and cold and the misunderstood beef-on-weck." Budin suggested that the basketball team be called the Buffalo Wings, that the mayor begin wearing a button that says DO YOUR THING WITH WINGS, and that a huge statue of a chicken wing (medium hot) be placed in the convention center.

When I telephoned Budin to inquire about the response to his suggestion, he said it had not been overwhelming. He told me, in fact, that he had embarked on a new campaign to improve Buffalo's reputation.

Budin said that a lot of people believed that the city's image suffered from its name. I remembered that his Sunday-magazine piece had ended "Buffalo, thy name is chicken wing." Surely he was not suggesting that the name of the city be changed to Chicken Wing, New York. What should be changed, he told me, is not the name but its pronunciation. He has taken to pronouncing the first syllable as if it were spelled "boo"—so that Buffalo rhymes with Rue de Veau. "It has a quality to it that lifts it above the prosaic 'Buffalo,'" he said.

Maybe, but I suspect that it's only a matter of time before Budin tells some corporate executive in Memphis or Cincinnati that he is calling from Boofalo and the executive says, "Has the snoo melted yet?"

On my last evening in Buffalo—just before the Katzes and I drove out on Niagara Falls Boulevard to try the wings at a place called Fat Man's Got 'Em, and just before Judy Katz gave me final instructions about the bucket of wings I was planning to take back to New York from Santora's the next day ("Get the big bucket. Whatever's left over will be fine the next morning")—I met a man named John Young, who told me, "I am actually the creator of the wing." Young, who is black, reminded me that black people have always eaten chicken wings. What he invented, he said, was the sauce that created Buffalo chicken wings—a special concoction he calls mambo sauce. He said that chicken wings in mambo sauce became his specialty in the middle sixties, and that he even registered the name of his restaurant, John Young's Wings 'n Things, at the county courthouse before moving to Illinois, in 1970. "If the Anchor Bar was selling chicken wings, nobody in Buffalo knew it then," Young said. "After I left here, everybody started chicken wings." Young, who had returned to Buffalo a few months before our talk, told me that those who had copied the dish must be saying, "Oh, man! The original King of the Wings is back. He's fixin' to do a job on you." In fact, Young said, he was pleased to see so many people in Buffalo make money off his invention—a magnanimous sentiment that I had also heard expressed by both Frank and Dom Bellissimo. "I could have formed a company and went across the country," Young told me. "It's still not too late."

The wings Young invented were not chopped in half—a process he includes in the category of "tampering with them." They were served breaded with the mambo sauce covering them. In John Young's Wings 'n Things, as well as in a restaurant called Bird Land, run by Young's brother Paul, they are still served that way—sometimes accompanied by the blue-cheese dressing and celery that were undoubtedly inspired by Teressa Bellissimo. It is true, a local poultry distributor told me, that John Young as well as Frank Bellissimo started buying a lot of chicken wings in the middle sixties, but there is no reason for the distributor to have saved the sales receipts that might indicate who was first. First with what? Was the Buffalo chicken wing invented when Teressa Bellissimo thought of splitting it in half and deep-frying it and serving it with celery and blue-cheese dressing? Was it invented when John Young started using mambo sauce and thought of elevating wings into a specialty? How about the black people who have always eaten chicken wings? The way John Young talks, black people may have been eating chicken wings in thirteenth-century Spain. How is it that historians can fix the date of the Battle of the Boyne with such precision? How can they be so certain of its outcome?

1980

*"I'll start with the knight in shining armor,
then have the maiden rare and radiant."*

THE HOMESICK RESTAURANT

SUSAN ORLEAN

In Havana, the restaurant called Centro Vasco is on a street that Fidel Castro likes to drive down on his way home from the office. In Little Havana, in Miami, there is another Centro Vasco, on Southwest Eighth—a street that starts east of the Blue Lagoon and runs straight to the bay. The exterior of Miami's Centro Vasco is a hodgepodge of wind-scoured limestone chunks and flat tablets of Perma-stone set in arches and at angles, all topped with a scalloped red shingle roof. Out front are a gigantic round fountain, a fence made from a ship's anchor chain, and a snarl of hibiscus bushes and lacy palm trees. The building has had a few past lives. It was a speakeasy in the twenties, and for years afterward it was an Austrian restaurant called the Garden. The owners of the Garden were nostalgic Austrians, who, in 1965, finally got so nostalgic that they sold the place to a Cuban refugee named Juan Saizarbitoria and went back to Austria. Saizarbitoria had grown up in the Basque region of Spain, and he had made his way to Cuba in the late thirties by sneaking onto a boat and stowing away inside a barrel of sardines. When he first arrived in Havana, he pretended to be a world-famous jai-alai player, and then he became a cook at the jai-alai club. In 1940, he opened Centro Vasco, and he made it into one of the most popular restaurants in Havana. Having lost the restaurant to Castro, in 1962, Juan Saizarbitoria moved to Miami and set up Centro Vasco in exile. Along with a couple of funeral homes, it was one of the few big Cuban businesses to come to the United States virtually unchanged.

The first Centro Vasco in America was in a small building on the edge of Miami. After a year or so, Saizarbitoria bought the Garden from the departing Austrians. He didn't have enough money to redecorate, so he just hung a few paintings of his Basque homeland and of the Centro Vasco he'd left behind in Havana; otherwise, the walls remained covered with murals of the Black Forest and rustic Alpine scenes. The restaurant prospered: it became a home away from home for Miami's Cubans in exile. Soon there was money to spend, so a room was added, the parking lot was expanded, awnings were replaced. In-

side, the walls were redone in a dappled buttery yellow, and the memories of Austria were lost forever under a thick coat of paint. Until then,
there might have been no other place in the world so layered with different people's pinings—no other place where you could have had a
Basque dinner in a restaurant from Havana in a Cuban neighborhood
of a city in Florida in a dining room decorated with yodeling hikers and
little deer.

These days, Centro Vasco is an eventful place. During a week I spent
there recently, I would sometimes leaf back and forth through the
reservation book, which was kept on a desk in the restaurant's foyer.
The pages were rumpled, and blobbed with ink. Los Hombres Em-
presa, luncheon for twelve. Beatriz Barron, bridal shower. The Velgaras,
the Torreses, and the Delgados, baby showers. A birthday party for
Carmen Bravo and an anniversary party for Mr. and Mrs. Gerardo
Capo. A paella party for an association of Cuban dentists. A fund-
raiser for Manny Crespo, a candidate for judge. Southern Bell, a luncheon for twenty-eight people; someone had written next to the
reservation, in giant letters, and underlined, "NO SANGRIA." The
Little Havana Kiwanis Club cooking contest had been held in the
Granada Room; the finals for Miss Cuba en Exilio had taken place on
the patio. There were dinner reservations for people who wanted a bowl
of *caldo Gallego,* the white-bean soup they used to eat at Centro Vasco
in Havana; lunches for executives of Bacardi rum and for an adventur-
ous group of Pizza Hut executives from Wisconsin; hundreds of reservations for people coming on Friday and Saturday nights to hear the
popular Cuban singer Albita; a twice-annual reservation for the Cen-
tauros, 1941 alumni of a medical school in Havana; a daily reservation
for a group of ladies who used to play canasta together in Cuba and relocated their game to Miami thirty years ago.

    Juan Saizarbitoria goes through the book with me. This is not the
Juan of the sardine barrel; he died four years ago, at the age of eighty-
two. This is one of his sons—Juan Jr., who now runs the restaurant with
his brother, Iñaki. The Saizarbitorias are a great-looking family. Juan
Jr., who is near sixty, is pewter-haired and big-nosed and pink-cheeked;
his forehead is as wide as a billboard, and he holds his eyebrows high,
so he always looks a little amazed. Iñaki, fifteen years younger, is

rounder and darker, with an arching smile and small, bright eyes. Juan Jr.'s son, Juan III, is now an international fashion model and is nicknamed Sal. He is said to be the spitting image of sardine-barrel Juan, whom everyone called Juanito. Before Sal became a model, he used to work in the restaurant now and then. Old ladies who had had crushes on Juanito in Havana would swoon at the sight of Sal, because he looked so much like Juanito in his youth. Everyone in the family talks a million miles a minute—the blood relatives, the spouses, the kids. Juan Jr.'s wife, Totty, who helps to manage the place, once left a message on my answering machine that sounded a lot like someone running a Mixmaster. She knows everybody, talks to everybody, and seems to have things to say about the things she has to say. Once, she told me she was so tired she could hardly speak, but I didn't believe her. Juanito was not known as a talker; in fact, he spoke only Basque, could barely get along in Spanish, and never knew English at all. In Miami, he occasionally played golf with Jackie Gleason, to whom he had nothing to say. Some people remember Juanito as tough and grave but also surprisingly sentimental. He put a drawing of the Havana Centro Vasco on his Miami restaurant's business card, and he built a twenty-foot-wide scale model of it, furnished with miniature tables and chairs. It hangs over the bar in the Miami restaurant to this day.

On a Friday, I come to the restaurant early. The morning is hot and bright, but inside the restaurant it's dark and still. The rooms are a little old-fashioned: there are iron chandeliers and big, high-backed chairs; amber table lamps and white linen; black cables snaking from amplifiers across a small stage. Pictures of the many presidential candidates who have come here trolling for the Cuban vote are clustered on a wall by the door.

Now the heavy door of the restaurant opens, releasing a flat slab of light. Two, three, then a dozen men stroll into the foyer—elegant old lions, with slick gray hair and movie-mogul glasses and shirtsleeves shooting out of navy-blue blazer sleeves. Juan comes over to greet them, and then they saunter into the far room and prop their elbows on the end of the bar that is across from Juanito's model of the old Centro Vasco. These are members of the Vedado Tennis Club, which had been one of five exclusive clubs in Havana. Immediately after the revolution, the government took over the clubs and declared that from then on all Cuban citizens could use them, and just as immediately the club members left the country. Now the Vedado members meet for lunch on the first Friday of every month at Centro Vasco. Meanwhile, back in Havana, the old Vedado clubhouse is out of business—a stately wreck on a palm-shaded street.

The Vedado members order Scotch and martinis and highballs. The bartender serving them left Cuba just three months ago. They themselves left the Vedado behind in 1959, and they are as embittered as if they'd left it yesterday. A television over the bar is tuned to CNN, and news about the easing of the Cuban embargo makes a blue flash on the screen.

A buoy-shaped man with a droopy face is standing at the other end of the bar. He is Santiago Reyes, who had been a minister in the Batista regime, the bartender tells me.

Santiago Reyes winks as I approach him, then kisses my hand and says, "My sincere pleasure, my dear." He bobs onto a bar stool. Four men quickly surround him, their faces turned and opened, like sunflowers. Santiago Reyes's words pour forth. It's Spanish, which I don't understand, but I hear a familiar word here and there: "embargo," "United States," "Miami," "Castro," "yesterday," "government," "Cuba," "Cuba," "Cuba." Across the room, the Vedado members chat in marbled voices. There are perhaps thirty-five of them here now, out of a total of a few hundred, and there will never be more. There has never been anything in my life that I couldn't go back to if I really wanted to. I ask if Little Havana is anything like the real Havana.

One gray head swivels. "Absolutely not at all," he says. "Miami was a shock when we got here. It was like a big farm. Plants. Bushes. It was quite something to see."

I say that I want to go to Havana.

"While you're there, shoot Fidel for me," the man says, smoothing the lapels of his blazer.

I say that I think I would be too busy.

He tips his head back and peers over the top of his glasses, measuring me. Then he says, "Find the time."

The tennis club sits down to *filete de mero Centro Vasco*. The food here is mostly Basque, not Cuban: *porrusalda* (Basque chicken-potato-and-leek soup), and *rabo encendido* (simmered oxtail), and *callos a la*

Vasca (Basque tripe). Juanito made up the menu in Havana and brought it with him to Miami. It has hardly changed; the main exception is the addition of a vegetarian paella that the cook concocted for Madonna one night when she came here for a late dinner after performing in Miami.

I wander into the other dining room. At one table, Dr. Salvador Lew, of radio station WRHC, is having lunch with a couple who have recently recorded a collection of Latin American children's music. They are talking and eating on the air—as Dr. Lew does with one or more different political or cultural guests every weekday. The live microphone is passed around the table, followed by the garlic bread. From one to two every day, at 1550 AM on the radio dial, you can experience hunger pangs.

Iñaki and Totty sit at a round table near Dr. Lew, having a lunch meeting with two Colombians. The four are discussing a plan to market the restaurant to Colombians, who are moving into the neighborhood in droves. More and more, the Cubans who left Havana after Castro's arrival are now leaving Little Havana, with its pink dollhouses guarded by plaster lions, and its old shoe-box-shaped apartment buildings hemmed in by sagging cyclone fences—Little Havana, which is nothing like big Havana. The prosperous Cubans are moving to the pretty streets off Ponce de Leon Boulevard, in Coral Gables, which looks like the elegant Miramar section of Havana; or to Kendall, near the newest, biggest Miami malls; or to breezy golf-course houses on Key Biscayne. Centro Vasco, which had been an amble from their front doors and a home away from home, is now a fifteen-minute drive on a six-lane freeway—a home away from home away from home.

Totty and Iñaki think a lot about how to keep Centro Vasco going in the present. They have plans to open a Little Havana theme park behind the restaurant: there would be cigar and rum concessions and a huge map of Cuba, made out of Cuban soil, and a mural showing the names of American companies that want to do business in Cuba as soon as the embargo is lifted and Castro leaves. Totty and Iñaki have already added more live music on weekends in order to draw young people who were probably sick of hearing their parents talk about old Havana, and who otherwise might not want to spend time somewhere so sentimental and old-fashioned, so much part of another generation. Now performers like Albita and Malena Burke, another popular singer, draw them in. And even that has its ironies, because the music that Malena Burke and Albita perform here and have made so popular with young Cuban Americans is *son* and *guajira* and *bolero*—the sentimental, old-fashioned music of the prerevolutionary Cuban countryside. Totty and Iñaki have also come up with the idea that Centro Vasco ought to have a special Colombian day. As I sit down at their table, they and the Colombians are talking about something that ends with Iñaki saying, "Barbra Streisand, okay, she has a great, great, great voice, but she doesn't dance! She just stands there!"

The Colombians nod.

"Anyway," Totty says, "for the special Colombian day we'll have a Colombian menu, we'll decorate, it'll be so wonderful."

One of the Colombians clears his throat. He is as tanned as toast and has the kind of muscles you could bounce coins off. He says to Totty, "The perfect thing would be to do it on Cartagena Independence Day. We'll do a satellite feed of the finals from the Miss Colombia beauty pageant." He lifts his fork and pushes a clam around on his plate. "I think this will be very, very, very important to the community."

"Perfect," Totty says.

"We'll decorate," Iñaki says.

Totty says, "We'll make it so it will be just like home."

I told everyone that I wanted to go to Havana. The place had hung over my shoulder ever since I got to Miami. What kind of place was it, that it could persist so long in memory, make people murderous, make them hungry, make them cry?

"If you go, then you should go to the restaurant and look at the murals," Iñaki said. "If they're still there. There's one of a little boy dressed up in a Basque costume. White shirt, black beret, little lace-up shoes. If it's still there. Who knows? Anyway, the little Basque boy was me."

Juan laughed when I said I was going. I asked what it had been like on the day Castro's people took the restaurant away, and he said, "I was working that day, and two guys came in. With briefcases. They said they were running the restaurant now. They wanted the keys to the safe, and then they gave me a receipt for the cash and said they'd call me. They didn't call."

Was he shocked?

"About them taking the restaurant? No. Not really. It was like dying. You know it's going to happen to you eventually—you just don't know exactly what day."

One night at dinner, I tried to persuade Jauretsi, Juan's youngest daughter, to go with me, and she said, "It would be a scandal, the daughter of Centro Vasco going to Cuba. Seriously, a scandal. No way." I was eating *zarzuela de mariscos,* a thick seafood stew, with Jauretsi, Totty, and Sara Ruiz, a friend of mine who left Cuba fifteen years ago. Juan came over to our table for a moment, between seating guests. All the tables were full now, and grave-faced, gray-haired, black-vested waiters were crashing through the kitchen doors backward, bearing their big trays. Five guys at the table beside us were eating paella and talking on cellular phones; a father was celebrating his son's having passed the bar exam; a thirtyish man was murmuring to his date. In the next room, the Capos's anniversary party was under way. There was a cake in the foyer depicting the anniversary couple in frosting—a huge sheet cake, as flat as a flounder except for the sugary mounds of the woman's bust and the man's frosting cigar. The guests were the next generation, whose fathers had been at the Bay of Pigs and who had never seen Cuba themselves. The women had fashionable haircuts and were carrying black quilted handbags with bright gold chains. The young men swarmed together in the hall, getting party favors—fat cigars, rolled by a silent man whose hands were mottled and tobacco-stained.

"If you go to Havana, see if the food is any good now," Juan said to me.

"I heard that there is only one dish on the menu each night," Totty said.

Sara, my émigré friend, said she used to go to Centro Vasco all the time after Castro took it over. Now she was eating a bowl of *caldo Gallego,* which she said she had hankered for ever since the Saizarbitorias's restaurant was taken away. "In the Havana Centro Vasco, the food isn't good anymore," she said. "It's no good. It's all changed." You have to pay for the food in United States dollars, not Cuban pesos, she said, but you don't have to leave a tip, because doing so is considered counterrevolutionary.

The Basque boy is still there, in Havana. His white shirt is now the color of lemonade, though, because after the revolution the murals on the walls of Centro Vasco were covered with a layer of yellowish varnish to preserve the old paint.

My waiter in Havana remembered Juanito. "He left on a Thursday," the waiter said. "He told me about it on a Wednesday. I was at the restaurant working that day." I was at Centro Vasco, sitting at a huge round table with a Cuban friend of Sara's, eating the *caldo Gallego* that made everybody so homesick, but, just as I'd been warned, it wasn't the same. The waiter whispered, "We need a Basque in the kitchen, but we don't have any Basques left," and then he took the soup away. The restaurant looks exactly like Juanito's model—a barnlike Moorish-style building, with an atrium entryway. The government has had it for thirty-five years now and has left it just as Juanito left it, with a fish tank and a waterfall in the foyer, and, inside, thronelike brown chairs, and cool tile floors, and the murals—Basques playing jai alai and rowing sculls and hoisting boulders and herding sheep—wrapping the room. As I had been told, business is done in dollars. People with dollars in Cuba are either tourists or Cubans who have some business on the black market or abroad. When my new Cuban friend and I came in, a Bruce Willis movie was blaring from the television in the bar. At a table on one side of ours, a lone Nicaraguan businessman with clunky black eyeglasses was poking his spoon into a flan, and at the table on our other side a family of eight were singing and knocking their wine goblets together to celebrate the arrival of one of them from Miami that very day.

I myself had been in Havana for two days. On the first, I went to the old Centro Vasco, where Juanito had started: not the place where he had moved the restaurant when it became prosperous, the one he'd built a model of to hang over the Miami bar, but the original one— a wedge-shaped white building on the wide road that runs along Havana's waterfront. The wedge building had been Havana's Basque center—the *centro Vasco*—and it had had jai-alai courts and lodgings and a dining room, and Juanito, the pretend world-famous jai-alai player, had started his cooking career by making meals for the Basques who came.

That was years ago now, and the place is not the same. My new friend drove me there, and we parked and walked along the building's long, blank eastern side. It was once an elegant, filigreed building. Now its ivory paint was peeling off in big, plate-size pieces, exposing one or two or three other colors of paint. Near the door, I saw something on the sidewalk that looked like a soggy paper bag. Close up, I saw that it was a puddle of brown blood and a goat's head, with a white striped muzzle and tiny, pearly teeth. My friend gasped, and said that it was probably a Santería ritual offering, common in the countryside but hardly ever seen on a city street. We looked at it for a moment. A few cars muttered by. I felt a little woozy. The heat was pressing on my head like a foot on a gas pedal, and the goat was pretty well cooked.

Inside the building, there were burst-open bags of cement mix, two-by-fours, bricks, rubble. An old barber chair. A fat, friendly, shirtless man shoring up a doorway. On the wall beside him were a mural of Castro wearing a big hat and, above that, a scene from the first day of the revolution, showing Castro and his comrades wading ashore from a cabin cruiser. This room had been the old Centro Vasco's kitchen, and its dining room had been upstairs. Now the whole building is a commissary, where food is prepared and is then sent on to a thousand people working for the government's Construction Ministry.

After a minute, a subdirector in the Ministry stepped through the rubble—a big, bearish man with shaggy blond hair and an angelic face. He said the workers' lunch today had been fish with tomato sauce, bologna, boiled bananas, and rice and black beans. He wanted us to come upstairs to see where the old Centro Vasco dining room had been, and as we made our way there he told us that it had been divided into a room for his office and a room where the workers' gloves are made and their shoes are repaired. He had eaten there when it was the old Centro Vasco, he added. It had had a great view, and now, standing at his desk, we could see the swooping edge of the Gulf of Mexico, the hulking crenellated Morro Castle, the narrow neck of the Bay of Havana, the wide coastal road, the orange-haired hookers who loll on the low gray breakwater, and then acres and acres of smooth blue water shining like chrome in the afternoon light. The prettiness of the sight made us all quiet, and then the subdirector said he had heard that some Spanish investors were thinking of buying the building and turning it back into a restaurant. "It's a pity the way it is now," he said. "It was a wonderful place."

That night, my friend and I ate dinner at a *paladar,* a kind of private café that Cubans are now permitted to own and operate, provided that it has no more than twelve chairs and four tables and is in their home. This one was in a narrow house in Old Havana, and the kitchen was the kitchen of the house, and the tables and the chairs were set in the middle of the living room. The owner was a stained-glass artist by trade, and he sat on a sofa near our table and chatted while we ate. He said that he loved the restaurant business, and that he and his wife were doing so well that they could hardly wait until the government permitted more chairs, because they were ready to buy them.

I went back to Centro Vasco one more time before leaving Cuba—not the old place, in the wedge building, but the new, Moorish one, in a section of Havana called Vedado, which is now a jumble of houses and ugly new hotels but for decades had been a military installation. I wanted to go once more to be sure I'd remember it, because I didn't know if I'd ever be back again. I went with my new friend and her husband, who was sentimental about the restaurant in the Vedado, because during the revolution he had fought just down the street from it. While he was driving us to Centro Vasco, he pointed to where he'd been stationed, saying, "Right—here! Oh, it was wonderful! I was preparing a wonderful catapult mechanism to launch hand grenades." In front of the restaurant someone had parked a milky-white 1957 Ford Fairlane, and some little boys were horsing around near it. On the sidewalk, four men were playing dominoes at a bowlegged table, and the *clack, clack* of the tiles sounded like the tapping of footsteps on the street. The same apologetic waiter was in the dining room, and he brought us plates of *gambas a la plancha* and *pollo frito con mojo criollo* and *tortilla Centro Vasco*. The restaurant was nearly empty. The manager came and stood proudly by our table, and so did the busboys and the other waiters and a heavy woman in a kitchen uniform who had been folding a huge stack of napkins while watching us eat. Toward the end of the meal, someone came in and warned us that our car was going to be lifted and carried away. I thought he meant that it was being stolen, but he meant that it was being relocated: Castro would be driving by soon, and, because he was worried about car bombs, he became nervous if he saw cars parked on the street.

As we were leaving, the waiter stopped us at the door. He had a glossy eight-by-ten he wanted to show me—a glamorous-looking photograph of Juan Jr.'s wedding. He said that it was his favorite keepsake. The Saizarbitorias had left nearly everything behind when they left Cuba. Juan was allowed to take only a little bit of money and three changes of clothes. In Miami, Juan's daughter Mirentxu had remarked to me on how strange it was to have so few family mementos and scrapbooks and pictures—it was almost as if the past had never taken place. I admired the wedding picture for a minute. Then the waiter and I talked a little about old Juanito. I couldn't tell whether the waiter knew that Juanito had died, so I didn't say anything. Meanwhile, he told me that a friend of his had once sent him a napkin from Centro Vasco in Miami, and he had saved it. He said, "I've had so many feelings over these years, but I never imagined that Juanito would never come back."

There had been one other Centro Vasco, but it wasn't possible for me to visit it. It had been the first Centro Vasco that Juanito opened in the United States, on the corner of Ponce de Leon and Douglas Road, in a building that straddled the border between Miami and Coral Gables— a place that might have been satisfactory except that the two cities had different liquor laws. If you wanted a drink, you had to be sure to get a table on the Miami side. The border had come to be too much trouble, so Juanito moved to Southwest Eighth Street, and eventually the old building was torn down.

But I did go back to the Centro Vasco on Southwest Eighth one more time after I came back from Cuba. It was a Saturday night, and it was busy: people were coming for dinner and to hear Malena Burke sing. I wanted to tell the Saizarbitorias about my trip, to tell them that the Basque boy was still there and that the food wasn't very good, but that the restaurant was just as they had left it and, in spite of the thirty-three years that had passed, was still in fine shape. Then I realized that I didn't know whether they would be glad or sorry about what I would tell them. In Havana, everyone I met talked constantly about the future, about what might happen when the United States lifted its embargo and when Castro retired, both of which events they expected soon. To the people I met in Cuba, the present seemed provisional and the past nearly forgotten, and their yearning was keen—charged with anticipation. In Miami, the present moment is satisfying, and thought is given to the future, but the past seems like the richest place—

frequently visited, and as familiar and real and comforting as an old family home.

The music wasn't to start until after midnight, so for a long time I stood in the foyer and watched people parade in: the executive of a Latin American television network, in a tight white suit and high white shoes; an editor from a Spanish soap-opera magazine; a Puerto Rican singer who had just performed at Dade County Auditorium, followed by her entourage; another singer, named Franco, who called out to someone while he and I were talking, "Hey, man, you look great! I thought you were dead!"; and dozens of good-looking couples speaking in bubbly Spanish, and all wearing something that glistened or sparkled or had a satiny shine. Toward midnight, Sherman Hemsley, of *The Jeffersons*, came in with a television producer, and Iñaki wrote "Cherman Jemsli Del Show Los Jeffersons" on a little slip of paper for Malena, so that when she pointed him out in the audience she'd know what to say.

Malena came onstage at one in the morning. She began with a ballad that had been made famous in Cuba in the fifties by a singer called La Lupe, who used to get so emotional when she reached the crescendo that she hurled things at the audience—usually her shoes and her wig. The room had been roaring before Malena came out, but now it was hushed. Malena had left Cuba just a few months earlier. Someone told me that the tears she sheds when she's singing about lost love are really real. By then, I was sitting at a table in the back of the room with Totty. I had some snapshots with me that I had taken in Havana for the family, because I'd thought they might like to see the old home again. Just as I was about to slide the pictures across the table to Totty, the singer sobbed to her crescendo, so I decided to wait until another day.

1996

THE MAGIC BAGEL

CALVIN TRILLIN

My wife and I came up with differing interpretations of a conversation I had with our older daughter, Abigail, not long after a dimsum lunch in Chinatown. Abigail, who lives in San Francisco, was in New York to present a paper at a conference. As a group of us trooped back toward Greenwich Village, where she'd grown up and where my wife, Alice, and I still live, Abigail and I happened to be walking together. "Let's get this straight, Abigail," I said, after we'd finished off some topic and had gone along in silence for a few moments. "If I can find those gnarly little dark pumpernickel bagels that we used to get at Tanenbaum's, you'll move back to New York. Right?"

"Absolutely," Abigail said.

When I reported that exchange to Alice, she said that Abigail was speaking ironically. I found it difficult to believe that anybody could be ironic about those bagels. They were almost black. Misshapen. Oniony. Abigail adored them. Both of my daughters have always taken bagels seriously. My younger daughter, Sarah, also lives in California—she's in Los Angeles—and she often complains about the bagels there being below her standards. For a while, I brought along a dozen bagels for Sarah whenever I went to L.A., but I finally decided that this policy was counterproductive. "If a person prefers to live in California, which happens to be thousands of miles from her very own parents," I told her, "it seems to me appropriate that such a person eat California

bagels. I understand that in some places out there if you buy a dozen wheat-germ bagels you get one bee-pollen bagel free."

Abigail, it should be noted, always had bagel standards at least as high as Sarah's. I have previously documented the moment when I realized that she was actually a New Yorker (until she was four or five, I had somehow thought of her as being from the same place I'm from, Kansas City): we were back in Missouri visiting my family, and she said, "Daddy, how come in Kansas City the bagels taste like just round bread?" In other words, she knew the difference between those bagel-shaped objects available in American supermarkets and the authentic New York item that had been hand-rolled and boiled in a vat and then carefully baked by a member in good standing of the Bakery and Confectionery Workers International Union. My sadness at the evidence that she wasn't actually from my hometown was offset by my pride in the evidence that she was precocious.

Would Proust have been ironic about the madeleine, particularly if he had fetched up in a place where you couldn't get a decent madeleine if your life depended on it? When my daughters were children, bagels were not only their staple food but also the food of important rituals. On Sunday mornings, I often took them to Houston Street, on the Lower East Side. At Russ & Daughters, which is what New Yorkers call an appetizer store, we would buy Nova Scotia salmon—a transaction that took some time, since the daughters (of Joel Russ, the founder, who stared down at us from a splendid portrait on the wall) had to quit slicing fish now and then to tell me in glorious detail how adorable my girls were. Then we'd go next door to Ben's Dairy to get cream cheese and a delicacy known as baked farmer's cheese with scallions. Then we were at Tanenbaum's, a bakery that was probably best known for a large, dark loaf often referred to as Russian health bread. We were not there for Russian health bread.

"So you think she's just humoring her old dad?" I asked Alice, when we discussed the conversation I'd had with Abigail on the way back from Chinatown.

"I do."

Alice was probably right. I understood that. Abigail enjoys living in California, and she's got a job there that she loves. Children grow up and lead lives of their own. Parents are supposed to accept that. Still, I decided that I'd look around for those pumpernickel bagels. As my father used to say, "What could it hurt?"

It wasn't my first try. When the pumpernickel bagels disappeared, I immediately made serious inquiries. Without wanting to cast blame, I have to say that the disappearance occurred on Mutke's watch. Mutke's formal name is Hyman Perlmutter. In the early seventies, he bought Tanenbaum's Bakery and transformed it into the downtown branch of a bakery he ran eight or ten blocks away called Moishe's. For some time, Mutke carried Tanenbaum's full inventory. Then one day—I don't remember precisely when, but Abigail and Sarah were still living at home—the pumpernickel bagels were no longer there. Confronted with the facts, Mutke was sanguine. Those particular bagels weren't available anymore, he explained, but, as a special order, he could always provide me with a dozen or two just like them. Eventually, he did. I pulled one out of the bag. It was a smooth bagel, uniformly round. It was the color of cappuccino, heavy on the milk. It was a stranger to onions. It was not by any means Abigail's bagel.

I realize now, of course, that I gave up too easily. Sure, I stopped by to try the pumpernickel anytime I heard of a promising new bagel bakery—even if it was uptown, a part of the city I don't venture to unnecessarily. But I didn't make a systematic search. How was I to know that bagels can be instrumental in keeping families intact? This time, I was going to be thorough. I had read in Molly O'Neill's *New York Cook Book* about a place in Queens where bagels were made in the old-fashioned way. I figured that there must be similar places in Brooklyn neighborhoods with a large population of Orthodox Jews—Williamsburg, maybe, or Borough Park. I was prepared to go to the outer boroughs. But I thought it made sense to start back on Houston Street.

The area where Abigail and Sarah and I used to make our Sunday rounds has seen some changes over the years. The old tenement streets used to seem grim. Now they sport patches of raffish chic. On Orchard Street, around the corner from our Sunday-morning purveyors, stores that have traditionally offered bargains on fabrics and women's clothing and leather goods are punctuated by the sort of clothing store that has a rack of design magazines and a coffee bar and such a spare display of garments that you might think you're in the studio apartment of someone who has bizarre taste in cocktail dresses and no closet to keep them in. These days, the Lower East Side is a late-night destination—both Orchard and Ludlow have bars too hip to require a sign—and a cool place to live. After spending years listening to customers tell him that he ought to move Russ & Daughters uptown, Mark Federman, the son of one of the daughters, is renovating the apartments above the store and expressing gratitude that his grandfather held on to the building.

Ben's Dairy has closed, and Moishe's Bakery has moved to a tiny place around the corner. But Russ & Daughters has been carefully preserved to look pretty much the way it did when the founder himself still had his arms deep in the herring barrel. I figured Mark might have some information I could use, and he was bound to be sympathetic to the project: his daughter, Niki, recently graduated from college and moved to San Francisco. "Do you think Niki might come back, too, if we found the bagels?" I asked, as Mark and I edged ourselves into the tiny office he shares with his wife, Maria.

"I don't think she'd come back for bagels," he said. "Maybe for an apartment upstairs."

Maria shook her head. "I already offered," she said.

Mark said that he knew precisely the bagel I was talking about, but that he had no idea where to find it. He phoned his mother, who's retired, in Florida. "Do you remember when Tanenbaum next door used to have this sort of gnarly—" he began, and then started to laugh. "Not an old woman," he said. "I'm asking about bagels." Apparently, his mother remembered the gnarly old woman quite well. Not the bagels.

Although Russ & Daughters carries bagels these days, Mark insisted that he didn't have the expertise to be much help in tracing a particular baker; locating an obscure source of belly lox would have been more his line of country. Still, he made a couple of calls, including one to Mosha's Bread, a wholesale operation in Williamsburg, which has been turning out pumpernickel since the late nineteenth century. (Mosha's Bread, it almost goes without saying, has no connection with Moishe's Bakery.) As I was about to leave Russ's, the boss of Mosha's, who turned out to be a woman named Cecile Erde Farkas, returned Mark's call. Mark introduced himself, and before he could explain my quest he began to sound like someone on the receiving end of a sales pitch. "To tell you the truth, I don't sell much bread," I heard him say, and then, "Here's what I could use—a good babka. I could sell the hell out of a good babka . . . plain, yeah, and chocolate."

There was a message on my answering machine that evening from Mark. He had reached a friend of his named Danny Scheinin, who ran

Kossar's, a distinguished purveyor of bialys, for decades before selling out a year or two ago. "Danny says he thinks Tanenbaum got that bagel from somebody named Poznanski," Mark said when I got back to him. "Also, he says it wasn't a real bagel."

"Not a real bagel!"

"I don't know exactly what he means," Mark said. "Talk to him."

When I reached Scheinin, I found out that what he'd meant was this: In the old days, there was a sharp split between bagel bakeries and bread bakeries. The bagel bakers had their own local, No. 338. They didn't bake bread and bread bakers didn't make bagels. Originally, of course, bagels were made only with white flour. But some bread bakers who trafficked in pumpernickel would twist some bread dough into bagel shapes and bake them. By not going through the intermediate boiling that is part of the process of making an authentic bagel, they stayed out of another local's jurisdiction. Scheinin was confident that Abigail's bagel had been made that way for Tanenbaum's by a bread baker named Sam Poznanski, in Williamsburg, who died some years ago. As far as Scheinin knew, the bakery still existed, under the management of Poznanski's wife. He gave me the number. "Tell her Danny from the bialys said to call," he told me.

Mrs. Poznanski, I have to say, did not seem terribly engaged by my quest. The longest answer she gave was when I asked her if Poznanski's had quit making the pumpernickel bagel when her husband died, and she said, "No. Before." Still, she confirmed that the object of Abigail's adoration was from Poznanski's and that it was not boiled. This was hard news to take. It sounded perilously close to saying that the bagel we were searching for was just round bread. But what bread!

The bread/bagel split was confirmed by Herb Bostick, a business agent of Local 3 of the Bakery and Confectionery Workers International Union, which by now has absorbed No. 338 into a local that mixes bagel bakers and bread bakers and cake bakers together the way someone faced with baking a pie at the last minute might mix in bits of whatever kinds of flour happened to be in the cupboard. What Bostick said was in line with what I'd learned from Cecile Farkas, of Mosha's, with whom I'd arranged a meeting after her babka pitch to Mark. She'd told me that for years her late father offered pumpernickel bagels that were baked without being boiled first. "Then they weren't real bagels?" I'd said.

"If my daddy called them bagels they were bagels," Mrs. Farkas said.

I hadn't had to journey to the outer boroughs to see Cecile Farkas. By chance, she was doing a bread promotion at a store on Twenty-third

Street. She turned out to be a chatty woman in her sixties, who told me that she had joined Mosha's only when her father became elderly; she'd been trained as an electrical engineer. That didn't surprise me. Mark Federman had been a lawyer. A family business is no respecter of degrees. Mrs. Farkas told me that her own daughter, having earned her master's in career counseling, plans to launch Mosha's West. Would Mosha's West be a few blocks closer to Manhattan than the original Mosha's? No. Her daughter lives in San Francisco. Cecile Farkas said that with only a few hours' notice, Mosha's could duplicate the sort of bagel Abigail craves. "It would be my pleasure," she said.

"If that happens and Abigail moves back to New York, you would have done a mitzvah," I said. "It would be written next to your name in the Book of Life."

Mrs. Farkas shrugged off any thought of reward. "It would be my pleasure," she repeated. I had recognized her as a person of character the moment she'd told me that whatever her daddy said was a bagel was a bagel.

I tried to present the situation to Alice in an objective way: "I suppose you think that if Mosha's really did succeed in duplicating the bagel and I told Abigail that it was readily available in the neighborhood and I didn't trouble her with the really quite arcane information that it's not, technically speaking, a bagel, I would be acting completely contrary to everything we tried to teach her about honesty and integrity."

"Yes," Alice said.

"I thought you might."

She's right, of course. I know that. Lately, though, it has occurred to me that there were areas I left unexplored in my conversation with Mrs. Poznanski. It's true that she expressed no interest whatsoever in bagels, but what if I got Mark Federman to agree to carry those little pumpernickel numbers—not instead of Mrs. Farkas's babkas, I hasten to say, but in addition to Mrs. Farkas's babkas. Would the Russ & Daughters account be enough to propel Poznanski's back into the bagel business? This is assuming, of course, that Sam Poznanski's recipe still exists. All in all, it's a long shot. Still, I'm thinking of making a trip to Williamsburg. What could it hurt?

2000

A RAT IN MY SOUP

PETER HESSLER

"Do you want a big rat or a small rat?" the waitress asked. I was getting used to making difficult decisions in Luogang, a small village in southern China's Guangdong province. I'd come here on a whim, having heard that Luogang had a famous restaurant that specialized in the preparation of rats. Upon arrival, however, I discovered that there were two celebrated restaurants—the Highest Ranking Wild Flavor Restaurant and the New Eight Sceneries Wild Flavor Food City. They were next door to each other, and they had virtually identical bamboo-and-wood décors. Moreover, their owners were both named Zhong—but then everybody in Luogang seemed to be named Zhong. The two Zhongs were not related, and competition between them was keen. As a foreign journalist, I'd been cajoled to such an extent that, in an effort to please both Zhongs, I agreed to eat two lunches, one at each restaurant.

The waitress at the Highest Ranking Wild Flavor Restaurant, who was also named Zhong (in Chinese, it means "bell"), asked again, "Do you want a big rat or a small rat?"

"What's the difference?" I said.

"The big rats eat grass stems, and the small ones eat fruit."

I tried a more direct tack. "Which tastes better?"

"Both of them taste good."

"Which do you recommend?"

"Either one."

I glanced at the table next to mine. Two parents, a grandmother, and a little boy were having lunch. The boy was gnawing on a rat drumstick. I couldn't tell if the drumstick had belonged to a big rat or a small rat. The boy ate quickly. It was a warm afternoon. The sun was shining. I made my decision. "Small rat," I said.

The Chinese say that people in Guangdong will eat anything. Besides rat, a customer at the Highest Ranking Wild Flavor Restaurant can order turtledove, fox, cat, python, and an assortment of strange-looking local animals whose names do not translate into English. All of them are kept live in pens at the back of the restaurant and are killed only when a customer orders one of them. Choosing among them involves considerations beyond flavor or texture. You order cat not just because you enjoy the taste of cat but because cats are said to impart a lively *jingshen* (spirit). You eat deer penis to improve virility. Snakes make you stronger. And rat? "It keeps you from going bald," Zhong Shaocong, the daughter of the owner of the Highest Ranking Wild Flavor Restaurant, told me. Zhong Qingjiang, the owner of the New Eight Sceneries Wild Flavor Food City, went further. "If you have white hair and eat rat regularly, it will turn black," she said. "And if you're going bald and you eat rat every day, your hair will stop falling out. A lot of the parents around here feed rat to a small child who doesn't have much hair, and the hair grows better."

Earlier this year, Luogang opened a "restaurant street" in the newly developed Luogang Economic Open Zone, a parkland and restaurant district designed to draw visitors from nearby Guangzhou city. The government invested $1,200,000 in the project, which enabled the two rat restaurants to move from their old, cramped quarters in a local park into new, greatly expanded spaces—about 1,800 square feet for each establishment. The Highest Ranking Wild Flavor Restaurant, which cost $42,000 to build, opened in early March. Six days later, the New Eight Sceneries Wild Flavor Food City opened, on an investment of $54,000. A third restaurant—a massive, air-conditioned facility, which is expected to cost $72,000—will open soon. A fourth is in the planning stages.

On the morning of my initiation into rat cuisine, I visited the construction site of the third facility, whose owner, Deng Ximing, was the only local restaurateur not named Zhong. He was married to a Zhong, however, and he had the fast-talking confidence of a successful entrepreneur. I also noticed that he had a good head of hair. He spoke of the village's culinary tradition with pride. "It's more than a thousand years old," he said. "And it's always been rats from the mountains—we're not eating city rats. The mountain rats are clean, because up there they aren't eating anything dirty. Mostly, they eat fruit—oranges, plums, jackfruit. People from the government hygiene department have been here to examine the rats. They took them to the laboratory and checked them out thoroughly to see if they had any diseases, and they found nothing. Not even the slightest problem."

Luogang's restaurant street has been a resounding success. Newspapers and television stations have reported extensively on the benefits of the local specialty, and an increasing number of customers are making the half-hour trip from Guangzhou city. Both the Highest Ranking Wild Flavor Restaurant and the New Eight Sceneries Wild Flavor Food City serve, on average, three thousand rats every Saturday and Sunday, which are the peak dining days. "Many people come from faraway places," Zhong Qingjiang told me. "They come from Guangzhou, Shenzhen, Hong Kong, Macao. One customer came all the way from America with her son. They were visiting relatives in Luogang, and the family brought them here to eat. She said you couldn't find this kind of food in America."

In America, needless to say, you would be hard-pressed to find twelve thousand fruit-fed rats anywhere on any weekend, but this isn't a problem in Luogang. On my first morning in the village, I watched dozens of peasants come down from the hills, looking to get a piece of the rat business. They came on mopeds, on bicycles, and on foot. All of them carried burlap sacks of squirming rats that had been trapped on their farms.

"Last year, I sold my oranges for fifteen cents a pound," a farmer named Zhong Senji told me. "But this year the price has dropped to less than ten cents." Like many other peasants, Zhong decided that he could do a lot better with rats. Today, he had nine rats in his sack. When the sack was put on a scale in the rear of the Highest Ranking Wild Flavor Restaurant, it shook and squeaked. It weighed in at just under three pounds, and Zhong received the equivalent in yuan of $1.45 per pound, for a total of $3.87. In Luogang, rats are more expensive than pork or chicken. A pound of rat costs nearly twice as much as a pound of beef.

At the Highest Ranking Wild Flavor Restaurant, I began with a dish called Simmered Mountain Rat with Black Beans. There were plenty of other options on the menu—among them, Mountain Rat Soup, Steamed Mountain Rat, Simmered Mountain Rat, Roasted Mountain Rat, Mountain Rat Curry, and Spicy and Salty Mountain Rat—but the waitress had enthusiastically recommended the Simmered Mountain Rat with Black Beans, which arrived in a clay pot.

I ate the beans first. They tasted fine. I poked at the rat meat. It was clearly well done, and it was attractively garnished with onions, leeks, and ginger. Nestled in a light sauce were skinny rat thighs, short strips of rat flank, and delicate, toylike rat ribs. I started with a thigh, put a chunk of it into my mouth, and reached for a glass of beer. The beer helped.

The restaurant's owner, Zhong Dieqin, came over and sat down. "What do you think?" she asked.

"I think it tastes good."

"You know it's good for your health."

"I've heard that."

"It's good for your hair and skin," she said. "It's also good for your kidneys."

Earlier that morning, I'd met a peasant who told me that my brown hair might turn black if I ate enough rat. Then he thought for a moment and said that he wasn't certain if eating rat had the same effect on foreigners that it did on the Chinese—it might do something entirely different to me. The possibility seemed to interest him a great deal.

Zhong Dieqin watched me intently. "Are you sure you like it?" she asked.

"Yes," I said, tentatively. In fact, it wasn't bad. The meat was lean and white, without a hint of gaminess. Gradually, my squeamishness faded, and I tried to decide what, exactly, the flavor of rat reminded me of. But nothing came to mind. It simply tasted like rat.

After a while, Zhong Dieqin excused herself, and the waitress drifted away. A young man came over and identified himself as the restaurant's assistant manager. He wanted to know whether I had come to Luogang specifically to report on the restaurants. I said that I had. "Did you register with the government before you came here?" he asked.

"No."

"Why not?"

"Because it's too much trouble."

"You should have done that—those are the rules," he said. There was a wariness in his voice, which I recognized as part of a syndrome that is pervasive throughout China: Fear of a Foreign Writer.

"I don't think the government cares very much if I write about restaurants," I said.

"They could help you," he said. "They would give you statistics and arrange interviews."

"I can find my own interviews. And if I registered with the government I would have to take all of the government officials out to lunch." A scene appeared in my mind: a gaggle of Communist cadres, middle-aged men in cheap suits, all of them eating rat. I put my chopsticks down.

The assistant manager kept talking. "A lot of foreigners come to our China to write about human rights," he said.

"That's true."

He looked at me hard. "Have you come here to write about human rights?"

"Have I asked you any questions about human rights?"

"No."

"Well, then, it would be hard for me to write a story about human rights. I'm writing a story about Luogang's rat restaurants. It's nothing sensitive."

"You should have registered with the government," he said stubbornly.

Next door, at the New Eight Sceneries Wild Flavor Food City, the Zhongs were more media-savvy. They asked if I had brought along a television crew. They looked disappointed when I said that I hadn't. Then the floor manager brightened and asked me how I'd liked their competition.

"It was fine," I said.

"What did you eat?"

"Simmered Mountain Rat with Black Beans."

"You'll like ours better," she said. "Our cook is better, the service is quicker, and the waitresses are more polite."

I decided to order the Spicy and Salty Mountain Rat. This time, when the waitress asked about my preference in sizes, I said, pleased with my boldness, "Big rat."

"Come and choose it."

"What?"

"Pick out the rat you want."

I followed one of the kitchen workers to a shed behind the restaurant, where cages were stacked atop one another. Each cage contained more than thirty rats. The shed did not smell good. The worker pointed at a rat.

"How about this one?" he said.

"Um, sure."

He put on a glove, opened the cage, and picked up the chosen rat. It was about the size of a softball. "Is it okay?" he said.

"Yes."

"Are you certain?"

The rat gazed at me with beady eyes.

I nodded.

Suddenly, the worker flipped his wrist, swung the rat into the air by the tail, and let go. The rat made a neat arc. There was a soft thud when its head struck the cement floor. There wasn't much blood. The worker grinned. "You can go back to the dining room now," he said. "We'll bring it out to you soon."

"Okay," I said.

Less than fifteen minutes later, the dish was at my table, garnished with carrots and leeks. The chef came out of the kitchen to join the owner, Zhong Qingjiang, the floor manager, and a cousin of the owner to watch me eat. "How is it?" the chef asked.

"Good."

"Is it too tough?"

"No," I said. "It's fine."

In truth, I was trying hard not to taste anything. I had lost my appetite in the shed, and now I ate quickly, washing every bit down with beer. I did my best to put on a good show, gnawing on the bones as enthusiastically as possible. When I finished, I sat back and managed a smile. The chef and the others nodded with approval.

The owner's cousin said, "Next time you should try the Longfu Soup, because it contains tiger, dragon, and phoenix."

"What do you mean by 'tiger, dragon, and phoenix'?" I asked warily. I didn't want to make another trip to the shed.

"It's not real tigers, dragons, and phoenixes," he assured me. "They're represented by other animals—cat for the tiger, snake for the dragon, and chicken for the phoenix. When you mix them together, there are all kinds of health benefits. And they taste good, too."

2002

RAW FAITH

BURKHARD BILGER

If it's all the same to you, Mother Noella Marcellino would rather you didn't call her the cheese nun. It's true that she makes cheese— a New England variation on the unctuous Saint-Nectaire of Auvergne. And, yes, she lives in a Benedictine cloister, the Abbey of Regina Laudis, in Bethlehem, Connecticut. Were you to point out that she just finished filming a documentary in France called *The Cheese Nun,* you would not be incorrect. Yet when Noella thinks of herself, which seems to happen only rarely, she does so in terms both more scientific and more spiritual: as an authority on cheese molds, or as a singer of gospel and Gregorian chant. One of her best friends was a blues musician, but that can give rise to its own misconceptions. She was a little miffed, a few years ago, when a French newspaper ran a story headlined SHE DOES RESEARCH BY DAY AND SINGS BLUES IN THE CHURCHES OF THE JURA BY NIGHT.

Mother Noella has spent twenty-nine of her fifty-one years in the abbey. Although she has occasionally been given permission to travel, she must spend all other nights and many hours of daily prayer behind the wooden scrims and walls of the cloister. In 1985, she took her final vows to remain at Regina Laudis for the rest of her life, earning the title of Mother. Yet her secular interests have only widened and deepened over the years. This winter she is completing a Ph.D. in microbiology, even as she helps shepherd the country through a culture war of an unusual sort: a war of cheese.

The United States has long produced more cheese than any other country: eight and a half billion pounds in 2001 alone, enough to stuff the Sears Tower, like an enormous celery stick, four times over. But for nearly a century that tower of curd has been a purely industrial product—formulated, manufactured, extruded, and dispensed with the kind of machinery usually reserved for making plastic. Only in the past fifteen years has a generation of former lawyers and first-time farmers, dot-com dropouts and back-to-the-landers, begun to develop true artisanal cheeses. "American cheesemaking is where winemaking was in the late 1970s," the food writer Clark Wolf says. "Every time you taste something new, you're shocked at how much better it is." Cheesemakers like Willow Smart, in Milton, Vermont, are creating their own rural traditions—Smart treats her sheep homeopathically and uses llamas to protect them from coyotes—and rivaling Europeans for the first time. Outside Louisville, Kentucky, Judy Schad, of Capriole Farms, makes some of the finest goat cheeses in the world. "The French have seven hundred years of experience, they've got experimental cheese stations, and their milk supply is subsidized," Schad says. "But my Mont St. Francis can kick a French Muenster all the way across the Atlantic."

One essential ingredient in this success is easy to isolate: the raw milk in many artisanal cheeses, unlike the pasteurized milk used by Kraft or Borden, is alive with billions of bacteria. These cultures transform the cheese as it ages, breaking down fats and proteins and giving off esters and other compounds that are the building blocks of flavor and aroma. Of course, bacteria can have less salubrious effects, too: well into the last century, raw milk was a prime breeding ground for tuberculosis and typhoid. Consequently, the Food and Drug Administration has required that all store-bought milk be pasteurized (heated to 145 degrees for thirty minutes, or to 161 degrees for fifteen seconds) and, since 1947, that all raw-milk cheeses be aged for at least sixty days. The assumption has been that pathogens can't survive in the dry, acid environment of an aged cheese. But six years ago a small study in South Dakota found that *Escherichia coli* could survive the sixty-day limit in cheddar, and the FDA took part in a study to verify the results. Raw-milk cheese, the study warned, might have to be aged for more than sixty days to be safe—if it can be made safely at all.

The news was even more upsetting to Europeans than it was to Americans. Unaged raw-milk cheese is considered a birthright in France and Italy, yet even before the FDA's research was complete, the United States began pushing for an international ban on raw-milk cheese. Cheesemakers responded by circulating petitions and forming advocacy groups, including a European raw-milk alliance and the International Coalition to Preserve the Right to Choose Your Cheese (now called the Cheese of Choice Coalition). They argued that raw milk is often healthier than pasteurized milk, and that cheese-borne illnesses are extremely rare. But it was hard to sway regulators with talk of tradition and "good bacteria." What was needed was an ally of impeccable character and scientific standing, someone to whom cheesemakers could bring their microbial troubles and ask for guidance. What was needed was a cheese nun.

On a gusty morning in April, Mother Noella strode across the University of Connecticut campus at Storrs, her habit flapping and billowing behind her, her gait both stiff-backed and rollicking. Beneath her white wimple, her plump cheeks were flushed and she peered out with a kind of cockeyed glee. She'd warned me before the ride to the campus that she had a lazy eye, but I thought she was joking until I saw her squinting at the side-view mirror. "Don't be nervous," she said, grabbing the wheel as the car lurched into gear. "That's my blind side anyway." Now, after an eventful parallel-parking session, we were going to meet her doctoral adviser, David Benson. "You should have seen me on some of those nights commuting back to the abbey," she said. "Midnight in downtown Hartford, after experiments with ether—that's when it got really interesting."

She let out a raucous laugh and bustled up the stairs of the molecular-and-cell-biology building, toward the labs that have served her as a kind of second cloister for the past ten years. She went past orange biohazard and radioactivity signs, past a virus lab that was off limits to pregnant women, and into a room cluttered with old beakers and calcium-crusted instruments. "The FBI was all over the building next door after September 11," Benson said, ushering us into his office. "Someone left a sample of anthrax in one of the freezers." He showed us a computer slide show, "Cheese Fungi: Cat Fur and Toad Skin," full of fuzzy and warty-looking cheese rinds, frighteningly magnified. Then Noella took me over to her cubicle. She leafed through a pile of papers on the desk and pulled out a monograph from a recent issue of *Applied and Environmental Microbiology*. N. Marcellino was listed as the first author. "There it is," she said, pointing to a page-long list of molds, each associated with a French region and cheese. "There's a story behind every one of those molds."

For nearly a year in the mid-1990s, Noella traveled through France on a Fulbright scholarship. She had wanted to study the history and ecology of French cheese caves, but the field proved so vast that she decided to focus on a single mold: *Geotrichum candidum*, the wrinkly white mold that encases some of the greatest French cheeses. How much, she wondered, did the mold vary from one cave to another? To find out, she crisscrossed the countryside in a secondhand Fiat. She would pull up to a ramshackle farm, introduce herself to a wary local cheesemaker, and ask for a sterile flask's worth of his milk. If she was lucky, and he realized that she wasn't after his secret recipe, he might take her into the underground chamber or natural cave where he ripened his cheese. "It helped that I was a nun," she says. "But it helped even more that I was a cheesemaker."

After nine months and nearly thirty thousand kilometers, Noella had collected 180 samples. It took another two years to characterize the molds with genetic and biochemical tests, but the results more than justified the effort: the samples contained dozens of distinct strains of *G. candidum*. Noella had been making and selling cheese at the abbey for twenty years by then. She had always thought that there were good molds (like the white rind on Brie) and there were bad molds (like the bluish fuzz on old bread). But her research showed that those categories concealed whole bestiaries. Each strain had its own appetites, its own ecology, its own biochemical effects. And each mold produced a different cheese.

A Frenchman would hardly be surprised by such diversity—Charles de Gaulle acknowledged it forty years ago when he said, "How can anyone be expected to govern a country with 246 cheeses?" But to Americans it is a revelation. Decades of pasteurized and processed cheese have all but wiped clean our memory of cheese as a living culture, formed and flavored by the grasses in a pasture, the yeasts in the air, the bacteria in a barrel, the molds in a cave. But the new cheesemakers tend to be quick studies.

Last year, at a meeting of the American Cheese Society, in Louisville, Mother Noella and Mother Telchilde, who tends the abbey's cows and has a Ph.D. in animal science, were asked to share their research results. "We brought our microscopes," Noella says. "We thought we could set up in the hall and show the cheesemakers some molds for an hour and a half or so." They ended up sitting in the hotel for seven hours. Cheesemakers came with hunks of rind and tales of infestation. They brought wheels of cheese that had been eaten through by scopulariopsis—an invasive fungus—and rinds that were overgrown by *poils de chat,* the dreaded hair-of-the-cat mold. "It was so touching," Noella says. "These American cheesemakers had no one else to turn to."

For the cheesemakers, though, the true heartaches weren't over cheeses that had gone bad; they were over cheeses that they would never make—at least, not legally. Toward the end of the conference, Noella gave a talk in which she mentioned that her favorite cheese in the world is a Mont d'Or. Made in the high valleys of the Massif du Mont d'Or, or the border between France and Switzerland, this raw-milk cheese is so magnificently molten when ripe that it must be held together by strips of local spruce. Like many of the world's finest cheeses, Mont d'Or can't be sold in America; by the time the cheese has aged sixty days, it has dissolved into a puddle.

After Noella's talk, a young Canadian cheesemaker with bleached-blond hair took her aside. Would she and Mother Telchilde like to come with him? He had something they might like to see. He led them to the hotel's restaurant and through the kitchen, past teams of cooks and servers preparing for the evening rush, to the chef's private office in the back. A few other guests joined them, and the sommelier brought a loaf of bread and a bottle of Bordeaux. Someone closed the door, and then the Canadian pulled out a small wrapped package and placed it on the table. "It was the Mont d'Or," Noella recalls. "He had made it himself and hidden it away like contraband. It was his offering to us."

The existence of a raw-milk underground has long been an open secret to certain epicures. The oozing Pont l'Évêque or Livarot, sold with a nudge and a wink at gourmet cheese shops; the reeking Epoisses, triple-wrapped and stashed in a Prada bag on the way through customs—these are emblems of devil-may-care sophistication nearly as clichéd as the flask of hooch in a Southern judge's chambers. What has changed, in recent years, is the fact that some of these cheeses are now homegrown. Clark Wolf used to make a point of going to a certain farmstead whenever he was visiting friends in upstate New York. "There was a guy there who was making contraband raw-milk Camembert," Wolf recalls. "It was incredibly good, but we always wondered if we'd be dead the next day." The story conjures up images of back-alley cheese exchanges, of men running through forests carrying wheels of Brie on their shoulders, hounds baying at their heels. But when I tracked down the cheesemaker in question he'd gone on to computer programming. He was in the kitchen one day stirring curd, he said, when he saw a car with a federal insignia pull up outside. Okay, he thought, this is it. When the knock on the door came, it turned out to be a land surveyor, but the cheesemaker had had enough. "You just can't live like that," he said. "You can't be an outlaw forever."

In 1983, a reporter at the *Times* published an exposé on contraband cheese: he had gone to eight food shops in Manhattan and had found unaged raw-milk Camemberts and Bries in every one. After that, the FDA quickly clamped down on cheese importers. Yet no arrests were made or fines levied, and within a few years the market quietly revived. This spring, at Murray's Cheese shop, in Greenwich Village, a raw-milk Camembert was perched on a mound of its pasteurized cousins, with a small sign stuck into it: "Get this before the FDA does." Other cheesemongers claim that heat-treated cheeses are really made of raw milk, just to inflate the price. Online, Fromages.com will send raw-milk cheeses from France to anyone with a credit card. When my shipment arrived by FedEx, the deliverywoman handed over the refrigerated box with evident relief. "Here's your *fromage*," she said, wrinkling her nose.

The cheeses were delectable, but it was hard to tell how much they owed to raw milk and how much to mere mystique. So one afternoon not long ago, I went to visit Max McCalman, the *maître fromager* at the restaurant Picholine, the hushed inner sanctum of lactophilia in Manhattan. McCalman is lean and phlegmatic, with heavy brows, rumpled skin, and cheekbones so narrow that his eyes seem almost to round the corner. When he talks about cheese, he falls into an intense monotone, as if he were reciting an argument endlessly rehearsed while cutting more than 150,000 pounds of cheese (at last count) into one-ounce portions. McCalman prefers the term "uncompromised milk" to "raw milk," and bears toward his charges the doomed and anxious love of a kindly orphanage director. "Cheese has suffered enough," he says. "People just don't understand it. They don't know what it is."

We were sitting at the back of the restaurant, in a small room with mahogany wine racks on four sides. In the corner was McCalman's high-tech cheese cave: a large refrigerator kept at an unvarying forty-eight degrees Fahrenheit, with around 85 percent humidity. On a butcher block in the center of the room, and on two carts alongside, the night's cheese selections were laid out: more than fifty noble slabs, towers, and pyramids, marbled and crumbling, like the ruins of an ancient metropolis. McCalman reached over and cut wedges from two Reblochon-style cheeses, one of pasteurized milk, the other of raw. We had done a few of these comparisons already, with the pasteurized invariably tasting milder, gummier, and less complex. But this time the difference was more elemental. The pasteurized version wasn't bad, with its musty orange rind and rich ivory pâte. But the raw-milk Reblochon seemed to bypass the taste buds and tap directly into the brain, its sweet, nutty, earthy notes rising and expanding from register to register, echoing in the upper palate as though in a sound chamber. I thought of something one of the founders of the Cheese of Choice Coalition had said when I asked her what difference raw milk could possibly make: "One is a cheese; the other is an aria by Maria Callas."

McCalman smiled sadly at the compromised Reblochon, as if at a three-legged dog. "I like all of our cheeses," he said. "Even the pasteurized." But when I asked him how old the raw-milk variety was, he frowned. "I don't know," he said. "Maybe it hasn't been aged sixty days, but we're not over here counting." To eat a cheese like this was to participate in the preservation of a dying culture, he said. "It's like the military policy: Don't ask, don't tell."

There are those, it is true, who lack the courage and the conviction to risk their lives for a dairy product. But then raw-milk advocates don't expect them to. Not really. McCalman says that Picholine serves about a ton of cheese every month, most of it unpasteurized, yet, in seven years as *maître fromager*, he hasn't heard "so much as one complaint of a tummy ache." It's one of the perverse ironies of FDA policy, he says, that raw-milk cheese is actually better for us than pasteurized: easier to digest and better at fending off contaminants.

To Mother Noella, the best symbol of this paradox is the sawed-off whiskey barrel in which she makes her cheese. Built from a few oak boards bound by a crude iron hoop, the barrel violates any number of food-safety principles and FDA regulations, but her local dairy inspector has learned to let it slide. It's more than a matter of tradition, Noella says; it's a triumph of rustic microbiology.

Standing in the abbey's dairy several weeks ago, Noella gazed down into the barrel's open mouth, at the glistening surface of what looked like an enormous flan. "Cheese is the collective memory of France," she told me, quoting a cheesemaker she once met. "No matter how extravagant or irrational its rituals seem, they usually have some practical purpose." Earlier that morning, before Mass, two sisters had filled the barrel with fresh milk—still warm from the cows and butter-yellow from the spring grasses they had eaten. A few milliliters of rennet had gone in, and its enzymes, distilled from the lining of a calf's fourth stomach, had done their work: the milk's proteins, once as long and loose as a skein of wool, were knitted into an elegant matrix, riddled with pockets of watery whey.

I reached down and fished out a hunk of curd. At this stage, it tasted as bland as poached egg white. But beneath the surface, bacteria were furiously consuming lactose and converting it into lactic acid. As the pH plummeted, the acid would fend off *E. coli* and other pathogens that can't tolerate an acid environment. Most cheesemakers—even artisanal ones—add commercial cultures to their milk, just to help the process along. But Noella relies only on what's already in the barrel. Like everyone at the abbey, she starts out with next to nothing and builds a rich existence from it.

When Noella left home, in 1969, her name was Martha Marcellino. She was the youngest daughter in a family of gifted, headstrong Italians—her brother John (Jocko) Marcellino co-founded the fifties-revival group Sha Na Na—and after four years of Catholic high school she was hungry for "the most radical place" she could find. She opted for Sarah Lawrence, which at the time gave neither exams nor grades. But, after a year of watching her classmates skip lectures and feed LSD to their cats, she was ready for something a little more structured. She had no idea how radical her choice would be.

"You don't come ready-made to be a cloistered nun," she says. "When you step behind that grille, it's a shock to the body. It's like, Oh my God, what have I done?" On her first trip to the abbey, on a weekend retreat in 1970, she was most impressed by the nuns' faith—the way they held to their vows, and to strict obedience, yet somehow seemed free. The abbey is a medieval place with a modern soul. The nuns are worldly and educated. (A number of them hold advanced degrees; one is a former movie star who gave Elvis his first on-screen kiss.) Yet their living areas are walled off from outsiders, and they sustain themselves on what they can grow and make on their 360-acre farm. Seven Latin services punctuate the day, and in between the nuns work as beekeepers, cowherds, and blacksmiths; they make their own pottery, grow and blend their own herbal teas, raise their own hogs, and sell some of their products in a gift shop. As a postulant, Noella was given the task of milking the Holsteins. (The abbey now has Dutch Belted cows, which give richer milk and look a bit like they're wearing habits themselves—black with a pure-white band around the belly.) Then, in 1977, she was asked to make the abbey's cheese.

At first, the abbey's pigs feasted on her mistakes. "It takes time to get it right, so the pigs had a lot of cheese," she says. "I learned that flies could lay eggs and you would get maggots. Who knew? And I was using boards and bricks to press the cheese, so I'd get these big, spongy, horrible things. So again: pigs." Noella used to tell the abbess that she was praying for an old Frenchwoman to come and show her how it was done. When Lydie Zawislak came to visit the abbey, it seemed like an act of Providence. Zawislak was from the Auvergne, in the Massif Central, and her grandmother had taught her how to make Saint-Nectaire. "We just spent day and night making butter and cheese," Noella says. The barrel was Zawislak's idea, as was the wooden paddle for stirring curd, with a cross-shaped hole in the center. Within a year, Noella was re-creating Saint-Nectaire in nearly every particular, even the color and taste of its rind. The molds of the Massif Central apparently had close cousins in the hills of Connecticut.

Noella might have gone on making cheese without a thought to its microbiology, but in 1985 an unaged cheese made with raw milk was blamed for twenty-nine fatalities—mostly stillbirths—in Southern California. The cheese was contaminated with *Listeria monocytogenes*, a bacterium that is often associated with food poisoning, which causes fever, aching muscles, and brief but violent stomach illness. When the FDA subsequently cracked down on dairies across the country, one of the first victims was Noella's wooden cheese barrel: the local inspector insisted that she trade it in for a stainless-steel vat. The nuns could simply have stopped selling their cheese and gone on making it the old way. Instead, they complied with the inspector and set about learning to defend their traditions scientifically. Four nuns were asked to get doctorates in key disciplines: microbiology, animal science, plant science, and agronomy.

"It was just terrifying," Noella says. "I had been a nun for twelve years, I didn't even have a bachelor's degree, and my first course was algebra and trigonometry, things I'd avoided in high school." To make matters worse, not long after the inspector's visit something went horribly wrong at the abbey's dairy. Instead of shrinking as they aged, the cheeses were swelling to the size of footballs and sometimes exploding. Noella took samples of milk and curd and tested them at the university. Then she swabbed every inch of the dairy kitchen, the equipment, the cows' udders and the milkers' hands, and ran tests again. The milk was clean enough to drink—its bad bacteria were too scarce to do any harm. But soon after it went into the vat, it became infested with *E. coli*. Noella next made two batches of cheese—one in a stainless-steel vat, the other in a wooden barrel—and inoculated them with *E. coli*. The results were as clear as they were counterintuitive. In the cheese from the sterile vat, *E. coli* populations thrived even after the cheese had ripened; in the cheese from the wooden barrel, they gradually died off.

"What was happening was that good bacteria were growing in the wood," Noella explained when she told me this story at the dairy. "It was like a sourdough culture that you keep on using, and it was driving off the *E. coli*." She reached into the barrel and dredged up a ragged white slab of curd, then plopped it into a round beech-wood mold. The curd had been cut and stirred, releasing its pockets of whey and settling to the bottom. Now it had to be pressed by hand in order to fill the mold to capacity, then placed in a mechanical press. Noella bent over and pushed the heels of her hands into the curd, leaning into the motion until pale streams of whey trickled from the mold. Years of this kind of work, of squeezing udders every morning and carrying buckets of milk up and down stairs, had given her carpal tunnel syndrome in both wrists, and she had already had surgery a number of times. "The instinct is to move around," she said, keeping her hands steady despite the pain. "But it's better not to. '*Restez là*,' Lydie always said." Stay where you are.

This past spring, Mother Noella, Mother Telchilde, and a committee of other cheese experts began to map out a scientific strategy for defending raw-milk cheese. The whiskey-barrel story may have convinced Noella's inspector, but she knew that it wouldn't pass muster with the FDA. The agency leans toward zero tolerance in matters of food safety, and it makes no exceptions for cloisters. Government scientists have finished the first half of their cheese study, and the news isn't good. They've made raw-milk cheddar under typical dairy conditions and inoculated it with strains of *E. coli* that have been associated with outbreaks. The doses were roughly a hundred to ten thousand times higher than would ordinarily be found in a natural cheese, so it is not surprising that the bacteria survived the aging process. But the FDA spokesman I talked to seemed to draw broader conclusions. "Sixty days does not render the product pathogen-free," he said.

The next phase of the study will show whether lower doses of bacteria fare as well. But in a sense the FDA already has an answer. Government statistics show that cheese is among the safest foods on the market—far less likely to make you sick than chicken, beef, pork, eggs, fish, or even vegetables. It's true that most of the cheeses covered by that statistic were pasteurized. Yet between 1948 and 1988 aged raw-milk cheese caused only one outbreak of disease in the United States, while pasteurized cheese caused five outbreaks. Catherine Donnelly, a professor of food microbiology at the University of Vermont and an expert on *Listeria*, spent a year reviewing the epidemiological literature at the behest of the Cheese of Choice Coalition. "Aged raw-milk cheeses have enjoyed a remarkable safety record," she concluded this spring. When an outbreak does occur, it's usually caused by a cheese that became contaminated after it was pasteurized.

Pasteurization has its place, of course. For a raw-milk cheese to be safe, it has to go straight from cow to curd to consumer, with impeccable hygiene every step of the way. That's fine for a French farmer with a village market down the road, or for an American with a few Jerseys and a lot of FedEx boxes. But it's not so good for Kraft. Cheesemaking will always be an industrial business in America—the geography as much as the culture dictates it. There's no margin for holding raw milk in a tanker while it crosses South Dakota, no guarantee that one sloppy farmer won't taint a thousand cheeses when his milk is mixed in at the factory.

The real question, then, is how and where to make exceptions. Should an American cheesemaker be able to make a Mont d'Or if her standards are high enough? Most scientists agree that after sixty days almost any cheese is safe. But before that the risks begin to rise. "People always say, 'Where are the bodies?' " Rusty Bishop, the director of the Wisconsin Center for Dairy Research, says. "The bodies are in

France." In the past seven years, ten people have died after being in-
fected by *Listeria* in unaged French cheeses, and many thousands more
have suffered stomach illnesses. Unlike an aged cheddar, a Mont d'Or
is high in moisture and low in acidity—an ideal breeding ground for
bacteria, good and bad. "I mean, there is nothing about those cheeses
that would inhibit pathogens," Donnelly says.

Still, a curious thing happens when you talk to cheese experts. They
start by gravely intoning morbidity statistics and bacteria counts. But as
soon as you ask whether they themselves would eat an unaged cheese
their worries seem to evaporate. "Absolutely!" Richard Koby, a lawyer
for the Cheese Importers Association of America, told me. "And I've
gotten sick before." Bishop says that he regularly eats unaged cheese in
France, but he jokes that he always disinfects it with plenty of wine.
And Donnelly, who keeps a boat called *Sailmonella* on Lake Cham-
plain, could bring herself to pass up raw-milk cheese only when she was
pregnant. "You know what?" she says. "It's really good."

It comes down to defining reasonable risk—something Americans
have never been very good at. On the same day that Max McCalman
worried about the demise of raw-milk cheese, restaurants around the
city were serving oysters on the half shell. Raw shellfish causes fifty
times as many illnesses as cheese, yet diners have learned to live with
that risk. They weigh guaranteed pleasure against potential pain, and if
it's fall or winter, when oysters are least likely to be contaminated, they
casually order a dozen. If the FDA were to allow it, we might develop
the same offhand calculus for cheese. We'd come to trust certain farm-
steads, whether their cheeses are aged or not, and when in doubt choose
pasteurized cheese. The alternative would be to stick to Cheez Whiz,
and its worrisome list of chemical additives, or avoid cheese entirely. If
you can't stand a little risk, as one microbiologist put it, shoot the cow.

Inside the abbey's cheese cave—a corner of a basement in the house beside the dairy—the walls are lined with wooden racks filled with ripening wheels. The air smells of wet earth, but it's really something more
peculiar: geosmin, a chemical compound produced by *G. candidum*.
Noella showed me where the mold grew on some of the older cheeses,
wrinkling the surface as if it were a fine linen shirt. Then she took down
a younger wheel, still plump and yellow but topped with a wispy crop
of white hairs. She put the wheel under a microscope and twiddled the

knobs for a moment, then moved aside to let me see. A field of ghostly dandelions hovered into view, each crowned with a perfect sphere of black spores. "They're beautiful," I told her, and she laughed. "That's the spirit. But if you were making Reblochon you'd kill yourself."

This was the hair-of-the-cat mold, the cheesemaker's bane. The spores in a single stalk could infest a cave within a matter of hours, leaping from wheel to wheel on the lightest currents of air. Wherever they landed, they would take root in the curd, digesting proteins and secreting bitter peptides. "They call it *la bête noire*," Noella said. She had once known a woman in the French Alps whose Reblochon was so badly infested that she called in an expert from the local dairy school. This was in the Haute-Savoie, where cheesemakers trace a cross in their curd before cutting it, and science is never far removed from religion. "I can't help you," the expert said. "You've been visited by *un mauvais sort*"—a bad spell. The only remedy was to call in a priest and have him exorcise the cave.

And yet in the right place, on the right wheel of cheese, the same mold could change from a curse to a blessing. In Noella's cheese, the bitter peptides would be digested by *G. candidum,* and the two molds would join forces in breaking down fats and proteins, transforming the chewy curd into a tender pâte. Like a continent evolving in rapid motion, the ripening rind would be invaded by wave after wave of new species, turning from gold to gray to a mottled brown. The cat hairs would sprout up like ancient ferns, then topple and turn to a velvet compost for their successors. The penicillium molds would arrive, their stalks too fine to be seen under a standard microscope, and put down pillowy patches of the palest gray. Then, at last, a faint-pink blush would spread across the surface like a sunset: *Trichothecium roseum,* the flower of the molds.

"Saint Benedict had a vision, just before he died, in which he saw the whole world in a ray of light," Noella said. "For me, that's what it's like to see through a microscope. You look at the rind of a cheese and there's a whole world there." Every dairy, every cheese cave, has its own specific ecology. Every handful of soil, no matter how ordinary, contains more biodiversity than a rain forest. That was the great lesson of her doctoral research. In just seven French dairies, she found eighteen unique strains of *G. candidum.* (The abbey's strain is more vigorous than all but one of them. "I'm so proud of my fungus," Noella said.) Most dairies never tap into this native genius. They dose their milk with prepackaged bacteria and spray their cheeses with generic molds, never guessing that their local soil may hold the secret to the next Roquefort or Gruyère—to an American cheese as inimitable as a Baldwin apple or a Concord grape.

Noella pulled a perfectly ripe wheel from the shelf and put it under the microscope. Cheesemaking is a kind of Eucharist, she likes to think, transforming the simplest material into a transcendent food— "milk's leap toward immortality," as the essayist Clifton Fadiman put it. But ripening is really more like prayer. You repeat an ancient formula as faithfully as possible, then you wait for something extraordinary to happen—for a visitation that is never guaranteed.

It's tempting to imagine what wonders Noella might conjure given the same freedom as the French. But that's too much to hope for, even for a nun. "I can't sit around here dreaming about new cheeses," she said. Beneath the microscope's lens, the last wave of settlers was arriving: four pearlescent spheres, perched on twitchy, hairlike legs, traversing the fields of mold like Conestoga wagons. "Cheese mites," Noella said. She took a straw brush and swept the surface clean, then handed the wheel to me. "Don't worry," she said. "They say they always pick the best cheese."

2002

"You think I'm a raw-foodist by choice?"

NIGHT KITCHENS

JUDITH THURMAN

The abbot's garden at the temple of Daisen-in, in Kyoto, is a rectangle of raked gravel bordered by a white wall on one of its long sides, and by the wooden porch of an old pavilion on the other, where the monks meditate. From behind the wall, a camellia bush throws off its scent. The grooves made by the rake run horizontally, like steady but freehand rulings on a blank page, until they eddy around two conical mounds, each about a foot tall. One evening last June, just after the temple had closed, I joined the sitting meditation, the hour-long *zazen*, held on the porch and open to the public twice a week. There were five other sitters, all Japanese, one a young mother who had her children in tow, two plump boys and a little girl, and I could hear them squirming at the end of the row (the wood creaks)—once or twice the presiding monk spoke to them in a low voice, breaking the silence. But after a while, with an impressive show of stoicism, they managed to keep still.

I had been to Daisen-in earlier that week, and at my first sight of the mounds I surprised myself by bursting into tears, perhaps because, for all its austerity, the garden is an image of release: of the moment at which, after an intractable struggle, you get permission from yourself to let the inessential go.

The temples I had come to Japan to visit were of a different sort, though they, too, had a Zen foundation. They were the workshops where tofu is handmade by artisans faithful to the old tradition. Here I should admit that, to a Western palate—mine, at least, unable, despite my best efforts at Daisen-in, to transcend an incorrigible greed for new sensations—even the greatest artisanal tofu didn't produce the kind of epiphany that my first mouthful of white truffle, or of a fruity tomato, or of corn rushed from a field into the pot did. But tofu has been the dietary mainstay of monastic life in Japan for about a millennium—it was imported from China and Korea, along with Buddhism—and it has never lost the soulful, exalted aura of its provenance. In that respect, its relation to the bean curd sold in plastic tubs at American supermarkets is that of a Communion wafer to a rice cracker. Westerners tend

to regard tofu as a convenient and perhaps necessary but vaguely pathetic substitute for some less wholesome, more morally dubious carnal
indulgence—a rare burger, say. They may even be a bit disdainful of a
dish (as they would be of an individual) that, by their standards, lacks an
identity, or begs for a disguise. Every tribe, however, has an ancestral
food that its exiles yearn for, and that its children can't live without: its
manna, which is often soft and white. When a tofu master offers you a
slice of bean curd he has just unmolded, he is inviting you to partake, in-
sofar as a stranger can, of what it means to be Japanese.

Okutan is a place congenial to such reflections. It is the oldest tofu
riyori in Kyoto. The original restaurant was established almost four hundred years ago within the walls of the Nazenji temple, and the current
proprietor, Yasuie Ishii, is the fifteenth generation of his family to preside
there. He is now in his sixties, but as a young man he bought a villa and
its outbuildings—a cluster of thatched pavilions—near the temple of
Kiyomizu-dera, with the idea of one day opening a second Okutan. This
newer branch sits on the hilly site of a village once owned by the temple's
lord. Guests eat at low tables in a tatami room cantilevered over the garden—a lush glade of cherry, cedar, and maple trees. *Mukashi dofu* is the
first course on the set menu: a dish from the monastic repertoire. A
kneeling waitress prepares it at your table. She sets a clay crock on a charcoal brazier, adds two or three small bricks of *momengoshi* ("cotton"
tofu—well drained of moisture and firm in consistency), pours some hot
water over them from a kettle, and, after they have simmered for a few
minutes (they are not supposed to steep, as they do in the classic hot pot,
yudofu), she ladles them into a bowl. You then help yourself to a sprinkling of scallions and seven hand-ground spices, and a spoonful of enriched fish stock that contains algae from Hokkaido. The courses that
follow observe the principle set by the first: exquisitely bland bean curd,
devoid of the bitter or metallic aftertaste that, in the commercial product
or its milk, is masked by additives; and served with a refined sauce or
paste that sets off its plainness the way a fanciful bijou sets off the elegance of a couture dress. Yet nothing else at Okutan, or perhaps in Japan,
rivals the purity of *shima dofu*—an ivory-colored attar of bean curd that
arrives on a turquoise plate, with a coral drop of sea-urchin (*uni*) purée,
and whose creation is an almost mystical rite.

I was having lunch with a Japanese friend—a native of Kyoto—and
after the meal Mr. Ishii introduced himself to us. We chatted briefly

about a mutual acquaintance, Hiroko Tanaka, who had arranged the interview. Madam Tanaka is a lithe woman of sixty who dresses in kimonos and wears her dark hair swept high off her pale forehead in a classic pompadour. A fan, a cell phone, and a pack of cigarettes are all tucked neatly into her obi. She has a dancer's carriage and the stage presence of a beauty who has spent her life being looked at. Her theatre was the world of the geisha house. Like many retired geishas (who are called *geikos* in Kyoto), she opened a bar on one of the cobbled backstreets off the river, in the Gion quarter, and she trains a small troupe of teenage protégées— *maikos*—in the arts and protocol of her former profession.

Though Mr. Ishii is a busy man, he devoted the better part of an afternoon to giving us a course in soybean history and gastronomy. This engaging lesson took place in his tofu kitchens and in his private museum of beans, which is housed in a crypt beneath the restaurant. Beans, he explained, are the seedpods of legumes, which grow on every continent except Antarctica, and *Glycine max* (soya) is one of some twenty thousand species, the majority of which are poisonous. Mr. Ishii has managed to obtain (and, in some cases, to finesse through customs, with the help of airline-pilot friends) about five thousand specimens, along with their flowers, which he displays, mostly for his own enjoyment, in glass bottles and vitrines. He also took us to his studio, in one of the thatched pavilions, where he edits photographs taken on a life of travels to the remote, mostly tropical places where one finds exotic bean stalks like the locust tree and the Calabar. I wondered about this extravagant politesse, until my friend received a cell-phone call from Madam Tanaka. Ishii-san, she said, had once been her admirer. But not even a celebrated geisha could get him off the subject of tofu.

Histories vary, but according to Mr. Ishii the art of extracting a milky liquid from the soybean and turning it into a cheap and versatile solid food by means of a curdling agent—a salt or an acid—was invented in China about two thousand years ago. The Chinese called the dish *dofu* (*do* = curdled; *fu* = bean), a name as basic as the nutrient it described. About seven hundred years later, a delegation of monks studying Chinese Buddhism brought the technique back to Japan with them. Tofu was exclusive to the upper classes (nobles and samurai) and the vegetarian clergy for about five centuries, in part because the labor required to pulverize dried soybeans (*daizu*) by hand, with a mortar and pestle, was too costly. But the advent of the millstone made tofu accessible to common people, and its place in the national diet and psyche has been compared to that of bread in France, or of potatoes in Eastern Europe—a difference being that one cannot live by bread or potatoes alone, whereas tofu (discounting one study, not cited by Mr. Ishii, that links its consumption by middle-aged Japanese American men to an increased incidence of brain atrophy in old age) is an almost uniquely perfect food: low in calories, high in protein, rich in minerals, devoid of cholesterol, eco-friendly, and complete in the amino acids necessary for human sustenance.

The workshop where Okutan's tofu is made occupies a multichambered grotto beneath the dining rooms that has the chaste and contemplative atmosphere of a chapel. Apart from the plumbing and electrical fixtures, almost no alloyed metal or industrial materials have been used in the construction of the kitchen or are used in the cooking process, as if they might profane the tofu with their modernity. Nearly all the accoutrements—even the sink—are handmade of cedar, and the stove is a slab of lava. In the kitchen's inner sanctum—the salt room—the regimen of purism is absolute. Adobe walls of clay mixed with rice straw are sheathed in bamboo; the ceiling is tented in thatch; the floor is cobbled with sea stones; and, though the dim light is electric, the bulbs are disguised by old wrought-iron lanterns. Here, Mr. Ishii explained, he distills his *nigari*—the coagulating agent. Salt from the mountains of China is wrapped in straw and suspended from a wooden tripod over a weathered cypress barrel. It absorbs humidity from the walls and exudes its moisture in an almost imperceptible drip, filling the barrel at the rate of three centimeters a year. Every six months, he adds more salt to the bundles, and if their hemp bindings break he replaces them. Otherwise, they have been hanging undisturbed since he courted Madam Tanaka, about thirty years ago.

Shima dofu, however, is the one variety of bean curd at Okutan that isn't curdled with *nigari*. It is an exceedingly expensive delicacy (about fifty dollars for a few thin slices), and on special occasions Mr. Ishii delivers a provision to the emperor's palace, molded with the imperial mark, a sixteen-petaled chrysanthemum. A dish of great antiquity, it comes from one of tofu's early landfalls in Japan, Ishigakijima—a small island southwest of Okinawa, 150 miles from Korea. Mr. Ishii learned the art of making *shima dofu* in his youth, from two old women there.

If you would like to try whipping up a batch at home, here is the recipe. Negotiate a contract for organic soybeans with a reliable farmer whose fields lie on the slopes of Mt. Hira, in the Shiga Prefecture, where the soil and the water are unpolluted. Make sure that the farmer harvests the beans as late as possible—preferably in December. (Green summer soybeans become *edamame,* and most commercial soybeans are harvested in the fall. The extra time on the stalk intensifies the flavor.) Pick the beans over carefully, throwing out those eaten by worms— a desirable sign that the farmer isn't cheating with a little DDT. Soak them overnight in very cold spring water. The beans will swell. Rinse them in more of the same, and grind them with a granite mortar, using all your strength, for two hours. Drain the pulp in a bamboo colander, and put the white soy juice you obtain—*gojiu*—to cook on a stone hearth. Let it bubble, subside, and bubble again, several times. (Heating *gojiu,* otherwise known as soy milk, is an essential process that deactivates a toxic substance found in most legumes which blocks digestion.)

Sometime well before you reach this point, however—perhaps while you are waiting for the delivery of your soybeans—hire a boat, and locate the tiny island of Hateruma on your charts (it isn't that far from Ishigakijima). The island is inhabited only by several hundred farmers, who raise sugarcane. Off the coast there is a coral reef (perhaps the sugar farmers can tell you where to find it). You will need a depth finder in good working order, because when the tide is at its lowest ebb you are going to moor the boat and gather the seawater—as Mr. Ishii does—that cascades from the reef, which has an exceptionally rich and complex mineral content. This primordial bouillon is your curdling agent. Add some to the strained *gojiu* (time and failure will teach you the precise amount), stirring with a wooden paddle, and turn the thickened curds into the slatted, four-by-ten-inch cedar boxes that you have lined with a fine-grained cheesecloth. Cover them, weight the covers with blocks of lava—about ten pounds per box—and leave them to drain. Do not, under any circumstances, cool your *shima dofu,* as you would common tofu, by unmolding it in a tank of water, which slimes the skin and dilutes the flavor. What is that flavor? Sublimely unsensational, like a perfectly clarified consommé—which keeps the spirit but discards the substance of the earthy ingredients and patient toil that have gone into it.

Traditional tofu-making in Japan is a nocturnal occupation. At Okutan the staff starts at 4 A.M., but many artisans show up for work around 2, and it is probably a good guess that behind the only lighted windows blazing in a darkened town soybeans are being soaked, ground, boiled, strained, reboiled, curdled, pressed, drained, cooled, sliced, and packaged. So at five o'clock one morning, I rolled off my futon in a lovely old *ryokan*, the Yoyokaku, near the beach in Karatsu, ready for research.

Karatsu is a small provincial city in the Saga Prefecture, about four hours by train from Kyoto, on the spectacularly eroded west coast of Kyushu Island. It is a former whaling port known for its pottery-dun-colored vessels used in the tea ceremony, which are a legacy of Japan's invasions of Korea and of the Korean artisans who returned with their samurai conquerors to settle there in the sixteenth century. The city is also famous for a rowdy, picturesque harvest festival, the *Kunchi*, which features a parade of gigantic floats and a week of revelry and feasting every November. But off-season it is a quiet backwater, rife with the sort of intrigue that makes for an old-fashioned novel of manners.

By the time I had found my shoes at the front door of the Yoyokaku and had unlocked my bicycle, the sun was up. I pedaled across a bridge linking the beaches to the mainland, and past Ka-ratsu Castle—a fortified seventeenth-century pagoda that is imposing at a distance, though deplorably restored—which guards the entrance to a bay dotted with misty and misshapen islands. The town was still shuttered, although a few fishmongers and flower sellers were setting up their wares. Downtown Ka-ratsu is Kyoto in miniature: a grid of low, mostly ramshackle timber-and-stucco houses that converges on two glass-vaulted pedestrian arcades, Gofukumachi and Kyomachi.

My destination was a tiny restaurant in Kyomachi, which has a gingko counter with ten seats, framed by parchment walls decorated in drippy ink by an inebriated artist. You have to reserve well in advance, and be on time for an early meal (breakfast or brunch), because the service ends at noon, when the exhausted workers go home to sleep. The cuisine consists almost entirely of artisanal tofu made nightly, on the premises, by Yoshimasa Kawashima, an oenophile, chef, organic farmer, philosopher of gastronomy, and devotee of flower arranging and the tea ceremony, whose family has been making tofu in Karatsu for nine generations. He, however, has created his own signature product, *zaru dofu*, a melting, ethereal confection with a mousselike consistency that is eaten with a spoon. It starts out like other artisanal tofu, but one of Kawashima's secrets is his *nigari*—magnesium chloride, which is trickier to use though milder than the more common calcium chloride, which leaves a saline aftertaste. As the creamy curds of *zaru dofu* are setting, they are scooped from the vat and mounded softly into shallow bamboo colanders, where they drain, and in which they are packaged for sale. These appealingly rustic receptacles give Kawashima's delicacy its name (*zaru* means "basket"). It is served in some of Tokyo's best restaurants and exported to New York by air twice a week, where diners unable to make the twenty-hour journey to Karatsu can try some at Megu, in Tribeca.

That morning, the breakfast menu included white, green, and black *zaru dofu* (the green is a pale celery, and the black a mauvish blue, like a berry gelato) served half a dozen ways: with soft rice and wasabi; with pinches of sea salt or sesame seeds and dribbles of olive oil or tamari; and in a bowl of the thick and fragrant house miso. A side dish of homemade plum pickles accompanied a seared bream, which had probably still been alive when I left the inn. The fish course was followed by a square of "silken" tofu, *kinugoshi*, deep-fried, but custardy on the inside—a contrast in texture that reminded me of crème brûlée (if you can imagine eating crème brûlée with chopsticks). The soybean lees (*okara*) dissolved on the tongue, like the fine shavings of a mild root or nut. *Okara* is the residue of the separation process—the stage at which the boiled soybean pulp is pressed in cheesecloth. It looks like sawdust or wheat germ, and it is often fed to animals or used as fertilizer, but Kawashima considers it worthy to be savored with a sprinkling of fish powder, minced carrot, and Japanese mushrooms. There were two soy-milk desserts: a gelatinous sweet made with sesame paste and a pot of quivering blancmange.

Kawashima is a large presence in Karatsu: a local boy made good, whose fame, or at least whose tofu, has reached America. At a smoky café with dark woodwork and a polished bar that seemed to have been modeled vaguely on a Greenwich Village coffeehouse, the customers were happy to tell me what they thought of him. One was a stocky, middle-aged woman who had come in for a jolt of caffeine after her tango lesson. She lit a cigarette, as did the waitress and a white-haired gentleman in a business suit. He fled, however, when another woman arrived and settled down with a cigar. The echo of ribald female laughter in the hazy gloom gave the place the atmosphere of a coven. No one seemed surprised that I had flown seven thousand miles to eat *zaru dofu*, but they gave me to understand that Kawashima was a "character," and "very rich"—he had bought "a big estate," a much envied property in the hills, and a beach house, too. There were forty other tofu makers in the town, but it was hard work, and none of the others made as much money, they said. I tried to buy them a round of espresso, but they wouldn't hear of it. The tango dancer pressed me to accept her fan.

I had also heard around the Yoyokaku that Kawashima owed at least some of his fame to another local luminary, Takashi Nakazato, one of Japan's greatest potters and the scion of a Karatsu dynasty going back thirteen generations, whose patriarch, Taroumon Nakazato, is a Living National Treasure. Nakazato is a noted gastronome who has helped to make a number of reputations, particularly those of sushi chefs and sake brewers. His original enthusiasm for Kawashima's *zaru dofu* piqued the interest of the press. But the two men had quarreled, it was said, over some matter of etiquette, and their falling-out seemed to enthrall the town. When I met Nakazato, he was at work on a huge urn in a serene, barnlike studio with high rafters and mullioned windows. The light was streaming in, and his assistants were silently prepping a rack of pots for firing. Their master is a slight man of sixty-eight, with a noble head, and his intense containment—a stillness of eye and body while his deft hands move—gives him a sagelike aura. When I asked Nakazato about Kawashima, he slowly looked up from his wheel. "I love food," he said laconically. "I know a young sushi chef in the pine forest. Do you know the pine forest? You should go there." There was a long pause. "There is lots of great tofu in Japan."

Kawashima bounded into the restaurant at about eight, as his pretty wife, Keiko, was clearing away the Nakazato pottery on which breakfast is served—rust-and-ash-colored vessels with a dark underglaze and a primal beauty. Tofu-making may have a Zen gestalt, but Kawashima— a sporty fifty-eight year old with a goatee and a crewcut—doesn't make a monklike impression. He is the sort of character the French call a *gaillard*—a bon vivant bristling with rakish vigor. One keeps up with him at a fast trot. His cottage-scale factory and offices occupy a warren of rooms in a somber two-hundred-year-old house, with blackened beams, that survived demolition when the arcade was built, and seems out of synch with its festive swags of plastic wisteria. At the back of a rather cramped, unlovely industrial kitchen, baskets of *zaru dofu* were moving down a conveyor belt, getting wrapped and labeled. (The tofu is handmade and strictly organic, but the packaging is mechanized, and a small fleet of white delivery vans was waiting at the loading dock.) Kawashima's younger brother was dressed in kitchen whites, stirring soy milk in a metal vat. It was warm but hadn't been curdled yet, and he offered me some from the ladle. Its taste was slightly beany, yet elemental, with an ineffable sweetness, as if it came not from a plant but from a breast.

"I've started showing up late," Kawashima told me. "At around three, to give my brother some breathing room. He's learning the ropes, and the only way you do that is by yourself." Kawashima's elder son has also decided to become a tofu maker, after a brief stint at Gateway Computers. "I didn't oblige him," Kawashima says. "I told him, on the contrary, to get away from home, the way I did. In my late teens, I left Karatsu for Fukuoka"—the nearest large city—"and worked at another tofu place, to see how they did things.

"I studied *chabana*, flower arranging, and learned to make tea—my business for ten years. When I came home, I wanted to create something new with tofu." A sudden loud clatter made me start: Kawashima had just pulled down a steel trapdoor in the ceiling, and he shooed me up the ladder. Under the eaves, he has built a tearoom for himself.

In the next two hours, making the rounds with Kawashima, I got to see quite a bit of his enterprise and its fruits. Having asked me if I liked dogs, he took me to his beach house—a Hamptons-style bungalow in an upscale enclave near the castle—where we played with his St. Bernard. Then we drove ten miles out of town, through strawberry fields, and up into the hills, where Kawashima owns several acres. We fed the fat koi in his pond, and tramped through the woods to admire his Shinto shrine, an altar guarded by two gaping stone dogs, one of which catches evil intentions, while the other spits out good luck. I helped him open the elaborately engineered stone sluices that irrigate his kitchen garden, where he stopped to do a little puttering. His wife doesn't like the country, he confided, so this is his bachelor kingdom, and he bought it with his "pocket money," because she also wouldn't like him spending the profits of their business on it. All his crops—tomatoes, melons, eggplants, cherries, a few beans (for *edamame*), and some white lettuce—are organically grown, as is the rice that he is seeding, experimentally, in a blanket of cotton, to keep down the weeds.

Though I normally don't start drinking at ten in the morning, I had the excuse that it was nine in the evening (of the night before) by my body clock, and Kawashima is a persuasive host. "I think I was born to make people happy," he said. So, having tasted some of his homemade plum wine, we sat at the kitchen table of his farmhouse, chasing our aperitif with a bottle of excellent Chapelle-Chambertin '96, while Kawashima reminisced, as oenophiles do, about the great vintages he has owned and drunk—an '81 Pétrus, some venerable Lafites—and what he ate with them. His memory stirred, he ducked into a walk-in wine cellar the size of a bank vault, and came back, looking very pleased, with a Château d' Yquem '21. I wrestled with my conscience before urging him, with feigned conviction, not to open it.

The farmhouse is built in the traditional style, with shoji windows and a tiled roof curling up at the edges, though its amenities are from a glossy shelter magazine. It sits on a rise overlooking a valley of terraced rice paddies that were simmering under an opaque sky and waiting for the spring rains—a timeless scene only somewhat spoiled by a fretwork of electric pylons. A little farther up the slope, Kawashima has added a luxurious bath pavilion that, like his kitchen, is a sybaritic gadgeteer's paradise. (The plumbing responds to voice commands.) The tub is in a sort of turret penthouse with glass walls which faces a deep forest furrowed by ravines and inhabited by wild boar and monkeys. When Kawashima is soaking there, he says, he sometimes sees a constellation of impudent simian eyes staring at him through the glass.

I doubted that *zaru dofu*, or any other sort of tofu, not even *shima dofu*, would have enough character to hold its own with a great Burgundy like the one we were drinking. But wine and bean curd, Kawashima's twin passions, are more compatible than you might think. To prove the point, he served us a little *amuse-gueule* that he devised for wine-tastings: a wedge of dense and pungent saffron-colored *miso zuke dofu*, which is a block of *momengoshi* steeped in fermented miso, wrapped in *konbu* (a form of kelp with a thick, ridged leaf which, in its dried form, resembles a slice of rubber tire tread), and aged for months. At last, some tofu with bite: an alarming, even macho one, like that of a Roquefort at the limit of ripeness.

If you don't speak Japanese, traveling alone in provincial Japan is not for the timid: the lingua franca is pantomime. I mastered the greetings, which change according to the time of day; a few adjectives (though I got into trouble with *oishii*—delicious—which may have a lewd connotation in the wrong context); and I learned to count. So finding the Yoyokaku had been a stroke of luck. The motherly proprietress, Harumi Okochi, whose husband's family have been innkeepers in Karatsu for more than a century, is a former English teacher with a nuanced command of the language and of the local society and folklore. Her library overlooks a rock garden and a waterfall, and after I had bathed in the *ryokan*'s communal tub and wrapped myself in a blue-and-white *yukata*, she poured me some tea and we sat reading poetry—paeans to tofu. She asked me if I knew the *Manyoshu* ("Assembly of Ten Thousand Leaves"), an anthology of literary treasures collected in the eighth century. "Some of its earliest verse," she said, "was written on Kashiwajima, an island you can see from the tower of the castle, and the fishermen there may have been among the first Japanese to make bean curd. According to legend, their tofu was so hard that it could break stones. That is what they still call it: *ishiwari*—stone-breaking—*dofu*. Though I have lived here all my life, I have never tasted it."

Kashiwajima is a worn, whale-shaped lump of volcanic rock boiling with greenery. Its love poets were the soldiers of a lonely garrison, watching the sea for Korean war galleys, thirteen hundred years ago, and pining for their wives. One afternoon, I hired a launch from a pier near the castle. It bounced across the swell while I clung to the guardrail with white knuckles. Mrs. Okochi, who had changed from a kimono into a pair of cotton trousers, sat primly unperturbed in the cabin, watching for flying fish, and holding a beautifully wrapped box of sweets from the inn, which she'd thought to bring as a gift for the chief tofu maker, Hiromi Takahira, who had agreed to reopen her workshop for us at an ungodly hour: 3 P.M. The little marina was deserted, though from somewhere nearby we heard the sounds of karaoke. There wasn't a teahouse or a store in sight, so we meandered around the waterfront until we found the workshop, in a corrugated shed on one of the piers. Pampas grass, wild hollyhocks, and thistle were growing by the front door, and the place, like the island generally, had a melancholy air. Kashiwajima has always been dependent on the sea, but in recent times it has lost many of its young people to jobs on the mainland. The elders who remain, however, are a hardy lot. An *uni* fisherman with white hair and a deep tan, who squatted in a doorway on sinewy haunches while mending his nets, was looking for a wife, he told Mrs. Okochi, eyeing her hopefully. "You should meet my sister," he added, waving down an elderly cyclist laden with buoys and baskets—Kashiwajima's last female abalone diver. She was pedaling home in a ratty wetsuit and a faded bonnet, toothless and cheerful, though also a little embarrassed, she told Mrs. Okochi, to be seen with such a puffy face. That, she explained, is what happens when you plug your ears and hold your breath long enough to catch a snap-jawed mollusk clinging to a reef thirty feet down.

At the workshop, Mrs. Takahira, a seventy-one-year-old fisherman's widow with a round face and a radiant complexion (tofu and hard labor are her beauty secrets, she said) welcomed us with a deep bow. The windows of the shed were open, and the sea breeze carried a scent of rain, wildflowers, and algae. Before her marriage, she told us, she worked on her parents' farm, growing soybeans, and then she became a nurse in Karatsu. After her husband died and her two sons left home, they told her to stop making tofu for herself—it was too much trouble. But about five years ago she decided that the island should exert "more of an effort to show the world that we exist," she said. "In the olden days, we were known for our *ishiwari dofu*. People made it for funerals and weddings, and it was eaten in a fish broth. Now they're too busy. I started thinking that maybe it could be revived. A few friends said they would help, and the Karatsu town council gave us some marketing advice. There are sixteen of us, and we take shifts."

Stone-breaking tofu got its name, according to Mrs. Takahira, because one day an islander walking home dropped her basket and spilled her tofu. "It didn't crumble, but the stone it fell on did," she said. "You can believe that or not, but it's very concentrated. We use five times as many soybeans for the same amount of tofu as other makers do, and organic Japanese *daizu* is three times as expensive as American beans, so we don't make much profit. They passed a law saying you can't use the local ocean water as a *nigari* anymore—because of the pollution—so we buy evaporated natural sea salt from Ō-shima, and that's what makes it so hard. But too much salt turns your tofu bitter, and if you overcook it, it stinks."

The only concession Mrs. Takahira makes to convenience, or age, is to pulverize the soybeans in an electric grinder. Otherwise, her tofu-making is powered entirely by muscle. She presses the *okara* with wooden rolling pins, then squeezes it like an Old World washerwoman wringing linen sheets. Each of the molds is compressed for forty minutes with a twenty-pound weight that she slings about with one hand as if it were a can of tuna fish. When she turns out the bricks of bean curd, their surface is crackled, like parched desert clay. Their texture is a bit grainy, and they offer some faint resistance to a knife. They are thoroughly *oishii*, though, with an intense soy flavor and the definitive, though unplaceable, sweetness that artisanal tofu seems to share, and which, like the scent of lotus blossoms in a folktale, signals the presence of an unseen divinity.

2005

"The little sad faces next to some items mean they don't taste very good."

THE POUR

*"It's a naïve domestic Burgundy without any breeding,
but I think you'll be amused by its presumption."*

"Are you the gentleman who thinks he ate his check?"

DRY MARTINI

ROGER ANGELL

The martini is in, the martini is back—or so young friends assure me. At Angelo and Maxie's, on Park Avenue South, a thirtyish man with backswept Gordon Gekko hair lowers his cell as the bartender comes by and says, "Eddie, gimme a Bombay Sapphire, up." At Patroon, a possibly married couple want two dirty Tanquerays—gin martinis straight up, with the bits and leavings of a bottle of olives stirred in. At Nobu, a date begins with a saketini—a sake martini with (avert your eyes) a sliver of cucumber on top. At Lotus, at the Merc Bar, and all over town, extremely thin young women hold their stemmed cocktail glasses at a little distance from their chests and avidly watch the shining oil twisted out of a strip of lemon peel spread across the pale surface of their gin or vodka martini like a gas stain from an idling outboard. They are thinking Myrna Loy, they are thinking Nora Charles and Ava Gardner, and they are keeping their secret, which is that it was the chic shape of the glass—the slim narcissus stalk rising to a 1939 World's Fair triangle above—that drew them to this drink. Before their first martini ever, they saw themselves here with an icy mart in one hand, sitting on a bar stool, one leg crossed over the other, in a bar small enough so that a cigarette can be legally held in the other hand, and a curl of smoke rising above the murmurous conversation and the laughter. Heaven. The drink itself was a bit of a problem—that stark medicinal bite—but mercifully you can get a little help for that now with a splash of scarlet cranberry juice thrown in, or with a pink-grapefruit-cassis martini, or a green-apple martini, or a flat-out chocolate martini, which makes you feel like a grown-up twelve years old. All they are worried about—the tiniest dash of anxiety—is that this prettily tinted drink might allow someone to look at them and see Martha Stewart. Or that they're drinking a variation on the cosmopolitan, that Sarah Jessica Parker–*Sex and the City* craze that is so not in anymore.

Not to worry. In time, I think, these young topers will find their way back to the martini, to the delectable real thing, and become more fashionable than they ever imagined. In the summer of 1939, King George VI and Queen Elizabeth visited President Franklin Delano Roosevelt at Hyde Park—it was a few weeks before the Second World War began—and as twilight fell FDR said, "My mother does not approve of cocktails and thinks you should have a cup of tea." The king said, "Neither does my mother." Then they had a couple of rounds of martinis.

I myself might have had a martini that same evening, at my mother and stepfather's house in Maine, though at eighteen—almost nineteen—I was still young enough to prefer something sweeter, like the yummy, Cointreau-laced sidecar. The martini meant more, I knew that much, and soon thereafter, at college, I could order one or mix one with aplomb. As Ogden Nash put it, in "A Drink with Something in It":

> There is something about a Martini,
> A tingle remarkably pleasant;
> A yellow, a mellow Martini;
> I wish I had one at present.
> There is something about a Martini,
> Ere the dining and dancing begin,
> And to tell you the truth,
> It is not the vermouth—
> I think that perhaps it's the gin.

In John O'Hara's 1934 novel, *Appointment in Samarra,* the doomed hero, Julian English, and his wife, Caroline, observe Christmas with his parents, as usual. They live in the Pennsylvania coal town of Gibbsville, but the Englishes are quality, and before their festive dinner Julian's father, Dr. William English, mixes and serves up midday martinis; then they have seconds.

In the 1940 classic movie comedy *The Philadelphia Story*, the reliable character actor John Halliday plays Katharine Hepburn's reprobate father, who has returned home unexpectedly on the eve of her wedding. Standing on a terrace in the early evening, he mixes and pours a dry martini for himself and his deceived but accepting wife (Mary Nash) while, at the same time, he quietly demolishes his daughter's scorn for him and some of her abiding hauteur. It's the central scene of the ravishing flick, since it begins Tracy Lord's turnabout from chilly prig Main Line heiress to passably human Main Line heiress, and the martini is the telling ritual: the presentation of sophistication's Host. Hepburn had played the same part in the Broadway version of the Philip Barry play, a year before, which also required that martini to be mixed and poured before our eyes. Sitting in the dark at both versions, I was entranced by the dialogue—only Philip Barry could have a seducer-dad convincingly instruct his daughter in morals—but at the same time made certain that the martini was made right: a slosh of gin, a little vermouth, and a gentle stirring in the pitcher before the pouring and the first sips. Yes, okay, my martini-unconscious murmured, but next time maybe a little more ice, Seth.

This is not a joke. Barry's stage business with the bottles and the silver stirring spoon in one moment does away with a tiresome block of explanation about the Lords: he's run off with a nightclub singer and she's been betrayed, but they have shared an evening martini together before this—for all their marriage, in fact—and soon they'll be feeling much better. In the movie, which was directed by George Cukor, the afternoon loses its light as the drink is made and the talk sustained, and the whole tone of the drama shifts. Everyone is dressed for the coming party, and the martini begins the renewing complications. Sitting in the theater, we're lit up a little, too, and ready for all that comes next—the dance, the scene by the pool—because the playwright has begun things right.

Cocktails at Hyde Park or on Philadelphia's Main Line sound aristocratic, but the Second World War changed our ways. In the Pacific, where I was stationed, a couple of Navy fighter pilots told me a dumb story they'd heard in training, about the tiny survival kit that was handed out to flight-school graduates headed for carrier duty. OPEN ONLY IN EXTREME EMERGENCY, it said—which seemed to be the case of a pilot north of Midway whose Grumman quit cold a hundred miles away from his flattop. After ditching, he climbed into his inflatable raft, regarded the empty horizon that encircled him, and opened the kit. Inside was a tiny shaker and a glass, a stirring straw, a thimbleful of gin, and an eyedropper's worth of vermouth. He mixed and stirred, and was raising the mini cocktail to his lips when he became aware that vessels had appeared from every quarter of the Pacific and were making toward him at top speed. The first to arrive, a torpedo boat, roared up, and its commanding officer, shouting through his megaphone, called, "*That's not the right way to make a dry martini!*"

Dryness was all, dryness was the main debate, and through the peacetime 1940s and '50s we new suburbanites tilted the Noilly Prat bottle with increasing parsimony, as the martini recipe went up from three parts gin and one part dry vermouth to four and five to one, halted briefly at six to one, and rose again from there. George Plimpton recently reminded me about the Montgomery—a fifteen-to-one martini named after the British field marshal, who was said never to go into battle with less than these odds in his favor. What was happening, of course, was an improvement in the quality of everyday gin. The Frankenstein's-laboratory taste of Prohibition gin no longer needed a sweetener to hide its awfulness: just a few drops of Tribuno or Martini & Rossi Extra Dry would suffice to soften the ginny juniper bite.

Preciousness almost engulfed us, back then. Tiffany's produced a tiny silver oil can, meant to dispense vermouth. Serious debates were mounted about the cool, urban superiority of the Gibson—a martini with an onion in it—or the classicism of the traditional olive. Travelers came home from London or Paris with funny stories about the ghastly martinis they'd been given in the Garrick Club or at the Hotel Regina bar. And, in a stuffy little volume called *The Hour,* the historian and *Harper's* columnist Bernard De Voto wrote, "You can no more keep a Martini in the refrigerator than you can keep a kiss there. The proper union of gin and vermouth is a great and sudden glory; it is one of the happiest marriages on earth and one of the shortest."

We appreciated our martinis, and drank them before lunch and before dinner. I recall an inviting midtown restaurant called Cherio's, where the lunchtime martini came in chalice-sized glasses. Then we went back to work. "Those noontime cocktails just astound me," a young woman colleague of mine said recently. "I don't know how you did it." Neither do I, anymore. My stepfather, E. B. White, sometimes took a dry manhattan at lunch, but his evening martini was a boon forever. Even when he'd gotten into his seventies and early eighties, I can remember his greeting me and my family at the Bangor airport late on a summer afternoon and handing me the keys to the car for the fifty-mile drive back to the coast. Sitting up front beside me, he'd reach for his little picnic basket, which contained a packet of Bremner Wafers, some Brie or Gouda cheese and a knife, and the restorative thermos of martinis.

At home, my vermouth mantra became "a little less than the absolute minimum," but I began to see that coldness, not dryness, was the criterion. I tried the new upscale gins—Beefeater's and the rest—but found them soft around the edges and went back to my everyday Gordon's. In time, my wife and I shifted from gin to vodka, which was less argumentative. At dinners and parties, I knew all my guests' preferences: the sister-in-law who wanted an "upside-down martini"—a cautious four parts vermouth to one of gin—and a delightful neighbor who liked her martinis so much that when I came around to get whiskey or brandy orders after dinner she dared not speak their name. "Well, maybe just a little gin on some ice for me," she whispered. "With a dab of vermouth on top."

We drank a lot, we loved to drink, and some of us did not survive it. Back in college, the mother of a girl I knew would sometimes fix herself a silver shaker of martinis at lunchtime and head back upstairs to bed. "Good night," she'd say. "Lovely to see you."

I met entire families, two or three generations, who seemed bent on destroying themselves with booze. John Cheever, the Boccaccio of mid-century America, wrote all this in sad and thrilling detail. What seems strange now about celebrated stories of his like "The Country Husband," "The Sorrows of Gin," and "The Swimmer" is how rarely the martini is mentioned, and how often it's just called gin. Alcohol was central to this landscape, its great descending river.

It's my theory—a guess, rather—that martini drinking skipped a generation after Vietnam and marijuana came along. Many thousands of earlier suburban children, admitted to the dinner table or watching their parents' parties from the next room, saw and heard the downside of the ritual—the raised voices and lowered control—and vowed to abandon the cocktail hour when they grew up. Some of them still blame martinis for their parents' divorces. Not until their children arrived and came of age did the slim glass and the delectable lift of the drink reassert itself, and carry us back to the beginning of this story.

I still have a drink each evening, but more often now it's Scotch. When guests come to dinner, there are always one or two to whom I automatically offer Pellegrino or a Coke: their drinking days are behind them. Others ask for water or wait for a single glass of wine with the meal. But if there's a friend tonight with the old predilection, I'll mix up a martini for the two of us, in the way we like it, filling a small glass pitcher with ice cubes that I've cracked into quarters with my little pincers. Don't smash or shatter the ice: it'll become watery in a moment. Put three or four more cracked cubes into our glasses, to begin the chill. Put the gin or the vodka into the pitcher, then wet the neck of the vermouth bottle with a quickly amputated trickle. Stir the martini vigorously but without sloshing. When the side of the pitcher is misted like a January windowpane, pour the drink into the glasses. Don't allow any of the ice in the pitcher to join the awaiting, unmelted ice in the glass. (My friend likes his straight up, so I'll throw away the ice in his glass. But I save it in my own, because a martini on the rocks stays cold longer, and I've avoided the lukewarm fourth or fifth sip from the purer potion.) Now stir the drink inside the iced glass, just once around. Squeeze the lemon peel across the surface—you've already pared it, from a fat, bright new lemon—and then run the peel, skin-side down, around the rim of the glass before you drop it in. Serve. Smile.

2002

THE RED AND THE WHITE

CALVIN TRILLIN

Before we get onto the question of whether experienced wine drinkers can actually tell the difference between red wine and white, I should probably tell you a little something about my background in the field. I have never denied that when I'm trying to select a bottle of wine in a liquor store I'm strongly influenced by the picture on the label. (I like a nice mountain, preferably in the middle distance.) When I was growing up, in Kansas City, Missouri, I didn't know about people drinking wine at meals that were not being eaten in celebration of a major anniversary. I assume that my neighbors would have been as startled as I to hear about such carryings-on. Years later, after I'd moved to New York, a newspaperman in my home town did me a great favor, and when I wondered aloud what I could get for him, a friend in New York—a sophisticated friend, who considered himself something of a gourmet, now that I think of it—said that a case of wine was always appreciated. I phoned the newspaperman's son-in-law in Kansas City to ask if he could find out, discreetly, what sort of wine was particularly fancied in his in-laws' house, and the son-in-law got back to me with a question of his own: "Does Wild Turkey count?" These days, I do drink wine, although if I'm at a meal at which drink orders are being given by the glass, I am likely to say to the waiter, "What sort of fancy beer do you have on tap?"

I have spent a certain amount of time in the company of wine cognoscenti, but I wouldn't claim that I have distinguished myself on those occasions. Many years ago, for instance, a winemaker I know was kind enough to invite me to the "barrel tasting" of California wines that used to be held annually at the Four Seasons restaurant, in New York—an event that was considered a very hot ticket in the wine game. At the table, many glasses of wine were put in front of us. Then someone who had his mouth very close to the microphone talked about each wine in what I believe scholars would call excruciating detail—the type of vines that had been grafted together to produce it, for instance, and how long it had been in stainless-steel vats or oak barrels. Displaying manners that I thought would have made my mother proud, I drank what was placed before me—not noticing, as I glanced around to see whether more food was ever going to appear, that everyone else was just sipping. I have since heard two or three versions of what transpired that evening, but they do not differ in whether or not I fell asleep at the table. Particularly considering my performance at the Four Seasons that evening, it's perfectly possible that some people asked to sum up my knowledge of and attitude toward wine might respond "Ignorance, tempered slightly by philistinism."

On the other hand, I have, in a manner of speaking, worked in the wine industry for a number of years. An old friend named Bruce Neyers makes wine in the Napa Valley. I think it would be too much to say that I'm an adviser to Bruce in his business, unless suggesting that he put a mountain on his label counts. Thanks to the miracle of the fax machine, though, I act as a sort of volunteer copy editor of the announcements that he sends out to his regular customers—what people in the trade would call his "offering letters." Bruce, a wry man who grew up in Wilmington, Delaware, and assumed through college that he would spend his life as a research chemist for DuPont, tends to discuss wine in straightforward terms even when he's addressing the sort of wine fiends who do close readings of offering letters. Still, I can't claim that I know precisely what he means when he writes, say, "The malo-lactic fermentation went to completion." What I bring to my editing task is not expertise in viticulture but a long experience in such matters as comma placement.

If Bruce shows up at my house during a business trip to New York, he is usually carrying some wine, a custom that reflects both his natural generosity and his concern about what he otherwise might be forced to drink. He has never considered my scenery-selection strategy a completely satisfactory way to build a cellar. He has particularly grim memories of a Chardonnay that attracted me with a view of mountains that are apparently near enough the grape-growing region of the Hungarian Danube to be depicted in the middle distance. He doesn't ask in advance if I'd prefer red or white—presumably because he knows that the question would give me the opportunity to say, "But can anybody really tell the difference?"

Why? Because, as best I can remember, it was from Bruce or one of his acquaintances in the Napa Valley that I first heard about the color test given at the University of California at Davis, whose Department of Viticulture and Enology is renowned in the wine world. I got the impression that the Test was often given to visitors from the wine industry, but since this was about twenty years ago, such details are hazy. I was definitely told, though, that the folks at Davis poured wine that was at room temperature into black glasses—thus removing the temperature and color cues that are a large part of what people assume is taste—and that the tasters often couldn't tell red wine from white. After Bruce returned from a short course at Davis in the mid-1970s, he had someone at the Joseph Phelps winery, where he then worked, set up a red-white test with black glasses. Bruce got three out of five.

I suppose I am programmed to expect that sort of result. I was raised by a man who, although he had never tasted coffee in his life, once told me that blindfolded I couldn't tell the difference between coffee with milk and coffee without milk. It has never occurred to me that the software drummers who are in the habit of saying to the bartender "J&B on the rocks" or "Ketel One with a twist" might actually be able to recognize their favorite booze in a blind tasting. Many years ago, when a friend in England began raising chickens and boasting of the gloriously distinctive taste of their eggs, I secretly replaced the freshly gathered eggs in his larder with eggs from a London supermarket, and I try to remind him at least semiannually that he raved about the next omelette to come out of the kitchen. In temperament and genes as well as in geographic origin, I'm from the Show Me state.

For years, I was likely to mention the Davis test whenever the subject of wine connoisseurship came up, even if I happened to be drinking a glass of beer at the time. A couple of years ago, for instance, a pleasant young man who was showing us around a winery owned by an acquaintance of mine in New York State mentioned that, as part of his final year at the Culinary Institute of America, he had gone to Davis for a six-week wine course. Naturally, I asked him how he did on the Test. He changed the subject. But at the end of the tour, after we'd all downed a friendly glass of wine or two and become better acquainted, he suddenly turned to me and said, quietly, "I got three out of seven."

I know what you're thinking: Is it possible that a self-confessed beer-swilling ignoramus got interested in the Davis test simply as a way of debunking wine connoisseurship? As another wine-business friend likes to point out, wine is way beyond any other subject in inspiring in the American layman an urge to refute the notion of expertise. (Modern art must come in second.) I'd like to think that I'm above that sort of thing. I took it for granted that experts could explain not only why certain red wines and certain white wines would be difficult for even a connoisseur to tell apart but also why that did not call into question the legitimacy of wine expertise—and could do so, if necessary, in excruciating detail.

Also, it's not as if wine connoisseurship lacks informed criticism from people who are not beer-swilling ignoramuses. Marc Dornan, of the Beverage Testing Institute, for instance, says to anyone who asks him that rating wines on a hundred-point scale, which is now common practice, is "utterly pseudoscientific." Tim Hanni, a Master of Wine, believes that most commentary about wines fails to take into account the biological individuality of consumers; he claims that he can predict what sort of wine appeals to you according to such factors as how heavily you salt your food and whether your mother suffered a lot from morning sickness while carrying you. Hanni has said for years that the matching of a particular wine with a particular food is a scam, there being "absolutely no premise historically, culturally, or biologically for drinking red wine with meat." As a way of illustrating the role played by anticipation in taste, Frédéric Brochet, who is a researcher with the oenology faculty of the University of Bordeaux, recently asked some experts to describe two wines that appeared by their labels to be a distinguished *grand cru classe* and a cheap table wine—actually, Brochet had refilled both bottles with a third, midlevel wine—and found his subjects mightily impressed by the supposed *grand cru* and dismissive of the same wine when it was in the *vin ordinaire* bottle.

An urge to refute the notion of expertise certainly seemed to be reflected in the headline of an article from *The Times* of London about the research Brochet has been carrying on—CHEEKY LITTLE TEST EXPOSES WINE "EXPERTS" AS WEAK AND FLAT. The headline caught the tone of the article, by Adam Sage, which began, "Drinkers have long suspected it, but now French researchers have finally proved it: wine 'experts' know no more than the rest of us." The test of Brochet's that caught my eye consisted partly of asking wine drinkers to describe what appeared to be a white wine and a red wine. They were in fact two glasses of the same white wine, one of which had been colored red with flavorless and odorless dye. The comments about the "red" wine used what people in the trade call red-wine descriptors. "It is a well known psychological phenomenon—you taste what you're expecting to taste," Brochet said in *The Times*. "They were expecting to taste a red wine and so they did. . . . About two or three per cent of people detect the white wine flavour, but invariably they have little experience of wine culture. Connoisseurs tend to fail to do so. The more training they have, the more mistakes they make because they are influenced by the color of the wine."

Reading about Brochet's color experiment revived my interest in the Davis test. I was curious, for one thing, about whether there was a way to compare his results with the results the Davis people had collected over the years—although, as I understood it, the Davis testers, working in the straightforward tradition of the American West, told a subject that he was choosing between red and white rather than trying to sneak a bottle of adulterated white past him. I decided it might be time to visit Davis and collect some statistics on what the Test actually showed. I got the Department of Viticulture and Enology on the telephone and explained my interest to a friendly woman there who is employed to field inquiries from people like me. She told me that as far as she knew Davis had never conducted such a test.

"Imagine that!" Bruce Neyers said, when I told him of my chat with the folks at Davis. He found it unsurprising that an institution with an interest in the distinctions among wines would have difficulty recalling evidence that the most elementary distinction can often not be made. Like a lot of wine people I've spoken to about the Test over the years, Bruce thinks it would be easy enough to pick out some unusual wines that might muddy the difference between the taste of red and white; that is presumably what was done in the test he'd taken years ago at Phelps. But even a loaded test might be pounced on as evidence that the judgments of wine experts are, as Adam Sage put it in his *Times* piece, "little more than self-delusion." When I asked Bruce if he could round up some Napa Valley wine people to take the red-white test, assuming I couldn't track it down at Davis, he said they might want to remain anonymous, since there were probably better ways to begin a wine-industry résumé than "Although I can't distinguish red wine from white wine . . ."

If anybody at Davis knew about a red-white test, I'd been told, it would probably be Ann Noble, who, at the time I dropped in to see her, was just winding up a twenty-eight-year teaching career in the Department of Viticulture and Enology. Professor Noble's field is taste and smell, particularly smell. She has noted that as children we are taught to label colors but not smells. In an effort to correct that oversight, she not only conducted in her courses what she calls "a kindergarten of the nose" but also invented the Wine Aroma Wheel, which permits someone to describe the aroma of a wine in specific terms and to identify varietals by their smell. Someone with an aroma wheel knows, for instance, that a Pinot Noir can be distinguished from a Zinfandel because it has the smell of berry, berry jam (strawberry), vanilla, butter, and spiciness rather than the smell of berry, black pepper, raisin, soy, butter, and vanilla.

Professor Noble told me that the test I'd heard about sounded like an urban myth. She regularly tested her students at the end of the semester by asking them to identify wine in black glasses, she said. But what they were trying to name was the varietal, not the color. For a couple of years, she kept track of wrong answers, and she found that perhaps 5 to 10 percent of them were not simply the wrong varietal but a wrong varietal that was also the wrong color. Conceivably, it occurred to me, that test could have been embellished over the years to become the Davis test I'd heard about, although 5 or 10 percent amounted to a lot fewer wrong answers than I would have expected. Then Professor Noble told me that in the tests she gave her students they were, of course, reaching their conclusions by smell alone.

"Smell alone?" I said.

"This is only by smell," she said. "The minute you put it in your mouth, it's game over. The difference is night and day."

She could imagine some wines that would be less obvious—Beaujolais, for instance, has less tannin than most red wines—but basically she thought that the astringency of red wine would be a giveaway if you were allowed to taste as well as smell. She offered to demonstrate this on the spot, and after ducking across the hall into her lab she returned with two wines in black glasses for me to taste. I tried both of them, and then I said, "The first one was red and the second one was white."

Professor Noble seemed taken aback. "It was the other way around," she said.

She was kind enough to come up with some mitigating circumstances. "It could have been test anxiety," she said. Then she tasted the wines and added, "I should have gotten a different red wine. This is not as astringent as I thought." Then she said that the red was, in fact, a weird wine, from Georgia. She didn't mean Georgia as in Tbilisi, where wine consumption is among the highest in the world; she meant Georgia as in Waycross. Then she mentioned that I hadn't had a warm-up taste.

I tried to help her think of other excuses. I told her the sun was in my eyes. I thought I'd reserve my other standard excuse—the ball hit a pebble—just in case she suggested that we do the Test again.

Professor Noble said she'd ask around among other faculty members whose concerns were most likely to have included a red-white test, but by the weekend of the test that Bruce Neyers had agreed to set up she had e-mailed me that no one at Davis seemed to know about such a test. (Neither, it later turned out, did the people in charge of the Culinary Institute of America's six-week California course that our winery guide had apparently been referring to.) By chance, both of my sons-in-law, Brian and Alex, were in San Francisco that weekend, and they were willing to act as tasters. Both of them have some interest in wine. My daughters, neither of whom drinks much wine, opted out; when we discussed the test over dinner in San Francisco the night before we were to drive up to Bruce's house, someone suggested that the sort of wine descriptors my younger daughter would use if asked to taste two wines might be "yucky" and "yuckier." Both of my sons-in-law seemed pretty free of test anxiety. "I'm not worried about failing," Alex said, partway through dinner. "I'm worried about failing and Brian passing."

Rather than repeat the sort of test he'd taken years before, Bruce had avoided wines he considered particularly likely to fool the tasters; he had gathered eight French wines that he thought of as typical products of the grapes they'd been made from. Not wanting to skew the results, I didn't mention what Ann Noble had told me about the way to increase your odds—take about three sips instead of one, building up the astringency of the tannin if it's red wine to produce a drying sensation in your mouth that would be hard to miss. As Bruce stood where he couldn't be observed and poured the wine into black glasses, he said that a couple of visiting wine retailers from Springfield, Missouri, sometimes known as the Gateway to the Ozarks, had dropped in just before we arrived and identified eight out of eight wines. Although he insisted he was telling the truth, I figured he was trying to make Brian and Alex nervous with some sort of Napa Valley version of trash talk, and I tried to keep them calm. "I want you to know that I'm totally evenhanded on this," I said to them. "Either one of you guys can be humiliated. I don't care which one it is."

As it turned out, they both did pretty well. Each person, wearing sunglasses as an added security measure, was asked to go through the wines twice—once trying to identify the color by smell, and then by taste. Alex got seven out of eight both times. Brian got only four by taste, but he got six by smell. By taste, both of them misidentified as white a Sancerre rouge made from Pinot Noir grapes in the Loire Valley. That was also one of two wines misidentified when tasted by another guest, Larry Bain, a San Francisco restaurant proprietor considered by Bruce to be knowledgeable in oenological matters—which means that if your brother-in-law is particularly arrogant about the sophistication of his palate you might consider keeping a bottle of Reverdy Sancerre rouge on hand, along with a black glass and a pair of sunglasses.

And what other information did the test at Bruce's provide? Taking an average of the three participants I witnessed—if Bruce's earlier guests really were from Missouri, they will understand that I can't count anything I didn't see with my own eyes—I concluded that experienced wine drinkers can tell red from white by taste about 70 percent of the time, as long as the test is being administered by someone who isn't interested in trying to fool them. That made me wonder whether there were similar statistics somewhere in a file drawer in Davis. If the Test never existed, after all, what test was that young man who showed us around the New York State winery taking when he got three out of seven? What test did I keep hearing about in California all those years? I sometimes ponder these questions when I listen to wine talk while sipping the amber microbrew the waiter brought when I asked him if he had any fancy beers on tap. At least, I think it's an amber microbrew.

2002

"Sweets?"

THE RUSSIAN GOD

VICTOR EROFEYEV

In the beginning was the word. And the word was with God. And the word was "vodka." In the vast but secluded expanse of Russia, vodka gives and vodka takes away. At the start of the twentieth century, a third of the Russian Army was supported by the excise duties paid on the Smirnov brand alone. At the same time, vodka has inflicted more suffering on the country than any war has. Some fourteen thousand Russian soldiers were killed during the ten-year occupation of Afghanistan, but more than thirty thousand Russians die of alcohol poisoning every year. The yearly consumption of alcohol is higher here than anywhere else in the world (almost four gallons of pure alcohol per capita, at least half of it in the form of vodka), and vodka has scarred virtually every family, just as the Second World War and the repressions of Stalin's regime did. (The only thing I know about my mother's father, for instance—other than that he divorced my grandmother soon after they were married—is that he was an alcoholic.) The very mention of the word "vodka" triggers unpredictable behavior in Russians. It seems to punch a hole directly into the subconscious, setting off a range of odd gestures and facial expressions. Some people wring their hands; some grin idiotically or snap their fingers; others sink into sullen silence. But no one, high or low, is left indifferent. More than by any political system, we are all held hostage by vodka. It menaces and it chastises; it demands sacrifices. It is both a catalyst of procreation and its scourge. It dictates who is born and who dies. In short, vodka is the Russian god. And, in 2003, that god will celebrate his five hundredth birthday.

One day in the early 1970s, Andrei Gromyko, the Soviet foreign minister, was traveling back to Moscow from his government dacha in the village of Zavidovo. His driver that day was Leonid Brezhnev, the general secretary of the Communist Party. The two leaders were alone in the car, and Gromyko felt able to broach a sore subject. "Leonid Ilyich," he said, "something has to be done about vodka. The people are turning into alcoholics."

Brezhnev didn't answer. Five minutes later, Gromyko was regretting having raised the issue when Brezhnev suddenly replied, "Andrei, there's no way the Russian people can do without it."

I heard this anecdote from Mikhail Gorbachev—who had heard it from Gromyko himself—when I paid him a visit, earlier this year, to talk about the vodka anniversary. We sat in his sombre, English-style office on Leningrad Prospect, as his late wife, Raisa Maximovna, gazed down at us from a large oil portrait.

As everyone in Russia knows, Gorbachev disagreed with Brezhnev, and he became the only Russian leader in the history of vodka to launch a relentless campaign to eradicate it. "The statistics were appalling," he told me. "Injuries in the workplace, falling productivity, diminishing life expectancy, accidents on the roads and railways. In 1972, they discussed the problem in the Politburo, but deferred it. It was impossible to solve, because the state budget itself was 'drunk'—it relied on the income from vodka sales. Stalin set it up that way—temporarily, but there's nothing as permanent as a temporary decision. In Brezhnev's time, the 'drunken' component of the budget increased from 100 billion rubles to 170 billion—that was how much profit vodka brought to the state." He went on, "In the course of my career, I saw massive drunkenness in the Party. Brezhnev drank, especially at the beginning. Yeltsin even used the fact that he drank to attract women—'He's just the same as we are!' Women couldn't keep their hands out of his pants. But in the West they were afraid—he had his finger on the nuclear button."

In May 1985, just two months after Gorbachev became the Party's general secretary, he issued a decree entitled "On Measures to Overcome Drunkenness and Alcoholism." He began his war on vodka by testing the public's commitment with a survey that was carried out in two hundred of the country's leading factories. The factory workers responded that they were against prohibition but in favor of restrictions on the use of alcohol. In practice, however, the anti-alcohol campaign turned into one of Communism's typical "bureaucratic excesses." Gorbachev destroyed vodka factories; closed most liquor stores; banned the serving of alcohol at receptions in Soviet embassies abroad; and, finally, even bulldozed vineyards in the Crimea, Georgia, Moldavia, the Kuban, and Stavropol— all to the howls and moans of the drinking nation, which soon dubbed him "the mineral-water secretary." Although the campaign, according to Gorbachev, led to "wives finally getting to see their husbands"—the birthrate rose, and so did life expectancy—some people started hoarding sugar to make moonshine, thereby creating an extreme sugar shortage. Others poisoned themselves with more dangerous intoxicants, including brake fluid. I remember, in those days, coming across a sign in a village store not far from Kostroma, near the northern end of the Volga: EAU DE COLOGNE ON SALE FROM 2 P.M. In the restaurants in Kostroma itself, the waiters were surreptitiously serving liquor in teacups.

Perhaps because Gorbachev came from south Stavropol, an area of Russia where, atypically, people consume mostly wine, he had failed to appreciate the extent of vodka's psychological influence. In the 1980s, in a country where vodka had become a currency that was often more reliable than the ruble, and where drunkenness was a factor in more than 70 percent of murders, vodka proved to be stronger than the power structures that Gorbachev had at his command. When he saw the poisoning statistics, he told me, he gave up. Perhaps the statistics had been distorted, in order to undermine his authority, he suggested bitterly. But then he laughed and told an old joke on himself: "There was this long line for vodka, and one poor guy couldn't stand it any longer. 'I'm going to the Kremlin, to kill Gorbachev,' he said. An hour later, he came back. The line was still there, and everyone asked him, 'Did you kill him?' 'Kill him!' he said. 'The line for that's even longer than this one!' "

Little has been recorded about the actual invention of vodka, and there is really nothing surprising in that: in Russia, vodka is thought of as a sacred and eternal substance, impervious to historical interpretation. In 1977, American vodka companies accused the Soviet distillers who were trying to make it in the U.S. market of "inauthenticity," and the ensuing commercial scandal lent some impetus to the study of vodka's history. But the cruelest blow was struck later that year, when Poland, at the time a faithful member of the Warsaw Pact, declared that vodka was really a Polish drink and that Russians had no right to use the name "vodka" for the alcohol they were producing. Alarmed Soviet functionaries searched for someone who could reconstruct the genesis of the drink and settled on a historian named William Pokhlebkin, who soon produced a treatise showing that the Poles had begun making vodka several decades after the Russians. (Pokhlebkin was killed, two years ago, in his apartment in the town of Podolsk, some twenty-five miles south of Moscow; one rumor has it that the murderer was a vengeful Pole.)

Some historians compare the Russian national dependence on vodka to the Tatar yoke, and there's a certain historical irony to the analogy. According to legend, vodka was first produced by monks at the Chudov Monastery, in the Kremlin, in the late fifteenth century, around the same time that the Russians finally freed themselves of Tatar rule. At first, the monks worked with alcohol imported from Genoa, through the Crimean port of Feodosiya. Later, it became common to make vodka out of the local grain alcohol, which was produced from rye or wheat and soft spring water. Almost everything about this story seems overly symbolic: the involvement of men of God, the name of the monastery, which no longer exists (*chudov* means "miraculous"), and its setting in the Russian capital. Evidently, many of the documents relating to the birth of vodka were destroyed in the mid-seventeenth century by the Russian Orthodox Church, which later declared vodka an invention of the Devil. (This despite the fact that Russian clergymen themselves have always had a healthy respect for the drink.)

The act of mixing alcohol with water could be a carryover from Mediterranean culture—in particular from the ancient Greeks, who mixed their wine with water—but it is more likely that the mixture was initially intended as a disinfectant for the treatment of wounds. Vodka quickly escaped the grip of medicine, however, and transubstantiated into the "burnt wine" some Swedes reminisced about after an expedition to Moscow in 1505. A few decades later, that burnt wine had set all of Russia aflame. The drink became so popular that by 1533 the Russian state had farmed out vodka production to local tavern owners, who—although they had to kiss the cross and swear to tell the truth—were soon wallowing in corruption. In the centuries before, when people had drunk mead, drunkenness was reserved for occasions of "revelry"; vodka transformed that revelry into the status quo.

The good times were short-lived. In 1648, a tavern revolt broke out in Moscow and then spread to other towns. The situation was dire. A third of the male population was in debt to the taverns, and for several years the peasants had been so drunk that they hadn't bothered to cultivate the land. In an attempt to put things right, the state assumed a monopoly on the sale of vodka, which meant that the vodka distillers' profits fell. This was when vodka acquired its long-term doppelgänger—home brew. People learned how to make a vodkalike drink at home and, in defiance of all prohibitions, continue to make it to this day. (Rural populations consume as many as four and half bottles of home brew for every bottle of vodka.) So far, the state has abrogated its own monopoly six times (the last time under Yeltsin, in 1992), and then reinstated it (in 1993, Yeltsin took fright at the rapid criminalization of the vodka sector), but each reversal has only tightened the grip of dipsomania.

"I feel sorry for the Russian people, who drink so much!" Tsar Alexander III told his minister of finance, Sergei Witte. In 1894, Witte launched a wide-reaching initiative to improve the quality of vodka, and thereby firm up the state monopoly. Dmitry Mendeleyev, the god of Russian chemistry, was brought in to do the job. Until then, vodka had been made simply, by processing equal volumes of alcohol and water with a number of trace additives to soften the taste. (Stolichnaya, for instance, has a small amount of sugar.) The water-alcohol mixture was then filtered, using charcoal. Mendeleyev observed that when alcohol and water were combined there was a mysterious contraction of the total mixture. (500 milliliters of water and 500 milliliters of alcohol produce 941 milliliters of vodka.) In order to obtain what he asserted was the optimum proportion of alcohol—40 percent—Mendeleyev said, water and alcohol needed to be measured not by volume but by weight. At the same time, the Russian physiologist Nikolai Volovich determined that the most beneficial dose of vodka to stimulate the working of the heart and to cleanse the blood was fifty grams a day. Temperance societies began to form across the country, but before they could have an effect the First World War began, and prohibition was introduced.

Prohibition remained in force during the 1917 Revolution and the civil war that followed, though followers of Reds and Whites alike took advantage of the mêlée to loot the vodka warehouses and drink to excess. (Pokhlebkin, in his treatise, jocularly suggested that the Reds won because they guarded the warehouses better and punished drunkenness by shooting.) Prohibition was repealed under Lenin in the mid-1920s, in a bid for popularity. He authorized the production of *rykovka,* a milder form of vodka, which was 30 percent alcohol. (It was named after the finance minister at the time, Aleksei Rykov.) But after Lenin died, vodka returned to its full strength, and its sale helped pay for the socialist industrialization of the USSR.

When the war against Hitler began, every Russian soldier at the front was given a daily "commissar's ration" of a hundred grams, as stipulated by the ministry of defense. Vodka manufacturers claim that the drink was as important as Katyusha rocket launchers in the victory over Nazism, because it bolstered the Russian army's spirits. But Vladimir Nuzhny, a professor of narcology and one of Russia's best-known theoreticians of alcoholism, thinks otherwise. Those hundred grams were a disaster for the entire postwar generation, he told me. Alcohol dependence soared, and the result was a downward spiral of dissolution that continued into the 1960s. When the monopoly on vodka production was abolished again, in the early 1990s, the vodka sector was thrown into chaos: the rich New Russians, who kick-started the motor of Russian "bandit" capitalism, were essentially old-fashioned bootleggers.

Mendeleyev not only created the classic standard for Russian vodka; he also gave the concoction its name. For several centuries, official documents had referred to vodka as "grain wine." To this day, there are probably more euphemisms for vodka than for anything other than the male sex organ. Its aliases range from "hot water," "the mono-polka," "the bubble," "crankshaft," "the bitter stuff," and "the white stuff" to the classic Soviet "half liter" and "quarter bottle" (also known as a "daughter"). Etymologically, the word "vodka" is derived from *voda*, the Russian word for "water." (The addition of the letter "k" makes it diminutive.)

The word appeared in standard Russian dictionaries in the mid-nineteenth century, but the upper classes and the urban middle class still regarded the drink as uncultured, almost obscene. Vodka was consumed primarily by the lower classes (hence the Russian idiom "drunk as a cobbler"). This was a result both of the quality of the vodka available (most of it was made from wood alcohol and smelled strongly of fuel oil) and of the barbarous "tavern" fashion in which it was consumed (it was illegal in taverns to eat food with liquor). Until the late nineteenth century, vodka was not even bottled—there weren't enough bottles—and it was measured by the *vedro*, or pail (equal to twenty-five pints).

The secret of the word "vodka" lies in its effect on the masses—in the mixture of lust and shame it inspires. The alcoholic views vodka as a woman; he is afraid to reveal his feelings for her, and is at the same time incapable of restraining them. The very mention of her name creates an atmosphere of conspiracy and mystical exaltation that provokes a kind of pagan stupor. In its essence, vodka is a brazen and shameless thing.

Vodka is unlike other forms of alcohol in that there is no justifiable excuse for drinking it. The Frenchman will praise the aroma of cognac, and the Scotsman will laud the flavor of whiskey. Vodka, however, is colorless, odorless, and tasteless. At the same time, it is an acrid and irritating drink. The Russian gulps his vodka down, grimacing and swearing, and immediately reaches for something else to "smooth it out." The result, not the process, is what's important. You might as well inject vodka into your bloodstream as drink it.

But then that's not entirely true, as all Russians, with the exception of the estimated 5 percent of the adult population that doesn't drink, can tell you. Vodka is like a song—it may have banal lyrics and a simple melody, but the combination, like that of alcohol and water, is more than the sum of its parts. In respectable society these days, vodka is served at a table set with a range of dishes perfected in minute detail by the old Russian landowners. The vodka ceremony has its own traditions ("No eating after the first glass"), its superstitions and catchphrases ("Vodka is the aunt of wine"), its schedule (ordinary Russian drunks are distinguished from alcoholics by the fact that they wait until five in the afternoon to start drinking), and its accoutrements (fish, salted gherkins, pickled mushrooms, jellied meat, and sauerkraut)—not to mention its toasts, which are the perfect excuse for consuming alcohol while simultaneously focusing on the general conversation. Every Russian knows that drinking vodka with *pelmeni*, a kind of meat dumpling, can induce a high not far short of nirvana.

Vodka has taken control of the will and conscience of a substantial sector of the Russian population. If you add up all the time that Russians have devoted to vodka and gather together all the vodka-fueled impulses of the soul—the fantasies, the dreams, the weeklong binges, the family catastrophes, the shamefaced hangovers, the murders, suicides, and fatalities (favorite Russian pastimes include choking on your own vomit and falling out of a window)—it becomes clear that behind the official history of the Russian state there exists another dimension. Despite all the misadventures and tragedies of Russian alcoholism, the spotlight here belongs to the inexplicable, almost universal delight that Russians take in the notion of drunken disorder. That delight has been recorded over the centuries in the accounts of astounded foreign travelers, such as the Dutch diplomat Balthazar Coet, who visited Moscow in 1676 and wrote, "We saw only the scandalous behavior of debauchees, glorified by the thronging crowd for their proficiency in drunkenness." We encounter the same philosophy in the samizdat bestseller from the Brezhnev era, Venedikt Erofeyev's *Moscow to the End of the Line,* a manifesto of indiscriminate social dissidence and a frank apologia for the metaphysics of drunkenness. "Everybody in Russia who was ever worth anything, everybody who was ever any use to the country," the book asserts, "every one of them drank like swine."

Drinking vodka is a social activity. When John Steinbeck was in Moscow, the story has it, it took him a while to understand that the three fingers two friendly guys waved at him were an invitation to split a bottle of vodka three ways; he ended up drinking *à trois* with them in a doorway anyway, apparently with no regrets. But the vodka-drinking ritual also involves a harsh questioning of human conventions. It demands freedom from history, from responsibility, from health, even from life itself. This condition of free fall, of moral weightlessness and philosophical incorporeality, represents both an attack on the "rational" West and a haughty assertion of Russian truth.

Gorbachev is of the opinion that "vodka has done more harm than good to the Russian people," but Evgeny Popov, a contemporary Russian writer who comes from hard-drinking Siberia, holds the opposite view.

In conversation in the bar of Moscow's Central Writers' House, Popov claimed that vodka has helped the Russian people counter the stress of living in a less than perfect nation. Vodka has provided access to a private life that is closed to the state, a place where it is possible to relax, to forget your troubles, to engage in sex with the illusion of free choice. Nowhere else has the relationship between literature and drink been as intense as it is in Russia. The revolutionary Nikolai Nekrasov, the émigré Aleksandr Kuprin, the leading Stalinist writer Aleksandr Fadeyev, the Nobel Prize winner Mikhail Sholokhov, and the man who is probably the best Russian writer of the twentieth century, Andrei Platonov, have all had love affairs with the bottle. As Popov told me, "Vodka makes it easier to think up literary plots."

The philosophy of vodka has its dark corner of violence. Russian despots with a sadistic streak, like Peter the Great and Stalin, have taken pleasure in forcing their guests to drink more than they could handle. Other hosts force-feed their guests vodka in order to reduce the social distance between them, to humiliate and deride or take advantage. Vodka is capable not only of generating bravado but also of inducing the excruciating feeling of remorse and self-abasement that is one of the essential elements of the ambivalent Russian personality. Hence the question that the Russian alcoholic traditionally asks his drinking companion: "Do you respect me?" The drinking Russian suffers from a marked divergence between his sober impulses and his drunken ones. It is not easy to govern an entire people in this state.

A vodka museum will open in Moscow next year, and a large festival is being planned to mark the five hundredth anniversary of the drink, but no one was able to provide me with a satisfactory explanation for why that anniversary is being celebrated in 2003. I decided to try asking the distillers themselves. I started by attempting to infiltrate Moscow's largest vodka factory, which produces the high-quality brand Crystall. But it proved to be an almost impregnable fortress—I had to get state backing just to enter the production premises. The gloomy brick factory building was erected beside the river Yauza during Witte's state-vodka monopoly in 1901. Because the famous Molotov cocktails were produced there during the Second World War, it became a target for German bombing raids. The factory was damaged, but it survived, continuing to supply the front with both Molotov cocktails and vodka. It now produces up to five million bottles a month, and the sight of alcohol pouring into numberless bottles there immediately summoned up the vision of the million Russian throats that empty those bottles every day. Inside, the Crystall factory has the sublime atmosphere of a cathedral. It is absolutely sterile. There is almost no smell of alcohol, and the employees wear white coats. The vodka is produced on a specialized production line, developed in Italy and Germany, in which alcohol is mechanically mixed with water (taken from the main Moscow water supply but specially filtered), and then the vodka is bottled, sealed, and packed into boxes. Most of the machine operators are women, because, as my female guide told me, women are more suited to monotonous work. The factory's melancholic director, Aleksandr Timofeyev, who has since been fired, was exceedingly courteous and evasive in conversation. The only thing I managed to get out of him was a confession that he himself didn't drink, so he didn't really know much about vodka. He sent me off as soon as he could with a very fine bottle.

To get answers, you have to go to the top, a truism that was confirmed by my conversation with Sergei Viktorovich Zevenko, who was known, when I saw him earlier this year, as the "vodka king." Zevenko was the director of Rosspirtprom, the government-run company that currently controls 40 percent of vodka production in Russia and oversees more than a hundred high-quality vodka factories. But he told me he had been drunk only once in his life, right after high school, when he was seeing off a friend who was joining the army. Now, at the age of thirty-four, he recalled the episode with disgusted laughter: "It took me an entire week to recover. It was a severe shock to my system."

Zevenko had a complicated life. His competitors envied his sovereign status. His efforts to persuade Russians to eschew the cheaper forms of vodka, which are more likely to cause fatal liver disease, for the higher-quality, state-controlled varieties had earned him, among New Russians, the status of "a temporary man." He himself said that there was a six-million-dollar price on his head: even in the corridors of the Rosspirtprom headquarters, he was accompanied by two bodyguards, and he drove through town with six submachine gunners in tow. He could relax only when he was abroad. The private companies that produce vodka (the vodka monopoly these days exists primarily on paper) had offered to pay him two million dollars a year to organize their operations, but he said that he'd work only for the state.

I met with Zevenko in his spacious office, in a high-rise on Kutuzovsky Prospect, overlooking the Moscow River. He was lean and fit, in a black sweater and slim black trousers. He looked nothing at all like an old-time Soviet bureaucrat or even a Putin-era politician. Like Gorbachev, he was from Stavropol, and he told me in his southern-Russian accent that he had never been a Soviet man—"I didn't like marching in formation"—although he had once been a member of the Komsomol. Educated as a lawyer, he described himself as a manager.

Zevenko said that the lack of skilled personnel was the main problem facing Russia now. As he put it, 80 percent of Russians today are "rotten," and he looked to the children of the new social order, who he hoped would be capable of bringing Russia fully into the civilized world. We spoke of Russia's five-hundred-year failure to control its dependency. What could be done about it? The idea of subjugating vodka—of making it work for the state and contribute to the creation of a healthy nation—is a paradoxical one, and although Zevenko was prepared to fight for it, he was well aware that his efforts would never earn him much recognition. The vodka world was too turbulent and risky, not unlike the narcotics market, and Zevenko was a thorn in the side of those who didn't wish to see order imposed. He didn't believe that a real monopoly of vodka production was possible, he said, but he did hope to squeeze as much of the low-quality vodka out of the market as he could. I left his office feeling that new people really were being born in Russia, people who didn't expect gratitude for their efforts, either from the state or from the public. But the vodka world turned out to be as turbulent as Zevenko predicted; not long after our meeting, he, too, was fired and he disappeared from sight. Still, he was not alone in his views, and, odd as it may seem, vodka's official five hundredth anniversary—which was almost certainly proclaimed in order to give a boost to the vodka market—could actually mark the beginning of our long goodbye to the drink.

The narcotics specialist Vladimir Nuzhny criticized Gorbachev's campaign against alcohol for its "antiscientific" approach, but he also told me that capitalism, if it succeeds, could put an end to the Russian addiction. "The new generation of entrepreneurs don't drink vodka," he said. "Young people are already switching to beer. They have to make decisions with a clear head. The privately owned factories fire people for drunkenness. The next fifteen or twenty years could bring a serious change for the better. It all depends on the economy." Gorbachev had also said that the future lies "in an emphasis on beer and wine."

Vodka culture is dividing. The Moscow elite choose between imported drinks and high-quality vodka. They drink, but they don't get drunk. It is also slowly becoming fashionable not to drink at all. (In that sense, the teetotaler Putin sets an example for the whole country.) The provinces, though, lag behind, and in rural areas vodka is still a kind of second currency. The choice there is not between vodka and wine but between cheap vodka and home brew; expensive vodka is seen as an extravagance or a pretension. In short, the vodka god will not give up easily, but he may yet be tamed, perhaps even relegated to historical myth. Vodka has always teetered between heaven and hell. Gorky, in a memoir about his boyhood on the Volga, writes that the people drank for joy and they drank for sorrow; the Russian soul is versatile.

2002

Translated, from the Russian, by Andrew Bromfield

"*Not my favorite again!*"

THE KETCHUP CONUNDRUM

MALCOLM GLADWELL

Many years ago, one mustard dominated the supermarket shelves: French's. It came in a plastic bottle. People used it on hot dogs and bologna. It was a yellow mustard, made from ground white mustard seed with turmeric and vinegar, which gave it a mild, slightly metallic taste. If you looked hard in the grocery store, you might find something in the specialty-foods section called Grey Poupon, which was Dijon mustard, made from the more pungent brown mustard seed. In the early 1970s, Grey Poupon was no more than a hundred-thousand-dollar-a-year business. Few people knew what it was or how it tasted, or had any particular desire for an alternative to French's or the runner-up, Gulden's. Then one day the Heublein Company, which owned Grey Poupon, discovered something remarkable: if you gave people a mustard taste test, a significant number had only to try Grey Poupon once to switch from yellow mustard. In the food world, that almost never happens; even among the most successful food brands, only about one in a hundred have that kind of conversion rate. Grey Poupon was magic.

So Heublein put Grey Poupon in a bigger glass jar, with an enameled label and enough of a whiff of Frenchness to make it seem as if it were still being made in Europe (it was made in Hartford, Connecticut, from Canadian mustard seed and white wine). The company ran tasteful print ads in upscale food magazines. They put the mustard in little foil packets and distributed them with airplane meals—which was a brand-new idea at the time. Then they hired the Manhattan ad agency Lowe Marschalk to do something, on a modest budget, for television. The agency came back with an idea: A Rolls-Royce is driving down a country road. There's a man in the backseat in a suit with a plate of beef on a silver tray. He nods to the chauffeur, who opens the glove compartment. Then comes what is known in the business as the "reveal." The chauffeur hands back a jar of Grey Poupon. Another Rolls-Royce pulls up alongside. A man leans his head out the window. "Pardon me. Would you have any Grey Poupon?"

In the cities where the ads ran, sales of Grey Poupon leaped 40 to 50 percent, and whenever Heublein bought airtime in new cities sales jumped by 40 to 50 percent again. Grocery stores put Grey Poupon next to French's and Gulden's. By the end of the 1980s, Grey Poupon was the most powerful brand in mustard. "The tagline in the commercial was that this was one of life's finer pleasures," Larry Elegant, who wrote the original Grey Poupon spot, says, "and that, along with the Rolls-Royce, seemed to impart to people's minds that this was something truly different and superior."

The rise of Grey Poupon proved that the American supermarket shopper was willing to pay more—in this case, $3.99 instead of $1.49 for eight ounces—as long as what they were buying carried with it an air of sophistication and complex aromatics. Its success showed, furthermore, that the boundaries of taste and custom were not fixed: that just because mustard had always been yellow didn't mean that consumers would use only yellow mustard. It is because of Grey Poupon that the standard American supermarket today has an entire mustard section. And it is because of Grey Poupon that a man named Jim Wigon decided, four years ago, to enter the ketchup business. Isn't the ketchup business today exactly where mustard was thirty years ago? There is Heinz and, far behind, Hunt's and Del Monte and a handful of private-label brands. Jim Wigon wanted to create the Grey Poupon of ketchup.

Wigon is from Boston. He's a thickset man in his early fifties, with a full salt-and-pepper beard. He runs his ketchup business—under the brand World's Best Ketchup—out of the catering business of his partner, Nick Schiarizzi, in Norwood, Massachusetts, just off Route 1, in a low-slung building behind an industrial-equipment-rental shop. He starts with red peppers, Spanish onions, garlic, and a high-end tomato paste. Basil is chopped by hand, because the buffalo chopper bruises the leaves. He uses maple syrup, not corn syrup, which gives him a quarter of the sugar of Heinz. He pours his ketchup into a clear glass ten-ounce jar, and sells it for three times the price of Heinz, and for the past few years he has crisscrossed the country, peddling World's Best in six flavors—regular, sweet, dill, garlic, caramelized onion, and basil—to specialty grocery stores and supermarkets. If you were in Zabar's on Manhattan's Upper West Side a few months ago, you would have seen him at the front of the store, in a spot between the sushi and the gefilte fish. He was wearing a World's Best baseball cap, a white shirt, and a red-stained apron. In front of him, on a small table, was a silver tureen filled with miniature chicken and beef meatballs, a box of toothpicks, and a dozen or so open jars of his ketchup. "Try my ketchup!" Wigon said, over and over, to anyone who passed. "If you don't try it, you're doomed to eat Heinz the rest of your life."

In the same aisle at Zabar's that day two other demonstrations were going on, so that people were starting at one end with free chicken sausage, sampling a slice of prosciutto, and then pausing at the World's Best stand before heading for the cash register. They would look down at the array of open jars, and Wigon would impale a meatball on a toothpick, dip it in one of his ketchups, and hand it to them with a flourish. The ratio of tomato solids to liquid in World's Best is much higher than in Heinz, and the maple syrup gives it an unmistakable sweet kick. Invariably, people would close their eyes, just for a moment, and do a subtle double take. Some of them would look slightly perplexed and walk away, and others would nod and pick up a jar. "You know why you like it so much?" he would say, in his broad Boston accent, to the customers who seemed most impressed. "Because you've been eating bad ketchup all your life!" Jim Wigon had a simple vision: build a better ketchup—the way Grey Poupon built a better mustard—and the world will beat a path to your door. If only it were that easy.

The story of World's Best Ketchup cannot properly be told without a man from White Plains, New York, named Howard Moskowitz. Moskowitz is sixty, short and round, with graying hair and huge gold-rimmed glasses. When he talks, he favors the Socratic monologue—a series of questions that he poses to himself, then answers, punctuated by "ahhh" and much vigorous nodding. He is a lineal descendant of the legendary eighteenth-century Hasidic rabbi known as the Seer of Lublin. He keeps a parrot. At Harvard, he wrote his doctoral dissertation on psychophysics, and all the rooms on the ground floor of his food-testing and market-research business are named after famous psychophysicists. ("Have you ever heard of the name Rose Marie Pangborn? Ahhh. She was a professor at Davis. Very famous. This is the Pangborn kitchen.") Moskowitz is a man of uncommon exuberance and persuasiveness: if he had been your freshman statistics professor, you would today be a statistician. "My favorite writer? Gibbon," he burst out when we met not long ago. He had just been holding forth on the subject of sodium solutions. "Right now I'm working my way through the Hales history of the Byzantine Empire. Holy shit! Everything is easy until you get to the Byzantine Empire. It's impossible. One emperor is always killing the others, and everyone has five wives or three husbands. It's very Byzantine."

Moskowitz set up shop in the 1970s, and one of his first clients was Pepsi. The artificial sweetener aspartame had just become available, and Pepsi wanted Moskowitz to figure out the perfect amount of sweetener for a can of Diet Pepsi. Pepsi knew that anything below 8 percent sweetness was not sweet enough and anything over 12 percent was too sweet. So Moskowitz did the logical thing. He made up experimental batches of Diet Pepsi with every conceivable degree of sweetness— 8 percent, 8.25 percent, 8.5, and on and on up to 12—gave them to hundreds of people, and looked for the concentration that people liked the most. But the data were a mess—there wasn't a pattern—and one day, sitting in a diner, Moskowitz realized why. They had been asking the wrong question. There was no such thing as the perfect Diet Pepsi. They should have been looking for the perfect Diet Pepsis.

It took a long time for the food world to catch up with Howard Moskowitz. He knocked on doors and tried to explain his idea about the plural nature of perfection, and no one answered. He spoke at food-industry conferences, and audiences shrugged. But he could think of nothing else. "It's like that Yiddish expression," he says. "Do you know it? 'To a worm in horseradish, the world is horseradish!'" Then, in 1986, he got a call from the Campbell's Soup Company. They were in the spaghetti-sauce business, going up against Ragú with their Prego brand. Prego was a little thicker than Ragú, with diced tomatoes as opposed to Ragú's purée, and, Campbell's thought, it had better pasta adherence. But, for all that, Prego was in a slump, and Campbell's was desperate for new ideas.

Standard practice in the food industry would have been to convene a focus group and ask spaghetti eaters what they wanted. But Moskowitz does not believe that consumers—even spaghetti lovers— know what they desire if what they desire does not yet exist. "The mind," as Moskowitz is fond of saying, "knows not what the tongue wants." Instead, working with the Campbell's kitchens, he came up with forty-five varieties of spaghetti sauce. These were designed to differ in every conceivable way: spiciness, sweetness, tartness, saltiness, thickness, aroma, mouth feel, cost of ingredients, and so forth. He had a trained panel of food tasters analyze each of those varieties in depth. Then he took the prototypes on the road—to New York, Chicago, Los Angeles, and Jacksonville—and asked people in groups of twenty-five to eat between eight and ten small bowls of different spaghetti sauces over two hours and rate them on a scale of one to a hundred. When Moskowitz charted the results, he saw that everyone had a slightly different definition of what a perfect spaghetti sauce tasted like.

If you sifted carefully through the data, though, you could find patterns, and Moskowitz learned that most people's preferences fell into one of three broad groups: plain, spicy, and extra-chunky, and of those three the last was the most important. Why? Because at the time there was no extra-chunky spaghetti sauce in the supermarket. Over the next decade, that new category proved to be worth hundreds of millions of dollars to Prego. "We all said, 'Wow!'" Monica Wood, who was then the head of market research for Campbell's, recalls. "Here there was this third segment—people who liked their spaghetti sauce with lots of stuff in it—and it was completely untapped. So in about 1989–90 we launched Prego extra-chunky. It was extraordinarily successful."

It may be hard today, fifteen years later—when every brand seems to come in multiple varieties—to appreciate how much of a breakthrough this was. In those years, people in the food industry carried around in their heads the notion of a platonic dish—the version of a dish that looked and tasted absolutely right. At Ragú and Prego, they had been striving for the platonic spaghetti sauce, and the platonic spaghetti sauce was thin and blended because that's the way they thought it was done in Italy. Cooking, on the industrial level, was consumed with the search for human universals. Once you start looking for the sources of human variability, though, the old orthodoxy goes out the window. Howard Moskowitz stood up to the Platonists and said there are no universals.

Moskowitz still has a version of the computer model he used for Prego fifteen years ago. It has all the coded results from the consumer taste tests and the expert tastings, split into the three categories (plain, spicy, and extra-chunky) and linked up with the actual ingredients list on a spreadsheet. "You know how they have a computer model for building an aircraft," Moskowitz said as he pulled up the program on his computer. "This is a model for building spaghetti sauce. Look, every variable is here." He pointed at column after column of ratings. "So here are the ingredients. I'm a brand manager for Prego. I want to optimize one of the segments. Let's start with Segment 1."

In Moskowitz's program, the three spaghetti-sauce groups were labeled Segment 1, Segment 2, and Segment 3. He typed in a few commands, instructing the computer to give him the formulation that would score the highest with those people in Segment 1. The answer appeared almost immediately: a specific recipe that, according to Moskowitz's data, produced a score of 78 from the people in Segment 1. But that same formulation didn't do nearly as well with those in Segment 2 and Segment 3. They scored it 67 and 57, respectively. Moskowitz started again, this time asking the computer to optimize for Segment 2. This time the ratings came in at 82, but now Segment 1 had fallen ten points, to 68. "See what happens?" he said. "If I make one group happier, I piss off another group. We did this for coffee with General Foods, and we found that if you create only one product the best you can get across all the segments is a 60—if you're lucky. That's if you were to treat everybody as one big happy family. But if I do the sensory segmentation, I can get 70, 71, 72. Is that big? Ahhh. It's a very big difference. In coffee, a 71 is something you'll die for."

When Jim Wigon set up shop that day in Zabar's, then, his operating assumption was that there ought to be some segment of the population that preferred a ketchup made with Stanislaus tomato paste and hand-chopped basil and maple syrup. That's the Moskowitz theory. But there is theory and there is practice. By the end of that long day, Wigon had sold ninety jars. But he'd also got two parking tickets and had to pay for a hotel room, so he wasn't going home with money in his pocket. For the year, Wigon estimates, he'll sell fifty thousand jars—which, in the universe of condiments, is no more than a blip. "I haven't drawn a paycheck in five years," Wigon said as he impaled another meatball on a toothpick. "My wife is killing me." And it isn't just World's Best that is struggling. In the gourmet-ketchup world, there is River Run and Uncle Dave's, from Vermont, and Muir Glen Organic and Mrs. Tomato Head Roasted Garlic Peppercorn Catsup, in California, and dozens of others—and every year Heinz's overwhelming share of the ketchup market just grows.

It is possible, of course, that ketchup is waiting for its own version

of that Rolls-Royce commercial, or the discovery of the ketchup equivalent of extra-chunky—the magic formula that will satisfy an unmet
need. It is also possible, however, that the rules of Howard Moskowitz,
which apply to Grey Poupon and Prego spaghetti sauce and to olive oil
and salad dressing and virtually everything else in the supermarket,
don't apply to ketchup.

Tomato ketchup is a nineteenth-century creation—the union of the
English tradition of fruit and vegetable sauces and the growing American infatuation with the tomato. But what we know today as ketchup
emerged out of a debate that raged in the first years of the last century
over benzoate, a preservative widely used in late-nineteenth-century
condiments. Harvey Washington Wiley, the chief of the Bureau of
Chemistry in the Department of Agriculture from 1883 to 1912, came
to believe that benzoates were not safe, and the result was an argument
that split the ketchup world in half. On one side was the ketchup establishment, which believed that it was impossible to make ketchup without benzoate and that benzoate was not harmful in the amounts used.
On the other side was a renegade band of ketchup manufacturers, who
believed that the preservative puzzle could be solved with the application of culinary science. The dominant nineteenth-century ketchups
were thin and watery, in part because they were made from unripe tomatoes, which are low in the complex carbohydrates known as pectin, which
add body to a sauce. But what if you made ketchup from ripe tomatoes,
giving it the density it needed to resist degradation? Nineteenth-century
ketchups had a strong tomato taste, with just a light vinegar touch. The
renegades argued that by greatly increasing the amount of vinegar, in
effect protecting the tomatoes by pickling them, they were making a
superior ketchup: safer, purer, and better-tasting. They offered a money-
back guarantee in the event of spoilage. They charged more for their
product, convinced that the public would pay more for a better ketchup,
and they were right. The benzoate ketchups disappeared. The leader
of the renegade band was an entrepreneur out of Pittsburgh named
Henry J. Heinz.
    The world's leading expert on ketchup's early years is Andrew F.
Smith, a substantial man, well over six feet, with a graying mustache
and short, wavy black hair. Smith is a scholar, trained as a political sci-

entist, intent on bringing rigor to the world of food. When we met for lunch not long ago at the restaurant Savoy in Soho (chosen because of the excellence of its hamburger and French fries, and because Savoy makes its own ketchup—a dark, peppery, and viscous variety served in a white porcelain saucer), Smith was in the throes of examining the origins of the croissant for the upcoming *Oxford Encyclopedia of Food and Drink in America,* of which he is the editor in chief. Was the croissant invented in 1683 by the Viennese, in celebration of their defeat of the invading Turks? Or in 1686 by the residents of Budapest, to celebrate their defeat of the Turks? Both explanations would explain its distinctive crescent shape—since it would make a certain cultural sense (particularly for the Viennese) to consecrate their battlefield triumphs in the form of pastry. But the only reference Smith could find to either story was in the *Larousse Gastronomique* of 1938. "It just doesn't check out," he said, shaking his head wearily.

Smith's specialty is the tomato, however, and over the course of many scholarly articles and books—"The History of Home-made Anglo-American Tomato Ketchup," for *Petits Propos Culinaires,* for example, and "The Great Tomato Pill War of the 1830's," for *The Connecticut Historical Society Bulletin*—Smith has argued that some critical portion of the history of culinary civilization could be told through this fruit. Cortés brought tomatoes to Europe from the New World, and they inexorably insinuated themselves into the world's cuisines. The Italians substituted the tomato for eggplant. In northern India, it went into curries and chutneys. "The biggest tomato producer in the world today?" Smith paused, for dramatic effect. "China. You don't think of tomato being a part of Chinese cuisine, and it wasn't ten years ago. But it is now." Smith dipped one of my French fries into the homemade sauce. "It has that raw taste," he said, with a look of intense concentration. "It's fresh ketchup. You can taste the tomato." Ketchup was, to his mind, the most nearly perfect of all the tomato's manifestations. It was inexpensive, which meant that it had a firm lock on the mass market, and it was a condiment, not an ingredient, which meant that it could be applied at the discretion of the food eater, not the food preparer. "There's a quote from Elizabeth Rozin I've always loved," he said. Rozin is the food theorist who wrote the essay "Ketchup and the Collective Unconscious," and Smith used her conclusion as the epigraph of his ketchup book: ketchup may well be "the only true culinary expression of the melting pot, and . . . its special and unprecedented ability to provide something for everyone makes it the Esperanto of cuisine." Here is where Henry Heinz and the benzoate battle were so important: in defeating the condiment old guard, he was the one who changed the flavor of ketchup in a way that made it universal.

There are five known fundamental tastes in the human palate: salty, sweet, sour, bitter, and umami. Umami is the proteiny, full-bodied taste of chicken soup, or cured meat, or fish stock, or aged cheese, or mother's milk, or soy sauce, or mushrooms, or seaweed, or cooked tomato. "Umami adds body," Gary Beauchamp, who heads the Monell Chemical Senses Center, in Philadelphia, says. "If you add it to a soup, it makes the soup seem like it's thicker—it gives it sensory heft. It turns a soup from salt water into a food." When Heinz moved to ripe tomatoes and increased the percentage of tomato solids, he made ketchup, first and foremost, a potent source of umami. Then he dramatically increased the concentration of vinegar, so that his ketchup had twice the acidity of most other ketchups; now ketchup was sour, another of the fundamental tastes. The post-benzoate ketchups also doubled the concentration of sugar—so now ketchup was also sweet—and all along ketchup had been salty and bitter. These are not trivial issues. Give a baby soup, and then soup with MSG (an amino-acid salt that is pure umami), and the baby will go back for the MSG soup every time, the same way a baby will always prefer water with sugar to water alone. Salt and sugar and umami are primal signals about the food we are eating—about how dense it is in calories, for example, or, in the case of umami, about the presence of proteins and amino acids. What Heinz had done was come up with a condiment that pushed all five of these primal buttons. The taste of Heinz's ketchup began at the tip of the tongue, where our receptors for sweet and salty first appear, moved along the sides, where sour notes seem the strongest, then hit the back of the tongue, for umami and bitter, in one long crescendo. How many things in the supermarket run the sensory spectrum like this?

A number of years ago, the H. J. Heinz Company did an extensive market-research project in which researchers went into people's homes and watched the way they used ketchup. "I remember sitting in one of those households," Casey Keller, who was until recently the chief growth officer for Heinz, says. "There was a three-year-old and a six-year-old, and what happened was that the kids asked for ketchup and Mom brought it out. It was a forty-ounce bottle. And the three-year-old went to grab it himself, and Mom intercepted the bottle and said, 'No, you're not going to do that.' She physically took the bottle away and doled out a little dollop. You could see that the whole thing was a bummer." For Heinz, Keller says, that moment was an epiphany. A typical five-year-old consumes about 60 percent more ketchup than a typical forty-year-old, and the company realized that it needed to put ketchup in a bottle that a toddler could control. "If you are four—and I have a four-year-old—he doesn't get to choose what he eats for dinner, in most cases," Keller says. "But the one thing he can control is ketchup. It's the one part of the food experience that he can customize and personalize." As a result, Heinz came out with the so-called EZ Squirt bottle, made out of soft plastic with a conical nozzle. In homes where the EZ Squirt is used, ketchup consumption has grown by as much as 12 percent.

There is another lesson in that household scene, though. Small children tend to be neophobic: once they hit two or three, they shrink from new tastes. That makes sense, evolutionarily, because through much of human history that is the age at which children would have first begun to gather and forage for themselves, and those who strayed from what was known and trusted would never have survived. There the three-year-old was, confronted with something strange on his plate—tuna fish, perhaps, or brussels sprouts—and he wanted to alter his food in some way that made the unfamiliar familiar. He wanted to subdue the contents of his plate. And so he turned to ketchup, because, alone among the condiments on the table, ketchup could deliver sweet and sour and salty and bitter and umami, all at once.

Last February, Edgar Chambers IV, who runs the sensory-analysis center at Kansas State University, conducted a joint assessment of World's Best and Heinz. He has seventeen trained tasters on his staff, and they work for academia and industry, answering the often difficult question of what a given substance tastes like. It is demanding work. Immediately after conducting the ketchup study, Chambers dispatched a team to Bangkok to do an analysis of fruit—bananas, mangoes, rose apples, and sweet tamarind. Others were detailed to soy and kimchi in South Korea, and Chambers's wife led a delegation to Italy to analyze ice cream.

The ketchup tasting took place over four hours, on two consecutive mornings. Six tasters sat around a large, round table with a lazy Susan in the middle. In front of each panelist were two one-ounce cups, one filled with Heinz ketchup and one filled with World's Best. They would work along fourteen dimensions of flavor and texture, in accordance with the standard fifteen-point scale used by the food world. The flavor components would be divided two ways: elements picked up by the tongue and elements picked up by the nose. A very ripe peach, for example, tastes sweet but it also smells sweet—which is a very different aspect of sweetness. Vinegar has a sour taste but also a pungency, a vapor that rises up the back of the nose and fills the mouth when you breathe out. To aid in the rating process, the tasters surrounded themselves with little bowls of sweet and sour and salty solutions, and portions of Contadina tomato paste, Hunt's tomato sauce, and Campbell's tomato juice, all of which represent different concentrations of tomatoness.

After breaking the ketchup down into its component parts, the testers assessed the critical dimension of "amplitude," the word sensory experts use to describe flavors that are well blended and balanced, that "bloom" in the mouth. "The difference between high and low amplitude is the difference between my son and a great pianist playing 'Ode to Joy' on the piano," Chambers says. "They are playing the same notes, but they blend better with the great pianist." Pepperidge Farm shortbread cookies are considered to have high amplitude. So are Hellman's mayonnaise and Sara Lee poundcake. When something is high in amplitude, all its constituent elements converge into a single gestalt. You can't isolate the elements of an iconic, high-amplitude flavor like Coca-Cola or Pepsi. But you can with one of those private-label colas that you get in the supermarket. "The thing about Coke and Pepsi is that they are absolutely gorgeous," Judy Heylmun, a vice president of Sensory Spectrum, Inc., in Chatham, New Jersey, says. "They have beautiful notes—all flavors are in balance. It's very hard to do that well. Usually, when you taste a store cola it's"—and here she made a series of *pik! pik! pik!* sounds—"all the notes are kind of spiky, and usually the citrus is the first thing to spike out. And then the cinnamon. Citrus and brown spice notes are top notes and very volatile, as opposed to vanilla, which is very dark and deep. A really cheap store brand will have a big, fat cinnamon note sitting on top of everything."

Some of the cheaper ketchups are the same way. Ketchup aficionados say that there's a disquieting unevenness to the tomato notes in Del Monte ketchup: tomatoes vary, in acidity and sweetness and the ratio of solids to liquid, according to the seed variety used, the time of year they are harvested, the soil in which they are grown, and the weather during the growing season. Unless all those variables are tightly controlled, one batch of ketchup can end up too watery and another can be too strong. Or try one of the numerous private-label brands that make up the bottom of the ketchup market and pay attention to the spice mix; you may well find yourself conscious of the clove note or overwhelmed by a hit of garlic. Generic colas and ketchups have what Moskowitz calls a hook—a sensory attribute that you can single out, and ultimately tire of.

The tasting began with a plastic spoon. Upon consideration, it was decided that the analysis would be helped if the ketchups were tasted on French fries, so a batch of fries were cooked up and distributed around the table. Each tester, according to protocol, took the fries one by one, dipped them into the cup—all the way, right to the bottom—bit off the portion covered in ketchup, and then contemplated the evidence of their senses. For Heinz, the critical flavor components—vinegar, salt, tomato ID (overall tomatoness), sweet, and bitter—were judged to be present in roughly equal concentrations, and those elements, in turn, were judged to be well blended. The World's Best, though, "had a completely different view, a different profile, from the Heinz," Chambers said. It had a much stronger hit of sweet aromatics—4.0 to 2.5—and outstripped Heinz on tomato ID by a resounding 9 to 5.5. But there was less salt, and no discernible vinegar. "The other comment from the panel was that these elements were really not blended at all," Chambers went on. "The World's Best product had really low amplitude." According to Joyce Buchholz, one of the panelists, when the group judged aftertaste, "it seemed like a certain flavor would hang over longer in the case of World's Best—that cooked-tomatoey flavor."

But what was Jim Wigon to do? To compete against Heinz, he had to try something dramatic, like substituting maple syrup for corn syrup, ramping up the tomato solids. That made for an unusual and daring flavor. World's Best Dill Ketchup on fried catfish, for instance, is a mar-

velous thing. But it also meant that his ketchup wasn't as sensorily complete as Heinz, and he was paying a heavy price in amplitude. "Our
conclusion was mainly this," Buchholz said. "We felt that World's Best
seemed to be more like a sauce." She was trying to be helpful.

There is an exception, then, to the Moskowitz rule. Today there are
thirty-six varieties of Ragú spaghetti sauce, under six rubrics—Old
World Style, Chunky Garden Style, Robusto, Light, Cheese Creations,
and Rich & Meaty—which means that there is very nearly an optimal
spaghetti sauce for every man, woman, and child in America. Measured
against the monotony that confronted Howard Moskowitz twenty
years ago, this is progress. Happiness, in one sense, is a function of how
closely our world conforms to the infinite variety of human preference.
But that makes it easy to forget that sometimes happiness can be found
in having what we've always had and everyone else is having. "Back
in the seventies, someone else—I think it was Ragú—tried to do an
'Italian'-style ketchup," Moskowitz said. "They failed miserably." It was
a conundrum: what was true about a yellow condiment that went on
hot dogs was not true about a tomato condiment that went on hamburgers, and what was true about tomato sauce when you added visible
solids and put it in a jar was somehow not true about tomato sauce
when you added vinegar and sugar and put it in a bottle. Moskowitz
shrugged. "I guess ketchup is ketchup."

2004

TASTES FUNNY

"You certainly have a peculiar sense of humor."

"... It is a pleasant accompaniment to fish, shellfish, and the lighter meats, but its delicate flavor is perhaps even more appreciated at the end of the meal with melon or dessert."

BUT THE ONE ON THE RIGHT—

DOROTHY PARKER

I knew it. I knew if I came to this dinner, I'd draw something like this baby on my left. They've been saving him up for me for weeks. Now, we've simply got to have him—his sister was so sweet to us in London; we can stick him next to Mrs. Parker—she talks enough for two. Oh, I should never have come, never. I'm here against my better judgment. Friday, at eight-thirty, Mrs. Parker vs. her better judgment, to a decision. That would be a good thing for them to cut on my tombstone: Wherever she went, including here, it was against her better judgment. This is a fine time of the evening to be thinking about tombstones. That's the effect he's had on me, already, and the soup hardly cold yet. I should have stayed at home for dinner. I could have had something on a tray. The head of John the Baptist, or something. Oh, I should not have come.

Well, the soup's over, anyway. I'm that much nearer to my Eternal Home. Now the soup belongs to the ages, and I have said precisely four words to the gentleman on my left. I said, "Isn't this soup delicious?"; that's four words. And he said, "Yes, isn't it?"; that's three. He's one up on me.

At any rate, we're in perfect accord. We agree like lambs. We've been all through the soup together, and never a cross word between us. It seems rather a pity to let the subject drop, now we've found something on which we harmonize so admirably. I believe I'll bring it up again; I'll ask him if that wasn't delicious soup. He says, "Yes, wasn't it?" Look at that, will you; perfect command of his tenses.

Here comes the fish. Goody, goody, goody, we got fish. I wonder if he likes fish. Yes, he does; he says he likes fish. Ah, that's nice. I love that in a man. Look, he's talking! He's chattering away like a veritable magpie! He's asking me if I like fish. Now does he really want to know, or is it only a line? I'd better play it cagey. I'll tell him, "Oh, pretty well." Oh, I like fish pretty well; there's a fascinating bit of autobiography for him to study over. Maybe he would rather wrestle with it alone. I'd better steal softly away, and leave him to his thoughts.

I might try my luck with what's on my right. No, not a chance there. The woman on his other side has him cold. All I can see is his shoulder. It's a nice shoulder, too; oh, it's a nice, *nice* shoulder. All my life, I've been a fool for a nice shoulder. Very well, lady; you saw him first. Keep your Greek god, and I'll go back to my Trojan horse.

Let's see, where were we? Oh, we'd got to where he had confessed his liking for fish. I wonder what else he likes. Does he like cucumbers? Yes, he does; he likes cucumbers. And potatoes? Yes, he likes potatoes, too. Why, he's a regular old Nature-lover, that's what he is. I would have to come out to dinner, and sit next to the Boy Thoreau. Wait, he's saying something! Words are simply pouring out of him. He's asking me if I'm fond of potatoes. No, I don't like potatoes. There, I've done it! I've differed from him. It's our first quarrel. He's fallen into a moody silence. Silly boy, have I pricked your bubble? Do you think I am nothing but a painted doll with sawdust for a heart? Ah, don't take it like that. Look, I have something to tell you that will bring back your faith. I do like cucumbers. Why, he's better already. He speaks again. He says, yes, he likes them, too. Now we've got that all straightened out, thank heaven. We both like cucumbers. Only he likes them twice.

I'd better let him alone now, so he can get some food. He ought to try to get his strength back. He's talked himself groggy.

I wish I had something to do. I hate to be a mere drone. People ought to let you know when they're going to sit you next to a thing like this, so you could bring along some means of occupation. Dear Mrs. Parker, do come to us for dinner on Friday next, and don't forget your drawn-work. I could have brought my top bureau drawer and tidied it up, here on my lap. I could have made great strides towards getting those photographs of the groups on the beach pasted up in the album. I wonder if my hostess would think it strange if I asked for a pack of cards. I wonder if there are any old copies of *St. Nicholas* lying about. I wonder if they wouldn't like a little help out in the kitchen. I wonder if anybody would want me to run up to the corner and get a late paper.

I could do a little drinking, of course, all by myself. There's always that. Oh, dear, oh, dear, oh, dear, there's always that. But I don't want to drink. I'll get *vin triste*. I'm melancholy before I even start. I wonder what this stiff on my left would say, if told him I was in a fair way to get *vin triste*. Oh, look at him, hoeing into his fish! What does he care whether I get *vin triste* or not? His soul can't rise above food. Purely physical, that's all he is. Digging his grave with his teeth, that's what he's doing. Yah, yah, ya-ah! Digging your grave with your tee-eeth! Making a god of your stom-mick! Yah, yah, ya-ah!

He doesn't care if I get *vin triste*. Nobody cares. Nobody gives a damn. And me so nice. All right, you baskets, I'll drink myself to death, right in front of your eyes, and see how you'll feel. Here I go. . . . Oh, my God, it's Chablis. And of a year when the grapes failed, and they used Summer squash, instead. Fifteen dollars for all you can carry home on your shoulder. Oh, now, listen, where I come from, we feed this to the pigs. I think I'll ask old Chatterbox on my left if this isn't rotten wine. That ought to open up a new school of dialectics for us. Oh, he says he really wouldn't know—he never touches wine. Well, that fairly well ends that. I wonder how he'd like to step to hell, anyway. Yah, yah, ya-ah! Never touches wi-yine! Don't know what you're miss-sing! Yah, yah, ya-ah!

I'm not going to talk to him any more. I'm not going to spend the best years of my life thinking up pearls to scatter before him. I'm going to stick to my Chablis, rotten though it be. From now on, he can go his way, and I'll go mine. I'm better than he is. I'm better than anybody at this table. Ah, but am I really? Have I, after all, half of what they have? Here I am lonely, unwanted, silent, and me with all my new clothes on. Oh, what would Louiseboulanger say if she saw her gold lamé going unnoticed like this? It's life, I suppose. Poor little things, we dress, and we plan, and we hope—and for what? What is life, anyway? A death sentence. The longest distance between two points. The bunch of hay that's tied to the nose of the tired mule. The—

Well, well, well, here we are at the *entrecôte*. Button up your *entrecôte*, when the wind is free—no, I guess not. Now I'll be damned if I ask old Loquacity if he likes meat. In the first place, his likes and dislikes are nothing to me, and in the second—well, look at him go after it! He must have been playing hard all afternoon; he's Mother's Hungry Boy, tonight. All right, let him worry it all he wants. As for me, I'm on a higher plane. I do not stoop to him. He's less than the dust beneath my chariot wheel. Yah, yah, ya-ah! Less than the du-ust! Before I'd be that way! Yah, yah, ya-ah!

I'm glad there's red wine now. Even if it isn't good, I'm glad. Red wine gives me courage. The Red Badge of Courage. I need courage. I'm in a thin way, here. Nobody knows what a filthy time I'm having. My precious evening, that can never come again, ruined, ruined, ruined, and all because of this Somewhat Different Monologist on my left. But he can't lick me. The night is not yet dead, no, nor dying. You know, this really isn't bad wine.

Now what do you suppose is going on with the Greek god on my right? Ah, no use. There's still only the shoulder—the nice, *nice* shoulder. I wonder what the woman's like, that's got him. I can't see her at all. I wonder if she's beautiful. I wonder if she's Greek, too. When Greek meets immovable body—you might be able to do something with that, if you only had the time. I'm not going to be spineless any longer. Don't think for a minute, lady, that I've given up. He's still using his knife and fork. While there's hands above the table, there's hope.

Really, I suppose out of obligation to my hostess, I ought to do something about saying a few words to this macaw on my left. What shall I try? Have you been reading anything good lately, do you go much to the play, have you ever been to the Riviera? I wonder if he would like to hear about my Summer on the Riviera; hell, no, that's no good without lantern slides. I bet, though, if I started telling him about That One Night, he'd listen. I won't tell him—it's too good for him. Anybody that never touches wine can't hear that. But the one on the right—he'd like that. He touches wine. Touches it, indeed! He just threw it for a formidable loss.

Oh, look, old Silver Tongue is off again! Why, he's mad with his own perfume! He's rattling away like lightning. He's asking me if I like salad. Yes, I do; what does he want to make of that? He's telling me about salad through the ages. He says it's so good for people. So help me God, if he gives me a talk on roughage, I'll slap his face. Isn't that my life, to sit here, all dressed up in my best, and listen to this thing talk about romaine? And all the time, right on my right—

Well, I thought you were never going to turn around. . . . You haven't? You have? . . . Oh, Lord, I've been having an awful time, too. . . . Was she? . . . Well, you should have seen what I drew. . . . Oh, I don't see how we could. . . . Yes, I know it's terrible, but how can we get out of it? . . . Well . . . Well, yes, that's true. . . . Look, right after dinner, I'll say I have this horrible headache, and you say you're going to take me home in your car, and—

1929

"He has some food issues."

CURL UP AND DIET

OGDEN NASH

Some ladies smoke too much and some ladies drink too much and some
    ladies pray too much,
But all ladies think that they weigh too much.
They may be as slender as a sylph or a dryad,
But just let them get on the scales and they embark on a doleful
    jeremiad;
No matter how low the figure the needle happens to touch,
They always claim it is at least five pounds too much;
No matter how underfed to you a lady's anatomy seemeth,
She describes herself as Leviathan or Behemoth;
To the world she may appear slinky and feline,
But she inspects herself in the mirror and cries, Oh, I look like a sea lion;
Yes, she tells you she is growing into the shape of a sea cow or manatee,
And if you say, No, my dear, she says you are just lying to make her feel
    better, and if you say, Yes, my dear, you injure her vanatee,
And in any case her eyes flow like faucets,
And she goes out and buys some new caucets.
Once upon a time there was a girl more beautiful and witty and
    charming than tongue can tell,
And she is now a dangerous raving maniac in a padded cell,
And the first indication her friends and relatives had that she was
    mentally overwrought
Was one day when she said, I weigh a hundred and twenty-seven, which
    is exactly what I ought.
Oh, often I am haunted
By the thought that somebody might some day discover a diet that
    would let ladies reduce just as much as they wanted,
Because I wonder if there is a woman in the world strong-minded
    enough to shed ten pounds or twenty,
And say, There now, that's plenty;
And I fear me one ten-pound loss would only arouse the craving for
    another,

So it wouldn't do any good for ladies to get their ambition and look like
    somebody's fourteen-year-old brother,
Because, having accomplished this with ease,
They would next want to look like somebody's fourteen-year-old
    brother in the final stages of some obscure disease,
And the more success you have the more you want to get of it,
So then their goal would be to look like somebody's fourteen-year-old
    brother's ghost, or rather not the ghost itself, which is fairly solid,
    but a silhouette of it,
So I think it is very nice for ladies to be lithe and lissome,
But not so much so that you cut yourself if you happen to embrace or
    kissome.

1935

QUICK, HAMMACHER,
MY STOMACHER!

OGDEN NASH

Man is a glutton.
He will eat too much even though there be nothing to eat too much of
    but parsnips or mutton.
He will deprecate his paunch
And immediately afterward reach for another jowl or haunch.
People don't have to be Cassandras or Catos
To know what will happen to their paunches if they combine hot
    biscuits and strawberry shortcake and French-fried potatoes,
Yet no sooner has a man achieved a one-pound loss
Than he gains two through the application to an old, familiar dish of a
    new, irresistible sauce.
Thus cooks aggravate men's gluttony
With capers and hollandaise and chutney.

They can take seaweed or pemmican
And do things to it in a ramekin.
Give them a manatee that has perished of exposure
And they will whip you up a casserole of ambrosia,
Which is why a man who digs his grave with his teeth's idea of life
    beyond the grave is definite—
There's a divine chef in it.
Men are gluttons,
And everybody knows it except tailors, who don't leave room enough at
    the edge to move over the buttons.

1948

"Something this big."

NESSELRODE TO JEOPARDY

S. J. PERELMAN

CITY CRACKS DOWN ON RESTAURANTS
IN HOLLANDAISE SAUCE CLEAN-UP

"The sauce is loaded with dynamite when carelessly prepared," a Health Department spokesman declared yesterday. "It
has become one of the bureau's worst headaches. . . ."

Many temperamental chefs, it was learned, resent the
Health Department's infringement on their culinary art. One
chef, for example, refused to tell an inspector how he made the
sauce because it was a "secret technique" that he had learned in
France.

Several weeks later, five persons contracted food poisoning
at the restaurant because of the hollandaise. The Health Department then demanded to know the chef's secret and found
that his technique consisted of straining the sauce through a
cheesecloth bag that must be squeezed with the hands.

—*The Times*

Whenever I turn over the whole grotesque affair in my mind, trying to rationalize the baffling complex of events that overtook
me on the French Riviera this autumn, I always ask myself the same
questions. What would have happened if Destiny, unpredictable jade,
had drawn my laggard feet to some hotel other than the Villa Heliotrope? What if Anglo-Saxon shyness had sealed Colin Rentschler's
lips and he had not impulsively come to the aid of a fellow American in
hazard? Would I ever have met that elegant assassin, Colonel Firdausi,
of the Turkish secret police, or cowered in the hold of a rusty Greek
steamer bound for the Piraeus, or given chase at midnight to a music-
hall juggler over the roofs of Montparnasse? In short, why should I,
timid recluse, have been wantonly singled out for a supporting role in a
nightmare as fantastic as the riddle of the cheesecloth bag, a problem to
shame the wildest conceits of an Eric Ambler or a Carol Reed? And
why—except that it is highly traditional—do I ask these questions all
over again when I should be getting on with my story?

To begin at the beginning, I'd been down at Fez, in North Africa, all summer, working on a book of favorite recipes of famous people like Tennessee Williams, Paul Bowles, Truman Capote, and Speed Lamkin, and my nerves were at sixes and sevens. I felt completely drained, used up; I'd pretty well exhausted my emotional bank balance doing the necessary research, and I knew it was touch and go unless I immured myself in some quiet pied-à-terre where I could slough off superficialities and organize my material. I shan't burden you with tedious autobiographical details, but perhaps I ought to explain that my people (poor bourgeois dears) left me a goodish bit of money. Praise be to Allah— and the automobile wax my father invented—I don't have to fret excessively about the sordid aspects of life, and hence I've applied myself to living graciously, which I do think is all that matters, really. I mean I sometimes wonder if a properly chilled Gibson or a superb *coq au vin* isn't basically more important than these grubby wars and revolutions everyone's being so hopelessly neurotic about. Not that money's actually vital to my existence, mind you; one art I've mastered is how to make do with the absolute minimum. Given fair seats at the ballet, half a dozen friends with country houses from whom I can scrounge weekends, a few custom-tailored suits, some decent hand-lasted shoes—it's a weakness, I know, but I'm fixated on good leather—and three months a year at Montreux or Bordighera, and I can live in a hole in the wall at the Crillon and rub along on a gigot and a crisp salad.

Anyhow, I'd finally fetched up at the Villa Heliotrope, a modest little establishment on the Estérel coast west of Cannes, and everything was proving utterly ideal. The cuisine wasn't too repugnant, and if *Madame la Patronne* occasionally used overmuch musk on her embonpoint, she at least rationed it in her seasoning. Well, one evening I came in to dinner with a truly pagan appetite. (Ardent sun-worshipper that I am, I'd spent the entire day on the *plage,* baking a glorious golden brown.) I had just dispatched Madame's creditable *rôti* and was attacking the dessert when the chap at the next table cleared his throat.

"Easy does it," he said abruptly. "I wouldn't bolt that Nesselrode if I were you."

"Why the devil not?" I snapped, glaring around at him. Bolting's sort of a sacrament with me, I suppose, and I didn't much fancy the high-handed line he'd taken.

"Because it's lumpy," he said. "They forgot to strain it." I tasted a soupçon and found he was right. I turned back for another look at my neighbor. His lean, dark face showed good bone structure, and there was something about his trench coat and the gravy on his hat that bespoke the inspector of a metropolitan health department.

"Look here," I said, mystified. "You knew that pudding was lumpy?"

"It's my business to know things like that, friend," he said with an opaque smile. As he rose and passed me, a card fluttered down beside my plate. It bore the legend COLIN RENTSCHLER, and, below, INSPECTOR, NEW YORK HEALTH DEPARTMENT. I was pretty thoughtful the rest of the meal. Something curious was shaping up, and while I'm not especially intuitive, I felt Colin Rentschler might have some connection with it.

I was seated on the terrace that evening, sipping a final pousse-café before turning in, when his loose-jointed figure settled into the adjoining chair. After a rather watchful silence, he made some inconsequential remark about the ecru-colored sky's portending the advent of the mistral, the dry northerly wind characteristic of Provence. "Odd ecru-colored sky, that," he observed. "Shouldn't wonder if it portends the advent of the mistral, the dry northerly wind characteristic of Provence."

"Yes," I agreed. "Sinister shade, isn't it? It reminds me of—well, of hollandaise sauce that's gone a trifle bad."

I heard the sharp, sudden intake of his breath, followed by a little click as he expelled it. When he spoke again, it was in a tight, strangled whisper that put shudders up my spine. "Then you know," he said. He glanced quickly over his shoulder and leaned forward, his eyes merciless as snails. "Listen. Pierre Moustique has been seen in Istanbul."

"Good God!" I murmured. Like everyone else, of course, I knew that New York gourmets were in a grip of terror due to a wave of hollandaise poisoning, and that Moustique, the chef who had betrayed his secret technique of squeezing the sauce through a cheesecloth bag with his bare hands, had escaped to Canada in a hamper of towels, but in the shimmering heat of Morocco I had lost touch with later developments, and my allusion to the evening sky had been made in all innocence. Before I could extricate myself, nonetheless, Fate, in the guise of a health inspector, had altered my future with a single decisive stroke.

"It's incredible"—Rentschler shrugged—"but then so is life. Last Thursday afternoon, Anna Popescu, a Moldavian seamstress in the Kadikoy quarter of Istanbul bearing a Nansen passport, reported that a chef closely resembling Moustique had approached her to repair a rent in a cheesecloth bag, offering ninety piastres. When she hesitated, he fled." His harsh voice stabbed at me, insistent as the cicadas in the Mediterranean night. "Schneider, until we can lay Moustique by the heels and analyze that bag which its poisoned meshes spell finis for unwary epicures, death will lurk in every frond of broccoli. I have two tickets on the morning plane for Istanbul. Are you the man to share a desperate adventure?"

I picked up my glass and, twirling the stem meditatively, swallowed it in a single gulp. A mad, foolhardy errand, I thought, and still the challenge to gamble for consummate stakes awoke a tocsin in my blood. I spat out a spicule of glass, arose, and extended my hand. "Done and done, Rentschler," I said coolly. "I've always taken my liquor mixed and my peril neat, and I see no reason to switch now. Next stop, the Golden Horn!"

Colonel Firdausi, deputy director of the Turkish secret police, hoisted a polished cordovan boot to the edge of his desk and, extracting the monocle from his eye, carefully scraped a bit of *shish kebab* from the sole. As he dusted his delicate, saurian hands with a handkerchief strongly redolent of attar of roses, motes of halvah danced in the slanting beam of sunlight above his head.

"This is a very interesting tale you tell me, gentlemen," he said with a smile. Colonel Firdausi's smile could have refrigerated a whole chain of Turkish frozen-food stores. "But I do not see precisely why you come to me. Surely you do not imply Pierre Moustique is still in Istanbul?"

"I imply that and more." Rentschler's left forefinger traced what was seemingly an idle pattern on the dusty arm of his chair, and then I realized with a start that he was scribbling a message to me. "Watch this man's mouth," it read, in Italian. "It is willful, sensual, that of a sybarite who will not cavil at resorting to violence if he is bilked." My colleague chuckled thinly, his steady gaze meeting Firdausi's square. "I imply, my dear Colonel, that he is in this selfsame room at the moment."

"You cease to amuse me, Monsieur." The Turkish official rapped the bell before him peremptorily. "The interview is ended. My secretary—"

"One second," cut in Rentschler. "Have you ever heard of the Club Libido, in Pera? No? Allow me to refresh your memory. The principal chanteuse at the Libido is Marie Farkas, a naturalized Transylvanian traveling under a League of Nations passport."

"Neither you nor Marie could possibly hope to surprise me," returned Firdausi icily. "I have been sleeping with the lady fifteen years."

"And therefore enjoy considerable seniority over me," admitted Rentschler. "Nevertheless, she has been fickle enough to confide that on your last two nuptial flights you wore a chef's cap, with the name of Pierre Moustique inscribed on the headband in indelible pencil."

"Inconstancy, thy name is woman," reflected Firdausi. "Ah, well, there is no use dissembling with such adversaries." Reaching into his tunic, he withdrew a green cheesecloth bag and tossed it pettishly on the blotter. "Is this what you are looking for?" As Rentschler's hand shot forward, it struck the ice-blue barrel of the colonel's automatic. "Tchk, tchk, impetuous boy," chided Firdausi. "Be so good, both of you, as to lace your fingers over your heads. Thank you. Now, Messieurs, exposition is wearisome, so I will be succinct."

"I will be succincter," Rentschler put in. "The real Colonel Firdausi is reposing at this instant in the Bosporus, in a burlap sack weighted with stale nougat. You are about to bind us back to back in a similar pouch and deposit us alongside him, as a warning to meddlers not to interfere in matters that do not concern them. Need I point out, though, Moustique, that you cannot possibly hope to get away with it?"

"Of course not," agreed the other, withdrawing from his tunic a capacious burlap sack. "Still, in the brisk interplay of Near Eastern intrigue, these little—ah—involutions are mandatory. *Au 'voir*, gentlemen."

Forty-five minutes later, trussed up in the sack, we were jolting in a dray over the cobblestones fringing the waterside. Despite our extreme discomfort and the danger confronting us, however, my companion exhibited no hint of the disquiet that pervaded me. Listening to his tranquil comparison of the respective merits of the pickles obtainable at Lindy's and the Russian Tea Room, one might easily have imagined him in his own club. At length, my endurance crumbled.

"Dash it all, man!" I burst forth. "Here's one pickle your precious department won't get us out of!"

"No, but Victor Hugo will," he said evenly. "I take it you've read *Les Misérables?*"

"This is hardly the time for a literary quiz," I interjected.

"You will recall," said Rentschler imperturbably, "that at an equally crucial pass Jean Valjean confounded Papa Thenardier and his gang by sawing through his bonds with a watch spring concealed in a penny. Tug manfully at your wrists." I complied, and, to my stupefaction, found myself liberated. The next thing I knew, Rentschler and I were racing through a maze of warehouses and cranes; I remember a ship's gangway clangorous with roustabouts shifting cargo, a lightning descent into a labyrinth of hatches, and, over the bellow of the siren, my colleague's unruffled explanation that we were stowaways aboard the Thessalonian *Schizophrene,* bound for the Piraeus and Trieste. Actually, we never went to either; a few hours later, Rentschler nudged me and we stole back on land. The whole thing had been a clever feint, for, as he pointed out, nobody was chasing us and there was no reason to slip out of the country illicitly. That night, seated in the aircraft droning toward London, I dully wondered what fresh complications lay in wait for us. But Fate and the stewardess, a shapely Philadelphian named Dougherty traveling under a nylon bust support, gave me back only an inscrutable smile.

Thin fingers of fog drifted across the West India Dock Road, tracing an eerie filigree across the street lamp under which Rentschler and I stood shivering in our mackintoshes. From time to time, almond-eyed devotees of the poppy, furtively hugging poppy-seed rolls, slid past us in their bast shoes, bent on heaven knows what baleful missions. For more than three hours, we had been breathlessly watching the draper's shop across the way, and I still had no clue as to why. Rentschler, shrewd judge of human foibles that he was, must have sensed my perplexity, for at last he broke silence.

"In the split second you saw that bag of Moustique's, Schneider," he queried, "did any thought occur to you?"

"Why, yes," I said, surprised. "I remember thinking there was only one shop in Europe that handles cheesecloth of that type—Arthur

Maggot's Sons, in the West India Dock Road. But I still can't fathom why we've spent three hours casing it."

"No particular reason," he rejoined. "It's just the kind of patient, plodding labor the public never gives one credit for in this profession. Come on, let's move in."

Bartholomew Maggot shrugged his vulpine shoulders irascibly and, applying a pinch of Copenhagen snuff to his nostril, opened the cash register and sneezed into it. A half hour's questioning had merely aggravated his normally waspish temper, and it was dishearteningly plain that we had reached an impasse. Rentschler, notwithstanding, refused to yield.

"This man who asked you to appraise his cheesecloth bag yesterday," he persisted. "You say he was hooded and smelled of attar of roses, but surely you must have noticed something unusual about him."

"No, sir, I did not," growled the draper. "Wait a bit, though, there *was* something. His lapel had a few grains of rice powder on it—the sort those French music-hall artistes wear."

"You've a sharp pair of eyes in your head, Maggot," complimented the inspector. "It's a pity we don't know where they came from."

"Why, this one came from Harrod's," explained Maggot, removing it. "It's glass, as you see, and has a little Union Jack in it. The other—"

"No, no, the grains," Rentschler interrupted testily. "Haven't you any idea which music hall uses that type of powder?"

"Let me see," said Maggot slowly. "The cove was carrying a theatrical valise with the name of Pierre Moustique, Bobino Theatre, Rue de la Gaité, Paris, France, painted on it in white letters, but I didn't really pay much mind."

"Humph," muttered Rentschler. His quick, deductive mind had caught something of importance in the other's words. "A very good evening to you, Mr. Maggot, and now, Schneider, to Paris *en grand vitesse*. Are you hungry? I think I can promise a ragout spiced with melodrama and served piping hot." I have often thought the world lost a major poet when Colin Rentschler joined the New York Health Department.

The mingled scent of caporal, cheap perfume, and garlic hung like a pall over the motley audience jamming the stalls of the Bobino, the

Left Bank's most popular vaudeville. A succession of weight-lifters, trained dogs, diseuses, and trick cyclists had displayed their enchantments, and now, as the curtain rose on the final turn and M. l'Inconnu, the masked juggler, strode into the glare of the footlights, my heart began beating like a trip hammer. Those delicate, saurian hands, the heavy odor of attar of roses—I racked my memory vainly, trying to recollect where I had met them before. A buzz of excited speculation rose from the patrons surrounding us; rumor ran rife that l'Inconnu was an unfrocked chef from New York, a quondam Turkish police official, a recent arrival from Limehouse, but none knew for sure. Yet some sixth sense told me that Rentschler, his hawk's profile taut in the darkness beside me, was close to the answer.

"Messieurs et dames!" The guttural voice of Pierre Moustique suddenly set my every nerve atingle. "I now attempt a feat to dizzy the imagination, keeping *trois boules* [three balls] suspended in the air simultaneously!" From the depths of his cape, he brought forth a green cheesecloth bag and spun three mothballs into swift rotating motion.

Rentschler sprang up with a choked cry. "*Gobe-mouche* that I am! Blockhead!" he exclaimed. "Don't you see, Schneider? That's why the hollandaise laid those diners low—he used that very bag to squeeze the sauce, indifferent to the fact that it had contained mothballs! Seal the exits! Stop that man!" But it was too late; with a snarled imprecation, Moustique sprang toward the wings. In the shrill hubbub that ensued, I inexplicably found myself dancing a java with a comely grisette; then Rentschler, flinging people aside like ninepins, was pulling me through a skylight and we were hurtling across the rooftops after our quarry. In reality, my associate explained as we hurtled, Moustique had left the Bobino in a cab, but protocol precluded our following him in any such mundane fashion.

"He's heading for the Ritz," panted the inspector. "A group of asparagus connoisseurs are holding their annual feed there tonight, which the columns of *Le Figaro* have been full of it for a week. Superfluous to add that if this blackguard, who is cooking for them under a nom de plume, compounds his lethal dressing, why the poor bastards will be stretched out in windrows. I've a pretty—good—hunch, though," he panted on, clearing the Rue du Cherche-Midi with a bound, "that we're about to tie a kink in his mayonnaise whip."

Well, we didn't. Two minutes afterward, Rentschler tripped over a loose gargoyle and dashed out his brains in the Quai Voltaire. I pressed on to the Ritz, but I must have crept in through the wrong dormer, because I wound up at a too, too marvelous gala at the Vicomtesse de Noailles'. Edith and Osbert and Sacheverell were there, and they gave me a simply divine recipe for my book. It's called Continental Upside-down Chowchow, and here's what you do. You take a double handful of exotic locales . . .

1951

"Believe me, if there are any compliments I'll pass them on to you."

EAT, DRINK, AND BE MERRY

PETER DE VRIES

E arly last winter, I tipped the scales at 200 pounds, whereas the Metropolitan Life Insurance Company prefers something in the neighborhood of 180 for men of my height and frame. Friends implored me to delete the difference, citing the connection between weight and longevity, and recommending various diets for soundness of body and length of days. However, though persuaded to reduce, I decided to give other methods, such as massage, a try first. To this end I permitted myself to be methodically flailed at weekly intervals by a giant Swede. I lost no weight, but the strenuousness of the Swede's exertions suggested it might be otherwise with him. After two months, during which my body underwent no change whatever except to turn the color of eggplant, I took up walking.

I went for brisk hikes about the Connecticut countryside, where I live, armed with a stick to fend off the numerous dogs in whom apparently boiled an accumulated resentment toward a man remembered as someone barreling down the road in a Pontiac to their constant peril. I got more exercise out of swinging the cane than out of walking—the first day or two, one mongrel in particular followed me all over the blasted heath—but my exertions were as fruitless as the Swede's.

I did extract from these all-weather rambles a certain lyric sustenance. I had a sense that, for housewives glancing from their cottage windows and for passing motorists, I pulled the whole scene together by offering to the eye that solitary figure for which all landscapes cry; of representing, as I strode cross-lots or climbed a stile, abiding values. Superimposed on this was another, terribly peculiar sensation. I had the conviction that I was losing girth, not at the waist but around my head. I wore on these expeditions a gray Homburg, relatively new, the only hat in my possession. Because my head is narrow, a hat that fits in terms of front and back is often loose enough at the sides for me to insert two fingers there, so that every hat I have owned has been both large and small for me. This Homburg seemed, on the moors, to grow roomier with every step I took. Since, like its predecessors, it was a doubtful fit to begin with, and since it was my wont to swing along at a brisk gait, each jar of my heels brought the hat a little farther down on my head, the way you bring an axe head down on its helve by pounding the end of the handle on a stump. On certain days I would arrive home with the hat resting on my ears, an effect that made for poor visibility and once almost cost me my life, when I started to cross a road in the dusk and was narrowly missed by a motorist who had not yet turned his lights on.

That was the day on which I had fixed to weigh myself. It had been two weeks since I began the walks, and I had refrained from checking. I gingerly boarded the bathroom scales and looked. There was some change but not much: I had gained four pounds.

The reason was not hard to find. I returned from these excursions ravenous, and as a result (taking the fueling of a furnace as a metaphor for caloric consumption) I had been shoveling it in as fast as I had been burning it up—or, rather, a little faster.

At about this time there fell into my hands a document containing some computations made by Dr. L. H. Newburgh, of the medical school of the University of Michigan, who has done work in the metabolism of obesity. A man weighing 250 pounds, he writes, "will have to climb twenty flights of stairs to rid himself of the energy contained in one slice of bread." A horizontal walk of a mile will reduce the man's weight "only 12½ grams (less than ½ ounce). He must walk 36 miles to rid himself of one pound of adipose tissue—how disappointing!"

On the basis of Dr. Newburgh's findings, I figured that the only way for me to make appreciable inroads on myself by walking would be to commute on foot between Westport and New York City, a discipline almost certain to be neutralized by Gargantuan snacks at Norwalk, Port Chester, and most other points along the way.

The inevitable remained.

There are numerous diets currently being recommended, published, and discussed. One is the familiar du Pont executives' diet, which I tried first. Its motif is meat. For lunch the first day, I had a pair of lamb chops with accessories too dismal to mention. For dinner, I had a plank steak. Steaks and chops two or even three times a day are, in addition to an ideal way of sustaining the requisite high protein intake, a neat formula for bankruptcy, unless you happen to be a du Pont executive. I realized, as the long, carnivorous days went by, that I was eating myself and my family into destitution, and switched to another feeding plan.

This one permitted me, implacably, for breakfast half a grapefruit, one boiled egg, and black coffee. To eat that at 7 A.M. and practice rigid self-denial until lunch at one o'clock is to engage in what theologians call mortification of the flesh. Noon, in fact, often found me close to that crystalline fatigue in which the early Christian anchorites are said to have had their visions. I carried in my wallet a checklist of low-calorie foods with which to assuage the worst pangs of my hunger. An item on the list was tangerines. I once ate seven at a sitting, pips and all. Another was cottage cheese, of which I sometimes devoured an entire container. One Saturday, my wife returned from shopping to find me hunched over an eighteen-ounce jar of it, a flying spoon in my hand.

"What are you gorging yourself for?" she asked.

"I'm on a diet," I said. "You know that."

It is possible to rationalize having dinner at someone else's home as a legitimate holiday from one's diet. My wife and I had a dinner invitation for Saturday of my second week on the more plebeian regimen. My wife caught a heavy cold on Friday, and Saturday morning I heard her canceling the engagement by phone. I rushed up and wrested the instrument from her grasp. "I'll be there," I told the hostess. "I won't *hear* of upsetting your plans any more than necessary!"

The hostess told me to come at "sevenish."

"Sevenish, then," I said, hanging up.

I was at her door at six-twenty, slavering. She served fish, roast duck and red cabbage, candied yams, tossed salad, and cherries jubilee, all of which I had the courtesy to eat without demurrer.

It takes only one good table bacchanal to undo a whole week's calorie budgeting. Since all this dieting was going on during the winter, when we were receiving or giving hospitality every Saturday or Sunday evening, I found myself faced with continuing complications. (I felt it as ungracious to diet before guests as before hosts.) I began a third diet without wholly abandoning the other, then still another while retaining features of its predecessors. Soon I had three or four diets going simultaneously, and became bewildered and discouraged. I weighed 205, then

207. I resolved that when the winter was over, I would buckle down in earnest. But once the round of al-fresco summer gaieties was under way, I was, far from mortifying my flesh, mortified by it. A British acquaintance whom I hadn't seen for several years greeted me on a recent visit with "Getting a bit thick in the flitch, aren't you, old man?"

The phrase "thick in the flitch" plunged me into a depression that lasted for weeks. It was, indeed, one of those periods of gloom when a man seeks relief in every anodyne—the pleasures of reading, companionship, and certainly food and drink. And it was in this interval that I came across a magazine article setting forth a viewpoint new to me on excess weight. The article was entitled "Obesity: Its Emotional Causes." It was written by the head of a Midwestern clinic who has done a great deal of research in the field and who claims that food is an escape for people who are emotionally upset. I at once took inventory of myself along the lines the author laid down. The only thing I could find that was upsetting me was my physical condition—my excess weight. It followed that I was eating too much because I was overweight.

The sinister hopelessness of this dilemma convinced me that it must be absurd, but I was presently routed from that refuge by the recollection of a parallel case I know of involving a man who is given to a kindred indulgence—that of the bottle. Chief among the "realities" to which he is unable to face up is the realization of the wasted, bibulous years behind him. Hence he has reached a point where it is, in large measure, liquor that is driving him to drink. He is living to a ripe old age in this vicious circle, too. My own circle, it seemed to me, was equally vicious. Or was it, I wondered. Was "vicious" quite the right word for it?

Well, come to think of it, maybe not. When all is said and done, what is there like a good dinner, prefaced by a few cocktails, washed down with a properly chilled wine, and topped off with a cup of well-brewed coffee and a spot of brandy, to assuage life's pains, obscure its vanities, and make one forget, for an hour, the melancholy of expanding girth? The answer is, nothing. Friends are, of course, another major ameliorative, and I can only regret that mine continue to talk about diet in the way they do, with a lot of scientific jargon and in a sort of Oxford Group testimonial fashion. It's a subject on which my own words carry, as the months go by, less and less weight.

1952

NOTES FROM THE OVERFED

AFTER READING DOSTOEVSKI AND THE NEW
WEIGHT WATCHERS MAGAZINE ON THE SAME PLANE TRIP

WOODY ALLEN

I am fat. I am disgustingly fat. I am the fattest human I know. I have nothing but excess poundage all over my body. My fingers are fat. My wrists are fat. My eyes are fat. (Can you imagine fat eyes?) I am hundreds of pounds overweight. Flesh drips from me like hot fudge off a sundae. My girth has been an object of disbelief to everyone who's seen me. There is no question about it, I'm a regular fatty. Now, the reader may ask, are there advantages or disadvantages to being built like a planet? I do not mean to be facetious or speak in paradoxes, but I must answer that fat in itself is above bourgeois morality. It is simply fat. That fat could have a value of its own, that fat could be, say, evil or pitying, is, of course, a joke. Absurd! For what is fat after all but an accumulation of pounds? And what are pounds? Simply an aggregate composite of cells. Can a cell be moral? Is a cell beyond good or evil? Who knows—they're so small. No, my friend, we must never attempt to distinguish between good fat and bad fat. We must train ourselves to confront the obese without judging, without thinking this man's fat is first-rate fat and this poor wretch's is grubby fat.

Take the case of K. This fellow was porcine to such a degree that he could not fit through the average door frame without the aid of a crowbar. Indeed, K. would not think to pass from room to room in a conventional dwelling without first stripping completely and then buttering himself. I am no stranger to the insults K. must have borne from passing gangs of young rowdies. How frequently he must have been stung by cries of "Tubby!" and "Blimp!" How it must have hurt when the governor of the province turned to him on the Eve of Michaelmas and said, before many dignitaries, "You hulking pot of *kasha!*"

Then one day, when K. could stand it no longer, he dieted. Yes, dieted! First sweets went. Then bread, alcohol, starches, sauces. In short, K. gave up the very stuff that makes a man unable to tie his shoelaces without help from the Santini Brothers. Gradually he began to slim down. Rolls of flesh fell from his arms and legs. Where once he looked roly-poly, he suddenly appeared in public with a normal build. Yes, even an attractive build. He seemed the happiest of men. I say "seemed," for eighteen years later, when he was near death and fever raged throughout his slender frame, he was heard to cry out, "My fat! Bring me my fat! Oh, please! I must have my fat! Oh, somebody lay some avoirdupois on me! What a fool I've been. To part with one's fat! I must have been in league with the Devil!" I think that the point of the story is obvious.

Now the reader is probably thinking, Why, then, if you are Lard City, have you not joined a circus? Because—and I confess this with no small embarrassment—I cannot leave the house. I cannot go out because I cannot get my pants on. My legs are too thick to dress. They are the living result of more corned beef than there is on Second Avenue— I would say about twelve thousand sandwiches per leg. And not all lean, even though I specified. One thing is certain: if my fat could speak, it would probably speak of man's intense loneliness—with, oh, perhaps a few additional pointers on how to make a sailboat out of paper. Every pound on my body wants to be heard from, as do Chins Four through Twelve inclusive. My fat is strange fat. It has seen much. My calves alone have lived a lifetime. Mine is not happy fat, but it is real fat. It is not fake fat. Fake fat is the worst fat you can have, although I don't know if the stores still carry it.

But let me tell you how it was that I became fat. For I was not always fat. It is the Church that has made me thus. At one time I was thin—quite thin. So thin, in fact, that to call me fat would have been an error in perception. I remained thin until one day—I think it was my twentieth birthday—when I was having tea and cracknels with my uncle at a fine restaurant. Suddenly my uncle put a question to me. "Do you believe in God?" he asked. "And if so, what do you think He weighs?" So saying, he took a long and luxurious draw on his cigar and, in that confident, assured manner he has cultivated, lapsed into a coughing fit so violent I thought he would hemorrhage.

"I do not believe in God," I told him. "For if there is a God, then tell me, Uncle, why is there poverty and baldness? Why do some men go through life immune to a thousand mortal enemies of the race, while others get a migraine that lasts for weeks? Why are our days numbered and not, say, lettered? Answer me, Uncle. Or have I shocked you?"

I knew I was safe in saying this, because nothing ever shocked the man. Indeed, he had seen his chess tutor's mother raped by Turks and would have found the whole incident amusing had it not taken so much time.

"Good nephew," he said, "there is a God, despite what you think, and He is everywhere. Yes! Everywhere!"

"Everywhere, Uncle? How can you say that when you don't even know for sure if we exist? True, I am touching your wart at this moment, but could that not be an illusion? Could not all life be an illusion? Indeed, are there not certain sects of holy men in the East who are convinced that *nothing* exists outside their minds except for the Oyster Bar at Grand Central Station? Could it not be simply that we are alone and aimless, doomed to wander in an indifferent universe, with no hope of salvation, nor any prospect except misery, death, and the empty reality of eternal nothing?"

I could see that I made a deep impression on my uncle with this, for he said to me, "You wonder why you're not invited to more parties! Jesus, you're morbid!" He accused me of being nihilistic and then said, in that cryptic way the senile have, "God is not always where one seeks Him, but I assure you, dear nephew, He is everywhere. In these cracknels, for instance." With that, he departed, leaving me his blessing and a check that read like the tab for an aircraft carrier.

I returned home wondering what it was he meant by that one simple statement "He is everywhere. In these cracknels, for instance." Drowsy by then, and out of sorts, I lay down on my bed and took a brief nap. In that time, I had a dream that was to change my life forever. In the dream, I am strolling in the country when I suddenly notice I am hungry. Starved, if you will. I come upon a restaurant and I enter. I order the open-hot-roast-beef sandwich and a side of French. The waitress, who resembles my landlady (a thoroughly insipid woman who reminds one instantly of some of the hairier lichens), tries to tempt me into ordering the chicken salad, which doesn't look fresh. As I am conversing with this woman, she turns into a twenty-four-piece starter set of silverware. I become hysterical with laughter, which suddenly turns to tears and then into a serious ear infection. The room is suffused with a radiant glow, and I see a shimmering figure approach on a white steed. It is my podiatrist, and I fall to the ground with guilt.

Such was my dream. I awoke with a tremendous sense of well-being. Suddenly I was optimistic. Everything was clear. My uncle's statement reverberated to the core of my very existence. I went to the

kitchen and started to eat. I ate everything in sight. Cakes, breads, ce-
reals, meat, fruits. Succulent chocolates, vegetables in sauce, wines,
fish, creams and noodles, éclairs, and wursts totaling in excess of sixty
thousand dollars. If God is everywhere, I had concluded, then He is in
food. Therefore, the more I ate the godlier I would become. Impelled
by this new religious fervor, I glutted myself like a fanatic. In six
months, I was the holiest of holies, with a heart entirely devoted to my
prayers and a stomach that crossed the state line by itself. I last saw my
feet one Thursday morning in Vitebsk, although for all I know they are
still down there. I ate and ate and grew and grew. To reduce would have
been the greatest folly. Even a sin! For when we lose twenty pounds,
dear reader (and I am assuming you are not as large as I), we may be
losing the twenty best pounds we have! We may be losing the pounds
that contain our genius, our humanity, our love and honesty, or, in the
case of one inspector general I knew, just some unsightly flab around
the hips.

   Now, I know what you are saying. You are saying this is in direct
contradiction to everything—yes, everything—I put forth before. Suddenly I am attributing to neuter flesh, values! Yes, and what of it? Because isn't life that very same kind of contradiction? One's opinion of
fat can change in the same manner that the seasons change, that our
hair changes, that life itself changes. For life is change and fat is life,
and fat is also death. Don't you see? Fat is everything! Unless, of course,
you're overweight.

                                                                    1968

"The Trout Babette was awful,
but the Heimlich maneuver was excellent."

TWO MENUS

STEVE MARTIN

KING'S RANSOM
Paducah, Kansas
Fine dining at its best.

Fried-butter Appetizer
Butter, cream, fat, lard, shortening, palm oil, drawn-butter dip.

Greaseballs
Four greaseballs served flaming hot in your hands (grease, balls).

♥ *Cow Organs Charlton Heston*
Steaming entrails and freshly slaughtered virgin cow brains, marinated in lard. Find the bullet and eat free!

Maybelle's Vegetarian Special
Ham, ham hocks, pork rinds, butter, eggs. Ask for Bac-O-Bits!

Double Height Rib-eye Steak
Cooked in its own juice while alive, served with hot buttered metal screws, cardboard.

Egg-yolk Omelette à la Mitt
Yellow hearts of egg folded into an omelette. Cooked and served inside a boxing glove.

Our Banana Split
Fried ice cream, butter, double-cream-infused banana, whipped cream, cherries in red dye no. 2, triple-fudge chocolate sauce, pancakes, cow fat.

♥ Heartwise!

SYNERGY
Beverly Hills, California
Phone: Yeah, right.

Air Salad
Dehumidified ocean air on a bed of fileted basil.

Egg-white Omelette
Egg whites, pumpkin seeds, Vitamin C, nonfat cheese buttons, aerated yogi urine.

Spaghetti à la Nerf
Our natural eggless spaghetti, cooked in desalted Caspian Sea water, simmered in oliveless olive oil, and sprinkled with parsley skins. As light as a Nerf ball!

Filet of Sole
Sole.

Chilean Sea Bass
The Patagonian toothfish is overfished, so try our soya-based lo-fat substitute, swimming in hot water. Soy, water, gelatin added for viscosity. Garlic vapor. A natural face-lift dish.

Our Banana Split
One banana lying in its own skin, covered in chocolate, on a bed of arugula. A cheesecloth mouth condom is supplied to enable you to taste the chocolate without swallowing.

Hemlock Tea
Try our depoisoned herbal infusion.

2000

"I wonder would you be good enough, the next time you get your
adrenaline flowing, to bring me a glass of iced tea."

THE ZAGAT HISTORY OF MY LAST RELATIONSHIP

NOAH BAUMBACH

AASE'S

Bring a "first date" to this "postage stamp"–size bistro. Tables are so close you're practically "sitting in the laps" of the couple next to you, but the lush décor is "the color of love." Discuss your respective "dysfunctional families" and tell her one of your "fail-safe" stories about your father's "cheapness" and you're certain to "get a laugh." After the "to die for" soufflés, expect a good-night kiss, but don't push for more, because if you play your cards right there's a second date "right around the corner."

BRASSERIE PENELOPE

"Ambience and then some" at this Jamaican-Norwegian hybrid. Service might be a "tad cool," but the warmth you feel when you gaze into her baby blues will more than compensate for it. Conversation is "spicier than the jerk chicken," and before you know it you'll be back at her one-bedroom in the East Village, quite possibly "getting lucky."

THE CHICK & HEN

Perfect for breakfast "after sleeping together," with "killer coffee" that will "help cure your seven-beer/three-aquavit hangover." Not that you need it—your "amplified high spirits" after having had sex for the first time in "eight months" should do the trick.

DESARCINA'S

So what if she thought the movie was "pretentious and contrived" and you felt it was a "masterpiece" and are dying to inform her that "she doesn't know what she's talking about"? Remember, you were looking for a woman who wouldn't "yes" you all the time. And after one bite of chef Leonard Desarcina's "duck manqué" and a sip of the "generous" gin margaritas you'll start to see that she might have a point.

GORDY'S

Don't be ashamed if you don't know what wine to order with your seared minnow; the "incredibly knowledgeable" waiters will be more than pleased to assist. But if she makes fun of "the way you never make eye contact with people," you might turn "snappish" and end up having your first "serious fight," one where feelings are "hurt."

PANCHO MAO

"Bring your wallet," say admirers of Louis Grenouille's pan-Asian-Mexican-style fare, because it's "so expensive you'll start to wonder why she hasn't yet picked up a tab." The "celeb meter is high," and "Peter Jennings" at the table next to yours might spark an "inane political argument" where you find yourself "irrationally defending Enron" and finally saying aloud, "You don't know what you're talking about!" Don't let her "stuff herself," as she might use that as an excuse to go to sleep "without doing it."

RIGMAROLE

At this Wall Street old boys' club, don't be surprised if you run into one of her "ex-boyfriends" who works in "finance." Be prepared for his "power play," when he sends over a pitcher of "the freshest-tasting sangria this side of Barcelona," prompting her to visit his table for "ten minutes" and to come back "laughing" and suddenly critical of your "cravat." The room is "snug," to say the least, and it's not the best place to say, full voice, "What the fuck were you thinking dating him?" But don't overlook the "best paella in town" and a din "so loud" you won't notice that neither of you is saying anything.

TATI

Prices so "steep" you might feel you made a serious "career gaffe" by taking the "high road" and being an academic rather than "selling out" like "every other asshole she's gone out with." The "plush seats" come in handy if she's forty-five minutes late and arrives looking a little "preoccupied" and wearing "a sly smile."

VANDERWEI'S

Be careful not to combine "four dry *sakes*" with your "creeping feeling of insecurity and dread," or you might find yourself saying, "Wipe that damn grin off your face!" The bathrooms are "big and glamorous," so you won't mind spending an hour with your cheek pressed against the "cool tiled floor" after she "walks out." And the hip East Village location can't be beat, since her apartment is "within walking distance," which makes it very convenient if you should choose to "lean on her buzzer for an hour" until she calls "the cops."

ZACHARIA AND SONS & CO.

This "out of the way," "dirt cheap," "near impossible to find," "innocuous" diner is ideal for "eating solo" and ensuring that you "won't run into your ex, who has gone back to the bond trader." The "mediocre at best" burgers and "soggy fries" will make you wish you "never existed" and wonder why you're so "frustrated with your life" and unable to sustain a "normal," "healthy" "relationship."

2002

*"Really, couldn't we have
one with less joie de vivre?"*

YOUR TABLE IS READY

JOHN KENNEY

You do not seize control at Masa. You surrender it. You pay to be putty. And you pay dearly. . . . Lunch or dinner for two can easily exceed $1,000.

—From the *Times*'s review of Masa, a sushi
restaurant that was given four stars

Am I very rich? Since you ask, I will tell you. Yes, I am. I happen to be one of the more successful freelance poets in New York. The point being, I eat where I like. And I like sushi. As does my wife, Babette.

Unfortunately, we were running late. This worried me. I had been trying to get a reservation at Masa since 1987, seventeen years before it opened, as I knew that one of the prerequisites of dining there was a knowledge of the future. I also knew of the restaurant's strict "on-time" policy. Babette and I arrived exactly one minute and twenty-four seconds late. We know this because of the Swiss Atomic clock that diners see upon arrival at Masa.

The maître d' did not look happy. And so we were asked, in Japanese, to remove our clothes, in separate dressing cabins, and don simple white robes with Japanese writing on the back that, we soon found out, translated as "We were late. We didn't respect the time of others." Babette's feet were bound. I was forced to wear shoes that were two sizes too small. The point being, tardiness is not accepted at Masa. (Nor, frankly, should it be.)

The headwaiter then greeted us by slapping me in the face and telling Babette that she looked heavy, also in Japanese. (No English is spoken in the restaurant. Translators are available for hire for $325 per hour. We opted for one.)

And so it was that Babette, Aki, and I were led to our table, one of only seven in the restaurant, two of which are always reserved—one for former Canadian prime minister Pierre Trudeau, who died five years ago, and the other for the actress and singer Claudine Longet, who accidentally shot and killed her boyfriend, the skier Spider Sabich, in 1976.

There are no windows in Masa. The light is soft, and, except for the tinkling of a miniature waterfall and the piped-in sound of an airplane losing altitude at a rapid rate, the place is silent. We sat on hemp pillows, as chairs cost extra and we were not offered any, owing to our tardiness.

Thirty-five minutes later, we met our waitstaff: nine people, including two Buddhist monks, whose job it is to supervise your meal, realign your chakras, and, if you wish, teach you to play the oboe. Introductions and small talk—as translated by Aki (which, we later learned, means "Autumn")—lasted twenty minutes. I was then slapped again, though I'm not sure why.

Before any food can be ordered at Masa, one is required to choose from an extensive water menu (there is no tap water at the restaurant). With Aki's help, we selected an exceptional bottle of high-sodium Polish sparkling water known for its subtle magnesium aftertaste (a taste I admit to missing completely). Henna tattoos were then applied to the bases of our spines. Mine depicted a donkey, Babette's a dwarf with unusually large genitals.

Then it was time to order—or to be told what we were having, as there is no menu. Babette and I had been looking forward to trying an inside-out California roll and perhaps some yellowtail. Not so this night. I was brought the white-rice appetizer and Babette was brought nothing. Aki said this was not uncommon, and then told us a story about his brother, Akihiko ("Bright Boy"), who has, from the sound of it, a rather successful motor-home business outside Kyoto.

I noticed another guest a few tables away being forced to do push-ups while the waitstaff critiqued his wife's outfit. Aki saw me looking at them and translated the words on the back of their robes: "We were twenty minutes late. We are bad."

It was then that our entrées arrived and we realized why this restaurant is so special. Before us were bay scallops, yellow clams, red clams, and exotic needlefish, all lightly dusted with crushed purple *shiso* leaves. Unfortunately, none of these dishes was for us. They were for the waitstaff, who enjoyed them with great gusto while standing beside our table. They nodded and smiled, telling us, through Aki, how good it all tasted. Aki told us that this was very common at fine Japanese restaurants and urged us to be on time in the future, even though he said we would never be allowed on the premises again. He then gave us a brochure for a motor home. Babette and I were strongly advised to order more water.

For dessert, I ordered nothing, as I was offered nothing. Babette was given a whole fatty red tuna wrapped in seaweed, served atop a bowl of crushed ice and garnished with a sign reading HAPPY ANNIVER-SARY, BARBARA (*sic*).

Our bill came to $839. Aki said we were lucky to get out for so little and then begged us to take him with us when we left. We caught a cab and got three seats at the bar at Union Square Café.

2005

"You might as well take a seat, Mr. Gallagher. There's a Reuben sandwich ahead of you."

"Its DNA is consistent with meat loaf."

SMALL PLATES

HORN OF MODERATION

STEVENSON

"May I suggest, sir, that you brace yourself for a disappointment."

BOCK

WILLIAM SHAWN

S hortly, now, pictures of goats will be hung up in the drinking places and bock beer will make its traditional spring appearance for the first time in fourteen years. It used to be a common saying that bock and the circus arrived together, but the circus doesn't come until April 6 or thereabouts this year and the date for bock is March 25. The brewers have an agreement not to release it earlier than that, and if you get any before then somebody is fudging. As in the old days, they've calculated to brew just enough to last two weeks. And as in the old days, the custom is being kept up for sentimental reasons, to stimulate business at a slack time, and to give the drinkers something to talk about. Originally, bock was logical, though. That was in the old, old days. Before modern refrigeration, beer couldn't be brewed in the summer, so the first appearance of the winter's brew, usually some time in May, was always celebrated in Germany with beer festivals, and bock was the choice and special brew made for the occasion. It was and is a lager of extra strength which has been aged longer and which is richer in malt extract and hence darker than light beer but lighter than dark. The bock these days could be put out any time the brewers agreed upon, but they've set upon March 25.

Practically everybody knows that *Bock* means "goat" in German, but nobody seems to know how the brew got the name of bock. There are many legends. One is that two rival German brewers agreed to drink it out one night to see whose beer was the stronger. After several hours, one of them had to go out for a breath of air, and got bowled over by a goat.

The brewer inside saw him fall and yelled "I win!" The other explained that it was a goat, and the name stuck. Another is that at the ancient beer festivals, there was a ritual which required that the guests be butted in the leathern breeches as they stood up to toast their host. Mr. Mülhäuser, *Braumeister* at Ruppert's, thinks the name is derived from *Einbeck*, or *Ainpock*, which was a famous brew of the eleventh century, and which was emulated in the sixteenth century by Duke William V of Bavaria when he started a *Brauhaus* for his own ducal beer. Mr. Mülhäuser thinks the name started then.

The old-time posters used to get pretty fanciful about their goats. They were pictured as drinking, dancing, walking arm-in-arm, and drawing a wagon made from a beer keg, surmounted by a lovely lady. Of the new posters, we are told that Trommer's will probably be most like the old ones. It's going to be done in four colors, showing a gnome on a goat which is hurdling a keg. Piel's will have a gnome, too, riding a bucking goat and holding up a stein. Schaefer's—who, by the way, claim an American bock-making record of ninety-two years, except for the prohibition interlude—will have just the head of a goat, smiling. The brewers are a little worried over the state ruling that their names, strictly, can't appear on their posters when they're displayed in places that serve hard liquor as well as beer, but some of them will probably take a chance.

1934

"More, please. Americans overeat, and, by God, I'm an American!"

DIAT

GEOFFREY T. HELLMAN

In an article on a visit we made to the Ritz a few weeks ago, we noted that Louis Diat, the head chef, was so wrought up about the forthcoming demise of that institution that Mr. Stack, its president, counseled us not to disturb him. Among other things, we wanted to ask him about the invention of vichyssoise, of which, as we mentioned, he was the originator. We let the matter slide until the other day, and then phoned Mr. Stack to see how the land lay. He told us to come on over and take a chance. This we did, and in a small office near the kitchen we found the celebrated chef, a mustached man of sixty-five with curly gray hair and large, black, bushy eyebrows, seated at an old roll-top desk. He received us cordially enough, but he was unmistakably downcast. We brought up vichyssoise at once, and he told us about its birth. "In the summer of 1917, when I had been at the Ritz seven years," he said, "I reflected upon the potato-and-leek soup of my childhood, which my mother and grandmother used to make. I recalled how, during the summer, my older brother and I used to cool it off by pouring in cold milk, and how delicious it was. I resolved to make something of the sort for the patrons of the Ritz." Diat worked out a soup involving a potato-and-leek purée strained twice to make it extra smooth, heavy cream, and, on the surface, a sprinkling of finely chopped chives. He named it *crème vichyssoise glacée,* after Vichy, then famous only as a spa, which is not far from his home town, Montmarault. Charles M. Schwab, dining in the Ritz Roof Garden, ordered it the first day it was on the menu, and asked for a second helping. Diat put it on the menu every evening that summer, and every summer thereafter. He took it off during the cold weather, but the hotel got so many requests for it in all temperatures, and at lunch as well as dinner, that in 1923 he put it on a year-round lunch-and-dinner basis, where it has remained ever since. "Mrs. Sara Delano Roosevelt, the President's mother, who had had it here, once called me up at five in the afternoon and asked me to send eight portions to her house," Mr. Diat told us. "I sent her two quarts and gave her the recipe, which I have since published in *Cooking à la*

Ritz." Diat has also written *French Cooking for Americans* and has just finished a third book, *Sauces: French and Famous.* The Ritz printed its menus in French until 1930, when the Hotel Association of New York City, of which it is a member, suggested that its restaurant business, then suffering from the depression, might pick up if it switched to English. It switched, and Mr. Diat's soup, in its fourteenth year, became "cream vichyssoise glacée," a kind of compromise.

Vichyssoise is only one of several hundred dishes Diat has originated. These include Chicken Gloria Swanson (sautéed chicken cooked in white wine and cream, served with creamed mushrooms and sliced cooked tomatoes, and garnished with rice and truffles); Breast of Guinea Hen Jefferson (guinea hen with ham, creamed tomatoes, *beignets* of wild rice, and a whiskey sauce); Lobster Albert (stuffed lobster gratiné, with mushrooms and a sauce half American, half *bonne femme*); Lobster Washington (like Newburg, but cooked with whiskey instead of sherry); Fillet of Sole Lincoln (cooked with oysters, shrimps, and sauce *bonne femme*); Pears Mary Garden (stewed pears with raspberry ice and raspberry sauce); Pears Geraldine Farrar (ditto with orange ice and apricot sauce); and Coeur Flottant Grace Moore (a vanilla-and-chocolate-mousse concoction). "I named the guinea-hen dish, which includes tomatoes, after Jefferson because around the end of the eighteenth century, when Americans still thought tomatoes were poison, Jefferson, who had eaten them in France, recommended them, and they were then adopted here," Mr. Diat said. "New desserts I generally named after our lady customers—the way to pay tribute to a lady is to make a special sweet for her. Lobster Albert I named after Albert Keller, the late president of the Ritz. Mr. Keller treated me like a brother. Of the eighty men on my kitchen staff, he knew fifty by name. When we buried him, eleven years ago, I said to myself, 'We are burying the Ritz.'"

Mr. Diat, whose father owned a shoe store, owes a great deal more than vichyssoise to his mother and grandmother—such as the correct way to prepare onion soup and potatoes *paysanne.* At the age of eight, he was getting up early to make soup before starting off to school. From his mother, he learned how to cook tarts, and from his grandmother how to broil chicken over charcoal, slowly. "They are very particular in the country in France," he said. At fourteen, he was apprenticed to the chef of a pastry shop in Moulins, near Vichy. At eighteen, after tours of duty at the Hotels Bristol and du Rhin, in Paris, he became *chef potager* at the Paris Ritz. At twenty-one, he became assistant to the head sauce cook of the London Ritz. He has been chef of the Carlton House since the day it opened, October 23, 1910, and of the Ritz since the day *it* opened, seven and a half weeks later. Until six months ago, when his doctor told him to take it easy, he worked fourteen hours a day, six days a week, and spent seven or eight hours at the hotel on Sunday, his day off. From 1916 to 1929, he lived in New Rochelle, with his wife and daughter, and in that period he used to come in on Sunday morning, return home for lunch, and then make another trip to the city, so that he would be on the job at dinnertime. From 1929 until last January, his home was on Central Park West, and commuting was out, but now he's back in an apartment in Hartsdale, with his wife. His daughter some years ago married George J. Lawrence, a junior officer of the Bowery Savings Bank. Currently, Mr. Diat gets the 7:27 out of Hartsdale every weekday morning, and arrives at his office about 8:15. He then spends an hour and a half on the telephone, placing orders for supplies with a dozen or more food dealers, and the rest of the morning touring the kitchen, giving his assistants an occasional word of advice or a helping hand, conferring with the banquet manager and the headwaiters, and correcting the proofs of the next day's menus. Afternoons, he mostly sticks to his desk and writes. He has assembled eighty pages of notes on the Paris, London, and New York Ritzes for a projected article or book; he hasn't decided which it will be. He has a brother seventeen years his junior, who is chef of the Hotel Plaza-Athénée, in Paris. His older brother, Jules, the one with whom he cooled his mother's and grandmother's potato soup, is dead. Jules, who was a teacher, had a son who was active in the French underground and died at Belsen. "My nephew was a very good *saucier*," Mr. Diat told us. "He was *chef saucier* of the French Pavilion at the New York World's Fair. The Boches killed him. He was a lovely fellow."

A waiter came in with Mr. Diat's lunch—lamb, rice, cauliflower, cottage cheese, stewed peaches—and he advised us that his eating habits, apart from tasting new dishes of his invention, are simple and have always been: a roll and a cup of coffee for breakfast; lunch about as we saw it; clear soup, green salad, and compote of fruit for dinner. We rose to go, and he put a hand on our arm. "I am not of the school of Escoffier," he said, "but of the schools of M. Jules Tissier, of the Bristol, in

Paris; of M. Georges Gimon, of the Paris Ritz; and of M. Emile Mal-
ley, of the London Ritz. I remember the day I came to America. It was
October 8, 1910. There was a nice blue sky. Everything was so nice that
I applied for citizenship the first week of November. But today! When
we lost Mr. Keller, and then Robert Walton Goelet, we lost the Ritz. I
will compare a hotel with a man. A man is in the prime of life, in full
vigor, at forty. So is a hotel, or should be. You know, if I am heartbro-
ken today, it is because everything has gone wrong. I explained my grief
to the Honorable William Waldorf Astor—he came to my office to see
me when he was over here from England and looked into the Astor Estate's disposition of the Ritz—and he was so upset he almost fell out of
his chair. I have been invited to go to the new Carlton House as super-
vising chef, but I don't know. I will go away for at least six months, either to California or to France, to forget about the Ritz. I don't want to
be in New York when they break this place up. When Queen Marie of
Romania came here for a supper party in the Oval Room, she said, 'Oh,
it is like my palace!' "

1950

"What wine goes best with vodka?"

4 A.M.

JAMES STEVENSON

There aren't too many appealing places to go in Manhattan at four in the morning. The streets are desolate; the few cars that are moving seem secretive, bent on melancholy errands; pedestrians are rare and nervous-looking. Dawn is a long way off. We were driving around the city at that hour last week, stopping at stoplights that didn't matter, listening to country-and-western on the radio, and rummaging through the familiar trash barrel of our minds, plucking at ratty memories, poking at old wounds inflicted and received, sorting out yearnings, examining the imminence of doom—the usual dog's breakfast of rumination. It was, in addition, damn cold: you could feel each and every bone in your fingers. We drove through places that we used to like. Washington Market, years ago, would be just ending its day around this hour, still smelling great, with bits of celery and lettuce on the wet cobblestones. (Kaput.) A sign on the World Trade Center (which did the old market in) was lit, proclaiming the view from the 107th floor. Of what, we wondered. The really good thing to see was gone. We went around Battery Park, spotted a fireboat in the darkness (that was nice), and huge new office buildings, such as American Express (not nice), then swung down Fulton Street toward the river and parked.

The old fish market was full of light. Flames jumped from bonfires in oil drums, cinders flying crazily, into the night sky; there was the rumble of trucks, the shouting of men, the clatter of dollies, the thudding of boxes on the pavement. Bundled-up men in rubber boots moved about, interweaving with the trucks and dollies; nobody bumped into anybody. Nobody seemed angry; everybody seemed to have a role with enough to do but not too much, and time to make a wisecrack or hail a friend. The smell was rich and splendid. The fish, extracted from the sea, had reached the next stage here: packed fin to fin on ice in boxes. The boxes were being put on dollies, wheeled down the grimy pavement, hurled into trucks. In one crowded shed, a colossus of a fish was lying on its personal bed of ice.

"What's that?" we asked a stocky man who had a cigar butt between his teeth.

"Grouper," he replied, around the butt. "Three hundred pounds."

"How did you get it in here?" we asked.

The man removed the cigar from his mouth and replied, "With a crane." He was very pleased with his answer.

Farther down, a man called to us, "I got porgies! I got blues!"

"Just looking," we said.

A huge man in a tattered windbreaker selected a skinny black fish from a box, picked it up, and studied it. Then he put it back and took a billfold from his hip pocket. He opened the billfold and counted the money in it.

At a place with oysters and clams and mussels, we stood and listened to the sound that a big bag of clams makes when it is dropped on the pavement. It is not easy to duplicate (*kah-chunk-ka-ch-ch-unk?*), but it is worth listening to.

A man standing by several enormous, smooth, deep-purple-skinned tuna—decapitated and de-tailed—was periodically shouting "Hey!" in a cheerful voice to nobody in particular. It seemed to be the opening part of a sales pitch, but since nobody was around, he never completed the commercial. But he appeared content.

Not far away, some small fish had fallen out of a box on a dolly and landed on the ground. Men danced around, crouching, swiftly stabbing the escapees with sharp hooks and flipping them back into the box.

"You want shad?" asked a man in the shad area, addressing an elderly buyer.

"Nah," said the old man. "I got shad yesterday."

We went out on the dock behind the market and exchanged a few words with some crewmen who had just about finished unloading the catch—white plastic bags of scallops—from the *Felicia*, about ninety feet overall, painted orange above the hull, just in from ten days off Long Island. In a long shed on the other side of the dock, a black man stood on an elevated platform surrounded by huge blocks of ice—blocks suitable for building pyramids. There was a machine for grinding the ice, but at the moment it was idle.

It was still as cold as a tuna on ice, so we went across South Street to a parked truck that sold coffee, and bought a cup. The hot cardboard warmed our fingers superbly, and we walked over to the biggest bonfire we could find. It was in a metal oil drum that had slits and odd-shaped openings around the bottom, so it glowed like a Halloween pumpkin. Three or four men stood around it, throwing on slats of wooden crates and cardboard boxes. The fire roared upward, the flames almost reaching the South Street Viaduct, overhead. A yellow dawn was starting behind the Brooklyn Bridge. We edged toward the warming fire, and hoped the day would not arrive too soon.

1977

SLAVE

ALEX PRUD'HOMME

When Albert Yeganeh says "Soup is my lifeblood," he means it. And when he says "I am extremely hard to please," he means that, too. Working like a demon alchemist in a tiny storefront kitchen at 259-A West Fifty-fifth Street, Mr. Yeganeh creates anywhere from eight to seventeen soups every weekday. His concoctions are so popular that a wait of half an hour at the lunchtime peak is not uncommon, although there are strict rules for conduct in line. But more on that later.

"I am psychologically kind of a health freak," Mr. Yeganeh said the other day, in a lisping staccato of Armenian origin. "And I know that soup is the greatest meal in the world. It's very good for your digestive system. And I use only the best, the freshest ingredients. I am a perfectionist. When I make a clam soup, I use three different kinds of clams. Every other place uses canned clams. I'm called crazy. I am not crazy. People don't realize why I get so upset. It's because if the soup is not perfect and I'm still selling it, it's a torture. It's *my* soup, and that's why I'm so upset. First you clean and then you cook. I don't believe that 99 percent of the restaurants in New York know how to clean a tomato. I tell my crew to wash the parsley *eight* times. If they wash it five or six times, I scare them. I tell them they'll go to jail if there is sand in the parsley. One time, I found a mushroom on the floor, and I fired the guy who left it there." He spread his arms, and added, "This place is the only one like it in . . . in . . . the whole earth! One day, I hope to learn something from the other places, but so far I haven't. For example, the other day I went to a very fancy restaurant and had borscht. I had to send it back. It was *junk.* I could see all the chemicals in it. I never use chemicals. Last weekend, I had lobster bisque in Brooklyn, a very well-known place. It was *junk.* When I make a lobster bisque, I use a whole lobster. You know, I never advertise. I don't have to. All the big-shot chefs and the kings of the hotels come here to see what *I'm* doing."

As you approach Mr. Yeganeh's Soup Kitchen International from a distance, the first thing you notice about it is the awning, which proclaims HOMEMADE HOT, COLD, DIET SOUPS. The second thing you notice is an aroma so delicious that it makes you want to take a bite out of the air. The third thing you notice, in front of the kitchen, is an electric signboard that flashes, say, "Today's Soups . . . Chicken Vegetable . . . Mexican Beef Chili . . . Cream of Watercress . . . Italian Sausage . . . Clam Bisque . . . Beef Barley . . . Due to Cold Weather . . . For Most Efficient and Fastest Service the Line Must . . . Be Kept Moving . . . Please . . . Have Your Money . . . Ready . . . Pick the Soup of Your Choice . . . Move to Your Extreme . . . Left After Ordering."

"I am not prejudiced against color or religion," Mr. Yeganeh told us, and he jabbed an index finger at the flashing sign. "Whoever follows that I treat very well. My regular customers don't say anything. They are very intelligent and well educated. They know I'm just trying to move the line. The New York cop is very smart—he sees everything but says nothing. But the young girl who wants to stop and tell you how nice you look and hold everyone up—*yah!*" He made a guillotining motion with his hand. "I tell you, I hate to work with the public. They treat me like a slave. My philosophy is: the customer is always wrong and I'm always right. I raised my prices to try to get rid of some of these people, but it didn't work."

The other day, Mr. Yeganeh was dressed in chefs' whites with orange smears across his chest, which may have been some of the carrot soup cooking in a huge pot on a little stove in one corner. A three-foot-long handheld mixer from France sat on the sink, looking like an overgrown gardening tool. Mr. Yeganeh spoke to two young helpers in a twisted Armenian-Spanish barrage, then said to us, "I have no overhead, no trained waitresses, and I have the cashier here." He pointed to himself theatrically. Beside the doorway, a glass case with fresh green celery, red and yellow peppers, and purple eggplant was topped by five big gray soup urns. According to a piece of cardboard taped to the door, you can buy Mr. Yeganeh's soups in three sizes, costing from four to fifteen dollars. The order of any well-behaved customer is accompanied by little wax-paper packets of bread, fresh vegetables (such as scallions and radishes), fresh fruit (such as cherries or an orange), a chocolate mint, and a plastic spoon. No coffee, tea, or other drinks are served.

"I get my recipes from books and theories and my own taste," Mr. Yeganeh said. "At home, I have several hundreds of books. When I do research, I find that I don't know anything. Like cabbage is a cancer fighter, and some fish is good for your heart but some is bad. Every day, I should have one sweet, one spicy, one cream, one vegetable soup— and they *must* change, they should always taste a little different." He added that he wasn't sure how extensive his repertoire was, but that it probably includes at least eighty soups, among them African peanut butter, Greek moussaka, hamburger, Reuben, BLT, asparagus and caviar, Japanese shrimp miso, chicken chili, Irish corned beef and cabbage, Swiss chocolate, French calf's brain, Korean beef ball, Italian shrimp and eggplant Parmesan, buffalo, ham and egg, short rib, Russian beef Stroganoff, turkey cacciatore, and Indian mulligatawny. "The chicken and the seafood are an addiction, and when I have French garlic soup I let people have only one small container each," he said. "The doctors and nurses love that one."

A lunch line of thirty people stretched down the block from Mr. Yeganeh's doorway. Behind a construction worker was a man in expensive leather, who was in front of a woman in a fur hat. Few people spoke. Most had their money out and their orders ready.

At the front of the line, a woman in a brown coat couldn't decide which soup to get and started to complain about the prices.

"You talk too much, dear," Mr. Yeganeh said, and motioned to her to move to the left. "Next!"

"Just don't talk. Do what he says," a man huddled in a blue parka warned.

"He's downright rude," said a blond woman in a blue coat. "Even abusive. But you can't deny it, his soup is the best."

1989

ENDANGERED ENTRÉES

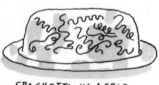

SPAGHETTI IN ASPIC

BRAISED CABBAGE CARS

CROWN ROAST
OF MONTEREY JACK

LEMON-COLLARED
CHICKEN ÉTOILE

crawford

UNDER THE HOOD

MARK SINGER

The other afternoon, at a parking lot on the Lower West Side, we put a 1988 Ford Taurus station wagon at Chris Maynard's disposal. Maynard removed two flat foil-wrapped packages from a canvas shoulder bag and then lifted the hood of the Ford. "Veal scaloppine," he said, "with Genoa salami, aged provolone cheese, and Spanish onion." He laid the packages on top of the car's fuel-injector housing, wedged each one into place with a cone-shaped wad of foil, slammed the hood shut, and said, "Now we'll just let that cook awhile."

He headed into traffic, up West Street, in the general direction of the Bronx and Tony's Delicatessen, birthplace of the corned-beef doughnut. Maynard has an open mind and is prone to serendipitous detours. Maybe he would get to Tony's and maybe he wouldn't; in either case, he was unlikely to stay hungry. On the front seat lay a set of bound galley proofs of *Manifold Destiny: The One! The Only! Guide to Cooking on Your Car Engine,* a soon-to-be-published collaboration between Maynard and Bill Scheller, who would have been along on the trip to the Bronx had he not been in the midst of a three-month detour to Spain.

Maynard and Scheller began to explore car-engine cooking five years ago, when they warmed up some smoked brisket on a drive from Montreal to Boston. After that, each time one of them got behind the wheel he did so with a broader sense of purpose and adventure than most of his fellow-motorists. Quickly, the two men branched into stuffed eggplant, poached fillet of sole, and baked apples. Last year, when they steered a Lincoln Town Car through the One Lap of America rally, a marathon eight-day drive around the republic, they got a concentrated chance to refine their techniques. Taking advantage of the Lincoln's spacious, eleven-by-thirteen-inch fuel-injector-housing surface and its piping-hot valve covers, they conducted successful experiments with ham steaks, pork tenderloins, and stuffed chicken breasts. They attracted a little publicity, and soon a cookbook became an inevitability.

Explicating a creation called Enzo's Veal ("in honor of the late Enzo Ferrari"), Maynard and Scheller write, "Start this in Manhattan and lunch will be ready in New Haven. Turn once, in Stamford." Despite such detailed instructions, they are aware that no two makes of engine behave identically. Chicken thighs that take three hours and forty-five minutes to cook under the hood of a Chrysler New Yorker may need about fifty minutes to become nicely browned inside an Olds Cutlass. *Manifold Destiny* preaches "the time-trusted method of temperature verification known as 'burn your finger.'" Repeatedly, the authors warn of the hazards of, say, sticking one's hands in the fan or doing something with a hot dog that would inhibit the free movement of the accelerator linkage. Maynard and Scheller dare to be poetic in naming dishes: Lead Foot Stuffed Cabbage, Pat's Provolone Porsche Potatoes, Thruway Thighs. Their chapter on Southern cooking offers a recipe for Blackened Roadfish. *Manifold Destiny* is dedicated to Molly and Pluggy, Scheller's half-Doberman/half-Labrador and Maynard's two-year-old Airedale, respectively. "Pluggy is my role model," Maynard said. "She's always ready for a good time."

Once, to accommodate a television crew, Maynard tried to cook an omelette in a Thunderbird, but the effort was subverted by a shoddy wrapping job and by "the Third World status of streets in New York City." This experience came to mind as he drove up the entrance ramp to the West Side Highway. "We may have seen that veal for the last time," he said as we rattled over the brick pavement. "Actually, the only thing I ever lost was a chicken breast—in Virginia. I was driving an '81 Toyota, usually a pretty good cooker. I put the breast on a little north of D.C., and somewhere near Richmond I pulled over to check and it was gone. Fortunately, I happened to be cooking a pork loin, too, so I ate that instead."

After one rubbernecking delay—a three-car pileup in the southbound lanes—we made our way up the Henry Hudson Parkway, then over to the Mosholu Parkway, and within twenty minutes we had arrived at Tony's Delicatessen, on Bainbridge Avenue. Beyond the generally endearing fact that Tony's is an Italian-owned place that serves Jewish food as well as Italian to a mainly Irish clientele, Maynard goes there specifically for the corned-beef doughnuts: deep-fried agglomerations of nothing your doctor would recommend—"oily enough to require an EPA variance on the Arctic tundra," according to Maynard and Scheller. It came as a disappointment to learn that there were none on the premises. Maynard was able to forestall starvation, however, because Manny Bonet, the chef at Tony's, is also the innovator of a triangular deep-fried concoction called the potato turnover.

Maynard ordered one of those and a cup of coffee. As he ate, we asked how he had discovered Tony's.

"I park my car a couple of blocks from here," he said. "Ironically, you can't cook in my car. It's a Volkswagen Rabbit, a diesel, with no good surface to attach anything to. The only thing that ever really worked was that first batch of smoked meat from Montreal. Driving from Philly to New York, I once tried to do some chicken breasts, but when I got to where I was going the chicken breasts were still sushi."

A cop car slowly cruised by, reminding Maynard that he had parked the Ford Taurus near a bus stop, in a less than strictly legal manner. He went outside, raised the hood, and said, "Mmm, smell that cooking!" Subtle hints of salami and onion hit our nostrils, followed by fresh Bx34 bus exhaust. "That's what I love about car-engine cooking," Maynard said. "Nothing beats stopping at a toll booth on the Garden State Parkway, checking under the hood, and having the smell of garlic and pork juice waft back at me."

Maynard's VW Rabbit was parked in a lot a block away, and he offered to show it to us. When we got there, however, he realized that he didn't have a key to get into the lot. That forced us to marvel at the Rabbit—missing right rear window, roof that had been walked on by a heavy person, graffiti on the hood—from a distance. A few doors down was Eddie's Delicatessen.

"They sell Irish bangers," said Maynard. "Want to check them out?"

Sure we did. They were in a freezer case—Irish Regular Pork Bangers and Irish White Breakfast Pudding. Each one looked as if it might fit neatly along the exhaust manifold of a Chevrolet Celebrity.

"How would I cook this sort of thing?" Maynard said, closing the freezer door. "I'd cook it in a frying pan on my stove. To be honest."

1989

PROTEIN SOURCE

MARK SINGER

Members of the New York Entomological Society paid forty-five dollars to attend the group's hundredth-anniversary dinner the other night at the Explorers Club. Among the items on the menu were cricket-and-vegetable tempura, mealworm balls in zesty tomato sauce, roasted Australian kurrajong grubs, and roast beef with gravy. Members of certain affiliated entomological organizations were asked to pay fifty-five dollars. Miscellaneous guests, including representatives of the media, had to cough up sixty-five dollars. Crews from all the major local television stations materialized, along with reporters from the BBC, CNN, TV Asahi (Japan), Christian Science Monitor Radio, Nickelodeon, Reuters, the Associated Press, *Scientific American,* the *Times,* the *Post, Newsday, U.S. News & World Report, Food Arts,* and a lot of other places.

Marialisa Calta, of *Eating Well,* had traveled all the way from northern Vermont. Her editor expected her to come back with a story, of course, but Marialisa Calta is more than a rote transcriber of such facts as that a hundred-gram portion of giant silk moth caterpillars provides 112.2 percent of the recommended daily adult allowance of riboflavin, 120 percent of the copper, and 197.2 percent of the iron. Marialisa Calta is a thoughtful human being. "I'm trying to free my mind from the cultural bias against eating bugs," she said. "Also, I'm Italian, and we supposedly eat anything."

A waiter in black tie and a wing collar passed by with a tray of hors d'oeuvres—mealworm ghanouj on fontina bruschetta. The mealworms, which had been simmered in red wine with salt and pepper, tasted fine. The ghanouj seemed a little gummy. Marialisa Calta suggested that we chase it with a live honeypot ant. On a nearby table was a petrilike dish of ants that looked familiar except that they had been feeding on peach nectar and the abdomen of each was a large, swollen, translucent sac. "Pick out a logy one," Marialisa said. "They're easier to catch." We picked out a logy one. It tasted sweet. Though there was a limit of one per person, we might have sampled another, but a cameraman from Channel 4 jostled us and made us spill our ginger ale.

We saw a man who we instinctively felt was Norman Cooper, the president of the National Pest Control Association—an intuition based mainly on the name tag he was wearing. Mr. Cooper's wife had obtained tickets to the latest August Wilson play, *Two Trains Running*, for that evening, he said, but he preferred to eat insects. Mr. Cooper is the president of ESCO, a.k.a. Exterminating Services Company—the largest pest-control firm in the metropolitan area. "We're concerned with insects as pests," he said, in a vaguely defensive tone. "My regard for the press in the past has not been the highest. I have seen them take scientific fact and distort it in order to make a sweeps-week rating higher. We've seen how they'll take a nonthreatening situation and blow it into a scare story. Of course, that's a generalization, but it's largely true."

Another waiter interrupted us, this time with a tray of fried mealworms and wax-worm fritters with plum sauce, and, when we looked up, some lower life forms had thrust a long lens and a microphone into Mr. Cooper's face.

We had a brief conversation with Robert Boyle, a writer and naturalist, who does a lot of trout fishing and fly-tying and has been eating insects for fifteen years—"not as much as I'd like but enough to repel friends." An open-minded friend of Mr. Boyle's who used to analyze bins of flour for the Army, testing them for their mealworm content, once recommended that he raise termites, "but not too close to the house." "Termites are something like 20 percent protein," Mr. Boyle said. "That's their wet weight. Dry, they might be closer to 50 percent."

Toni Schwed was also present. She is working on an anthology of "fiction, poetry, aphorisms, and cartoons—everything that's not nonfiction—about bugs," and has just published a book titled *Noah and Me*, about a psychotherapist for animals.

On the buffet line, we caught up with Mr. Cooper again, and he introduced us to some of his fellow pest-control professionals: Ivor Specterman, the general manager of ESCO; Bob Stien, of Acme Exterminating, in Manhattan; and Gil Bloom, of Standard Exterminating, in Queens.

Gil Bloom had some wisdom to convey about the press. "Like pest control, they serve a necessary function in society," he said. "They're not always loved, but they serve a purpose. We do our best to treat them as nontarget organisms. As exterminators, we tend to target only four-legged, six-legged, and, on occasion, eight-legged organisms. We don't normally go after two-legged creatures, although, if you were really interested, I could set you up with someone."

During dinner, we shared a table with Mr. Cooper and Dr. Muhammad Shadab, an entomologist on the staff of the American Museum of Natural History, where he specializes in making anatomically exact pointillist drawings of the reproductive organs of spiders. One of the centerpieces was a green-mesh-covered glass fishbowl containing a bed of aquamarine gravel and a large tarantula-colored tarantula. Dr. Shadab studied it for about two seconds before pronouncing it female.

From the buffet table we had picked up a couple of two-inch-long Thai water bugs—a species that, according to Lou Sorkin, the treasurer of the New York Entomological Society, has "the flavor of lettuce, seaweed, or Gorgonzola cheese, depending where you bite into it." Instead of eating them, we decided to keep them as souvenirs.

We asked Mr. Cooper whether the Thai water bug was the same insect that people encounter in dark, dank, scary New York City basements and refer to interchangeably as the water bug and the American cockroach—as opposed to the smaller, ubiquitous species of cockroach that is found in New York City kitchens and is known as the German cockroach (except in Germany, where it is known as the French cockroach, and in France, where it is known as the English cockroach).

"Yes," Mr. Cooper said, and he explained that the Thai water bug was a close relative of the North American scary-basement water bug.

Immediately, Dr. Shadab contradicted him. "No," Dr. Shadab said. "The American cockroach is not a true bug. In common language they are all bugs, but a true bug has different wings and mouthparts. A true bug—like the bedbug—has a piercing mouth so that it can suck the juices out of plants and sometimes animals. Now, that's a true bug. A roach is a roach."

A Thai water bug sat untouched on Mr. Cooper's plate.

"Do people ever eat roaches?" he was asked.

"No," Dr. Shadab said.

"Well, perhaps," Mr. Cooper said. "But not knowingly."

1992

A SANDWICH

NORA EPHRON

The hot pastrami sandwich served at Langer's Delicatessen in down-town Los Angeles is the finest hot pastrami sandwich in the world. This is not just my opinion, although most people who know about Langer's will simply say it's the finest hot pastrami sandwich in Los An-geles because they don't dare to claim that something like a hot pastrami sandwich could possibly be the best version of itself in a city where until recently you couldn't get anything resembling a New York bagel, and the only reason you can get one now is that New York bagels have deterio-rated.

Langer's is a medium-sized place—it seats 135 people—and it is decorated, although "decorated" is probably not the word that applies, in tufted brown vinyl. The view out the windows is of the intersection of Seventh and Alvarado and the bright-red-and-yellow signage of a His-panic neighborhood—bodegas, check-cashing storefronts, and pawn-shops. Just down the block is a spot notorious for being the place to go in L.A. if you need a fake ID. The Rampart division's main police station, the headquarters of the city's second-most-recent police scandal, is a mile away. Even in 1947, when Langer's opened, the neighborhood was not an obvious place for an old-style Jewish delicatessen, but in the early 1990s things got worse. Gangs moved in. The crime rate rose. The Langers—the founder, Al, now eighty-nine, and his son Norm, fifty-seven—were forced to cut the number of employees, close the restaurant nights and Sundays, and put coin-operated locks on the restroom doors. The open-ing of the Los Angeles subway system—one of its stops is half a block from the restaurant—has helped business slightly, as has the option of having your sandwich brought out to your car. But Langer's always seems to be just barely hanging on. If it were in New York, it would be a shrine, with lines around the block and tour buses standing double-parked out-side. Pilgrims would come—as they do, for example, to Arthur Bryant's in Kansas City and Sonny Bryan's in Dallas—and they would report on their conversion. But in Los Angeles a surprising number of people don't even know about Langer's, and many of those who do wouldn't be caught dead at the corner of Seventh and Alvarado, even though it's not a particularly dangerous intersection during daytime hours.

Pastrami, I should point out for the uninitiated, is made from a cut of beef that is brined like corned beef, coated with pepper and an assortment of spices, and then smoked. It is characterized by two things. The first is that it is not something anyone's mother whips up and serves at home; it's strictly restaurant fare, and it's served exclusively as a sandwich, usually on Russian rye bread with mustard. The second crucial thing about pastrami is that it is almost never good. In fact, it usually tastes like a bunch of smoked rubber bands.

The Langers buy their pastrami from a supplier in Burbank. "When we get it, it's edible," Norm Langer says, "but it's like eating a racquetball. It's hard as a rock. What do we do with it? What makes us such wizards? The average delicatessen will take this piece of meat and put it into a steamer for thirty to forty-five minutes and warm it. But you've still got a hard piece of rubber. You haven't broken down the tissues. You haven't made it tender. We take that same piece of pastrami, put it into our steamer, and steam it for almost three hours. It will shrink 25 to 30 percent, but it's now tender—so tender it can't be sliced thin in a machine because it will fall apart. It has to be hand-sliced."

So: tender and hand-sliced. That's half the secret of the Langer's sandwich. The other secret is the bread. The bread is hot. Years ago, in the 1930s, Al Langer owned a delicatessen in Palm Springs, and, because there were no Jewish bakers in the vicinity, he was forced to bus in the rye bread. "I was serving day-old bread," Al Langer says, "so I put it into the oven to make it fresher. Hot crispy bread. Juicy soft pastrami. How can you lose?"

Today, Langer's buys its rye bread from a bakery called Fred's, on South Robertson, which bakes it on bricks until it's ten minutes from being done. Langer's bakes the loaf the rest of the way, before slicing it hot for sandwiches. The rye bread, faintly sour, perfumed with caraway seeds, lightly dusted with cornmeal, is as good as any rye bread on the planet, and Langer's puts about seven ounces of pastrami on it, the proper proportion of meat to bread. The resulting sandwich, slathered with Gulden's mustard, is an exquisite combination of textures and tastes. It's soft but crispy, tender but chewy, peppery but sour, smoky but tangy. It's a symphony orchestra, different instruments brought together to play one perfect chord. It costs eight-fifty and is, in short, a work of art.

2002

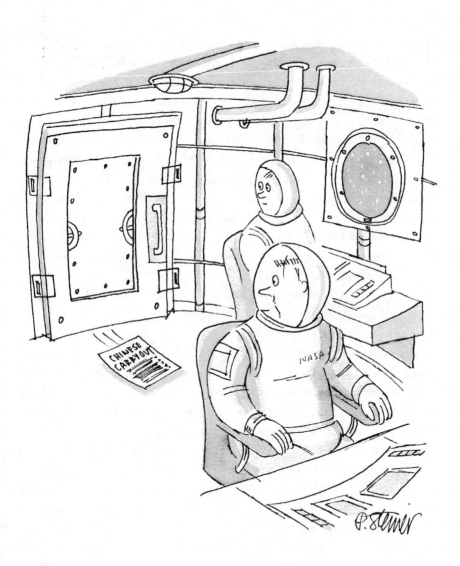

SEA URCHIN

CHANG-RAE LEE

July 1980. I'm about to turn fifteen and our family is in Seoul, the first time since we left, twelve years earlier. I don't know if it's different. My parents can't really say. They just repeat the equivalent of "How in the world?" whenever we venture into another part of the city, or meet one of their old friends. "Look at that—how in the world?" "This hot spell, yes, yes—how in the world?" My younger sister is very quiet in the astounding heat. We all are. It's the first time I notice how I stink. You can't help smelling like everything else. And in the heat everything smells of ferment and rot and rankness. In my grandfather's old neighborhood, where the two- and three-room houses stand barely head-high, the smell is staggering. "What's that?" I ask. My cousin says, "Shit."

"Shit? What shit?"

"Yours," he says, laughing. "Mine."

On the wide streets near the city center, there are student demonstrations; my cousin says they're a response to a massacre of citizens by the military down south in Kwangju. After the riot troops clear the avenues, the air is laden with tear gas—"spicy," in the idiom. Whenever we're in a taxi moving through there, I open the window and stick out my tongue, trying to taste the poison, the human repellent. My mother wonders what's wrong with me.

I don't know what's wrong. Or maybe I do. I'm bored. Maybe I'm craving a girl. I can't help staring at them, the ones clearing dishes in their parents' eateries, the uniformed schoolgirls walking hand in hand, the slim young women who work in the Lotte department store, smelling of fried kimchi and L'Air du Temps. They're all stunning to me, even with their bad teeth. I let myself drift near them, hoping for the scantest touch.

But there's nothing. I'm too obviously desperate, utterly hopeless. Instead, it seems, I can eat. I've always liked food, but now I'm bent on trying everything. As it is, the days are made up of meals, formal and impromptu, meals between meals and within meals; the streets

are a continuous outdoor buffet of braised crabs, cold buckwheat noodles, shaved ice with sweet red beans on top. In Itaewon, the district
near the United States Army base, where you can get anything you
want, culinary or otherwise, we stop at a seafood stand for dinner. Basically, it's a tent diner, a long bar with stools, a camp stove and fish
tank behind the proprietor, an elderly woman with a low, hoarse voice.
The roof is a stretch of blue poly-tarp. My father is excited; it's like
the old days. He wants raw fish, but my mother shakes her head. I can
see why: in plastic bins of speckled, bloody ice sit semi-alive cockles,
abalones, eels, conches, sea cucumbers, porgies, shrimps. "Get something fried," she tells him, not caring what the woman might think.
"Get something cooked."

A young couple sitting at the end of the bar order live octopus.
The old woman nods and hooks one in the tank. It's fairly small, the
size of a hand. She lays it on a board and quickly slices off the head
with her cleaver. She chops the tentacles and gathers them up onto a
plate, dressing them with sesame oil and a spicy bean sauce. "You have
to be careful," my father whispers, "or one of the suction cups can stick
inside your throat. You could die." The lovers blithely feed each other
the sectioned tentacles, taking sips of *soju* in between. My mother immediately orders a scallion-and-seafood pancake for us, then a spicy
cod-head stew; my father murmurs that he still wants something live,
fresh. I point to a bin and say that's what I want—those split spiny
spheres, like cracked-open meteorites, their rusty centers layered with
shiny crenellations. I bend down and smell them, and my eyes almost
water from the intense ocean tang. "They're sea urchins," the woman
says to my father. "He won't like them." My mother is telling my father
he's crazy, that I'll get sick from food poisoning, but he nods to the
woman, and she picks up a half and cuts out the soft flesh.

What does it taste like? I'm not sure, because I've never had anything like it. All I know is that it tastes alive, something alive at the
undragged bottom of the sea; it tastes the way flesh would taste if
flesh were a mineral. And I'm half gagging, though still chewing; it's
as if I had another tongue in my mouth, this blind, self-satisfied creature. That night I throw up, my mother scolding us, my father chuck-
ling through his concern. The next day, my uncles joke that they'll
take me out for some more, and the suggestion is enough to make me
retch again.

But a week later I'm better, and I go back by myself. The woman is there, and so are the sea urchins, glistening in the hot sun. "I know what you want," she says. I sit, my mouth slick with anticipation and revulsion, not yet knowing why.

2002

"If you could eat only one food for the rest of your life, what would it be?"

AS THE FRENCH DO

JANET MALCOLM

> With the left hand, hold an asparagus upright in the heart of an
> artichoke while a wall of the sauce is built around it with the
> right hand.
>
> —*The Alice B. Toklas Cookbook*

How can a sauce be a wall? Why does Toklas swerve from the hortatory to the passive in midsentence? To answer these questions, it is necessary to cook the dish called Hearts of Artichokes à la Isman Bavaldy, which Toklas offers as an example of French haute cuisine on pages 11 to 12 of her cookbook. It was, she tells us, one of the courses in a nine-course lunch for sixteen at a fashionable French home to which she and Gertrude Stein had been invited, and which included Aspic de Foie Gras, Salmon Sauce Hollandaise, Hare à la Royale, Pheasants Roasted with Truffles, Lobster à la Française, Singapore Ice Cream, cheese, and fruit.

"It does not take as long as it sounds to prepare this dish," Toklas writes of Hearts of Artichokes à la Isman Bavaldy, and she is right. The recipe is actually harder to read than the dish is to prepare. There are so many steps that one cannot take them in; one's eyes glaze over, one's thoughts wander. However, shopping for the ingredients (which Toklas doesn't list—you just bump into them as you read) refocuses the mind. The ingredients are: artichokes, asparagus, lemons, cardamom seeds, sweetbreads, shallots, coriander seeds, butter, flour, dry champagne, and bread crumbs.

You cook the artichokes in water to which lemon juice, cardamom seeds, and salt have been added, and then remove the leaves and put them aside. They are not part of the dish. ("The leaves can be scraped with a silver spoon and mixed with a little cream to be used in an omelette or under mirrored eggs," Toklas writes, trying to be helpful, but only adding to the forbidding length of the recipe.) Then you boil the asparagus until it is just tender, and cut each spear "within 2 inches of the tip."

Earlier, you have started to deal with the sweetbreads. Toklas says to soak them in cold water for an hour; boil them for twenty minutes with salt, shallots, coriander seeds; plunge them into cold water; "remove tubes and skin" (very messy); and, finally, put them through a strainer with a potato masher. I found that unworkable and made a mush of them in the Cuisinart. Next, you sauté the sweetbread mush in butter, and add flour and then champagne. "Cook gently until this sauce becomes stiff."

And now comes the improbable (and, as it proved, impossible) building of the wall of sauce. Toklas's wobbly sentence clearly expresses the anxiety of the moment and subtly enacts the disparity between what the two hands are doing: the left hand confidently clutching the asparagus spear, the right hand helplessly plastering its base with the sauce, which no amount of cooking can make into the cementlike substance needed to hold the spear upright when the left hand releases it. The recipe called for twelve artichoke hearts. I cooked six, and six times failed to keep the asparagus from drooping miserably into the pool of sauce gathering in and messily spilling out of the artichoke heart. There was no way to make the dish presentable.

Well, was it good? No. The champagne (two cups of it), and a final browning with buttered bread crumbs, muddied the delicate taste of the sweetbread, and the asparagus and artichoke hearts similarly had no reason for being together—they canceled out each other's virtue. Nor could you taste the cardamom and coriander seeds. The dish took about two hours to prepare, three minutes to serve to game friends, who politely pushed it around on their plates, and ten seconds to throw out.

But the first time I cooked from *The Alice B. Toklas Cookbook,* in 1954, the year of its publication, when it was given to me for my birthday by an arty friend, was to quite different effect. Seven years had yet to pass before the appearance of *Mastering the Art of French Cooking,* and, like most people living in pre-Julia America, I had never eaten real French food. Thus, when I took my first bite of the coq au vin I had made from Toklas's recipe, on page 149, I could hardly credit my senses. I was stunned by the suave deliciousness of what I had produced. In all my life, I had never eaten anything of such complex and rich, and yet clear and pure, flavor. It was a moment of astonished rapture, one that I will never forget.

When I decided to cook the dish again recently, I doubted that the moment would be repeated. In 2002, Americans no longer need to be told, as Toklas told us with great condescension in 1954, that "the French never add Tabasco, ketchup or Worcestershire sauce, nor do they eat any of innumerable kinds of pickles, nor do they accompany a meat course with radishes, olives or salted nuts. . . . To cook as the French do one must respect the quality and flavor of the ingredients." (When I first read these words, I was properly awed by them. I had not yet made Hearts of Artichokes à la Isman Bavaldy.)

But Toklas's coq au vin—or Cock in Wine, as she called it for the sake of her radish-eating American readers—remains wonderful. The combination of fowl, pork lardoons, butter, carrots, shallots, onions, wine, brandy, and mushrooms is as felicitous as the combination of artichokes, asparagus, and sweetbread mush is ridiculous. It differs in one respect from the usual coq-au-vin recipe: Toklas uses white wine instead of red for the sauce, and I, for one, think this is a good idea. But in either manifestation coq au vin remains one of the glories of French bourgeois cuisine. The butter and pork fat aren't good for the heart, but the dish is good for the soul.

Below, I reprint Toklas's appealingly short recipe—its brevity and the ordinariness of the ingredients were what attracted me to it in 1954—followed by a sort of hovering Jewish mother's version for use in 2002.

COCK IN WINE NO. I

Cut a young cock or a young chicken in serving pieces. In an enamel-lined pot melt 3 tablespoons butter, add ¾ cup diced side fat of pork, 6 small onions, 4 shallots and 1 medium-sized carrot cut in thin slices. Brown these in butter. Remove and place pieces of chicken in pot and brown over high heat. Add salt, pepper and 2 cloves of crushed garlic. Remove the browned pork fat, onions, shallots and carrot. Heat 3 table-spoons brandy, light and pour into pot. Sprinkle ¾ table-spoon flour into the pot. Stir with a wooden spoon for 2 or 3 minutes, then add 1 cup fresh mushrooms and 1 cup hot good dry white wine. Increase heat, add pork fat and vegetables. Cook uncovered for ¼ hour. Serve very hot.

COCK IN WINE NO. 2

Buy four pieces of chicken and as small a slab of pork fat or bacon as you can find. Fill a cup to the ³/₄ mark with pork fat you have diced into small pieces. Heat 1 tablespoon butter in a heavy enameled or stainless casserole, and sauté the pork pieces until brown. Remove to a side dish. Add another tablespoon of butter to the pot (if needed) and sauté 12 small white onions, 8 large quartered shallots, and 4 sliced carrots until lightly browned. Remove and add to the side dish with two cloves of crushed garlic. Rub chicken pieces with salt and pepper, and brown over medium-high flame in the fat left in pot; then remove. Pour 3 tablespoons brandy into pot and light. When flames subside, add ³/₄ tablespoon of flour and stir with a wooden spoon for about a minute over very low heat. Add one and a half to two cups dry white wine, then return chicken and vegetables and pork pieces to the pot. Cook covered over low heat for half an hour or until the chicken is properly done. While the chicken is cooking, sauté 4 or 5 sliced mushrooms in 1 tablespoon butter over high heat. Add them to the pot in the last five minutes of cooking. Taste the sauce—it will probably need salt. Serve with boiled new potatoes.

2002

"I'll have the barbecued half-pounder, with all the ramifications."

BLOCKING AND CHOWING

BEN McGRATH

If you are an offensive lineman, the Netherlands cafeteria, at Hofstra University, in Hempstead, where the New York Jets hold their training camp, has a couple of things going for it: the portions are unlimited, and the food doesn't cost anything. "Shit, if it's free it's for me, you know what I'm saying?" Randy Thomas said recently, dipping a piece of fried chicken into a puddle of blue-cheese dressing during his lunch break, between practices. Thomas, the Jets' starting right guard, has a fast metabolism, and he weighs three hundred pounds; his appetite can be expensive. "I'm known to eat, like, seventeen pieces of chicken," he says. "By the way I eat, you would think I'm a big fat slob. But I just keep myself lean."

"Lean" is a relative term in the Brobdingnagian world of an NFL cafeteria. Thomas is not quite the largest of the men who, for the past month, have lumbered into the Netherlands four times a day, like trucks rolling up to a gas station, dressed in sleeveless T-shirts, green shorts, and sandals, with their ankles, knees, and elbows wrapped in tape. Jumbo Elliott—"still the biggest guy on earth," according to the Jets' head coach, Herman Edwards—is three inches taller; Kareem McKenzie is twenty-five pounds heavier. But Thomas is the undisputed king of consumption, and when he pushes back his chair, raising his arms above his head after polishing off a plate of pecan pie, he reveals an ample midsection.

While there is no direct meal-by-meal oversight of Jets players' dining habits, the strength-and-conditioning coach, John Lott, has a few basic recommendations for some of his bigger, hungrier charges: avoid fried foods and sweets; drink water instead of soda. To this end, the cafeteria menu, prepared by the team trainer and a certified nutritionist, is color-coded by fat content: green for lentil soup; yellow for a mesquite-turkey club; red for meatloaf with gravy or fish-and-chips. Thomas was unaware of these traffic signals, but would probably not have heeded them anyway. "I don't worry about my fat," he says. "I just fuckin' eat. It makes me happy and comfortable and relaxed, you know?

'Cause if I'm hungry on the field I don't perform—I'm thinking about fuckin' eatin'."

Once the season begins, this week, the players are on their own for dinner—and for the all-important late-night "snack," which for Thomas means a dozen wings and eight fried jumbo chicken fingers. (The team continues to provide a buffet breakfast and lunch every day.) And while Thomas and his teammates savor the cafeteria grub—"These goddam chicken tenders are good, boy. They're addictive. They're so goddam *crunchy*"—they spend a certain amount of time at the training table trading restaurant tips for steak houses and all-you-can-eat buffets. Major's Steak House, on Long Island, is one favorite, and East-West, an all-you-can-eat Chinese restaurant in New Jersey, is another; Thomas ran afoul of the management at East-West two years ago when he put away sixteen lobster tails. ("I've fucked up some buffets, man," Thomas says.)

Coach Lott was a player himself, so he understands the urge to eat after a hard-fought game. (In his playing days, he weighed as much as 307 pounds.) "I really strongly advise the guys to go to town one night a week," he says. "If you hamstring them and say 'Don't eat this' or 'Don't eat that,' you will find a guy at three o'clock in the morning with a bucket of Kentucky Fried Chicken eating all he can because he's just going stir crazy." Still, Lott tries to set guidelines: "Instead of getting a Big Mac, get the grilled-chicken sandwich. And, hey, if you want a milk shake, get your milk shake."

In past years, the team has scheduled a series of educational seminars with the nutritionist, to recommend healthier alternatives to fast food. This season, the Jets are testing a new, more proactive approach: house calls. "Not everyone's married, and they don't live with their moms, so they're by themselves," Coach Lott said. "I'm going to have a couple of ladies cook prepared meals and bring them to their house. It's not going to be a lady preparing them sundaes; it's going to be a balanced meal." So far, four players have signed up (Randy Thomas, who is married, is not among them), but Lott expects more players to request lady service once the word spreads. "They won't have to think about it," he said. "They just go home and eat."

2002

"*Let me see if I have it correctly, sir. To hell with the appetizer. A chopped sirloin that damn well better be rare. No goddam relish tray. Who cares which salad dressing, since they all taste like sludge?*"

WHEN EDIBLES ATTACK

REBECCA MEAD

The guests at the Food Allergy Ball, a black-tie gala that took place at the Plaza Hotel last week, were drawn from that class of New York society which includes Fortune 500 CEOs and senior partners at corporate law firms and exclusive interior decorators: the fortunate few who are largely sheltered from many of life's afflictions. But food allergies—the symptoms of which can range from mild nausea at a bite of shrimp to convulsions brought on by the mere inhalation of a cashew fragment—can strike even the most pampered New Yorkers, and, more significantly, the children of the most pampered New Yorkers, for whom a rogue peanut-butter-and-jelly sandwich in the lunchroom can present a deadly threat. This fact helps explain why the Food Allergy Initiative, a nonprofit organization that was founded six years ago, has already raised a total of nine million dollars for research and education.

"If you're not going to do it for your kids, who are you going to do it for?" said Todd Slotkin, the Food Allergy Initiative's chairman and a senior executive at MacAndrews & Forbes Holdings. Slotkin's food-allergy activism was activated by the diagnosis of allergies in his twin sons as toddlers, after he unwittingly fed one of them a nut-laced cookie while on vacation in Nantucket. Slotkin suffers from the usual anxieties of parenthood—what are your kids doing, and who are they doing it with?—amplified to an excruciating degree. "My sons are eleven, and in a few years, I hear, they will start to kiss other people," he said as he tucked into a feast that began with a grilled-eggplant terrine (comprising twenty-one ingredients, all carefully enumerated on the menu), and explained that for his boys a make-out partner who had recently eaten a nut-studded brownie could prove fatal.

Sharyn Mann, the FAI's vice chairman and the mistress of ceremonies, was motivated by similar concerns: her daughter, Tamara, suffers from severe food allergies. Mann wore a strapless black gown and a spray of black feathers in her upswept hair, in keeping with the black-and-white décor inspired by Cecil Beaton's set designs for *My Fair Lady*. Mann had managed to enlist ten cast members of the show's

London revival to fly over and perform, and friends of Mann testified that her maternal vigilance was as impressive as her event production talents. "I was there the first time her daughter turned blue," said Wanda Dworman. "If she went anywhere, she couldn't eat anything outside of water or Jell-O." Dworman described how her own consciousness about allergic reactions was raised during a trip to Aspen, where a bee flew behind her wraparound sunglasses and stung her twice; and she was pleased to report that there were at least some restaurateurs who took the issue seriously. "A lot of places have nuts in bread, but there are restaurants, like Le Cirque and Daniel, that are very sympathetic to this," she said.

The guests of honor were Joseph Flom, the senior partner of Skadden, Arps, Slate, Meagher & Flom—and, according to Ronald Perelman, who introduced him, "my lawyer, my friend, and a member of my family"—and Flom's son Jason, the president of Lava Records. Jason Flom described how his aversion to nuts had caused him to make a hasty, gasping exit from the Chappaqua dinner table of former president Clinton not long ago, after it became clear that assurances from the waitstaff that the meal was nut-free depended on what your definition of "nut" was. Other politicians have also failed to grasp the seriousness of the food-allergy issue. Robert F. Kennedy, Jr., who is a board member of FAI, said that he had written to Jimmy Carter after Carter sent a letter to the airlines in defense of packaged peanuts as an in-flight snack.

The main course was beef goulash with garlic-chive spaetzle. The Plaza kitchen, having striven so hard to create an allergy-proof menu, was momentarily flummoxed by requests for a vegetarian alternative; eventually someone rustled up a plate or two of steamed baby vegetables, the kind of thing children only pretend to be allergic to. The seven different desserts—created by the restaurants Danube and Bouley, whose chef, David Bouley, was honored with the Joe Baum Lifetime Achievement Award—were delivered to dimmed lights, a drumroll, and a rousing trumpet voluntary.

Bouley, on receiving his award, cited "the right to have a fine culinary experience without fear," and the evening's menu demonstrated the possibility of having a fine culinary experience without nuts—although some guests admitted quietly that a nut or two could be a good thing. Rita Blake, who owns a company that makes what she described as "very, very, very high-end window treatments," said that a few handfuls of nuts had served as her dinner the previous night. Blake was sympathetic to those with food allergies, having developed an intolerance to shellfish a few years ago, but nonetheless defended the maligned foodstuff. "I love nuts," she said. "I think they are nature's perfect food. I give my dog raw almond butter with her vitamins."

2003

"If I told you the secret of making light, flaky piecrust, it wouldn't be much of a secret anymore, now would it?"

KILLING DINNER

GABRIELLE HAMILTON

It's quite something to go bare-handed up through a chicken's ass and dislodge its warm guts. Startling, the first time, how fragilely they are attached. I have since put countless suckling pigs—pink, the same weight and size as a pet beagle—into slow ovens to roast overnight so that their skin becomes crisp and their still-forming bones melt into the meat. I have butchered 220-pound sides of beef down to their primal cuts; carved the tongues out of the heads of goats; fastened baby lambs with crooked sets of teeth onto green applewood spits and set them by the foursome over hot coals; and boned the saddles and legs of rabbits, which, even skinned, look exactly like bunnies.

But when I killed my first chicken I was only seventeen and unaccustomed. I had dropped out of school and was staying in the basement of my father's house, in rural New Jersey, for very little rent. That fall, I spent a lot of time sitting outside on the log pile at dusk smoking hand-rolled cigarettes in my canvas jacket, watching the garden decay and thinking about death and the inherent beauty of the cycle of life. In my father's chicken coop, one bird was being badly henpecked. My dad said we should kill it and spare it the slow torture by its pen mates. I said I could do it. I said it was important to confront the death of the animal you had the privilege of eating, that it was cowardly to buy cellophane-wrapped packages of boneless, skinless breasts at the grocery store. My father said, "You can kill the damned thing when I get home from work."

From a remote spot on the back kitchen steps, he told me how to pull the chicken decisively out of the pen. I spoke to it philosophically about death, grasping it firmly yet calmly with what I hoped was a soothing authority. Then he told me to take it by the legs and hold it upside down. The chicken protested from deep inside its throat, close to the heart, a violent, vehement, full-bodied cluck. The crowing was almost an afterthought. To get it to stop, I started swinging it in full arm circles, as my dad instructed me. I windmilled that bird around and around the way I'd spun lettuce as a kid in the front yard, sending droplets of water out onto the gravel and pachysandra from the old-fashioned wire-basket spinner my mom used.

He said this would disorient the bird—make it so dizzy that it couldn't move—and that's when I should lay it down on the block and chop its head off, with one machinelike whack. In my own way, not like a machine at all, I laid it down on a tree stump, and while it was trying to recover I clutched the hatchet and came down on its neck. This first blow made a vague dent, barely breaking the skin. I hurried to strike it again, but lost a few seconds in my grief and horror. The second blow hit the neck like a boat oar on a hay bale. I was still holding its feet in one hand and trying to cut its head off with the dull hatchet in my other when both the chicken and my father became quite lucid, and not a little agitated. The chicken began to thrash, its eyes open, as if chastising me for my false promises of a merciful death. My dad yelled, "Kill it! Kill it! Aw, Gabs, kill the fucking thing!" from his bloodless perch. I kept coming down on the bird's throat—which was now broken but still issuing terrible clucks— stroke after miserable stroke, until I finally got its head off. I was blubbering through clenched teeth. My dad was animated with disgust at his dropout daughter—so morose and unfeminine, with the tips of her braids dyed aquamarine, and unable even to kill a chicken properly. As I released the bird, finally, and it ran around the yard, bloody and ragged but at least now silent, he screamed, "What kind of person are you?"

It was a solid minute before the chicken's nerves gave out and it fell over motionless in some dead brown leaves. I wiped my snot on my sleeve, picked up the bird from the frozen ground, tied its feet, and hung it on a low tree branch to bleed it. The other chickens in their pen, silhouetted against the dusk, retreated inside to roost for the night. My dad closed the kitchen door and turned on the oven. I boiled a blue enameled lobster pot full of water, and submerged the bird to loosen its feathers. Sitting out on the back steps in the yellow pool of light from the kitchen window, I plucked the feathers off the chicken, two and three at a time. Its viscera came out with an easy tug: a small palmful of livery, bloody jewels that I tossed out into the dark yard.

There are two things you should never do with your father: learn how to drive, and learn how to kill a chicken. I'm not sure you should sit across from each other and eat the roasted bird in resentful silence, either, but we did that, too, and the meat was disagreeably tough.

2004

CLANDESTINE CUISINE

Liver Surprise

16 parts macaroni and cheese
1 part liver

Mix. Serve in as festive
a manner as possible.

Cauliflower? What Cauliflower?

27 parts macaroni and cheese
1 part cauliflower

Combine ingredients. Arrange
portion on plate in the shape
of a bunny and act innocent.

Limas Incognito

43 parts macaroni and cheese
1 part lima beans

Grind the beans to a paste and
stir them into the macaroni. Do not
behave as if anything were amiss.

Land Mine o' Halibut

188 parts macaroni and cheese
1 part halibut

Mash the hell out of the halibut
and blend it in with the other stuff.
Sit back and hope for the best.

R. Chast

FICTION

"Peas and carrots, peas and carrots, always together . . .
but are they really happy?"

TASTE

ROALD DAHL

There were six of us to dinner that night at Mike Schofield's house in London: Mike and his wife and daughter, my wife and I, and a man called Richard Pratt.

Richard Pratt was a famous gourmet. He was president of a small society known as the Epicures, and each month he circulated privately to its members a pamphlet on food and wines. He organized dinners where sumptuous dishes and rare wines were served. He refused to smoke for fear of harming his palate, and when discussing a wine, he had a curious, rather droll habit of referring to it as though it were a living being. "A prudent wine," he would say, "rather diffident and evasive, but quite prudent." Or, "a good-humored wine, benevolent and cheerful—slightly obscene, perhaps, but nonetheless good-humored."

I had been to dinner at Mike's twice before when Richard Pratt was there, and on each occasion Mike and his wife had gone out of their way to produce a special meal for the famous gourmet. And this one, clearly, was to be no exception. The moment we entered the dining room, I could see that the table was laid for a feast. The tall candles, the yellow roses, the quantity of shining silver, the three wineglasses to each person, and, above all, the faint scent of roasting meat from the kitchen brought the first warm oozings of saliva to my mouth.

As we sat down, I remembered that on both Richard Pratt's previous visits Mike had played a little betting game with him over the claret, challenging him to name its breed and its vintage. Pratt had replied that that should not be too difficult, provided it was one of the great years. Mike had then bet him a case of the wine in question that he could not do it. Pratt had accepted, and had won both times. Tonight I felt sure that the little game would be played over again, for Mike was quite willing to lose the bet in order to prove that his wine was good enough to be recognized, and Pratt, for his part, seemed to take a grave, restrained pleasure in displaying his knowledge.

The meal began with a plate of whitebait, fried very crisp in butter, and to go with it there was a Moselle. Mike got up and poured the wine himself, and when he sat down again, I could see that he was watching Richard Pratt. He had set the bottle down in front of me so that I could read the label. It said GEIERSLAY OHLIGSBERG, 1945. He leaned over and whispered to me that Geierslay was a tiny village in the Moselle, almost unknown outside Germany. He said that this wine we were drinking was something unusual, that the output of the vineyard was so small that it was almost impossible for a stranger to get any of it. He had visited Geierslay personally the previous summer in order to obtain the few dozen bottles that they had finally allowed him to have.

"I doubt anyone else in the country has any of it at the moment," he said. I saw him glance again at Richard Pratt. "Great thing about Moselle," he continued, raising his voice, "it's the perfect wine to serve before a claret. A lot of people serve a Rhine wine instead, but that's because they don't know any better. A Rhine wine will kill a delicate claret, you know that? It's barbaric to serve a Rhine before a claret. But a Moselle—ah!—a Moselle is exactly right."

Mike Schofield was an amiable, middle-aged man. But he was a stockbroker. To be precise, he was a jobber in the stock market, and, like a number of his kind, he seemed to be somewhat embarrassed, almost ashamed, to find that he had made so much money with so slight a talent. In his heart he knew that he was not really much more than a bookmaker—an unctuous, infinitely respectable, secretly unscrupulous bookmaker—and he knew that his friends knew it, too. So he was seeking now to become a man of culture, to cultivate a literary and aesthetic taste, to collect paintings, music, books, and all the rest of it. His little sermon about Rhine wine and Moselle was a part of this thing, this culture that he sought.

"A charming little wine, don't you think?" he said. He was still watching Richard Pratt. I could see him give a rapid, furtive glance down the table each time he dropped his head to take a mouthful of whitebait. I could almost *feel* him waiting for the moment when Pratt would take his first sip, and look up from his glass with a smile of pleasure, of astonishment, perhaps even of wonder, and then there would be a discussion and Mike would tell him about the village of Geierslay.

But Richard Pratt did not taste his wine. He was completely engrossed in conversation with Mike's eighteen-year-old daughter, Louise. He was half turned toward her, smiling at her, telling her, so far as I could gather, some story about a chef in a Paris restaurant. As he spoke, he leaned closer and closer to her, seeming in his eagerness almost to impinge upon her, and the poor girl leaned as far as she could away from him, nodding politely, rather desperately, and looking not at his face but at the topmost button of his dinner jacket.

We finished our fish, and the maid came around removing the plates. When she came to Pratt, she saw that he had not yet touched his food, so she hesitated, and Pratt noticed her. He waved her away, broke off his conversation, and quickly began to eat, popping the little crisp brown fish quickly into his mouth with rapid jabbing movements of his fork. Then, when he had finished, he reached for his glass, and in two short swallows he tipped the wine down his throat, and turned immediately to resume his conversation with Louise Schofield.

Mike saw it all. I was conscious of him sitting there, very still, containing himself, looking at his guest. His round, jovial face seemed to loosen slightly and to sag, but he contained himself and was still and said nothing.

Soon the maid came forward with the second course. This was a large roast of beef. She placed it on the table in front of Mike, who stood up and carved it, cutting the slices very thin, laying them gently on the plates for the maid to take around. When he had served everyone, including himself, he put down the carving knife and leaned forward with both hands on the edge of the table.

"Now," he said, speaking to all of us but looking at Richard Pratt. "Now for the claret. I must go and fetch the claret, if you'll excuse me."

"You go and fetch it, Mike?" I said. "Where is it?"

"In my study, with the cork out—breathing."

"Why the study?"

"Acquiring room temperature, of course. It's been there twenty-four hours."

"But why the study?"

"It's the best place in the house. Richard helped me choose it last time he was here."

At the sound of his name, Pratt looked around.

"That's right, isn't it?" Mike said.

"Yes," Pratt answered, nodding gravely. "That's right."

"On top of the green filing cabinet in my study," Mike said. "That's the place we chose. A good draft-free spot in a room with an even temperature. Excuse me, now, will you, while I fetch it."

The thought of another wine to play with had restored his humor, and he hurried out the door, to return a minute later, more slowly, walking softly, holding in both hands a wine basket in which a dark bottle lay. The label was out of sight, facing downward. "Now!" he cried as he came toward the table. "What about this one, Richard? You'll never name this one!"

Richard Pratt turned slowly and looked up at Mike; then his eyes traveled down to the bottle, nestling in its small wicker basket, and he raised his eyebrows, a slight, supercilious arching movement of the brows, and with it a pushing outward of the wet lower lip, suddenly imperious and ugly.

"You'll never get it," Mike said. "Not in a hundred years."

"A claret?" Richard Pratt asked, condescending.

"Of course."

"I assume, then, that it's from one of the smaller vineyards?"

"Maybe it is, Richard. And then again, maybe it isn't."

"But it's a good year? One of the great years?"

"Yes, I guarantee that."

"Then it shouldn't be too difficult," Richard Pratt said, drawling his words, looking exceedingly bored. Except that, to me, there was something strange about his drawling and his boredom: between the eyes a shadow of something evil, and in his bearing an intentness that gave me a faint sense of uneasiness as I watched him.

"This one is really rather difficult," Mike said. "I won't force you to bet on this one."

"Indeed. And why not?" Again the slow arching of the brows, the cool, intent look.

"Because it's difficult."

"That's not very complimentary to me, you know."

"My dear man," Mike said, "I'll bet you with pleasure, if that's what you wish."

"It shouldn't be too hard to name it."

"You mean you want to bet?"

"I'm perfectly willing to bet," Richard Pratt said.

"All right, then, we'll have the usual. A case of the wine itself."

"You don't think I'll be able to name it, do you?"

"As a matter of fact, and with all due respect, I don't," Mike said. He was making some effort to remain polite, but Pratt was not bothering overmuch to conceal his contempt for the whole proceeding. And yet, curiously, his next question seemed to betray a certain interest.

"You like to increase the bet?"

"No, Richard. A case is plenty."

"Would you like to bet fifty cases?"

"That would be silly."

Mike stood very still behind his chair at the head of the table, and he was still carefully holding the bottle in its ridiculous wicker basket. There was a trace of whiteness around his nostrils now, and his mouth was shut very tight.

Pratt was lolling back in his chair, looking up at him, the eyebrows raised, the eyes half closed, a little smile touching the corners of his lips. And again I saw, or thought I saw, something distinctly disturbing about the man's face, that shadow of intentness between the eyes, and in the eyes themselves, right in their centers, where it was black, a small, slow spark of shrewdness, hiding. "So you don't want to increase the bet?"

"As far as I'm concerned, old man, I don't give a damn," Mike said. "I'll bet you anything you like."

The three women and I sat quietly, watching the two men. Mike's wife was becoming annoyed; her mouth had gone sour and I felt that at any moment she was going to interrupt. Our roast beef lay before us on our plates, slowly steaming.

"So you'll bet me anything I like?"

"That's what I told you. I'll bet you anything you damn well please, if you want to make an issue out of it."

"Even ten thousand pounds?"

"Certainly I will, if that's the way you want it." Mike was more confident now. He knew quite well that he could call any sum Pratt cared to mention.

"So you say I can name the bet?" Pratt asked again.

"That's what I said."

There was a pause while Pratt looked slowly around the table, first at me, then at the three women, each in turn. He appeared to be reminding us that we were witness to the offer.

"Mike!" Mrs. Schofield said. "Mike, why don't we stop this nonsense and eat our food. It's getting cold."

"But it isn't nonsense," Pratt told her evenly. "We're making a little bet."

I noticed the maid standing in the background holding a dish of vegetables, wondering whether to come forward with them or not.

"All right, then," Pratt said. "I'll tell you what I want you to bet."

"Come on, then," Mike said, rather reckless. "I don't give a damn what it is—you're on."

Pratt nodded, and again the little smile moved the corners of his lips, and then, quite slowly, looking at Mike all the time, he said, "I want you to bet me the hand of your daughter in marriage."

Louise Schofield gave a jump. "Hey!" she cried. "No! That's not funny! Look here, Daddy, that's not funny at all."

"No, dear," her mother said. "They're only joking."

"I'm not joking," Richard Pratt said.

"It's ridiculous," Mike said. He was off balance again now.

"You said you'd bet anything I liked."

"I meant money."

"You didn't *say* money."

"That's what I meant."

"Then it's a pity you didn't say it. But anyway, if you wish to go back on your offer, that's quite all right with me."

"It's not a question of going back on my offer, old man. It's a no-bet anyway, because you can't match the stake. You yourself don't happen to have a daughter to put up against mine in case you lose. And if you had, I wouldn't want to marry her."

"I'm glad of that, dear," his wife said.

"I'll put up anything you like," Pratt announced. "My house, for example. How about my house?"

"Which one?" Mike asked, joking now.

"The country one."

"Why not the other one as well?"

"All right, then, if you wish it. Both my houses."

At that point, I saw Mike pause. He took a step forward and placed the bottle in its basket gently down on the table. He moved the salt-cellar to one side, then the pepper, and then he picked up his knife, studied the blade thoughtfully for a moment, and put it down again. His daughter, too, had seen him pause.

"Now, Daddy!" she cried. "Don't be *absurd*! It's too silly for words. I refuse to be betted on like this."

"Quite right, dear," her mother said. "Stop it at once, Mike, and sit down and eat your food."

Mike ignored her. He looked over at his daughter and he smiled, a slow, fatherly, protective smile. But in his eyes, suddenly, there glimmered a little triumph. "You know," he said, smiling as he spoke, "you know, Louise, we ought to think about this a bit."

"Now, stop it, Daddy! I refuse even to listen to you! Why, I've never heard anything so ridiculous in my life!"

"No, seriously, my dear. Just wait a moment and hear what I have to say."

"But I don't want to hear it."

"Louise! Please! It's like this. Richard, here, has offered us a serious bet. *He* is the one who wants to make it, not me. And if he loses, he will have to hand over a considerable amount of property. Now, wait a minute, my dear, don't interrupt. The point is this. *He cannot possibly win.*"

"He seems to think he can."

"Now, listen to me, because I know what I'm talking about. The expert, when tasting a claret—so long as it is not one of the famous, great wines like Lafite or Latour—can only get a certain way towards naming the vineyard. He can, of course, tell you the Bordeaux district from which the wine comes, whether it is from St. Emilion, Pomerol, Graves, or Médoc. But then each district has several communes, little counties, and each county has many, many small vineyards. It is impossible for a man to differentiate between them all by taste and smell alone. I don't mind telling you that this one I've got here is a wine from a small vineyard that is surrounded by many other small vineyards, and he'll never get it. It's impossible."

"You can't be sure of that," his daughter said.

"I'm telling you I can. Though I say it myself, I understand quite a bit about this wine business, you know. And anyway, heavens alive, girl, I'm your father and you don't think I'd let you in for—for—for something you didn't want, do you? I'm trying to make you some money."

"Mike!" his wife said sharply. "Stop it now, Mike, please!"

Again he ignored her. "If you will take this bet," he said to his daughter, "in ten minutes you will be the owner of two large houses."

"But I don't want two large houses, Daddy."

"Then sell them. Sell them back to him on the spot. I'll arrange all that for you. And then, just think of it, my dear, you'll be rich! You'll be independent for the rest of your life!"

"Oh, Daddy, I don't like it. I think it's silly."

"So do I," the mother said. She jerked her head briskly up and down as she spoke, like a hen. "You ought to be ashamed of yourself, Michael, ever suggesting such a thing! Your own daughter, too!"

Mike didn't even look at her. "Take it!" he said eagerly, staring hard at the girl. "Take it, quick! I'll guarantee you won't lose."

"But I don't like it, Daddy."

"Come on, girl. Take it!"

Mike was pushing her hard. He was leaning toward her, fixing her with two hard, bright eyes, and it was not easy for the daughter to resist him.

"But what if I lose?"

"I keep telling you, you can't lose. I'll guarantee it."

"Oh, Daddy, must I?"

"I'm making you a fortune. So come on now. What do you say, Louise? All right?"

For the last time, she hesitated. Then she gave a helpless little shrug of the shoulders and said, "Oh, all right, then. Just so long as you swear there's no danger of losing."

"Good!" Mike cried. "That's fine! Then it's a bet!"

"Yes," Richard Pratt said, looking at the girl. "It's a bet."

Immediately, Mike picked up the wine, tipped the first thimbleful into his own glass, then skipped excitedly around the table filling up all the others. Now everyone was watching Richard Pratt, watching his face as he reached slowly for his glass with his right hand and lifted it to his nose. The man was about fifty years old and he did not have a pleasant face. Somehow, it was all mouth—mouth and lips—the full, wet lips of the professional gourmet, the lower lip hanging downward in the center, a pendulous, permanently open taster's lip, shaped open to receive the rim of a glass or a morsel of food. Like a keyhole, I thought, watching it; his mouth is like a large, wet keyhole.

Slowly he lifted the glass to his nose. The point of the nose entered the glass and moved over the surface of the wine, delicately sniffing. He swirled the wine gently around in the glass to release the bouquet. His concentration was intense. He had closed his eyes, and now the whole top half of his body, the head and neck and chest, seemed to become a kind of huge, sensitive smelling-machine, receiving, filtering, analyzing the message from the sniffing nose.

Mike, I noticed, was lounging in his chair, apparently unconcerned, but he was watching every move. Mrs. Schofield, the wife, sat prim and upright at the other end of the table, looking straight ahead, her face tight with disapproval. The daughter, Louise, had shifted her chair away a little, and sidewise, facing the gourmet, and she, like her father, was watching closely.

For at least a minute, the smelling process continued; then, without opening his eyes or moving his head, Pratt lowered the glass to his mouth and tipped in almost half the contents. He paused, his mouth full of wine, getting the first taste; then he permitted some of it to trickle down his throat, and I saw his Adam's apple move as it passed by. But most of it he retained in his mouth. And now, without swallowing again, he drew in through his lips a thin breath of air, which mingled with the fumes of the wine in the mouth and passed on down into his lungs. He held the breath, blew it out through his nose, and finally began to roll the wine around under the tongue, and chewed it, actually chewed it with his teeth, as though it were bread.

It was a solemn, impressive performance, and I must say he did it well.

"Um," he said, putting down the glass, running a pink tongue over his lips. "Um—yes. A very interesting little wine—gentle and gracious, almost feminine in the aftertaste."

There was an excess of saliva in his mouth, and as he spoke he spat an occasional bright speck of it onto the table.

"Now we can start to eliminate," he said. "You will pardon me for doing this carefully, but there is much at stake. Normally I would perhaps take a bit of a chance, leaping forward quickly and landing right in the middle of the vineyard of my choice. But this time—I must move cautiously this time, must I not?" He looked up at Mike and he smiled, a thick-lipped, wet-lipped smile. Mike did not smile back.

"First, then, which district in Bordeaux does this wine come from? That is not difficult to guess. It is far too light in the body to be from either St. Emilion or Graves. It is obviously a Médoc. There's no doubt about *that*.

"Now—from which commune in Médoc does it come? That also, by elimination, should not be too difficult to decide. Margaux? No. It cannot be Margaux. It has not the violent bouquet of a Margaux. Pauillac? It cannot be Pauillac, either. It is too tender, too gentle and wistful for a Pauillac. The wine of Pauillac has a character that is almost imperious in its taste. And also, to me, a Pauillac contains just a little pith, a curious, dusty, pithy flavor that the grape acquires from the soil of the district. No, no. This—this is a very gentle wine, demure and bashful in the first taste, emerging shyly but quite graciously in the second. A little arch, perhaps, in the second taste, and a little naughty also, teasing the tongue with a trace, just a trace, of tannin. Then, in the aftertaste, delightful—consoling and feminine, with a certain blithely generous quality that one associates only with the wines of the commune of St. Julien. Unmistakably this is a St. Julien."

He leaned back in his chair, held his hands up level with his chest, and placed the fingertips carefully together. He was becoming ridiculously pompous, but I thought that some of it was deliberate, simply to mock his host. I found myself waiting rather tensely for him to go on. The girl Louise was lighting a cigarette. Pratt heard the match strike and he turned on her, flaring suddenly with real anger. "Please!" he said. "Please don't do that! It's a disgusting habit, to smoke at table!"

She looked up at him, still holding the burning match in one hand, the big, slow eyes settling on his face, resting there a moment, moving away again, slow and contemptuous, and, bending her head, she blew out the match, but continued to hold the unlighted cigarette in her fingers.

"I'm sorry, my dear," Pratt said, "but I simply cannot have smoking at table."

She didn't look at him again.

"Now, let me see—where were we?" he said. "Ah, yes. This wine is from Bordeaux, from the commune of St. Julien, in the district of Médoc. So far, so good. But now we come to the more difficult part— the name of the vineyard itself. For in St. Julien there are many vine-yards, and as our host so rightly remarked earlier on, there is often not much difference between the wine of one and the wine of another. But we shall see."

He paused again, closing his eyes. "I am trying to establish the 'growth,'" he said. "If I can do that, it will be half the battle. Now, let me see. This wine is obviously not from a first-growth vineyard—nor even a second. It is not a great wine. The quality, the—the—what do you call it?—the radiance, the power, is lacking. But a third growth— that it could be. And yet I doubt it. We know it is a good year—our host has said so—and this is probably flattering it a little bit. I must be care-ful. I must be very careful here."

He picked up his glass and took another small sip.

"Yes," he said, sucking his lips, "I was right. It is a fourth growth. Now I am sure of it. A fourth growth from a very good year—from a great year, in fact. And that's what made it taste for a moment like a third- or even a second-growth wine. Good! That's better! Now we are closing in! What are the fourth-growth vineyards in the commune of St. Julien?"

Again he paused, took up his glass, and held the rim against that sagging, pendulous lower lip of his. Then I saw the tongue shoot out, pink and narrow, the tip of it dipping into the wine, withdrawing swiftly again—a repulsive sight. When he lowered the glass, his eyes re-mained closed, the face concentrated, only the lips moving, sliding over each other like two pieces of wet, spongy rubber.

"There it is again!" he cried. "Tannin in the middle taste, and the quick astringent squeeze upon the tongue. Yes, yes, of course! Now I have it! This wine comes from one of those small vineyards around Beychevelle. I remember now. The Beychevelle district, and the river and the little harbor that has silted up so the wine ships can no longer use it. Beychevelle . . . Could it actually be a Beychevelle itself? No, I don't think so. Not quite. But it is somewhere very close. Château Tal-bot? Could it be Talbot? Yes, it could. Wait one moment."

He sipped the wine again, and out of the side of my eye I noticed Mike Schofield and how he was leaning farther and farther forward over the table, his mouth slightly open, his small eyes fixed upon Richard Pratt.

"No. I was wrong. It is not a Talbot. A Talbot comes forward to you just a little quicker than this one; the fruit is nearer to the surface. If it is a '34, which I believe it is, then it couldn't be a Talbot. Well, well. Let me think. It is not a Beychevelle and it is not a Talbot, and yet—yet it is so close to both of them, so close, that the vineyard must be almost in between. Now, which could that be?"

He hesitated, and we waited, watching his face. Everyone, even Mike's wife, was watching him now. I heard the maid put down the dish of vegetables on the sideboard behind me, gently, so as not to disturb the silence.

"Ah!" he cried. "I have it! Yes, I think I have it!"

For the last time, he sipped the wine. Then, still holding the glass up near his mouth, he turned to Mike and he smiled, a slow, silky smile, and he said, "You know what this is? This is the little Château Branaire-Ducru."

Mike sat tight, not moving.

"And the year, 1934."

We all looked at Mike, waiting for him to turn the bottle around in its basket and show the label.

"Is that your final answer?" Mike said.

"Yes, I think so."

"Well, is it or isn't it?"

"Yes, it is."

"What was the name again?"

"Château Branaire-Ducru. Pretty little vineyard. Lovely old château. Know it quite well. Can't think why I didn't recognize it at once."

"Come on, Daddy," the girl said. "Turn it round and let's have a peek. I want my two houses."

"Just a minute," Mike said. "Wait just a minute." He was sitting very quiet, bewildered-looking, and his face was becoming puffy and pale, as though all the force was draining slowly out of him.

"Michael!" his wife called sharply from the other end of the table. "What's the matter?"

"Keep out of this, Margaret, will you please."

Richard Pratt was looking at Mike, smiling with his mouth, his eyes small and bright. Mike was not looking at anyone.

"Daddy!" the daughter cried, agonized. "But, Daddy, you don't mean to say he's guessed it right!"

"Now, stop worrying, my dear," Mike said. "There's nothing to worry about."

I think it was more to get away from his family than anything else that Mike then turned to Richard Pratt and said, "I'll tell you what, Richard. I think you and I better slip off into the next room and have a little chat?"

"I don't want a little chat," Pratt said. "All I want is to see the label on that bottle." He knew he was a winner now; he had the bearing, the quiet arrogance, of a winner, and I could see that he was prepared to become thoroughly nasty if there was any trouble. "What are you waiting for?" he said to Mike. "Go on and turn it round."

Then this happened: the maid, the tiny, erect figure of the maid, in her white-and-black uniform, was standing beside Richard Pratt, holding something out in her hand. "I believe these are yours, sir," she said.

Pratt glanced around, saw the pair of thin horn-rimmed spectacles that she held out to him, and for a moment he hesitated. "Are they? Perhaps they are. I don't know."

"Yes sir, they're yours." The maid was an elderly woman—nearer seventy than sixty—a faithful family retainer of many years' standing. She put the spectacles down on the table beside him.

Without thanking her, Pratt took them up and slipped them into his top pocket, behind the white handkerchief.

But the maid didn't go away. She remained standing beside, and slightly behind, Richard Pratt, and there was something so unusual in her manner and in the way she stood there, small, motionless, and erect, that I, for one, found myself watching her with a sudden apprehension. Her old, gray face had a frosty, determined look, the lips were compressed, the little chin was out, and the hands were clasped together tight before her. The curious cap on her head and the flash of white down the front of her uniform made her seem like some tiny, ruffled, white-breasted bird.

"You left them in Mr. Schofield's study," she said. Her voice was unnaturally, deliberately polite. "On top of the green filing cabinet in his study, sir, when you happened to go in there by yourself before dinner."

It took a few moments for the full meaning of her words to penetrate, and in the silence that followed I became aware of Mike and how he was slowly drawing himself up in his chair, and the color coming to his face, and the eyes opening wide, and the curl of the mouth, and the dangerous little patch of whiteness beginning to spread around the area of the nostrils.

"Now, Michael!" his wife said. "Keep calm now, Michael, dear! Keep calm!"

1951

"Hi. My name is Don. I'll be introducing you to Mark, who will be taking your drink order, and after that to Gloria, who will be your waitress."

"This giblet gravy is lumpy."

TWO ROAST BEEFS

V. S. PRITCHETT

"When one says that what one is still inclined to call civilization is passing through a crisis," says Mr. Plymbell in his very expensive antique shop, raising a white and more than Roman nose and watching the words go off one by one on the air and circle the foreign customer, "one is tempted to ask oneself whether or not a few possibly idle phrases that one let fall to one's old friend Lady Hackthorpe at a moment of national distress in 1940 are not, in fact, still pertinent. One recalls observing, rightly or wrongly, at that time that one was probably witnessing not the surrender of an heroic ally but the defeat of sauces. Béarnaise, hollandaise, madère—one saw them overrun. One can conceive of the future historian's inquiring whether the wars of the last ten years, and indeed what one calls 'the peace,' have not been essentially an attack on gastronomy, on the stomach and palate of the human race."

After a pause, a small medallion of distaste is stamped on his white imperial face. Plymbell is obviously one whose loose clothes have once been better filled and whose stomach has known better days. He adds, "Of course, it may or may not have escaped your notice that the British nation have made a not unremarkable attempt to do 'the thing' fairly. One could offer the modest example of one's daily luncheon. . . ."

Plymbell's lunch is a study.

For several years now, at two minutes before half past twelve every day, Plymbell is first in the queue in the foyer outside the locked glass doors of Polli's Restaurant, a few yards from his shop. On one side of the glass Plymbell floats—handsome, Roman, silver-haired, as white-skinned and consequent as a turbot of fifty; on the other side of the glass, in the next aquarium, stands Polli with the key in his hand waiting for the clock to strike the half hour—a man liverish and suspended in misanthropy like a tench in the weed of a canal. Plymbell stares clean through Polli to the sixty empty tables beyond; Polli stares clean through the middle of Plymbell into the miasma of the restaurant keeper's life. Two fish gaze with the indifference of creatures who have accepted the fact that neither of them is edible. What they want, what the whole of England is crying for, is not fish but red meat, and to get meat at Polli's one has to be there at half past twelve, on the dot.

First customer in is Plymbell. He has his table, in the middle of this chipped Edwardian place, with his back to one of those white pillars that give it the appearance of a shop-soiled wedding cake mounted on a red carpet, and he faces the serving hatch. Putting up a monocle to his more annoyed eye, he watches the chef standing over his pans, and while he watches he taps the table with lightly frantic fingers. Polli's waiters are old men, and the one who serves Plymbell has the dejected smirk of a convict.

Plymbell hardly glances at the farcical menu and never looks at the waiter when he coldly gives his order. "Two soups," says Plymbell. "Two roast beefs . . . Cheese and biscuits," he adds. "Bring me mine now and you can bring the second order in a quarter of an hour, when my secretary arrives."

It is a daily scene. Plymbell's waiter comes forward with his dishes like one hurrying a funeral in a hot country, feebly averting his nose from the mess he is carrying on his dish. He scrapes his serving spoons and, at the end, eyes his customer with criminal scorn. Plymbell's jaws move over this stuff with a slow social agony. In fifteen minutes he has eaten his last biscuit, and is wetting his finger to pick up the small heap of crumbs he has worked to one side of his plate. Plymbell looks at his watch.

Exactly at this moment Plymbell's assistant comes in. Shabby, thin, with wrinkled cotton stockings and dressed in black, a woman of forty-five, Miss Tell scrapes on poor shoes to the table. She carries newspapers in a bundle under an arm and a basket in her hand. He looks carefully away from her as she alights like some dingy fly at the other side of the table. It is astonishing to see a man so well dressed lunching with a woman so bowed and faded. But presently she does a conjuring trick. Opening her bundle, Miss Tell puts a newspaper down on the roll of bread on her side plate and then picks it up again. The roll of bread has gone. She has slipped it into her lap. A minute passes while she wriggles to and fro like a laying hen, and then she drops the roll into the basket by the leg of her chair.

Plymbell is looking away from her while she does this and, his lips hardly moving, he speaks one word.

"What?" is the word.

She replies also with one word—the word naturally varies—cringing toward him, looking with fear, trying to get him to look at her.

"Sausages," she may whisper.

"How many?" Plymbell asks. He still does not look at her.

"Half pound," she says. On some fortunate days: "A pound."

Plymbell studies the domed skylight in the ceiling of the restaurant. The glass is still out; the boards put there during the war when a bomb blew out the glass have not been replaced. Meanwhile the waiter brings a plate of soup to Miss Tell. She stares at the soup without interest. When the waiter goes, she lifts the plate across the table and puts it in Plymbell's place, and then lowers her head in case other customers have seen. Plymbell has not seen, because he has been gazing at the ceiling, but, as if absent-mindedly, he picks up a spoon and begins to drink Miss Tell's soup, and when he has finished, puts her plate back on her side of the table, and the waiter takes it away.

For several years now Plymbell has been lunching at Polli's. He used to lunch there before the war with Lady Hackthorpe. She was a handsome woman—well-cut clothes, well-cut diamonds, brilliantly cut eyes, and sharply cut losses. She took a cut of everything. Plymbell bought and sold for her, decorated her house. She had several slices off him.

Miss Tell used to go home to her parents in the evening and say, "I don't understand it. I make out her bill every month and he says 'Miss Tell, give me Lady Hackthorpe's bill,' and tears it up."

Miss Tell lived by what she did not "understand." It was an appetite.

After 1940, no more Lady Hackthorpe. A bomb cut down half of her house and left a Hepplewhite bed full of broken glass and ceiling plaster on the first floor, and a servant's washstand on the floor above. Lady Hackthorpe went to Ireland.

Plymbell got the bed and a lot of other things out of the house into his shop. Here again, there was something Miss Tell did not "understand." She was supposed to "keep the books straight." Were Lady Hackthorpe's things being "stored" or were they being "returned to stock"?

"I mean," Miss Tell said, "if anyone was killed when a thing is left open it's unsatisfactory."

Plymbell listened and did not answer. He was thinking of other things. The war on the stomach and the palate had begun. Not only had

Lady Hackthorpe gone. Plymbell's business was a function of Lady Hackthorpe's luncheons and dinners, and other people's, too. He was left with his mouth open in astonishment and hunger.

"Trade has stopped now," Miss Tell said one night when she ducked into the air-raid shelter with her parents. "Poor Mr. Plymbell never goes out."

"Why doesn't he close the business, Kitty?" Miss Tell's mother said.

"And leave all that valuable stock?" said Mr. Tell. "Where's your brain?"

"I never could fathom business," said Mrs. Tell.

"It's the time to pick up things," said Mr. Tell.

"That's a way to talk when we may all be dead in a minute," said Mrs. Tell.

Mr. Tell said something about prices being bound to go up, but a huge explosion occurred and he stopped; it was embarrassing to use the words "go up."

"And this Lady Hackthorpe—is she *friendly* with this Plymbell?" said old Mrs. Tell when the explosion settled in as part of the furniture of their lives.

"*Mr.* Plymbell," Miss Tell corrected her mother. Miss Tell had a poor, fog-colored London skin and blushed in a patch across her forehead. "I don't *query* his private life."

"He's a man," sighed Mrs. Tell. "To hear you talk he might be the Fairy Prince or Lord Muck himself. Listen to those guns. You've been there fifteen years."

"It takes two to be friendly," said Miss Tell, who sometimes spoke like a poem. "When one goes away it may be left open one way or another, I mean, and that"— Miss Tell searched for a new word but returned to the old one, the only one that ever, for her, met the human case, "and that," she said, "is unsatisfactory."

"You're neurotic," her mother said. "You never have any news."

And then Miss Tell had a terrible thought. "Mum!" she cried, dropping the poetic accent she brought back from the West End every night, "where's Tiger? We've left him in the house."

Her mother became swollen with shame.

"You left him," accused Miss Tell. "You left him in the kitchen." She got up. "No one's got any heart. I'm going to get him."

"You stay here, my girl," said Mr. Tell.

"Come back, Kitty," said Mrs. Tell.

But Miss Tell (followed across the garden, as it seemed to her, by an airplane) went to the house. In her panic Mrs. Tell had left not only the cat, she had left her handbag and her ration books on the kitchen table. Miss Tell picked up the bag, and then kneeled under the table looking for Tiger. "Tiger, dear! Tiger!" she called. He was not there. It was at this instant that the airplane outside seemed to have followed her into the house, for the place suddenly closed in, then expanded and became hot, rose up in the air and fell down in cartloads upon the kitchen table. When Miss Tell was dug out alive and unhurt, black with dust, six hours later, Mr. and Mrs. Tell were dead in the garden.

When Plymbell recalls his experiences in the war for the inquiring foreign customer, he says there were times when one was inclined to ask oneself whether the computed odds of something like 897,000 to 1 in favor of one's nightly survival were not, perhaps, an evasion of a private estimate one had arrived at without any special statistical apparatus— that it was fifty-fifty, and even providential. It was a point, he said, one recollected making to one's assistant at the time, when she came back.

Miss Tell came back to Plymbell's at lunchtime one day a fortnight after she had been dug out. She was singular: she had been saved by looking for her cat. Mr. Plymbell was not at the shop, or in his rooms above it. In the vainglory of her escape she went round to Polli's. Plymbell was more than halfway through his meal when he saw her come in. She was wearing no hat on her dusty black hair, and under her black coat, which so often had ends of cotton on it, she was wearing navy-blue trousers. Plymbell winced: it was the human aspect of war that was so lowering; he saw at once that Miss Tell had become a personality. Watching the wag of her narrow shoulders as she walked, he saw she had caught the general immodesty of the "bombed out."

Without being invited, she sat down at his table and put herself sideways, at her ease, crossing her legs to show her trousers. Her face had filled out into two little puffs of vanity on either side of her mouth, as if she were eating or were containing a yawn. The two rings of age on her neck looked like a cheap necklace. Lipstick was for the first time on her lips. It looked like blood.

"One inquired in vain," said Plymbell with condescension. "I am glad to see you back."

"I thought I might as well pop round," said Miss Tell.

Mr. Plymbell was alarmed; her note was breezy. "Aren't you coming back?"

"I haven't found Tiger," said Miss Tell.

"Tiger?"

Miss Tell told him her story.

Plymbell saw that he must try and put himself for a moment in his employee's situation and think of her grief. "One recalls the thought that passed through one's mind when one's own mother died," he said.

"They had had their life," said Miss Tell petulantly.

A connoisseur by trade, Plymbell was disappointed by the banality of Miss Tell's remark. What was grief? It was a hunger. Not merely personal, emotional, and spiritual; it was physical. Plymbell had been forty-two when his mother died, and he, her only child, had always lived with her. Her skill with money, her jackdaw eye had made the business. The morning she died in hospital he had felt that a cave had been opened inside his body under the ribs, a cave getting larger and colder and emptier. He went out and ate one of the largest meals of his life.

While Miss Tell, a little fleshed already in her tragedy, was still talking, the waiter came to the table with Plymbell's allowance of cheese and biscuits.

Plymbell remembered his grief. "Bring me another portion for my secretary," he said.

"Oh no, not for me," said Miss Tell. She was too dazed by the importance of loss to eat. "I couldn't."

But Polli's waiter had a tired, deaf head. He came back with biscuits for Miss Tell.

Miss Tell looked about the restaurant until the waiter left and then coquettishly she passed her plate to Plymbell. "For you," she said. "I couldn't."

Plymbell thought Miss Tell ill-bred to suggest that he would eat what she did not want. He affected not to notice and gazed over her head, but his white hand had already taken the plate, and in a moment, still looking disparagingly beyond her, in order not to catch her eye, Mr. Plymbell bit into one of Miss Tell's biscuits. Miss Tell was smiling slyly.

After he had eaten her food, Mr. Plymbell looked at Miss Tell with a warmer interest. She had come to work for him in his mother's time, more than fifteen years before. Her hair was still black, her skin was now gray and yellow with a lilac streak on the jaw, there were sharp stains like poor coffee under her eyes. These were brown with a circle of gold in the pupils, and they seemed to burn as if there were a fever in their shadows. Her black coat, her trousers, her cotton blouse were cheap, and even her body seemed to be thin with cheapness. Her speech was awkward, for part of her throat was trying to speak in a refined accent and the effect was half arrogant, half disheartened. Now, as he swallowed the last piece of biscuit, she seemed to him to change. Her eyes were brilliant. She had become quietly a human being.

What is a human being? The chef whom he could see through the hatch was one; Polli, who was looking at the menu by the cash desk, was another; his mother, who had made remarkable ravioli; people like Lady Hackthorpe, who had given such wonderful dinner parties before the war; that circle which the war had scattered and where he had moved from one lunch to the next in a life that rippled to the sound of changing plates that tasted of sauces now never made. These people had been human beings. One knew a human being when the juices flowed over one's teeth. A human being was a creature who fed one. Plymbell moved his jaws. Miss Tell's sly smile went. He looked as though he was going to eat *her*.

"You had better take the top room at the shop," he said. "Take the top room if you have nowhere to live."

"But I haven't found Tiger," Miss Tell said. "He must be starving."

"You won't be alone," said Plymbell. "I sleep at the shop."

Miss Tell considered him. Plymbell could see she was weighing him against Tiger in her mind. He had offered her the room because she had fed him.

"You have had your lunch, I presume," said Plymbell as they walked back to the shop.

"No— I mean yes. Yes, no," said Miss Tell secretively, and again there was the blush like a birthmark on her forehead.

"Where do you go?" said Plymbell, making a shameful inquiry.

"Oh," said Miss Tell defensively, as if it were a question of chastity. "Anywhere. I manage. I vary." And when she said she varied, Miss Tell looked with a virginal importance first one way and then the other.

"That place starves one," said Plymbell indignantly. "One comes out of there some days and one is weak with hunger."

Miss Tell's flush went. She was taken by one of those rages that shake the voices and the bones of unmarried women, as if they were going to shake the nation by the scruff of its neck. "It's wrong, Mr. Plymbell. The government ought to give men more rations. A man needs food. Myself, it never worries me. I never eat. Poor mother used to say, 'Eat, girl, eat.' " A tear came to Miss Tell's right eye, enlarged it and made it liquid, burning, beautiful. "It was funny, I didn't seem to fancy anything. I just pick things over and leave them."

"I never heard of anyone who found the rations too much," said Mr. Plymbell with horror.

"I hardly touch mine since I was bombed out," said Miss Tell primly, and she straightened her thin, once humble body, raised her small bosom, which was ribbed like a wicker basket, gave her hair a touch or two, and looked with delicate resolution at Plymbell. "I sometimes think of giving my ration books away," she said in an offhand way.

Plymbell gaped at the human being in front of him. "Give them away!" he exclaimed. *"Them?"* he said. "Have you got more than one?"

"I've got Father's and Mother's, too."

"But one had gathered that the law required one to surrender the official documents of the deceased," said Plymbell, narrowing his eyes suggestively. His heart had livened, his mouth was watering.

A warm, enticing shamelessness, the conceit, even the voluptuousness, of sin were upon Miss Tell. She moved her erring shoulders, her eyes became larger, her lips drooped. "It's wicked of me," she said.

Plymbell took her thin elbow in his hand and contained his anxiety. "I should be very careful about those ration books. I shouldn't mention it. There was a case in the paper the other day."

They had reached the door of the shop. "How is Lady Hackthorpe?" Miss Tell asked. "Is she still away?"

Miss Tell had gone too far; she was being familiar. Plymbell put up his monocle and did not reply.

A time of torture began for Plymbell when Miss Tell moved in. He invited her to the cellar on the bad nights, but Miss Tell had become lightheaded with fatalism and would not move from her bed on the top floor.

In decency Plymbell had to remain in his bed and take shelter no more. Above him slept the rarest of human beings, as Plymbell conceived human beings—a creature who had three ration books, a woman who was technically three people. He feared for her at every explosion. His mouth watered when he saw her: the woman with three books who did not eat and who thought only of how hungry Tiger must be. If he could have turned himself into a cat!

At one point Plymbell decided that Miss Tell was like Lady Hackthorpe with her furniture; Miss Tell wanted money. He went to the dark corner behind a screen between his own office and the shop, where sometimes she sewed. When he stood by the screen he was nearly on top of her. "If," he said in a high, breaking voice that was strange even to himself, "if you are ever thinking of *selling* your books . . ."

He had made a mistake. Miss Tell was mending and the needle was pointing at him as she stood up. "I couldn't do that," she said. "It is forbidden by the law." And she looked at him strictly.

Plymbell gaped before her hypocrisy. Miss Tell's eyes became larger, deeper, and liquid in the dusk of the corner where she worked. Her chin moved up in a number of amused, resentful movements; her lips moved. Good God, thought Plymbell, is she eating? Her thin arms were slack, her body was inert. She continued to move her dry lips. She leaned her head sideways and raised one eye. Plymbell could not believe what he saw. Miss Tell was plainly telling him: "Yes, I *have* got something in my mouth. It is the desire to be kissed."

Or was he wrong? Plymbell was not a kissing man. His white, demanding face was indeed white with passion, and his lips were shaped for sensuous delicacy, but the passion of the gourmet, the libidinousness of the palate gave him his pallor. He had felt desire, in his way, for Lady Hackthorpe, but it had been consummated in bisques, in crêpes, in *flambées*, in *langouste* done in many manners, in *ailloli*, in bouillabaisse and vintage wines. That passion had been starved, and he was perturbed by Miss Tell's signal. One asks oneself (he reflected, going to his office and considering reproachfully his mother's photograph, which stood on his desk)—one asks oneself whether or not a familiar adage about Nature's abhorrence of a vacuum has not a certain relevance, and indeed whether one would not be justified in coining a vulgar phrase to the effect that when one shuts the front door on Nature, she comes in at the back. Miss Tell was certainly the back; one might call her the scullery of the emotions.

Plymbell lowered his pale eyelids in a flutter of infidelity, unable honestly to face his mother's stare. Her elderly aquiline nose, her close-curled silver hair tipped with a touch of fashionable idiocy off the forehead, her too-jeweled, hawking, grabbing, slapdash face derided him for the languor of the male symptom, and at the same time, with the ratty double-facedness of her sex, spoke sharply about flirtations with employees. Plymbell's eyes lied to her image. All the same, he tried to calm himself by taking a piece of violet notepaper and dashing off a letter to Lady Hackthorpe. Avocado pear, he wrote, whitebait (did she think?), *bœuf bourguignon*, or what about *dindonneau* in those Italian pastes? It was a letter crisp, in his fashion, with the glittering stare of lust. He addressed the envelope, and, telling Miss Tell to post it, Plymbell pulled down the points of his slack waistcoat and felt saved.

So saved that when Miss Tell came back and stood close to his desk, narrow and flat in her horrible trousers, and with her head turned to the window, showing him her profile, Plymbell felt she was satirically flirting with his hunger. Indignantly he got up and, before he knew what he was doing, he put his hand under her shoulder blade and kissed her on the lips.

A small frown came between Miss Tell's eyebrows. Her lips were tight and set. She did not move. "Was that a bill you sent to Lady Hackthorpe?" she asked.

"No," said Plymbell. "A personal letter."

Miss Tell left his office.

Mr. Plymbell wiped his mouth on his handkerchief. He was shocked by himself; even more by the set lips, the closed teeth, the hard chin of Miss Tell; most of all by her impertinence. He had committed a folly for nothing and he had been insulted.

The following morning Plymbell went out on his weekly search for food, but he was too presumptuous for the game. In the coarse world of provisions and the black market, the monocle was too fine. Plymbell lacked the touch; in a long day all he managed to get was four fancy cakes. Miss Tell came out of her dark corner and looked impersonally at him. He was worn out.

"No offal," he said in an appalled, hoarse voice. "No offal in the whole of London."

"Ooh," said Miss Tell, quick as a sparrow. "I got some. Look." And she showed him her disgusting, bloodstained triumph on its piece of newspaper.

Never had Miss Tell seemed so common, so flagrant, so lacking in sensibility, but, also, never had she seemed so desirable. And then, as before, she became limp and neutral and she raised her chin. There were the unmistakable crumb-licking movements of her lips. Plymbell saw her look sideways at him as she turned. Was she inviting him to wipe out the error of the previous day? With one eye on the meat, Plymbell made a step toward her, and in a moment Miss Tell was on him, kissing him, openmouthed and with frenzy, her fingernails in his arms, and pressing herself to him to the bone.

"Sweetbreads," she said. "For you. I never eat them. Let me cook them for you."

An hour later she was knocking at the door of his room and carrying a loaded tray. It was laid, he was glad to notice, for one person only. Plymbell said, "One had forgotten what sweetbreads were."

"It was nothing. I have enjoyed your confidence for fifteen years," said Miss Tell in her poetic style. And the enlarged eyes looked at him with an intimate hunger.

That night, as usual, Plymbell changed into a brilliant dressing gown, and, standing before the mirror, he did his hair, massaging with the fingers, brushing first with the hard ivory brush and then with the soft one. As he looked into the glass, Miss Tell's inquiring face kept floating into it, displacing his own.

"Enjoyed my confidence!" said Plymbell. "The devil she has! What is she up to? What does she want?"

In her bedroom Miss Tell turned out the light, drew back the curtains, and looked into the London black and at the inane triangles of the searchlights. She stood there listening. "Tiger, Tiger," she murmured. "Where are you? Why did you go away from me? I miss you in my bed. Are you hungry? I had a lovely dinner ready for you—sweetbreads. I had to give it to him because you didn't come."

In answer, the hungry siren went like the wail of some monstrous, disembodied Tiger, like all the dead cats of London restless beyond the grave.

Miss Tell drew the curtains and lay down on her bed. "Tiger," she said crossly, "if you don't come tomorrow, I shall give everything to him. He needs it. Not that he deserves it. Filling up the shop with that woman's furniture, storing it free of charge, writing her letters, ruining himself for her. I hate her. I always have. I don't understand him and her, how she gets away with it, owing money all round. She's got a hold—"

The guns broke out. They were like an open declaration of war upon Lady Hackthorpe.

Tiger did not come back, and rabbit was dished up for Plymbell. He kissed Miss Tell a third time. It gave him the agreeable sensation that he was doing something for the war. After the fourth kiss, Plymbell became worried. Miss Tell had mentioned stuffed veal. She had spoken of mushrooms. He had thoughtlessly exceeded in his embrace. He had felt for the first time in his life—voluptuousness; he had discovered how close to eating kissing is, and as he allowed his arm to rest on Miss Tell's lower-class waist, he had had the inadvertent impression of picking up a cutlet in his fingers. Plymbell felt he had done enough for the vanity of Miss Tell. He was in the middle of this alarmed condition when Miss Tell came into his office and turned his alarm to consternation.

"I've come to give my notice," she said in her poetic style.

Plymbell was appalled. "What is wrong, Miss Tell?" he said.

"Nothing's wrong," said Miss Tell. "I feel I am not needed."

"Have I offended you?" said Plymbell suspiciously. "Is it money?"

Miss Tell looked sharply. She was insulted. "No," she said. "Money is of no interest to me. I've got nothing to do. Trade's stopped."

Plymbell made a speech about trade.

"I think I must have got"—Miss Tell searched for a word and lost her poetic touch—"browned off," she said, and blushed. "I'll get a job in a canteen. I like cooking."

Plymbell in a panic saw not one woman but three women leaving him. "But you are cooking for me," he said.

Miss Tell shrugged.

"Oh yes, you are. Miss Tell—be my housekeeper."

Good God, thought Plymbell afterward, so that was all she wanted. I needn't have kissed her at all.

How slowly one learns about human nature, he thought. Here was a woman with one simple desire: to serve him—to slave for him, to stand in queues, to cook, to run his business, do everything. And who, to crown all, did not eat.

"I shall certainly not kiss her again," he said.

At this period of his life, with roofs leaving their buildings and servants leaving their places all round him, Plymbell often reflected guardedly upon his situation. There was, he had often hinted, an art in keeping servants. He appeared, he noted, to have this art. But would he keep it? What was it? Words of his mother's came back to him: "Miss Tell left a better job and higher wages to come to me. This job is more flattering to her self-importance." "Never consider them, never promise; they will despise you. The only way to keep servants is to treat them like hell. Look at Lady Hackthorpe's couple. They'd die for her. They probably will."

Two thousand years of civilization lay in those remarks.

"And never be familiar." Guiltily, he could imagine Lady Hackthorpe putting in her word. As the year passed, as his nourishment improved, the imaginary Lady Hackthorpe rather harped on the point.

There was no doubt about it, Plymbell admitted, he *had* been familiar. But only four times, he protested. And what is a kiss, in an office? At this he could almost hear Lady Hackthorpe laughing, in an insinuating way, that she hardly imagined there could be any question of his going any further.

Plymbell, now full of food, blew up into a temper with the accusing voices. He pitched into Miss Tell. He worked out a plan of timely dissatisfaction. His first attack upon her was made in the shop in the presence of one of the rare customers of those days.

"Why no extra liver this week, Miss Tell? My friend here has got some," he said.

Miss Tell started, then blushed on the forehead. It was, he saw, a blush of pleasure. Public humiliation seemed to delight Miss Tell. He made it harder. "Why no eggs?" he shouted down the stairs, and on another day, as if he had a whip in his hand, "Anyone can get olive oil." Miss Tell smiled and looked a little sideways at him.

Seeing he had not hurt her in public, Plymbell then made a false move. He called her to his room above the shop and decided to "blow her up" privately.

"I can't *live* on fish," he began. But whereas, delighted to be noticed, she listened to his public complaints in the shop, she did not listen in his room. By his second sentence, she had turned her back and wandered to the sofa. From there she went to his writing table, trailing a finger on it.

She was certainly not listening. In the middle of his speech and as his astounded, colorless eyes followed her, she stopped and pointed through the double doors where his bedroom was and she pointed to the Hepplewhite bed.

"Is that Lady Hackthorpe's, too?" she said.

"Yes," said Plymbell, off his guard.

"Why do you have it up here?" she said rudely.

"Because I like it," said Plymbell, snubbing her.

"I think four-posters are unhealthy," said Miss Tell, and circled with meandering impertinence to the window and looked out onto the street. "That old man," she said, admitting the vulgar world into the room, "is always going by."

Plymbell raised his eyebrows; they would have gone higher only with difficulty.

Miss Tell shrugged at the window and considered the bed again across the space of two rooms. Then, impersonally, she made a speech. "I never married," she said. "I have been friendly but not married. One great friend went away. There was no agreement, nothing said, he didn't write and I didn't write. In those cases I sympathize with the wife, but I wondered when he didn't communicate. I didn't know whether it was over or not over, and when you don't know, it isn't satisfactory. I don't say it was anything, but I would have liked to know whether it was or not. I never mention it to anyone."

"Oh," said Plymbell.

"It upset Dad," said Miss Tell, and of that she was proud.

"I don't follow," said Plymbell. He wanted to open the window and let Miss Tell's private life out.

"It's hard to describe something unsatisfactory," said Miss Tell. And then "Dad was conventional."

Mr. Plymbell shuddered.

"Are you interested?" asked Miss Tell.

"Please, please go on," said Plymbell.

"I have been 'the other woman' three times," said Miss Tell primly.

Plymbell put up his monocle, but as far as he could judge, all Miss Tell had done was make a public statement. He could think of no reply. His mind drifted. Suddenly he heard the voice of Miss Tell again, trembling, passionate, raging as it had been once before, at Polli's, attacking him.

"She uses you," Miss Tell was saying. "She puts all her rubbish into your shop, she fills up your flat. She won't let you sell it. She hasn't paid you. Storage is the dearest thing in London. You could make a profit, you would turn over your stock. Now is the time to buy, Dad said. . . ."

Plymbell picked up his paper.

"Lady Hackthorpe," explained Miss Tell, and he saw her face, small-mouthed and sick and shaking with jealousy.

"Lady Hackthorpe has gone to America," Plymbell said in his snubbing voice.

Miss Tell's rage had spent itself. "If you were not so horrible to me, I would tell you an idea," she said.

"Horrible? My dear Miss Tell," said Mr. Plymbell, leaning back as far as he could in his chair.

"It doesn't matter," said Miss Tell, and she walked away. "When is Lady Hackthorpe coming back?" she said.

"After the war, I suppose," said Plymbell.

"Oh," said Miss Tell, without belief.

"What is your idea?"

"Oh no. It was about lunch. At Polli's. It is nothing," said Miss Tell.

"Lunch," said Plymbell with a start, dropping his eyeglass. "What about lunch?" And his mouth stayed open.

Miss Tell turned about and approached him. "No, it's unsatisfactory," said Miss Tell. She gave a small laugh and then made the crumb movements with her chin.

"Come here," commanded Plymbell. "What idea about lunch?"

Miss Tell did not move, and so he got up, in a panic now. A mad suspicion came to him that Polli's had been bombed, that someone—perhaps Miss Tell herself—was going to take his lunch away from him. Miss Tell did it down again. Miss Tell came and sat on the arm of his chair.

"Nothing," she said, looking into his eyes for a long time and then turning away. "You have been horrible to me for ten months and thirteen days. You know you have." Her back was to him.

Slices of pork, he saw, mutton, beef. He went through a nightmare that he arrived at Polli's late, all the customers were inside, and the glass doors were locked. The headwaiter was standing there refusing to open. Miss Tell's unnourished back made him think of this. He did no more than put his hand on her shoulder, as slight as a chicken bone, and as he did so, he seemed to hear a sharp warning snap from Lady Hackthorpe. "Gus," Lady Hackthorpe seemed to say, "what are you doing? Are you mad? Don't you know why Miss Tell had to leave her last place?" But Lady Hackthorpe's words were smothered. A mere touch—without intention on Plymbell's part—had impelled Miss Tell to slide backward onto his lap.

"How have I been horrid to you?" said Plymbell, forgetting to put inverted commas round the word "horrid."

"You know," said Miss Tell.

"What was this idea of yours," he said quietly, and he kissed her neck. "No, no," she said, and moved her head to the other side of his neck. There was suddenly a sound that checked them both. Her shoe fell off. And then an extraordinary thing happened to Plymbell. The sight of Miss Tell's foot without its shoe did it. At fifty, he felt the first indubitable symptom. A scream went off inside his head—Lady Hackthorpe nagging him about some man she had known who had gone to bed with his housekeeper. "Ruin," Lady Hackthorpe was saying.

"About lunch—it was a good idea," Miss Tell said tenderly into his collar.

But it was not until three in the morning that Miss Tell told Plymbell what the idea was.

And so, every weekday, there is the modest example of Mr. Plymbell's daily luncheon. The waiter takes the empty soup plate away from Miss Tell and presently comes forward with the meat and vegetables. He scrapes them off his serving dish onto her plate. She keeps her head lowered for a while, and then, with a glance to see if other customers are looking, she lifts the plate over to Mr. Plymbell's place. He, of course, does not notice. Then, absently, he settles down to eat her food. While he does this, he mutters, "What did you get?" She nods at her stuffed basket and answers. Mr. Plymbell eats two lunches. While this goes on, Miss Tell looks at him. She is in a strong position now. Hunger is the basis of life and, for her, a great change has taken place. The satisfactory has occurred.

For two or three years have passed. Letters from America have come to the shop. Lady Hackthorpe is talking about cutting her American losses and coming back. On the one hand (Plymbell clearly sees), there is civilization, there are all those sauces; on the other, there is a woman with those ration books, not merely a human being—in Plymbell's sense of the word—but three human beings.

Miss Tell has put it plainly: "If that woman comes in here, out I go."

It is bad enough when Lady Hackthorpe sends food parcels, but Plymbell has been able to hide two of them and eat the contents secretly. He has failed, though, to think of any way of hiding Lady Hackthorpe. Blatancy is her life. The only plan that has occurred to Plymbell is one he tries out on the occasional foreign customer.

"There are times," the speech runs, "when one is inclined to indite a brief but cogent epistle to any valued friend one may, hypothetically, have in lands less corrupted by necessity than one's own, making the possibly disloyal suggestion that they postpone their return to their native hearth until what one can only call the war on the stomach has been, to use a vulgarism, mopped up. One is saddled with degradation; one hardly cares to be observed positively enjoying."

Miss Tell has heard this speech once or twice. All she wants, she says, is to see the letter with her own eyes and post it herself. She wants to make sure, as well, that he has mentioned selling the furniture. It is the only unsatisfactory thing left.

1952

*"I think I speak for my entire generation when I say,
'Yes, I will have another drink.'"*

THE SORROWS OF GIN

JOHN CHEEVER

It was a Sunday afternoon, and from her bedroom Amy could hear the Beardens coming in, followed a little while later by the Farquarsons and the Parminters. She went on reading *Black Beauty* until she felt in her bones that they might be eating something good. Then she closed her book and went down the stairs. The living-room door was shut, but through it she could hear the noise of loud talk and laughter. They must have been gossiping or worse, because they all stopped talking when she entered the room.

"Hi, Amy," Mr. Farquarson said.

"Mr. Farquarson spoke to you, Amy," her father said.

"Hello, Mr. Farquarson," she said. By standing outside the group for a minute, until they had resumed their conversation, and then by slipping past Mrs. Farquarson, she was able to swoop down on the nut dish and take a handful.

"Amy!" Mr. Lawton said.

"I'm sorry, Daddy," she said, retreating out of the circle, toward the piano.

"Put those nuts back," he said.

"I've handled them, Daddy," she said.

"Well, pass the nuts, dear," her mother said sweetly. "Perhaps someone else would like nuts."

Amy filled her mouth with the nuts she had taken, returned to the coffee table, and passed the nut dish.

"Thank you, Amy," they said, taking a peanut or two.

"How do you like your new school, Amy?" Mrs. Bearden asked.

"I like it," Amy said. "I like private schools better than public schools. It isn't so much like a factory."

"What grade are you in?" Mr. Bearden asked.

"Fourth," she said.

Her father took Mr. Parminter's glass and his own, and got up to go into the dining room and refill them. She fell into the chair he had left vacant.

"Don't sit in your father's chair, Amy," her mother said, not realizing that Amy's legs were worn out from riding a bicycle, while her father had done nothing but sit down all day.

As she walked toward the French doors, she heard her mother beginning to talk about the new cook. It was a good example of the interesting things they found to talk about.

"You'd better put your bicycle in the garage," her father said, returning with the fresh drinks. "It looks like rain."

Amy went out onto the terrace and looked at the sky, but it was not very cloudy, it wouldn't rain, and his advice, like all the advice he gave her, was superfluous. They were always at her. "Put your bicycle away." "Open the door for Grandmother, Amy." "Feed the cat." "Do your homework." "Pass the nuts." "Help Mrs. Bearden with her parcels." "Amy, please try and take more pains with your appearance." She looked at them through the glass doors. Her mother was wearing the red stole that matched the window curtains, but it didn't conceal the fact that the zipper on her dress was broken. Her father was wearing the gray flannel suit that had belonged to Uncle Robert before he died. She could never understand how a man as rich and successful as her father—a vice-president in charge of distribution—could go around wearing the clothes of a dead man. It made her sick. Mrs. Farquarson had big, white, doughy legs, and she was wearing tennis shorts, so you could see how ugly her legs were.

They all stood, and her father came to the door and called her. "We're going over to the Parminters' for supper," he said. "Cook's here, so you won't be alone. Be sure and go to bed at eight like a good girl. And come and kiss me good night."

After their cars had driven off, Amy wandered through the kitchen to the cook's bedroom beyond it and knocked on the door. "Come in," a voice said, and when Amy entered, she found the cook, whose name was Rosemary, in her bathrobe, reading the Bible. Rosemary smiled at Amy. Her smile was sweet and her old eyes were blue. "Your parents have gone out again?" she asked. Amy said that they had, and the old woman invited her to sit down. "They do seem to enjoy themselves, don't they? During the four days I've been here, they've been out every night, or had people in." She put the Bible face down on her lap and smiled, but not at Amy. "Of course, the drinking that goes on here is all sociable, and what your parents do is none of my business, is it? I worry about drink more than most people, because of my poor sister. My poor sister drank too much. For ten years, I went to visit her on Sunday afternoons, and most of the time she was non compos mentis. Sometimes I'd find her huddled up on the floor with one or two sherry bottles empty beside her. Sometimes she'd seem sober enough to a stranger, but I could tell in a second by the way she spoke her words that she'd drunk enough not to be herself any more. Now my poor sister is gone, I don't have anyone to visit at all."

"What happened to your sister?" Amy asked.

"She was a lovely person, with a peaches-and-cream complexion and fair hair," Rosemary said. "Gin makes some people gay—it makes them laugh and cry—but with my sister it only made her sullen and withdrawn. When she was drinking, she would retreat into herself. Drink made her contrary. If I'd say the weather was fine, she'd tell me I was wrong. If I'd say it was raining, she'd say it was clearing. She'd correct me about everything I said, however small it was. She died in Bellevue Hospital one summer when I was working in Maine. She was the only family I had."

The directness with which Rosemary spoke had the effect on Amy of making her feel grown, and for once politeness came to her easily. "You must miss your sister a great deal," she said.

"I was just sitting here now thinking about her. She was in service, like me, and it's lonely work. You're always surrounded by a family, and yet you're never a part of it. Your pride is often hurt. The Madams seem condescending and inconsiderate. I'm not blaming the ladies I've worked for. It's just in the nature of the relationship. They order chicken salad, and you get up before dawn to get ahead of yourself, and just as you've finished the chicken salad, they change their minds and want crabmeat soup."

"My mother changes her mind all the time," Amy said.

"Sometimes you're in a country place with nobody else in help. You're tired, but not too tired to feel lonely. You go out onto the servants' porch when the pots and pans are done, planning to enjoy God's creation, and although the front of the house may have a fine view of the lake or the mountains, the view from the back is never much. But there is the sky and the trees and the stars and the birds singing and the pleasure of resting your feet. But then you hear them in the front of the house, laughing and talking with their guests and their sons and daughters. If you're new and they whisper, you can be sure they're talking about you. That takes all the pleasure out of the evening."

"Oh," Amy said.

"I've worked in all kinds of places—places where there were eight or nine in help and places where I was expected to burn the rubbish myself, on winter nights, and shovel the snow. In a house where there's a lot in help, there's usually some devil among them—some old butler or parlor maid—who tries to make your life miserable from the beginning. 'The Madam doesn't like it this way,' and 'The Madam doesn't like it that way,' and 'I've been with the Madam for twenty years,' they tell you. It takes a diplomat to get along. Then there is the rooms they give you, and every one of them I've ever seen is cheerless. If you have a bottle in your suitcase, it's a terrible temptation in the beginning not to take a drink to raise your spirits. But I have a strong character. It was different with my poor sister. She used to complain about nervousness, but, sitting here thinking about her tonight, I wonder if she suffered from nervousness at all. I wonder if she didn't make it all up. I wonder if she just wasn't meant to be in service. Toward the end, the only work she could get was out in the country, where nobody else would go, and she never lasted much more than a week or two. She'd take a little gin for her nervousness, then a little for her tiredness, and when she'd drunk her own bottle and everything she could steal, they'd hear about it in the front part of the house. There was usually a scene, and my poor sister always liked to have the last word. Oh, if I had had my way, they'd be a law against it! It's not my business to advise you to take anything from your father, but I'd be proud of you if you'd empty his gin bottle into the sink now and then—the filthy stuff! But it's made me feel better to talk with you, sweetheart. It's made me not miss my poor sister so much. Now I'll read a little more in my Bible, and then I'll get you some supper."

The Lawtons had had a bad year with cooks—there had been five of them. The arrival of Rosemary had made Marcia Lawton think back to a vague theory of dispensations; she had suffered, and now she was being rewarded. Rosemary was clean, industrious, and cheerful, and her table—as the Lawtons said—was just like the Chambord. On Wednesday night after dinner, she took the train to New York, promising to return on the evening train Thursday. Thursday morning, Marcia went into the cook's room. It was a distasteful but a habitual precaution. The absence of anything personal in the room—a package of cigarettes, a fountain pen, an alarm clock, a radio, or anything else that could tie the old woman to the place—gave her the uneasy feeling that she was being deceived, as she had so often been deceived by cooks in the past. She opened the closet door and saw a single uniform hanging there and, on the closet floor, Rosemary's old suitcase and the white shoes she wore in the kitchen. The suitcase was locked, but when Marcia lifted it, it seemed to be nearly empty.

Mr. Lawton and Amy drove to the station after dinner on Thursday to meet the 8:16 train. The top of the car was down, and the brisk air, the starlight, and the company of her father made the little girl feel kindly toward the world. The railroad station in Shady Hill resembled the railroad stations in old movies she had seen on television, where detectives and spies, bluebeards and their trusting victims, were met to be driven off to remote country estates. Amy liked the station, particularly toward dark. She imagined that the people who traveled on the locals were engaged on errands that were more urgent and sinister than commuting. Except when there was a heavy fog or a snowstorm, the club car that her father traveled on seemed to have the gloss and the monotony of the rest of his life. The locals that ran at odd hours belonged to a world of deeper contrasts, where she would like to live.

They were a few minutes early, and Amy got out of the car and stood on the platform. She wondered what the fringe of string that hung above the tracks at either end of the station was for, but she knew enough not to ask her father, because he wouldn't be able to tell her. She could hear the train before it came into view, and the noise excited her and made her happy. When the train drew in to the station and stopped, she looked in the lighted windows for Rosemary and didn't see her. Mr. Lawton got out of the car and joined Amy on the platform. They could see the conductor bending over someone in a seat, and finally the cook rose. She clung to the conductor as he led her out to the platform of the car, and she was crying. "Like peaches and cream," Amy heard her sob. "A lovely, lovely person." The conductor spoke to her kindly, put his arm around her shoulders, and eased her down the steps. Then the train pulled out, and she stood there drying her tears. "Don't say a word, Mr. Lawton," she said, "and I won't say anything." She held out a small paper bag. "Here's a present for you, little girl."

"Thank you, Rosemary," Amy said. She looked into the paper bag and saw that it contained several packets of Japanese water flowers.

Rosemary walked toward the car with the caution of someone who can hardly find the way in the dim light. A sour smell came from her. Her best coat was spotted with mud and ripped in the back. Mr. Lawton told Amy to get in the back seat of the car, and made the cook sit in front, beside him. He slammed the car door shut after her angrily, and then went around to the driver's seat and drove home. Rosemary reached into her handbag and took out a Coca-Cola bottle with a cork stopper and took a drink. Amy could tell by the smell that the Coca-Cola bottle was filled with gin.

"Rosemary!" Mr. Lawton said.

"I'm lonely," the cook said. "I'm lonely, and I'm afraid, and it's all I've got."

He said nothing more until he had turned in to their drive and brought the car around to the back door. "Go and get your suitcase, Rosemary," he said. "I'll wait here in the car."

As soon as the cook had staggered into the house, he told Amy to go in by the front door. "Go upstairs to your room and get ready for bed."

Her mother called down the stairs when Amy came in, to ask if Rosemary had returned. Amy didn't answer. She went to the bar, took an open gin bottle, and emptied it into the pantry sink. She was nearly crying when she encountered her mother in the living room, and told her that her father was taking the cook back to the station.

When Amy came home from school the next day, she found a heavy, black-haired woman cleaning the living room. The car Mr. Lawton usually drove to the station was at the garage for a checkup, and Amy drove to the station with her mother to meet him. As he came across the station platform, she could tell, by the lack of color in his face, that he had had a hard day. He kissed her mother, touched Amy on the head, and got behind the wheel.

"You know," her mother said, "there's something terribly wrong with the guest-room shower."

"Damn it, Marcia," he said, "I wish you wouldn't always greet me with bad news!"

His grating voice oppressed Amy, and she began to fiddle with the button that raised and lowered the window.

"Stop that, Amy!" he said.

"Oh, well, the shower isn't important," her mother said. She laughed weakly.

"When I got back from San Francisco last week," he said, "you couldn't wait to tell me that we need a new oil-burner."

"Well, I've got a part-time cook. That's good news."

"Is she a lush?" her father asked.

"Don't be disagreeable, dear. She'll get us some dinner and wash the dishes and take the bus home. We're going to the Farquarsons'."

"I'm really too tired to go anywhere," he said.

"Who's going to take care of me?" Amy asked.

"You always have a good time at the Farquarsons'," her mother said.

"Well, let's leave early," he said.

"Who's going to take care of me?" Amy asked.

"Mrs. Henlein," her mother said.

When they got home, Amy went over to the piano.

Her father washed his hands in the bathroom off the hall and then went to the bar. He came into the living room holding the empty gin bottle. "What's her name?" he asked.

"Ruby," her mother said.

"She's exceptional. She's drunk a quart of gin on her first day."

"Oh dear!" her mother said. "Well, let's not make any trouble now."

"Everybody is drinking my liquor," her father shouted, "and I am Goddamned sick and tired of it!"

"There's plenty of gin in the closet," her mother said. "Open another bottle."

"We paid that gardener three dollars an hour and all he did was sneak in here and drink up my Scotch. The sitter we had before we got Mrs. Henlein used to water my bourbon, and I don't have to remind you about Rosemary. The cook before Rosemary not only drank everything in my liquor cabinet but she drank all the rum, kirsch, sherry, and wine that we had in the kitchen for cooking. Then, there's that Polish woman we had last summer. Even that old laundress. *And* the painters. I think they must put some kind of a mark on my door. I think the agency must have checked me off as an easy touch."

"Well, let's get through dinner, and then you can speak to her."

"The hell with that!" he said. "I'm not going to encourage people to rob me. *Ruby!*" He shouted her name several times, but she didn't answer. Then she appeared in the dining-room doorway, wearing her hat and coat.

"I'm sick," she said. Amy could see that she was frightened.

"I should think you would be," her father said.

"I'm sick," the cook mumbled, "and I can't find anything around here, and I'm going home."

"Good," he said. "Good! I'm through with paying people to come in here and drink my liquor."

The cook started out the front way, and Marcia Lawton followed her into the front hall to pay her something. Amy had watched this scene from the piano bench, a position that was withdrawn but that still gave her a good view. She saw her father get a fresh bottle of gin and make a shaker of martinis. He looked very unhappy.

"Well," her mother said when she came back into the room. "You know, she didn't look drunk."

"Please don't argue with me, Marcia," her father said. He poured two cocktails, said "Cheers," and drank a little. "We can get some dinner at Orfeo's," he said.

"I suppose so," her mother said. "I'll rustle up something for Amy." She went into the kitchen, and Amy opened her music to "Reflets d'Automne." "COUNT," her music teacher had written. "COUNT and lightly, lightly . . ." Amy began to play. Whenever she made a mistake, she said "Darn it!" and started at the beginning again. In the middle of "Reflets d'Automne" it struck her that *she* was the one who had emptied the gin bottle. Her perplexity was so intense that she stopped playing, but her feelings did not go beyond perplexity, although she did not have the strength to continue playing the piano. Her mother relieved her. "Your supper's in the kitchen, dear," she said. "And you can take a popsicle out of the deep freeze for dessert. Just one."

Marcia Lawton held her empty glass toward her husband, who filled it from the shaker. Then she went upstairs. Mr. Lawton remained in the room, and, studying her father closely, Amy saw that his tense look had begun to soften. He did not seem so unhappy any more, and as she passed him on her way to the kitchen, he smiled at her tenderly and patted her on the top of the head.

When Amy had finished her supper, eaten her popsicle, and exploded the bag it came in, she returned to the piano and played "Chopsticks" for a while. Her father came downstairs in his evening clothes, put his drink on the mantelpiece, and went to the French doors to look at his terrace and his garden. Amy noticed that the transformation that had begun with a softening of his features was even more advanced. At last, he seemed happy. Amy wondered if he was drunk, although his walk was not unsteady. If anything, it was more steady.

Her parents never achieved the kind of rolling, swinging gait that she saw impersonated by a tightrope walker in the circus each year while the band struck up "Show Me the Way to Go Home" and that she liked to imitate herself sometimes. She liked to turn round and round and round on the lawn, until, staggering and a little sick, she would whoop "I'm drunk! I'm a drunken man!" and reel over the grass, righting herself as she was about to fall and finding herself not unhappy at having lost for a second her ability to see the world. But she had never seen her parents like that. She had never seen them hanging on to a lamppost and singing and reeling, but she had seen them fall down. They were never indecorous—they seemed to get more decorous and formal the more they drank—but sometimes her father would get up to fill everybody's glass and he would walk straight enough but his shoes would seem to stick to the carpet. And sometimes, when he got to the dining-room door, he would miss it by a foot or more. Once, she had seen him walk into the wall with such force that he collapsed onto the floor and broke most of the glasses he was carrying. One or two people laughed, but the laughter was not general or hearty, and most of them pretended that he had not fallen down at all. When her father got to his feet, he went right on to the bar as if nothing had happened. Amy had once seen Mrs. Farquarson miss the chair she was about to sit in, by a foot, and thump down onto the floor, but nobody laughed then, and they pretended that Mrs. Farquarson hadn't fallen down at all. They seemed like actors in a play. In the school play, when you knocked over a paper tree you were supposed to pick it up without showing what you were doing, so that you would not spoil the illusion of being in a deep forest, and that was the way *they* were when somebody fell down.

Now her father had that stiff, funny walk that was so different from the way he tramped up and down the station platform in the morning, and she could see that he was looking for something. He was looking for his drink. It was right on the mantelpiece, but he didn't look there. He looked on all the tables in the living room. Then he went out onto the terrace and looked there, and then he came back into the living room and looked on all the tables again. Then he went back onto the terrace, and then back over the living-room tables, looking three times in the same place, although he was always telling her to look intelligently when she lost her sneakers or her raincoat. "Look for it, Amy," he was always saying. "Try and remember where you left it. I can't buy you a new raincoat every time it rains." Finally he gave up and poured himself a cocktail in another glass. "I'm going to get Mrs. Henlein," he told Amy, as if this were an important piece of information.

Amy's only feeling for Mrs. Henlein was indifference, and when her father returned with the sitter, Amy thought of the nights, stretching into weeks—the years, almost—when she had been cooped up with Mrs. Henlein. Mrs. Henlein was very polite and was always telling Amy what was ladylike and what was not. Mrs. Henlein also always wanted to know where Amy's parents were going and what kind of a party it was, although it was none of her business. She always sat down on the sofa as if she owned the place, and talked about people she had never even been introduced to, and asked Amy to bring her the newspaper, although she had no authority at all.

When Marcia Lawton came down, Mrs. Henlein wished her good evening. "Have a lovely party," she called after the Lawtons as they went out the door. Then she turned to Amy. "Where are your parents going, sweetheart?"

"I don't know," Amy said.

"But you must know, sweetheart. Put on your thinking cap and try and remember. Are they going to the club?"

"No," Amy said.

"I wonder if they could be going to the Trenchers'," Mrs. Henlein said. "The Trenchers' house was lighted up when we came by."

"They're not going to the Trenchers'," Amy said. "They hate the Trenchers."

"Well, where are they going, sweetheart?" Mrs. Henlein asked.

"They're going to the Farquarsons'," Amy said.

"Well, that's all I wanted to know, sweetheart," Mrs. Henlein said. "Now get me the newspaper and hand it to me politely. *Politely*," she said, as Amy approached her with the paper. "It don't mean anything when you do things for your elders unless you do them politely." She put on her glasses and began to read the paper.

Amy went upstairs to her room. In a glass on her table were the Japanese flowers that Rosemary had brought her, blooming stalely in water that was colored pink from the dyes. Amy went down the back stairs and through the kitchen into the dining room. Her father's cocktail things were spread over the bar. She emptied the gin bottle into the pantry sink and then put it back where she had found it. It was too late to ride her bicycle and too early to go to bed, and she knew that if she got anything interesting on the television, like a murder, Mrs. Henlein would make her turn it off. Then she remembered that her father had brought her home from his trip west a book about horses, and she ran cheerfully up the back stairs to read her new book.

It was after two when the Lawtons returned. Mrs. Henlein, asleep on the living-room sofa dreaming about a dusty attic, was awakened by their voices in the hall. Marcia Lawton paid her, and thanked her, and asked if anyone had called, and then went upstairs. Mr. Lawton was in the dining room, rattling the bottles around. Mrs. Henlein, anxious to get into her own bed and back to sleep, prayed that he wasn't going to pour himself another drink, as they so often did. She was driven home night after night by drunken gentlemen. He stood in the door of the dining room, holding an empty bottle in his hand. "You must be stinking, Mrs. Henlein," he said.

"Hmm," she said. She didn't understand.

"You drank a full quart of gin," he said.

The lackluster old woman—half between wakefulness and sleep—gathered together her bones and groped for her gray hair. It was in her nature to collect stray cats, pile the bathroom up to the ceiling with interesting and valuable newspapers, rouge, talk to herself, sleep in her underwear in case of fire, quarrel over the price of soup bones, and have it circulated around the neighborhood that when she finally died in her dusty junk heap, the mattress would be full of bankbooks and the pillow stuffed with hundred-dollar bills. She had resisted all these rich temptations in order to appear a lady, and she was repaid by being called a common thief. She began to scream at him.

"You take that back, Mr. Lawton! You take back every one of those words you just said! I never stole anything in my whole life, and nobody in my family ever stole anything, and I don't have to stand here and be insulted by a drunk man. Why, as for drinking, I haven't drunk enough to fill an eyeglass for twenty-five years. Mr. Henlein took me to a place of refreshment twenty-five years ago, and I drank two Manhattan cocktails that made me so sick and dizzy that I've never liked the stuff ever since. How dare you speak to me like this! Calling me a thief and a drunken woman! Oh, you disgust me—you disgust me in your ignorance of all the trouble I've had. Do you know what I had for Christmas dinner last year? I had a bacon sandwich. Son of a bitch!" She began to weep. "I'm glad I said it!" she screamed. "It's the first time I've used a dirty word in my whole life and I'm glad I said it. Son of a bitch!" A sense of liberation, as if she stood at the bow of a great ship, came over her. "I lived in this neighborhood my whole life. I can remember when it was full of good farming people and there was fish in the rivers. My father had four acres of sweet meadowland and a name that was known far and wide, and on my mother's side I'm descended from patroons, Dutch nobility. My mother was the spit and image of Queen Wilhelmina. You think you can get away with insulting me, but you're very, very, very much mistaken." She went to the telephone and, picking up the receiver, screamed, "Police! Police! Police! This is Mrs. Henlein, and I'm over at the Lawtons'. He's drunk, and he's calling me insulting names, and I want you to come over here and arrest him!"

The voices woke Amy, and, lying in her bed, she perceived vaguely the pitiful corruption of the adult world; how crude and frail it was, like a piece of worn burlap, patched with stupidities and mistakes, useless and ugly, and yet they never saw its worthlessness, and when you pointed it out to them, they were indignant. But as the voices went on and she heard the cry "Police! Police!" she was frightened. She did not see how they could arrest her, although they could find her fingerprints on the empty bottle, but it was not her own danger that frightened her but the collapse, in the middle of the night, of her father's house. It was all her fault, and when she heard her father speaking into the extension telephone in the library, she felt sunk in guilt. Her father tried to be good and kind—oh, she knew he never meant to be anything else—and, remembering the expensive illustrated book about horses that he had brought her from the West, she had to set her teeth to keep from crying. She covered her head with a pillow and realized miserably that she would have to go away. She had plenty of friends from the time when they used to live in New York, or she could spend the night in the park or hide in a museum. She would have to go away.

"Good morning," her father said at breakfast. "Ready for a good day!" Cheered by the swelling light in the sky, by the recollection of the manner in which he had handled Mrs. Henlein and kept the police from coming, refreshed by his sleep, and pleased at the thought of playing golf, Mr. Lawton spoke with feeling, but the words seemed to Amy offensive and fatuous; they took away her appetite, and she slumped over her cereal bowl, stirring it with a spoon. "Don't slump, Amy," he said. Then she remembered the night, the screaming, the resolve to go. His cheerfulness refreshed her memory. Her decision was settled. She had a ballet lesson at ten, and she was going to have lunch with Lillian Towele. Then she would leave.

Children prepare for a sea voyage with a toothbrush and a Teddy bear; they equip themselves for a trip around the world with a pair of odd socks, a conch shell, and a thermometer; books and stones and peacock feathers, candy bars, tennis balls, soiled handkerchiefs, and skeins of old string appear to them to be the necessities of travel, and Amy packed, that afternoon, with the impulsiveness of her kind. She was late coming home from lunch, and her getaway was delayed, but she didn't mind. She could catch one of the late-afternoon locals; one of the cooks' trains. Her father was playing golf and her mother was off somewhere. A part-time worker was cleaning the living room. When Amy had finished packing, she went into her parents' bathroom and flushed the toilet. While the water murmured, she took a twenty-dollar bill from her mother's desk. Then she went downstairs and left the house and walked around Blenhollow Circle and down Alewives Lane to the station. No regrets or goodbyes formed in her mind. She went over the names of the friends she had in the city, in case she decided not to spend the night in a museum. When she opened the door of the waiting room, Mr. Flanagan, the stationmaster, was poking his coal fire. "It's Amy Lawton," he said, without turning around.

"Yes."

"You know," he said, "I *felt* it was you. You never come in here, do you, except to get some gum out of the machine and get weighed, and yet just as I was poking my fire, it came to my mind that Amy Lawton was going to step into the waiting room. It's second sight. I can feel things before they happen."

"I want to buy a ticket to New York," Amy said.

"One-way or round-trip?"

"One-way, please."

Mr. Flanagan went through the door into the ticket office and raised the glass window. "I'm afraid I haven't got a half-fare ticket for you, Amy," he said. "I'll have to write one."

"That's all right," she said. She put the twenty-dollar bill on the counter.

"And in order to change that," he said, "I'll have to go over to the other side. Here's the four-thirty-two coming in now, but you'll be able to get the five-ten." She didn't protest, and went and sat beside her cardboard suitcase, which was printed with European hotel and place names. When the local had come and gone, Mr. Flanagan shut his glass window and walked over the footbridge to the northbound platform and called the Lawtons'. Mr. Lawton had just come in from his game and was mixing himself a cocktail. "I think your daughter's planning to take some kind of a trip," Mr. Flanagan said.

It was dark by the time Mr. Lawton got down to the station. He saw his daughter through the station window. The girl sitting on the bench, the rich names on her paper suitcase, touched him as it was in her power to touch him only when she seemed helpless or when she was very sick. Someone had walked over his grave! He shivered with longing, he felt his skin coarsen as when, driving home late and alone, a shower of leaves on the wind crossed the beam of his headlights, liberating him for a second at the most from the literal symbols of his life—the buttonless shirts, the vouchers and bank statements, the order blanks, and the empty glasses. He seemed to listen—God knows for what. Commands, drums, the crackle of signal fires, the music of the glockenspiel—how sweet it sounds on the Alpine air—singing from a tavern in the pass, the honking of wild swans; he seemed to smell the salt air in the churches of Venice. Then, as it was with the leaves, the power of her figure to trouble him was ended; his goose-flesh vanished. He was himself. Oh, why should she want to run away? Travel—and who knew better than a man who spent three days of every fortnight on the road—was a world of overheated plane cabins and repetitious magazines, where even the coffee, even the champagne, tasted of plastics. How could he teach her that home sweet home was the best place of all?

1953

"What have we here? The gastronomic equivalent of war?"

THE JAGUAR SUN

ITALO CALVINO

"Oaxaca" is pronounced "Wa*h*aka." Originally, the hotel where we were staying had been the Convent of Santa Catalina. The first thing we noticed was a painting in a little room leading to the bar. The bar was called Las Novicias. The painting was a large, dark canvas that portrayed a young nun and an old priest standing side by side; their hands, slightly apart from their sides, almost touched. The figures were rather stiff for an eighteenth-century picture; the painting had the somewhat crude grace characteristic of Colonial art, but it conveyed a distressing sensation, like an ache of contained suffering.

The lower part of the painting was filled by a long caption, written in cramped lines in an angular, italic hand, white on black. The words devoutly celebrated the life and death of the two characters, who had been chaplain and abbess of the convent (she, of noble birth, had entered it as a novice at the age of eighteen). The reason for their being painted together was the extraordinary love (this word, in the pious Spanish prose, appeared charged with ultraterrestrial yearning) that had bound the abbess and her confessor for thirty years, a love so great (the word in its spiritual sense sublimated but did not erase the physical emotion) that when the priest came to die, the abbess, twenty years younger, in the space of a single day fell ill and literally expired of love (the word blazed with a truth in which all meanings converge), to join him in Heaven.

Olivia, whose Spanish is better than mine, helped me decipher the story, suggesting to me the translation of some obscure expressions, and these words proved to be the only ones we exchanged during and after the reading, as if we had found ourselves in the presence of a drama, or of a happiness, that made any comment out of place. Something intimidated us—or, rather, frightened us, or, more precisely, filled us with a kind of uneasiness. So I will try to describe what I felt: the sense of a lack, a consuming void. What Olivia was thinking, since she remained silent, I cannot guess.

Then Olivia spoke. She said, "I would like to eat *chiles en nogada.*"

And, walking like somnambulists, not quite sure we were touching the ground, we headed for the dining room.

In the best moments of a couple's life, it happens: I immediately reconstructed the train of Olivia's thought, with no need of further speech, because the same sequence of associations had unrolled in my mind, though in a more foggy, murky way. Without her, I would never have gained awareness of it.

Our trip through Mexico had already lasted over a week. A few days earlier, in Tepotzotlán, in a restaurant whose tables were set among the orange trees of another convent's cloister, we had savored dishes prepared (at least, so we were told) according to the traditional recipes of the nuns. We had eaten a *tamal de elote*—a fine semolina of sweet corn, that is, with ground pork and very hot pepper, all steamed in a bit of corn husk—and then *chiles en nogada*, which were reddish brown, somewhat wrinkled little peppers, swimming in a walnut sauce whose harshness and bitter aftertaste were drowned in a creamy, sweetish surrender.

After that, for us, the thought of nuns called up the flavors of an elaborate and bold cuisine, bent on making the flavors' highest notes vibrate, juxtaposing them in modulations, in chords, and especially in dissonances that would assert themselves as an incomparable experience—a point of no return, an absolute possession exercised on the receptivity of all the senses.

The Mexican friend who had accompanied us on that excursion, Salustiano Velazco by name, in answering Olivia's inquiries about these recipes of conventual gastronomy, lowered his voice as if confiding indelicate secrets to us. It was his way of speaking—or, rather, one of his ways; the copious information Salustiano supplied (about the history and customs and nature of his country his erudition was inexhaustible) was either stated emphatically like a war proclamation or slyly insinuated as if it were charged with all sorts of implied meanings.

Olivia remarked that such dishes involved hours and hours of work and, even before that, a long series of experiments and adjustments. "Did these nuns spend their whole day in the kitchen?" she asked, imagining entire lives devoted to the search for new blends of ingredients, new variations in the measurements, to alert and patient mixing, to the handing down of an intricate, precise lore.

"Tenían sus criadas," Salustiano answered. ("They had their ser-

vants.") And he explained to us that when the daughters of noble families entered the convent they brought their maids with them; thus, to satisfy the venial whims of gluttony, the only cravings allowed them, the nuns could rely on a swarm of eager, tireless helpers. And as far as they themselves were concerned, they had only to conceive and compare and correct the recipes that expressed their fantasies confined within those walls: the fantasies, after all, of sophisticated women, bright and introverted and complex, women who needed absolutes, whose reading told of ecstasies and transfigurations, martyrs and tortures, women with conflicting calls in their blood, genealogies in which the descendants of the conquistadores mingled with those of Indian princesses or slaves, women with childhood recollections of the fruits and fragrances of a succulent vegetation, thick with ferments, though growing from those sun-baked plateaus.

Nor should sacred architecture be overlooked, the background to the lives of those religious; it, too, was impelled by the same drive toward the extreme that led to the exacerbation of flavors amplified by the blaze of the most spicy chiles. Just as Colonial Baroque set no limits on the profusion of ornament and display, in which God's presence was identified in a closely calculated delirium of brimming, excessive sensations, so the curing of the hundred or more native varieties of hot peppers carefully selected for each dish opened vistas of a flaming ecstasy.

At Tepotzotlán, we visited the church the Jesuits had built in the eighteenth century for their seminary (and no sooner was it consecrated than they had to abandon it, as they were expelled from Mexico forever): a theatre-church, all gold and bright colors, in a dancing and acrobatic baroque, crammed with swirling angels, garlands, panoplies of flowers, shells. Surely the Jesuits meant to compete with the splendor of the Aztecs, whose ruined temples and palaces—the royal palace of Quetzalcoatl!—still stood, to recall a rule imposed through the impressive effects of a grandiose, transfiguring art. There was a challenge in the air, in this dry and thin air at an altitude of two thousand meters: the ancient rivalry between the civilizations of America and Spain in the art of bewitching the senses with dazzling seductions. And from architecture this rivalry extended to cuisine, where the two civilizations had merged, or perhaps where the conquered had triumphed, strong in the condiments born from their very soil. Through the white hands of novices and the brown hands of lay sisters, the cuisine of the new Indo-

Hispanic civilization had become also the field of battle between the aggressive ferocity of the ancient gods of the mesa and the sinuous excess of the baroque religion.

On the supper menu we didn't find *chiles en nogada*. From one locality to the next the gastronomic lexicon varied, always offering new terms to be recorded and new sensations to be defined. Instead, we found *guacamole*, to be scooped up with crisp tortillas that snap into many shards and dip like spoons into the thick cream (the fat softness of the *aguacate*—the Mexican national fruit, known to the rest of the world under the distorted name of avocado—is accompanied and underlined by the angular dryness of the tortilla, which, for its part, can have many flavors, pretending to have none); then *guajolote con mole poblano*—that is, turkey with Puebla-style *mole* sauce, one of the noblest among the many *moles*, and most laborious (the preparation never takes less than two days), and most complicated, because it requires several different varieties of *chile*, as well as garlic, onion, cinnamon, cloves, pepper, cumin, coriander, and sesame, almonds, raisins, and peanuts, with a touch of chocolate; and finally *quesadillas* (another kind of tortilla, really, for which cheese is incorporated in the dough, garnished with ground meat and refried beans).

Right in the midst of chewing, Olivia's lips paused, almost stopped, though without completely interrupting their continuity of movement, which slowed down, as if reluctant to allow an inner echo to fade, while her gaze became fixed, intent on no specific object, in apparent alarm. Her face had a special concentration that I had observed during meals ever since we began our trip to Mexico. I followed the tension as it moved from her lips to her nostrils, flaring one moment, contracting the next (the plasticity of the nose is quite limited—especially for a delicate, harmonious nose like Olivia's—and each barely perceptible attempt to expand the capacity of the nostrils in the longitudinal direction actually makes them thinner, while the corresponding reflex movement, accentuating their breadth, then seems a kind of withdrawal of the whole nose into the surface of the face).

What I have just said might suggest that in eating Olivia became closed into herself, absorbed with the inner course of her sensations; in reality, on the contrary, the desire her whole person expressed was that of communicating to me what she was tasting: communicating with me through flavors, or communicating with flavors through a double set of taste buds, hers and mine. "Did you taste that? Are you tasting it?" she was asking me, with a kind of anxiety, as if at that same moment our incisors had pierced an identically composed morsel and the same drop of savor had been caught by the membranes of my tongue and of hers. "Is it cilantro? Can't you taste cilantro?" she insisted, referring to an herb whose local name hadn't allowed us to identify it with certainty (was it coriander, perhaps?) and of which a little thread in the morsel we were chewing sufficed to transmit to the nostrils a sweetly pungent emotion, like an impalpable intoxication.

Olivia's need to involve me in her emotions pleased me greatly, because it showed that I was indispensable to her and that, for her, the pleasures of existence could be appreciated only if we shared them. Our subjective, individual selves, I was thinking, find their amplification and completion only in the unity of the couple. I needed confirmation of this conviction all the more since, from the beginning of our Mexican journey, the physical bond between Olivia and me was going through a phase of rarefaction, if not eclipse: a momentary phenomenon, surely, and not in itself disturbing—part of the normal ups and downs to which, over a long period, the life of every couple is subject. And I couldn't help remarking how certain manifestations of Olivia's vital energy, certain prompt reactions or delays on her part, yearnings or throbs, continued to take place before my eyes, losing none of their intensity, with only one significant difference: their stage was no longer the bed of our embraces but a dinner table.

During the first few days I expected the gradual kindling of the palate to spread quickly to all our senses. I was mistaken: aphrodisiac this cuisine surely was, but in itself and for itself (this is what I thought to understand, and what I am saying applies only to us at that moment; I cannot speak for others or for us if we had been in a different humor). It stimulated desires, in other words, that sought their satisfaction only within the very sphere of sensation that had aroused them—in eating new dishes, therefore, that would generate and extend those same desires. We were thus in the ideal situation for imagining what the love between the abbess and the chaplain might have been like: a love that, in the eyes of the world and in their own eyes, could have been perfectly chaste and at the same time infinitely carnal in that experience of flavors gained through secret and subtle complicity.

Complicity: the word, the moment it came into my mind—referring not only to the nun and the priest but also to Olivia and me—heartened me. Because if what Olivia sought was complicity in the almost obsessive passion that had seized her, then this suggested we were not losing—as I had feared—a parity between us. In fact, it had seemed to me during the last few days that Olivia, in her gustatory exploration, had wanted to keep me in a subordinate position: a presence necessary, indeed, but subaltern, obliging me to observe the relationship between her and food as a confidant or as a compliant pander. I dispelled this irksome notion that had somehow or other occurred to me. In reality, our complicity could not be more total, precisely because we experienced the same passion in different ways, in accord with our temperaments: Olivia more sensitive to perceptive nuances and endowed with a more analytical memory, where every recollection remained distinct and unmistakable, I tending more to define experiences verbally and conceptually, to mark the ideal line of our journey within ourselves contemporaneously with our geographical journey. In fact, this was a conclusion of mine that Olivia had instantly adopted (or perhaps Olivia had been the one to prompt the idea and I had simply proposed it to her again in words of my own): the true journey, as the introjection of an "outside" different from our normal one, implies a complete change of nutrition, a digesting of the visited country—its fauna and flora and its culture (not only the different culinary practices and condiments but the different implements used to grind the flour or stir the pot)—making it pass between the lips and down the esophagus. This is the only kind of travel that has a meaning nowadays, when everything visible you can see on television without rising from your easy chair. (And you mustn't rebut that the same result can be achieved by visiting the exotic restaurants of our big cities; they so counterfeit the reality of the cuisine they claim to follow that, as far as our deriving real knowledge is concerned, they are the equivalent not of an actual locality but of a scene reconstructed and shot in a studio.)

All the same, in the course of our trip Olivia and I saw everything there was to be seen (no small exploit, in quantity or quality). For the following morning we had planned a visit to the excavations at Monte Albán, and the guide came for us at the hotel promptly with a little bus. In the sunny, arid countryside grow the agaves used for mescal and tequila, and *nopales* (which we call prickly pears) and cereus—all thorns—and jacaranda, with its blue flowers. The road climbs up into the mountains. Monte Albán, among the heights surrounding a valley, is a complex of ruins: temples, reliefs, grand stairways, platforms for human sacrifice. Horror, sacredness, and mystery are consolidated by tourism, which dictates preordained forms of behavior, the modest surrogates of those rites. Contemplating these stairs, we try to imagine the hot blood spurting from the breast split by the stone axe of the priest. Three civilizations succeeded one another at Monte Albán, each shifting the same blocks: the Zapotecs building over the works of the Olmecs, and the Mixtecs doing the same to those of the Zapotecs. The calendars of the ancient Mexican civilizations, carved on the reliefs, represent a cyclic, tragic concept of time: every fifty-two years the universe ended, the gods died, the temples were destroyed, every celestial and terrestrial thing changed its name. Perhaps the peoples that history defines as the successive occupants of these territories were merely a single people, whose continuity was never broken even through a series of massacres like those the reliefs depict. Here are the conquered villages, their names written in hieroglyphics, and the god of the village, his head hung upside down; here are the chained prisoners of war, the severed heads of the victims.

The guide to whom the travel agency entrusted us, a burly man named Alonso, with flattened features like an Olmec head (or Mixtec? Zapotec?), points out to us, with exuberant mime, the famous bas-reliefs called Los Danzantes. Only some of the carved figures, he says, are portraits of dancers, with their legs in movement (Alonso performs a few steps); others might be astronomers, raising one hand to shield their eyes and study the stars (Alonso strikes an astronomer's pose). But for the most part, he says, they represent women giving birth (Alonso acts this out). We learn that this temple was meant to ward off difficult childbirths; the reliefs were perhaps votive images. Even the dance, for that matter, served to make births easier, through magic mimesis—especially when the baby came out feet-first (Alonso performs the magic mimesis). One relief depicts a cesarean operation, complete with uterus and fallopian tubes (Alonso, more brutal than ever, mimes the entire female anatomy, to demonstrate that a sole surgical torment linked births and deaths).

Everything in our guide's gesticulation takes on a truculent significance, as if the temples of the sacrifices cast their shadow on every act and every thought. When the most propitious date had been set, in accordance with the stars, the sacrifices were accompanied by the revelry of dances, and even births seemed to have no purpose beyond supplying new soldiers for the wars to capture victims. Though some figures are shown running or wrestling or playing football, according to Alonso these are not peaceful athletic competitions but, rather, the games of prisoners forced to compete in order to determine which of them would be the first to ascend the altar.

"And the loser in the games was chosen for the sacrifice?" I ask.

"No! The winner!" Alonso's face becomes radiant. "To have your chest split open by the obsidian knife was an honor!" And in a crescendo of ancestral patriotism, just as he had boasted of the excellence of the scientific knowledge of the ancient peoples, so now this worthy descendant of the Olmecs feels called upon to exalt the offering of a throbbing human heart to the sun to assure that the dawn would return each morning and illuminate the world.

That was when Olivia asked, "But what did they do with the victims' bodies afterward?"

Alonso stopped.

"Those limbs— I mean, those entrails," Olivia insisted. "They were offered to the gods, I realize that. But, practically speaking, what happened to them? Were they burned?"

No, they weren't burned.

"Well, what then? Surely a gift to the gods couldn't be buried, left to rot in the ground."

"*Los zopilotes,*" Alonso said. "The vultures. They were the ones who cleared the altars and carried the offerings to Heaven."

The vultures. "Always?" Olivia asked further, with an insistence I could not explain to myself.

Alonso was evasive, tried to change the subject; he was in a hurry to show us the passages that connected the priests' houses with the temples, where they made their appearance, their faces covered by terrifying masks. Our guide's pedagogical enthusiasm had something irritating about it, because it gave the impression he was imparting to us a lesson that was simplified so that it would enter our poor profane heads, though he actually knew far more, things he kept to himself and took care not to tell us. Perhaps this was what Olivia had sensed and what, after a certain point, made her maintain a closed, vexed silence through the rest of our visit to the excavations and on the jolting bus that brought us back to Oaxaca.

Along the road, all curves, I tried to catch Olivia's eye as she sat facing me, but, thanks to the bouncing of the bus or the difference in the level of our seats, I realized my gaze was resting not on her eyes but on her teeth (she kept her lips parted in a pensive expression), which I happened to be seeing for the first time not as the radiant glow of a smile but as the instruments most suited to their purpose: to be dug into flesh, to sever it, tear it. And as you try to read a person's thoughts in the expression of his eyes, so now I looked at those strong, sharp teeth and sensed there a restrained desire, an expectation.

As we reentered the hotel and headed for the large lobby (the former chapel of the convent), which we had to cross to reach the wing where our room was, we were struck by a sound like a cascade of water flowing and splashing and gurgling in a thousand rivulets and eddies and jets. The closer we got, the more this homogeneous noise was broken down into a complex of chirps, trills, caws, clucks, as of a flock of birds flapping their wings in an aviary. From the doorway (the room was a few steps lower than the corridor), we saw an expanse of little spring hats on the heads of ladies seated around tea tables. Throughout the country a campaign was in progress for the election of a new president of the republic, and the wife of the favored candidate was giving a tea party of impressive proportions for the wives of the prominent men of Oaxaca. Under the broad, empty vaulted ceiling, three hundred Mexican ladies were conversing all at once; the spectacular acoustical event that had immediately subdued us was produced by their voices mingled with the tinkling of cups and spoons and of knives cutting slices of cake. Looming over the assembly was a gigantic full-color picture of a round-faced lady with her black, smooth hair drawn straight back, wearing a blue dress of which only the buttoned collar could be seen; it was not unlike the official portraits of Chairman Mao Tse-tung, in other words.

To reach the patio and, from it, our stairs, we had to pick our way among the little tables of the reception. We were already close to the far exit when, from a table at the back of the hall, one of the few male guests rose and came toward us, arms extended. It was our friend Salustiano Velazco, a member of the would-be president's staff and, in that capacity, a participant in the more delicate stages of the electoral campaign. We hadn't seen him since leaving the capital, and to show us, with all his ebullience, his joy on seeing us again and to inquire about the latest stages of our journey (and perhaps to escape momentarily that atmosphere in which the triumphal female predominance compromised his chivalrous certitude of male supremacy) he left his place of honor at the symposium and accompanied us into the patio.

Instead of asking us about what we had seen, he began by pointing out the things we had surely failed to see in the places we had visited and could have seen only if he had been with us—a conversational formula that impassioned connoisseurs of a country feel obliged to adopt with visiting friends, always with the best intentions, though it successfully spoils the pleasure of those who have returned from a trip and are quite proud of their experiences, great or small. The convivial din of the distinguished gynaeceum followed us even into the patio and drowned at least half the words he and we spoke, so I was never sure he wasn't reproaching us for not having seen the very things we had just finished telling him we had seen.

"And today we went to Monte Albán," I quickly informed him, raising my voice. "The stairways, the reliefs, the sacrificial altars . . ."

Salustiano put his hand to his mouth, then waved it in midair—a gesture that, for him, meant an emotion too great to be expressed in words. He began by furnishing us archeological and ethnographical details I would have very much liked to hear sentence by sentence, but they were lost in the reverberations of the feast. From his gestures and the scattered words I managed to catch ("*Sangre . . . obsidiana . . . divinidad solar*"), I realized he was talking about the human sacrifices and was speaking with a mixture of awed participation and sacred horror—an attitude distinguished from that of our crude guide by a greater awareness of the cultural implications.

Quicker than I, Olivia managed to follow Salustiano's speech better, and now she spoke up, to ask him something. I realized she was repeating the question she had asked Alonso that afternoon: "What the vultures didn't carry off—what happened to that, afterward?"

Salustiano's eyes flashed knowing sparks at Olivia, and I also grasped then the purpose behind her question, especially as Salustiano assumed his confidential, abettor's tone. It seemed that, precisely because they were softer, his words now overcame more easily the barrier of sound that separated us.

"Who knows? The priests . . . This was also a part of the rite— I mean among the Aztecs, the people we know better. But even about them, not much is known. These were secret ceremonies. Yes, the ritual meal . . . The priest assumed the functions of the god, and so the victim, divine food . . ."

Was this Olivia's aim? To make him admit this? She insisted further, "But how did it take place? The meal . . ."

"As I say, there are only some suppositions. It seems that the princes, the warriors also joined in. The victim was already part of the god, transmitting divine strength." At this point, Salustiano changed his tone and became proud, dramatic, carried away. "Only the warrior who had captured the sacrificed prisoner could not touch his flesh. He remained apart, weeping."

Olivia still didn't seem satisfied. "But this flesh—in order to eat it . . . The way it was cooked, the sacred cuisine, the seasoning—is anything known about that?"

Salustiano became thoughtful. The banqueting ladies had redoubled their noise, and now Salustiano seemed to become hypersensitive to their sounds; he tapped his ear with one finger, signaling that he couldn't go on in all that racket. "Yes, there must have been some rules. Of course, that food couldn't be consumed without a special ceremony . . . the due honor . . . the respect for the sacrificed, who were brave youths . . . respect for the gods . . . flesh that couldn't be eaten just for the sake of eating, like any ordinary food. And the flavor . . ."

"They say it isn't good to eat?"

"A strange flavor, they say."

"It must have required seasoning—strong stuff."

"Perhaps that flavor had to be hidden. All other flavors had to be brought together, to hide that flavor."

And Olivia asked, "But the priests . . . About the cooking of it— they didn't leave any instructions? Didn't hand down anything?"

Salustiano shook his head. "A mystery. Their life was shrouded in mystery."

And Olivia—Olivia now seemed to be prompting him. "Perhaps that flavor emerged, all the same—even through the other flavors."

Salustiano put his fingers to his lips, as if to filter what he was saying. "It was a sacred cuisine. It had to celebrate the harmony of the elements achieved through sacrifice—a terrible harmony, flaming, incandescent . . ." He fell suddenly silent, as if sensing he had gone too far, and as if the thought of the repast had recalled him to his duty, he hastily apologized for not being able to stay longer with us. He had to go back to his place at the table.

Waiting for evening to fall, we sat in one of the cafés under the arcades of the *zócalo*, the regular little square that is the heart of every old city of the colony—green, with short, carefully pruned trees called *almendros*, though they bear no resemblance to almond trees. The tiny paper flags and the banners that greeted the official candidate did their best to convey a festive air to the *zócalo*. The proper Oaxaca families strolled under the arcades. American hippies waited for the old woman who supplied them with *mescalina*. Ragged vendors unfurled colored fabrics on the ground. From another square nearby came the echo of the loudspeakers of a sparsely attended rally of the opposition. Crouched on the ground, heavy women were frying tortillas and greens.

In the kiosk in the middle of the square, an orchestra was playing, bringing back to me reassuring memories of evenings in a familiar, provincial Europe I was old enough to have known and forgotten. But the memory was like a trompe l'oeil, and when I examined it a little it gave me a sense of multiplied distance, in space and in time. Wearing black suits and neckties, the musicians, with their dark, impassive Indian faces, played for the varicolored, shirtsleeved tourists—inhabitants, it seemed, of a perpetual summer—for parties of old men and women, meretriciously young in all the splendor of their dentures, and for groups of the really young, hunched over and meditative, as if waiting for age to come and whiten their blond beards and flowing hair; bundled in rough clothes, weighed down by their knapsacks, they looked like the allegorical figures of winter in old calendars.

"Perhaps time has come to an end, the sun has grown weary of rising, Cronos dies of starvation for want of victims to devour, the ages and the seasons are turned upside down," I said.

"Perhaps the death of time concerns only us," Olivia answered. "We who tear one another apart, pretending not to know it, pretending not to taste flavors anymore."

"You mean that here—that they need stronger flavors here because they know, because here they ate . . ."

"The same as at home, even now. Only we no longer know it, no longer dare look, the way they did. For them there was no mystification: the horror was right there, in front of their eyes. They ate as long as there was a bone left to pick clean, and that's why the flavors . . ."

"To hide that flavor?" I said, again picking up Salustiano's chain of hypotheses.

"Perhaps it couldn't be hidden. *Shouldn't* be. Otherwise, it was like not eating what they were really eating. Perhaps the other flavors served to enhance that flavor, to give it a worthy background, to honor it."

At these words I felt again the need to look her in the teeth, as I had done earlier, when we were coming down in the bus. But at that very moment her tongue, moist with saliva, emerged from between her teeth, then immediately drew back, as if she were mentally savoring something. I realized Olivia was already imagining the supper menu.

It began, this menu, offered us by a restaurant we found among low houses with curving grilles, with a rose-colored liquid in a hand-blown glass: *sopa de camarones*—shrimp soup, that is, immeasurably hot, thanks to a quantity of *chiles* we had never come upon previously, perhaps the famous *chiles jalapeños.* Then *cabrito*—roast kid—every morsel of which provoked surprise, because the teeth would encounter first a crisp bit, then a bit that melted in the mouth.

"You're not eating?" Olivia asked me. She seemed to concentrate only on savoring her dish, though she was very alert, as usual, while I had remained lost in thought, looking at her. It was the sensation of her teeth in my flesh that I was imagining, and I could feel her tongue lift me against the roof of her mouth, enfold me in saliva, then thrust me under the tips of the canines. I sat there facing her, but at the same time it was as if a part of me, or all of me, were contained in her mouth, crunched, torn shred by shred. The situation was not entirely passive, since while I was being chewed by her I felt also that I was acting on her, transmitting sensations that spread from the taste buds through her whole body. I was the one who aroused her every vibration—it was a reciprocal and complete relationship, which involved us and overwhelmed us.

I regained my composure; so did she. We looked carefully at the salad of tender prickly-pear leaves (*ensalada de nopalitos*)—boiled, seasoned with garlic, coriander, red pepper, and oil and vinegar—then the pink and creamy pudding of *maguey* (a variety of agave), all accompanied by a carafe of *sangrita* and followed by coffee with cinnamon.

But this relationship between us, established exclusively through food, so much so that it could be identified in no image other than that of a meal—this relationship which in my imaginings I thought corresponded with Olivia's deepest desires—didn't please her in the slightest, and her irritation was to find its release during that same supper.

"How boring you are! How monotonous!" she began by saying, repeating an old complaint about my uncommunicative nature and my habit of giving her full responsibility for keeping the conversation alive—an argument that flared up whenever we were alone together at a restaurant table, including a list of charges whose basis in truth I couldn't help admitting but in which I also discerned the fundamental reasons for our unity as a couple; namely, that Olivia saw and knew how to catch and isolate and rapidly define many more things than I, and therefore my relationship with the world was essentially via her. "You're always sunk into yourself, unable to participate in what's going on around you, unable to put yourself out for another, never a flash of enthusiasm on your own, always ready to cast a pall on anybody else's, depressing, indifferent—" And to the inventory of my faults she added this time a new adjective, or one that to my ears now took on a new meaning: "Insipid!"

There: I was insipid, I thought, without flavor. And the Mexican cuisine, with all its boldness and imagination, was needed if Olivia was to feed on me with satisfaction. The spiciest flavors were the complement—indeed, the avenue of communication, indispensable as a loudspeaker that amplifies sounds—for Olivia to be nourished by my substance.

"I may seem insipid to you," I protested, "but there are ranges of flavor more discreet and restrained than that of red peppers. There are subtle tastes that one must know how to perceive!"

The next morning we left Oaxaca in Salustiano's car. Our friend had to visit other provinces on the candidate's tour, and offered to accompany us for part of our itinerary. At one point on the trip he showed us some recent excavations not yet overrun by tourists. A stone statue rose barely above the level of the ground, with the unmistakable form that we had learned to recognize on the very first days of our Mexican archeological wanderings: the *chacmool,* or half-reclining human figure, in an almost Etruscan pose, with a tray resting on his belly. He looks like a rough, good-natured puppet, but it was on that tray that the victims' hearts were offered to the gods.

"Messenger of the gods—what does that mean?" I asked. I had read that definition in a guidebook. "Is he a demon sent to earth by the gods to collect the dish with the offering? Or an emissary from human beings who must go to the gods and offer them the food?"

"Who knows?" Salustiano answered, with the suspended attitude he took in the face of unanswerable questions, as if listening to the inner voices he had at his disposal, like reference books. "It could be the victim himself, supine on the altar, offering his own entrails on the dish. Or the sacrificer, who assumes the pose of the victim because he is aware that tomorrow it will be his turn. Without this reciprocity, human sacrifice would be unthinkable. All were potentially both sacrificer and victim—the victim accepted his role as victim because he had fought to capture the others as victims."

"They could be eaten because they themselves were eaters of men?" I added, but Salustiano was talking now about the serpent as symbol of the continuity of life and the cosmos.

Meanwhile I understood: my mistake with Olivia was to consider myself eaten by her, whereas I should be myself (I always had been) the one who ate her. The most appetizingly flavored human flesh belongs to the eater of human flesh. It was only by feeding ravenously on Olivia that I would cease being tasteless to her palate.

This was in my mind that evening when I sat down with her to supper. "What's wrong with you? You're odd this evening," Olivia said, since nothing ever escaped her. The dish they had served us was called *gorditas pellizcadas con manteca*—literally, "plump girls pinched with butter." I concentrated on devouring, with every meatball, the whole fragrance of Olivia—through voluptuous mastication, a vampire extraction of vital juices. But I realized that in a relationship that should have been among three terms—me, meatball, Olivia—a fourth term had intruded, assuming a dominant role: the name of the meatballs. It was the name *gorditas pellizcadas con manteca* that I was especially savoring and assimilating and possessing. And, in fact, the magic of that name continued affecting me even after the meal, when we retired together to our hotel room in the night. And for the first time during our Mexican journey the spell whose victims we had been was broken, and the inspiration that had blessed the finest moments of our joint life came to visit us again.

The next morning we found ourselves sitting up in our bed in the *chacmool* pose, with the dulled expression of stone statues on our faces and, on our laps, the tray with the anonymous hotel breakfast, to which we tried to add local flavors, ordering with it mangoes, papayas, cherimoyas, guayabas—fruits that conceal in the sweetness of their pulp subtle messages of asperity and sourness.

Our journey moved into the Maya territories. The temples of Palenque emerged from the tropical forest, dominated by thick, wooded mountains: enormous ficus trees with multiple trunks like roots, lilac-colored *macuilis, aguacates*—every tree wrapped in a cloak of lianas and climbing vines and hanging plants. As I was going down the steep stairway of the Temple of the Inscriptions, I had a dizzy spell. Olivia, who disliked stairs, had chosen not to follow me and had remained with the crowd of noisy groups, loud in sound and color, that the buses were disgorging and ingesting constantly in the open space among the temples. By myself, I had climbed to the Temple of the Sun, to the relief of the jaguar sun, to the Temple of the Foliated Cross, to the relief of the quetzal in profile, then to the Temple of the Inscriptions, which involves not only climbing up (and then down) a monumental stairway but also climbing down (and then up) the smaller, interior staircase that leads down to the underground crypt. In the crypt there is the tomb of the king-priest (which I had already been able to study far more comfortably a few days previously in a perfect facsimile at the Anthropological Museum in Mexico City), with the highly complicated carved stone slab on which you see the king operating a science-fiction apparatus that to our eyes resembles the sort of thing used to launch space rockets, though it represents, on the contrary, the descent of the body to the subterranean gods and its rebirth as vegetation.

I went down, I climbed back up into the light of the jaguar sun— into the sea of the green sap of the leaves. The world spun, I plunged down, my throat cut by the knife of the king-priest, down the high steps onto the forest of tourists with super-8s and usurped, broad-brimmed sombreros. The solar energy coursed along dense networks of blood and chlorophyll; I was living and dying in all the fibers of what is chewed and digested and in all the fibers that absorb the sun, consuming and digesting.

Under the thatched arbor of a restaurant on a riverbank, where Olivia had waited for me, our teeth began to move slowly, with equal rhythm, and our eyes stared into each other's with the intensity of serpents'—serpents concentrated in the ecstasy of swallowing each other in turn, as we were aware, in our turn, of being swallowed by the serpent that digests us all, assimilated ceaselessly in the process of ingestion and digestion, in the universal cannibalism that leaves its imprint on every amorous relationship and erases the lines between our bodies and *sopa de frijoles, huachinango a la veracruzana,* and *enchiladas.*

Translated, from the Italian, by William Weaver

1983

"Julia Child says it's delicious, James Beard loves it, Craig Claiborne is crazy about it, but Stanley J. Tischler, Jr., hates it."

THERE SHOULD BE A NAME FOR IT

MATTHEW KLAM

Lynn's roasting a chicken. She takes out garlic, chili powder, and a lime. "What's that for?" I say.

"There are pine nuts above your head," she says. I hand them down to her. Now she butters the pan. She's got the coriander in a bag, cloves, curry, and two oranges. Then other green herbs. Jesus Christ, I'm thinking, all that crap for the chicken.

"All that's for the chicken?"

"What?"

"What? That." I'm pulling on my eyebrow hair. It's a nervous habit, but I feel like plucking these long curly ones. "All that goes on the chicken?"

She rinses off her hands and says, "This is a recipe from my mom."

It's early summer. It's afternoon, and the kitchen is the brightest room in this house. It's like a greenhouse in here, very sunny. The house itself is small and cheap, though 150 years ago somebody planted a sycamore on the front lawn. Protected from the wind and fed by sun and water, the plant grew into a giant. The limbs stretch up—it's like an elephant, white tusks against the sky.

"Up we go," she says, upending the chicken. She pulls a little waxpaper bag from inside it like an envelope and drops it in the sink.

"What the hell is that?" I say. Lynn wipes her forehead with her wrist. She takes the bag out of the sink and tears it open, spilling the contents into her hand. It's meat—it looks like tongues.

"Oh, my God."

"It's chicken livers. See?"

She flicks them with her finger. It's three glistening pieces of purple meat, but not at all like steak. They look like they were alive five minutes ago. She holds one. She seems to enjoy touching it.

"Okay, get rid of it." Lynn puts the bag and the livers in the garbage. She says, "You make it with onions. My mother loves it."

"Yeah."

This is the whole chicken, an entire animal. Like, I haven't exactly seen this done before by a person my age. We're both kids. We don't know how to cook this stuff. In all the time we've been living together, Lynn's never cooked a whole chicken.

I'm leaning close enough to her that I can smell her shampoo. Her hair is thick and reddish brown, full and shiny, and her skin is the color of creamy tan suede. Mexican mother, Irish father. You know how they airbrush the skin of ladies in *Playboy*? I see Lynn's body every day, I look at her skin up close, I've had my eye an inch above her stomach or her shoulder or her calf, and it's perfect. It's golden skin. Every morning after her shower, Lynn comes and stands in front of me—I'm either getting dressed or making notes for work—then she turns around and I rub cream across her shoulders, underneath the bra straps, bright-white fabric against her tan skin.

She cuts the fat off the chicken, that makes sense, but with scissors, of all things. She holds it like a little playmate, flipping it over, rocking it under the faucet. She washes out the hole in it, pouring some little pieces of red guts into the sink, shaking out the dried blood or cartilage that runs down and sticks in the drain. Disgusting. Then she tears off a piece of brown paper bag and folds it, dabbing the outside of the chicken.

"What are you doing?" I ask.

"It gets the old oil out of the skin."

"Old oil? What, like sweat?"

"No, not like sweat," she says. "Like sweat? Chickens don't sweat."

"I know."

"I'm cooking you dinner and you're gonna stand here and give me shit?"

"No! No way. This is gonna be great."

I love her. Man! I really do. She's a pistol. It's not placating love, it's really passionate love. Uncharted territory, yes, definitely. But that's what love is—undefined.

"Move aside, termite," she says to me, grabbing the bottle of olive oil.

"Termite," I say. "Good one."

I love how she says that—"Are you gonna give me shit?" That's great. The answer is yes, I am.

Lynn's awesome, though. She knows what she's thinking, and she knows what you're thinking. She's got you. She's a keeper, as they say. I want to keep her.

"It's not disgusting, Jack. It makes it taste better."

"Sounds good," I say. I mean, whatever this girl touches turns to gold.

Say something bad happened to her, and we have no control over it. All of a sudden there's a situation. Hang on, let me start this over.

It's hard to explain—poor kid—a month ago Lynn had to get an abortion. What a lead balloon. What a joke. It ain't no joke.

"Give me that," she says, pointing at the pepper, and I hand it to her. She rubs chili powder on the skin. Now the paprika, now salt, now some other stuff.

In Spanish, the word is *aborto*, a foreign word that even I can master and pretty easy for Celia, Lynn's mother, to yell at her a few times over the phone. *"Aborto! Aborto! Clak-ata-clak-ata-clak-ata."*

Lynn called home. It was night, we were lying in bed, and I heard everything from my side. I wanted to help, but what could I do? You don't interfere with a family. Lynn nodded into the phone, picked up a pencil and stared at it.

"Mom. We already decided."

"God damn it!" I heard Celia say. "You slut. You and your jackass boyfriend."

After two minutes, Lynn hung up. She didn't say anything.

"Jackass boyfriend?" I said.

"She said to tell you she hates you."

"Thanks."

In my mind, I saw Celia stomping barefoot through her newly carpeted house with the antenna phone and her 1950s bouffant hairdo and ten pounds of eye shadow, shaking her fist, saying, "Goddam jackass," meaning me, blaming it on me.

Lynn and I have a normal sex life. Whatever that means. Sex is never normal with anyone, it's bizarre, it's wiggly meats, but Lynn was a virgin when we met. And then a couple of months went by, and we were invited to her parents' for Christmas.

We drove from Colorado to Ohio. It's twenty-two hours by car. You know how it is when you go on a road trip—you're going to a new place together. After five or six hours, the inside of the car smelled like BO; my ass began to hurt; my legs felt like concrete; there were sunflower seeds all over the floor. More miles, and soon we were spitting the shells on each other. Two o'clock in the morning, shit-bag road stop, I'm buying cigarettes in Michigan. Lynn's standing next to me in a pink pajama top and jeans, sunflower-seed shells in her hair, which is all sticking up in knots in the back from her sleeping on it. She gave me two candy fireballs, her hand was warm and clammy. Outside, no cars passed by. It was silent. It wasn't particularly cold for December. There was the gas station and then nothing for miles.

We stood in the unfamiliar light of the store in the middle of nowhere, lost. It was at about that time that I felt anything could happen. Me and my girlfriend, Lynn, on our first road trip together. When you're twenty-three, a road trip is the highlight of your life. I held onto her hand. It's the same person, and she's great, but she seemed different all of a sudden, three-dimensional. Like a person you've just met for the first time, and would like to get to know. As we drove off, the car went over a speed bump and out of the corner of my eye I saw Lynn's boobs shake.

They put me in the guest room in the basement. The room had white wicker furniture and green-and-silver jungle wallpaper. Mold in the squishy rug. We'd packed our clothes into the same suitcase, and as I dug through it for my contact-lens holder I came across a bunch of Lynn's underwear. I took a pair out and held them up to the light, little flowered cotton panties. They had a lacy edge. They were clean and cute and smelled like powder. Eleven o'clock at night I'm sitting on the bed in the dank basement, white wicker furniture and green jungle wallpaper, the underwear crumpled against my nose and mouth, tracing swirl patterns in the stucco ceiling. I really loved her. Two floors above me my girlfriend lay sleeping, down the hall from her mother and father. I never put pressure on Lynn, for I knew that would be wrong, and yet she must've felt safe. We'd begun to build up trust. This is the part where Lynn loses her virginity. It was the holiday season. The stage was set.

Lunchtime, Celia had made a Mexican specialty, a casserole, a savory thing, cheap cuts of fatty meat, bone chips, dog lips, and I went into the bathroom to get a stain off my pants. Lynn came in to help me and we both ended up naked from the waist down. She got up on the sink, both of us a little self-conscious, trying to be quiet, except I was so excited my feet itched, the thing so hard it felt like it was pulling off me of its own power. Lynn's, like, kicking my jeans, she was, like, Don't come inside me, she was, like, drooling, her eyes rolled back into her head, kind of grunting, her legs around my waist. And there were her parents—Celia and Phil sitting outside the door sopping up the orange grease on their plates from their Mexican lasagna. Man, it was something. Lynn said, "I'm supposed to be a virgin, you bastard. My mother is in the next room. Stop it right now. Stop it before I faint," laughing. "Somebody, help." I almost fainted myself, both of us leering and hot as monkeys.

It's terrible the way kids work off their parents.

That week was the best sex I ever had in my life: Celia knocking on the door to Lynn's room during afternoon-naptime, me beneath the blanket, Lynn saying, "I'll be right out, Mom, I'm getting dressed," Celia saying, "Where's Jack, honey?" *and really not knowing where I was!* See? That's why I love the Midwest. Such a dreamy lack of a clue. That's what happens in the Ohio River Valley, even to a transplanted Mexican with citizenship. I'm from New York, where dead people are not that dumb. These folks are idiots. I mean innocent. Other friends of their family would come by, I'd run down to the basement to bring up extra chairs and I'd feel it dribbling in my pants. Once the first one was out of the way, we did it every time Phil and Celia turned their backs. Every time they went to the food store. They had to go back to the food store so many times because we were eating everything in the refrigerator and losing weight at the same time. Their whole house must still smell from our spooge. I picture that dumpy suburban street—the snow melting in rivers of mud everywhere, her dad walking around in that stupid fisherman hat, the smell of new wall-to-wall carpet everywhere in their house—and I get an exciting feeling inside. It's like the first time we did it all over again.

Lynn holds the chicken's weight in one hand and rubs a stick of butter around it with the other, like a deodorant stick, almost. She sprinkles it with lime, rubbing gently with her other hand around its back and rump. It makes me squeamish sitting there, like it might get up all of a sudden and tap my shoulder, but Lynn's got a pretty sure grip on it. She grabs it by the cavity, sticks it on its back in the pan, and throws in a bunch of herb leaves and pine nuts. Then she cuts up an onion and an orange with the skin still on.

My officemate Amy told me, after she had her baby, how similar an uncooked chicken felt in her hands to the body of her little daughter. She said how she held it, rubbing olive oil on it, under the wings, around the thighs, with soft loose pink skin, the small, protective rib cage. It was the same weight and size as her baby. She said even the elbows had a similar feel in her wet hands. She said it was too funny, so she loaded her camera, little naked Elizabeth lying next to the chicken on Amy's leather coat, and all the groceries piled up around them. She stood on a chair and got the two little birds on film.

Lynn is standing at the sink now, measuring out rice, and looking at me with those bright-green eyes that say, "I know what I'm doing here." She looks like an angel. My knees begin to buckle, and I just want to put her down on the kitchen floor and start the trouble all over again. I want to bare her breast and nod on her nipple. I'm her baby. She's my baby. Everybody's somebody's baby. Let's make a baby.

Lynn says, "What else besides rice?"

"Do you want salad?" I say.

In April, we put a garden in the backyard. The land behind our house is flat. It gets both sun and shade. The grass is long and lush and light green, and right now there are some dandelions. It'll need mowing soon. The garden was our team project, although the day we rented the tiller Lynn was sick and I did everything, and I'd just as soon have Fritos over a vegetable any day of the week. But we both like looking at the garden.

After dinner we go and check out the garden, walking between the rows, careful of where we step. Sometimes she'll pull weeds. When it gets dark we lie on the cold metal basement doors and watch the sky. Above us, the clouds are silently on the move, backlit by the moon. The smell of cut grass is everywhere. The sweet smell and the crickets, and the slick noise of lawn sprinklers hissing in the dark. Grass smells good. There should be a name for it.

"I'll get the salad," I say. There's a basket we use for the vegetables. I take it off the top of the refrigerator.

"I'll do it," Lynn says. "I'm in the mood." She pulls the basket out of my hands and goes out the back door, the glass doorknob banging against the wall.

The sun is going down. Flat, ginger-colored light is sprayed against every surface inside the kitchen, across the counters and the refrigerator door and the walls that are the color of yellow wine. I hear her say hello to Whiskey, the cat. The people next door own him. Stupid name for a cat.

It's Tuesday. It's almost seven. Time to eat.

We said we'd get a cat but what I really want is a dog—dogs are better—but cats are less permanent. If we had to move, you could give the cat away, or leave it. No one would do that to a dog, and anyway it's against the law. A dog would starve to death.

Our difficulties began one night three months ago. I know the exact night. Lynn came home from class and said, "I just got my period. It's so early this month." She said something cute like "You don't have to worry about rubbers for a while." I do worry about rubbers. They are my downfall. We did it that night, no rubber. There was an instant—I remember it—when I was deciding whether or not to actually go for it. I followed a certain line of reasoning, and remembered what she said, twinkled over the risks, and then blew my nuts out. It was great. I really enjoyed myself, oink oink, drowning in it. But then her period disappeared the next day. Or I should say it never came.

She was ovulating.

Let me lay this out again. She ovulated that night, thus the dot of blood. Then we did it. Bingo. You morons, you fucking biologists.

We were pregnant. It was April. I'd just turned twenty-four. I'd never been near an abortion clinic. And Colorado's not the laid-back, liberal-Jew neck of the woods I come from. This here's the American West. I work for a software designer, but I've seen guys in spurs all duded up like *Deliverance* on a Friday night.

I felt desperate and called my parents. My mom told me how in Florida a pro-life group stood outside a women's clinic with a bullhorn, yelling, "If you come out now we'll shoot you, but your unborn child will be spared!" Congress had just blocked the abortion pill for the eighty-second time. She told me that what we were doing was okay. Her voice made me homesick.

The thing about New York City is everything's so jam-packed. It's the crowds, there are so many bums, dead people practically lying on the street. In the winter you die from the cold wind, in the summer you die from the heat. The breeze stinks, the people smell like piss, there's the traffic. It's impossible to park. Everybody's in a rotten mood. No place to hide.

In Colorado, the sun always shines. The sky is usually blue, and when we hang our clean clothes on the line in the backyard they dry in an hour. When you smell them they're crisp and smell like air. The mountains are to the west of town. This is a new town, 120 years old. They shot indigenous peoples to settle this town. You drive up into the Rockies and see powdery snow on the side of the road. Toward the eastern part of Colorado, there are cornfields that go clear across the Midwest, I think. That yonder there is Kansas, I reckon. Anyway, it's flat, and kind of stunning from inside a car, cows and fields and vistas slashing out in every direction, and the sky above you is a flawless ceiling. God, you think, this would be perfect, if only . . . If only I had more money, if only it were a couple of years from now, if only Lynn and I were married, or were ready to get married, if I had more friends here—but old friends—or decent places to hang out at, or more of a feeling of what's next.

They wouldn't let us come in to the clinic yet. She wasn't far enough along. We had to wait almost two weeks to have it done. Seven and a half weeks is the magic number, for all you peckerheads taking notes. Anything less, it's a speck of unremovable dust. Lynn ate saltines before she got out of bed every day, and I brought her a cold glass of club soda. Our friend Tina taught her that.

I'd walk in, hand her the saltines, and sit and look at this girl I've been sleeping next to for months and months—five months by then— and I hated her. She was sick now, and I was sick of her, I hated her little puffy knocked-up ass, she looked like a worried old hag, and out of nowhere I'm just not so sure of anything. Why I all of a sudden don't love her. Because there's something about her that I'm definitely not too sure about. What if she turns into her mother? Celia's a joke.

They say a pregnant woman looks radiant. Lynn went around for two weeks, agitated and angry and with an upset stomach, but she really did look radiant—it was like a cosmetics expert had done something to her face. Her cheeks were flushed all day and her eyes were as bright as green candy. I can't explain the difference. I kept catching myself staring. For those two weeks she was nauseous and pissed off. Added to that, I was still in training for my job, we were not married or engaged or anything, and Lynn really didn't know, ha ha, was she maybe ready to be a mother? Maybe she wasn't and maybe she was. Is twenty-two too young? She toyed with the idea while lolling around in the bath, conditioning her hair. Well, I knew. I'm sure. Please ask me.

Out the window now the sun is setting. It's the summer of 1995. I see Lynn is crouched between the vegetables, picking peas and pulling up weeds.

This garden is a pretty thought—it's the nicest thing I've ever done. We have snap peas growing along one row. I read in the paper that they like to climb so I built a trellis beside the row, criss-cross lattice-wood slats, about two feet tall. I painted it white. We have eggplants, squash, tomatoes, and yellow flowers, and next year we'll plant tubers. When I hate Lynn, or when I can't stand to look at her or be near her, when I feel disgusting, when I wish God would just erase me, I look at the garden. When she gets angry or yells about something terrible I did and we're fighting, I look out the window at that thing we made, the garden, at the lawn when it's been mowed and raked and looks like a putting green, cool and flat and smells sweet. You want to lie down on it and tear the grass up with your hands. Sometimes I think I'm just about ready to kill her.

How come I never do what I'm supposed to do? How come everything I do is such a fucking disaster? Doesn't anybody get what they want? And that line of hers about how she might want to have it. She came out of the bathtub with a towel on her head, fluffing her hair. "Honey," she said. She never called me "honey" before in her life. "Honey, I've been thinking about our child." I could feel all the blood draining from my head. White flecks on the edges of my vision. There was a narrow window of opportunity there, before I calmed myself, where different pictures whizzed into my mind. Space travel, that sort of thing. I told her, You have it alone, honey darling, in your little purple dreamworld—I'll be in Australia by the time the thing comes out.

There's the great Colorado sky, there's the grass, there's the clothes on the line, fruit hanging ripe in the trees, the smell of wet cut grass. The land ripping out flat to the Mississippi with the sun leering on top in every direction. And you're standing above it, a million miles from bumper-to-bumper commuter-nightmare New York. You're not there anymore, though, you're here, at the foot of the Rockies, cow-town college town on the American prairie. Great American steer farm. Steroid-fat cows. Transistor radios in barns, cows chewing all night long.

There were five of us in the room during the procedure: the doctor, her assistant, the hand-holder, me, and, of course, Lynn. She was the star. This was her show. Then it would finally be over. The hand-holder was a therapist, trained in female personal crisis. She was never more than a foot from Lynn all day that long day.

The staff was ready to go. A stainless-steel machine is used by the doctor to vacuum it out, and the doctor needed Lynn's okay to begin. The whole thing was supposed to take five minutes.

Lynn got weepy from nerves, and we all waited while she collected herself. Everyone was anxious to get on with it. I bet Lynn was, too. I held her hand and kissed it, she wasn't even looking at me, she stared up at some poster on the ceiling. The sound, the way she cried, choking a little, the way you do when you're sobbing lying on your back, so the spit runs down your throat, swallowing, laughing underneath the crying for how absurd the scene was—even Lynn could see it—lying there with her legs propped up in the air, all these fucking people around her holding her hands and her knees and her privates, watching her like she was—ha ha!—about to give birth (sorry). Boo-hoo. But in my mind I keep coming back to that sound, not loud, not shrill, that crying, it was almost a noise an animal would make. How much trouble Lynn was having even crying right then, without strangling on her own spit. Is there a way to describe how much I wanted to get the fuck out of there? I wanted to shout, God of New York, turn off that sound, get me out of this room before I'm seared and split open, before I develop breasts myself. The other half of my brain, though, recorded her voice for all time.

"You're okay," Lynn said to nobody, to herself. "You're okay." She'd planned to get through it without tears.

Then it was quiet and she told the doctor to go ahead, and the doctor nodded to her assistant. The assistant turned on the machine, and the machine made a sound like any vacuum.

Lynn is outside, bent over the row of peas. The chicken is sitting over there in the pan. I guess it's ready to bake. She put garlic, butter, lime juice, chili powder, chopped nuts, oranges, cloves, parsley, coriander, half a banana, and paprika on it. What's left? Jean Naté? A cigar up the butt? The rice is cooking away in a pot. The chicken sits there like a drag queen, waiting to get roasted.

When it was over Lynn went into another room and fell asleep. The therapist came over and said, "You were so good today. Guys aren't usually so good."

I nodded. The woman looked at me sweetly. I guess I was good. So what. Maybe it wasn't the norm for her. Or was she just looking for a tip? My voice, though, was so much deeper than everybody else's in the room. Whatever I said that day came out sounding like a frog croak.

Like a belch. My voice was unnaturally deep. I nodded as much as possible. Other than an arrest for drunk driving in college, it was the most nodding I'd ever done in one five-hour stretch.

"What are you doing?" I yell to Lynn out the window. She's bent over the rosebush. Her head is down and her shoulders are rounded, as though she's concentrating on something small.

Lynn says, "There are beetles on the roses."

I look over at the roasting pan again. "Do we cook this thing or what? I'm getting hungry. What temperature do you set it at?" No answer. She's busy with the roses.

"Lynn, you didn't turn the oven on. I'm going to come out there and pull you in by your hair."

Her hair is hanging around her face. She's looking down. "Relax," she says. "The oven is on. What time is it?" I can feel myself getting annoyed so I take ten deep breaths, counting the numbers slowly, saying the word "relax" as I breathe out.

"Damn it, Lynn, I can't hear you." She looks up finally.

"It has to cook for an hour," she says. "And you have to move the rack."

The pan is heavier than I thought. She said move the rack. What does that mean, up or down? I grab it and then drop it, hot rack, and then the roasting pan, too, onto the oven door.

"Fuck it."

"What's going on?" she says.

"The rack is on fire."

"Of course it is, Jack, it's three hundred and fifty degrees in there. Did you burn yourself? Better put cold water on it."

I stand over the sink and let the water run on my fingers. There's a welt on my palm. I am a moron. She says, "Didn't you ever hear of an oven mitt?"

Man. My fucking hand. Did I ever hear of an oven mitt? What is that, sarcasm?

She says, "Do you want to try something weird?" Out the window I see her looking up toward me, her face flushed from leaning over for so long. "Should we put dandelions in the salad? Look at this," she says, holding up a bunch of dandelions from our lawn in a little bouquet. "Mexicans kill for these, the little leaves," she says. "And they fry the flowers." I never ate dandelions before. And who cares.

"Is that too weird?" she says.

"Hey, yeah," I say, drying my burned hand gingerly on my T-shirt. "Momma had a baby and the head popped off." When I was a kid, we used to pick a dandelion and say this when we flicked the head off the stem. The water in the rice pot foams over the sides.

"Excuse me, Momma didn't have a baby and the head popped off," I say, correcting myself.

I walk over and grab a towel, move the rack down, push the chicken in, and close the oven. The door goes *sping* against the metal. It's 7:02. Nothing comes to mind. Outside she looks up at the window.

"Is that a joke?" she says.

At this angle the sun cuts right through the house. It's orange, purple, rose-colored light, blasting right through the house and spilling against everything.

"Fuck you," she says.

It's about time somebody said it. I can hear the familiar sound of it ringing in the background.

"You can never keep anything to yourself," she says.

"What?" I say.

"In your head," she says, standing at the doorway. "Forget it." Over in the rice pot, there isn't any water left. So the bottom is cooking way too fast. It's, like, black. I use a coffee cup and dump some water in. It sizzles, a cloud of steam comes up. One more cup of water. The rice starts cooking again. My eyes are tearing. In a few seconds the whole wet mess is bubbling away. I feel like I scorched my face.

Lynn's basket is overflowing with greenery and edible dandelions.

"Get out of my way," she says. "You are an animal."

"I'm sorry. Why did I say that? Is it too late to take it back?"

"What's wrong with you?" she says.

Lynn goes over to the oven with a dish towel and slides the roasting pan out. She carries it past me, not even hot yet, out the back door and I hear it go *gong* against the metal basement doors. I step up to the window. The chicken's in the grass, onions, carrots, sliced oranges—the whole thing.

Lynn is standing in front of me now. The dish towel is wound around her hand.

"Cool," I say. "How symbolic."

She says, "I think we need therapists."

"What can I say? I'm sorry," I tell her.

"Why don't you get down on your knees."

I say, "I will if you want." No one moves.

"You're mad at me," she says. "How can you be mad at me?"

"I'm sorry. Jesus Christ. It's my fault."

She shakes her head, staring at me. "Now what?"

"I'm too hungry," I say. "I can't make any big decisions."

"What the hell happened to your face?" she says.

Outside, I pick up the roasting pan out of a pile of leaves. Lynn comes up beside me and puts the chicken back in it, and we shovel up the vegetables and carry everything over to the garbage and throw it all away, even the cracked enamel pot. Whiskey is already there at the fence, meowing and sniffing around.

"Go on, Whiskey," I say. "Not for you."

"Make sure the lid's on tight," she says to me. "I don't want to clean this up a second time from some raccoon."

Let's say, for the sake of something, that I never loved her, that what we have here is a housing arrangement, with scenes of nude touching, that we joined for a little comfort, that it's missing some key element of normal love. It's not normal, it's more like high-school love, or freshman-year-in-college kind of love, the kind you're glad to stick with as long as it's great, as long as it doesn't start ruining your life. The very, very flawed kind. That's my idea of love, actually, the perfect first two weeks, early on, when all you care about is love.

We get a pizza. We pay the man. We eat the salad she picked and lie on the rug in the living room, eating pizza, watching TV, together on the floor. We have no furniture—we aren't there yet. The vibe between us is two people very tired and in shock, but amiable. I put some cream on my face. The welt on my hand throbs. I'd rather have pizza anyway, chicken sucks. I love her. Who else would accept me in this condition?

I should say I'll make dinner tomorrow night.

"I can make dinner tomorrow night."

"You gonna make some chicken?" she says.

"White Christmas lasagna," I say. "With spinach and salad and bread."

"Sounds good," she says. "Move over," sliding toward me. She slings her leg over both of mine, sticking her face in my neck. "This way," she says, and I move to accommodate her. I can feel Lynn's warm, clean breath on my skin. What a feeling, from one person to another.

"I don't understand anything," she says. Her eyes close. Her breath slows.

Lynn gets up from beside me and takes the dinner plates with her. I must be insane. She gives me what I need, and I love her. Hollow but true. I have to remember these things, about her and about the chicken in the grass—is that how it works? Perfect. Stupid. Shared. Turn off the TV now. Turn off the lights.

1997

SPUTNIK

DON DeLILLO

The Demings were home this afternoon, busy at various tasks in
their split-level house, a long low two-tone colonial with a picture
window, a breezeway, and bright siding.

Erica was in the kitchen making Jell-O chicken mousse for dinner.
Three cups chicken broth or three chicken-bouillon cubes dissolved in
three cups boiling water. Two packages Jell-O lemon gelatine. One teaspoon salt. One-eighth teaspoon cayenne. Three tablespoons vinegar.
One and a third cups whipped-topping mix. Two-thirds cup mayonnaise. Two cups finely diced cooked chicken. Two cups finely chopped
celery. Two tablespoons chopped pimiento.

Then boil and pour and stir and blend. Fold spiced and chilled
gelatine into chicken thing. Spoon into nine-by-five-inch loaf pan.
Chill until firm. Unmold. Garnish with crisp lettuce and stuffed olives
(if desired). Makes six entrée salads.

Do not reuse this bottle for storing liquids.

Erica did things with Jell-O that took people's breath away. Even
now, as she prepared the chicken mousse for final chilling, there were
nine parfait glasses in the two-tone Kelvinator. This was dessert for the
next three evenings. Each glass was tilted at a forty-five-degree angle
either against the wall of the refrigerator or against another object. This
tilting method, handed down from her grandmother and her mother,
allowed Erica to do Jell-O desserts in a number of colorful diagonal
stripes, working the combinations among half a dozen flavors. She
might put black-raspberry Jell-O, slightly thickened, into a parfait
glass. She puts the glass in the fridge, tilting it at forty-five degrees.
After the gelatine chills and fully thickens she folds in a swath of lime
Jell-O, and then maybe orange, and then strawberry or black cherry. At
the end of the process she has nine multistriped desserts, all different,
all so vividly attractive.

Doing things with Jell-O was just about the best way to improve
her mood, which was oddly gloomy today—she couldn't figure out why.

From the kitchen window she could see the lawn, neat and

trimmed, low-hedged, open and approachable. The trees at the edge of the lawn were new, like everything else in the area. All up and down the curving streets there were young trees and small new box shrubs and a sense of openness, a sense of seeing everything there is to see at a single glance, with nothing shrouded or walled or protected from the glare.

Nothing shrouded or secret except for young Eric, who sat in his room, behind drawn fiberglass curtains, jerking off into a condom. He liked using a condom because it had a sleek metallic shimmer, like his favorite weapons system, the Honest John, a surface-to-surface missile with a warhead that carried yields of up to fifteen kilotons.

Avoid contact with eyes, open cuts, or running sores.

He sat sprawled in a butterfly chair and thought nobody could ever guess what he was doing, especially the condom part. Nobody could ever guess it, know it, imagine it, or associate him with it. But what happens, he thought, if you die someday and it turns out that everything you've ever done in private becomes general knowledge in the hereafter? Everybody automatically knows everything you ever did when you thought you were totally and sneakily and safely unseen.

Prolonged exposure to sun may cause bursting.

They put thermal pads on the Honest John to heat the solid fuel in preparation for firing. Then they remove the pads and launch the missile from a girderlike launch rail in a grassy field somewhere in the Free World. And the missile's infallible flight, the way it sweeps out precise volumes of mathematical space, it's so saintly and sun-tipped, swinging out of its apex to dive to earth, and the way the fireball halos out above its column of smoke and roar, like some nameless faceless whatever. It made him want to be a Catholic.

Plus she'd have three chicken-mousse salads for leftovers later in the week.

Out in the breezeway husband Rick was simonizing their two-tone Ford Fairlane convertible, brand-new, like the houses and the trees, with whitewall tires and stripes of jet-streak chrome that fairly crackled when the car was in motion.

Erica kept her Jell-O molds in the seashell-beige cabinet over the range. She had fluted molds, ring molds, crown molds in a number of sizes, she had notes and diagrams, mold techniques, offer forms for special decorative molds that she intended to fill out and mail at her earliest convenience.

If swallowed, induce vomiting at once.

Eric stroked his dick in a conscientious manner, somber and methodical. The condom was feely in a way he'd had to get used to, rubbery dumb and disaffecting. On the floor between his feet was a photo of Jayne Mansfield with her knockers coming out a sequined gown. He wanted to sandwich his dick between her breasts until it went *whee*. But he wouldn't just walk out the door when it was over. He would talk to her breasts. Be tender and lovey. Tell them what his longings were, his hopes and dreams.

There was one mold Erica had never used, sort of guided-missile-like, because it made her feel uneasy somehow.

The face in the picture was all painted mouth and smudgy lashes, and at a certain point in the furtherance of his business Eric deflected his attention from the swooping breasts and focused on the facial Jayne, on her eyebrows and lashes and puckered lips. The breasts were real, the face was put together out of a thousand thermoplastic things. And in the evolving scan of his eros, it was the masking waxes, liners, glosses, and creams that became the soft moist mechanisms of release.

Intentional misuse by deliberately inhaling contents can be harmful or fatal.

Erica wore a swirly blue skirt and buttercup blouse that happened to match the colors of their Fairlane.

Rick was still in the breezeway, running a shammy over the chromework. This was something, basically, he could do forever. He could look at himself in a strip of chrome, warp-eyed and hydrocephalic, and feel some of the power of the automobile, the horsepower, the decibel rumble of dual exhausts, the pedal tension of Ford-O-Matic drive. The sneaky thing about this car was that, yes, you drove it sensibly to the dentist and occasionally carpooled with the Andersons and took Eric to the science fair but beneath the routine family applications was the crouched power of the machine, top down, eating up the landscape.

Danger. Contents under pressure.

One of Erica's favorite words in the language was "breezeway." It spoke of ease and breeze and being contemporary and having something others did not. Another word she loved was "crisper." The Kelvinator had a nice roomy crisper and she liked to tell the men that such-and-such was in the crisper. Not the refrigerator, the crisper. The carrots are in the crisper, Rick. There were people out there on the Old Farm Road, where the front porches sag badly and the grass goes unmowed and the Duck River Baptists worship in a squat building that sits in the weeds on the way to the dump, who didn't know what a crisper was, who had iceboxes instead of refrigerators, or who had refrigerators that lacked crispers, or who had crispers in their refrigerators but didn't know what they were for or what they were called, who put tubs of butter in the crisper instead of lettuce, or eggs instead of carrots.

He came in from the breezeway.

"The carrots are in the crisper, Rick."

He liked to nibble on a raw carrot after he'd waxed and buffed the car.

He stood looking at the strontium-white loaf that sat on a bed of lettuce inside a cake pan in the middle of the table.

"Wuff, what is it?"

"It's my Jell-O chicken mousse."

"Hey, great," he said.

Sometimes she called it her Jell-O chicken mousse and sometimes she called it her chicken-mousse Jell-O. This was one of a thousand convenient things about Jell-O. The word went anywhere, front or back or in the middle. It was a push-button word, the way so many things were push-button now, the way the whole world opened behind a button that you pushed.

May cause discoloration of urine or feces.

Eric sidled along the wall and slipped into the bathroom, palming the sloppy condom. He washed it out in the sink and then fitted it over his middle finger and aimed the finger at his mouth so he could blow the condom dry. And in the movie version of his life he imagined how everything is projected on a CinemaScope screen, all the secret things he did alone over the years, and now that he is dead it's all available for public viewing and all his dead relatives and friends and teachers and ministers can watch him with his finger in his mouth, more or less, and a condom on his finger, and he is panting rhythmically to dry it off.

He heard his mother call his name.

He had to wash it and reuse it because this was the only one he had, borrowed from another boy, Danny Anderson, who'd taken it from his father's hiding place, under the balled socks, and who swore he'd never used it himself—a thing that wouldn't be fully established until both boys were dead and Eric had a chance to see the footage.

To avoid suffocation keep out of reach of small children.

Eric hid the rubber in his room, pressed into a box of playing cards. He took a long look at Jayne Mansfield's picture before he slipped it into the world atlas on his desk. He realized that Jayne's breasts were not as real-looking as he'd thought in his emotionally vulnerable state, dick in hand. They reminded him of something, but what? And then he saw it. The bumper bullets on a Cadillac.

He went into the kitchen and opened the fridge, just to see what was going on in there. The bright colors, the product names and logos, the array of familiar shapes, the tinsel glitter of things in foil wrap, the general sense of benevolent gleam, of eyeball surprise, the sense of a tiny holiday taking place on the shelves and in the slots, a world unspoiled and ever renewable. But there was something else as well, faintly unnerving. The throb, perhaps. Maybe it was the informational flow contained in that endless motorized throb. Open the great white vaultlike door and feel the cool breezelet of systems at work, converting current into power, talking to each other day and night across superhuman spaces, a thing he felt outside of, not yet attuned to, and it confused him just a bit.

Except their Kelvinator wasn't white, of course. Not on the outside, anyway. It was Bermuda pink and dawn gray.

He looked inside. He saw the nine tilted parfait glasses and felt a little dizzy. He got disoriented sometimes by the tilted Jell-O desserts. It was as if a science-fiction force had entered the house and made some things askew while sparing others.

They sat down to dinner and Rick carved the mousse and doled out portions. They drank iced tea with a slice of lemon wedged to the rim of each glass, one of Erica's effortless extra touches.

Rick said to Eric, "Whacha been up to all afternoon? Big homework day?"

"Hey, Dad. Saw you simonizing the car."

"Got an idea. After dinner we'll take the binoculars and drive out on the Old Farm Road and see if we can spot it."

"Spot what?" Erica said.

"The baby moon. What else? The satellite they put up there. Supposed to be visible on clear nights."

It wasn't until this moment that Erica understood why her day had felt shadowed and ominous from the time she opened her eyes and stared at the mikado-yellow walls with patina-green fleecing. Yes, that satellite they put into orbit a few days ago. Rick took a scientific interest and wanted Eric to do the same. Sure, Rick was surprised and upset, just as she was, but he was willing to stand in a meadow somewhere and try to spot the object as it floated over. Erica felt a twisted sort of disappointment. It was theirs, not ours. It flew at an amazing rate of speed over the North Pole, *beep beep beep*, passing just above us, evidently, at certain times. She could not understand how this could happen. Were there other surprises coming, things we haven't been told about them? Did they have crispers and breezeways? It was not a simple matter, adjusting to the news.

Rick said, "What about it, Eric? Want to drive on out?"

"Hey, Dad. G-g-g-great."

A pall fell over the table, displacing Erica's Sputnik funk. She thought Eric's occasional stuttering had something to do with the time he spent alone in his room. Hitting the books too hard, Rick thought. He was hitting something too hard, but Erica tried not to form detailed images.

Do not puncture or incinerate.

The boy could sit in the family room and watch their super-console TV, which was compatible with the knotty-pine paneling, and he could anticipate the dialogue on every show. Newscasts, ball games, comedy hours. He did whatever voice the announcer or actor used, matching the words nearly seamlessly, and he never stuttered.

All the other kids ate Oreo cookies. Eric ate Hydrox cookies, because the name sounded like rocket fuel.

One of her kitchen gloves was missing—she had many pairs—and she wanted to believe Eric had borrowed it for one of his chemistry assignments. But she was afraid to ask. And she didn't think she looked forward to getting it back.

Yesterday he'd dunked a Hydrox cookie in milk, held it dripping over the glass, and said thickly, "Is verry gud we poot Roosian moon in U.S. sky."

Then he took a bite and swallowed.

The men went out to find the orbiting satellite. Erica cleared the table, put on her rubberoid gloves, and began to do the dishes. Rick had kidded her about the gloves a number of times. The kitchen was equipped with an automatic dishwasher, of course. But she felt com-

pelled as a homemaker to do a preliminary round of handwashing and
scouring, because if you don't get every smidge of organic murk off the
fork tines and out of the pans before you run the dishwasher, it could
come back to haunt you in the morning.

Flush eyes with water and call physician at once.

And the gloves protected her from scalding water and the touch of
food scraps. Erica loved her gloves. The gloves were indestructible, basically, made of the same kind of materials used in countertops and TV
tubes, in the electrical insulation in the basement and the vulcanized
tires on the car. The gloves were important to her despite the way they
felt, clammy but also dry, a feeling that defied innate contradiction.

All the things around her were important. Things and words.
Words to believe in and live by.

Breezeway

Crisper

Sectional

Car pools

Bridge parties

Broadloom

When she finished up in the kitchen she decided to vacuum the
living-room rug but then realized this would make her bad mood
worse. She'd recently bought a new satellite-shaped vacuum cleaner
that she loved to push across the room because it hummed softly and
seemed futuristic and hopeful, but she was forced to regard it ruefully
now, after Sputnik, a clunky object filled with self-remorse.

Stacking chairs

Scatter cushions

Storage walls

Room divider

Fruit juicer

Cookie sheet

She thought she'd lift her spirits by doing something for the church
social on Saturday to pep up the event a little.

Do not use in enclosed space.

She would prepare half a dozen serving bowls of her Jell-O an-
tipasto salad. Six packages of Jell-O lemon gelatine. Six teaspoons salt.
Six cups boiling water. Six tablespoons vinegar. Twelve cups ice cubes.
Three cups finely cut salami. Two cups finely cut Swiss cheese. One and

a half cups chopped celery. One and a half cups chopped onion. Twelve tablespoons sliced ripe olive.

She remembered coming home one day about six months ago and finding Eric with his head in a bowl of her antipasto salad. He said he was trying to eat it from the inside out to test a scientific theory of his. The explanation was so crazy and unconvincing that it was weirdly believable. But she didn't believe it. She didn't know what to believe. Was this a form of sexual curiosity? Was he pretending the Jell-O was a sort of lickable female body part? And was he engaged in an act of unnatural oral stimulation? He had jellified gunk all over his mouth and tongue. She looked at him. She had people skills. Erica was a person who related to people. But she had to put on gloves just to talk to him.

She set to work in the kitchen now, listening all the while for the reassuring sound of her men coming home, car doors closing in the breezeway, the solid clunk of well-made parts swinging firmly shut.

1997

BREAKFAST SPECIAL

2 EGGS, COFFEE, TOAST, ORANGE JUICE, A SET OF STAINLESS STEEL COOKING POTS, A 3-IN-1 POWER DRILL, AND A PAIR OF LADIES' CORDUROY CARGO PANTS WITH REINFORCED SEAMS.

39.95

MANKOFF

"Enough yin. More yang."

ENOUGH

ALICE McDERMOTT

Begin, then, with the ice-cream dishes, carried from the dining room into the narrow kitchen on a Sunday night, the rest of the family still sitting contented around the lace-covered table, her father's cigarette smoke just beginning to drift into the air that was still rich from the smell of the roast, and the roasted potatoes, the turnips and carrots and green beans, the biscuits and the Sunday-only perfume of her mother and sisters. Carried just two dishes at a time because this was the good set, cabbage roses with gold trim. Two bowls at a time, silver spoons inside, carried carefully and carefully placed on the drain-board beside the soapy water where the dinner plates were already soaking, her mother being a great believer in soaking, whether children or dishes or clothes, or souls. Let it soak: the stained blouse, the bruised knee, the sin—sending them into their rooms with a whole rosary to pray, on their knees, and a full hour in which to do it.

She was the youngest child, the third girl, with three brothers, and since the boys were excused and the kitchen too small, their mother said, to hold a pair of sisters in it together, this final task, the clearing of the ice-cream dishes, was hers alone. Two at a time, she gathered the plates while the others sat, contented, limp, stupefied with food, while she herself felt her stomach straining against the now tight waist of her good dress, felt her legs grown heavy from all she had eaten. Sunday dinner was the only meal they had with their father, who worked two jobs to keep them all fed (that was the way it was put by Mother and Father both, without variance), and the bounty of the spread seemed to be their parents' defiant proof of the man's long week of labor. They always ate too much at Sunday dinner and they always had dessert. Pie on the first Sunday of the month, then cake, ice cream, stewed fruit—one Sunday after the other and always in that same rotation. Ice cream being the pinnacle for her, stewed fruit the depths from which she would have to rise, through pie (if mincemeat, hardly a step in the right direction, if blueberry, more encouraging), then cake—always yellow with eggs and dusted with powdered sugar—and then at last, again, ice cream, store-bought or homemade, it hardly made a difference to she who was told once a month that a lady takes a small spoonful, swallows it, and then takes another. She does not load the spoon up and then run the stuff in and out of her mouth, studying each time the shape her lips have made ("Look how cross-eyed she gets when she's gazing at it"). A lady doesn't want to show her tongue at the dinner table.

Carefully, she collected the bowls and carried them two by two into the narrow kitchen. She placed one on the drainboard and then lifted the spoon out of the other and, always, with a glance over her shoulder, licked the spoon, front and back, and then raised the delicate bowl to her chin and licked that, too, licked the cabbage roses and the pale spaces in between, long strokes of the tongue from gold-edged rim to gold-edged rim and then another tour around the middle. Place it down softly and pick up the next. The creamy dregs spotting her nose and her cheeks, vanilla or chocolate, peach or strawberry—strawberry the best because her brothers and a sister always left behind any big pieces of the fruit. Heel of her hand to the sticky tip of her nose (lick that, too) and then back into the dining room again for the next two bowls. Oh, it was good, as good as the whole heaping bowl that had been filled by her father at the head of the table, passed hand to hand by her sisters and brothers, and set before her.

Extrapolate, then, from the girlhood ritual (not to say, of course, that it ended with her girlhood) to what came to be known as her trouble with the couch. Trouble on the couch would have been more accurate, she understood later, when she had a sense of humor about these things that at the time had no humor in them at all. But such precision was the last thing her family would have sought, not in these matters. Her trouble with the couch, it was called. Mother walking into what should have been the empty apartment except that the boiler at the school had broken and the pastor had sent them all home and here she was with the boy from upstairs, side by side on the couch, her two cheeks flushed fever pink and her mouth a bleary, full-blown rose, and her mother would have her know (once the boy had slipped out the door) that she wasn't born yesterday and Glory Be to God fourteen years old was a fine age to be starting this nonsense and wasn't it a good thing that tomorrow was Saturday and the confessionals at church would be fully manned. She'd had a good soaking in recriminations all that evening and well into Saturday afternoon, when she finished the rosary the priest himself had prescribed, the end coming only after she returned from the Communion rail on Sunday morning and her mother caught and held her eye. A stewed-fruit Sunday no doubt.

Her oldest sister found her next, on the couch with her high-school sweetheart, midafternoon once again—their mother, widowed now, off working in an office—and the first four buttons of her dress undone, the lace bodice of her pale-pink slip all exposed. And then not a month or two later that same sister found her there with another boy, his head in her lap and his hand brushing up and down from her ankle to her knees.

Then there was that Saturday night during the war when her oldest brother, too drunk to go home to his new wife on the next block, let himself in and found her stretched out on the couch in the embrace of some midshipman who, it was clear, despite their quick rearranging of clothes, had his fingers tangled up in her garter. There were buttons undone that time, too, and yet again when she was spied on by the second sister, who never did marry herself but who had an eyeful, let me tell you—a marine, this time, his mouth, to put it delicately, where her corsage should have been and her own hands twisted into his hair as if to hold him there—which led to such a harangue about her trouble with the couch that, finally, even her old mother was moved to say that there was a war on, after all.

Later, her best girlfriend joked that maybe she would want to bring that couch along with her on her wedding night. And joked again, nine months to the week later, when her first son was born, that she didn't seem to need that old couch after all.

There were seven children born altogether, the first followed and each of the others preceded by a miscarriage, so that there were thirteen pregnancies in all, every loss mourned so ferociously that both her husband and her mother advised, each time, not to try again, each birth celebrated with a christening party that packed the small house—made smaller by the oversize floral couch and high-backed chairs and elaborate lamps she had chosen—and spilled out into the narrow yard and breezeway, where there would be dancing, if the weather allowed. A phonograph placed behind the screen in the kitchen window and the records going all through the long afternoon, and on into the evening. You'd see her there after the last guest had gone, the baby on her shoulder and maybe another child on her hip, dancing to something slow and reluctant and melancholy ("One for my baby, and one more for the road"). Lipstick and face powder on the white christening gown that night, as well as the scent of the party itself, cigarette smoke and perfume and the cocktails on her breath.

She was a mother forever rubbing a licked finger to her children's cheeks, scrubbing at the pink traces of her own kisses, forever swelling up again with the next birth. Kids in her lap and her arms wrapped around them even after their limbs had grown longer than her own. The boys, before she knew it, lifting her off her feet when she took them in her arms.

She was forty-six when she gave birth to the last, and he was eighteen and on a weekend home from college when he recognized, for the first time in his life, what the sighs and the stirrings coming from his parents' bedroom on that Saturday morning actually signified. (He did a quick calculation of their ages, just to be sure he had it right, and then thought, *Still?*, amazed and a little daunted.) For the rest of the weekend, he imagined ways he might rib them about it, although he couldn't bring himself to come out with anything, knowing full well that even the most good-natured mention of what went on behind their bedroom door could get him the back of his father's hand—or, worse yet, cause a blush to rise from his own cheeks well before he'd managed to raise any kind of glow in theirs.

And there was the Christmas, some years later, when one of them had given their parents a nostalgic collection of forties music and, listening to Bing Crosby sing in his slow, sleepy way, "Kiss me once and kiss me twice (and kiss me once again)," hadn't their mother said, for all assembled to hear, "If you don't turn this off, I'm going to have to find a place to be alone with your father." And hadn't he and his siblings, every one of them well versed by then in matters of love and sex, sat dumbfounded, calculating, no doubt . . . seventy-one, seventy-two . . . still?

Shades of the trouble with the couch, she took her husband's hand in his last days and unbuttoned her blouse and didn't seem to care a bit who saw her, doctor or nurse, son or daughter or grandchild—or older sister who'd never married herself and couldn't help but say, out in the waiting room, "Now, really." She leaned forward, now and again, to whisper to him, even after he was well past hearing, her open lips brushing both the surgical tape that secured the respirator in his mouth and the stubbly gray beard of his cheek.

Growing plump in her widowhood, though she was the first to admit she'd never been what you would call thin, she traveled in busloads of retirees—mostly widows, although there was the occasional man or two—only missing a museum trip or a foliage tour or a luncheon (with a cocktail) at this or that historic site or country inn if a grandchild was in need of minding. What she could do best—her own daughters marveled at it, who else would have the patience—was sit for hours and hours at a time with a colicky baby over her shoulder or a worn-out toddler on her knee and talk or sing. She told nonsense stories, more sound than substance, or sang every tune in her lifetime repertoire, from Beatles songs to ancient hymns, hypnotizing the children somehow (her sons and daughters were sure of it) into sleep, or sometimes just a dazed contentedness, tucked under her arm or under her chin, seconds, minutes, then hours ticking by, the bars of summer or winter, late-afternoon or early-morning sunlight moving across them, across the length of a room, and neither of them, adult or child, seeming to mark the time gone by.

But take a look in your freezer after she's gone, the daughters reported to one another and to the better-liked sisters-in-law as well. Nearly a full gallon eaten—or all but a final spoonful so she didn't have to put the carton in the trash and give herself away. She's welcome to it, of course, but at her age it's a weight thing. She needs to watch her weight. It's the deceptiveness, too, don't you see. What does she eat when she's alone?

Alone, in an apartment now, ever since the night a stranger crept up the breezeway, broke the kitchen window, and made off with her purse, the portable TV, and the boxed silver in the dining room, which had been her mother's, she licked chocolate pudding from the back of a spoon, sherbet, gelato, sorbet, ice cream, of course. She scraped the sides of the carton, ran a finger around the rim.

On visits to her out-of-state children she'd get up in the night, stand by the light of the refrigerator, take a few tablespoons from the gallon, or a single ice-cream bar, but always end up going back for more. A daughter-in-law found her one morning, 2 A.M., with the last chocolate/vanilla ice-cream cup and a tiny wooden spoon—leftovers from the grandchild's birthday party she had made the trip specifically to attend—and gave her such a lecture, as she put it when she got home, that you'd think she'd been shooting heroin.

It was the weight that concerned them, said her children, conferring. They were afraid it was the weight that was keeping her these days from those senior trips she used to love, from the winter vacations in Florida she'd once looked forward to. Now that the grandchildren were grown out of the need for a sitter, she should be doing more of those things, not fewer. They solicited a talking-to for their mother from her doctor, who instead reminded them all that she was past eighty and healthy enough and free to do, or not do, what she liked.

They took to stopping by to see her, on lunch hours, or before going to the grocery store, keeping their car keys in their hands, and urging her to turn off the television, to plan something, to do something. Her grandchildren, driving cars now, asked her out to their kinds of places, treated her to frothy lattes topped with whipped cream that would repeat on her the rest of the afternoon and on into the evening, despite bicarbs and antacids, until she brought herself to tell them when they called, "Thank you, dear, but I'm quite content at home."

Peach, strawberry, and reliable vanilla. Rocky road and butter pecan and mint chocolate chip. Looking at ninety and still, still, the last thing she feels at the end of each day is that longing to wrap her legs around him, around someone. The pleasure of the taste, of loading up a spoon and finishing it bit by bit, and then taking another spoonful and another—one kind of pleasure, enhanced by stealth and guilt, when it is someone else's carton, someone else's home in the middle of the night, another kind when it's her own and she carries her bowl, in full light, to the couch before the television in the living room. Forbidden youthful passion and domestic married love, something like that, anyway, if you want to extrapolate. If you want to begin with the ice-cream dishes licked clean by a girl who is now the old woman past all usefulness, closing her eyes at the first taste. If you want to make a metaphor out of her lifelong cravings, something she is not inclined to do. Pleasure is pleasure. A remnant of strawberries, a young man's hands, a newborn in your arms, or your own child's changing face. Your lips to the familiar stubble of your husband's cheek. Your tongue to the last vein of fudge in the empty carton. Pleasure is pleasure. If you have an appetite for it, you'll find there's plenty. Plenty to satisfy you—lick the back of the spoon. Take another, and another. Plenty. Never enough.

2002

THE BUTCHER'S WIFE

LOUISE ERDRICH

Here's an odd and paradoxical truth: A man's experience of happiness can later kill him. Though he appeared to be no more than an everyday drunk, Delphine Watzka's father, Roy, was more. He was a dangerous romantic. In his life, he had loved deeply, even selflessly, with all the profound gratitude of a surprised Pole. But the woman he had loved and married, Minnie Watzka, née Kust, now existed only in the person of her daughter, Delphine, and in photographs. Minnie had died when Delphine was very young, and afterward Roy indulged in a worship of those photographs. Some nights, he lit a line of votive candles on the dresser and drank steadily and spoke to Minnie until, from deep in his cups, she answered.

During the first years after Minnie's death, Roy bounced in and out of drink with the resilience of a man with a healthy liver. He remained remarkably sloshed even through Prohibition by becoming ecumenical. Hair tonic, orange-flower water, cough syrups of all types, even women's monthly elixirs fueled his grieving rituals. Gradually, he destroyed the organ he'd mistaken for his heart. By the time Delphine reached her twelfth year, her father's need to drink was produced less by her mother's memory than by the drink itself. After that, she knew her father mainly as a pickled wreck. Home was chaos. Now Delphine was a grown woman and he was completely failing. In the spring of 1936, she quit secretarial school and moved back from the Twin Cities to their Minnesota farm to care for him.

As Delphine walked into town for supplies, she thought of her mother. She possessed only one tiny locket photo of Minnie, and while she was away she had found herself missing the other photographs. It was in that fit of longing to see her mother's face that Delphine entered Waldvogel's Meats, and met Eva Waldvogel.

The first true meeting of their minds was over lard.

"I'll take half a pound," Delphine said. She was mentally worn out by her father's insistence that since he was dying anyway he might as well kill himself more pleasurably with schnapps. All day long he'd been drunk underneath the mulberry trees, laughing to himself and trying to catch the fruit in his mouth. He was now stained purple with the juice.

"There's lard and there is lard." Eva reached into the glass case that was cooled by an electric fan. "My husband was trained back in Germany as a master butcher, and he uses a secret process to render his fat. Taste," she commanded, holding out a small pan. Delphine swiped a bit with the tip of her finger.

"Pure as butter!"

"We don't salt it much," Eva whispered, as though this were not for just anyone to overhear. "But it won't keep unless you have an icebox."

"I don't have one," Delphine admitted. "Well, I did, but my dad sold it while I was away."

"Who is he, may I ask?"

Delphine liked Eva's direct but polite manners and admired her thick bun of bronze-red hair stuck through with two yellow lead pencils. Eva's eyes were a very pale, washed-out blue with flecks of green. There was, in one eye, an odd golden streak that would turn black when the life finally left her body, like a light going out behind the crack in a door.

"Roy Watzka," Delphine said slowly.

Eva nodded. The name seemed to tell her all that she needed to know. "Come back here." Eva swept her arm around the counter. "I'll teach you to make a mincemeat pie better than you've ever eaten. It's all in the goddam suet."

Delphine went behind the counter, past an office cascading with papers and bills, past little cupboards full of clean aprons and rags, and a knickknack shelf displaying figures made of German porcelain. She and Eva entered the kitchen, which was full of light from big windows set into the thick walls. Here, for Delphine, all time stopped. As she took in the room, she experienced a profound and fabulous expansion of being.

There was a shelf for big clay bread bowls and a pull-out bin containing flour. Wooden cupboards painted an astounding green matched the floor's linoleum. A heavy, polished meat grinder was bolted to the counter. The round table was covered with a piece of oilcloth with squares. In each red-trimmed square was printed a bunch of blue grapes or a fat pink-gold peach, an apple or a delicate green pear. On the windowsills, pots of geraniums bloomed, scarlet and ferociously cheerful.

Suddenly extremely happy, Delphine sat in a solid, square-backed chair while Eva spooned roasted coffee beans into a grinder and then began to grind them. A wonderful fragrance emerged. Delphine took a huge breath. Eva, her hands quick and certain, dumped the thin wooden drawer full of fresh grounds into a pale-blue speckled enamel coffeepot. She got water from a faucet in her sink, instead of from a pump, and then she put the coffee on the stove and lit the burner of a stunning white gas range with chrome trim swirled into the words "Magic Chef."

"My God," Delphine breathed. She couldn't speak. But that was fine, for Eva had already whipped one of the pencils out of her hair and taken up a pad of paper to set down the mincemeat recipe. Eva spoke English very well but her writing was of the old, ornate German style, and she wasn't a good speller. Delphine was grateful for this tiny flaw, for Eva appeared so fantastically skilled a being, so assured—she was also the mother of two sturdy and intelligent sons—that she would have been an unapproachable paragon to Delphine otherwise. Delphine—who had never really had a mother, much less a sister, who cleaned up shameful things in her father's house, who had been toughened by cold and hunger and was regarded as beneath notice by the town's best society, and yet could spell—stole confidence from the misspelled recipe.

The next time Delphine visited the Waldvogels' store, she noted the jangle of a cheerful shop bell. She imagined that it was only the first of many times that she would ring the bell as she entered the shop. This did not prove to be the case. By the next time Delphine came to the shop, she had already attained a status so familiar that she entered by the back door.

Delphine placed her order, as before, and, as before, Eva asked her to come in and sit down for a coffee. There was no cleanser on Eva's shelf that would be strong enough for the work Delphine had to do to make Roy's place habitable again, and Eva wanted to concoct something of her own.

"First off, a good vinegar-and-water washdown. Then I should order the industrial-strength ammonia for you, only be careful with the fumes. Maybe, if that doesn't work, a very raw lye."

Delphine shook her head. She was smitten with shame, and could not tell Eva that she was afraid her father might try to drink the stuff. Eva sipped her coffee. Today, her hair was bound back in a singular knot, in the shape of a figure eight, which Delphine knew was the ancient sign for eternity. Eva rose and turned away, walked across the green squares of linoleum to punch down the risen dough. As Delphine watched, a strange notion popped into her head, the idea that perhaps the most strongly experienced moments—such as this one, when Eva turned, and the sun met her hair, and for that one instant the symbol blazed out— those particular moments were eternal. They actually went somewhere— into a file of moments that existed beyond time's range and could not be pilfered by God.

Well, it *was* God, wasn't it, Delphine went on stubbornly, who had made time and thereby created the end of everything? Tell me this, Delphine wanted to say to her new friend, why are we given the curse of imagining eternity when we can't experience it, when we ourselves are so finite? She wanted to say it, but suddenly grew shy, and it was in that state of concentrated inattention that she first met Eva's husband, Fidelis Waldvogel, Master Butcher.

Before she actually met him, she sensed him, like a surge of electric power in the air when the clouds are low. Then she felt a heaviness. A field of gravity moved through her body. She was trying to rise, to shake the feeling, when he suddenly filled the doorway.

It was not his size. He was not extraordinarily tall or broad. But he shed power, as though there were a bigger man crammed into him. One thick hand hung down at his side like a hook; the other balanced on his shoulder a slab of meat. That cow's haunch weighed perhaps a hundred pounds or double that. He held it lightly, although the veins in his neck throbbed, heavy-blooded as a bull's. He looked at Delphine, and his eyes were white-blue. Their stares locked. Delphine's cheeks went fever red, and she looked down first. Clouds moved across the sun, and the red mouths of the geraniums on the windowsill yawned. The shock of his gaze caused her to pick up one of Eva's cigarettes. To light it. He looked away from her and conversed with his wife. Then he left without asking to be introduced.

That abruptness, though rude, was more than fine with Delphine. Already, she didn't want to know him. She hoped that she could avoid him. It didn't matter, so long as she could still be friends with Eva, and hold the job that she soon was offered, waiting on customers.

So it was. From then on, Delphine used the back door, which led past the furnace and the washtubs, the shelves of tools, the bleached aprons slowly drying on racks and hooks. She walked down the hallway cluttered with papers and equipment and lifted from a hook by the shop door the apron Eva had given her, blue with tiny white flowers. From then on, she heard the customer bell ring from the other side of the counter.

Within a week, Delphine had met most of the regular customers. Then she met Tante Marie-Christine, who was not a customer but Fidelis's sister. One afternoon, Tante swept in with just one clang of the bell, as though the bell itself had been muted by her elegance. She went right around to the case that held the sausage, wrenched it open, fished out a ring of the best bologna, and put it in her purse. Delphine stood back and watched—actually, she stood back and envied the woman's shoes. They were made of a thin, flexible Italian leather and were cleverly buttoned. They fit Tante's rather long, narrow feet with a winsome precision. She might not have had a captivating face—for she resembled her brother, replicated his powerful neck and too-stern chin, and the eyes that on him were commanding on her were a ghostly blue that gave Delphine the shivers—but her feet were slim and pretty. She was vain about them, and all her shoes were made of the most expensive leather.

"Who are you?" Tante asked, rearing her head back and then swirling off in her fur coat without deigning to accept an answer. The question hung in the air long after Tante had gone back to invade Eva's kitchen. "Who are you?" is a question with a long answer or a short answer. When Tante dropped it in the air like that, Delphine was left to consider its larger meaning as she scrubbed down the meat counters and prepared to mop the floor.

Who are you, Delphine Watzka, you drunkard's child, you dropout secretary, you creature with a belly of steel and a heart that longs for a mother? Who are you, *what* are you—born a dirty Pole in a Polack's dirt? You with a cellar full of empty bottles and a stewed father lying on the floor? What makes you think you belong anywhere near this house, this shop, and especially my brother Fidelis, who is the master of all that he does?

When Tante swept back out with a loaf of her sister-in-law's fresh bread under her arm and grabbed a bottle of milk, Delphine wrote it all down on a slip: "Tante took a bottle of milk, a ring of number-one bologna, and a loaf of bread." And she left it at that. When Tante found out that Delphine had written the items down, she was furious. Tante didn't take things. By her reckoning, she was owed things. She had once given her brother five hundred dollars to purchase equipment, and although he had paid her back she continued to take the interest out in ways that were intended to remind him of her dutiful generosity.

Eva's two boys, Franz and Louis, did not like Tante. Delphine could see that. Not that she knew all that much about children. She had not been around them often. But as these boys belonged to Eva, she was interested in who they were.

At fourteen, Franz was strong and athletic, with one of those proud, easygoing American temperaments that are simultaneously transparent and opaque. His inner thoughts and feelings were either nonevident or nonexistent; she couldn't tell which. He always smiled at her and said hello, with only the faintest of German accents. He played football and was, in fact, a local hero. The second boy was more reclusive. Louis had a philosophical bent and a monkish nature, though he'd play with tough abandon when he could. His grades were perfect for one year, and abysmal the next, according to his interests. He had inherited his mother's long hands, her floss of red-gold hair, her thin cheeks, and eyes that looked out sometimes with a sad curiosity and amusement, as if to say, What an idiotic spectacle. Louis was polite, though more restrained than his brother. He anxiously accomplished errands for his father, but he clearly doted on his mother. Eva often stroked his hair, so like her own, with its curls clipped. When she held him close and kissed him, he pulled away, as boys had to, but did it gently, to show that he didn't want to hurt her feelings.

Nineteen thirty-six was a year of extremes. That winter, Minnesota had endured a bout of intense cold. Now it sucked in its breath and wilted in a brutal heat. As the heat wave wore on, cleaning became more difficult. Eva Waldvogel, who prided herself on triumphing over anything that circumstance brought her way, could not keep the shop functioning with the efficiency she usually demanded. Now that Delphine was around Eva from the early morning on, she could see how her friend suffered. Eva's face was pale with the daily effort and sometimes she announced that she had to lie down, just for a minute, and rest. When Delphine checked on her, she often found Eva in such a sunken dead shock of slumber that she didn't have the heart to wake her. After an hour or two, Eva woke anyway, in a frenzy of energy, and pushed herself again.

They mopped down the floors of the slaughter room with bleach every single day. The meat cases were run on full cold, yet they were lukewarm and the meat within had to be checked constantly for rot. They bought only the smallest amount of milk to sell because it often soured during the drive to the store. They kept little butter or lard. The heat kept getting worse. The boys slept outside on the roof in just their under-shorts. Eva dragged a mattress and sheets up there, too, and slept with them while Fidelis stayed downstairs, near his gun, for fear of a break-in.

When Delphine walked to work, just an hour after sunrise, the air was already stiff and metallic. If it broke, it would break violently, Fidelis said, to no one in particular. As he systematically sharpened the blades of his knives and saws, his back turned, he started singing, and Delphine re-alized, with a strange shock, that his voice was very beautiful. The heat made her flustered, and his voice dismayed her, so pure in a room that was slippery with blood. Sharply, she banged a ham down on the metal counter, and he went silent. It was a relief not to have to listen.

The sky went dark, the leaves turned brown, and nothing happened. Rain hung painfully nearby in an iron-gray sheet that stretched across the sky, but nothing moved. No breeze. No air. Delphine washed her face and donned the limp apron by the door. Late in the day, she stripped the wax off the linoleum in order to apply a new coat. The floor was already dry when she flipped the cardboard sign in the entry window from OPEN to CLOSED. Now, in a special bucket, she mixed the wax and with a long brush painted the floor, back to front, in perfect swipes. She painted her-self right up to the counter, put a box in the doorway so that the boys would not ruin the drying surface. She retreated. Hung up her apron, said a quick goodbye, and went home to swelter. Early the next morning, be-fore the store opened, she'd return and apply another coat. Let it dry while she drank her morning coffee with Eva. Then, between customers, she'd polish that linoleum to a mighty finish with a buffing rag and elbow grease. That's what she had planned, anyway, and all that she had planned did occur, but over weeks and under radically different circumstances.

The next morning, while Delphine sat in the kitchen, the heat pushed at the walls. The strong black coffee sent her into a sweat. She drank from a pitcher of water that Eva had set on the table.

"Listen." Eva had been awake most of the night, doing her weekly baking in the thread of cool air. "I don't feel so good."

She said this in such an offhand way that Delphine hardly registered the words, but then she repeated herself as though she did not remember having said it. "I don't feel so good," Eva whispered. She put her elbows on the table and her hands curled around her china cup.

"What do you mean you don't feel so good?"

"It's my stomach. I get pains. I'm all lumped up." Beads of sweat trembled on her upper lip. "They come and go." Eva drew a deep breath and held it, then let it out. *There.* She pressed a dish towel to her face, blotted away the sweat. "Like a cramp, but I'm never quite over the monthly. . . . That comes and goes, too."

"Maybe you're just stopping early?"

"I think so," Eva said. "My mother . . ." But then she shook her head and smiled, spoke in a high, thin voice. "Don't you hate a whiner?"

She jumped up awkwardly, banging herself against the counter, but then she bustled to the oven, moved swiftly through the kitchen, as though motion would cure whatever it was that had gripped her. Within moments, she seemed to have turned back into the unworried, capable Eva.

"I'm going out front to start polishing the floor," Delphine said. "By now, in this heat, it's surely dry."

"That's good," Eva said, but as Delphine passed her to put her coffee cup in the gray soapstone sink, the butcher's wife took one of Delphine's hands in hers. Lightly, her voice a shade too careless, she said the words that even in the heat chilled her friend.

"Take me to the doctor."

Then she smiled as though this were a great joke, lay down on the floor, closed her eyes, and did not move.

Fidelis had left early on a delivery, and he could not be found. He wasn't home, either, when Delphine returned from the doctor's. By then, she had Eva drugged with morphine in the backseat, and a sheaf of instructions telling her whom to seek. What could possibly be done. Old Dr. Heech was telephoning the clinic to tell a surgeon he knew there to prepare for a patient named Eva Waldvogel.

Delphine found Louis and gave him a note for Fidelis. Louis dropped it, picked it up, his lithe boy's fingers for once clumsy with fright. He ran straight out to the car and climbed into the backseat, which was where Delphine found him, holding Eva as she sighed in the fervent relief of the drug. She was so serene that Louis was reassured and Delphine was able to lead him carefully away, terrified that Eva would suddenly wake, in front of the boy, and recognize her pain. From what Delphine had gathered so far, Eva must have been suffering for many months now. Her illness was remarkably advanced, and Heech in his alarm, as well as his fondness for Eva, scolded her with the violent despair of a doctor who knows he is helpless.

As Delphine led Louis back to the house, she tried to stroke his hair. He jerked away in terror at the unfamiliar tenderness. It was, of course, a sign to him that something was really wrong with Eva.

"Fidelis," Delphine had written in the note, "I have taken Eva to the clinic to the south called the Mayo, where Heech says emergency help will be found. She passed out this morning. It is a cancer. You can talk to Heech."

It was on the drive down to the Mayo Clinic that Delphine first really listened to the butcher's singing; only this time it was in her mind. She replayed it like a comforting record on a phonograph as she kept her foot calmly on the gas pedal of Dr. Heech's DeSoto and the speedometer hovered near eighty miles an hour. The world blurred. Fields turned like spoked wheels. She caught the flash of houses, cows, horses, barns. Then there was the long stop-and-go of the city. All through the drive, she replayed the song that Fidelis had sung just the morning before, in the concrete of the slaughter room, when she had been too crushed by the heat to marvel at the buoyant mildness of his tenor. *"Die Gedanken sind frei,"* he had sung, and the walls had spun each note higher, as if he were singing beneath the dome of a beautiful church. Who would think that a slaughterhouse would have the acoustics of a cathedral?

The song wheeled in her thoughts as she drove, and using what ragtag German she knew, Delphine made out the words: *"Die Gedanken sind frei, / Wer kann sie erraten, / Sie fliehen vorbei, / Wie nächtliche Schatten"*— "Thoughts are free . . . they fly around like shadows of the night." The dead crops turned, row by row, in the fields, the vent blew the hot air hotter, and the wind boomed into the open windows. Even when it finally started to rain, Delphine did not roll the windows back up. The car was moving so fast that the drops stung like BBs on the side of her face and kept her alert. Occasionally, behind her, Eva made sounds. Perhaps the morphine, as well as dulling her pain, had loosened her self-control, for in the wet crackle of the wind Delphine heard a moan that could have come from Eva. A growling, as though her pain were an animal she had wrestled to earth.

The first treatment after Eva's surgery consisted of inserting into her uterus several hollow metal bombs, cast of German silver, containing radium. During the weeks that Eva spent in the hospital, the tubes were taken out, refilled, and reinserted several times. By the time she was sent home, she smelled like a blackened pot roast.

"I smell burned," she said, "like bad cooking. Get some lilac at the drugstore." Delphine bought a great purple bottle of flower water to wash her with, but it didn't help. For weeks, Eva passed charcoal and blood, and the smell lingered. The cancer spread. Next, Dr. Heech gave her monthly treatments of radium via long twenty-four-karat-gold needles, tipped with iridium, that he pushed into the new tumor with forceps so as not to burn his fingers. She took those treatments in his office, strapped to a table, dosed with ether for the insertion, then, after she woke, with a hypodermic of morphine. Delphine sat with her, for the needles had to stay in place for six hours.

"I'm a damn pincushion now," Eva said once, rousing slightly. Then she dropped back into her restless dream. Delphine tried to read, but shooting pains stabbed her own stomach when the needles went in; she even had a sympathetic morphine sweat. But she kept on going, and as she approached the house each day she said the prayer to God that she'd selected as the most appropriate to the situation: "Spit in your eye." The curse wasn't much, it didn't register the depth of her feeling, but at least she was not a hypocrite. Why should she even pretend to pray? That was Tante's field.

Tante had mustered a host of pious Lutheran ladies, and they came around every few afternoons to try to convert Eva, who was Catholic. Once Eva became too weak to chase them off, Delphine did whatever she could think of to keep them from crowding around the bed like a flock of turkey vultures in a gloating prayer circle. Feeding them was her best strategy, for they filed out quickly enough when they knew that there was grub in the kitchen. After they'd gorged on Eva's pain and her signature linzer torte, the recipe for which she'd given to Delphine, Tante would lead them away one small step at a time.

Delphine bleached the bloody aprons. She scrubbed the grimy socks. The boys' stained drawers and their one-strap overalls. She took their good suits out of mothballs and aired and pressed them. She sprinkled Fidelis's thick white cotton shirts with starch and every morning she ironed one for him, just as Eva had done. She took on the sheets, the sweat, the shit, and the blood, always blood. The towels and the tablecloths. Doing this laundry was a kind of goodbye gift. For once Eva left,

Delphine would be leaving, too. Fidelis had others to help him. Tante, Delphine was sure, would find stepping in to care for the boys and her brother a perfect showcase for her pieties.

For all that he was a truly unbearable souse, no one in town disliked Roy Watzka. There were several reasons for this. First, his gross slide into abandon had been triggered by loss. That he had loved to the point of self-destruction fed a certain reflex feature in many a female heart, and he got handouts easily when strapped. Women made him sandwiches of pork or cold beans, and wrapped them carefully for him to eat when coming off a binge. Another reason was that Roy Watzka, during those short, rare times when he was sober, had a capacity for intense bouts of hard labor. He could work phenomenally. Plus, he told a good tale. He was not a mean drunk or a rampager, and it was well known that, although she certainly put up with more than a daughter should ever have to, he did love Delphine.

Eva liked him, or felt sorry for him, anyway, and she was one of those who had always given him a meal. Now that she was in trouble, Roy showed up for a different purpose. He came to the shop almost every afternoon, sometimes stinking of schnapps. But, once there, he'd do anything. He'd move the outhouse, shovel guts. Before he left, he'd sit with Eva and tell her crazy stories about the things that had happened to him as a young man: the pet hog he'd trained to read, how to extract the venom from a rattlesnake, the actual wolf-man he'd once known who taught him words in the Lycanthropian language, or the Latin names of flowers and where they came from. Listening sometimes, Delphine was both glad of Roy's adept distractions and resentful. Where had he learned these things? In bars, he said. She'd cleaned up after him all her life and never had he talked to her like this.

Delphine and Eva sat together on broken chairs in Eva's garden, each with a bottle of Fidelis's earth-dark, home-brewed beer held tight between their feet. They were protected from the mosquitoes by citronella burning in a bucket and sprigs of basil which Eva snapped off and thrust into their hair. Delphine wore a wash dress and an apron and a pair of low green pumps. Eva wore a nightgown and a light woolen shawl, with her feet bare in Japanese thongs. The slugs were naked. Antlered and feeble, they lived in the thickness of hay and the shredded newspapers that Eva had put down for mulch. They had already eaten many of the new seedlings from the topmost leaves down to the ground, and Eva had vowed to destroy them.

"Their last feast," she said, gesturing at her bean plants as she poured a little beer into a pie plate. "Now they are doomed."

The beer was chilled from the glass refrigerator case in the store, newly installed. It seemed a shame to waste it on slugs. The two women sipped it slowly as the sun slanted through the margins of the stock pens.

"Maybe we should simply have shriveled them with salt," Delphine said. But then she had a thought: we are close to Eva's own death, and can afford to make death easy on the helpless. She said nothing.

Eva's garden, Delphine had decided, reflected the dark underside of her organizational genius. It was everything raw and wild that Eva was not. It had grown rich on junk. Pot scrapings, tea leaves, and cucumber peelings all went into the dirt, buried haphazardly, sometimes just piled. Everything rotted down beneath the blistering Minnesota sun. Eva's method was to have no method. Give nature its head. She had apple trees that grew from cores. Rosebushes, bristling near the runner that collected steer's blood, were covered with blooms so fat and hearty that they looked sinister. The boys' dog dug up old bones that some former dog had buried and refused to rebury them. It would be awful in the spring, Delphine thought, when the snow melted away, to see the litter of femurs and clavicles, the knobs and knuckles. As if the scattered dead, rising to meet the Judgment, had had to change and swap their parts to fit.

Delphine had always had a tendency to think about fate, but she did so more often now that Eva's sickness put her constantly in mind of mortality, and also made her marvel at how anyone managed to live at all. Life was a precious feat of daring, she saw, improbable, as strange as a feast of slugs.

Eva bent over, flipped out a small pocket of earth with her trowel, and tamped in her quarter-full beer bottle as a trap. "Die happy," she encouraged. Delphine handed over her own three-quarters-drunk bottle, too. This one Eva planted by a hill of squash that would overpower the rest of the garden by fall, though she would not be there to see it. She settled back against the crisscrossed canvas webbing of her chair and forked open another bottle. It was a good day, a very good day for her.

"I'm going," Delphine said, but she continued to sit with Eva through sunset and on into the rising dark. It was as if they knew that no moment of the weeks to come would be this peaceful and that they would both, in fearful nights, remember these hours. How the air turned blue around them and the moths came out, invisible and sightless, flapping against the shuttered lamp at the other end of the yard.

Delphine shut her eyes, and her mind grew alert. All around her, she felt how quickly things formed and were consumed. It was going on beyond the wall of her sight, out of her control. She felt as though she could drift away like a boat of skin, never to return, leaving only her crumpled dress and worn green shoes.

She heard Eva's voice.

"I wish it were true, what I read—that the mind stays intact. The brain. The eyes to read with."

Delphine had sometimes thought that her friend didn't care if she became an animal or a plant, if all this thinking and figuring and selling of pork and blood meal were wasted effort. She treated her death with scorn or ridicule. But with that statement Eva revealed a certain fear she'd never shown before. Or a wistfulness.

"Your mind stays itself," Delphine said, as lightly as she could. "There you'll be, strumming on your harp, looking down on all the foolish crap people do."

"I could never play the harp," Eva said. "I think they'll give me a kazoo."

"Save me a cloud and I'll play a tune with you," Delphine said.

It wasn't very funny, so they laughed all the harder, laughed until tears started in their eyes, then they gasped and fell utterly silent.

"The boys are playing in the orchard. The men are already half lit," Delphine reported. It was the first weekend in September, a holiday. Eva struggled and Delphine helped her to sit up and look out the window of the little room off the kitchen, where Fidelis had set up her bed. Eva smiled faintly, then fell back, nodding at the sight.

"Men are such fools," she whispered. "They think they're so smart hiding the Everclear in the gooseberry bush."

There was no saving her. They were well beyond that now. But even though the last few days were nightmarish Eva refused to die in a morbid way. She sometimes laughed freakishly at pain and made fun of her condition, more so now, when the end was close.

They'd closed the shop at noon. Now everyone in town was celebrating. Fidelis had the old chairs and table out in the yard and on the table he had a summer sausage and a beer sausage, a watermelon, bowls of crackers, and beer in a tub of ice underneath the tomato plants, to wash down the high-proof alcohol that Eva knew he was hiding. Over and over the men sneaked their arms into the gooseberry fronds. With a furtive look at the house, they'd tip the bottle to their lips. Even Fidelis, normally so powerful and purposeful, acted like a guilty boy.

The men's voices rose and fell, rumbling with laughter at the tall tales they told, stern with argument at the outrages committed by the government, and sometimes they even fell silent and gazed stuporously into the tangled foliage. Roy was out there, trying to nurse along a beer, not gulp. As always, Fidelis was at the center of the gathering, prodding everbolder stories out of the men or challenging them to feats of strength.

In the kitchen, Delphine cut cold butter into flour for a pastry. She had decided to make pies for the holiday supper—the men would need them to counteract the booze. The potatoes were boiling now, and she had a crock of beans laced with hot mustard, brown sugar, and blackstrap molasses. There were, of course, sausages. Delphine added a pinch of salt, rolled her dough in waxed paper, and set it in the icebox. Then she started on the fruit, slicing thin moons from the crate of peaches, peeling out the brownest bits of rosy flesh. It's nearly time, she thought, nearly time. She was thinking of Eva's pain. Delphine's sense of time passing had to do only with the duration of a dose of opium wine, flavored with cloves and cinnamon, or of the morphine that Dr. Heech had taught her to administer, though he warned her not to give too much, lest by the end even the morphine lose its effect.

Hearing Eva stir, Delphine set aside her pie makings. She put some water on to boil, to sterilize the hypodermic needle. Last night, she'd prepared a vial and set it in the icebox, the 1:30 solution, which Heech had told her she was better than any nurse at giving to Eva. Delphine was proud of this. The more so because she secretly hated needles, abhorred them, grew sickly hollow when she filled the syringe, and felt the prick in her own flesh when she gave the dose to Eva.

Now she knew, when she checked on Eva, not so much by the time elapsed as by the lucid shock of agony in Eva's stare, her mouth half open, her brows clenched, that she would need the relief very soon, as soon as the water had boiled. Delphine thought to divert her friend by massaging her sore hands.

Eva groaned as Delphine worked the dips between her knuckles, and then her forehead smoothed, her translucent eyelids closed over, she began to breathe more peacefully and said, softly, "How are the damn fools?"

Delphine glanced out the window and observed that they were in an uproar. Sheriff Hock had now joined them, and Fidelis was standing, gesturing, laughing at the big man's belly. Then they were all comparing their bellies. In the lengthening afternoon light, Fidelis's face was slightly fuzzy with the unaccustomed drink, and with the fellowship of other men, too, for lately he had been isolated in Eva's struggle to die.

"They're showing off their big guts to each other," Delphine said.

"At least not the thing below," Eva croaked.

"Oh, for shame!" Delphine laughed. "No, they've kept their peckers in. But something's going on. Here, I'm going to prop you up. They're better than burlesque."

She took down extra pillows from the shelves, shoved the bed up to the window, and propped Eva where she would see the doings in the yard. Now it looked like they were making and taking bets. Bills were waved. The men weren't stumbling drunk, but loud drunk. Roaring with jokes. All of a sudden, with a clatter, the men cleared the glasses and bottles, the crackers and the sticks of sausage, the bits of cheddar and the plates off the table. And then the Sheriff, a former actor who'd played large characters in local productions, lay down upon it on his back. He was longer than the table, and he balanced there, like a boat in dry dock, his booted feet sticking absurdly straight up and his head extended off the other end. His stomach made a mound. Now on the other side of the table, directly beneath Eva's window, stood Fidelis. He'd unbuttoned the top buttons of his white shirt and rolled his sleeves up over his solid forearms.

Suddenly, Fidelis bent over Sheriff Hock in a weight lifter's crouch and threw his arms fiercely out to either side. Delicately, firmly, he grasped in his jaws a loop that the women now saw had been specially created for this purpose in Sheriff Hock's thick belt.

There was a moment in which everything went still. Nothing happened. Then a huge thing happened. Fidelis gathered his power. It was as if the ground itself flowed up through him, and flexed. His jaws flared bone-white around the belt loop, his arms tightened in the air, his neck and shoulders swelled impossibly, and he lifted Sheriff Hock off the table. With the belt loop in his teeth, he moved the town's Falstaff. Just a fraction of an inch. Then Fidelis paused. His whole being surged with a blind, suffusing ease. He jerked the Sheriff higher, balancing now, half out of the crouch.

In that moment of tremendous effort, Delphine saw the butcher's true face—his animal face, his ears flaming with heat, his neck cords popping—and then his deranged eye, straining out of its socket, rolled up to the window to see if Eva was watching. That's when Delphine felt a thud of awful sympathy. He was doing this for Eva. He was trying to distract her, and Delphine suddenly understood that Fidelis loved Eva with a helpless and fierce canine devotion, which made him do things that seemed foolish. Lift a grown man by the belt with his teeth. A stupid thing. Showing clearly that all his strength was nothing. Against her sickness, he was weak as a child.

Once Fidelis had dropped the Sheriff, to roars of laughter, Delphine went back into the kitchen to fetch the medicine. She opened the door of the icebox. Looked once, then rummaged with a searching hand. The morphine that Fidelis had labored with vicious self-disregard to pay for and which Delphine had guarded jealously was gone. The vial, the powder, the other syringe. She couldn't believe it. Searched once again, and then again. It wasn't there, and already Eva was restless in the next room.

Delphine rushed out and beckoned Fidelis away from the men. He was wiping down his face and neck, the sweat still pouring off him.

"Eva's medicine is gone."

"Gone?"

He was not as drunk as she'd imagined, or maybe the effort of lifting the Sheriff had sobered him.

"Gone. Nowhere. I've looked. Someone stole it."

"Heiliges Kreuz Donnerwetter . . ." he began, whirling around. That was just the beginning of what he had to say, but Delphine left before he got any further. She went back to Eva and gave her the rest of the opium wine. Spoon by spoon it went down; in a flash it came back up. "What a mess," Eva said. "I'm worse than a puking baby." She tried to laugh, but it came out a surprised, hushed groan. And then she was gasping, taking the shallow panting breaths she used to keep herself from shrieking.

"Bitte . . ." Her eyes rolled back and she arched off the bed. She gestured for a rolled-up washcloth to set between her teeth. It was coming. It was coming like a mighty storm in her. No one could stop it from breaking. It would take hours for Delphine to get another prescription from Dr. Heech, wherever he happened to be celebrating the holiday, and then to find the pharmacist. Delphine yelled out the garden door to Fidelis, and then sped out the other way. As she ran, a thought came into her mind. She decided to act on it. Instead of steering straight for Heech she gunned the shop's truck and stopped short at Tante's little closet of a house, two blocks from the Lutheran church, where Tante prayed every Sunday that the deplorable Catholic her brother had married desist from idolatry—saint worship—before her two nephews were confirmed.

"Was wollen Sie?"

When Tante opened the door to Delphine, her face had all the knowledge in it, and Delphine knew she'd guessed right. Delphine had remembered her clucking over the dose of the drug with her prayer friends in whispered consultation as they pressed up crumbs of lemon pound cake with their fingers.

"Wo ist die Medizin?" Delphine said, first in a normal tone of voice.

Tante affected Hochdeutsch around Delphine and made great pretense of having trouble understanding her. When Tante gave only a cold twist of a smile, Delphine screamed: "Where is Eva's medicine?" Delphine stepped in the door, shoved past Tante, and dashed to the refrigerator. On the way there, with an outraged Tante trailing, she passed a table with a long slim object wrapped in a handkerchief. Delphine grabbed for it on instinct, unrolled it, and nearly dropped the missing hypodermic.

"Where is it?" Delphine's voice was deadly. She turned, jabbing the needle at Tante, and then found herself as in a stage play advancing with an air of threat. The feeling of being in a dramatic production gave her leave to speak the lines she wished had been written for the moment.

"Come on, you rough old bitch, you don't fool me. So you're a habitual fiend on the sly!"

Delphine didn't really think that, but she wanted to make Tante so indignant that she would tell her where the morphine was. But when Tante gaped and couldn't rally her wits to answer, Delphine, disgusted, went to the little icebox, rooted frantically through it. With a savage permission, she tossed out all of Tante's food, even the eggs, and then she turned and confronted Tante. Her brain was swimming with desperation.

"Please, you've got to tell me. Where is it?"

Now Tante had gained control. She even spoke English.

"You will owe me for those eggs."

"All right," Delphine said. "Just tell me."

But Tante, with the upper hand, enjoyed her moment.

"They are saying that she is addicted. This cannot be. The wife of my brother? It is a great shame on us."

Delphine now saw that she had been stupid to antagonize the only person who could provide morphine quickly. She'd blown her cover and now she regretted her self-indulgence, grew meek.

"Oh, Tante," she sighed, "you know the truth, don't you? Tante, our Eva will probably not make it, and she is suffering terribly. You see her only when she's comfortable, so of course how can you possibly know how the agony builds? Tante, have mercy on your brother's wife. There is no shame in keeping her comfortable—the doctor has said so."

"I think," Tante said, her black figure precise, "the doctor doesn't really know. He feels too sorry for her, and she is addicted, that is for sure my good friend Mrs. Orlen Sorven can tell this."

"Tante, Tante, for the love of God . . ." Delphine begged from her heart. She thought of falling on her knees. Tante's frozen little mouth twitched.

"It doesn't matter, anyway. I have thrown it down the sinkhole."

Delphine turned and saw that on the edge of Tante's porcelain sink a clean-washed vial and the bottle that had held the powder were drying in the glow of sun. And when she saw this, she lost all control and didn't quite know what she was doing. She was strong, suddenly phenomenally strong, and when she grabbed Tante by the bodice, jerked her forward, and said, into her face, "Okay. You come and nurse her through this. You'll see," Tante found herself unable to resist, her struggles feeble against Delphine's surging force as she dragged her to the car, stuffed her inside, then roared off and dumped her at the house.

"I don't have time to go in there. You help her. You stay with her. You," she shrieked, roaring the engine. Then she was gone and Tante, with the smug grimness of a woman who has at last been allowed to take charge, entered the back door.

It did take hours, and in those hours, Delphine did pray. She prayed as though she meant what she said. She prayed her heart out, cussed and swore, implored the devil, made bargains, came to tears at the thwarted junctures where she was directed to one place and ended up at another. It proved impossible to track down either Heech or the pharmacist. She was returning empty-handed, driving back to the house, weeping angrily, when she saw her father stumbling along the road, his pants sagging, his loose shirt flopping off his hunched, skinny shoulders. As she drew near, she looked around to see if anyone else was watching, for an all-seeing rage had boiled up in her and she suddenly wanted to run him over. She put the truck in low gear and followed him, thinking how simple it would be. He was drunk again and wouldn't even notice. Then her life would be that much easier. But as she drew alongside him, she was surprised to meet his eyes and see that they were clear. He shuffled anxiously around to the side door; she saw that he had a purpose: out snaking himself booze at a time like this. Only the bottle in his hand was not the usual schnapps but a brown square-shouldered medicine bottle labeled SUL-PHATE OF MORPHIA, for which he'd broken into the drugstore and sawed through the lock of the cabinet where the pharmacist kept the drugs he had to secure by law.

As Delphine slammed on the brakes, jumped from the truck, and ran to the house, she heard it from outside, the high-pitched keen of advanced agony, a white-silver whine. She rushed in, skidded across a litter of canning smashed down off the shelves, and entered the kitchen. There was Tante, white and sick with shock, slumped useless in the corner of the kitchen, on the floor. Louis and Franz, weeping and holding onto their mother as she rummaged in the drawer for a knife. The whole of her being was concentrated on the necessity. Even young, strong Franz couldn't hold her back.

"Yes, yes," Delphine said, entering the scene. She'd come upon so many scenes of mayhem in her own house that now a cold flood of competence descended on her. With a swift step, she stood before Eva. "My friend," she said, plucking the knife away, "not now. Soon enough. I've got the medicine. Don't leave your boys like this."

Then Eva, still swooning and grunting as the waves of pain hit and twisted in her, allowed herself to be lowered to the floor.

"Get a blanket and a pillow," Delphine said, kindly, to Franz. "And you," she said to Louis, "hold her hand while I make this up, and keep saying to her, 'Mama, she's making the medicine now. It will be soon. It will be soon.'"

2001

"Today's big story is eggplant."

BARK

JULIAN BARNES

On the feast day of Jean-Étienne Delacour, the following dishes were prepared on the instructions of his daughter-in-law, Mme Amélie: bouillon, the beef that had been boiled in it, a grilled hare, a pigeon casserole, vegetables, cheese, and fruit jellies. In a spirit of reluctant sociability, Delacour allowed a dish of bouillon to be placed before him; he even, in honor of the day, raised a ceremonial spoonful to his lips and blew graciously, before lowering it untouched. When the beef was brought in, he nodded at the servant, who laid in front of him, on separate plates, a single pear and a slice of bark that had been cut from a tree some twenty minutes earlier. Delacour's son, Charles, his daughter-in-law, his grandson, his nephew, his nephew's wife, the curé, a neighboring farmer, and Delacour's old friend André Lagrange made no observation. Delacour, for his part, civilly kept pace with those around him, eating one-quarter of the pear while they consumed their beef, one-quarter alongside the hare, and so on. When the cheese was brought in, he took out a pocketknife and cut the tree bark into slices, then chewed each piece slowly to oblivion. Later, as aids to sleep, he took a cup of milk, some stewed lettuce, and a rennet apple. His bedroom was well ventilated and his pillow stuffed with horsehair. He ensured that his chest was not weighed down with blankets, and that his feet would remain warm. As he settled his linen nightcap around his temples, Delacour reflected contentedly on the folly of those around him.

He was now sixty-one. In his earlier days, he had been both a gambler and a gourmand, a combination that had frequently threatened to inflict penury on his household. Wherever dice were thrown or cards turned, wherever two or more beasts could be induced to race against one another for the gratification of spectators, Delacour was to be found. He had won and lost at faro and hazard, backgammon and dominoes, roulette and rouge et noir. He would play pitch and toss with an infant, bet his horse on a cockfight, play two-pack patience with Mme V—— and solitaire when he could find no rival or companion.

It was said that his gourmandism had put an end to his gambling. Certainly, there was no room in such a man for both of these passions to express themselves fully. The moment of crisis had occurred when a goose reared to within days of slaughter—a goose he had fed with his own hand, and savored in advance, down to the last giblet—was lost at a hand of piquet. For a while, Delacour sat between his two temptations like the proverbial ass between two bales of hay; but, rather than starve to death like the indecisive beast, he acted as a true gambler and let a toss of the coin decide the matter.

Thereafter, his stomach and his purse both swelled, while his nerves became calmer. He ate meals fit for a cardinal, as the Italians say. He would discourse on the point of esculence of every foodstuff from capers to woodcock; he could explain how the shallot had been introduced into France by the returning Crusaders, and the cheese of Parma by M. le Prince de Talleyrand. When a partridge was placed in front of him, he would remove the legs, take a bite from each in a considered manner, nod judicially, and announce which leg the partridge had been accustomed to rest its weight on while sleeping. He was also a familiar of the bottle. If grapes were offered as a dessert, he would push them away with the words "I am not in the habit of taking my wine in the form of pills."

Delacour's wife had approved his choice of vice, since gourmandism is more likely to keep a man at home than gambling. As the years passed, her silhouette began to ape that of her husband. They lived plumply and easily until one day, fortifying herself in the midafternoon while her husband was absent, Mme Delacour choked to death on a chicken bone. Jean-Étienne cursed himself for having left his wife unattended; he cursed his gourmandism, her complicity in which had led to her death; and he cursed fate, chance, whatever governs our days, for having lodged the chicken bone at just such a murderous angle in her throat.

When his initial grief began to recede, he accepted lodging with Charles and Mme Amélie. He began a study of the law, and could often be found absorbed in the Nine Codes of the Kingdom. He knew the rural code by heart and comforted himself with its certainties. He could cite the laws concerned with the swarming of bees and the making of compost; he knew the penalties for ringing church bells during a storm and for selling milk that had come into contact with copper pans; word for word, he recited ordinances governing the behavior of wet nurses, the pasturing of goats in forests, and the burial of dead animals found on the public highway.

For a while, he continued with his gourmandizing, as if to do otherwise would be faithless to the memory of his wife; but, though his stomach was still in it, his heart was not. What led to his abandonment of his former passion was the municipality's decision, in the autumn of 18—, that, as a matter of hygiene and general beneficence, a public bathhouse should be built. That a man who had greeted the invention of a new dish as an astronomer would the discovery of a new star should be brought to temperance and moderation by a matter of soap and water moved some to mockery and others to moralizing. But Delacour had always given little heed to the opinions of others.

The municipality, in order to excite interest in the project, had devised a scheme based upon an Italian idea. The sum to be raised was divided into forty equal lots; each of the subscribers was obliged to be over forty years of age. Interest would be paid at the rate of 2.5 percent per annum, and upon the death of an investor the interest accruing to his share would be divided among the remaining subscribers. Simple mathematics led to a simple temptation: the last surviving investor would, from the thirty-ninth death until his own, enjoy an annual interest equal to the full sum of his original stake. The loans would terminate upon the death of the final subscriber, when the capital would be returned to the nominated heirs of the forty investors.

The death of Delacour's wife had brought him a small legacy, and Mme. Amélie proposed that it might be both a prudent and a civic gesture for him to invest it in the building of the baths. When she first mentioned the scheme to her husband, he was doubtful. "You do not think, my dear, that it might awaken my father's old passion?"

"It can scarcely be called gambling when there is no possibility of losing."

"That is surely what all gamblers constantly claim."

But Delacour approved his daughter-in-law's suggestion. He followed the progress of the subscription keenly. As each new investor came forward, he entered the man's name in a pocket book, adding his date of birth and general remarks upon his health, appearance,

and genealogy. When a landowner fifteen years his senior joined the
scheme, Delacour was merrier than he had been at any time since the
death of his wife. After a few weeks, the list was filled, whereupon he
wrote to the thirty-nine other subscribers suggesting that since they
had all, as it were, enlisted in the same regiment, they might choose
to distinguish themselves by some sartorial mark, such as a ribbon in
the coat. He also proposed that they institute a supper to be held annually for subscribers—he had almost written "survivors."

Few looked favorably on either proposal; some did not even reply;
but Delacour continued to view his fellow-subscribers as comrades in
arms. If he met one in the street, he would salute him warmly, inquire
about his health, and exchange a few general words, perhaps about
cholera. With his friend Lagrange, who had also subscribed, he would
pass long hours at the Café Anglais, playing actuary with the lives of
the other thirty-eight.

The municipal baths had not yet been declared open when the first
subscriber died. Jean-Étienne, at supper with his family, proposed a
toast to the overoptimistic and now lamented septuagenarian. Later,
he took out his pocket book, made an entry, with a date, and drew a
long black line underneath.

Mme Amélie commented to her husband on the high spirits of
her father-in-law, which seemed to her inappropriate.

"Death in general is his friend," Charles replied. "It is only his
own death that should be considered his enemy."

Mme Amélie briefly wondered if this was a philosophical truth or
an empty platitude. She had an amiable nature, and worried little
about her husband's actual opinions. She was more concerned about
the manner in which he delivered them, which was increasingly beginning to resemble that of his father.

Along with a large engraved certificate of subscription, investors
also received the right to use the baths gratis "for the full period of investment." Few were expected to do so, since those wealthy enough to
subscribe were certainly wealthy enough to own a bathtub. But Delacour took to invoking his right, first on a weekly, then on a daily, basis.
Some regarded this as an abuse of the municipality's benevolence, but
Delacour was unswayed. His days now followed a fixed pattern. He

would rise early, eat a single fruit, drink two glasses of water, and walk
for three hours. Then he would visit the baths, where he soon became
familiar with the attendants; as a subscriber, he was allowed a special
towel reserved for his use. Afterward, he would make his way to the
Café Anglais, where he would discuss the matters of the day with his
friend Lagrange. The matters of the day, in Delacour's mind, rarely
amounted to more than two: any foreseeable diminution of the subscribers' list, and the lax application of various laws by the municipality. It had, in his opinion, insufficiently advertised the scale of reward
for the destruction of wolves: twenty-five francs for a she-wolf in cub,
eighteen francs for a she-wolf not in cub, twelve for a male wolf, six
for a cub, the amounts to be paid within a week following verification
of the evidence.

Lagrange, whose mind was of a contemplative rather than a the-
oretical cast, considered this complaint. "And yet I do not know of
anyone," he commented mildly, "who has observed a wolf in the last
eighteen months."

"The more reason that the populace should be prompted to vigilance."

Delacour next denounced the lack of stringency and frequency
with which wine was tested for adulteration. By Article 38 of the law
of July 19, 1791, still applicable, a fine of up to a thousand francs and
imprisonment for a period of up to one year might be imposed upon
those who mixed litharge, fish glue, extract of campeche wood, or
other noxious substances with the wine they sold.

"You drink only water," Lagrange pointed out. He raised his own
glass and peered at the wine within. "Besides, if our host were to embark on such practices, it might very happily reduce the list of subscribers."

"I do not intend to win in such a fashion."

Lagrange was disturbed by the harshness of his friend's tone.
"Win," he repeated. "You can win, if you call it 'winning,' only by my
death."

"That I shall regret," Delacour said, evidently unable to conceive
of an alternative outcome.

After the Café Anglais, Delacour would return home and read works
on physiology and diet. Twenty minutes before supper, he would

cut himself a fresh slice of tree bark. While others ate their life-shortening concoctions, he would expatiate upon general threats to health and the lamentable impediments to human immortality.

These impediments gradually reduced the list of subscribers. With each death, Delacour's good cheer increased, and so did the strictness of his regimen. Exercise, diet, sleep; regularity, temperance, study. One work of physiology indicated, with veiled phrasing and a sudden burst of Latin, that a reliable mark of health in the human male was the frequency with which he engaged in sexual connection. Both total abstinence and excessive indulgence were potentially harmful, although not as harmful as certain practices associated with abstinence. But a moderate frequency—for example, exactly once per week—was deemed to be salutary.

Delacour, convinced of this practical necessity, rendered up excuses to his dead wife and entered into an arrangement with a maid at the baths, whom he visited once a week. She was grateful for the money he left, and once he had discouraged displays of affection he looked forward to their exchanges. He decided that, when the thirty-ninth subscriber died, he would give her a hundred francs, or perhaps a little less, in recognition of her life-prolonging services.

More investors died; Delacour entered their terminal dates in his pocket book and smilingly toasted their departures. On one such evening, Mme. Amélie, after retiring, said to her husband, "What is the reason for living if it is only to outlive others?"

"Each of us must find his own reason," Charles replied. "That is his."

"But do you not find it strange that what seems to afford him the most joy nowadays is the death of other mortals? He takes no customary pleasure in life. His days are ordered as if in obedience to the strictest duty—and yet duty to what, duty to whom?"

"The subscription was your proposal, my dear."

"I did not foresee, when I proposed it, the effect that it might have upon his character."

"My father's character," Charles replied sternly, "is unchanged. He is an old man now, and a widower. Naturally, his pleasures are diminished and his interests have altered somewhat. Yet he applies the same vigor of mind and the same logic to what interests him now as he did to what interested him before. His character has not changed," Charles repeated, as if his father were being charged with senility.

André Lagrange, had he been asked, would have agreed with Mme Amélie. Once a voluptuary, Delacour had become an ascetic; once an advocate of tolerance, Delacour had developed a severity toward his fellow men.

Seated at the Café Anglais, Lagrange listened to a peroration concerning the inadequate enforcement of the eighteen articles governing the cultivation of tobacco. Then there was a silence, a sip of water was taken, and Delacour continued, "Every man should have three lives. This is my third."

Bachelorhood, marriage, widowerhood, Lagrange supposed. Or perhaps gambling, gourmandism, the tontine. But Lagrange had been contemplative for long enough to recognize that men were often provoked to universal statements by some everyday event whose significance was being exaggerated. "And her name?" he asked.

"It is strange," Delacour said, "how, as life proceeds, the dominant sentiments may change. When I was young, I respected the priest, I honored my family, I was full of ambition. As for the passions of the heart, I discovered, when I met the woman who was to become my wife, that a long prologue of love led finally, with the sanction and approval of society, to those carnal delights that we hold so dear. Now that I have grown older, I am less persuaded that the priest can show us the best way to God, my family often exasperates me, and I have no ambition left."

"That is because you have acquired a certain wealth and a certain philosophy."

"No, it is more that I judge the individual rather than the social rank he fills. The curé is a pleasant companion but a theological fool; my son is honest but tedious. Observe that I do not claim virtue for this change in my understanding. It is merely something that has happened to me."

"And carnal delight?"

Delacour sighed and shook his head. "When I was a young man, in my Army years, before meeting my late wife, I naturally accommodated myself with the sort of women who made themselves available. Nothing in those experiences of my youth told me of the possibility that carnal delight might lead to feelings of love. I imagined—no, I was sure—that it was always the other way round."

"And her name?"

"The swarming of bees," Delacour replied. "As you know, the law is clear. So long as the owner follows his bees as they swarm, he has the right to reclaim and take possession of them again. But if he has failed to follow them then the proprietor of the ground on which they alight has legal title to them. Or take the case of rabbits. Those rabbits that pass from one warren to another become the property of the man on whose land the second warren is situated, unless this proprietor has enticed them thither by means of fraud or artifice. As with pigeons and doves. If they fly to common land, they belong to whosoever may kill them. If they fly to another dovecote, they belong to the owner of that dovecote, provided, again, that he has not enticed them thither by fraud or artifice."

"You have quite lost me." Lagrange looked on benignly, familiar with such perambulations from his friend.

"I mean that we make such certainties as we can. But who can foresee when the bees might swarm? Who can foresee whither the dove might fly, or when the rabbit might tire of its warren?"

"And her name?"

"Jeanne. She is a maid at the baths."

"Jeanne who is a maid at the baths?" Everyone knew Lagrange for a mild man. Now he stood up quickly, kicking his chair backward. The noise reminded Delacour of his Army days, of sudden challenges and broken furniture.

"You know her?"

"Jeanne who is a maid at the baths? Yes. And you must renounce her."

Delacour did not understand. That is to say, he understood the words but not their motive or purpose. "Who can foresee whither the dove might fly?" he repeated, pleased with this formulation.

Lagrange was leaning over him, knuckles on the table, almost trembling, it seemed. Delacour had never seen his friend so serious or so angry. "In the name of our friendship you must renounce her," he said.

"You have not been listening." Delacour leaned back in his chair, away from his friend's face. "At the start it was simply a matter of hygiene. I insisted on the girl's docility. I wanted no caresses in return— I discouraged them. I paid her little attention. And yet, in spite of all this, I have come to love her. Who can foresee—"

"I have been listening, and in the name of our friendship I insist."

Delacour considered the request. No, it was a demand, not a request. He was suddenly back at the card table, faced with an opponent who for no evident reason had raised his bid tenfold. At such moments, assessing the inexpressive fan in his opponent's hands, Delacour had always relied on instinct, not calculation.

"No," he replied quietly, as if laying down a small trump.

Lagrange left.

Delacour sipped his glass of water and calmly reviewed the possibilities. He reduced them to two: disapproval or jealousy. He ruled out disapproval: Lagrange had always been an observer of human behavior, not a moralist who condemned its vagaries. So it must be jealousy. Of the girl herself, or of what she represented: health, longevity, victory? Truly, the subscription was driving men to strange behavior. It had made Lagrange overexcited, and he had gone off like a swarm of bees. Well, Delacour would not follow him. Let him land wherever he chose.

Delacour continued with his daily routine. He did not mention Lagrange's defection to anyone, and he constantly expected him to reappear at the café. He missed their discussions, or at least Lagrange's attentive presence; but gradually he resigned himself to the loss. He began to visit Jeanne more frequently. She did not question this, and listened as he talked of legal matters she rarely understood. Having previously been warned against impertinent expressions of affection, she remained quiet and tractable, but did not fail to notice that his caresses had become gentler. One day, she informed him that she was with child.

"Twenty-five francs," he replied automatically. She protested that she was not asking for money. He apologized—his mind had been elsewhere—and asked if she was confident that the child was his. On hearing her assurance—or, more exactly, the tone of her assurance, which had none of the vehemence of mendacity—he offered to have the baby placed with a wet nurse and to provide an allowance for it. He kept to himself the surprising love he had come to feel for Jeanne. To his mind, it was not really her affair; it concerned him, not her, and he also felt that, were he to express what he felt, it might depart, or

become complicated in a way that he did not desire. He let her understand that she could rely upon him; that was enough. Otherwise, he
enjoyed his love as a private matter. It had been a mistake to tell Lagrange; doubtless it would be a mistake to tell anyone else.

A few months later, Lagrange became the thirty-sixth member of
the tontine to die. Since Delacour had told no one of their quarrel, he
felt obliged to attend the funeral. As the coffin was being lowered, he
remarked to Mme Amélie, "He did not take sufficient care of himself."

When Delacour looked up, he saw Jeanne, standing at the back of
a group of mourners on the other side of the grave, her dress now full
in front of her.

The law relating to wet nurses was, in his view, ineffective. The
declaration of January 19, 1715, was plain enough. Wet nurses were
forbidden to suckle two infants at the same time, on pain of correc-
tional punishment for the woman and a fine of fifty francs for her
husband; they were obliged to declare their own pregnancies as soon
as the second month was reached; they were also forbidden to send
infants back to the parental home, even in cases of nonpayment, but
were obliged, instead, to continue their service and be reimbursed by
the police tribunal. Yet everyone knew that such women could not always be trusted. They made arrangements for additional infants; they
lied about the advancement of their pregnancies; and, if there was a
dispute over payment between parents and wet nurse, it was not unknown for the child not to survive the following week. Perhaps he
should permit Jeanne to feed the child herself after all, since that was
what she wanted.

At their next encounter, Delacour expressed surprise at her presence at the graveside. Lagrange had never, as far as he knew, exercised
the right to use the municipal baths.

"He was my father," she replied.

Of Paternity and Filiation, he thought. Decree of March 23,
1803, promulgated April 2nd. Chapters 1, 2, and 3.

"How?" was all he could say.

"How?" she repeated.

"Yes, how?"

"In the usual manner, I am sure," the girl said.

"Yes."

"He used to visit my mother as . . ."

"As I visit you."

"Yes. He was much taken with me. He wished to acknowledge me, to make me . . ."

"Legitimate?"

"Yes. My mother did not want this. There was a dispute. She feared he would try to steal me. She guarded me. Sometimes he would spy on us. When she was dying, my mother made me promise never to receive him or to have contact with him. I promised. I did not think that . . . that the funeral amounted to contact."

Jean-Étienne Delacour sat on the girl's narrow bed. Something was slipping in his mind. The world was making less sense than it should. This child, provided it survived the hazards of accouchement, would be Lagrange's grandchild. What he chose not to tell me, what Jeanne's mother kept from him, what I, in my turn, have not told Jeanne. We make the laws but the bees swarm anyway, the rabbit seeks a different warren, the pigeon flies to another's dovecote.

"When I was a gambler," he said finally, "people disapproved. They thought it was a vice. I never thought so. To me it seemed the application of logical scrutiny to human behavior. When I was a gourmand, people judged it an indulgence. I never thought so. To me it seemed a rational approach to human pleasure."

He looked at her. She seemed to have no idea what he was talking about. Well, that was his own fault. "Jeanne," he said, taking her hand. "You need have no fear for your child. No fear of the kind your mother had. It is not necessary."

"Yes, sir."

At supper, he listened to his grown-up son's prattle and declined to correct numerous idiocies. He chewed on a sliver of tree bark, but without appetite. Later, his cup of milk tasted as if it had come from a copper pan, his stewed lettuce stank of the dunghill, his rennet apple had the texture of a horsehair pillow.

In the morning, when they found him, his linen nightcap was grasped in a rigid hand, though whether he had been about to put it on, or whether for some reason he had just chosen to remove it, no one could tell.

2002

"Dinner is scrambled."

ABOUT THE TYPE

This book was set in Adobe Caslon. William Caslon released his first typefaces in 1722. His types were based on seventeenth-century Dutch old style designs, which were then used extensively in England. Because of their incredible practicality Caslon's designs met with instant success. Caslon's types became popular throughout Europe and the American colonies; printer Benjamin Franklin hardly used any other typeface. The first printings of the American Declaration of Independence and the Constitution were set in Caslon. For her Caslon revival, designer Carol Twombly studied specimen pages printed by William Caslon between 1734 and 1770. Ideally suited for text, Adobe Caslon is right for magazines, journals, book publishing, and corporate communications.